Since 1969, Antonia Fraser has written many acclaimed historical works which have been international bestsellers. These include the biographies *Mary Queen of Scots* (James Tait Black Memorial Prize), *Cromwell: Our Chief of Men, King Charles II*, and *The Gunpowder Plot: Terror and Faith in 1605* in 1996 (St Louis Literary Award; CWA Non-Fiction Gold Dagger). Four highly praised books focus on women in history: *The Weaker Vessel: Woman's Lot in Seventeenth-Century England* (Wolfson Award for History, 1984), *The Warrior Queens: Boadicea's Chariot* (1988), *The Six Wives of Henry VIII* (1992) and *Marie Antoinette: The Journey* (Franco-British Society, 2001). Antonia Fraser is the editor of the series *Kings and Queens of England* (Weidenfeld & Nicolson), and wrote the volume *King James VI of Scotland, I of England.* She was made CBE in 1999, and awarded the Norton Medlicott Medal by the Historical Association in 2000. She was married to Harold Pinter, who died on Christmas Eve 2008: her bestselling memoir of their life together *Must You Go?* was published in 2010. Her most recent books include *Love and Louis XIV: The Women in the Life of the Sun King, Perilous Question: The Drama of the Great Reform Bill*, and *My History: A Memoir of Growing Up* published by Weidenfeld & Nicolson. Visit her website at www.antoniafraser.com

By Antonia Fraser

Mary Queen of Scots

Cromwell: Our Chief of Men

King James VI of Scotland, I of England
(*Kings and Queens* series)

King Charles II

The Weaker Vessel: Woman's Lot
in Seventeenth-Century England

The Warrior Queens: Boadicea's Chariot

The Six Wives of Henry VIII

The Gunpowder Plot: Terror and Faith in 1605

Marie Antoinette: The Journey

Love and Louis XIV: the Women in the
Life of the Sun King

Must You Go?

Perilous Question: The Drama of the
Great Reform Bill

My History: A Memoir of Growing Up

King Charles II

ANTONIA FRASER

W&N
WEIDENFELD & NICOLSON

A W&N PAPERBACK

First published in Great Britain in 1979
by Weidenfeld & Nicolson
First published in paperback in 1993
by Mandarin Paperbacks
Reprinted in 1998 by Arrow Books

This paperback edition published in 2002
by Weidenfeld & Nicolson,
an imprint of the Orion Publishing Group,
Carmelite House, 50 Victoria Embankment,
London EC4Y 0DZ

An Hachette UK company

9 10

A CIP catalogue record for this book
is available from the British Library.

ISBN 978-0-7538-1403-1

Set in Monotype Garamond by
Butler and Tanner Ltd, Frome and London
Printed and bound in Great Britain by
Clays Ltd, St Ives plc

MIX
Paper from
responsible sources
FSC® C104740

www.orionbooks.co.uk

For my mother and Harold
the first readers
with love

Contents

Illustrations

Author's Note

First and foremost this book has been a labour of love. I have always been fascinated by the character of King Charles II, sharing the view of Queen Victoria, who told Dean Stanley that, for all his moral failings, she regarded Charles II as one of the most attractive of her predecessors. I wanted to discover for myself whether he merited this long-held sympathy.

Romantic curiosity was the start. Curiosity of a different sort spurred me on when I was working on the life of Oliver Cromwell. What happened next to the 'young gentleman', as Cromwell himself sometimes described the exiled Charles II? The Restoration of 1660 is such a convenient starting-point for historical studies: it is sometimes forgotten that Charles II was already thirty at the time of his return, with one whole dramatic existence behind him. I have hoped in my biography to span both periods of his life before and after 1660 and show their relation to each other.

Thirdly, as a historical work, this biography is in the nature of a re-assessment, based on the workings of many scholars in the field. There are surprisingly few biographies of any note of Charles II compared to some popular figures; paradoxically, we have been extremely fortunate in our historians of the period. Osmund Airy's life (1901) should still be mentioned and Sir

Arthur Bryant's biography, concentrating on the reign itself (1931, revised 1955), is enduringly splendid. The most recent life, by Maurice Ashley (1972), is especially strong on the tortuous diplomacy of the period. Since that date there has been still more research made public – and such valuable additions to our knowledge will undoubtedly continue to flow forth. In making my reassessment I gratefully acknowledge my debt to all scholars of the period, past and present. Finality is impossible – fortunately, in my opinion, for who would wish the last word on King Charles II to have been spoken?

I have taken the usual liberties in correcting spelling and punctuation where it seemed necessary to make sense to the general reader today. For the same reason I have ignored the fact that the calendar year was held to start on 25 March during this period and have used the modern style of dates starting on 1 January throughout. There was a ten-day difference in dating between England and the Continent during this period – England used Old Style (O.S.) and the Continent New Style (N.S.); once again, to avoid confusion, I have dated letters according to their source, occasionally giving both dates where necessary. Charles II was, of course, King of Great Britain, as we should term it today, but I have often used the term England to denote this area, as people did at the time.

I wish to thank Her Majesty the Queen for gracious permission to work in the Royal Archives at Windsor, Sir Robert Mackworth-Young, the Royal Librarian, and Miss Langton of the Royal Library. I also wish to thank Dr Stephen R. Parks, Curator of the Osborn Collection, Yale University; the Director of the Pierpont Morgan Library, New York; Mr Richard W. Couper, President and Chief Executive, and Mr James W. Henderson, Director of Research Libraries, of the New York Public Library; Mr T. I. Rae, Keeper of the Department of Manuscripts, National Library of Scotland; and Dr A. L. Murray, Assistant Keeper of the Scottish Record Office, for allowing me to see the various manuscripts in their care.

I am most grateful to the following for assistance in different ways, representing the extraordinary variety displayed in the life of King Charles II: Lord Aberdare; Mr Howard Adams; Lt-Col.

David Ascoli; Mr E. K. Barnard of the Cathedral Office, Portsmouth; Mr Neal Beck, Secretary of the King Charles Spaniel Club; Lord Clifford of Chudleigh; Lt-Col. A. Colin Cole, Garter King of Arms; Mr C. R. H. Cooper, Keeper of Manuscripts, and Mr M. V. Roberts of Enquiry Services, Guildhall Library; Mr Timothy Crist; Dr Chalmers Davidson; Mr Barry Denton of Northampton; Sir John Dewhurst, former President of the Royal College of Obstetricians and Gynaecologists; Mr J. F. Downes of Hook Norton; Mr Peter Foster, Surveyor of the Fabric of Westminster Abbey; Mr Eric J. Freeman, Librarian of the Wellcome Institute for the History of Medicine; Mr. J. R. Goulsbra, Secretary of the Royal Hospital, Chelsea; Mr John Gross; Mr Nigel Hamilton; Mr J. W. Hele, High Master of St Paul's School; Dr Albert E. J. Hollaender; Squadron-Leader L. R. Horrox; Mr Cyril Humphris; Mr Jonathan Israel; Mr Simon Jenkins; Mr R. C. Latham; Mr Raphael Loewe for translating the Sasportas letter; Mrs D. Maclaine, Secretary of the Cavalier King Charles Spaniel Club; Mr N. H. MacMichael, Keeper of the Muniments, Westminster Abbey; Mrs W. E. Macready, Honorary Secretary, Société Jersiaise; Sir Iain Moncrieffe of that Ilk; Dr G. C. R. Morris; Mr Ferdinand Mount; Mrs P. M. O'Connor, Honorary Secretary, Marlipins Museum, Shoreham; Miss Jane O'Hara-May; Mr Richard Ollard; Mrs Julia Parker for her horoscope of King Charles II; Mr George Pinker; Mr Anthony Powell; Lady Violet Powell; Mr John Sales, Curator of the Bridport Museum; Mr Edgar Samuel; Mr A. Schishca; Mr Arthur M. Schlesinger, Jr; Dr Jan Den Tex; Miss Audrey Williamson; Professor I. Tishby of Jerusalem for permission to quote from the unpublished letter of Rabbi Jacob Sasportas; and Mr Steen Vedel for the unpublished diary of his ancestor Corfitz Braëm.

Professor J. P. Kenyon read the manuscript at an early stage and made many helpful criticisms. Peter Earle and Gila Falkus also read the manuscript and made suggestions. Dr Maurice Ashley kindly read the proofs. I was delighted to get to know Sir Arthur Bryant through our shared interest in King Charles II, and to receive his encouragement. Anne Somerset gave me vital assistance in checking references and making good any omissions; my daughter, Flora Fraser, carried on the good work. Above all, Christopher Falkus of Weidenfeld's was a tower of strength at every stage.

Lastly I should like to thank my secretary Mrs Charmian Gibson, Mrs Patsy Parsons, and Mrs V. Williams and her staff for heroic typing.

ANTONIA FRASER

PART ONE

The Hopeful Prince

'A great and a hopeful Prince'
CLARENDON

CHAPTER ONE

Heaven Was Liberal

'This year Heaven was liberal to his Majesty in giving him a son to inherit his dominions.'

Richard Perrinchief, *The Royal Martyr*

When in the summer of 1630 a healthy son was born to the King and Queen of England, it seemed that their happiness was complete. Henrietta Maria, wife of Charles, the first Stuart monarch of that name, had presented him with an heir. King Charles was twenty-nine years old, his French wife twenty. He loved her passionately.

It had not always been so: at the time of their marriage five years earlier the young King had preferred the companionship of his father's favourite, the dazzling Duke of Buckingham. The death of Buckingham had brought the little Queen into her husband's confidence and favour, never to leave it. Their married love was now total. Only a family – an heir – was needed, and the last traditional ambition of a royal couple would be fulfilled. Unfortunately their first child, Charles James, was a weakling who was born and died in May 1629.

Almost exactly a year later, on 29 May 1630, at noon with Venus the star of love and fortune shining high over the horizon, Henrietta Maria gave birth to a second son, also named Charles. Unlike his brother, this baby was enormous and healthy, and, even in that age of appalling infant mortality, clearly destined to survive. Verses on a contemporary engraving referred to the brothers as two sweet May-flowers, only one of which remained 'in our garden, fresh to grow'. The child of 1629 was shown being borne away to celestial spheres.

Of happy 1630 it was written in contrast, 'This year Heaven was liberal to his Majesty in giving him a son to inherit his dominions.'[1] And as the bells rang out, later giving way to bonfires in the summer night, the King proceeded immediately to St Paul's for a service of thanksgiving. It was incidentally the patronal feast of St Augustine of Canterbury, he who had brought Christianity to the Angles: it must be said that the appearance of Venus would prove the more relevant portent of the young Prince's character.

As the good news spread outwards across the King's widespread dominions, so the spokesmen of his power rejoiced. In far-off Scotland, from which his Stuart father James had come, the King's deputies lit fires; in Ireland too there was official rejoicing; across the water the Court of Louis XIII were content to hear that a daughter of Bourbon France had fulfilled the natural function of a Queen.

The child thrived. At the time it seemed like the end of a fairy-tale.

Only a few years later, it would become apparent that Charles had been born at the zenith of his unfortunate father's short arc of happiness. Far from marking the end of a fairy-tale, the birth of the future Charles II marked the beginning of the most troubled period that man could remember in the history of the realm. By the time Charles was eight years old, war had broken out with his father's northern kingdom; by the time he was twelve, the whole of England was plunged in civil war. A few years more and the young Prince himself was penniless and a fugitive.

At the time poets were fascinated by the presiding presence of Venus at the Prince's birth. One of the most graceful expressions of this preoccupation was given by Robert Herrick in his 'Pastoral' on the occasion, set by Nicholas Lanier for presentation to the King:

> And that his birth should be more singular,
> At noon of day, was seen a silver star,

Bright as the wise men's torch, which guided them
To God's sweet babe, where born at Bethlehem;...

Later astrologers were morbidly obsessed by the significance of that delusive star in his chart.* So paradoxically dreadful were the early fortunes of Charles Stuart the second, compared to the golden expectations at his birth, that they would ponder helplessly on the subject. If the heavens themselves had been misleading, was it a wonder that mere mortals had erred in predicting for him a destiny both splendid and serene?

It was fortunate that the young father and mother, as they gazed into a cradle garnished with taffeta and ribbons, could not foresee even their own future: separation, violent death for one, desolate widowhood for the other. Yet Charles I and Henrietta Maria might have been comforted by knowing the end of the story. The fairy-tale element persisted. The boy himself would pass through every vicissitude known to a prince in such stories, but ultimately he would survive them all.

Unlike his father, unlike his grandfather Henri Quatre, unlike his great-grandmother Mary Queen of Scots, unlike his great-grandfather Lord Darnley, unlike his brother James and his exiled descendants, Charles II would die in his own royal bed. And he would die as the dominating monarch his father, grandfather James and brother all dreamt of being without success. He would die master in his own house, confessing the religion his mother was harried for practising and for which Mary Stuart was executed and James II driven out. He would die the last absolute King of Great Britain.

So perhaps the auspicious star, whose celestial rays duly ornamented the medal commemorating his 'singular birth', was not so delusive after all.

The marriage of this baby's parents in May 1625 had brought

* For the astrologically minded – as most of Charles' contemporaries were – it is of interest to note that he was born with the Sun in Gemini, Virgo on the ascendant, the Moon and Venus both in Taurus. The celestial picture is thus dominated by Mercury, denoting a quick intelligence and a certain restlessness of temperament; there is also an earthly love of pleasure, a stubborn loyalty, and, with Mars in Leo, physical courage.[2]

HENRI IV
King of France
and Navarre
b. 1553
d. 1610
= 1. Marguerite de Valois
2. Marie de Medici

LOUIS XIII
King of France
b. 1601
d. 1643
= Anne of Austria

Elisabeth
b. 1602
d. 1644
= Philip IV
King of Spain

LOUIS XIV
b. 1638
d. 1715
= Maria Teresa
Infanta of Spain

Philippe
duc d'Orléans
b. 1640
d. 1701
= Henriette-Anne
of England

Maria Teresa
b. 1638
d. 1683
= Louis XIV

HOUSE OF STUART

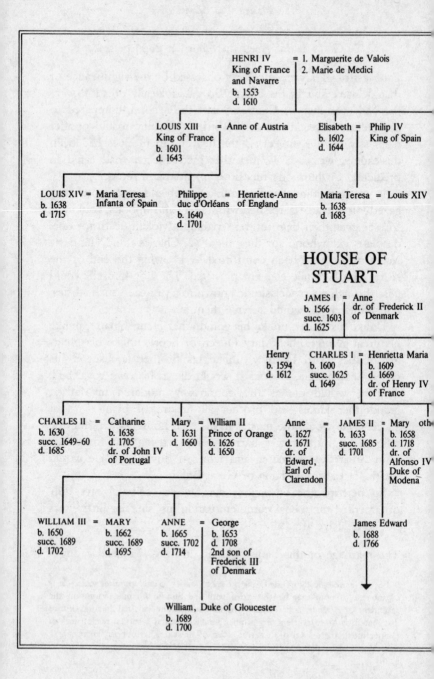

JAMES I
b. 1566
succ. 1603
d. 1625
= Anne
dr. of Frederick II
of Denmark

Henry
b. 1594
d. 1612

CHARLES I
b. 1600
succ. 1625
d. 1649
= Henrietta Maria
b. 1609
d. 1669
dr. of Henry IV
of France

CHARLES II
b. 1630
succ. 1649–60
d. 1685
= Catharine
b. 1638
d. 1705
dr. of John IV
of Portugal

Mary
b. 1631
d. 1660
= William II
Prince of Orange
b. 1626
d. 1650

Anne
b. 1627
d. 1671
dr. of
Edward,
Earl of
Clarendon
= JAMES II
b. 1633
succ. 1685
d. 1701
= Mary
b. 1658
d. 1718
dr. of
Alfonso IV
Duke of
Modena

oth

WILLIAM III
b. 1650
succ. 1689
d. 1702
= MARY
b. 1662
succ. 1689
d. 1695

ANNE
b. 1665
succ. 1702
d. 1714
= George
b. 1653
d. 1708
2nd son of
Frederick III
of Denmark

William, Duke of Gloucester
b. 1689
d. 1700

James Edward
b. 1688
d. 1766

HOUSE OF BOURBON

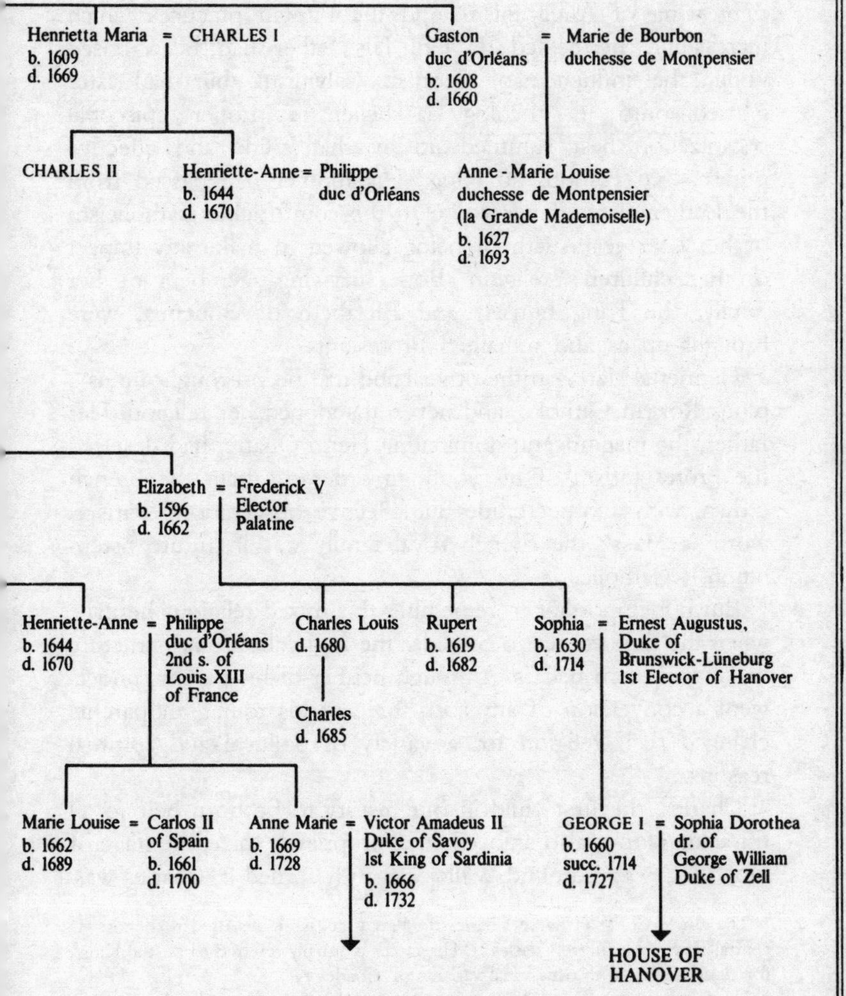
Henrietta Maria = CHARLES I
b. 1609
d. 1669
Gaston = Marie de Bourbon
duc d'Orléans
duchesse de Montpensier
b. 1608
d. 1660
CHARLES II
Henriette-Anne = Philippe
duc d'Orléans
b. 1644
d. 1670
Anne-Marie Louise
duchesse de Montpensier
(la Grande Mademoiselle)
b. 1627
d. 1693
Elizabeth = Frederick V
Elector
Palatine
b. 1596
d. 1662
Henriette-Anne = Philippe
duc d'Orléans
2nd s. of
Louis XIII
of France
b. 1644
d. 1670
Charles Louis
d. 1680
Charles
d. 1685
Rupert
b. 1619
d. 1682
Sophia = Ernest Augustus,
Duke of
Brunswick-Lüneburg
1st Elector of Hanover
b. 1630
d. 1714
Marie Louise = Carlos II
of Spain
b. 1662
d. 1689
b. 1661
d. 1700
Anne Marie = Victor Amadeus II
Duke of Savoy
1st King of Sardinia
b. 1669
d. 1728
b. 1666
d. 1732
GEORGE I = Sophia Dorothea
dr. of
George William
Duke of Zell
b. 1660
succ. 1714
d. 1727
HOUSE OF
HANOVER

together a disparate pair – at any rate in terms of religion. The King* was not only the supreme governor of the Protestant Church in his own country, but was emotionally committed to Anglicanism as such. He eschewed equally the Roman Catholic tenets which lay, as it were, beyond the right wing of Anglicanism, and the Puritan practices which increasingly permeated its left. His father had been raised under the influence of Scottish Calvinism, but had later grafted onto its theology a belief in proper episcopal organization best summed up by that crude and effective phrase, 'No Bishop, no King.' His mother had passed from the Lutheranism of her youth to the comfortable Catholicism of her later years without being allowed to make any impact on her children's religion. Both surviving members of her family, the King himself and Elizabeth of Bohemia, were brought up as and remained Protestants.

Henrietta Maria on the other hand had been brought up as a pious Roman Catholic, and never abandoned her religion. Her father, the magnificent, dominating Henri Quatre, had deserted the Protestantism of his youth in order to attain the French crown, with another crude but effective observation, 'Paris is worth a Mass': the French royal family was in future ostentatiously Catholic.

But it is important to remember this mixed religious heritage when the time comes to consider the foundations and structure of Charles' own beliefs. Although neither of his parents underwent a conversion of any sort, three of his four grandparents changed their religion for a variety of political and spiritual reasons.

Charles, the first child in our history to be born heir to all three kingdoms, also enjoyed an appropriately mixed heritage of blood.† Or, as Edmund Waller elegantly turned it, Charles was

* The single Christian name Charles, in Part One, is always used to denote its central figure, the future Charles II. His father is usually referred to as 'the King', for clarity's sake, with occasional variants of 'Charles I'.

† His father was the second son of James VI and I, only succeeding his brother, the legendary and lamented Henry Prince of Wales, as heir on his death in 1612; in any case both princes were born before James ascended the English throne in 1603, uniting the three crowns of Scotland, England and Ireland.

A Prince on whom such different lights did smile,
Born the divided world to reconcile!

Historic names sparkle like jewels – some of them slightly flawed gems – in Charles' genealogical tree. Through his father he descended from Scottish James, canny, intellectual and somewhat boorish; the improbable son of that ill-fated enchanter Mary Queen of Scots and the degenerate Darnley. James had married a Danish Princess, Anne, daughter of Frederick II and Sophie of Mecklenbergh-Schwerin. The union brought a good strong strain of northern blood, Scandinavian and German, into the British royal family, which proved most helpful. Neither Tudors nor Stuarts had proved conspicuously fertile in the last hundred years: but James and Anne between them produced a quiverful of children.

The effect of this family was to transform what might otherwise have been a miserable marriage into a perfectly acceptable partnership by royal standards. Anne, easy-going if rather frivolous by nature, was quickly despised for her girlish tastes by the infinitely cleverer James. In any case the King had been since boyhood romantically inclined towards his own sex. As the years wore on, and especially after the arrival of the Scottish court in the luxurious atmosphere of London, King and Queen went their separate ways. James turned to favourites, including George Villiers, created Duke of Buckingham; Anne turned 'to favour and to prettiness', including such laudable if extravagant projects as the patronage of Inigo Jones. But James was a devoted father. That bond at least kept the royal pair together.

The blood which Charles inherited through his mother was half French and half Italian. Henrietta Maria,* as the daughter

* As she will be known, according to the English custom, and to distinguish her from her daughter, later Duchesse d'Orléans and Madame de France, who will be called Henriette-Anne (baptized Henrietta, the name Anne being added later as a compliment to Anne of Austria). The Queen herself naturally used the French version of her name, signing herself as Henriette Marie throughout her life; but the English at the time often found the whole name too confusing to cope with and she sometimes appears merely as Mary. One of the Royalist watchwords at the Battle of Naseby, when Charles I was fighting for survival, was 'For God and Queen Mary'.

of the late King of France, by no means considered herself bettered by marrying the King of England: for Charles I to have the great Henri Quatre as a father-in-law was surely an honour in itself. But Charles II would find it a more dubious advantage to be the grandson of Henri of Navarre. Indeed how bitterly at times he must have regretted those blithe words of his progenitor on the subject of Paris and the Mass, as people often do come to loathe the *panache* of their famous ancestors, too frequently quoted against them. Whenever changes of religion were either suggested or imputed to Charles, his relationship to Henri Quatre, that celebrated worldly convert, was always stressed; at other times he was besought to emulate his grandfather in heroism, or at least to remember whose grandson he was.

Charles was, then, by blood one-quarter Scots, one-quarter Danish, one-quarter French and one-quarter Italian. Further back, the marriage of the cousins Mary Queen of Scots and Darnley increased the proportion of Scottish noble blood; while Mary's Guise mother supplemented his French inheritance. For the thin but vital trickle of English – Tudor – blood which had ensured his family's succession to the English throne, it was necessary to go back five generations to his great-grandmother's grandmother, Margaret Tudor, daughter of Henry VII. And even that Tudor blood was itself basically Welsh.

It was no wonder that King James had swept aside contemporary discussions of heredity when he ascended the English throne, preferring to delve into a mythological past where creatures like Brute, first King of all the Britons, flourished. *Titus Britannicus*, a eulogy of Charles by Aurelian Cook appearing shortly after his death, referred to him as having all the blood-royal of the Christian world in his veins – British, Saxon, Danish, Norman and Scottish from his father, Bourbon of France, Austrian of Spain and Medici of Florence from his mother.[3] It was English blood itself which was lacking.

Nevertheless, in his tastes, Charles remained a very typical Englishman all his life: his enjoyments united him with, rather than divided him from, his subjects. In his case, blood was evidently less important than those early formative years, rated so highly by the Jesuits and modern psychology. These were spent in carefree, nurturing England.

The victory of environment over heredity was the more remarkable because of Charles' striking physical appearance, which was even more foreign than his actual blood. First, he had an abnormal darkness of complexion, a truly saturnine tint. This darkness was the subject of comment from the first. His mother wrote jokingly to her sister-in-law that she had given birth to a black baby and to a friend in France that 'he was so dark that she was ashamed of him'. She would send his portrait 'as soon as he is a little fairer'.[4] But Charles never did become fairer. Later the sobriquet 'the Black Boy' would be used, still commemorated in English inn signs.

There was definitely a strain of very dark, swarthy Italian blood in the French royal family, inherited through Marie de Medici, which might and did emerge from time to time. Anne of Austria, wife of Henrietta Maria's brother Louis XIII, was said to have given birth to a baby having the 'colour and visage of a blackamoor', which died a month after its birth. In 1664 another Queen of France, wife of Charles' first cousin Louis, was supposed to have given birth to a black child.[5] There was even a 'fanatic' fantasy at the time of the Popish Plot in the late 1670s, that Charles had been fathered on Henrietta Maria by a 'black Scotsman' – a neat combination of two prejudices of the time, against the Catholics and the Scots. So it became convenient to refer to the then King as that 'black bastard'.[6]

Of the many grandchildren of Marie de Medici, Charles was the only one to look purely Italian; the rest being in general both frailer and paler. But his appearance was certainly a complete throwback to his Italian ancestors, the Medici Dukes of Tuscany. Directly descended as he was from Lorenzo the Magnificent there is a striking resemblance in their portraits. Bishop Burnet,* alluding to Charles' Italianate appearance and

* Burnet, the Scottish-born Bishop of Salisbury, was the author of the *History of My Own Time*, first published in 1723 (after his death); frequent allusions to it will be made in this work since Burnet provides many fascinating sidelights on the period. Nevertheless, allowance must always be made for his highly prejudiced pro-Whig and anti-Catholic views.

intending to make a political point concerning tyranny, compared the King to a statue of Tiberius.[7] Marvell was presumably describing the same phenomenon when he described Charles as

> Of a tall stature and of sable hue
> Much like the son of Kish, that lofty Jew.

Charles' second most striking physical attribute was that same tall stature. About two yards high, said the Parliamentary posters seeking his capture after the Battle of Worcester; six feet two inches, stated another, and he may have been as much as six feet three inches tall. Since a man of six feet two would be outstanding in a crowd today, the effect of Charles' salient height may be imagined in an age when the average male height, due to diet and disease, was so much less than in our own time. On his sea voyage towards his Restoration in May 1660, Charles marked his own height in his cabin with a knife; afterwards numerous sight-seers measured themselves against the spot, but even the tallest could not reach it.[8] As with his relationship to Henri Quatre, Charles must have lived to curse his eminence. The problems of tall men today in aeroplanes, cars and beds are as nothing compared to the problem which faced Charles fleeing after the Worcester defeat, compelled to try and disguise the one physical attribute which no make-up can conceal.

At first sight this height may seem a surprising phenomenon, since Charles I was short and Henrietta Maria positively tiny: she was termed 'the little Queen' – not always in tenderness. But his grandmother Anne of Denmark was tall, with a large bone structure: she had what would now be thought of as typical Scandinavian looks, with tow-coloured hair and a ruddy complexion. It would seem therefore that Charles' individual appearance was a combination of those two bloods least associated with him in the popular imagination – Danish and Italian.

The result, attractive as it may be by modern standards, was not much admired at the time. Charles was considered rather peculiar-looking, as he himself was the first to admit, with typical self-deprecation: 'Odd's fish, I am an ugly fellow,' he observed to the painter Lely after inspecting his own portrait. His curling and sensual mouth, so beguiling in our day, was considered particularly hideous, almost a deformity. Big mouths were definitely not the fashion: 'large and ugly' wrote Madame de Motteville with firmness of this particular feature, when describing Charles at the age of sixteen in her memoir of his mother.[9]

And fair hair itself was in principle preferred to dark. For one matter, there was a contemporary suspicion that beneath a saturnine appearance there lurked a saturnine character, something generally defined as melancholy and not particularly pleasant. Lord Mulgrave, for example, who was brought up at Court, thought it worth making the point that Charles being swarthy *and* cheerful was an exception to the rule.[10]

It took time for Charles to prove to the world that an attractive, good-humoured fellow lurked under his dark skin. Even his mother wrote that he was an ugly baby, and so large that at four months he might have been a year old. Charles succeeded in charming much of the world despite rather than because of the oddities of his physical appearance.

In a picture painted when Charles was a few months old, his proud parents flank their offspring. The King stands, a dignified figure, if not yet possessed of that hieratic appearance of dramatic suffering uncovered by Van Dyck. This franker portrait shows Charles' father with blunter features, of no great distinction, with a strong resemblance to those of James I.

Henrietta Maria's appearance also needed the help of a great artist and courtier to flower on the canvas. There is general agreement about the quality of her looks: when she was young, her attraction lay in her animation and in particular her sparkling black eyes, which, combined with her doll-like figure, made her at the time of her marriage 'a most absolute delicate lady', in the words of Simonds D'Ewes. But there was something simian about her. Her arms were disproportionately long, and, as she grew older and more unhappy, she lost weight rapidly, which did not suit her. By the birth of Henriette-Anne in 1644 she had become a sad, small monkey of a person, whose wide mouth looked almost grotesque. It was left to Pepys, at the Restoration, to describe Henrietta Maria – at fifty – as 'a very little plain old woman'.[11]

Those days lay far in the future. The young couple in the portrait are boldly delighted with their new treasure.

As has been related, the first child of Charles I and Henrietta Maria died at birth. All the circumstances of this sad event were unfortunate, including the fact that the baby was premature and the local midwife called into Greenwich Palace inadequate. But the Queen determined to put the tragedy behind her: 'As to my loss, I wish to forget it.'[12] After all, she had now had the reality of her husband's love, and it must have been some secret comfort to her that during the labour he had urged that, if there was any choice to be made, the mother rather than the child should be saved.

Henrietta Maria concentrated her energies on recovering, and replacing the lost child as soon as possible. To that end, she took herself off to the spa at Tunbridge Wells, whose waters were renowned for their good effects on gynaecological problems. (This spa, incidentally, makes constant appearances in the court history of the seventeenth century, as high-born but barren ladies, not the least of them Charles' own wife, Catharine of Braganza, sought there the cure to their troubles.) But the conception of Charles was more romantic than such planning might indicate. The Queen grew restless, cut short her visit to Tunbridge Wells, and moved with her entourage to Oatlands Palace, near Weybridge. The King, hearing of this, paid Oatlands a surprise visit. It was here that Charles was conceived. By mid-October the Queen knew she was pregnant again: in one of the last letters of his life the King addressed Charles in a moving phrase: 'You are the son of our love....'[13]

This time a midwife was sent over from France by Marie de Medici. She also despatched a useful chair, and a charm against miscarriage in the shape of a heart: Henrietta Maria wore the charm constantly, worrying when she forgot to put it on. It was also decided that this birth should take place at St James's Palace, so much quieter than the official royal residence at Whitehall. London in those days had a heavily eastward slant: thus the setting of this red-brick hunting lodge, built by Henry VIII, was quite pastoral in the early seventeenth century. Not only did it have a fine view of the St James's deer park – that park on which Charles himself later lavished so much care – but, being surrounded by other open spaces and fields, St James's Palace was cut off from the bustle of Westminster.

Here a bed with hangings of green satin was made ready at a cost of nearly seven hundred pounds. Luxurious beds were one of the major outlays of the time, as will be seen in the magnificent beds caparisoned for Charles himself, his wife and mistresses – rather as expensive cars are bought today.

Finally, Queen Henrietta Maria reached that 'happy hour for herself and us', as one contemporary put it.[14] Her labour began at about four o'clock in the morning. Shortly before noon, the baby was born in one of the Tudor rooms to the south of Colour Court, fronting St James' Court.* Almost immediately, according to the custom of the time, he was taken from his mother and given to a wet-nurse to be fed. Rockers stepped forward to the royal cradle: that too was according to the custom of the time, the only thing of note about them being the fact that they were Protestants. It had been part of Henrietta Maria's marriage contract, carefully laid down, that her children should not be nursed by Catholics. But the King presented the successful midwife, who, being French, probably *was* a Catholic, with £1,000.

The baptism, which took place on 27 June, was also according to the rite of the English Church. The ceremony was performed by the Bishop of London, the King's friend William Laud. It was a significant and appropriate choice. Although it would be another three years before he was created Archbishop of Canterbury, already Laud's name was synonymous with the repression of Puritanism within the English Church. Laud was nearing sixty, but his whole preferment had come since the accession of King Charles I: he had been made a Privy Councillor and had recently taken part in a harsh judgement against the Puritan Leighton in the Star Chamber.

* Few traces remain today of Henry VIII's palace other than the Gatehouse, parts of the Chapel Royal and the old Presence Chamber. The present Marlborough House was then Friary Court, where Henrietta Maria installed her Capuchin confessors.

For the baptism, the Lord Mayor of London presented a silver font. The Duchess of Richmond stood proxy for the godmother, the Queen of France, and, as a tribute to her principal's status, was fetched in a coach drawn by six plumed horses: her retinue (both sexes) arrived wearing white satin set off by crimson silk stockings. The baby's wet-nurse received a chain of rubies from Marie de Medici, the dry-nurse being given a silver plate; the six (Protestant) cradle-rockers were given a selection of silver spoons, cups and salt-cellars. From a less successful relation, the Elector Palatine, the husband of his aunt Elizabeth, the baby received a jewel.[15]

Charles began his life in the traditional long white clothes of linen and satin. But, unlike English babies of the time, he was not swaddled. Aristocratic French mothers did not approve of this habit of rolling up the baby like a tiny mummy – the Huguenot heiress Charlotte de la Trémouille, wife of the Earl of Derby, fought the same battle in her nursery at about the same date. Psychologists who have recently pointed out the dangers of deprivation of physical contact in the new-born would be happy to think that the baby Charles was allowed to lie freely (and he undoubtedly showed every sign of enjoying physical contact uninhibitedly in his later years).

The next step was to dress the child in tiny linen shirts (still preserved in the Royal collection). In 1631 he was handed over to the Countess of Dorset, who became his official governess, and given his own miniature establishment. Unlike the first choice of governess, the Catholic Countess of Roxburgh, she was an impeccable Anglican. The Countess of Dorset replaced the dry- and wet-nurses he had enjoyed since birth. One of these foster-mothers, Mrs Christabella Wyndham, was to feature in Charles' life in another interesting connection. Later the early experience was recalled most favourably by Charles' foster-sister Elizabeth Elliott. It had been the greatest happiness that could befall her, she wrote at the Restoration, 'to suck the same breast with so great a monarch'; she therefore petitioned the monarch for some financial recognition of the fact.[16]

The nursery of King Charles and Queen Henrietta Maria, once established, was soon filled with healthy and charming children. For all her fragility Henrietta Maria proved a most efficient child-bearer, after her first bad experience. With speed and love that nursery made for ever famous by Van Dyck was created. The Queen bore a total of nine children in fourteen years, of whom six survived infancy, a gratifyingly high proportion by the standards of the time, when even petted royalty would consider themselves lucky to provide so many healthy heirs.

Mary, the Princess Royal, the ringleted girl with rosebud mouth and slightly droopy, chubby cheeks, who stands at the fore of the most famous Van Dyck picture, was born in November 1631. James Duke of York followed in October 1633, and Elizabeth, Van Dyck's grave-eyed child, on the Feast of the Holy Innocents in 1635. At the time the coincidence puzzled the local panegyrists: as her *Carmen Natalitum*, produced by Corpus Christi College, Cambridge, put it, 'Hast thou dared to be born on the day when infancy was a crime?'[17] Later, in view of her early death, commentators found it sadly appropriate. Henry Duke of Gloucester was born in 1639, and Henriette-Anne in 1644.

These were the survivors. But of course the royal nursery was not without its tragedies. A baby Katharine died at birth. Princess Anne, Van Dyck's delicious infant, stretching out one fat arm to the world, died a little later of consumption. Bishop Fuller described her affecting death-bed, and how he said a short prayer over the child: '"Lighten mine eyes, O Lord, lest I sleep the sleep of death." ... This done the little lamb gave up the ghost.'[18]

For Charles it was a loving childhood. Like many children throughout history down to our own day, he formed an attachment to an odd toy 'without which in his arms he would never go abroad or lie in his bed'.[19] In his case the object was a piece of wood, which led courtiers to predict either that blockheads would one day be his favourites or else that he would rule with the club – wrongly in both cases. Like many children of his own time, the Prince was also obliged to wear uncomfortable iron supports for his legs until one of his nurses braved the King's wrath and hid them. For all this, by the grim standards of childhood of the time, Charles enjoyed a great deal of uncritical affection.

He was also expected to demonstrate love and care to others. As one of the speakers in Herrick's 'Pastoral' upon his birth had it:

> And I a sheep-hook will bestow,
> To have his little Kingship know,
> As he is Prince, he's Shepherd too.

Henrietta Maria, with the awakening of her deep protective feeling for her husband, had noticed the damage done by his stiff manner, to which a speech impediment contributed. Courtiers and populace alike were unnecessarily antagonized. She wanted her eldest son 'to be bred to wonderful civility' in contrast. The little Prince, by nature affectionate and affable, found the lesson an easy one to learn. The result, wrote Bishop Burnet with his usual carping tone where Charles was concerned, was that the adult man was 'civil rather to an excess'; there was 'a softness and a gentleness in him, both in his air and his expression'; in this he outdid even his brother James, in whom the same lesson had been inculcated.[20]

But it is difficult to see that in this case Burnet's disapproval was justified. For the rest of his life Charles displayed the radiant civility of a happy nature to all comers, in marked contrast to the dreadful public awkwardness of his father, whose natural charm was only seen in his immediate family circle. The quality enabled him to endure the indignities of his exile, on the one hand, and on the other hand in better days to transform himself into that popular monarch summed up by Evelyn as 'debonair and easy of access ... down to the spaniels who dwelt in his bedchamber'. Elizabeth of Bohemia summed it up: 'Though he be my nephew, I must say this truth of him, that he is extremely civil. . .'[21]

That was one keynote of his upbringing. The other, unquestionably if at first sight surprisingly, was the high moral tone of the royal family as a whole. In this respect the nurseries merely echoed the prevailing attitudes at court. Unlike almost any other seventeenth-century monarch, King Charles I was absolutely faithful to his wife, and the Queen equally devoted. Any court is essentially a chameleon, taking its colour from its principal figure: King Charles I was extravagant, building up an incomparable art collection which unfortunately he could ill afford, but he was not wanton.

In short, Charles in youth was surrounded with security: he was granted the supreme blessing of a happy childhood.

By the mid-1630s Queen Henrietta Maria had already sufficient anxious reason to hope that the son would not repeat the character of the father she loved so much. Beneath the level of official rejoicing, there had been certain grumblings at the birth of Charles. If there was one bad fairy at his christening it was a Puritan sprite. Puritans resented the fact that the Catholic Queen had proved herself fertile: hopes had been pinned on the accession of one of Elizabeth of Bohemia's enormous brood of children. As her brother's heir before the birth of Charles, Elizabeth was in those days regarded as a Puritan sympathizer, her children as Protestant white hopes.

As the children moved on their cheerful round, winters at St James's Palace, happy summers at any one of a number of royal palaces such as Greenwich, Hampton Court and Oatlands, their father was playing out his part in a very different kind of drama. It is difficult to date precisely that moment at which the King's troubles began in earnest. His first great Parliamentary defeat, ending in the acceptance of the Petition of Right, had taken place in June 1628, two years before Charles' birth. In August the King suffered a personal as well as a political blow when his favourite, the Duke of Buckingham – already under pressure from Parliament – was assassinated. Thus Charles had been born into a time of tranquillity only if, in the words of the intelligent Puritan sympathizer Lucy Hutchinson, 'that quietness may be call'd peace, which was rather like the calm and smooth surface of the sea, whose dark womb is already impregnated of a horrid tempest'.[22]

The King had accepted the Petition of Right with reluctance and only because the acute financial demands of his foreign policy left him no choice but to conciliate Parliament. He was obliged to make certain concessions concerning arbitrary arrests and taxation in order to continue to operate as he wished in the foreign sphere. But at the same time he was extremely careful to make it clear that his personal prerogative, that vexed but vital attribute of a British monarch, had been left intact.

The exact nature of the royal prerogative, which like a phoenix rose again in the reign of his son from the ashes of the Commonwealth, was a subject of running debate throughout the seventeenth century. But in 1628 no-one denied its actual existence. In practice the King was generally allowed the sole right to direct foreign policy. More vaguely, he claimed to be able to wield certain special powers, beyond those possessed by King and Parliament in concert – but here, with the theory of it all, argument began, and would not end with his death, nor with the death of his eldest son. It was more to the point, once again speaking practically, that the King had the power to prorogue or to dissolve Parliament without the agreement of the Commons. Prorogation was a form of suspension and did not necessitate a fresh election before Parliament met again. Dissolution on the other hand implied an election and with it the possibility of a differently constituted House of Commons. But neither prorogation nor dissolution bound the King to recall Parliament within a specified period of time.

In the spring of 1629 King Charles I dissolved Parliament after a series of unruly scenes and, as he saw it, 'seditious' speeches from the MPs calling attention to such financial abuses as the levying of tunnage and poundage. Parliament did not sit again until 1640. In the meantime the King governed, or attempted to do so, by use of his prerogative powers without the assent of the Commons. Charles was therefore born into the second year of what was afterwards termed the Eleven Years' Tyranny.

With Parliament in abeyance, there was still no closed season for religious differences. The early 1630s were a time of constant abuse and counter-abuse in this respect. The Puritans can be roughly divided into the Independents (such as Oliver Cromwell), who believed in the primacy of conscience and a general tolerance of sects, and the Presbyterians (including many leading Scottish nobles); the latter believed, as the Greek root of their name indicates, in the authority of the elders, and thus the need for conformity. Both factions, while disagreeing with each other fiercely on matters of church organization, condemned any excrescences on the plain surface of the Church of England. The Puritan opposition in the House of Commons – and Lords – had included Independents as well as Presbyterians.

Their protests arose, as so many protests do, out of fear. Their particular fear was 'Popery' or 'Papistry', but since Roman Catholicism was in fact proscribed by the law in England, and the numbers of Catholics were diminishing, their precise target was the right wing of the English Church. The Puritan argument suggested that those guilty of High Church or 'Arminian' practices (named after a Dutch theologian) might turn into Catholics at any moment. The sulphurous path leading to the Roman Church was, in the opinion of Puritans, thoroughly adorned with such 'Arminian' trappings as surplices, altar rails, crucifixes and statues. These were to the Puritans horrifying and idolatrous symbols; even the celebration of Christmas was denounced as being a piece of Popish flummery.

It was in this sense that the Catholicism of Henrietta Maria, although strictly supervised by her husband, was always a potential source of weakness to the Crown. The Queen's Chapel in St James's, newly designed by Inigo Jones, was granted to her: here, angry subjects were aware, the Mass was being said daily. When William Prynne, the Puritan demonstrator, wrote about Henrietta Maria's frizzled locks, her odious dancing and so forth (small crimes to us if at all) he knew himself to be on safe ground with a great many of his contemporaries – because the Queen was a Catholic

The fabric of religious dispute was shot through with political colours even before the King dissolved Parliament in 1629; political and religious issues remained interwoven throughout the so-called Eleven Years' Tyranny. For example it was relevant that those Anglicans who supported the secular authority of the bishops, in Parliament tended to be more favourable to the King. This in turn persuaded the King that Puritanism was to be identified with attacks upon the monarchy as well as upon the Church.

In Scotland the ritual of the English Church had always been dourly regarded. At least old King James had known, none better, how to deal with that country, in which he had not only been born and brought up but also spent most of his adult life. King Charles I had been born there, but that was all. Neither by upbringing nor by temperament was he able to understand the Scottish nation, at once so arrogant and so sincere. When little Charles was three years old, his father paid a disastrous visit to Scotland. In the course of it he managed to remind the Scots by a series of tactless gestures, including an elaborate coronation ceremony, of exactly those religious observances which most disgusted them. The imposition of a new prayer book in 1637 was but a further proof of the King's total lack of comprehension of the very nature of his Scottish subjects.

The year 1637, by which, according to the Jesuit tradition, the young Charles' character had been formed for ever, was in other ways a year of destiny for Great Britain. In England, in the heart of the quiet Buckinghamshire countryside, John Hampden refused to pay that tax known as ship-money, on the grounds that the King had no right to levy taxes on his subjects at will: ship-money was normally levied on the coastal counties and no extra peril justified the extension. The King took the line that he was the best judge of any extra peril, and the law narrowly upheld him. In the same year William Prynne, along with two others, was mutilated and left in the stocks, for the crime of seditious libel. Early in the next year the Scots formed the greater National Covenant, a direct and stark answer to the imposition of the hateful new Prayer Book. Those who took its Oath pledged their lives to resist the recent innovations in the Church, which they declared to be contrary to the Word of God – and to the spirit of the Reformation. They vowed to defend 'the true religion' of Scotland. It was a document which in one form or another (for it was extended five years later) would haunt the King's son for the next twenty years.

The year 1637 was also that in which Van Dyck painted all five of the surviving royal children at the behest of their father –

that celebrated picture which focuses on the solid head of an enormous mastiff. After haggling over the payment and reducing it from £200 to £100, the King hung the portrait above the table in his Breakfast Chamber at Whitehall.

Like many weak but upright men, the King had pronounced views on everything, not only the nature of the Scottish Prayer Book, but also how his children should be painted. Even on canvas, they were not to be swaddled or over-protected. Two years earlier Van Dyck had irritated him by painting Charles in infant 'coats'. The picture was intended by Henrietta Maria for her sister the Duchess of Savoy, but it had taken some time to complete because one of the subjects, Mary, would never sit still for long enough. Normally boys at this period were put into jackets, lace collars and breeches at about five: the 'breeching' was made a little ceremony by the formal attendance of the tailor to measure his new client, and a miniature sword was generally thrown in, to the delight of the recipient. At the King's behest, Charles was painted in grown-up clothes, in contrast to his younger brother James; the picture probably ended up being hung by Henrietta Maria at Somerset House.[23]

In the spring of 1638, as the Scottish horizons grew dark with the clouds of approaching war, the young Charles was made a Knight of the Garter and Prince of Wales. The medal struck for the occasion – presciently – showed 'the Royal Oak' under a Prince's Coronet. He was also granted his own household, according to the serene routine of the time. Charles had made his first public appearance at the age of six in one of Inigo Jones' airy fantastic masques, *The King and Queen's Entertainment*. Now he was established with both a governor, the Earl of Newcastle, and a tutor, Dr Brian Duppa.

Both choices were indicative of the King's growing desire to bind to him men of proven loyalty in a time of mounting crisis. Newcastle, now in his forties, was being rewarded for his championship over a long period, a championship which was not entirely disinterested. As Clarendon put it, he 'loved monarchy, as it was the foundation and support of his own greatness'. That apart, Newcastle was an obvious choice, because he combined a love of sport (he was an expert horseman and authority on equitation) with a passion for the arts. Newcastle was 'active and full of courage': he particularly enjoyed pastimes such as fencing and dancing, while being at the same time 'amorous of poetry and music'.[24] One recognizes in this determination to enjoy the world in all its appealing aspects a pattern which his royal pupil would also display.

In any case, there need be no doubts as to the kind of advice which Newcastle pressed on the Prince by precept and example, since he took care to write it down.[25] His most famous piece of advice was to avoid being too devout, since one can be a good man and a bad king. Like another gubernatorial tip he gave Charles, 'Above all be civil to women', it cannot have had an unwelcome sound to his pupil's ears.

Dr Duppa had the capacity to exercise a very different kind of influence. At fifty he was a distinguished divine, a protégé of Laud, through whose patronage he had recently become Bishop of Chichester. By nature he was both learned and devout, but, as Newcastle bore witness, Duppa took care to 'hide the scholar in him' in order not to appear a tiresome pedant to Charles. The result was that Charles was undoubtedly fond of him – years later, as the newly restored King, he rushed to his old tutor's death-bed at Richmond and knelt to ask for his blessing. Nevertheless, the values which Charles carried into his adult life were those of Newcastle, not Duppa.

The tutor who succeeded Duppa, John Earle, later also Bishop of Salisbury, scored more success with the Prince by his unglossed mixture of piety and charity. Earle later went into exile with his pupil. Perhaps the charm of Earle's manner – his light, 'facetious' conversation – won the Prince's heart; more likely it was his lack of hypocrisy. As Bishop Burnet observed, Charles was ever on the look-out for pretence of this kind. At any rate, at the Restoration Earle was duly rewarded along with those others to whom Charles felt properly grateful.

It was important for Charles' future that his little world also included the orphaned Duke of Buckingham and his brother Lord Francis Villiers (killed in the Civil War). Indeed, it is impossible to understand the extraordinarily deep bond which existed between Charles and Buckingham in later years – despite the most reckless behaviour on Buckingham's part – unless one remembers this shared childhood. Buckingham shared all the memories of Charles' halcyon past, since after the assassination of his father he was taken with Francis Villiers into the royal household. The King made the gesture not only out of loyalty to his dead friend, but also because the boys' mother was a Catholic, and as such considered unsuitable to have guardianship of such important infants. So the two were 'bred up' by the King with his own children. For Charles to reject Buckingham would in a sense have been to abandon his own happiest memories.

Charles was a spirited and cheerful child. He was also a normal boy, as Henrietta Maria's first letter to 'her dear sone the Prince' reveals: 'Charles, I am sore that I must begin my first letter with chiding you, because I hear that you will not take physick, I hope it was only for this day and that tomorrow you will do it....' She threatened to tell Lord Newcastle.[26] Whether or not the threat worked, Charles' own first known letter is also on the vexed subject of 'physick'. To Lord Newcastle he wrote, at the age of nine, 'My Lord, I would not have you take too much physick, for it doth always make me worse and I think it will do the like with you...."[27]

In the Van Dyck portrait, Charles' steady gaze is central to the picture. He looks out, his cheeks still childishly round, the sensual mouth slightly more set, his hair dark and long, his eyes dark and enigmatic. It is a study of confidence. The accidents of childhood, a broken arm, a fever, jaundice, were surely the worst that could befall him. The Prince's world must have seemed as steady as the head of the dog on which he rests his hand.

It was not so, however. By the summer of 1639 his father the King was taking the high road to Scotland, armed on this occasion not with the Prayer Book but with the sword. The confrontation which ensued was subsequently known as 'the First Bishops' War', the specific cause of its outbreak being the resentment felt by the Scottish Presbyterians towards the Bishops' new Prayer Book. The Bishops' position was considered to be quite incompatible with the system of Presbyterian church government envisaged by the National Covenant. Nevertheless, beneath the open assault on the Bishops was concealed, at any rate in the opinion of Charles I, a covert attack on the royal authority. It was a situation covered by his father's famous dictum: 'No Bishop, no King'. So the drama commenced.

The King himself once correctly predicted his own eventual fate, when he took the so-called *Sortes Virgilianae* in a library at Oxford, at the request of Lord Falkland; this was a method of dipping at random into a book and discovering a text. The King hit upon Dido's fearful imprecation against Aeneas, the prophecy that he would be 'torn from his subjects' and his son's embrace' and 'fall untimely by some hostile hand'.[28] It would have been an advanced seer who was able in 1639 to visualize just how that might come about. Nevertheless, by the age of nine Charles' own life was permanently altered.

'The Prince ... hastens apace out of his childhood', wrote Duppa in September, 'and is likely to be a man betimes, and an excellent man if my presage deceive me not, and flattery and humoring him, the bane of Princes, do not spoil him.'[29] It was, however, not flattery which now threatened the Prince of Wales. Heaven had been liberal at his birth. But it would be over twenty years before Heaven showed itself liberal again.

CHAPTER TWO

'I Fear Them Not!'

'Seeing the sudden and quick march of the enemy towards you ... your Highness was pleased to tell me, you feared them not, and drawing a pistol ... resolved to charge them.'

Sir John Hinton, *Memoires*

As the early years of Charles' life had been golden, so the next were to be tarnished. A secure childhood gave way to a youth marked by a series of traumatic incidents.

Increasingly the King took his eldest son into his own care and company, and tried to associate him with his own decisions. This was partly the natural move of the time to take aristocratic boys out of female-dominated society. There was nothing particularly upsetting about that. But in Charles' case the situation was aggravated by the need to prove to the world at large that the Prince of Wales was in no way over-influenced by the Roman Catholic Queen.

Charles was also allowed – carefully supervised – his own little sorties. There was, for example, a visit to Cambridge in March 1641, a fairly typical royal visit not only by the standards of the time but also by our own, except for the youth of the royal visitor. At Peterhouse, Charles, accompanied by Buckingham, Francis Villiers and another high-born orphan, the Duke of Richmond, all chaperoned by Dr Duppa, received an honorary Master of Arts degree from the Vice-Chancellor. He also received two pairs of embroidered gloves from the same source and from the Provost of King's a Bible. So far so good. But in King's Chapel the Prince was considered to have failed by omitting to say his prayers into his hat according to the undergraduate custom. Dinner at Trinity Hall, however, passed without incident, and afterwards Charles watched two plays, including Abraham Cowley's *The Guardian*, enhanced by a Prologue addressed to him personally.

Finally he was allowed to join his father at Newmarket.

On the way back there was another stop at Cambridge, with the pleasant sound of the undergraduates of Trinity shouting 'Vivat Rex!' to greet his father's ears – although Cambridge was a town reputedly much permeated by Puritanism. Since the previous year, it had been represented in Parliament by Oliver Cromwell, a man already gaining notoriety for his views on the need to restrain monarchical authority in some way. In the Civil War itself, as the University towns polarized, it was to be Oxford which declared for the King, Cambridge becoming a Parliamentarian stronghold. But the visit began and ended pleasantly from Charles' point of view, since his father presented him with some sweetmeats for the return journey.

The first clearly traumatic incident occurred when Charles was ten years old. It concerned the trial of the King's servant Strafford. As other families in their intimate hearts are haunted by the early bankruptcy of the breadwinner, the abandonment by one beloved parent, or some other harsh, unassimilable tragedy, so this royal family of Stuart was to be haunted by the death of Strafford. Need he have died? Could he have been saved? Was there any point, ultimately, in the cruel sacrifice?

It is possible to discern in Charles himself a real Strafford complex, in modern phraseology. His father did much to augment it in the last years of his life, as the King became increasingly tormented by the memory of the (useless) betrayal. By August 1646 he was impressing on his son the 'negative direction which is never to abandon the protection of your friends under any pretension whatsoever'. (In the original draft of the letter, the King was even more explicit: 'Never to give way to the punishment of any for their faithful service to the Crown, upon whatever pretence, or for whatsoever cause.'[1]) But Charles' own recollections of Strafford, as well as his father's remorse, must have played their part.

The facts were as follows. Thomas Wentworth, later Earl of Strafford, had been sent to Ireland as Lord Deputy in 1633, to try and introduce some semblance of order into those Augean Stables. To a certain extent this man of 'deep policy, stern resolution and ambitious zeal to keep up the glory of his own greatness', as Lucy Hutchinson called him, had been successful.[2] To Charles he was more simply a benevolent figure who despatched him hawks from his mews in the name of his own son Will. But to the King, the memory remained of a tough statesman, one who had shown himself capable in the past of welding together a vociferous House of Commons and putting himself, in so far as anyone could in this age before official ministerial appointments and recognized political parties, at the head of a coherent group.

The military proceedings of 1639 against the Scots had ended in a stalemate, with both sides, King and Covenanters, agreeing to disband their forces, and neither in fact doing so. Already, in this critical situation, Strafford, who had returned from Ireland at the King's request, was moving into the position of the King's chief counsellor. When the King, hobbled by lack of money and lack of political support against the Scots, finally called Parliament in the spring of 1640, it was Strafford who advised him to do so. And when the King dissolved this assembly again in May – hence its historical name of the Short Parliament – it was with the aid of Strafford's practical management.

A further military action in the summer of 1640 resulted in the humiliation of the English forces by the Scots at Newburn, near Newcastle. None of this helped the King's cause against his English Parliamentary opponents: the Newburn rout in particular occurred just as the King, at York, was trying to avoid calling another English Parliament. It was easy for the Parliamentary opposition* to see that they had more in common with the so-called Scottish enemies than with the Crown.

* Political nomenclature is a perpetual headache in this period, when words such as 'opposition', 'party' and 'minister' did not bear the easily identifiable meanings they have since acquired. For example, since it was officially treason to oppose the King, there could be no official opposition as there is today. Nevertheless, it is impossible to avoid the language of one's own time altogether.

On 3 November that body to be known as the Long Parliament met for the first time. The intention of the opposition under the great Parliamentary leader John Pym was to demand the resolution of their manifold grievances against the Crown. One of the first of these grievances was embodied in the person of 'Black Tom Tyrant', as Strafford was bitterly designated. It was the Irish association which was fatal. The Irish troops which Strafford was discovered to be offering the King as aid against the Scots became in the minds of the excitable Commons a fearful force of Papist invaders. Strafford was to be the scapegoat of the whole corpus of the King's unsatisfactory policies.

There were various weapons at Parliament's command. Foremost amongst these was impeachment. This involved the bringing of charges against a particular person for crimes against the State: the 'articles of impeachment' could be prepared by either House, although Strafford, because he was a peer, had to be impeached at the bar of the House of Lords. Then there was the possibility of introducing an Act of Attainder against an individual, for high treason. The penalty for high treason was death, as well as the forfeiture of titles and offices. Like any other measure passed by Parliament, an Act of Attainder needed the assent of both houses before it became law – and of course the assent of the King himself.

Strafford was duly impeached at the instance of the House of Commons and in March 1641 there began his trial following that impeachment. Taking place in Westminster Hall, it would seem afterwards like a kind of awful dress rehearsal for the ordeal of the King, set on the same stage eight years later. Charles attended the seven weeks of proceedings daily. By virtue of his title as Prince of Wales, he sat to the right of his father's throne, wearing the full robes of his rank. The throne itself was left empty. The King did attend, but in order to remain incognito – in theory, if not in practice – stationed himself in a box; he was accompanied at times by the Queen, his brother-in-law the Elector Palatine, and his daughter Mary. For the time being all eyes were focused not on the master but on the servant: Strafford was positioned on a raised platform amidst the spectators. Proud of his service, confident in his own integrity, Strafford from time to time exchanged smiles across the crowded room with the King.

His confidence was misplaced. It was true that the trial itself failed, but immediately afterwards the old lion of Parliament, John Pym, with his young lions at his heels, called for an Act of Attainder. The House of Commons voted it through. All Strafford's 'sinewy' arguments that he had not committed treason were in vain.

The King too felt a misplaced confidence that he could save his servant. Strafford wrote a formal release to his master, offering to have his own life sacrificed 'towards that blessed agreement which God, I trust, shall for ever establish betwixt you and your subjects. ... Besides, to a willing man there is no injury done.' The King did not think it would come to that.[3]

He reckoned without that dread new European phenomenon, a politically activated mob. Rumour was in the hands of the people, Shakespeare's pipe:

> Of so easy and so plain a stop
> That the blunt monster with uncounted heads,
> The still-discordant wavering multitude, can play upon it.

This maddened mob was thronging round the palace of Whitehall, even breaking into its outer chambers.

It was true that there were rumours, rumours everywhere. As the people could be heard howling for the blood of the Catholic Queen, her cause was further damaged by the presence of another Catholic Queen, her own mother, under her roof: Marie de Medici had taken refuge in England from the various troubles of France a few years earlier. Certainly the wavering multitude had many tuneful rumours at their disposal: these included the story that a French (Catholic) army had landed at Portsmouth, inspired by Henrietta Maria, and that an Irish (Catholic) army had been ordered by Strafford to come to the King's assistance.

The King hesitated. On 2 May he married off Charles' nine-year-old sister Mary to the fifteen-year-old Prince of Orange, son of the Stadtholder of the Netherlands. It was hoped that Parliament, like a hungry dog smelling meat, would be appeased by the somewhat small bone of this Protestant but otherwise unremarkable match.* Parliament was not appeased. By 10 May the King could hesitate no longer. The royal assent to Strafford's execution was given.

The next day he decided to send Charles down to the House of Lords with a desperate yet somehow embarrassed message. Could not Strafford 'fulfil the natural course of his life in a close imprisonment'? If this could be done without 'the discontentment of my people' it would be 'an unspeakable contentment' to the King. But of course if nothing less than Strafford's life would satisfy this same people, then the King must say 'Fiat Justitia'. Even the postscript after the King's signature had a rather shabby sound to it: 'and if Strafford must die, it were charity to reprieve him until Saturday'.[4] Armed with this paper, the nine-year-old Prince of Wales did not succeed in convincing Parliament to stay its hand.

Strafford was executed the next day.

As Laud (himself imprisoned and subsequently executed) observed, Strafford was dead with 'more honour than any of them will gain which hunted after his life'. In particular, he was dead with more honour than his royal master was alive. Charles, the witness to all this, including those popular threats of harm to his mother which had probably precipitated his father's assent, was growing up with a vengeance.

About the time of Strafford's execution, Charles' first governor, Newcastle, resigned his charge. The new incumbent, the Marquess of Hertford, was an odd hangover of royal history. Twenty-five years earlier he had married in secret James I's cousin Arbella Stuart. The King was furious when he found out, suspecting Hertford of aiming at the succession. The marriage had been quashed, the couple imprisoned. That period of Hertford's past was long forgotten, but his very age made him an ineffective governor, compared to Newcastle. At the same time the House of Commons was becoming increasingly

* It was, nonetheless, a match of vast consequence for the future of the House of Stuart, since from the marriage issued a son, half Orange and half Stuart – the future William III.

aggressive on the subject of the Prince of Wales: the Puritan element questioned whether Charles should not be surrounded by more suitable attendants than those designated by his father and, above all, by his mother. It was the measure of the importance given to the role that John Hampden himself was said to desire the post of the Prince's governor, in order to instruct him in 'principles suitable as to what should be established as laws'.[5] As a counterpoint, the Scots from across the border were vociferous in their claim that the Prince, like his father, should spend more time in Scotland.

If ten years before it had been thought important that the very rockers of Charles' cradle should be Protestants, how much more vital was the religion of his tutors! When the King planned a new expedition – of negotiation and discussion – to Scotland in the summer of 1641, certain members of the House of Commons, including Oliver Cromwell, proposed that Hertford alone was inadequate to escort the Prince of Wales. He should be stiffened by two good Puritan lords in the shape of Lords Bedford, and Saye and Sele. Charles did not in fact accompany his father, but the controversy raged on. Two sets of proposals put by Parliament to the King, the Ten Propositions of June 1641 and the Nineteen Propositions a year later, made specific suggestions for the upbringing of Charles and the rest of the young royal family.

In October 1641 there were squabbles with the Commons about Charles' education: one faction demanded that only 'safe' people (religiously safe, not Popish) should be allowed near him. The arguments were still going on in January 1642. That was the month in which the King, failing in his attempt to arrest five Members of the Commons, was humiliatingly rebuffed by the Speaker of the House himself. So finally he left the capital.

The following six months of the year were spent by both sides, King and Parliament, in preparations for a war which no-one thought particularly desirable, but almost everyone now thought was inevitable. The King reacted to the Commons' threats concerning his son by keeping Charles more closely with him, rather than less. In any case, the role of the father was made heavier by the fact that Henrietta Maria left for the

Continent in February to try and raise money for arms by selling her jewels. There were happy periods of respite: another jaunt to Cambridge and a visit to the Ferrars family at nearby Little Gidding, where Charles ate apple pie and cheese in the pantry and they all played cards. But in general life was more serious, as the King prepared earnestly if sadly for the coming contest. A letter from Charles to his sister Mary in Holland, written in March from Royston, refers to the King as 'very much disconsolate and troubled, partly for my royal mother's and your absence, and partly for the disturbances of the kingdom'. (Mary had not travelled abroad at the time of her marriage, but did so a year later with Henrietta Maria.) It is a laborious composition, no doubt written under duress – what eleven-year-old boy ever wrote voluntarily to his younger sister? Only in the latter half does a hint of Charles' own cheerful temperament creep in: 'Dear sister, we are as much as we may merry, and more than we would sad, in respect we cannot alter the present distempers of these troublesome times.'[6]

Charles remained at his father's side for the next three years.

Thus the origins of the intense love which the son felt for the father, the reverence which Charles II would feel for the memory of Charles I, were to be found in this period of the King's greatest tribulation. The young Charles, in common with the rest of the Royalists, cannot have failed to admire his father for his dignity, the admirable spiritual quality which enabled the King to accept alterations in his personal circumstances with equanimity. At the same time Charles, like any other son, also had an opportunity to judge his father more harshly concerning his purely tactical behaviour. The fatal mixture of weakness and strength, in exactly the wrong proportions, was also observed first hand by Charles. So too was the use of deceit, justified by the need to preserve his royal rights.

Charles and his brother James were both at their father's side on that ominous day, 22 August 1642, when he raised the standard of war at Nottingham Castle. The vast royal banner loomed above their heads, so heavy that it needed twenty men to grapple with it – and incidentally so unstable that it had blown down that evening. The King's entourage included their Palatine cousin, the twenty-two-year-old Prince Rupert, a spirited young fellow with theories about warfare which would shortly be tested. The herald had difficulty in making out the exact text of the declaration of war, because the King had altered it by hand at the last moment; his speech was hard to follow. The confusion which ensued was matched by the uncertainty which many in England, Scotland and Ireland felt about the precise issues involved. Nevertheless, to the young Princes at least the issues probably seemed as simple as Clarendon would later describe them: 'The whole business of the matter was whether the King was above Parliament, or Parliament in ruling, above the King.'

Already Charles was enjoying the privileges ensured to him by his ancient chivalric title of Prince of Wales, a title which recalled the martial days of the Black Prince. The characteristic plumes, which had been assumed by the Black Prince after Crécy, were now to be the emblem of a troop of lifeguards made up of northern noblemen and gentlemen, under the nominal command of a twelve-year-old boy.

In July at York with his father, Charles was described as putting on a brave show, at the head of a fine company. On the field itself he was presented with a rich tent and a 'very goodly white horse, trapped most richly to the ground with velvet all studded with burning waves of gold'. Charles then put on a 'very curious gilt armour', and dashingly leapt onto the back of his new steed, to the general cheers of the onlookers. Later he was painted by William Dobson in those same trappings.*

The whole scene recalled the days of ritual chivalry. To many present the hopeful young Charles must have appeared as Hotspur once, 'his cuisses on his thighs, gallantly armed', vaulting with ease into his seat like feathered Mercury:

* At the sale of Charles I's belongings, this armour was purchased by Edward Annesley, Keeper of the Stores at the Tower of London: it is still to be seen there today. There are also two sets of small bronze cannons, bearing his mark as Prince of Wales; these were made pre-war.[7]

As if an angel dropp'd down from the clouds
To turn and wing a fiery Pegasus...

At Edgehill in the following October, the reality of Charles' first battle was different. For one thing, his own position was a good deal less prominent than that of the noble Hotspur. At this, the opening contest of the Civil War, Charles found himself treated once more as a child in tutelage. That was bad enough, with Charles' own regiment allowed the privilege of charging in the front line. But the efforts to protect his royal person, aggravating as they were, were also inadequate. With his brother, Charles had at least one and probably two narrow escapes in the course of the day, which rendered the Battle of Edgehill yet another scarring experience.

On the morning of the battle the two boys were left in the charge of Dr William Harvey, the famous physician, and told in effect to keep out of mischief. Gradually the traditional *ennui* of war became too much for Dr Harvey, who surreptitiously took a book out of his pocket. He was only restored to a sense of his surroundings by the impact of a cannon ball actually grazing the ground beside him. Then and only then did Dr Harvey hastily move his royal charges away to safety.

The evening's well-known incident is recounted in various different versions, but although the details vary, there is general agreement that the Prince of Wales and the Duke of York came within an ace of being captured.[8] Somehow, either with Sir Edward Hyde or Sir John Hinton (later Charles' own physician), the Princes found themselves cut off in a field, within a 'musket-shot' of the enemy. For a while they took refuge in a barn, which was being used as a field hospital for the Royalist wounded. Then, in the fading autumn light, a body of Parliamentary horse was seen riding down on them from the left. Fooled by the direction – because they did not understand how the various regiments had become rearranged in the course of the battle – the little royal party moved towards this body as though to saviours.

Suddenly the Parliamentarians were recognized for what they were. Hinton begged the Prince of Wales to retreat, at first humbly, at last 'somewhat rudely'. But 'I fear them not!' shouted Charles, whipping his pistol out of his holster and flourishing it hopefully in the faces of the enemy. He was resolved to charge. Suddenly one Parliamentary trooper broke ranks and rode towards them. Fortunately at this dramatic moment the Prince was rescued from the consequences of his own optimism, and of his aides' folly, by the appearance of a Royalist on a good mount; he proceeded to pole-axe the trooper.

James remembered the experience all his life (it features in his memoirs). Charles remembered it no less. Sir John Hinton, writing up his own account of it years later, presented it to King Charles II for his approval.[9]

For all this drama, and the palpable excitement of a struggle in which opponents were pitting themselves against each other for the first time, Edgehill was generally regarded as a draw, in modern terms. Or rather, both sides gingerly claimed victory. It was not immediately clear who had won what in the course of the Civil War: Marston Moor, for example, a name familiar to us as the first of the great Cromwellian victories based on superior cavalry tactics, was for an instant claimed as a Royalist triumph. This was partly due to the difficulty of communications on the battlefield itself – the Marston Moor report was founded on the success of a Royalist charge on one wing, while defeat lurked on the other – and partly to the general slowness and confusion of communications within the British Isles. But Edgehill, at least, was correctly assessed as indecisive.

Both sides recoiled to regroup their existing forces and recruit the vital new men needed for a more clinching outcome to their hostilities. The King headed with his sons for Oxford.

It was sometime after Edgehill that the ten-year-old Duke of York suddenly asked his father:

'When shall we go home?'

'We have no home,' replied the King.

It was a sad statement, one of those pronouncements which linger in the minds of children.[10]

In fact, it was not entirely true. There was the great Royalist city of Oxford awaiting them. The loyalty of Oxford was as carefully preserved as that of Cambridge was fractured. The famous dreaming spires of the University dreamt, if anything, of a monarchical victory. The King was quickly able to set up a Parliament of his own. Its acts would subsequently be castigated as illegal by that other, so-called true Parliament of Westminster. Nevertheless, at the time there were many Royalists who considered the Oxford Parliament, enjoying the King's backing, as the valid assembly.

Charles remained at his father's side during his various wartime peregrinations until a violent attack of measles laid him low. The disease also went to his eyes: he suffered from conjunctivitis for some time afterwards. But he had recovered sufficiently to attend the Battle of Cropredy Bridge in June 1644. After this the King learnt of the battle at Marston Moor in distant Yorkshire, now correctly assessed as a Parliamentary victory. Charles was also present at the second Battle of Newbury in October. Newbury was one of the few engagements of the Civil War in which Cromwell took part that did not result in an outstanding victory for Parliament. The reason was the divided Parliamentary command and the growing internal struggle between the political and military arms of the party – a struggle which would virtually incapacitate Parliament as a striking force for several months until the formation of the New Model Army the following spring. At the time the action was botched, and the King allowed to escape back to Oxford. Here he resided, more or less secure, for over a year.

In recognition of his growing stature, the Prince of Wales was now given his own Council of advisers. This Council included Sir Edward Hyde, Sir Arthur Capel (created Lord Capel), Lord Hopton and a selection of Royalists of proven loyalty or military expertise. Charles' new governor, the Earl of Berkshire, was probably also included. Berkshire was the least successful of Charles' three bear-leaders, but since Hertford had been called away to the West Country, where it was hoped that his wide lands would enable him to organize a substantial contribution to the royal armies, some substitute had to be found.

Berkshire was middle-aged and fussy. In any case, Charles was getting too old for governors. Kicking his heels in Oxford, he got into trouble with Berkshire for laughing during a sermon in St Mary's Church. The presence of a row of ladies sitting opposite him was not without significance. It would be a sad boy of fourteen who never laughed at a sermon, particularly with an appreciative audience: however, that was not the line that Berkshire took. He was seen to hit his young Prince on the head with his staff.

In appearance too the Prince of Wales was altering, developing. The miniature of Charles at thirteen by the court painter David Des Granges (who later accompanied him into exile) shows a face in which the heavy sensuality of the adult is beginning to mark the softness of the boy. In Dobson's martial portrait, the black heavy-lidded eyes are proud and the rounded cheeks characteristic of all the Stuart children are beginning to thin out. The chin is firm.

The other royal children were not faring so well. Mary, the child bride, was not happy in her adopted country. Elizabeth, because she was delicate, and Henry, because he was a baby, remained in the royal nurseries in London. Here the little captives – as they quickly became, cut off from both father and mother – suffered at first from the general lack of funds. At times there was hardly enough to eat. Later they were encumbered with alien Presbyterian attendants at the orders of Parliament.

Even marking time in Oxford, Charles, the eldest brother, was infinitely luckier. Now his freedom was to be extended. As the war news reaching Oxford worsened, the King began to feel that the moment to separate himself physically from his heir had arrived. We have Clarendon's authority that the King's concern at this point was to do with his own possible imprisonment, not his death. The King was convinced that his existence was essential to the continuance of Parliamentary government. But they might constrain him. Therefore it was important to have his heir outside their control: 'While his son was at liberty they would not dare to do him harm.'

Besides, an experience of responsibility 'out of his [the King's] own sight' would 'unboy' Charles.[11] And there was another advantage in using the Prince of Wales as a puppet commander in certain tricky situations where the Royalists were arguing with each other over the precise details of their authority. It was difficult to be jealous of the command of a titular overlord who was the King's son.

Already Charles had taken part in one of his father's Councils. Early in 1645 he was made nominal General of the Western Association – a conglomerate of the four most western counties. Here the royal cause was in unnecessary disarray due to internal disputes. Even more grandly, the Prince of Wales was made nominal Generalissimo of all the King's forces in England. Once again rivalries were at the root of the appointment: Charles' first cousin, Prince Rupert, desired and deserved a major new appointment to stiffen the western resistance; it was more acceptable to his enemies that he should receive it at the Prince of Wales' hands than at those of the King himself.

Much less magnificent were the actual circumstances of Charles' departure. Lord Hopton was sent ahead to prepare accommodation for him in Bristol. But there was so little money left in the royal coffers at Oxford that the whole operation had to be funded on the credit of Lord Capel. And it was Lord Capel who was put in command of the Prince's meagre retinue of guards – a single regiment of horse and a single regiment of foot – all that could be spared. Charles was given a new Council by the King to represent him in the West. It included Sir Edward Hyde and John (created Lord) Colepeper. The latter had played a part in the Oxford Parliament, advising more compromise with the King's opponents: he therefore had to be reconciled with Hyde before they could leave together for the West. Colepeper was a loyal man and a devoted negotiator, but, as will be seen, changeable in his opinions.

On 4 March 1645 Charles left Oxford, in the pouring rain, for the West. James, at eleven, was considered too young to go with him and remained cooped up in Oxford.

There could be no doubt that his recent experiences had turned Charles from a high-spirited but cosseted boy into a very different kind of animal. The exact nature of the animal was not yet known. Dr Earle, his tutor, had written of 'The Child' in his study *Microcosmography*, 'We laugh at his foolish sports, but his game is our earnest, and his drums, rattles and hobby-horses but the emblems and mockings of man's business."[12] Charles had passed abruptly from those martial games which enliven most childhoods to drums beaten in earnest, horses employed in the grim and sweaty vigour of the cavalry charge. Yet still he had stood aside, kept as a spectator, ready to watch but not yet ready to take part in man's business.

Now he would leave the parental and gubernatorial restraints of the university town, melancholy under its mantle of rain. Charles would never see his father again. But of that, as of the other griefs which lay ahead, the new General of the Western Association was fortunately unaware.

CHAPTER THREE
Present Miseries

> 'We have so deep a sense of the present miseries and calamities of this kingdom, that there is nothing that we more earnestly pray to Almighty God than that He would be pleased to restore unto it a happy peace.'
>
> Charles, Prince of Wales, to Sir Thomas Fairfax, 15 September 1645

It was the King's intention, which seemed feasible from Oxford, that Charles should remain in safety in Bristol. Having been set up as a puppet commander, he should continue to act as such. The puppet master was to be Sir Edward Hyde.

Reality was very different. Once the Prince of Wales reached the West, he was the target of all the complaints and hopeful suggestions of the western gentry, who simply could not believe that his presence would not of itself bring some solution to their problems. These problems were demonstrable.

'I expect nothing but ill from the West,' wrote Prince Rupert gloomily on 24 March, a week after the arrival of the Prince of Wales; 'Let them hear that Rupert says so.'[1]

It was an understandable point of view. The western gentry had made many loyal promises since the inception of the Civil War but had in fact raised neither men nor money. Now everyone was blaming everyone else for this unhappy state of affairs. Furthermore the two leading commanders in the West, Sir Richard Grenville and Sir John Berkeley, would neither of them agree to take orders from the other; even more unhelpfully, they both persisted in asserting their independence of the Royalist general George, Lord Goring.

Goring's impossibly capricious personality was partly to blame. His high-handed behaviour at Marston Moor the year before had contributed to the defeat of his own side. He was now drinking heavily. As for Grenville, he was enormously quarrelsome. His recent campaign, which he had conducted under the title of the King's General in the West, had also been inglorious. It only made matters worse that Grenville had probably enriched himself personally. Matters came to a head when he first refused to come to Goring's aid at Taunton in March, then proved most uncooperative when he did arrive. The combination of Goring and Grenville was a nasty one.

Into this hornets' nest stepped the Prince of Wales and his Council. In spite of Grenville's record – and in spite of the fact that he had also recently been wounded – the Council immediately appointed him as commander of the new army of the Western Association.

It was probably a blunder in the first place, although Grenville did at least show himself a stern disciplinarian towards his own troops, and had the advantage of being a proper Cornishman. But the mistake was rendered fatal when the King immediately wrote off from Oxford nullifying the appointment and setting up Goring instead. Throughout the summer the rival commanders battled for the acknowledgement of their claims.

The authority of Prince Rupert – the one man in the West who could have imposed some kind of unified command – was unintentionally undermined by the presence of the Prince of Wales and his Council, since many of the western gentry preferred to address themselves to this gentler fount of authority.

The character of Charles' puppet master, Sir Edward Hyde, also came into further prominence in the West. Hyde, later Earl of Clarendon, is a central figure in the story of Charles, in youth, early manhood and the first years of his restored kingship. The relationship drew to a close nearly twenty-five years after this western foray. It ended with Clarendon telling a middle-aged monarch 'twenty times a day' that he was lazy and not fit to govern.[2] It ended with an ageing statesman dismissed by an apparently ungrateful king. There are many comparisons to be made for the dismissal of an old friend and servant by his ascendant master, of which the most famous is that of Falstaff and Prince Hal. All these comparisons are unflattering to the master. It is worth noticing that, in the case of Charles and Hyde, part of the trouble between them existed from the first and was temperamental.

The temperament concerned was that of Hyde rather than Charles.

Sir Edward Hyde, with his neat little mouth and sharp straight nose, his upright Anglicanism, his unwavering political principles in a wavering age, was a man for whom the phrase 'generation gap' might actually have been invented. A world of experience separated him from his young charge, a fact he never attempted to conceal. He was in his thirties when he went to Bristol, over twenty years older than Charles. In Hyde's case they had been a long and active twenty years. Hyde was constitutionally incapable of playing the tolerant old retainer, the Colonel Sapp to Charles' King Rudolf of Ruritania. Besides, Hyde was not an old retainer: he was a brilliant and shrewd statesman; he did not exactly expect to find old heads on young shoulders, but he did expect those young shoulders to bow before the weight of advice given by the old on all occasions.

Originally a lawyer, in 1640 Hyde was to be found attacking prerogative courts, royal judges and Laudian bishops. He even voted for Strafford's attainder. Later Hyde became an advocate for a new kind of Royalism, based on an Anglican Church, both liberated and strengthened, and as such was transformed into not only a defender but also a firm friend of King Charles I. Throughout the difficult days of 1642 Hyde had constantly pressed the King to base his claim on those ancient rights which were his under the law; this would have the effect of emphasizing that it was Parliament, not the King, which represented a new type of arbitrary tyranny. Hyde's reliance on purely constitutional expedients from the first distinguished him from another whole section of the King's advisers, headed by his wife, who could not see the use of appealing to the law of the land, when they regarded the King himself as embodying this law. *Rex est lex* – as one saying had it.

This rift in royal circles widened into a chasm as the war

proceeded. Hyde, for example, had been instrumental in persuading the King to summon his Oxford Parliament. But naturally the legal-minded Hyde disapproved of his master's delicate secret negotiations with his Irish supporters: he foresaw correctly the danger to the King's reputation if they were uncovered. It was as much to take Hyde's keen nose off the scent of this correspondence as to safeguard his son that the King despatched his wise counsellor to Bristol.

Hyde therefore viewed himself as one deputed to supervise – and, where necessary, restrict – the young Prince of Wales. He was a man of extreme gravity of character even in his younger years, the sort of gravity which is quickly taken for pomposity by the young. Charles on the other hand was being encouraged to see himself as having a useful and expanding role to play. Hyde liked to guide by disapproval; Charles liked to learn by encouragement: it was never an ideal combination. From the first Hyde was not sufficiently tolerant, Charles not sufficiently appreciative. By April Charles was said by Hyde (in his later *History*) to be encouraging disrespect towards his Council at Bridgwater.[3] But it was neither necessary nor politic to try and swaddle the Prince for ever.

Some of Hyde's disapproval was certainly incurred by another fairly natural piece of youthful folly. In Bridgwater Charles encountered once more his former nurse, Mrs Christabella Wyndham, wife of the governor of the town. On the Continent Queen Henrietta Maria dangled the hand of her eldest son in marriage as a bait to raise money, now that her jewels were in danger of running out. Louise Henrietta, eldest daughter of the Prince of Orange (Mary's sister-in-law), was offered this fine prospect in return for Dutch money, but her father declined the honour. Earlier there had been plans to marry Charles to the wealthy Infanta Joanna of Portugal, or to the daughter of the Duc d'Orléans, the super-rich Anne-Marie Louise de Montpensier, known to history as La Grande Mademoiselle. But in the West Country Charles was showing more interest in sex than in marriage.

To Mrs Wyndham, in Bridgwater, should probably be accorded the honour of having seduced her former nurseling, the Prince of Wales. By the sexual standards of the time, to play such a gracious role in the life of a young prince was more of a privilege than an offence, as Madame de Beauvais played it for Louis XIV. Charles was nearly fifteen. Certainly by the time of his arrival in Jersey a year later he was a fully fledged man in the physical sense, capable of a proper love affair. That was not particularly precocious. In an age when princes were frequently married off before they reached their teens, early sexual maturity was desirable rather than the reverse.

In some ways Mrs Wyndham, 'a celebrated beauty and an opulent heiress', was a suitable choice.[4] Where Mrs Wyndham did overstep the mark, according to contemporary *mores*, was by showing gross familiarity to the Prince of Wales in public, including such spontaneous gestures as diving across a room and covering his face with kisses. In doing so, she greatly shocked and annoyed Hyde, who wrote about the whole episode quite lewdly in his *History*;[5] the simple act of seduction accomplished in private, might, one feels, have been discreetly glossed over. Furthermore Mrs Wyndham, in Hyde's view, distracted Charles from the conduct of his own business.

Complaints concerning Charles and his work are to be reiterated down the decades and Hyde is very often to be the source of the complaint. In his view Charles had hitherto been 'very little conversant with business, nor spent his time so well towards the improvement of his mind and understanding as might have been expected from his years and fortune' – a somewhat sour comment in view of the wartime conditions in which the Prince had been raised. Yet Charles did apply himself, as even Hyde admitted, 'with great ingenuity' to the affairs of the Council. Now Mrs Wyndham, besides her public fondlings, was also guilty of playing on Charles' affections in order to affect Council proceedings. It was her influence, wrote Hyde, that persuaded two members of the Prince's entourage, Sir Charles Berkeley and Robert Long, to demand to join the Council proper – positions to which they had no right because it was actually the King's Council (in the West) not the Prince's.[6]

So the petty feuds proliferated.

Elsewhere in England a revolutionary war machine, the New

Model Army, was being assembled by the King's enemies. Charles in the West devoured local specialities, such as cherry pie and cream, with relish; he also struggled to play some kind of useful political part, for all Hyde's strictures, in a situation which was rapidly becoming swamped by the rising tide of Royalist failure. At Bridgwater on 2 June he received a petition from that strange body of protesters known as the Clubmen. The aims of the Clubmen were out of the mainstream of the time: wishing to live in peace in their lands, but sometimes using force to bring about peace, they suffered at the hands of both Royalists and Roundheads. On this occasion they were petitioning against the 'intolerable rapine' committed against them by Goring's horse.

Charles on his own initiative behaved with both sympathy and wisdom. He wrote a shocked letter to Goring. He also tried to persuade the Clubmen not to take the law into their own hands.

On 14 June the New Model Army clashed with the King at Naseby, in Northamptonshire: this, their paramount victory, extinguished his military hopes. Not only that, but the King's secret papers, revealing his 'treacherous' Irish dealings, were discovered. For all the successes of Montrose in Scotland, the Royalist cause in England was virtually lost. A month later, to complete the pattern of disaster, Goring, that bird of ill omen, was totally defeated by Fairfax and the New Model Army at Langport not far from Bridgwater.

The Prince by this time had moved back to Bristol, and then after an outbreak of plague out again to 'fine sweet' Barnstaple. But he was clearly no longer as safe as he had formerly been in the West. He wrote an official letter to the Parliamentary general Sir Thomas Fairfax: 'We have so deep a sense of the present miseries and calamities of this kingdom, that there is nothing that we more earnestly pray to Almighty God than that He would be pleased to restore unto it a happy peace.'[7] But at this stage there was very little that anyone on the Royalist side, let alone a fifteen-year-old prince, could do. Once Prince Rupert had surrendered Bristol after a fierce siege, the question was not so much whether the Prince of Wales should be evacuated, but when he should go. Above all, it had to be resolved in which country he should take refuge.

It was a decision of some moment. And it dominated the Prince's councils, as well as his correspondence from his father, for the next six months. Should the Prince of Wales be sent to friendly France – where his mother had taken refuge, and was now living at the expense of her relations with his baby sister Henriette-Anne? Or to Scotland? Or to Ireland? Or even to Denmark – where Charles had another relative on the throne?

More was at stake than Charles' own safety. France, roughly speaking, represented the foreign Catholic interest, and the influence of Queen Henrietta Maria. Scotland stood for Presbyterianism (and therefore some kind of compromise on behalf of the Anglican King), but also for the British interest, since there it could legitimately be argued that the Prince of Wales was still on British soil. The problem of Ireland was that it was beset by so many different factions at this date, most of them represented by military forces of one size or another, that it was difficult to know whose interests would be served by the arrival there of the Prince of Wales. Perhaps distant Denmark was the best solution.

At first the King himself took the line that 'France must be the place, not Scotland nor Denmark'.[8] He dreaded making any kind of religious deal with the Scots. At the same time the King was obsessed that the Prince's mere presence in England might scupper his own dealings with the rebels. If there was any danger of Charles falling into their hands he should proceed immediately to France, where he should place himself under his mother's orders in absolutely everything – except religion. Should Charles be made prisoner nonetheless, he must on no account agree terms with his captors, even if the King's own life was threatened.

But the King's caveat about religion hardly satisfied the Council, who were frankly horrified at the idea of their Prince passing into any French Catholic hands, including those of his mother. Meanwhile there were public meetings in which the view was forcibly expressed that the Prince of Wales should not leave British soil. Later petitions in Cornwall specifically begged him not to go to France.

Throughout the autumn the Prince's entourage was pushed further and further west into Cornwall itself. From there it was decided to make a supreme effort to come to the relief of Exeter. Finally Charles reached Truro, on an extreme point of the peninsula.

Goring fled to France in November, to cause further trouble there. Grenville remained, to propose a scheme by which 'poor little Cornwall', as he termed his native region, should make a separate peace, and set up as a Royalist enclave under the Prince of Wales. The scheme, so agreeable to Grenville's Cornish susceptibilities, was, however, doomed from the start, since the Council pointed out quickly that such negotiations implied the abdication of King Charles I.

By December the King changed his mind about the Prince's refuge: Denmark was now his first choice. Once again the Council objected that the perils of reaching Denmark through winter seas, let alone the difficulty of finding a vessel to make the journey, far outweighed the advantages of that Protestant country as a refuge. Hyde remained strongly of the opinion that Scotland or Ireland (both British soil) were the obvious sites. The King began to bombard his son with letters to the contrary. The situation was further complicated by the fact that Queen Henrietta Maria herself had entered the fray. She was urgently demanding that her son should join her in France, in order to stir Cardinal Mazarin, the effective ruler of the country, to action on the King's behalf.

As the campaign in the West reached its last stages the feared General Cromwell, the victor of Naseby, plunged into it, storming Hopton at Torrington in February. The men who flocked to the triumphant Parliamentary banners at Totnes, west of Torquay, were addressed by the great man himself. The Council hastily decided to favour a retreat to the Scilly Isles – just off the Cornish coast. Anything rather than France, was their passionately held policy. Even Jersey, so close to the coast of France but still within the British dominions, was better than a foreign country, where the Prince of Wales would incur the double slur of being a papist and a pensionary. The King himself was becoming increasingly worried by the reckless way in which his spouse in France was prepared to sacrifice the integrity of the Church of England to gain (Presbyterian) Scottish support. He wrote off in anguish to his 'Dear Heart': 'I assure thee, I put little or no difference between setting up the Presbyterian government, or submitting to the Church of Rome.'[9]

It was as a last throw that in January 1646 the Prince of Wales formally appointed Lord Hopton as head of the western army, with Grenville under him to command the foot. Grenville immediately and predictably refused to serve in the subordinate position. Hyde described later how Charles did all he could to try and persuade Grenville not to persist in this destructive – and self-destructive – course. But when Grenville remained obdurate, Charles was obliged to have him committed to prison. Grenville's charismatic but perverse personality was one of the complications of Charles' Cornish existence.

On 15 February Hopton fought the final action of the campaign at Torrington; two days later Charles with his Council took refuge at Pendennis Castle, a fastness built by Henry VIII two hundred feet up on the Falmouth peninsula. For a moment the Council wistfully hoped it might be safe to keep him there; but the discovery of a plot to kidnap the Prince of Wales within the castle itself clinched the matter. It was a choice between retreat and capture.

At ten o'clock at night on Monday 2 March Charles went aboard the frigate *Phoenix* from Land's End, accompanied by Sir Edward Hyde, John Colepeper and the Earl of Berkshire. He landed at St Mary's in the Scilly Isles on the afternoon of 4 March. It was exactly a year since he had left Oxford. Ten days later Hopton signed the articles of surrender at Exeter.

The move, although master-minded by the Council, accorded with Charles' own desires. He too shared their reluctance to abandon the scene of action, lest he seem cowardly; but it would have been madness at this point to have ignored his father's reiterated and fervent pleas not to prejudice the whole position of the monarchy by falling into enemy hands. He did not wish as yet to go to France, despite Henrietta Maria's frantic requests. The Scilly Isles constituted a *pis aller*.

But in another sense the journey itself was delightful and the consequences for Charles' future character radical. For it was during this brief halcyon trip aboard the *Phoenix*, in the course of which the Prince insisted on taking the helm himself, that Charles discovered that joyous taste for the sea which never deserted him, and was to unite him emotionally to so many of his subjects.

'It is no paradox to say that England hath its root in the sea,' wrote Halifax.[10] Charles discovered his own roots lay there too. The Scillies consisted of tiny islands of which St Mary, the largest, was just over two miles long; they were graced by an exceptionally balmy climate. Everything here centred on the sea. Between the Scillies and Cornwall was said to lie the vanished kingdom of Lyonesse. Over its legendary site now sailed the young Prince in a series of excursions through the spring waters.

That was the pleasant side of the picture. On the other hand conditions on land were rough, food (mainly brought from France) inadequate, and, since no-one had been expecting the little court to arrive, accommodation lamentable. With her witty and evocative pen, Ann Lady Fanshawe, wife of Charles' secretary, described how her room was regularly dowsed by the spring tide. There was a shortage of fuel to dry themselves out. In former times her own footman would have been better lodged.[11] The court, less optimistic than the young Prince, fretted at the hardships and the inaction.

In the meantime the Parliamentary privateers, like sharks, began to menace the Prince's peace. The sea trips were curtailed. It was not long before the argument about where the Prince should now seek refuge began to rage all over again with renewed vigour. Hyde and Colepeper both voted for Jersey, still British soil. The Queen continued to advocate France. When Colepeper visited her to collect money and supplies, she pressed on him a letter full of apprehension about the Scilly Isles' exposed position. 'I shall not sleep in quiet until I hear that the Prince of Wales shall be removed from thence.'[12] As to the danger of the sea passage to France, she had an assurance from the French Queen that her son's safety would be guaranteed. And was not the King himself writing to her on every possible occasion concerning the safety of the Prince of Wales?

That of course was true. The King continued to desire that his heir should be outside the sphere of danger, where Parliament might capture him and use him either as a pawn or as a hostage with which to blackmail his father. A letter from the King at Oxford, dated 22 March, began, 'Hoping that this will find you safe with your mother ...' But it went on to say, 'I command you upon my blessing to be constant to your religion, neither hearkening to Roman superstitions, nor the seditious and schismatical doctrines of the Presbyterians and Independents.' On 30 March Parliament itself showed an awareness of the Prince of Wales' potential by formally inviting him to return. Charles replied tactfully that indeed he had a great and earnest desire to be amongst them, especially if it would lead to 'a blessed peace'.[13] But he seemed to be able to keep this great and earnest desire well under control: the next month he was still lingering in the Scillies.

The King, in beleaguered Oxford, was out of contact. At the end of April he fled from Oxford to what he mistakenly believed would be the protection of the Scottish army. As a result he was still further embroiled in political intrigue, still more out of touch with his son.

It was not until 16 April that Charles set sail again, and then the destination was Jersey, not France. There was not much the Queen could do about the decision except bewail it. At least she could take comfort from the fact that Charles was now extremely near the French mainland. (Jersey is only twelve miles away at its nearest point, but fifty miles from England.)

On the journey it was the Prince of Wales who took the helm of the frigate *Proud Black Eagle*. But the arrival in Jersey seemed like a triumph for the Hyde faction. Jersey, for all its proximity to France, had been first joined to the English crown under William the Conqueror. Its governor, Sir George Carteret, came of a notable island family, but had also earned his post by a distinguished career at sea: he had been appointed to this vital naval outpost by the King in 1643. Since Jersey was now one of the few areas of the British Isles where the royal writ ran without contest, it became the focus for loyal hopes. Perhaps the island would 'happily' be the means to reduce its 'Neighbour Rebells' by force, as a suggestion made in January had it? 'Or at least by your example of fidelity, to turn the hearts and affections not only of them but of many others in His Majesty's dominions...'[14]

To reward this fidelity, and promote it to further useful ends, the loyal islanders were granted the sight of Prince Charles dining in state. With great elegance, Charles accepted a gift of 1,500 *pistoles* (that is, money) from them – 'having not 20 in the world'. When the Prince of Wales attended church at St Helier on Sunday, 26 April, it was a brilliant and royal occasion. The church was carpeted and beflowered, every pillar decked with branches and garlands: the harvest of the Jersey spring. The beach itself was crowded as the drums beat and the colours flew. Soon Charles was able to set up a miniature court, according to the gracious tradition in which he had been raised; to the Jersiaises, as a result, he appeared 'un Prince grandement bénin' [benign].[15]

The feeling was mutual. That summer in Jersey left Charles with a particular affection for the place and its 'cheerful good-natured people', as Lady Fanshawe described them.[16] His residence was the old Elizabeth Castle set in the fine bay of St Helier. It had been built in the reign of the great Elizabeth, on the site of an ancient monastery, but its romantic eminence might have been constructed for the court of King Arthur. It was even cut off from the main island at high tide, being reached by a causeway. The castle itself was not in a very splendid state of repair. But Charles appreciated the heady spring climate, the fine walks in the interior of the island amidst elms and oaks, in contrast to the rocky, picturesque coast.

And he was able to pursue his new passion for sailing more or less without restriction, since the Parliamentary navy was unlikely to menace him so close to the French coast (and in any case the Jersiaises themselves were much given to privateering in a jolly, uninhibited way, which discouraged callers). A boat was built at St Malo; it was gaily painted, with twelve pairs of oars and two masts – the first of the many boats Charles would commission in a sea-mad life, a foretaste of those magnificent post-Restoration craft, the *Henrietta*, the *Monmouth* and so forth, on whose details he would lavish such care. (But it was Sir George Carteret who paid for it: Charles had not the wherewithal.)

Another pleasant aspect of that summer interlude was the relationship Charles formed with Marguerite Carteret, daughter of the Seigneur of Trinity Manor. This is Charles' first recorded love affair and his inamorata was about twenty, four years older than himself. The setting also seems appropriate. Sex and the sea were two splendid new discoveries.

Did their summer dalliance have more serious consequences than either intended? The figure of Marguerite's son James, occasionally claimed as Charles' first child, has to be considered. There are certainly legends surrounding the life of James de la Cloche (the surname derived from the man Marguerite subsequently married, Jean de la Cloche). When he applied to become a Jesuit novice at Rome, de la Cloche produced mysterious letters to substantiate his claim to royal origins. The story ran that he had been kept abroad in obscurity. At the English court in the mid-1660s, the King was supposed to have told him out of the blue that he had a better title to the throne than the Duke of Monmouth, because his mother was of higher rank than Lucy Walter.[17]

But all this is fairly suspect: the incident at the English court is quite uncharacteristic of the known behaviour of King Charles II on the subject of his bastards. On the one hand Charles showed absolutely no hesitation in acknowledging them, as witness his immediate recognition of James Crofts, the future Duke of Monmouth, born only a few years after the Jersey episode. On the other hand he was extremely careful never to make any kind of remark concerning their possible title to the throne, having troubles enough with the remarks of others on that subject. The obscurity surrounding James de la Cloche is likely to have originated with his mother's rank rather than with his father's – the assumption must be that he was an illegitimate son, born before her marriage, concealed to save her reputation. After the English King was restored to prosperity, stories of the youthful romance inspired either de la Cloche himself or his sponsors to try and take advantage of it. As for the mysterious letters, de la Cloche probably forged them.

Love and the sea, twin passions, did not preserve the peace of Charles' summer from continued storms over his residency. Queen Henrietta Maria had succeeded in suborning Charles' attendant John Colepeper when he visited her for money and supplies. He now agreed with the Queen that France was the obvious place. Colepeper arrived in Jersey from France shortly after the Prince of Wales and Hyde. But Hyde continued to maintain stoutly that it would be the greatest possible mistake for the Prince of Wales to desert British soil.

In the course of the summer the Prince of Wales was also won round to his mother's point of view. This was not solely due to the vehemence with which Colepeper argued the case, for he was a man notorious for arguing every case with passion, however often he changed his mind; nor was it due to the assistance of Lord Digby, a future Catholic, and another pro-French attendant, Lord Jermyn. It was the views of the King, now in the hands of the Scots, that weighed most heavily with his son. These were fully passed on by his mother. 'Dear Charles,' she wrote, 'you see the King's command to you and me. I have no doubt you will obey it, and suddenly.'[18]

The King had become convinced that Charles should join the Queen in France, particularly since he had heard rumours of schemes afoot to make the young Duke of York – a Parliamentary captive since the fall of Oxford – a puppet monarch. By 17 June the King was longing to hear that Charles was safe with his mother. Of course he was adamant that Charles must continue to protect the Church of England, stoutly and for ever. As the King wrote on 16 August, from Newcastle upon Tyne where the Scots held him, 'Take it as an infallible maxim from me, that, as the Church can never flourish without the protection of the Crown, so the dependency of the Church upon the Crown is the chiefest support of regal authority.'[19]

It was a strong directive, which lingered in Charles' mind throughout the years of exile. But that summer to neither King nor Prince did the maintenance of episcopacy seem incompatible with both Scottish and French aid. So the fateful decision was taken to embark at last for France.

Charles' departure from Jersey was delayed for two days by a storm, and when he did manage to leave on 25 June it was to an orchestral accompaniment of thunder, lightning and a 'pell-mell wind'.[20] The elements were noisier but scarcely heavier in their disapproval than those royal servants who continued to regard this French venture as a catastrophic error. It was the custom for Hyde, Hopton and Capel to come once a day to kiss the hands of the Prince of Wales; as the pro-French party of Colepeper, Digby and Jermyn gained ascendancy, the ceremony became increasingly embarrassing to all concerned. The pro-French lords took to lingering on the rocks by the waterfront, or on the bowling-green, until it was over.

When the Prince of Wales did embark, so fearful were Jermyn and Digby of Hyde's moral influence that they actually walked with the Prince to the ship, one either side.

There was no need.

Hyde had put every argument and failed. He had also correctly foreseen the suicidal divisions which the departure to France would spread within the Royalist ranks. But he had not been able to provide a viable alternative. For all the balmy delights of Jersey, the Prince of Wales really could not be expected to maintain his court there for ever. The military situation in Ireland had changed, to the King's disadvantage, and even if Charles had been able to make the sea voyage in safety, he was not certain of a proper welcome, let alone military backing. The possibility of Denmark, in so far as it had ever existed, had receded since the previous year: in any case, Denmark too was a foreign power, albeit a Protestant one.

Armed with these melancholy thoughts, Hyde continued to lurk in Jersey, a prophet without honour.

The Prince of Wales, more cheerfully, sailed off on his French adventure.

CHAPTER FOUR
Dependence

> If there lie man (ye Gods) I ought to hate
> Dependence and attendance be his fate.
>
> Abraham Cowley

France had expressed in advance a flattering desire for the company of the Prince of Wales. His reception there only confirmed the morbid suspicions nourished by the anti-French party in his entourage: France, in the shape of her effective representative Cardinal Mazarin, was playing a game of diplomatic dog-in-the-manger. True enough, the Cardinal had been extremely anxious to secure the Prince's person, when there was some danger of this prize falling into other hands. Now that danger was eliminated, the Cardinal intended to proceed extremely cautiously. It was one thing to offer a refuge to the first cousin of the King of France, joining his mother in penurious exile. It was quite another matter to set that same exile on his route homewards, at the head of French troops.

In order to launch such an operation, the Cardinal felt it his duty as a Frenchman to be absolutely sure his country would end up on the winning side. It was certainly not enough, in diplomatic terms, to draw a bow at venture.

It is only fair to state that France had her own controversies. The death of Louis XIII in 1643 had left his widow Anne of Austria as titular regent for her son. The responsibility of government was, however, born by Cardinal Richelieu and at his death devolved upon Cardinal Mazarin. But the two men were not totally comparable. Richelieu had been an aristocrat not only in style, but by birth. Much was made of Mazarin's lowly Italian blood by the French nobility and it became a convenient scapegoat for their dislike of his regime. His relationship with the widowed Queen was in contrast warm: it was rumoured that they were secretly married.

Two years after Charles reached France, Queen and Cardinal would have to face the first of the series of rebellions against their Regency which took their name – the wars of the Fronde – from the stone-bearing sling borne by their popular assailants. Not all Frondeurs, however, formed part of the mob. The second and third wars of the Fronde were headed by the Prince de Condé. At least the Stuarts did not inhabit a throne perilously surrounded by senior near-royal nobles: the murderous policy of the Tudors towards royal rivals had seen to that. The French throne was menaced not only by Condé, but by others, including the King's uncle, Gaston Duc d'Orléans.

And the French exchequer, full as it might be by the current English standards of exile, was not full by its own. France had been fighting the Spanish Hapsburgs for over ten years and as a result was maintaining armies as far apart as Spain, Italy and Flanders. Taxes were high, the people resentful. On the one hand, the Cardinal did not approve of the anti-monarchical standards flourishing across the channel. On the other hand, he could not spare men and money for a useless crusade.

If only the Cardinal could be sure that the monarchy in England would prevail! In vain the English Royalists exclaimed with increasing desperation that indeed the monarchy *would* prevail – provided that there was French assistance. The sagacious Cardinal shook his head. The news from England indicated that in purely worldly terms Parliament was the better bet of the two. The King had fled from Oxford to the Scots, only to find himself held in quasi-captivity. The so-called Newcastle Propositions presented to him in July would, if he had accepted them, have involved him in swearing the Covenant; they also represented the domination of the Presbyterians, not only in Scotland but in the English Parliament. For in 1643 the Oath of the National Covenant, which applied only to Scotland, had been reinforced by a new oath, the Solemn League and Covenant. According to this, the religion of England and Ireland was also to be reformed 'according to the Word of God'. It was a significant advance: the Scots were committed to imposing Presbyterianism on England. The English Parliamentary leaders had signed as well as the Scots.

Despite this, the Cardinal had to admit that the English royal family did have a moral claim on their French relations. The argument was of course circular. And it continued to rage, in one form or another, at times disguised by Mazarin's subtlety, at times exposed by the English Royalist disgust, throughout the first period of Charles' exile.

Charles' initial experience of France and French methods consisted of politely induced frustration. For himself he discovered that nasty truth best expressed by Abraham Cowley:

> If there lie man (ye Gods) I ought to hate
> Dependence and attendance be his fate.

Far from being greeted with open arms, Charles was not even officially received by his cousin, the young King Louis XIV, for several weeks after his arrival. Excuses of protocol (oh, the difficulties of two royalties greeting each other – at any rate in polite French eyes!) were used to stave off this moment of commitment. The Prince of Wales kicked his heels and resumed his long-interrupted relationship with his mother.

Henrietta Maria was living in the old palace of Saint-Germain, near but not too near Paris, and at some distance from the French court, which was established at the Palais Royal and had one of its country retreats at Fontainebleau. The exiled Queen was in no fit state to handle a relationship with an adolescent son. Distraught herself, she was incapable of spreading happiness and reassurance about her. Her problems ranged from the financial to the emotional. She was paid a small pension of twelve hundred francs a day by the French government, but sent most of it abroad; in the meantime her love and concern for her afflicted husband racked her daily. She corresponded ceaselessly with the King, in codes devised by Cowley, brought into her employ by Lord Jermyn. Another poet, Richard Crashaw, a Catholic convert, also formed part of her little entourage, but the presence of these bards, romantic-sounding as it might be, was hardly conducive to an easy establishment. Above all they were poor. Crashaw was described as 'a mere scholar and very shiftless'. The Queen needed rich and stable men about her, as Julius Caesar had once needed the sleek-headed who slept at night.

The lack of money was already chronic. Jewels and gold and silver objects, souvenirs of a vanished gold and silver age, departed regularly to be sold. The two-year-old Princess Henriette-Anne, smuggled out of the siege of Exeter in yet another dramatic escapade in the history of the Stuart children, was now in Paris, shivering and at times virtually starving with her mother. The spectacle of a foreign queen, who was also a daughter of France, living in such evident penury, enraged the emotional Parisians, who blamed Mazarin. In a rude rhyme the Cardinal was described as robbing the English Queen of her rings: *leur reine desolée/De ses bagues par toi volées*. . . .

Officially, Charles himself received no money at all. This was a matter of policy. It was thought to be injurious for the Prince of Wales to appear as a pensioner of a foreign government. Therefore 'a mean addition' was made to the sum paid to Henrietta Maria.[1] For funds Charles was expected to apply to her. It was of course a situation which was equally injurious in another way – to the relationship between mother and son.

Perhaps this relationship was doomed even if Henrietta Maria's agitated hands had not been left clutching the purse-strings. For one thing, the Prince of Wales could hardly be expected to regress into youth without demur. At sixteen he was of an age when many kings took over the reins of power. He had spent nearly four years following the flag of his father, and the last fifteen months in nominal independence fighting in Cornwall and elsewhere. He had presided over his own court at Jersey.

Henrietta Maria had also changed. She still had something in her face so charming that she was 'beloved of all', in the loyal words of Madame de Motteville.[2] But she was no longer the gay enchanting creature to whose bright eyes no one could refuse anything. She was a thin, hag-ridden, desperate woman, to whom a great many things had been refused in recent years. Her health had never really picked up after the difficult birth of Henriette-Anne. As for her character, that had never been perfect, but its faults had been exacerbated by suffering. One of Henrietta Maria's failings was an inordinate possessiveness towards her children, accompanied by a conviction that she had an absolute right to control not only their movements but also their emotions and opinions. These were – anticipating events – the traditional feelings of a widow; if Henrietta Maria had lived out her natural days in England in her sunny court, the beloved wife of a commanding monarch, this disagreeable tendency might never have manifested itself. As it was, she treated her eldest son as a child. But the Prince of Wales indubitably felt himself to be a man.

Nevertheless, the pattern of life which was now imposed upon him was at best adolescent. His childhood friend Buckingham was once more at his side. The two boys were allotted Thomas Hobbes to teach them mathematics. The worthy and agreeable Dr John Earle read with them for an hour a day. Dr Brian Duppa was also resurrected to brush up the Prince's education. Halifax, in his *Character of a Trimmer*, complained that one bad effect of the Civil War was that it forced Charles II to have a foreign education:[3] but he did not of course receive a foreign education as we should now understand the term. He simply continued his English education after a considerable interruption.

With due regard for his father's oft-repeated remarks concerning the Church of England, Charles paid ostentatious visits to Charenton, the headquarters of French Protestantism. As a matter of fact, Protestantism here took such a severe form that Hyde, still in Jersey, added Charles' apparent adherence to such an extreme sect to his list of other worries.

It was not until 14 August that Charles was received by his cousin Louis, then on the eve of his eighth birthday. All the French royal niceties were observed. Something in the French air was encouraging to such ceremonies. Besides, the elaborate formality of the reception was in itself an excuse and justification for the delay. The Prince of Wales rode on the same side of the coach as the young King, and on his right hand, 'no point of honour being forgotten and nothing omitted that could testify the close ties of consanguinity'.[4]

Customarily, such ceremonies lasted three days – no more, no less. So after three days Charles found himself back at Saint-Germain again, his cause no further forward. Those about him periodically began to mutter that they wished they were back in Jersey again.

It was hardly surprising under the circumstances that the two young men, Charles and Buckingham, got a reputation for idleness. At the time, their books must have appeared to them as a bundle of rather unattractive strangers. But it is also worth recording that somehow or other Charles acquired 'a great compass of knowledge': we know this not only from John Evelyn but from the normally critical Burnet.[5] Charles understood the 'mechanics of physic' and made himself an excellent chemist; he both loved and understood the art of navigation. This kind of expertise, including the mathematics involved, was not obtained by idleness. Like most young people, Charles did not want to be driven to study: but he was obviously capable of great application when his interest was aroused.

This was also the period blamed by the sober – and the priggish – in later years for inculcating Charles' taste for 'gallantry'. One would hardly have blamed the penniless and in effect jobless Charles if he had decided to taste the pleasures of the flesh in compensation for the general frustration of his existence. But there is in fact no particular evidence that he did so.

All the stories of Charles' 'debauchery' in exile must be treated with extreme caution. At the time it suited the Parliamentary book to spread such propaganda. Later the truth was embroidered, in the light of his subsequent career as a gallant monarch. The facts show him to have been really quite moderate in his tastes for a bachelor prince, by the standards of the time. He was certainly no byword for debauchery.

Certainly, as a boy of sixteen, the frolics which he enjoyed with Buckingham were comparatively mild. The one person who genuinely charmed him at this point, the delightful, tender Isabelle-Angélique, Duchesse de Châtillon, widow of the Admiral Coligny, was exactly the kind of woman to appeal to an inexperienced young man. Everyone adored Bablon, as she was nicknamed; her wit and softness captivated the entire French Court. Her numerous admirers included the Prince de Condé as well as the Duc de Nemours and England's own Lord Digby. It was in a sense a safe choice for a young man to make because Bablon's alluring qualities had been hailed with general approval. Contemporary rumours that Charles wanted to marry her are certainly not true – he was well aware of the use to which his hand in marriage had to be put – but he was much infatuated. Alas for the youthful Prince, the affair was all the more romantic for being Platonic.

When Henrietta Maria suggested that one solution to the royal finances would be to court the famous heiress the Grande Mademoiselle, Charles applied himself to the task with a kind of jolly gaucherie which hardly suggested the budding rake. Altogether he was not regarded as a very polished figure by the French court at this stage. According to Madame de Motteville, even his natural wit was not apparent because he hesitated and stammered (like his father and his uncle Louis XIII).[6] Unlike King Charles I, King Charles II showed no trace of this disability in later life, except for some nervousness as a public orator – so perhaps much of the stammer was due to adolescent dislike of the circumstances in which he found himself.

Anne-Marie Louise de Montpensier, known as the Grande Mademoiselle, was Charles' first cousin. Her grandfather, not her father, having been King, she was in reality only a 'Petit-Enfant de France', not an 'Enfant' like her aunt Henrietta Maria. But the golden glow cast by her Montpensier inheritance tended to make everyone in this period overlook the fact. Louis XIV had no sisters. Anne-Marie Louise rejoiced undisputed in her title of Mademoiselle. With Charles, she formed part of that web of cousinage, the grandchildren of Henri Quatre and Marie de Medici, whose relationships and alliances were to be spun about seventeenth-century Europe: of these grandchildren four would ultimately be paired off – Louis XIV and Maria Teresa, child of the French Princess Elisabeth and the King of Spain; Louis' brother Philippe and Charles' sister Henriette-Anne. But Charles and Anne-Marie wee not destined to be amongst that happy (or unhappy) number: they shared a birthday on 29 May (although Anne-Marie was three years older) but otherwise did not have a great deal in common.

For an heiress – and the Grande Mademoiselle was not only rich but the greatest heiress in Europe – she was not bad-looking, being tall, blonde and buxom. Physically at least, the Prince of Wales and this daughter of Gaston Duc d'Orléans by his wealthy first wife, Mademoiselle de Montpensier, would have made a splendid couple.

But beneath Anne-Marie's Amazonian appearance beat a sentimental heart. That again contrasted with quite a shrewd brain. This mixture of shrewdness and sentimentality meant that Anne-Marie put a certain price on her wealth, particularly when courted by an impoverished and exiled young cousin. That price was a properly convincing application of ardour to her conquest.

Weighed in the scales against the possibility of an august destiny, Charles' clumsy courtship, so evidently spurred on by his mother, made little progress. For one thing, he declared hopelessly that he really could not speak French. So the sweet nothings which Anne-Marie craved, to make her overlook her cavalier's lack of fortune, remained firmly stuck behind the language barrier. In the meantime, Charles did manage to communicate successfully with Bablon, but she, of course, was no heiress.

Even if Charles had spoken to his cousin with the tongues of men and of angels – in French – it is improbable that that fierce guardian of national interests, Mazarin, would have allowed such a rich prize to pass outside France. The Grande Mademoiselle herself believed that Charles would become a Catholic to marry her – truly a delusion. That step would be quite fatal to the salvation of the English monarchy, as even the unwise Lord Jermyn pointed out. But the original stumbling-block to the project was Charles' inability to apply himself to the main chance by the use of his romantic talents.

Like Madame de Motteville at the same period, Mademoiselle was quite pleased with what she saw: she admired Charles' upright figure in particular – how tall he was for his age. But she wrote firmly that, as far as anything else was concerned, the Prince of Wales was to her an object of pity, and that was all.[7]

The mixture of enforced idleness and poverty, stirred from time to time by a dash of bad news from England, made the court of Queen Henrietta Maria a fertile breeding-ground for quarrels and intrigues. These, which were to prove such an alarming feature of the English Royalist party in exile, ranged from the petty to the fundamental. The personalities of those involved contributed a further bitter tincture to the dose.

The character of Henry Lord Jermyn, Henrietta Maria's closest adviser, was either an unfortunate accident or an example of the Queen's lack of judgement in choosing her intimates. The Queen's contemporaries who were not her admirers tended to take the latter view, since Jermyn had been a pre-war courtier, not a politician, and owed most of his advancement to the Queen.

Unlike, for example, Hyde, Jermyn was very much the Queen's man. He had become her Master of the Horse in 1639. This royal and feminine path to advancement did not prevent Jermyn nourishing political ambitions: he was soon to be found demanding to be made Lord High Admiral. Jermyn was a man equipped neither with political experience nor, what was worse, with natural political understanding. Furthermore, he showed a dangerous lack of sensitivity about the religious obsession of others on the whole question of the Covenant and whether Charles would take it; he never quite grasped what all the fuss was about.

Yet this man was to become the main influence on Queen Henrietta Maria as the years went by and practical memories of her husband faded. So great was their intimacy that rumours of a stronger tie – amorous, even marital – persisted at least among Parliamentary propagandists. Widowed queens were of course a natural target for such stories; inevitably their very real need for consolation was assumed to take some sexual form by the scandalous. From there it was a small step to suppose a secret marriage had taken place. It has been seen that the same assumption was made of another widowed queen and her adviser: Anne of Austria and Mazarin. The trouble with Jermyn was not so much the intimacy of his connection with Henrietta Maria, if indeed it existed, as the quality of the man himself.

He was no Mazarin. Meddlesome, petty-minded and impatient, he encouraged the worst side of his royal mistress's character. Prolonged and wearisome would be the wails of complaint from that other Royalist faction, headed by Hyde, concerning Jermyn's character during the years of exile. But it is difficult to say that they were basically unjustified. The best thing that could be said about Jermyn was that he employed Cowley as his secretary. As against that, another poet, Marvell, referred to him angrily as having the bearing of a butcher. Neither attribute equipped him for the important role he was destined to play in Royalist counsels.

The calibre of another adviser, George Lord Digby (later Earl of Bristol), was not of the finest either. He was far too changeable by nature, if charming, a man 'of phantasticall humours' who, like Jermyn, adored interfering. Hyde accused him 'of perplexing and obstructing every thing in which he had no hand'. Even Digby's best quality in adversity, his optimism, could quickly turn to rashness.

In August Prince Rupert appeared at the Queen's court. Charles welcomed his cousin warmly. Nevertheless, the arrival of this experienced man of war only served to augment the disputes which had already arisen there because of clashes of personality. With the waiting and quarrelling, Charles' spirits sank. Except that he had youth and health, there was not much to be said for his two desultory years at the court of France.

Scotland was the dragon which threatened to upset the whole English situation. How to deal with this powerful yet irresolute monster? Throughout the summer and autumn of 1646 the King was still under so-called Scottish protection. In January the following year he was handed over to Parliament, and the Scots, regarded by many as traitors as a result, retreated back across their borders.

In June 1647 the King was abducted once more, albeit peacefully, at the hands of the Army; but in the autumn the Army leaders, headed by Cromwell, allowed the King to slip through their fingers. This was very likely deliberate. They were beginning to need support against their own extremists, the agitators in the Army ranks, and toyed with the possibility of working out some agreement with him. The King got as far as the Isle of Wight, where he was once more made a nominal prisoner, while all concerned awaited the next turn of events before deciding on his exact status. From Carisbrooke Castle in the Isle of Wight the King negotiated once more with the Scots – and incidentally the Irish as well, although that was kept a secret.

The Scots were by now unhelpfully divided amongst themselves. There were those who adhered strictly to the precepts set out in the National Covenant of 1638 and the Solemn League of 1643, and in principle wished to impose its oath upon everybody else: this would exclude even the mildest religious deviation. These Covenanters were headed by Argyll, dour, canny and for all his fanaticism a man of immense political perception. Temperamentally, the Covenanters were in sympathy with Parliament, particularly its Presbyterian members – their rigidity did not fit with the Independents' way of thinking. Then there was the group, also Presbyterian, which was more in sympathy with the King. Headed by the Duke of Hamilton and his brother, these men would come to be known as the Engagers after they had gone towards a private agreement, or Engagement, with Charles I. Hamilton was less tricky, but also less able, than Argyll. Thirdly, there were the followers of the great general Montrose: of all the Scots Montrose was a straightforward King's man.

Yet, for all their divisions, the Scots as a nation had enormous advantages as possible crusaders to rescue the King. They had an army. They were the King's subjects: there could therefore be no imputation of restoration by foreign help. On the other hand, the price of their help was liable to be religious demands of an exigent nature.

This problem of the price of the Scottish help was already

central to the question of the restoration of the English monarchy. As has been seen, Hyde had been ruminating unhappily over it in Jersey. It would continue to dominate Royalist counsels until the defeat of Worcester put an end to the dream.

Was the price – the taking of the Oath of Covenant – too high? Hyde, devoted son of the Church of England, always thought that it was. Like most pre-war English politicians, he disliked the Scots and did not trust them: an understandable point of view. When an emissary came from the Scots to test the reaction of the Prince of Wales to the Covenant, Hyde, still in Jersey, issued a stern directive: the price *was* too high.

The trouble was that King Charles I did not by any means maintain such a stern posture in his own dealings with the Scots. With hindsight and with history's more profound knowledge of his character, one is able to see that the King never indicated that the price was too high for one very good reason – because he had no intention of paying it. His restoration to power was for him an end in itself; from that, all blessings would flow, including the supreme blessing of declaring that all previous commitments, made to secure this position, would not now have to be honoured. Henrietta Maria did not find the price too high, simply because she did not understand the currency in which it would be paid. She did not take these strange Scottish oaths and covenants, which she barely bothered to comprehend, particularly seriously. It has been noted that quite early on she was urging her husband to entertain the notion of Scottish help.

By December the King's secret negotiations with Hamilton's party were moving towards that point where a Scottish army of rescue was proposed. A new undercover 'Engagement' was signed on 26 December by the King and the Scottish commissioners on the Isle of Wight. The King promised to condemn all those Independent non-conformist sects detested equally by the 'Engagers' and their Covenanter comrades. Presbyterianism was to be established for three years.

Abroad however the line was still taken that the Scots were but one possible arrow in the royal quiver, particularly in view of the fact that communications with the King on the Isle of Wight were sparse and unreliable. France, for all her family connections, was failing to show herself a noble champion, and the outbreak of the so-called 'Parliamentary' war of the Fronde in October 1648 would effectively put an end to hope in that direction. But France was not the only country in Europe where the Stuarts could claim cousinage. There was also Holland.

Here the eldest sister of Charles, Mary, and her youthful husband, the Prince of Orange, were loyally anxious to help her distressed father. Gradually the English exiles of independent mind were drifting away from the polite complications represented by France to the more vigorous possibilities now open to them in Holland and Flanders.

Yet here too the Prince of Orange was much restricted by his own circumstances in the aid he could propose for his father-in-law. His position as Stadtholder of Holland remained ambivalent: he was not, for example, an independent monarch of the rank of his father-in-law or even of some of the German princely rulers. Holland was only one of those provinces which together constituted the United Provinces of the Dutch Netherlands, each of which had its own Stadtholder. William was thus responsible to the States of Holland. On the other hand, those Princes of Orange who were appointed Captain General and Admiral General were also responsible to the States-General: this body was made up of delegations appointed by each province.

In 1647 Mary's husband William II succeeded his father, the talented Frederick Henry, at the age of twenty-one. Not all the Dutch approved of the help which the new Stadtholder wished to give his father-in-law. A Dutch counsellor would bewail the 'English labyrinth' in which it was feared the Prince of Orange would involve them through the fatal Stuart marriage – and with some reason.[8] Besides which, the Scottish Covenanters, not the Stuart Episcopalians, were temperamentally the natural allies of the Protestant Dutch. Nevertheless, William, together with the Duke of Lorraine, raised troops on his father-in-law's behalf – between five hundred and a thousand men – and encamped them at Borkum; he also chartered and equipped some ships at Amsterdam, and spent money buying munitions for the Scottish army.

It was natural under the circumstances that, like the other young and spirited Royalists, Charles Prince of Wales should prefer the prospect of action based on Holland to inaction based on France. By the beginning of 1648 Henrietta Maria herself had come round to that point of view and, still treating her son as one who could be despatched hither and thither without too much consultation, sent him off to Calais on the French border, to await developments. But here Mazarin stepped in once more and obstinately blocked the young Prince's progress. He must not leave France.

It was a time of exceptional frustration for Charles.

Meanwhile in England some at least of the Army and Parliamentary leaders were becoming ruefully aware of the underhand nature of their King. Very few in either category had abandoned the notion of a monarchy as such: negotiations with the King consisted in advancing various expedients for limiting his powers, and trying to work out some practical way in which his alleged tyranny could be held in check. As a result, certain members of the House of Commons decided to explore the notion of transferring the royal role into the hands of the Prince of Wales. Little was really known of Charles in England at this point: might he not prove more amenable to the idea of monarchy limited in its powers by Parliament? The answer from Charles was of course a firm negative – thereafter when these expedients were explored by Parliament it would be in terms of the younger princes: James, even Henry.

When rumours of the King's secret agreement with the Scots leaked out, the Army and the Independents in Parliament were together confirmed in their disgust. Negotiations with the King were formally broken off at the beginning of the year when a Vote of No Addresses was passed by Parliament.

In the meantime the King's intrigues appeared to have had a successful outcome: they had combined Royalists and Presbyterians in a further outbreak of fighting, which began with a Royalist insurrection in Wales and culminated in a Scottish invasion. This, the Second Civil War, was blamed by the Army leaders on the King's double-dealing: he earned from them the unpleasant sobriquet of 'the man of blood'. Charles' position was made clear by the fact that commissions were issued in his name to various Royalist commanders, including Langdale in the north and Byron in the north-west. A signature was however still the sole measure of contribution by the unhappy Prince.

By now the Engagers in Scotland were longing equally for the *éclat* of the Prince's presence. Charles, the boy who, at the age of twelve, had drawn his sword at Edgehill and shouted, 'I fear them not!', was still kept prudently in reserve, like a weapon of uncertain provenance.

Nevertheless, the moment of decision could not be much longer delayed. On 9 March a heated debate took place in the Prince's Council. The Queen had given way and agreed to his departure. Hyde's known views were overruled.

At the end of the meeting 'the Prince's resolution was taken without more ceremony to come into Scotland'. By 23 March his offer was known in Edinburgh and on 1 May the Duke of Hamilton, the Earl Lauderdale and three other Engagers formally requested the arrival of the Prince of Wales. On 30 May Charles himself wrote back in the most flattering terms that he was 'inexpressibly desirous of himself and impatient to be amongst them'.[9]

Nevertheless, the Prince of Wales did not arrive in Scotland. By August, when the Scottish army passed lumberingly into England, he had still not arrived. His part in the Second Civil War was totally, not to say fatally, mismanaged by his elders and advisers.

What now transpired, put briefly (although the expression of it was not brief at the time), was the re-emergence of all the old worries in Royalist circles about the Scots. Instead of permitting the Prince to depart, his advisers sent off renewed cautious enquiries concerning the use of an English prayer book in his private devotions, and similar questions which were surely of little import compared to the vast issue at stake – the defeat of the Parliamentary Army.

Perhaps it might after all be better to despatch the Prince to Ireland. . . . The old mildew of indecision concerning the relative merits of Scotland and Ireland as a jumping-off ground continued to blight the Royalist counsels during this critical summer. Yet a realistic appraisal of the Irish situation should have made its relative weakness clear.

Ireland was full of armies. The island itself was inhabited by an enormous variety of factions, in which religion and ethnic origin made many weird combinations – there were Anglican English, Anglican Anglo-Irish, Catholic Anglo-Irish, Catholic Irish and Presbyterian Scots, and that was not the end of it. Nearly all these bodies were represented at one time or another by an army, or at least combined into a military force. The presence of the Papal Nuncio further complicated matters by inspiring the view, at any rate in the breasts of Catholics, that Papal money might be enlisted. But the Pope, like the Presbyterians, demanded religious concessions.

Ireland was therefore a quagmire during this period, rather than the sort of solid ground from which a counter-offensive could be launched. Yet still the Royalists dithered and would not commit themselves to Scotland.

On 25 June Cardinal Mazarin, with the shadow of the impending war and the Fronde athwart him, released Charles. He had by now too many troubles of his own to wish to add to them by the presence of the English Prince of Wales. Now, if ever, was the moment at which Charles should have joined the Scottish Engagers under their leader the Duke of Hamilton. The Scots were about to invade England with a vast but ill-equipped army – it lacked any artillery, for instance. The propaganda value of the presence of the Prince of Wales at its head would have been immense, as the Scots themselves fully realized. It would have enabled this force to present itself as a monarchical army of liberation – rather than an invading body of England's unpopular neighbours, the Scots.

But Charles, on leaving France, had been re-routed to Holland by the news that part of the English fleet had revolted against Parliament. At first this seemed a wonderful portent of good things to come. At Helvoetsluys Charles found the rebellious sailors, and also his younger brother James, whom he had not encountered for over three years, since he left Oxford. Alas, the revolt of these ships proved an excessive blessing in terms of

Charles' fortunes. Not only did it provide an additional and fatal motive for delay in joining the Scottish army. It also provoked a coolness between the royal brothers which the Prince of Wales could well have done without, dependent as he was on his family for support.

The trouble was that the disaffected sailors turned out to be rebelling against naval discipline, law and order, rather than against Parliament itself. Yet already James, with joy, had placed himself at their head. Despite its rashness, one can at least sympathize with this action on the part of the fifteen-year-old Duke of York. He was after all titular High Admiral. James was here enjoying his first measure of liberty since his dramatic escape from Parliamentary captivity in April. He had carried out that escape, dressed in woman's clothes, specifically to avoid being used as a pawn against his father and elder brother, which had been Parliament's hope after Charles rejected their approaches. It was natural to wish to spread his wings. The revolt of the fleet offered the perfect opportunity.

But these wings his elder brother now proceeded smartly to clip. James was ejected from his self-appointed post of admiral 'much to his mortification'. He complained sulkily that he was once more being treated as a prisoner 'and not trusted with himself'.[10] Even more to the point, Charles sent packing a Colonel Bampfylde. This doubtful character, who had aided James in his escape, was now intriguing to put him in Charles' place; James would then sail the fleet on his own responsibility. The brothers had been extremely close as children, devoted companions in boyhood, sharing the intimacies of such experiences as Edgehill and the tricky Court years at Oxford. It was regrettable that this new phase in their relationship, when they met for the first time as adults, opened under a cloud.

Charles' precise attitude to his brother James is one of the most fascinating conundrums both of his own nature and of his reign. From 1649 onwards James was only a heartbeat away from the throne, such as it was. Just as Parliament had turned from the vision of a pliant Prince of Wales to that of an accommodating Duke of York, there would always be the danger of others during the years of exile toying with the same fantasy.

Rumours of Charles' illness and death always brought the provident and the toadies scurrying to James' side. It was sad but inevitable that Charles' new relationship with his brother had to be built upon suspicion as well as affection.

The fleet, which had arrived 'full of anger, hatred and disdain', was restored to discipline.[11] Lord Willoughby of Parham, who had the advantage of being a Presbyterian, was made Vice-Admiral. It was now time to resume the original plan of sailing for Scotland. Money and supplies continued to present difficulties and the Dutch were not in a particularly generous mood. Nevertheless, on 17 July Charles set sail and by 24 July the fleet was off Yarmouth.

Meanwhile, matters had already progressed in the north. Hamilton had actually crossed the border on 8 July. The Covenanters however did not join him and remained in Scotland, like so many Achilles sulking in their tents. In the absence of the Prince of Wales, gleeful Parliamentary propaganda put exactly that xenophobic construction upon the expedition which the wiser Royalists dreaded. The Parliamentary newspaper *Mercurius Britannicus* was able to write disdainfully of the Scots bringing 'their lice and Presbytery amongst us'.[12] Mere words of scorn might not have harmed the royal cause overmuch: the trouble was that northern Royalists, acting on the same anti-Scottish principle, simply did not join in with the so-called Scottish army of liberation as had been expected. The Scottish army's reputation for plunder, as it zig-zagged uneasily south, completed the disastrous picture. Rumours that the Scots would be rewarded with good English lands for their efforts were readily believed.

In the south, Charles, at the head of his newly acquired fleet, showed resolution and courage. It was born of a surge of new Royalist optimism, since he was in no position to appreciate how disastrously the northern situation was deteriorating. He tried first to save Colchester, which was being besieged by Fairfax. Then he sailed for the Downs, seizing a number of merchant ships on the way and exacting a useful ransom of £20,000 from the Common Council. Next he set up a blockade at the mouth of the Thames, penning in the Earl of Warwick and the rest of the Parliamentary fleet. Here another important ship absconded to his side; now in command of a fleet of eleven ships, carrying a total of nearly three hundred guns, Charles felt sufficiently confident to write to the House of Lords on behalf of his father.

It was certainly in Charles' mind that he might soon be in a position to rescue the King, still in his Isle of Wight fastness, if this naval superiority was maintained.

At this point the Scots reminded Charles strongly of their prior strategic claims. On 10 August an emissary from the Committee of the Estates, in the shape of the Earl of Lauderdale, arrived in order to persuade Charles to fulfil his promise and join them. Yet, even at this stage, both sides continued to argue out the points of dispute – mainly religious – between them. The Prince was informed in unvarnished terms that certain members of his train, such as Prince Rupert, the Marquess of Montrose and Lord Digby, would not be welcome among the Scots. And there was no question of the Prince being accompanied by his own Anglican (non-Covenanting) chaplains. The Prince must also promise to use the Presbyterian form of service.

It is true that the Prince and Lauderdale did establish a good personal relationship. This Lauderdale, a man of thirty, must be distinguished from the infinitely grosser and less attractive post-Restoration statesman he subsequently became. He was odd-looking, with a mass of uncouth red hair hanging down on either side of his face, but he was acute and quick-witted, despite his barbaric appearance. Nevertheless, for all his Caliban quality, Lauderdale would go down in history as the only Scot Charles actually liked. As for Lauderdale himself, from the first he formed 'a great opinion' of the Prince's 'power' – 'We are like to be very happy with him,' he wrote.[13]

For all this amity, no immediate resolution of the problem of the Covenant versus the Royal Anglican position was found.

Neither the Prince nor Lauderdale were aware that as these discussions on the finer points of Presbyterianism raged, General Cromwell was sweeping down on the hapless Scots. They had reached Lancashire; he approached them across the Pennines. It was a dramatic tactical manœuvre, the finest of Cromwell's career. It met its reward at the Battle of Preston on 17 August, at which Cromwell defeated the numerically far superior Royalists by pouncing on them from the rear.

Only the day before, Lauderdale had been finally called into the Prince's Council and told that his conditions would be accepted. It did not help that the scene in which concessions – too late – were made to the Scots was extremely unpleasantly handled. Prince Rupert, who was about to be excluded, found himself sitting next to Lauderdale, who was successfully demanding that exclusion.

The sacrifice and the humiliation were in vain. A few days later the news of the disastrous defeat at Preston made it clear that the Second Civil War was in effect at an end. And with it had perished the Engagers' authority in Scotland. It was now Lauderdale who was unable to return to a Scotland newly dominated by the Kirk, the Covenanters, and 'gley-eyed' (squinting) Argyll – all those uncontaminated by the recent débâcle.

The whole incident left a bitter taste behind it. Each party, Royalists and Scots, could argue that they had been let down by the other. This sour sediment was not a good omen for any future co-operation between them.

CHAPTER FIVE

The King's Son

> 'Almighty God, who do'st establish thrones of Princes, and the succession in those thrones, by giving thy judgements to the King, and thy righteousness to the King's Son...'
>
> 'Prayer for the Prince of Wales', *The Cavalier Soldier's Vade-Mecum*, 1648

In the light of the Scottish defeat at Preston, the immediate instinct of the Prince of Wales was to head back for Holland. There counsel could be taken, this new situation assessed and a new strategy devised. There was obviously no future in hanging about the shores of England. The Engagers were in total disarray. Nothing could be expected from the Covenanting Scots.

But Charles reckoned without his surly navy.

Seeing no reason whatsoever to depart without the fun of a fight, they crowded on deck of the royal ship and threatened to throw Lauderdale and John Colepeper overboard. It was their belief – quite unfounded – that this little clique intended to take the Prince away from them in a single ship. The only person they would heed was their Prince himself. Charles rose to the occasion. After a great deal of pacification at his hands – or the 'so kind words', as they were afterwards described – the sailors finally agreed to return to Holland.

Or so it was believed on the Prince's ship. In fact, two of the largest vessels continued to ignore orders and sailed defiantly in the direction of Lord Warwick and the Parliamentary Navy. This was an age when there were new chords of disobedience to be heard, amidst the general music of strife and war. It was a phenomenon from which neither side was immune. The year before, the ranks of the Parliamentary Army had threatened their officers in a bellicose manner; in 1649 the Levellers in the Burford mutiny would challenge the authority of Cromwell himself.

The royal ship was compelled to give chase to the deviants and an absurd and unnecessary engagement took place. The action would have been farcical if men's lives had not been at stake. Before the battle was joined the rival royal commanders, Sir William Batten and Prince Rupert, were already yapping at each other like jealous dogs. When Batten wiped the sweat off the back of his neck with a napkin Rupert took it as a signal to the enemy and threatened to shoot Batten for treachery if they were defeated.

The only person who continued to behave with calm and courage, as he had done throughout this long and trying summer, was Prince Charles. He refused to go below decks to protect himself, just as he had tried to remain on the scene of battle at Edgehill. This time he had his way. He told his attendant lords very firmly that dishonour meant more to him than his safety, and stayed on deck.

The sailors' action was particularly ill-advised since they had hardly any water aboard. In the end it was a propitious storm which saved them from the consequences of their rashness by deflecting the Parliamentary Navy from their challenge. And on 3 September, when there was a possibility of an encounter with Warwick's ships, they were saved by the determination of the Dutch States-General to remain neutral. The Dutch Admiral Tromp was ordered to station himself between the Royal Tweedledee and the Parliamentary Tweedledum.

So Charles returned at last to Holland.

For the next six months he was, with his brother James, more or less dependent on the personal charity of the Prince of Orange, the Dutch States-General having declined to provide further financial assistance for the crippled English Royalist cause. It was a curious time in Charles' life, during which cares were not unalleviated by pleasures. Like the phoney war which preceded the bombing of London at the beginning of the

Second World War, it was in some ways a period of calm and even relaxation, a prelude to, rather than a foretaste of, the searing experiences to follow.

The Hague itself was not a bad place in which to take up residence. It was cut off from the inhospitable North Sea by a stretch of dunes and had been designated the seat of the States-General, and of the provincial body, the States of Holland, at the end of the sixteenth century. When Prince Maurice of Nassau settled there in 1618 it became the royal residence as well. The cultural life of The Hague flourished. Not only literature, philosophy and the arts, but that inevitable seventeenth-century offshoot, theology, were part of the general cultural air of the city. While Amsterdam remained the commercial capital, bolstered up by the prosperity brought by commerce and industry, the lifeblood of the Dutch people – painters, philosophers and theologians – enjoyed the free and argumentative atmosphere of The Hague.

It was a time of development for Charles personally. At least he was free of his mother's apron strings. With James to care for, he moved to a position as head of the family – those members of it who were at liberty. Then there was his relationship with his sister Mary. It had to be faced that Mary, the pretty, ringleted child of Van Dyck's pictures, had not grown up into a particularly agreeable young woman. Marriage before she was ready for it and a troublesome mother-in-law – Amalia von Solms was fearfully strong-minded – had combined to inspire in Mary an undiplomatic dislike of her adopted country.

Poor Mary had inherited the tactlessness of both her parents. She refused to learn Dutch, hardly the mark of an amiable spouse, and made it clear that, in her eyes, France was preferable to Holland. As a result, she has been harshly treated by Dutch historians. Correctly, they have drawn attention to her deficiencies as Dutch consort. It is true that circumstances might explain the emergence of this outwardly chilly figure, indifferent to the susceptibilities of her adopted people. Princesses in those days however were not expected to undergo psychological difficulties. At least the English should regard her with more sympathy, since the consequence of all this was a true devotion to her brother Charles, both to his person and to his interests.

Nonetheless, it was distressing that the one member of his family in a position to aid Charles practically at this juncture was a square peg in a round hole. As it was, Charles found himself covering up for Mary, atoning for her unfortunate hauteur with his own civility. The Prince of Orange himself was a decent fellow who took his responsibilities to his in-laws seriously, not merely because it would suit him to have his wife's father back on the throne of England. After William II's premature death in 1650, Mary's lack of judgement – like that of her mother, similarly placed – grew worse, and her determination to aid Charles ostentatiously, at the expense of Holland, more pronounced. Once again it was Charles who indulged in graceful little gestures, such as addressing the Elector of Brandenburg as 'brother' (indicating an imaginary equality of rank between them, as opposed to the correct salutation of 'cousin').[1] His sister, on the other hand, did not care to study the art of how to please.

In general, Mary placed a quite pathetic reliance on her status as an English princess. It gave her a much needed sense of security to meditate on her royal rank: but that again was somewhat tactless in view of the fallen fortunes of the house of Stuart and their reliance on the good will of other European rulers, whether of equal status or not. Determined to emphasize that she remained the daughter of a king, Mary complained loudly that she ought to continue to take precedence over her sister-in-law Louise Henrietta of Orange when she married the Elector of Brandenburg. Mary's case was weak because the Elector was a supreme ruler, whereas the Prince of Orange was not. The new Electress should really have preceded her.

In the autumn of 1648 however the devotion of Mary helped to support Charles' growing feeling of authority in the family. This family was in the process of being extended, on one side of the blanket at least, by the pregnancy of Charles' mistress Lucy Walter. The character of this straightforward young lady later became surrounded by myths. The truth about Lucy, 'brown, beautiful and bold', as John Evelyn called her, was that she was neither a whore, as one legend suggests, nor the chosen bride of the Prince of Wales. She was not even of low birth, as Monmouth's enemies would declare in later years, in order to taunt him with the fact that other royal bastards – the son of Louise de Kéroüalle for example – were of superior antecedents on their mother's side. Lucy Walter's own mother was a niece of the Earl of Carbery; she herself came of a perfectly respectable Welsh family, hence her appealing, dark-eyed Celtic looks.[2]

Lucy Walter was not a whore. But she did belong to that restless and inevitably light-moralled generations of young ladies who grew up in the untrammelled times of the Civil War. Barbara Villiers, a far more celebrated mistress of Charles II, was another such. As their brothers, who had grown up frequently without fathers, became the undisciplined high-spirited bucks of the 1660s, so those young ladies who survived to the merrier times of the Restoration became the great ladies of the Court. But Evelyn added that Lucy Walter was 'insipid'. Perhaps he implied a lack of a survivor's instinct. For Lucy Walter died in 1658, to be buried in an unnamed grave in Paris. It thus became fashionable to blacken her birth as well as her character.

Lucy Walter probably ended up at The Hague via Paris, having been taken there by her uncle. She quickly adapted herself to the age in which she found herself. By September at The Hague she was probably the mistress of Robert Sidney (Charles had of course been absent for nearly two months); but she was also pregnant by Charles. Later these simple facts would become embroidered and re-embroidered with all the complicated threads of the succession politics of the 1670s as the circumstances of Monmouth's birth became a matter of political importance rather than light conjecture. (Even the republican Algernon Sidney was described as her lover – although he was in England throughout the period, guarding Dover Castle.)

The child afterwards known as James Duke of Monmouth but first called James Crofts, after his guardian Lord Crofts, was born on 9 April 1649. Therefore his conception must have taken place some time in July – that is, just before the Prince of Wales sailed off at the head of his rumbling fleet. It is important to bear the date in mind in view of the fantasies which would later cluster like brambles round the circumstances of this boy's birth.

These fantasies take two principal, and contradictory, forms. The first concerns Monmouth's paternity and suggests that he was not really Charles' son at all, but, seeing that Lucy was free with her favours, the offspring of Robert Sidney. This canard can be ignored for two reasons. First, Monmouth as a boy bore a striking resemblance to his father at the same age; later he enjoyed the highly characteristic looks of the Stuart family: the paternity over which the scandal-minded sniggered at his birth was never questioned in the periwigged duke, lounging at his royal father's Court. Secondly, Charles himself never questioned Monmouth's parentage. He assumed responsibility for the child from his birth and was inclined rather to remove him from his unsuitable mother's care than to consign him to a limbo of doubtful bastardy. Yet Charles did not acknowledge every child that came his way, as it were – the offspring of every pretty woman that had pleased his fancy. In the 1670s, as a secure monarch, he declined very firmly to acknowledge Barbara Palmer, the sixth child of Barbara Villiers, despite her mother's protests. It is unlikely that the perilously placed Prince of Wales was any more complaisant in 1648. Obviously Charles had every reason to believe that Monmouth was his son.

The other fantasy suggested that Monmouth, far from being another man's bastard, was actually the Prince of Wales' legitimate son. It is on this point that the date of the baby's conception becomes vital. It has been seen how tense and strife-torn were Charles' days in July. He was extinguishing the naval mutiny on the one hand, as he desperately strove to reach agreement with the Scots on the other. It is inconceivable that he should at this point have taken time off to contract a highly unsuitable – and secret – marriage. Charles was, on the contrary, only too aware that in a dwindling hand of cards his marriageability constituted about his only remaining ace. His parents, one way or another, had been attempting to play this card to their advantage since his childhood, as Dutch princesses, Spanish and Portuguese infantas, were considered; Charles was well aware of his own value in this respect. Indeed, when he finally elected to play the ace, after his Restoration, he did so after a very cool estimate of the advantages to himself which would thus accrue.

There is negative evidence on Lucy's side as well. Her liaison with Charles continued sporadically until 1650. Now known as Mrs Barlow, she was with him in Paris, witnessed by Evelyn, and possibly in Jersey. Thence she passed into other hands. Charles himself was absent from her side for nearly two years while he was in Scotland and England; during this time her second child, Mary, was born. Furthermore, Lucy contemplated wedding Sir Henry de Vic, the English resident in Brussels, with the full approval of Charles – an insane move, if she was actually proposing to commit bigamy.

For others than the lighthearted Lucy, life at The Hague that September had its complications and anxieties. In the streets, the followers of Prince Rupert and those of the pro-Scottish John Colepeper began to battle. Their feud was by no means ended by the failure of the summer's naval expedition. It was a particular piece of ill-fortune that at this critical juncture Prince Charles should be laid low by smallpox, since he represented the one figure of authority that everyone tacitly agreed to respect.

Hyde was back at his side. He had arrived at The Hague, exhausted from sea-sickness, having tried in vain to catch up with his Prince in France. But Hyde continued to preach against the Scottish involvement. On hearing of the previous Lauderdale agreement, disrupted by circumstances, he wrote to Henrietta Maria that, if another such concordat was proposed, he would have to move to another part of her service. He was thus hardly a figure of reconciliation.

The Prince, who still managed to appear in this attractive role, was out of action until November. On recovery, his first task was to sort out those same disorderly sailors, who were now drinking and rioting their way about the port of Rotterdam, to the general discontent of the Dutch and the English civilian exiles alike. Some crews actually returned with their vessels to the Parliamentary side; others were recaptured. Charles' method of dealing with them was to make the uncompromising Prince Rupert their admiral, and that despite a few remaining demands for the appointment of the Duke of York. Rupert's name has come down to our day trailing chivalric garlands: in his own time he was known less charmingly as 'Prince Robber'. He was certainly a man of action. Once he had thrown a mutineer or two overboard with his own hands, the Royalist Navy reluctantly recognized itself to be under control once more. With his brother Maurice as Vice-Admiral, Rupert set about restoring the reputation of the Navy as a striking force. The pair of Palatine princes captured a number of prizes, which helped to swell the pathetically depleted exchequer of the Prince of Wales.

But there had been vital months of delay and indecision. And time and tide round Carisbrooke Castle on the Isle of Wight had not waited for this happy resolution of the Royalist naval problems. Divisions between Parliament and Army grew daily more pronounced. One was represented by corrupt and often inefficient members, who nevertheless could still claim legality behind their authority; the other by the soldiers victorious in the recent war, who could and did claim right as well as might. There was hardly likely to be accord between them. In any case, the King still hoped to divide and so to rule again. On 18 September a Parliamentary delegation arrived at Newport on the Isle of Wight in a final effort to negotiate with him according to their notions of compromise. They were animated not only by a wish to fend off the encroachments of the Army on their own authority, but also, being principally Presbyterians, by a desire to subdue the Army's religious Independents.

The King showed himself in principle prepared to make concessions, but understandably refused to deny pardon to Princes Rupert and Maurice and certain other designated Royalists. As ever, he spoke up firmly for the use of bishops as a system of church government: 'Episcopacy,' he said, 'had been exercised by the Apostles.' Although these abortive negotiations were known as the Treaty of Newport in the language of the time, no such treaty in our sense ever existed. And the King made it clear in a private letter to the Duke of Ormonde that he had no intention of honouring it even if it had been concluded: Ormonde should pay no attention, he wrote, if he ever read of such an agreement.

In any case, Parliament itself was scarcely more constant. In October it rejected those terms already agreed, although negotiations were still in progress. As for the attitude of the Army, Cromwell lingered in Scotland. He had arrived as an invader, but then discovered the more pacific delights of theological conversation in Edinburgh.

People cannot help their personal predilections, although they may conceal them. It was one of Charles' difficulties that the Scots were naturally distasteful to him. But they were naturally agreeable to the English Independent general. Cromwell might fight the Scots, but he would always be able to strike up accord with them afterwards. To Cromwell, the Scots were not after all such bad fellows, particularly the Covenanters, like Argyll, who had not been involved in the recent holocaust. With Charles, the process was in exact reverse. He might make any number of agreements with them. But in his heart of hearts he could never like or even admire them. It is possible that during this Scottish sojourn of Cromwell's delicate feelers were put out, like the exploratory touch of a cat's paw, concerning the future of the King. If – only if – it came to a trial and if – only if – such a trial brought about a death sentence, how would the Scots ...? But Argyll to his dying day strenuously denied that any kind of pledge of complaisance towards their King's execution was given in advance by the Scots.

In the meantime of course the safety of the King was a subject of agonizing concern, rather than diplomatic feelers, to his wife and family abroad. Why not rescue him? There existed a force of upwards of a thousand Lorrainers: could this not be used to raid the Isle of Wight, as Henrietta Maria and Lord Jermyn continued to hope? The idea sounded more practicable than it actually was. There was the problem of transport. The Isle of Wight was distant, the Parliamentary Navy effective, and, since the King's guards did not intend that there should be another precipitate flight, there would be no connivance this time. Moreover, the King himself had given his parole, his word of honour, that he would not escape. He did not – as yet – consider himself to be absolved from that promise.

Towards the end of November, the Prince of Wales decided

THE NETHERLANDS IN THE SEVENTEENTH CENTURY
Amsterdam
The Hague
Delft
Rotterdam
ZEELAND
Breda
THE
Flushing
Hoogstraete
LANDS
Bruges
Antwerp
Dunkirk
Calais
BRABANT
FLANDERS
Brussels
SPANISH
NETHERLANDS
FRANCE

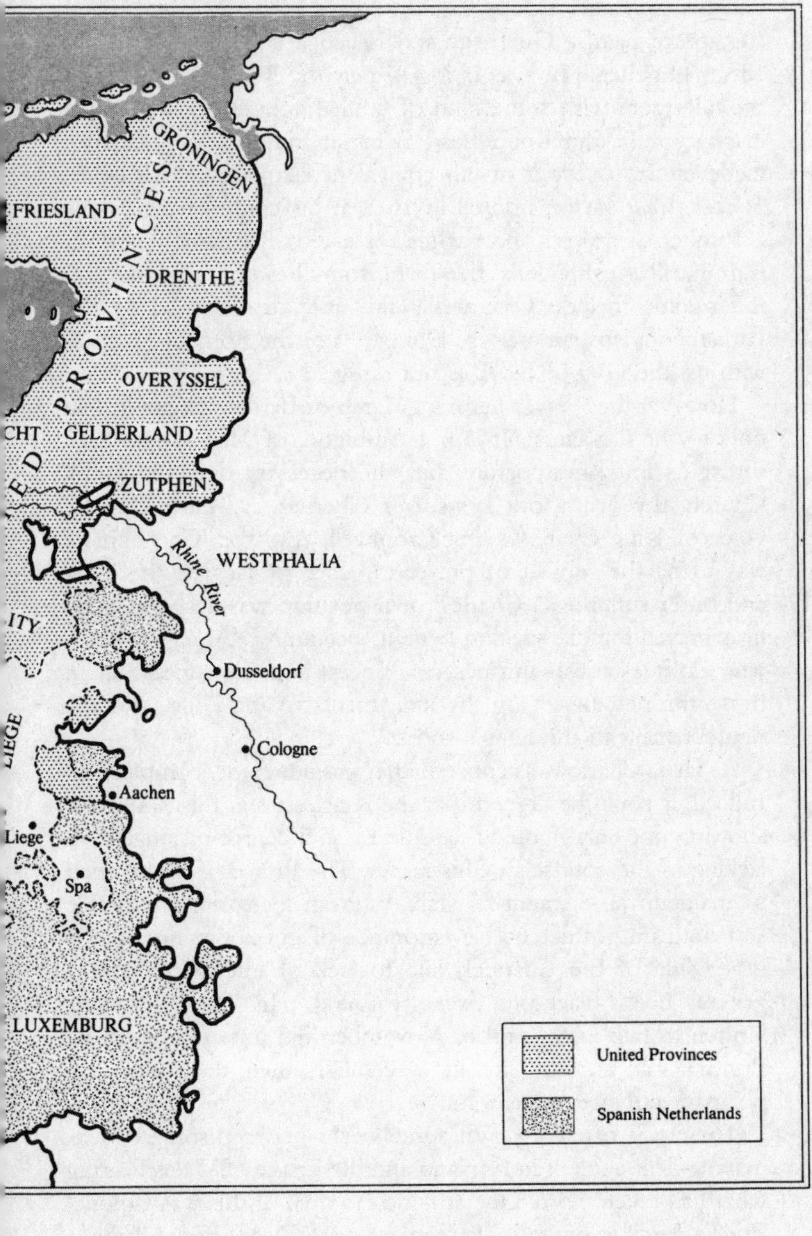
GRONINGEN
FRIESLAND
PROVINCES
DRENTHE
OVERYSSEL
CHT
GELDERLAND
ZUTPHEN
Rhine River
WESTPHALIA
ITY
Dusseldorf
LIEGE
Cologne
Aachen
Liege
Spa
LUXEMBURG
United Provinces
Spanish Netherlands

that the Lorrainer troops would be used to better effect trying to capture nearby Guernsey and issued a commission to that effect. In general, he was trying to rally the Royalist forces, and provide them with some kind of unified animus parallel to the inspiration of the Roundhead Army in time of war. Charles made efforts to work up an equivalent campaign: the *Cavalier Soldier's Vade-Mecum*, printed in 1648 at his command, contains a number of prayers and psalms for use by Royalist soldiers. It is, ironically, highly derivative from Roundhead propaganda, and the psalms include Cromwell's favourite, to be used as the Parliamentarian battle-cry at Dunbar: 'For the Lord of Hosts is with us: the God of Jacob is our refuge.'

However the 'Prayer before a March or Battle' was applicable only to the Cavaliers: 'It is not Ambition, or Malice, that hath thrust us into this posture, but the necessary defence of thy Church, thy Truth, our Laws, our Liberties. ...' Here was the voice of King Charles I, not Cromwell. And the King himself was to be the subject of prayer in order to alleviate 'his long and bitter sufferings'. Charles' own position was acknowledged in a prayer for his specific benefit, beginning, 'Almighty God, who do'st establish thrones of Princes, and the succession in those thrones, by giving thy judgements to the King, and thy righteousness to the King's son ...'[3]

As far as Charles was concerned, it was not empty compliment. Indeed, it could be argued that the King's son at this point was showing not only righteousness, but also a degree of judgement lacking in the counsels of his father. The Prince of Wales tried to maintain an element of stability in an increasingly unstable situation; unfortunately, his ignorance of developments on the other side of the Channel, due to lack of intelligence and a general news black-out, was profound. His father's letters, written to him at the end of November, did not arrive into the Prince's hands until late in December; then their text was poignant rather than relevant.

There was often a gap of some weeks between some epoch-making dénouement in England and the Prince of Wales hearing what had taken place. One striking example of this was Colonel Pride's forcible purge of Parliament on 6 December. All those members who did not bow to the Army's increasingly radical demands – including the trial of the King – were ejected: a 'rump' of under sixty members was left. This meant that the Army leaders, including Oliver Cromwell, the victor of the Second Civil War newly returned from Scotland, and his son-in-law Henry Ireton, were in virtual control, with the aid of this Rump Parliament to carry out their behests. On the day of Pride's Purge the King was taking freezing walks along the shore of the Solent, Henrietta Maria crouched in poverty and misery at the equally cold palace of Saint-Germain, and Charles himself was by now at Breda, an ancient stronghold at the confluence of the Mark and the Pra, just north of today's Belgian border. He had decided to make the move, as the situation in Holland grew increasingly impossible. For all the amity of the Prince of Orange, an individual, even a royal one, could do little. The Dutch were embarrassed and slightly hostile.

Charles' first choice had in fact not been Breda but the welcoming island of Jersey. There Henrietta Maria could join him. Their ultimate objective was Ireland, which could be more easily reached from Jersey. But Henrietta Maria's finances did not even permit her to get as far as Jersey. With her son, she could expect but little from the French Court at that time. It was true that the Peace of Westphalia in October had brought an official end to the Thirty Years' War, which had plagued the people and beggared the state exchequers (although France continued to fight Spain for another eleven years). In theory, European rulers were now free to get on with their interior business of government. But the granary of this particular peace contained within it the seeds of popular dissidence as well as those of absolutism. In France the first war of the Fronde, which broke out in October and lasted until March the following year, fully occupied Queen Anne and Cardinal Mazarin.

Breda lay in North Brabant, which was part of the Prince of Orange's personal patrimony; in addition the Brabantines tended to be Catholics, and would not therefore, like their Dutch neighbours, yearn after the Protestantism of the Parliamentary party. It was not a dull place. Later *A Briefe Relation*, a Commonwealth gazette, would call it a 'town smelling with delight, gallantry and wealth'. Its artisans were said to be eminent in 'the schools of Mars and Venus'.

Of Charles' counsellors at Breda not only Hyde, but the Marquess of Ormonde, still concentrated on the prospect of an Irish venture. The presence of Ormonde at the Prince's side at Breda was in itself reassuring. This splendid man of enormous vitality, head of the Anglo-Norman family of Butler, had been brought up in England under the guardianship of Archbishop Laud, but his vast estates were Irish: as he neatly put it, summing up the enduring Anglo-Irish situation, he himself was Irish 'by fortune though not by birth'. His blonde good looks called forth the admiration of Cromwell himself who, gazing at his portrait, observed approvingly that he looked more like a huntsman than a soldier. Ormonde was twenty years older than Charles (and would outlive him) and had a passion for hard work, coupled with a romantic admiration for King Charles I, which made him a wonderfully energetic and loyal servant. Indeed, Ormonde is one of the few consistently admirable and sympathetic soldiers-cum-statesmen throughout the Civil War period, Commonwealth, Protectorate and reign of Charles II. This in itself is a remarkable achievement, since many behaved admirably in some of these periods, but generally those who behaved admirably throughout did not also behave sympathetically.

For the time being, therefore, with the experienced Hyde and the stable Ormonde to head them, the pro-Irish party of Charles' advisers were in the ascendant.

As for Charles at Breda, he experienced for the first time the unpleasant fate of being a provider who could not provide, an experience which became disastrously familiar to him during the years of exile. Much was traditionally expected of a royal prince in the way of benevolence and charity – whatever his fortunes. Desperately, his suffering followers (who had of course suffered in the royal cause) assumed that their prince or monarch could still exercise his ancient role as a fatherly protector, at any rate in the financial sense. Increasingly, as far as Charles was concerned, that could not be. In December the Prince could not even borrow £200 from a banker at The Hague called Monsieur L'Empereur; he finally scrounged the money out of another banker called Boyet. In the meantime the demands of his pathetic co-Royalists – the 'Crowd of Fugitives who hung upon them [the Court] for bread' – swelled.[4] At Breda, where Charles existed with a greatly diminished household, these demands could only be met by the small subscriptions still forthcoming for the cause from the loyal Cavaliers.

At Breda in December there was stringency, a certain amount of hope, a great deal of waiting. Elsewhere the pace was moving faster and ever faster.

In December the Prince of Wales received at last renewed overtures from the Scots. The Committee of the Estates and the Kirk had at last agreed. The Committee's letter referred to Charles tactfully – or perhaps menacingly would be the right description – as their 'native Prince'; as such, he should urge his father to take the Oath of the Covenant, which had always been the price demanded by the Scots for their approval and assistance. There was certainly a note of menace in the Kirk's reference to Charles' own way of life, his need for 'prayer and understanding'. Both Committee and Kirk agreed that in this vital 'prayer and understanding' lay the true key to the King's recovery of his own throne. The Prince returned a negative answer.

Even if he had so wished, there was not much that Charles could have done at this point. During this same period, events were galloping to a crisis in England. Charles could not reach his father. He did not even know where his father was now held. That left 'prayer and understanding'. No doubt Charles did pray, if not according to the Scots' model. But his prayers did not prevent his father being removed from Carisbrooke on 1 December by the Army. The King was confined first of all at Hurst Castle, a grim and isolated fortress on the Hampshire bank of the Solent, near Lymington – he observed that he was leaving the best castle in England for the worst. A few days later, following Pride's Purge of the House of Commons, the Army officially seized power. On 17 December the King was taken at their orders to Windsor Castle.

About this time Charles at Breda was receiving his father's

letters written from Carisbrooke at the end of the previous month. The sentiments expressed therein were admirable, although the Army leaders, becoming rapidly convinced that there would be no peace for the weary English people while the King could continue to stir the pot, might have viewed them with cynicism.

'Son,' began the King, 'by what hath been said, you may see how long we have laboured in search of peace. Do not you be discouraged to tread those ways, to restore yourself to your right; but prefer the way of peace....' This particular letter was long and full of sage advice, couched in beautifully rounded phrases, the King being as ever a master of the graceful admonition. Its final words were prophetic. It is likely that they remained in the memory of the young Prince until the time came to implement them: 'The English people are a sober people,' wrote the King, 'however at present under some infatuation. We know not but this may be the last time we may speak to you or the world publicly.... To conclude, if God give you success, use it humbly and far from revenge. If He restore you upon hard conditions, whatever you promise, keep.'[5]

Charles returned to the Court at The Hague for Christmas, and it was a paradox that life there during that brief but festive season was extremely gay. In England Christmas had been visited with grim official disapproval, and banished from the calendar, as being Popish and undesirable. The House of Commons continued to sit. Shops were forbidden to close. It was supposed to be a day like any other. But at The Hague Charles flirted with his cousins, the numerous Palatine princesses, and admired in particular the vivacity of little Sophia.

It was not until 13 January that Charles was informed that the trial of his father was going ahead. The news was horrific enough – the trial of a reigning monarch by his subjects administered a shock wave throughout Europe in itself. But at this point Charles did not seriously envisage his father's life being in danger. Deposition, a lifetime's incarceration: these were the possibilities, frightful enough in themselves. Charles wrote immediately to General Sir Thomas Fairfax – widely and correctly rumoured to be far less intransigent on the subject of the King than his colleague Oliver Cromwell – and the Council of War.[6] He pointed out in the most urgent terms that he had no sources of information about the health and general condition of his father other than the 'common gazettes' – the newspapers which trickled across the Channel and into the Low Countries, often weeks late. The Army had not allowed his father at Windsor to receive the Prince's own emissary, who had been sent with the specific task of reporting on the King's state.

Now there had come to Charles' ears a rumour 'the mere thought of which seems so horrible and incredible' that it moved him to address the Council of War directly. He begged them to testify to their fidelity by reinstating their lawful King, and restoring peace to the kingdom. It should be appreciated that to Charles his correspondents were no more than a collection of enigmatic strangers, who had mysteriously seized power in his own country. He had never met Cromwell or the other insurgent leaders. Charles' complete ignorance of the make-up of the new men at the helm in England, although hardly his own fault, was to be a great disadvantage to him subsequently when trying to cope from abroad with the phenomenon of the Commonwealth. On this occasion he made a pathetic attempt to woo these new men with flattery: the restoration of peace, he wrote, would be 'an honour never before given to so small a number as you'.

The letter was of course perfectly useless, not to say irrelevant, in an England now totally dominated by the revolutionary junta. The Army leaders had ears, but they did not wish to hear. Their growing suspicions of each other added to their determination not even to be seen to hearken to outside pleadings. A letter written by Henrietta Maria during the previous autumn, asking to be allowed to be near her husband 'in the uttermost extremity', was not even opened – it lay sealed for thirty-three years.[7]

In his despair, Charles also tackled his theoretical friend and ally, France, once more. On 18 January he wrote to his cousin the King, and to Mazarin, begging them to remonstrate with these English plenipotentiaries. But there was little comfort to be derived from France: on 6 January the eight-year-old Louis and his brother Philippe d'Orléans, sleepy and ill-prepared, had been bundled away from Paris, where their palace was surrounded by the howling and contumacious Frondeur mob, to Saint-Germain. Their new abode was icy cold and ill-furnished: the nightmare trip was later blamed for Louis XIV's lifelong dislike of Paris. Peace was not made for three months – three crucial months, in which all influence of the French royal family was in abeyance, from the point of view of the English royal family. Letters of remonstrance, received too late to weigh very heavily, were the best Charles could get out of them.

On 20 January 1649 the trial of King Charles I opened in Westminster Hall – the sombre scene of Strafford's ordeal eight years earlier. Two days later the Prince of Wales seems to have realized for the first time that his father's life was actually in danger. His slowness to grasp the exact nature of the King's predicament is explained not only by difficulties of communication but also by the nature of the age in which he lived. Monarchs *were* put to death, it was true, but such events had been appalling rarities in European history. Although the King's own grandmother, Mary Queen of Scots, had been executed, so earth-shaking was the event felt to be that parallels were sought back in the Middle Ages to gloss it over with the patina of historical precedent; moreover, the deed had not been carried out by her own subjects, but by their neighbours.

On 23 January one of the Prince's attendants, Boswell, pleaded in French on the King's behalf in front of the States-General. Charles' own French was still considered too limping to carry out such a crucial task. He was horrified to have to tell them, began Boswell, that an English Prince came before them, seeking intercession for the life of the King his father. As a result of this personal appeal, two Dutch envoys, Albert Joachimi and Pauw Adriaen, set off for England, led by an emissary from the Prince in the shape of Sir Henry Seymour. It was the intention of the Dutch to ask for the trial to be delayed, at least, in favour of some kind of arbitration.

The mission was useless. By the time the Dutch reached England the King had already been condemned to death. Some of the most determined judges had already signed the death warrant by the Friday, 26 January – although certain names were not to be found amongst their number, including that of Fairfax. Representative of that (large) section of the English people who could not follow the revolutionaries down their messianic path any further, Fairfax had not even attended the trial. When his whereabouts were questioned, a masked woman called out from the public gallery that he had too much wit to be present. It later transpired that it was his wife. The same masked unknown, made fearless by her confidence in her own rectitude, had something to say when the charge against the King was proposed to be in the name of 'the Commons and Parliament assembled and all the good people of England'. She cried out once more, 'It's a lie, not half nor a quarter of the people!'[8]

On the Saturday, 27 January, the King was brought back into the court to hear the sentence of death read out.

The next day, at St James's Palace, to which he had been brought from Windsor and where he would spend the last days of his life, the King was allowed to receive Sir Henry Seymour, the Prince's messenger. The mission was accomplished through the good offices of the King's guard, Colonel Tomlinson – who was after the Restoration rewarded for this chink of humanity in the hitherto unbreachable Army wall by being let off trial for his life. Seymour was thus able to receive last messages for Charles, and the King's final letter to his wife.

On the next day, the last day of his life, the King was permitted to see those two touching little figures, Princess Elizabeth and Henry Duke of Gloucester, who had remained as captives in London since the collapse of their father's regime. It was fifteen months since they had set eyes on the King. Princess Elizabeth had grown into a delicate but intelligent girl of thirteen: the tears rained down her face as she clasped her father. That set her brother off crying too. It was a scene which wrung all who witnessed it, including the King's custodians.

Later that night the Princess wrote down the contents of the interview in full, the first and most affecting of all the many documents which form the martyrology of King Charles I.[9] The King spoke to the girl of her mother: she should tell Queen Henrietta Maria 'that his thoughts had never strayed from her, and that his love should be the same to the last'.

But even in such a poignant moment the King did not forget the future of the royal house he had tried in vain to serve, and had only succeeded in ruining. The interests of the true succession must remain paramount. There must be no young puppet kings in the hands of Parliament, agreeing to conditions which older and wiser heads would have rejected. Elizabeth was to tell James Duke of York that in future Charles was to be to him not only his elder brother but also his king. To the eight-year-old Harry, the King was even more explicit. Taking the boy onto his knee, he told him, 'Sweetheart, now they will cut off thy father's head.'

Then, as Harry continued to gaze steadily at his father, the King patiently explained the most important worldly message of all: 'Mark what I say, you must not be a king as long as your brothers Charles and James do live. For they will cut off your brothers' heads when they can catch them, and cut off thy head too at the last. And therefore I charge you, do not be made a king by them.'

The little boy sighed deeply and to his father's gratified surprise said very firmly, 'I will be torn in pieces first.' The King ended on a note of a martyr's holy pride: 'And that he doubted not but that the Lord would settle his throne upon his son ... and that we should all be happier than we could have been if he had lived.'

That son was in the meantime in a state of turmoil and despair. The only step he was not prepared to take on behalf of his father is the one sometimes ascribed to him in popular mythology – the presentation of a blank sheet of paper to the generals, bearing his signature, for them to name their own terms to save his father's life.[10] It had been dinned into Charles by the King that nothing was worth the sacrifice of the Church of England, whose preservation was bound up with that of the monarchy itself. If the generals had demanded a series of religious concessions, Charles knew well his father would not have wished to live on those terms.*

* The blank sheet of paper preserved in the Bodleian Library, Oxford, bearing the signature Charles P, said to be proof of the story, is in fact some kind of Irish military instruction.

Charles thrashed about him, looking for foreign aid. Letters were sent on behalf of Louis XIV to both Oliver Cromwell and to Fairfax, whose withdrawal from the proceedings had given rise to false hopes that he might head some northern or even Scottish-based rescue attempt. But it was symptomatic of the tense, icy, suspicious – and determined – atmosphere which prevailed among the remaining Army leaders in London, that the generals did not even dare open these letters, and those of the States-General, except in the presence of three hundred officers. In the same way the Dutch emissaries were heard on Monday, 29 January, in complete silence. Afterwards no comment was given. None was necessary. In England the Gadarene hours were rushing by towards the execution of the King.

Tuesday, 30 January, was the appointed day. Then, at the very last minute, there was a hitch. Curiously enough, it was the existence of Charles Prince of Wales which held up the proceedings and brought about that very delay which foreign supplication could not achieve.

It was suddenly realized that the execution of King Charles I was not enough. That would simply leave the junta and England itself with the spectre (or vision) of King Charles II. It would be a powerful case of 'The King is dead, long live the King'. For although the House of Lords had been abolished in early January, leaving the House of Commons with the self-appointed power to pass new statutes without the agreement of either Lords or King, no one had yet got round to the task of abolishing the monarchy itself. They had all been too much involved in the process of cutting off the King's head with the crown on it, in the jovial, blackguardly phrase ascribed to Oliver Cromwell. There was no time before the execution to pass through such a radical measure – in fact, the monarchy was not officially abolished until six weeks later – but something had to be done about the succession. Otherwise they might cut off the King's head to their heart's content, but the crown would merely be transferred by the devout monarchists to another head of the Royal Hydra, the head of the Prince of Wales.

In the course of that freezing January morning an urgent

measure was passed 'that no person whatsoever should presume to declare Charles Stewart (son of the late Charles) commonly called the Prince of Wales, or any other person, to be King, or chief magistrate, of England and Ireland....' Only then was it time for the King, wearing two shirts against the cold so that he should not shiver and be mistaken for a coward, to step out of a window in the Palace of Whitehall towards the ready scaffold.

'I go from a corruptible crown to an incorruptible crown,' the King told his chaplain, Bishop Juxon, 'where no disturbance can be, no disturbance in the world.' To the Bishop also he entrusted his last letter to his son, a long message of advice and blessing. It was a sad and sapient document, in which Charles was pressingly advised to take his stand on goodness and piety: how much better to be 'Charles le Bon' than 'Charles le Grand', how much better to be 'good than great'.[11] In the meantime the frantic boy in Holland, in ignorance of this last pacifist testament, was still searching for military support, believing correctly that one who was held by the sword would only be rescued by it. And otherwise would die by it.

Just after two o'clock in the afternoon that day the King went finally to his incorruptible crown. He was dressed all in black, but with the George, the insignia of the Garter, a jewel made of a single onyx. This he handed to Bishop Juxon, with the instruction that it should be given to the Prince of Wales together with the single word, 'Remember'. As his head left his body, cleft by the axe of the masked executioner whose identity would be for ever hidden from posterity for fear of vengeance, a great groan went up from the spectators: a groan which, like the deed itself, would never be forgotten by those who witnessed it. They had no need of onyx jewel or last instruction. They would remember.

It was not until 5 February that Charles, in Holland, learned that the corruptible crown was now his.

Immediately after the execution the ports had been sealed, in an effort to stop the intelligence reaching the Continent until the situation in England was stabilized under the new regime. The news itself seeped into Holland in that most horrid of all forms for those who are waiting: bad news received in a series of newspaper reports, at first unsubstantiated, later growing in circumstantial detail.

But Charles himself did not learn the news from these reports.

Once his advisers had to accept that the worst had happened, there was a terrible debate amongst them as to how they should tell him.[12] The method chosen provided a bitter contrast to that famous romantic night scene at Kensington Palace by which the young Victoria, two hundred years later, would learn, from the royal address of her courtiers, that she had become Queen.

Charles' chaplain, Stephen Goffe, used the same expedient. He entered the room and, after a slight hesitation, began: 'Your Majesty—'

To the agonized son, he needed to say no more. After the weeks of uncertainty, Charles burst into bitter weeping. To Goffe he could not speak. Eventually he made a sign for him to leave. For several hours, Charles II, King of England, Scotland and Ireland, otherwise Charles Stuart, son of that man of blood Charles Stuart the elder, remained quite alone.

PART TWO

Nothing but the Name

'The poor King, who has nothing of it
but the name. . . .'
REPORT TO EDWARD NICHOLAS, September 1649

CHAPTER SIX

A Candle to the Devil

'It's needful sometimes to hold a candle to the devil.'

A Briefe Relation, 21 April 1650

Of all his father's former dominions, it was only in Jersey that Charles II was now declared King. There he was proclaimed – actually in French – '*Vive le Roy Charles Second*' – on 16 February 1649, seventeen days after the execution. Up till then the dreadful rumours had not been believed.

In vain the drums of the devoted island rolled, the cannons roared, and the governor, Sir George Carteret, waved his hat, shouting the loyal slogan.[1] Throughout England itself there was a blankness, a silence, in which the Royalists felt as though they were in some hideous dream, unable to move; and even the Roundheads were shocked by the measures to which rebellion had brought them.

This apathy contrasted with the cheerful energy of the new men as they set about to design their Kingless, godly Commonwealth. While Parliament designed a new seal for itself, showing the House of Commons on one side and Britain – lopped off at the Scottish border – on the other, Jersey had a new seal designed for the new King. Nowhere else was it safe to do so. This rare object showed St George on its obverse mounted on a charger: a quixotic gesture from tiny Jersey.

From the point of view of this new King, the loyalty of Jersey was less crucial than the attitude of his lopped-off kingdom,

Scotland. The Scots as a whole remained monarchist; in any case, they were not disposed to have their monarchy abolished for them by the English. In Scotland Charles II was officially proclaimed King at the Mercat Cross of Edinburgh on reception of the news of his father's death. That at least was something.

The frontispiece to the cult book of the 'martyrdom' of King Charles I (*Eikon Basilike*) shows his son receiving his crown from two angels. How much of it was written by the King himself is debatable, but as Charles I's own account of his sufferings, *Eikon Basilike* had a wide readership in a Europe concussed by the English King's death. Charles II showed his own devotion to the book by having copies bound, with 'CR' and a death's head on the cover; these were presented to his intimates at The Hague.[2] Nevertheless, with the exception of Scotland (and Jersey), the two symbolic angels supporting the new King on the book's frontispiece were alone in their task.

Despite the shock which the late King's execution administered to other crowned heads, the impact did not prove conducive to action. In May the Elector of Brandenburg wrote with regard to Charles II, 'The occasion seems suitable for all Christian princes to come to the help of His Majesty, to avenge as befits, the dreadful and never-before-heard-of deed. . . .' The Elector went on to promise to try and persuade his own Diet to assist, since he himself had, alas, neither money nor men. From the Princess Regent of Hesse Cassel, Amelia Elizabeth, it was roughly the same sad story: she referred poignantly to the 'hateful deed and inexcusable prosecution', but troops and money were quite another matter. Wolfgang Wilhelm, Count of Neuburg, had a cosy feeling that 'God the Almighty, the righteous judge, will not allow such a criminal deed to go unpunished. . . .' But when it came to the question of himself carrying out this divine vengeance, he spoke of the burden of taxes and recent wars against his people. The Elector of Cologne only wished he could help with money, men or mustering-places. The Archbishop of Mainz deplored the murder of the late King but was still lacking 'the most desirable part' of his archiepiscopal lands as a result of recent conflicts. The Bishop of Würzburg professed himself bankrupted by the quartering troops. The Count of Hatzfeldt referred piteously to the subject of his own imprisonment in 1646.[3]

The various excuses given to the King's messenger, Johann Adam von Karpfen, and relayed by him dolefully back to Charles II, remind one of the lame explanations given in the parable of the wedding guests. But this is of course unfair to princes still genuinely suffering from the depredations of the Thirty Years' War, which had only ended officially six months before.

As these little fish declined the honour, Charles did not fare any better with the great powers. France was temporarily freed from the nightmare of civil war by April, but that did not imply an immediate ability to look outside her own boundaries, since domestic unrest continued. (Civil war broke out again in January 1650.) A mission to the Imperial Court in October by Sir Wolfgang William de Swan met with results similar to the unhappy round-up of the Electors. A delicate postscript to a letter from the Elector of Saxony, expressing as usual his regrets, enquired whether all the English had complied with the King's murder or just 'the meaner classes'? If merely the latter, perhaps Charles would win back the minds of his loyal subjects by 'friendliness' and the use of the United Kingdom?[4]

Friendliness, and the use of the United Kingdom, although excellent ideas in principle, were more difficult for the King to apply in exile than the Elector imagined. The use of the United Kingdom in particular raised up those twin religious spectres: the employment of Ireland brought with it a whiff of Popery; that of Scotland involved taking the Oath of the Covenant. The original Oath of the Covenant of 1638 had been reinforced by the Solemn League and Covenant in 1643. The death of one king and the accession of another had only exacerbated these problems. It is probable that a message was sent by Charles to Argyll in July, suggesting that he would join with the Scots – if the Solemn League and Covenant was *not* pressed upon him.[5] But the Covenanting Scots were still cock-a-hoop at the fall of the Engagers, and as a result more obdurate than ever on the need to take the oath as a price of their assistance.

Under the circumstances Ireland was once more considered to be the more alluring prospect. In preparation for the expedition there, it was decided to take Charles and his Court back to Jersey. He had returned to France in June and spent the summer at Saint-Germain. He landed at St Helier on 17 September, accompanied by the Duke of York. A contemporary diarist gives a sombre picture of the royal brothers at church in St Helier: the King in deep purple mourning, unrelieved except for the Star of the Garter on his cloak; James a tall, slight figure in black.[6] It was characteristic of the jumpiness of the time that there were fears for their assassination even within Jersey itself: attendants were ordered to wear swords; sentries were posted.

This new sojourn in the island – which was to last for five months – was of a very different nature from the King's previous jaunt three-and-a-half years earlier. Then he had been young in spirit, at the beginning of his ordeal. Now, in the words of his father's last letter, he had the advantage of wisdom over most princes, having spent the years of discretion in 'the experience of troubles and exercise of patience'. The late King had suggested that piety and other virtues, both moral and political, would develop more easily under such circumstances, as trees in winter thrive, rather than in 'warmth and serenity of times'.[7]

It was true. Charles' experience of troubles so early in his maturity had certainly brought out in him virtues which might otherwise have remained latent. The need to display public courage rather than private grief, this was implanted in Charles, along with the other qualities which would mark his exile – resilience, a splendid kind of grit, and, even in the most terrible situations, a sort of buoyancy evidently chosen as an alternative to despair. Lastly, he was beginning to display an ability to keep his own counsel. But of course other less admirable attributes may take root in the wintry soil of adversity. These include the ability to mislead or trick, the will to deceive – attributes which are sometimes essential for survival but can never win a chorus of praise for those who possess them. During the next eighteen months Charles would demonstrate, generally for the better, but also on occasion for the worse, what sort of man the experience of troubles had made of him.

In Jersey there were at least pleasures to be tasted. Some were the guileless pleasures common to monarchs down the ages (although hitherto denied to Charles), such as a review of the island troops, which took place on the sands. Charles was also able to indulge his love of riding and sailing. Both the King and the Duke of York had brought with them their dwarfs who acted as pages and playthings. The beautiful and bossy Mrs Christabella Wyndham was back again, ruling everyone, as Pepys heard later, 'like a Minister of State'.[8]

But money was, and continued to be, an obsessional concern. Before he left the island, Charles issued an order for a mint to be set up with a view to issuing coinage for the new reign: once more Jersey was the only place where his writ ran sufficiently for the order to have any kind of plausibility. Yet there were no resources for the mint to be established and in fact the order was never carried out.[9]

In November Charles was asking Sir George Carteret to expedite the arrival of the money voted to him for 'supply' by the island: he really had very little else to live on. The royal demesne in Jersey had to be sold. The King and the Duke of York themselves kept a very simple court, cutting down on the number of dishes served; their attendants would doubtless have preferred slightly more pomp, especially since certain of them existed on the consumption of the left-over dishes. Others were allotted board wages, to be paid when the money came in (and when would that be?). In general, the courtiers were in wretched straits.

And of course the quarrels broke out all over again. The personalities surrounding the King continued to clash. The presence of the veteran Sir Edward Nicholas – he was approaching sixty – in Charles' counsels was generally felt to be an asset: he was described by Hyde in his *History* as 'a very honest and industrious man, and always versed in business'.[10] He had been Secretary of State to Charles I, and was appointed in the same position to Charles II. The only trouble with Nicholas' honesty was that it filled him with natural distaste for court intrigues; that in turn did not necessarily make him the best man to deal with them. Like Hyde, he was an Anglican; like Hyde, he disapproved of the notion of further negotiations, covert or overt, with the Scots.

Less salubrious in Charles' inner circle was the presence of Lord Percy. Here was another devotee of Queen Henrietta Maria, and, when one considers the calibre of her other Cavalier, Lord Jermyn, it is evident that somehow the Queen did not attract men of judgement to her side. This was particularly regrettable when the men in question passed into her son's counsels. Despite his loyalty to the Queen, Percy was a Presbyterian, which put him in natural opposition to Hyde or Nicholas. Percy had also fought a duel with Prince Rupert during those bad days at The Hague the previous year. Not only religiously but also philosophically Percy advocated giving in to the demands of the Scots, on the grounds that they represented the power of the moment. Although Hyde described Percy angrily as an atheist, it was in fact a Hobbesian view. At least it was to Percy's credit that he had been a brave soldier; he had another talent – even his enemy Hyde praised his flair for economical household management.

The King's private secretary, Sir Robert Long, was an altogether more doubtful character. He had entered Charles' story as secretary to the Council of the Prince of Wales in the West Country, when, it will be recalled, he had caused trouble by demanding to sit on the Council proper. There had also been some unpleasant innuendoes concerning his loyalty, including a tale that he had been in touch secretly with the Parliamentary commander Essex; in a couple of years' time there would be more trouble, when he would be alleged to have shown the King's correspondence to Henry Ireton. But Long too enjoyed the favour of Henrietta Maria, which put him in the same camp as Percy and ranged him against Hyde and Nicholas.

Throughout the autumn, as preparations for the Irish venture were made, these disputes smouldered on, with the occasional spark flying. The King himself came in for criticism: he was not attending to his business sufficiently. It was a charge which was already familiar to Charles and we shall meet it again and again after the Restoration. During this troubled period Charles had a habit of meeting a situation in which nothing could be done with an assumption of indifference, even indolence, and for that he should not have been blamed. But the active members of his entourage fretted at the delays, and looked round for a scapegoat: the King's reputation for laziness was always conveniently to hand.

For better or for worse, the Irish plans were destined to come to nothing. The earnest little court at Jersey plotted and prepared and nagged throughout the autumn; all the while the victorious campaign of Oliver Cromwell had quite put an end to any possibility of the King landing there. It was in September at Drogheda, north of Dublin, and in October at Wexford, on the south-east tip of Ireland, that Cromwell instigated those fabled blood-baths which conquered Ireland, for the time being (and, incidentally, blackened his reputation for ever). Yet, owing to the perennial difficulty of communications, it was not until late in the year that the devastating news reached the King and his advisers.

At the orders of Parliament, Cromwell had set out to stop Ireland being used as a beachhead for an invasion of England on behalf of the Royalists. In that, he had succeeded only too triumphantly. Even if Prince Rupert's naval skills had enabled Charles to land in Ireland at one of the remaining unoccupied ports, such as Waterford, the King would have found little for his comfort on arrival. Cromwell had reduced the royal forces to a series of pitiful, isolated and beleaguered fortresses.

With hopes of Ireland gone, the situation in England was hardly more encouraging than it had been immediately after the execution. As one correspondent wrote in the spring of 1650, the King's party there was 'so poor, so disjointed, so severely watched' that they could do nothing on their own. The same source suggested that 'a good understanding' between the King's party and the Presbyterians might at least enable the English Royalists to rise again.[11]

It was a conclusion which could no longer be avoided.

The thin lips of the Covenanting Scots began to stretch in a new smile of welcome, confident that this time the King could not elude their rigid embrace.

Given that King Charles II had a moral duty to try and recover his throne as soon as possible, he had absolutely no alternative at the beginning of 1650 but to try Scotland once more. He was a monarch. He had inherited a kingdom. He must now seek to wrest that kingdom from its unlawful possessors. It was up to him to establish who, if anyone, could help him in the task. This explains, among other things, how Charles, having decided to try the Covenanters once more, also gave a commission to Argyll's sworn enemy, the Marquess of Montrose. As a result, Montrose landed at Kirkwall in the Orkney islands in January 1650.

At the time when it was made in Jersey, this decision represented an intelligible desire to utilize all available pro-monarchical forces within Scotland. If Montrose did well, he would strengthen the King's hand in his coming negotiations with the Covenanters. If he did *very* well, he might even make these same negotiations both abortive and unnecessary. But it was most unfortunate that Montrose landed at Kirkwall before he received a crucial letter from the King, written from Jersey and dated 12 January. In this letter Charles broke the news that he was once more contemplating meeting the terms of the Scots. Montrose, in his ignorance and innocence, campaigned in Scotland quite unaware of what was taking place elsewhere in Europe.

Montrose was a man of strong sensibilities, black and white loyalties. He had performed an important psychological role after the execution of King Charles I by transmitting some of his own enthusiasm for recovering the throne to the King's son: the arch-traitors who had murdered his beloved master could and would be defeated. He wrote to his new sovereign, 'As I never had passion upon earth so strong as that to do your King father service, so it shall be my study ... to show it redoubled for the recovery of you.'[12] That was the kind of servant of whom Charles stood in need in the dark days of 1649.

But Montrose was also excitable, a noble figure not only to his age, but to himself. Later Burnet wrote of him that he took upon him the deportment of a hero too much 'and lived as in a romance'. Hyde more calmly described him as 'a man of *éclat*' who lived in style with numerous servants.[13] It is a fact that the presence of a romantic character on the stage of history frequently upsets the balance of the whole plot. To a certain extent this was true of Charles' involvement with Montrose. Naturally Montrose's supporters took the King's new negotiations with the Covenanters much amiss. Montrose's correspondence with Charles was subsequently published in Paris, with the deliberate intention of disrupting relations between King and Covenanters. Yet Charles' intention at this point was hardly to betray Montrose – something for which he had no possible motive, uncertain as he was of the whole Covenanter situation. He did however entertain hopes that he might frighten the Covenanters by his use of Montrose: much as they loathed Montrose, they might be persuaded by jealousy to take some kind of corporate action with him. In corporate action in Scotland, the King was convinced – as were most sensible people – lay the true salvation.

Charles finally left Jersey on 13 February 1650. Warrants for the Court in Jersey towards the end of the previous year show one hundred pounds paid to Robert Long for parchment, paper, quills, wax and so forth.[14] That was the measure of the ceaseless correspondence which had preceded his embarkation. And the cost of the departure itself was not small. It certainly strained the slender Jersey exchequer. Now that he decided to take the plunge and meet the Scots again, Charles' intention was to make the bravest showing possible, if only to demonstrate that they might be dealing with a pauper, but they were also dealing with a King. He even went to the trouble of acquiring some new clothes – although clothes were never one of his ruling passions – because the rest of his wardrobe was 'so spotted and spoiled'. An embroidered suit with hatband and belt was ordered, and another plain riding suit, with an 'innocent [spotless] coat'.[15]

The King went first to meet his mother. How much – all tragic – had happened in the two years since their last encounter! Now the Queen Mother's own poverty was fearful: she relied on scarcely concealed acts of charity among the kinder of the French *noblesse*. For example, one princess, a former mistress of Henri Quatre, sent the poor lady a sheep whose stomach proved to be filled with gold coins. No doubt both the mutton and money were welcome, but it was a sad comedown for the daughter of the great Henri to be dependent on the sweetness of his former paramour. Even so, the main burden of Henrietta Maria's conversation was to beg her son never to sign the Covenant.

The new battle joined between the King and the Covenanters – a battle of words, and certainly of wits, from which in the end neither emerged triumphant, at least in the estimate of history – was joined at Breda on 26 March. Both parties arrived there on that date within a few hours of each other. The King's deliberate and delightful courtesy was from the first very much to the fore. He sent his own coach to receive the Scottish commissioners, which was one formal mark of extreme respect, and received them in his bed-chamber, which was another.

Regrettably, the three chief commissioners chosen, Alexander Brodie, Alexander Jaffray and the Earl of Cassilis, belonged to the sternest faction of the Covenanters. Three other commissioners, George Winram, Sir James Smith and the Earl of Lothian, who were made of softer stuff, were kept severely in the background. On 4 April the most domineering terms were laid before the young King at Breda. Not only was he himself to take the Oath itself, but he was also to swear to establish the Presbyterian form of worship in England and Ireland, as well as Scotland. Furthermore, he was to permit no other form of worship within his own household. King Charles I would have turned in his grave, and, commenting on it all afterwards, Henrietta Maria made almost the same point: 'Le feu Roy votre père avait un si grande horreur. . . .'[16]

The stipulation concerning the King's own household was a peculiar insult by the standards of the time; the demand was quite in excess of normal practice. Even Henrietta Maria was permitted Catholic chaplains and a chapel in the anti-Papist England of the 1620s, a country in which Catholicism was officially proscribed. On a grander scale, all church affairs were to be submitted to the authority of the Kirk; all treaties with Catholics were to be annulled, all previous commissions and declarations withdrawn.

Despite the loftiness of these claims, Charles was still prepared to accept them, as he told his brother-in-law the Prince of Orange – so far as Scotland itself was concerned. What he could not do was impose on 'his other kingdoms'. And he could not renege on his previous commitments.[17] The clause concerning previous treaties and commissions meant in effect ratting on the faithful Ormonde in Ireland and the fiery Montrose now in Orkney.

But the commissioners were adamant. Indeed, there could be no question of the terrible choice which faced Charles, since it was spelt out for him by the commissioners, who with great lack of charm referred to Montrose throughout as James Graham – shades of his father and 'Charles Stuart the elder'. As for Charles' previous dealings with James Graham: 'It will be your Majesty's wisdom to acknowledge the sin, and to humble yourself before God.'[18]

So the battle at Breda raged. People prophesied the outcome according to their hopes. Sir John Berkeley, one of Charles' aides, wrote that there could be no danger of an agreement, 'for they [the Scots] are resolved to insist upon things unreasonable, and we are not in a disposition to grant them [things] reasonable'. But Jermyn and Percy were more optimistic. It was at this point that one Royalist was quoted in an English newspaper as saying, 'It's needful sometimes to hold a candle to the devil....'[19]

The scales wavered to and fro and stayed, for the time being, level. But there were two new weights on the side of the Covenant which were to be of considerable significance in the final decision. First, the Engagers, or at least some of them, had returned to the fold of the Scottish counsels, and as a result Lauderdale, amongst others, was back at Breda. Lauderdale stressed the importance of Charles' physical presence in Scotland. His mere arrival there would 'dissipate those clouds'.[20] Once before Charles had been asked to lend his presence to a Scottish campaign, had not arrived in time and had been blamed in consequence. The fact that this Scot, whom Charles both liked and trusted, advocated agreement, was important.

Even more influential was the advice of the Prince of Orange. William's reflection on hearing the news of the Irish defeat must stand for a whole body of judicious monarchical opinion: 'It is obvious that God wishes him [Charles] to understand that Scotland is the only way to his restoration.' Under the circumstances, William urged Charles to go the whole hog – to follow Presbyterian worship himself while in Scotland.[21] William concerned himself with trying to make the Covenanters scale down their more unreasonable demands, through the medium of the Dutch Calvinists.

Charles took refuge in silence. This enabled both sides to rejoice in turn. One moment the Cavaliers were triumphant and describing the Presbyterians as 'drowned rats'; the next moment Argyll's star was sufficiently in the ascendant for him to hint that Charles might actually marry his daughter, Lady Anne Campbell, a decent but scarcely scintillating match.

The problem remained Montrose, now campaigning somewhere in the north of Scotland, and quite out of touch. But by this stage Charles understood perfectly well that he either had to accept the Covenanters' terms or abandon the hope of restoration for the time being. At last, on 27 April, Charles returned a formal and favourable answer to the commissioners' proposals. He would swear the Oath of the Covenant. He would grant everything demanded as regards Scotland herself, including the establishment of the Presbyterian Kirk and the ratification of the Scottish Parliament and its Acts.

He still would not accept Presbyterianism for England, the abandonment of the Catholic Irish treaty, the renunciation of Ormonde – in short, all those demands which were not strictly speaking pertinent to Scotland. He proposed that the Engagers should receive back both their estates and their public offices (for the time being they had to be content with their estates). But it was implicit in the agreement as it stood that Montrose no longer held the King's commission.

In Scotland Montrose heard the small glad news that the King had bestowed upon him the Garter and the vast bad news of the talks at Breda in one and the same letter. By the time the King wrote a rueful letter telling Montrose that he now had to look after himself, the Marquess had already been captured by the gleeful Covenanters. On 18 May he was led through the streets of Edinburgh like a captive in a Roman triumph. On 21 May (o.s.) he was executed.

He went to his death, they said, like a bridegroom. As the

ghost of Strafford haunts Charles I, Montrose's ghost continues to haunt the reputation of his master. It has been suggested in defence of Charles II that he received private assurances (which were broken) that Montrose would not be sacrificed. As a counter to this it has been pointed out that Argyll would never have given such assurances, knowing in advance that they would be broken, for he stood thereby to imperil the new treaty between King and Scots at its inception.[22] Both points are academic, if on balance it is likely that the assurances were *not* given, because Charles at Breda was playing for a larger stake than the single life of Montrose. He was gambling for his restoration and for that of the entire monarchical regime.

In view of Montrose's tragic end, it is natural to blame the King for his betrayal. But many survivors, partisans, guerrillas or exiled leaders without troops, behave in a manner unimaginable in the clear light of successful day. It was in the gloomier shades of desperation that Charles' treatment of Montrose took place: in this light it should be judged.

Immediately after agreeing to take the Oath of the Covenant Charles had to contend with the other unpleasant consequences of his new policy. First the Anglican Royalists in England felt understandable outrage and disdain at such a compromise. It was not for this that they had sacrificed lives and estates in the interests of the King in the past, nor for the Presbyterian interest that they intended to struggle on in the future, bowed under the crippling demands of sequestration and taxation. Thus a number of horrified Anglicans in England took no further part in the Royalist cause there. Having lit a candle to the devil, King Charles II could not expect other lights to shine as well.

Animated by the same profound horror, Hyde and his faction exclaimed against the dishonour of the deed. Hyde had gone on a mission to Spain seeking support, in order to avoid the contamination of the Covenanter intrigues. 'Oh my lady,' he wrote from Madrid to his friend Lady Morton, 'we are making haste out of Christianity and forgetting that there is another court to appear in when we are out of this.' To Nicholas he described the whole involvement as 'folly and atheism'. The most he could do was utter the pious ejaculation: 'If there be a judgement of Heaven upon him [Charles II], I can only pray it may fall as light on him as may be.'[23]

On 24 May (o.s.) Charles set sail for Scotland. In general, if he went with the disapproval of the English Anglicans, he went with the approval of Europe. Her sovereigns were well able to appreciate that he had little alternative but to travel north if he wished to recover his throne – being either disinclined or unable to help him themselves. As a Commonwealth spy wrote accurately of the King's Scottish expedition, 'They must needs go whom their Fates drive....'[24]

Charles' journey, and indeed his arrival in Scotland, was not auspicious. He was twenty-two days at sea, tormented by contrary winds, and it was only by 'a very great Providence' that he escaped the searching ships of the Commonwealth. The Providence consisted of a Scotch mist. A hundred years earlier it had been a Scotch mist which saved his great-grandmother, Mary Queen of Scots, from the navy of Queen Elizabeth, on her return from France. On that occasion John Knox had been inspired to compare the mist to the religious darkness which the young Queen was bringing with her. In this case it would have been plausible to suggest that it was the Covenanters who were about to confront Charles with the powers of religious darkness.

Even before he sailed, the Scottish Parliament had made some stringent new demands, believing, as *Mercurius Politicus* put it, that the King was now 'safely caught in the springe [trap] of the Kirk'.[25] Charles himself was unaware of this, but the unpleasant news caught up with him when a storm obliged his vessel to anchor just off Heligoland at the mouth of the Elbe. There were new arguments and disputes.

It was on 3 July, still on board ship, but by now at anchor at the mouth of the River Spey, on the north-east coast of Scotland, that Charles capitulated for the third and last time. For him personally it had been a painful progress, from the first agreement to negotiate, via the moderate terms proposed in April, to the final humiliation of accepting these new and pungent conditions. Even so, he did not give in without a final attempt to defend the laws of England against the encroachments of a Scottish Parliament. How could the establishment of Presbyterianism in England be lawful, since nothing had received the King's assent since 1649, when monarchy and the House of Lords had been abolished? This ploy was unsuccessful.

So it was that Charles II came at last to swear that great oath, so solemn to so many, so odious to many more, so invidious to a Stuart king. He took it in both forms. It began: 'I Charles King of Great Britain, France and Ireland, do assure and declare by my solemn oath, in the presence of Almighty God, the searcher of all hearts, my allowance and approbation of the National Covenant and Solemn League and Covenant above written. . . .' It ended menacingly on the subject of Presbyterian government and worship, as approved by the General Assembly of the Kirk and the Scottish Parliament: 'And I shall observe these in my own practice and family, and shall never make opposition to any of these, nor endeavour any alteration therein.'[26]

There can be no question that Charles swore the Oath in the cause of expediency and nothing else. As Buckingham, ever light-hearted where considerations of honour were concerned, had originally suggested, once he had sworn the Oath and secured Scotland, then he would proceed on his own sweet way.

In part, he had been brought to this cynical signature by the demands of *Realpolitik*. But the Covenanters themselves were also guilty. They had imposed upon their King demands which they knew he had absolutely no desire to fulfil (and had tried to impose some which were legally outside his power to grant, such as the commitment of England to Presbyterianism). This point was appreciated by the Covenanters themselves in their hearts. Alexander Jaffray, one of the commissioners, wrote in his Diary, 'We did both sinfully entangle and engage the nation ourselves and that poor, young Prince to whom we were sent, making him sign and swear a Covenant which we knew from clear and demonstrable reasons that he hated in his heart.'[27]

But that was after the event. At the time Kirk and politicians were delighted with the effects of their intransigence. They combined to keep a strict watch over their King: he was treated like a secret weapon not yet ready to be unveiled. The fishwives might burn their baskets on bonfires out of joy at the coming of their Prince, but they were not otherwise allowed to have any truck with him. And from the nobility it was 'none of the better sort', only 'Argyll's faction' who were granted access, according to a report given to Nicholas.[28]

As it was, Charles' first few weeks in Scotland were of unimaginable gloom and depression. In themselves, they were quite enough to prejudice him against Scotland, and its way of life, even if he had not already had dour experience of the Covenanters. It was true that much of what he saw was redolent of his family's history. He visited Falkirk – 'his own house', as one correspondent put it, since it had been built by his ancestor James V as a hunting lodge. But not all the architectural echoes of family history were as pleasing as this graceful palace, built in the French manner. Charles also visited Gowrie House at Perth, whose name spoke of that strange entanglement of King James VI and the aristocracy, the Gowrie conspiracy. Whatever the truth of it, King James had at least emerged with his life. 'God grant His Majesty be as fortunate' was one pious reflection concerning King Charles' own sojourn there.[29]

At Aberdeen his lodgings overlooked the Tolbooth. While Montrose's head had been exhibited in Edinburgh itself, the Scots had followed their ancient if barbarous custom of posting up other limbs in other towns as a warning. Montrose's hand was nailed to the Tolbooth. Even if the King did not see it, he must have been told of the grisly memento. The King's standard in Scotland was of black damask; it depicted joined hands between swords coming out of a cloud; the Latin motto referred to those whom piety, honour and virtue had made friends. Montrose's fate was a perpetual reminder of the sacrifice which, along with piety, honour and virtue, had gone to the making of this new friendship between himself and the Kirk.

Meanwhile, the Kirk itself, like Shylock, determined to extract the due and forfeit of its bond. So relentless was its treatment of the young King, pressing upon him, amongst other humiliations, the need to denounce both father and mother, that there must have been a measure of revenge in it against the whole royal house of Stuart. There was an actual day appointed to bewail the sins of the late King and the royal family. Perhaps, like Shylock again, the Kirk was seeking to 'feed fat the ancient grudge' it had against that family which had so sparingly accepted its precepts. Otherwise, the King yawned his way through the sermons, which were both infinitely long and very frequent. And the Scots' social life was as bleak as their church-going. Grace before a meal could stretch interminably: 'At dinners, they lay as fiercely about 'em as in the Pulpit.'[30]

Even without the sufferings outlined above, the Scots were probably not a people it was immediately possible to love, if you had been nurtured in the courts of England and France. Charles had already known poverty, but it was poverty due to keeping up the state of a bankrupt King. Even the English soldiers of the Commonwealth commented disdainfully in their letters home on the low standards of Scottish life: tables, windows, cupboards all with 'shut' written in large characters on them, and women who were so dirty and ill-favoured that they resembled those witches the Scots were so fond of burning. The mixture of religious fanaticism and low living did not endear itself to the newly acclaimed King of Scotland. He kept a perfect composure in public. But inside himself he brooded. To Dr King, Dean of Tuam (and thus a passionate Anglican), he observed in conversation, 'The Scots have dealt very ill with me – very ill.'[31] It was an ominous remark.

The final irony of all the King's Scottish experience was provided by the fact that, exactly two months after he swore the Oath of the Covenant at Speyside, the entire justification for the gesture, the Scottish army, was vanquished beneath the hooves of Cromwell's victorious cavalry at Dunbar. So that the Covenanter Scots, far from constituting that mighty host which would place the King on his English throne, became a spent and impotent force, as once the Engagers had been.

The Commonwealth command had not been idle while Charles disputed with the Kirk. Cromwell had returned from Ireland in the early summer, having quelled the country against future revolt, and almost immediately set out on a punitive expedition against Scotland. Officially it was described as a pre-emptive strike: the Commonwealth Army was marching purely in order to stop the Scots invading England on behalf of King Charles.

At the exact moment when King Charles, shackled by the Oath, set foot in Scotland, Cromwell's fortunes did not, for once, look particularly propitious. And throughout August 1650, an exceptionally wet and nasty month, even by the standard of such Scottish summers, the astute Scottish general David Leslie was able to taunt Cromwell by guerrilla methods. In the mountainous, rainy south of Scotland, Cromwell's tentless troops suffered; at the same time they found it impossible to come to grips with Leslie.

At this point the Scottish leaders were riding high. They had their young lion bound, the old beast of England hemmed in. They even found it in their fanatic hearts to instigate another series of purges of the armed forces, based on religion. The Act of Classes removed a number of bonny fighters from the Scottish ranks. At The Hague the reckless action was compared to that of the people of Jerusalem, fighting among themselves when Vespasian pressed the town.[32] Nevertheless, by the end of August the Scots had, in their own view, caught Cromwell and his exhausted forces, many of them sick, in a proper trap. He was confined on the coast road south, between the devil, in the shape of Leslie on the commanding heights above him, and the deep grey waters of the North Sea on his left.

King Charles, no more than an adjunct to the Scottish action, lounged at Perth. And it was here that he received the news that on 3 September Cromwell, in a dramatic escapade worthy of the most adventurous hero of romance, had not only eluded the trap, but had also defeated the vastly superior home forces. There is one story that Charles actually fell on his knees in thanksgiving when he received the news, and another that he threw his cap in the air for joy.[33] Both are probably apocryphal; but they symbolize the acute dislike and resentment the King now felt against the Scots.

In personal terms, Charles was infinitely more devastated by the news of the death of his sister Elizabeth, shortly after Dunbar.[34] The poor young Princess died in captivity at Carisbrooke Castle, only two days before permission arrived from Parliament for herself and her brother Henry to leave at last for the Continent. It was the final horror that little Henry was informed that his sister had died of grief because Charles had taken the Oath of the Covenant. In fact, she died of consumption; the poet Henry Vaughan aptly wrote of her as 'a rose-bud born in snow ... sprung to bow/To headless tempests, and the rage/Of an incensed, stormy age'.* She died with her cheek resting on the Bible her father had given her the day before his execution: 'Come unto Me, all ye that travail and are heavy laden, and I will give ye peace.'

In Scotland Charles was young and human enough to rejoice in his heart at the humiliation of his own persecutors. As for their reaction to this holocaust inflicted on them, its flavour may be judged by a letter to Charles from Robert Douglas, one of the moderators of the General Assembly, shortly afterwards. Douglas implied that the defeat had been in fact due to the 'Guiltiness' of the royal family: perhaps a new day of 'Humiliation' should be kept? Charles himself should seriously consider 'of the controversy that God hath against you and your family, for which His wrath seems not yet to be turned away ...', to say nothing of his own motives for subscribing to the Covenant: 'If self-interest and the gaining of a crown have been more in your eye than the advancing of religion and righteousness, it is an iniquity to be repented of and for which your Majesty ought to be humbled.'[35] There was no mention here of the fatal Act of Classes which had decimated the fighting force, nor the divisions among the Scots themselves.

Yet Charles could ill afford the luxury of *Schadenfreude* at the defeat of the Covenanters if he was still intent on his own

* She was buried simply in the Isle of Wight. In a more secure age it was Queen Victoria who had a monument of marble executed, still to be seen in St Thomas' Church there: 'Erected as a token of respect for her virtues and sympathy for her misfortunes by Victoria R.'

restoration. It was the gloomy truth that he must once again compromise and reconcile if he was to have any hope of succeeding. It was no wonder that when he was adjured to repent yet again, Charles observed wearily: 'I think I must repent me ever being born.'

CHAPTER SEVEN

Ravished at Worcester

'And now ravished at Worcester by numerous over-powering force, on that black and white day September the third, 1651.'

A True Narrative ... of His Majesty's Miraculous Escape

On 4 October 1650 King Charles rode carelessly out of Perth, 'as if going on hawking' – and only came to rest forty-two miles later. This attempt to escape his Covenanter captors, as they had virtually become, was known as the Start. It finished almost as soon as it began. The King pushed north to Dundee, paused at Cortachy and rested overnight somewhere near. But no Highland Royalist force emerged to join him. Two officers from his abandoned hosts at Perth soon caught up with him, finding the King to be 'in a nasty room on an old bolster above a mat of sedge and rushes over-wearied and very fearful'.[1]

Charles was taken to Huntly Castle, and by 6 October he was back at Perth, listening to yet another sermon. The Scottish leaders issued a cold instruction on the subject to their emissaries: 'You shall say how much we are grieved and amazed with His Majesty's sudden and unexpected behaviour. . . .'[2]

But the Start had a significance beyond a spontaneous gesture of defiance. It demonstrated in terms which the Kirk could not miss that Charles had reached the limits of his endurance where their demands were involved. Humanly, he was no longer capable of compromise. There had already been sufficient interference with his intimate entourage: Long and another of his attendants had taken themselves off to Dundee, where they were already in touch with the northern Royalists.

Charles' doctor, Alexander Fraizer, also played some part, by putting his master in touch with the 'Malignants', as the Episcopalian Royalists were described. Fraizer had the advantage of having known the King in both Jersey and France; other advantages he possessed he would deploy skilfully after the Restoration, for he could deliver a Court lady's child and cure its father of an amatory disease with equal deftness. In these rugged days, however, it was of more consequence that Fraizer had 'an unquiet and over-active spirit'; he was a natural intriguer rather than a successful one.

When Sir James Balfour came to Charles on 3 October with news of a whole lot of new purges which would be proposed, to include his own household, the King felt he had had enough, dug his heels into his horse and set off on his gallop to Angus and beyond. That, at any rate, is the most plausible explanation both of the Start and of the King's speedy arrest. It has been suggested that Buckingham first inspired and then betrayed the expedition; alternatively that he tried to stop it: but all this is to complicate the issue unnecessarily.[3] The King's apprehension was in fact made inevitable by the unplanned nature of the outing.

Charles' disgust with the Covenanters had been growing apace since Dunbar. On the very day of the battle he had written to Nicholas that it was difficult to conceive of the 'villainy' in Scotland – 'Indeed it has done me a great deal of good,' continued Charles, 'for nothing could have confirmed me more to the Church of England than being here, seeing their hypocrisy.'[4] Politically and strategically, it was madness on the part of the Covenanters to suppose they could defeat Cromwell without the help of all the pro-monarchical forces in Scotland: these obviously included the northern Royalists, whom they had so unhelpfully termed the Malignants, while putting their celebrated champion Montrose to death.

It was with a view to creating some kind of national unity, even at this late hour, that the project of the King's coronation was raised once more. In an age when the coronation of the sovereign has a ritual rather than a political significance, it is easy to forget the importance which the ceremony could still bear in the time of Charles II. This was twofold – foreign as well as domestic. The proposed crowning of Charles in Scotland had always been seen as a propaganda exercise to impress the European powers. It had been hoped to crown Charles at Edinburgh on 15 August 'if Cromwell does not prevent it....' There were happy rumours in Jersey that the solemnity had actually taken place.[5] For a few months at least Cromwell had adequately prevented it.

Now, as the autumn wore on, more colloquies on the subject took place. The Commonwealth gazette, *Mercurius Britannicus*, might refer to Charles as 'his little kingship', an English spy might mark Charles' correspondence 'from Proud Tarquin', and Cromwell refer to him in conversation as 'the young gentleman': none of these titles, sardonic and otherwise, replaced the esteem still given to a crowned head.

Domestically, there was a deliberate attempt to focus nationalist sentiment on Charles' person by referring to the ancient Kings of Scotland – Fergus and so forth, a line of over a hundred sovereigns – to which Charles was regarded as the natural successor. Fergus had probably not figured greatly in Charles' fantasies hitherto, but at Christmas Sir James Balfour gave him 'a great charter', inscribed with the royal genealogical descent, to assist such reveries.[6]

Enormous trouble was taken over the details of the coronation, which was appointed to take place on 1 January 1651 at the Cathedral at Scone. Still, the restraining hand of Presbyterianism was not lacking from the order of the day, or, as the author of an early life of Charles succinctly put it, 'A fresh farce was now necessary and his Majesty had a principal part to play in it.'[7] A committee was formed to draw up the procedure. The King was allowed to wear a prince's robe of considerable richness, and his train-bearers were taken from among the sons of the nobility – the right-minded members of it. He also sat under a canopy of crimson velvet. But the traditional ceremony of anointing – a crucial part of any previous coronation – was omitted as being sheer superstition.

For at the heart of the ceremony was a contradiction like a canker, and that marred it somewhat, in spite of all the determination to create enough magnificence to illumine a nation. Charles sat on the throne of Scone, as his forefathers had done. But it was noticeable that he received the crown from Argyll and the sceptre from the Earl of Crawford, both Covenanters. Shortly afterwards John Middleton, a leading 'Malignant' soldier who wished to return to the Covenanting fold, did penance in sack-cloth – a strange epilogue to a coronation.

Above all, Charles had to endure another of Robert Douglas' protracted sermons, the delivery of which, as Moderator of the General Assembly, Douglas took to be his due on this occasion. This particular effort was not only lugubrious but at times positively menacing. There were a number of solemn warnings about collapsing monarchies. These could fall for two principal reasons. First, 'The sins of former kings have made this a tottering crown'; Douglas added that the chief reason for the misfortunes of both Charles I and James VI and I was contained in their attitude to Presbyterianism. Secondly, a crown could simply totter through general troubles and commotions. Thus, 'A King when he getteth his Crown on his head, should think at the best, it is but a fading crown.'[8] It must have come as a pleasant surprise when Douglas announced at last the real theme of the coronation – to cleave the Scottish people to their young King.

At least the royal Household Book for Coronation Day shows some taste for magnificence: a vastly increased amount of meat and partridges was ordered, a total of ten calves' heads, and twenty-two salmon.[9] A quantity of damask napkins had been ordered well ahead, in December, fifty-four of which, for the King's table alone, were embroidered with 'CR' in anticipation of the ceremony.[10]

And to a certain extent the gambit worked. King Charles made a series of progresses in that part of eastern and northern Scotland not controlled by the Commonwealth troops. At Pittenweem, for example, a coal seaport on the East Fife peninsula, the burgh laid down an elaborate order for his reception, including the ringing of bells from the moment of his arrival onwards, the wearing of their best apparel by the baillies and their council, and the employment of one of 'my lord's best carpets' to cover the festive table. On this they proposed to keep in readiness 'of fine flour some great buns and other wheat bread of the best order', as well as eight or ten gallons of good strong ale. When the King finally left, cannons were fired.[11]

Elsewhere too he received a fine, even tumultuous reception. His regal peregrinations included visits to all the Fife coastal towns, on to St Andrews and Struthers House, thence back to Perth, north to Aberdeen via Dundee, as well as a tour of the garrisons of Stirling, Inchgarvie and Burntisland. He found time too for the now celebrated national pastime of golf (which had been enjoyed, incidentally, by both Mary Queen of Scots and James VI) and a jousting pastime named 'running at the glove'.

In general, Charles bent every effort to make this new deal towards national unity work. At Aberdeen in February he persuaded the ministers to assist General Middleton in recruitment (now that Middleton had used that sackcloth to purge himself of his previous association with Montrose). That was one coup. Another took place in March, when he persuaded the Scottish Parliament to approve the raising of troops generally in the Highlands. The Engagers were in principle allowed back.

And Charles' own reputation was growing in the world outside. In March his former tutor Newcastle, then in Antwerp, referred to him in glowing terms: 'A braver King certainly we have not had since the conquest ... his most excellent parts being bred in the school of calamity.' The character he was beginning to acquire was of one 'admirably active and intelligent in all his great affairs' – with only one proviso. He did not care enough for his own safety, being 'too forward to hazard his person in any attempt against the rebels'.[12] Even that was not a disastrous quality in a young prince, who had to conjure unity out of nowhere, virtually unaided, except by the magnetism of his own person.

And Charles showed that his natural talent for diplomacy had not deserted him in these more public displays, in his handling of the delicate matter of Argyll's daughter, Lady Anne Campbell.[13]

Argyll's ambitions in this respect have already been mentioned: when he arrived at Breda the previous year, with a present of six Flanders mares for the King's coach, one wit suggested that he also intended to unload on the King a seventh mare in the shape of his daughter. In Scotland, undeniably a bachelor, Charles could have found himself in an awkward situation.

It was not a question of the young lady's own attractions (Ann, Lady Halkett, a Scot herself, spoke up for her valiantly and said that she was as well behaved as anyone at the English court). What was at issue was the demonstrable folly of saddling England with a Scottish Queen, one not even of royal birth, the daughter of Argyll to boot. No possible advantage of Argyll's patronage could possibly outweigh the solecism of such a match, in terms of Charles' future in England. And that was after all where the whole Scottish venture was aimed. At the same time it would not do to offend Argyll either – and the power of his position at that time is best illustrated by the fact that Buckingham too dangled after the young lady's hand. Buckingham's courtships were always practical, never romantic – witness his ultimate marriage to the great northern heiress and daughter of the Parliamentary general Sir Thomas Fairfax.

For once it was Henrietta Maria who behaved with common sense and judgement, when Charles consulted her on the subject. There was nothing 'new and extraordinary' in the notion that such a well-born young lady as the daughter of Argyll should wed a King, tactfully wrote back this descendant of the great Henri Quatre. But was it wise to exclude the English altogether from *consultation* over the question of his marriage? In general, the 'imprudence or rather the madness' of Charles' taking of the Covenant had galvanized the widowed Queen. She warned courtiers who were not Catholics away from her side, saying that she was doing so in order to counterbalance her son's behaviour. Reasonably enough, she did not wish to forfeit all the Catholic support in Europe. The Argyll marriage project lapsed for lack of encouragement.[14]

Back in Scotland, the real problem of the time was not the character of the monarch, who was indeed proving himself right royally, nor at this moment even the character of the opposition.

The first known letter from Charles, Prince of Wales, to his governor the Earl (later Duke) of Newcastle.

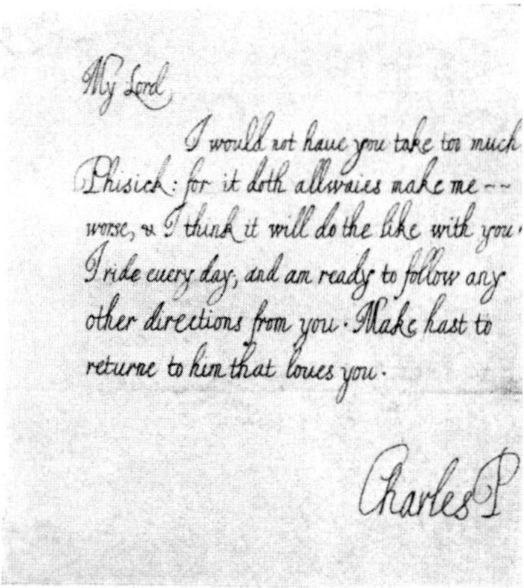
My Lord

I would not haue you take too much Phisick: for it doth allwaies make me -- worse, & I think it will do the like with you. I ride every day, and am ready to follow any other directions from you. Make hast to returne to him that loues you.

Charles P.

Queen Henrietta Maria and King Charles I with their eldest child Charles, Prince of Wales, by H.G. Pot, *c.* 1632.

The five children of Charles I, 1637, by Van Dyck. Left to right: Princess Mary, James, Duke of York, Charles, Prince of Wales, Princess Elizabeth and Princess Anne.

Right: Miniature of the Prince of Wales at the age of thirteen by David Des Granges.

Queen Henrietta Maria in the early 1630s, after Van Dyck.

Charles, Prince of Wales, wearing gilt armour now preserved in the Tower of London; by William Dobson.

Charles I and the Prince of Wales; engraving by Gerald Glover.

Edward Hyde, first Earl of Clarendon, by Lely.

The rare seal of Charles II issued in Jersey after his father's death; Jersey was the only part of the English dominions in which Charles II was proclaimed.

Mary, Princess of Orange and eldest sister of Charles II, 1659, by Adriaen Hanneman.

'La Grande Mademoiselle' (Anne-Marie Louise de Montpensier), first cousin of Charles II and the greatest heiress in Europe.

Whiteladies and Boscobel House in Shropshire, where Charles II hid after the battle of Worcester; he commissioned this commemorative painting, by Robert Streater, after the Restoration.

Worcester, showing the house from which Charles II escaped at the end of the battle; photo by the author.

The Royal Oak today, isolated in a field near Boscobel House (it was once part of a forest).

Charles II asleep in the lap of Major Carlos in the branches of the Boscobel Oak.

Charles II in farmer's clothes riding with Jane Lane from Bentley Hall to Abbot's Leigh. These are two of a set of five historical reconstructions of the royal adventures painted by Isaac Fuller some time after the Restoration. Much of the detail is accurate, but the King himself, only twenty-one at the time of his escape, looks far too old.

Charles II in exile, artist unknown but probably a Spanish painter working in Bruges (detail).

Right: Lucy Walter, known as Mrs Barlow, mistress of Charles II.

Miniature of James, later Duke of Monmouth, Charles II's illegitimate son by Lucy Walter, showing a strong resemblance to pictures of his father at the same age.

Cromwell, a man of over fifty, in precarious health, had taken the winter in Edinburgh badly: he was struck down again in the spring so severely that he saluted the (English) doctor who cured him with the words, 'He has plucked me out of the grave!' The problem was that, for all these progresses, for all this parade of unity, marked by the Scots Parliament appointing the King as commander in March, the people themselves simply did not join up in sufficient numbers to constitute a proper resurgent military force.

For at least a generation the Scottish national fabric had been torn and torn again by religious division. Such rents were not so easily mended. For thirteen years, more or less, the country had been at war, its terrain frequently fought over. The deep human instinct to live at peace, if peace was at all possible, was a much stronger impulse than the shallow new growth of national loyalty implanted by their young King.

Unfortunately there was no way of discovering this unpalatable truth except by trial and failure. In the early summer of 1651 King Charles still rode high. Argyll's influence diminished, his own authority increased. Charles' twenty-first birthday, 29 May 1651, was declared in the Scottish Parliament the day of 'the King's Majestic Majority'; that evening Fife at least was lit up with congratulatory bonfires, and the ordnance was heard blasting off from Burntisland and other Royalist garrisons. The English heard that Charles was 'very absolute' in following 'his own private counsels'. On 24 June the *Weekly Intelligence* (a Commonwealth gazette) reported that he was 'higher than his people as much in stature as authority'. And Charles' enormous physical energy was coming into its own. He thought nothing of riding, two or three times a week, between Stirling and Perth in order to display himself alternately at the head of his forces, and in Parliament. He rode up and down the lines of the army, wearing 'a soldier's dress' of buff, set off by a red sash and his precious George. As to his own commitment, he told them genially that he had only one life to lose.[15]

The question was rapidly arising: where and in what direction was this life, and indeed this army, to be deployed? The obvious decision was to march on England. Given that, the possibilities were twofold. Charles could either plan for England immediately or he could wend his way north, and join up firmly with the Highlanders and Royalists there. Having united all available Scottish forces, he could consider further southward action. Both these courses begged the question of the Cromwellian army still in Scotland, centred on Edinburgh and straddled about the south-east and south-west of the country. The Scots, as everyone realized at heart, were in no position to take on the English again after the defeat at Dunbar. Indeed, both courses open to the King presupposed the swelling of their forces by a large number of additional troops – without which they could scarcely hope to suffer anything but a new and even more humiliating version of the Dunbar catastrophe.

It is important to realize that any plan for a direct southward move was based on the illusion of English Royalist help, because this goes far to explain the ultimate failure of the disastrous Worcester expedition. The notion of English Royalist help was an illusion for the grim reason that by 1651 the English Royalist movement was in itself a myth.[16] Yet of this the King's intelligence, such as it was, was quite unaware. Communications had been cut for too long. It was impossible for the King's advisers, or indeed Charles himself, to appreciate the totality of the hold which a vigilant government now held over England itself. In many ways the country had become like a modern police state, with passes and permissions needed for any form of movement.

The activists fled, their estates confiscated. The feeble (and those disgusted by the King's taking of the Covenant) compounded. The only Royalists with any sort of liberty were those who had decided to sit out the times until better ones prevailed. These were scarcely the types to risk life and limb to join an invading Scottish army, as it would once again appear to be.

Of Royalist underground conspiracy, about the only movement with any vitality in it was the so-called Western Association; this had been formed, under the cover of a race-meeting in April 1650, by Colonel Francis Wyndham of Somerset and Sir

John Paulet of Hampshire. The sphere of its activities was remote from the vital north-western territories through which a Scottish army must pass to recruit English troops. The north-west was the traditional area of Royalist support, where many of the great magnates, such as the powerful Earl of Derby, had favoured the King. Yet the Northern Association, the alleged sister movement to that of the West Country, has been shown to be non-existent except on paper. An unsuccessful and easily quelled rising in Norfolk in December 1650 further depressed the Royalist spirits.

Back in Scotland however, Dean King reported that the King's power was absolute: 'all factions composed, the ambitious defeated, the army cheerful, accomplished, numerous'.[17] In June too, most hopeful sign of all, the pernicious Act of Classes was repealed. From the Scottish angle all the prognostications were cheerful. As far as can be made out, it was always the intention of the King to put this mood of optimism to good use and march on England. Strategically, it made as much sense as marching north; besides, there was always the uncertainty as to how long any alliance of former Malignants and present Covenanters would last. Then there was Charles' undoubted dislike of the Scots, not diminished by the fact that he had successfully united them under his personal banner. To put it mildly, he had no personal inducement to linger in a country which had treated him so ill.

Nevertheless, the Scots themselves were much less certain of the right course to take. At this point, an unexpected upsurge of the Commonwealth fortunes in Scotland transformed the situation. Hitherto the monarchical party had rested, militarily speaking, on the secure base of the Fife peninsula; apparently impregnable to Commonwealth assault, it enabled them to scurry about the north-east with more or less impunity. But on 24 June, at Inverkeithing just north of Edinburgh (close by the site of the modern Forth Bridge), the brilliant young Parliamentary commander John Lambert presented Cromwell with just the victory he needed. It is possible that David Leslie can also be blamed for not sending in enough troops in support. In any case, the bloodshed at Inverkeithing was even more lethal than that at Dunbar: the proportion of Scots killed in relation to the total force was greater.

The Fife débâcle removed from the Scots their other option of a northward encirclement. In a clever manœuvre Cromwell, now restored to health, reached Perth and cut off the Scots' supplies. Militarily speaking, Charles had probably been right from the first in desiring the southern expedition. Now he was certainly right in desiring to speed up the operation if it was to take place at all.

Still the Scots havered. Their army lurked uncertainly west of Fife, near Stirling, leaving the initiative to Cromwell. The Scots did not finally take the decision to plunge south, regardless, for several vital weeks. The actual march began as late as 31 July. The Duke of Hamilton (formerly Earl of Lanark, who had succeeded his brother, executed by Parliament) agreed that marching on England was probably the best course. Or at any rate he called it 'the least ill'. But he added, 'It appears very desperate to me.' Now the fatal divisions, the doom of Scottish society for so many years, began to appear in their ranks once again. Argyll, for example, retreated morosely from the scene and refused to join the army. At this the Engager Hamilton was full of glee: 'All the rogues have left us.'[18] But by the time Charles reached England he would need all the rogues he could get.

It was thus a listless and troubled force which crossed the border into England on 5 August.* Such energy as it had was unfortunately diverted into such idiotic channels as the dispute initiated, with typically bad timing, by Buckingham. The perky young Duke suddenly took it upon himself to object to command of the army being given to a Scot, although the King had the veteran Leslie at his side, as well as Middleton. When Charles tactfully referred to Buckingham's youth as a reason for denying him (Buckingham was actually two years older than Charles),

* Somehow King Charles II managed to pass on his own dislike of Scotland to generation after generation. He ordered the refurbishment of Holyrood Palace but never went to inspect the results. No reigning monarch visited Scotland again until 1822 – a gap of nearly two hundred years. Since the reign of Queen Victoria, of course, the royal family of Great Britain have more than atoned for this neglect.

the Duke sulked in the most childish and public manner, refusing to speak to Charles, refusing to come to the Council, and – supreme buffoon's touch – refusing to change his linen in protest.

These debilitations contrasted with the energy with which the Commonwealth acted to meet the Scottish menace. Once again, as in 1648, much care was taken to present the invaders as alien and predatory. *Mercurius Britannicus* was coached to make a display of anti-Scottish feeling; an issue of early August chose to recall to its readers every single Scottish invasion of England which had taken place since that of King Malcolm in 1071. The word 'un-English' was used to describe those who might be so unwary as to join the 'King of Scots'; stoning was suggested as a suitable fate for them.[19]

This so-called King of Scots was in fact proclaimed King of England at Penrith, a northern market town, and later at Rokeby, where a flourish of trumpets attended the ceremony. But it was significant that the important border town of Carlisle had refused to surrender to his call. And as their native country receded, all too many of the Scots decided to recede from the army back to it. Practically no-one in England joined the royal standard to replace them.

Government measures in England, including the cancellation of all public meetings, dealt efficiently with the emergency. Meanwhile, Cromwell, Lambert and Harrison, three of the toughest Parliamentary generals, were busy harrying the Scottish army in the rear: 'That mongrel Scotch Army', as Thomas Lord Bruce (a Royalist) disdainfully called it in his memoirs.[20] But it was not actually mongrel enough. The Catholics of Lancashire existed but they did not rise. The King was after all at the head of a band of Presbyterians.

Nothing seemed to go right. When the Earl of Derby, the great magnate of Lancashire, landed from the Isle of Man to bring his followers to the King's aid, he was instantly defeated at Wigan. Only the Earl himself, and a handful of his men, escaped to join the King further south. The presence of Commonwealth spies in the Royalist organization exacerbated its problems: Isaac Berkenhead, a supposed Royalist agent, betrayed the correspondence between the King and Lord Derby. Another spy, Thomas Coke, revealed so much of the Royalist network in England that about two thousand people were taken into custody, including potential leaders such as the Duke of Richmond and Lord Beauchamp.[21]

The King's fortunes got no better as he moved south. If anything, the patriotic revulsion of the English against the Scots increased. The Parliamentary commander of the town of Shrewsbury refused to surrender to 'the King', and addressed his refusal pointedly to the 'Commander-in-Chief of the Scottish Army'. There are many instances in contemporary records and memoirs of once loyal monarchists who simply stayed away from the doomed and by now straggling royal train as it wound its way through that English countryside. At Chirk Castle Sir Thomas Middleton not only declined to rouse North Wales on behalf of the King, but even refused to receive his letter.

The Duke of Hamilton had written, 'I confess I cannot tell you whether our hopes or fears are greatest, but we have one stout argument – despair; for we must either stoutly fight or die.' It was in this mood that King Charles, at the head of no more than sixteen thousand men, most of whom were by now utterly exhausted, arrived on August 22 at the city of Worcester.

Twelve days passed before the Commonwealth Army attacked. This period was spent by the King in desperate activity, trying to salvage something like victory from a hopeless situation.

Proud of its loyalty to the royal house, Worcester had been the first city to declare for Charles I in the Civil War. Graced by an incomparable cathedral, which loomed over the woody bank of the River Severn, it presented a fair sight, this city set in a flat green countryside of fertility, nearing the Marches of England and Wales. Here the King lodged in a small mediaeval house* and gave his mind to the reanimation of his dispirited men. It had been twenty-three days since they departed from Scotland. Their problems were not purely of the mind: they were exhausted by this seemingly endless yet unsuccessful progress through England, and their belongings were in tatters;

* Still to be inspected today, but now converted into a restaurant.

most of them lacked shoes and stockings altogether.

The city did have one advantage to set against all this; it occupied a naturally defensive position, situated on one river, the Severn, as it flowed down to Bristol, and defended by another, the Teme, which flowed into the Severn at a strategic point slightly south-east of the town. Beyond the river palisade were the heights blocking off Worcester from Evesham and, to the west, the Malvern Hills. This combination of river and hill might be turned to profit at the eleventh hour.

The day after his arrival the King held an assembly in the broad water-meadows below the cathedral. But the manifesto he issued showed that his prolonged march had still given him no opportunity to feel the pulse of English opinion; he was quite out of touch. For instance, he offered to settle religion according to the Covenant; he thought the difficulties of this were covered by promising arrears of pay to anyone who would desert the Commonwealth. The Act of Oblivion he offered to anyone except the actual regicides must also have seemed curiously unreal to those gathered in the water-meadows; they would have formed the perfectly correct conclusion that it was the King and the Scots who were going to need an Act of Oblivion before they were much older. At least Charles stressed the fact that the Scots would be returning to their own country once the matter at hand was concluded: government propaganda had underlined the fear that the Scots would be granted good English land.

But when the King tried to order a levy of all persons between sixteen and sixty, he was preaching to the wind. Soon Cromwell himself would be ranged against him with thirty thousand seasoned men. The government had even successfully ordered out the English militia against England's titular King. Any stray soldiers were far more inclined to join up with the winning side of the Commonwealth than with that of the beleaguered King.

Cromwell, supported by Lambert, Harrison and Fleetwood, had arrived from the north. But, with his usual strategic flair, he decided to cut off Worcester from the south and south-east in order to obviate the risk of the King reaching London. The royal party inside Worcester were like settlers within a defensive

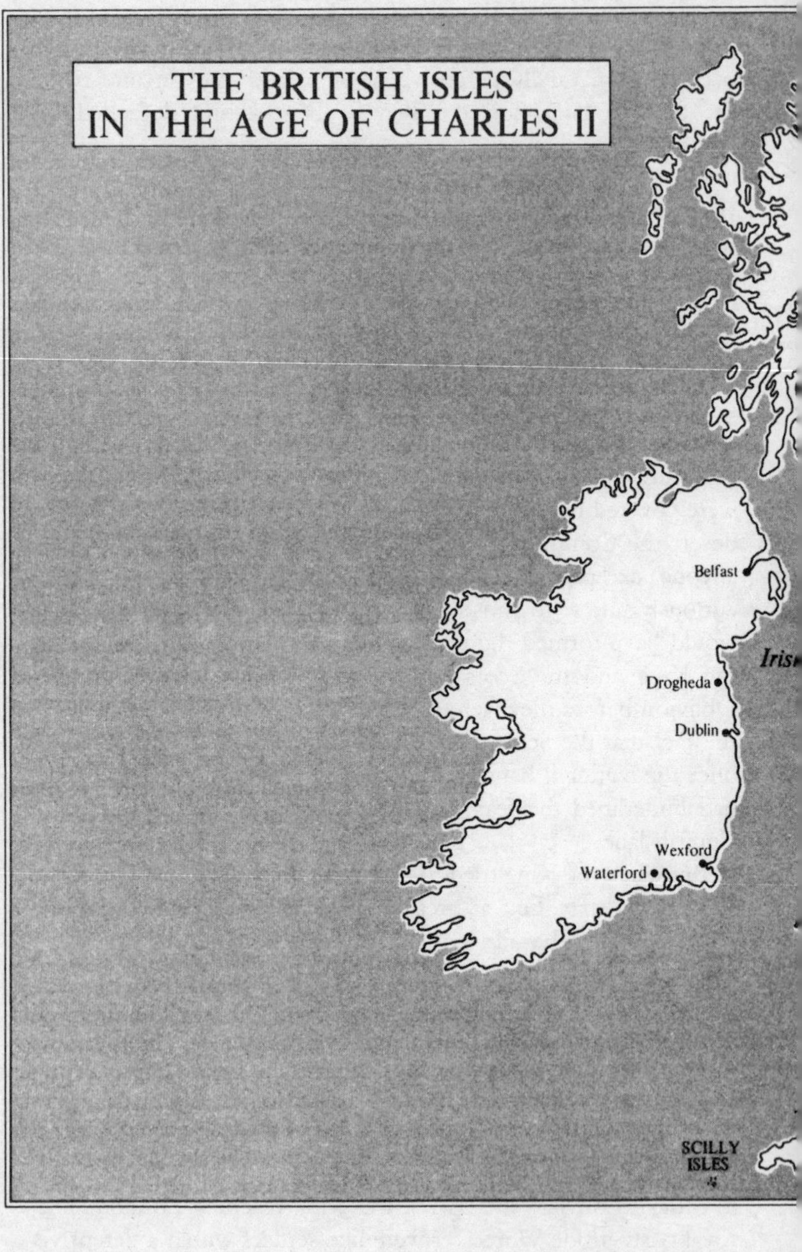
THE BRITISH ISLES
IN THE AGE OF CHARLES II
Belfast
Drogheda
Dublin
Wexford
Waterford
SCILLY
ISLES

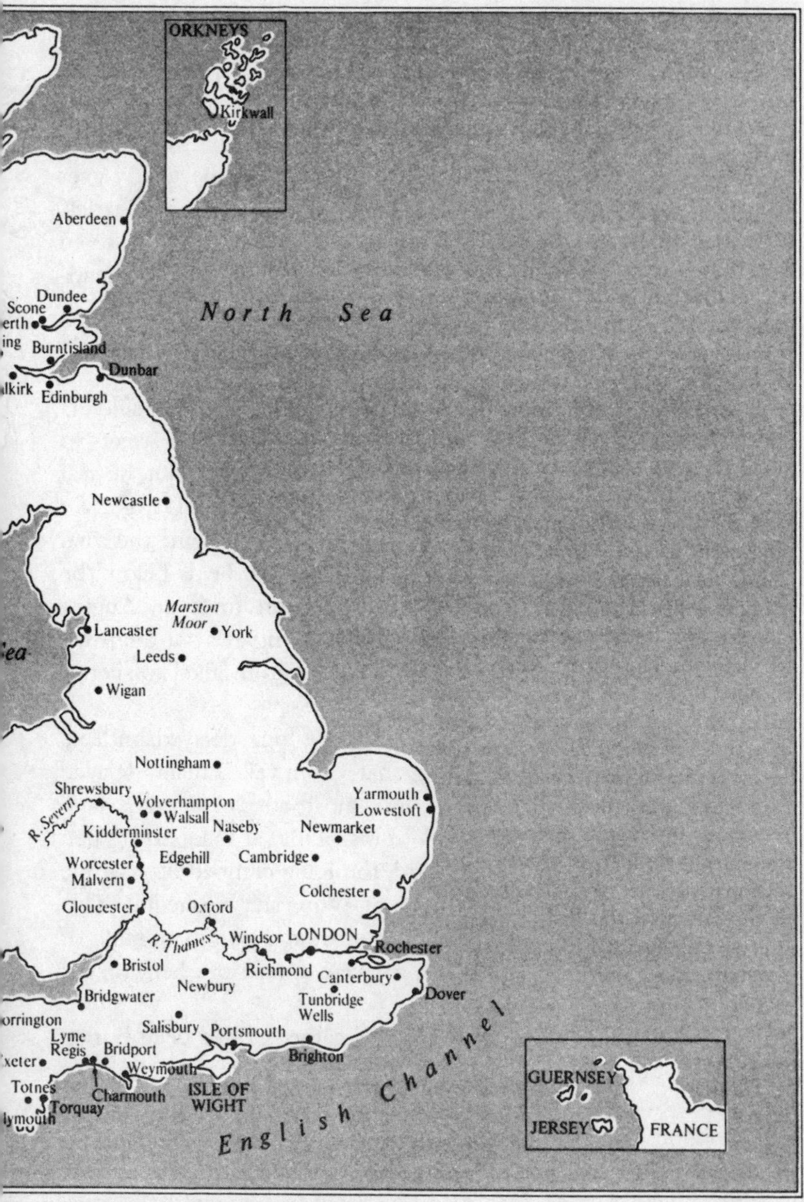

ORKNEYS
Kirkwall
Aberdeen
Dundee
Scone
erth
ing
Burntisland
Dunbar
lkirk
Edinburgh
North Sea
Newcastle
Marston Moor
York
Lancaster
Leeds
Wigan
Nottingham
Shrewsbury
R. Severn
Wolverhampton
Walsall
Kidderminster
Naseby
Newmarket
Yarmouth
Lowestoft
Worcester
Malvern
Edgehill
Cambridge
Colchester
Gloucester
Oxford
R. Thames
Windsor
LONDON
Rochester
Bristol
Richmond
Canterbury
Newbury
Bridgwater
Tunbridge Wells
Dover
orrington
Salisbury
Portsmouth
Lyme Regis
Bridport
Brighton
xeter
Weymouth
Totnes
Charmouth
ISLE OF WIGHT
Torquay
lymouth
English Channel
GUERNSEY
JERSEY
FRANCE

circle of their upturned wagons; they soon found themselves ringed by the Indians. In the absence of any possibility of rescue – no military here galloping up in the nick of time – the King hoped to break out of the ring. He was certainly very much in control of the campaign. Indeed, in this final throw (the first and last military command in the field he would ever hold), he showed both courage and ability. It was at Charles' orders that the four vital bridges guarding access to the town were blown up; it was not his fault that the order was inadequately carried out, so that one bridge, at Upton, survived in sufficiently good condition to be patched up and used by Lambert.

Otherwise, the King concentrated the bulk of his soldiers within the walled city, where he trusted to the narrow streets to provide a natural form of defensive fortification. But he did position three Scottish regiments under Thomas Dalyell, Sir William Keith and Major General Pitscottie to guard the vital confluence of the Severn and the Teme in the fields below the city to the west. Cromwell was in position from 29 August onwards, with the Cromwellian guns battering away at the town from the east; a bold night foray by Middleton failed to silence these guns.

The final Indian charge could not be long delayed; indeed, there are grounds for believing that Cromwell actually delayed the assault to coincide with his 'most auspicious day' – 3 September, the first anniversary of his victory at Dunbar.[22] When the first noise of firing was heard, the King climbed up the fine fourteenth-century square tower of Worcester Cathedral. This watchpost surveyed (and still surveys) an imposing panorama of water and wood, as the two rivers were spread out beneath his gaze.

It was an historic position. In this cathedral had been buried another unfortunate English monarch, John, and an unlucky prince, Arthur, he whose premature death after marriage to Catharine of Aragon had brought about the marital conflicts of Henry VIII. Just as in its own past Worcester had seen many battles, with Saxons, Danes and Normans jostling in its legends, so the cathedral too had its scars. The beautiful stained glass which had survived the Reformation had not survived the depredations of the Parliamentary troops after the Siege of Worcester in 1646, when cathedral and city were pillaged. The arrival of King Charles II incidentally provided a welcome doctrinal interruption in the Puritan services which had taken place there ever since.

The King was armed with a spy-glass and dressed in his now familiar uniform of a buff coat, and boots, with a red sash and the George round his neck. Below him he could see into the College Green, surrounded by mediaeval houses, and packed with horses, carts and men. Beyond that could be glimpsed others of his troops, and their colourful standards: in his own mind, at least, they were prepared to defend the city or die in the attempt. Beyond that again lay the marshes outside the city.

The Castle Hill, to the immediate south-west of Worcester, had a fort on it. Close and to the south-east lay the so-called Fort Royal (now a tasteful municipal park), whose top put an observer on a level with the cathedral itself. Perry Wood and Nunney Wood were situated beyond the Fort Royal. Bunns Hill lay roughly between the two high points, with Cromwell stationed below it. There the King could see the bridge of boats being towed up the Severn by Fleetwood, with the men milling around over it. Further away still, his own Scots, under Sir William Keith, guarded the Powick Bridge; they were determined to hold it valiantly.

It was the sight of the boats which inspired the King to his next move. Cromwell with most of his cavalry had crossed the Severn in support of Fleetwood. Determined as he was not to sit down under the certainty of defeat, the King concluded that this departure must have considerably weakened the main Commonwealth force to the south-east. He therefore ordered his own men to charge immediately out of the Sidbury Gate and attack them. And he himself promptly joined in the fray.

At first this brave essay was successful. The Royalists, covered by their own artillery, attacked up hill, and for three hours conducted themselves with an unparalleled energy and venom. Their King was there with them, on foot, fighting at their side, cheering them on. Once their meagre ammunition was exhausted, they still went on at push of pike, butting with their muskets where they were too closely engaged to use pikes. It was here that the gallant Duke of Hamilton fell, mortally wounded.* Some of the enemy's artillery was captured, and for a brief moment their troops fell back.

It has been proposed that, if the Scottish infantry south-west of the city had been supported at this juncture, victory might have been grasped. When Leslie was created Baron Newark after the Restoration, there was someone with a long enough memory to observe that he should have been hanged instead.[23] It is possible that Leslie failed to order support out of a general malaise, product of the dejection which had overcome him since his defeat at Dunbar. His subsequent behaviour at Worcester demonstrates that he was in no mood to believe victory possible and thus seize an unexpected initiative. Nevertheless, one cannot genuinely believe that the King had a chance at this stage, Leslie or no Leslie. The Parliamentary forces were superior in every respect – and numerically by this point nearly tripled those of the King.

As it was, Cromwell, when he took in what was happening outside the Sidbury Gate, immediately recrossed the Severn. The Commonwealth counter-attack was all too potent. It was with the greatest difficulty that the King, amongst others, got back to the Sidbury Gate at all: Charles had to crawl through the wheels of an upturned wagon. The oxen which had been pulling it lay dead in his path.

The loss of Fort Royal was disastrous. Now the Scots' own guns could be turned upon them with impunity; and Fleetwood was fast approaching the city from the west. Chaos outside the various gates of Worcester grew apace. And inside the city too doubts were mounting as to how long the city itself could be held. The Scots, let it never be forgotten, were far from home. At some point Leslie's nerve certainly collapsed: he was glimpsed in the mêlée 'as one amazed or seeking to fly he knew not whither'.[24]

* This expatriate Scot was buried under the high altar of the cathedral, where he lies to this day.

One man however who kept his head and his courage to the last was the King. There were many tributes to Charles' valour on that dreadful 'black and white day', as a contemporary narrative called it, when the King's men were 'ravished at Worcester by numerous overpowering force'.* A nameless Royalist officer, subsequently imprisoned at Chester, described him charging again and yet again: 'Certainly a braver Prince never lived, having in the day of the fight hazarded his person much more than any officer of his army, riding from regiment to regiment.' Charles was able to call every officer by name, and if God Himself had not preserved him, so the account ended, 'he must in all human reason needs have perished that day'.[26]

Once having beaten his way back into the city via the Sidbury Gate, the King stripped off his armour. To his disgust, he saw that some of the soldiers in the city streets were already throwing down their arms. Calling for a fresh horse, he rode amongst them, urging, pleading and commanding them to stand and fight.

'I had rather you would shoot me!' he cried. 'Rather than let me live to see the consequences of this day.'

It was too late. The cavalry were finished. 'Neither threats nor entreaty' would persuade them to make a fresh charge. Charles could not even get them to shut the gates of the city.[27]

Even so, it was not until several hours later, hours spent in vicious hand-to-hand fighting in blood-soaked streets whose gutters ran red with slaughter, that the King himself even contemplated escape. Afterwards, Cromwell, a man who did not exaggerate, described the Battle of Worcester to Parliament as 'as stiff a contest as ever I have seen'. Much of the vigour of the last resistance came at the initiative of the King himself.

All the evidence, both of his courage and of his carelessness of his own safety, indicates that the King was prepared to perish in the attempt. He told the Scottish soldiers cheerfully in high

* We may discount the usual sneer from Bishop Burnet, who was not of course an eye-witness of the battle and wrote many years afterwards. Extreme courage is the verdict of all those present – with the exception of Buckingham.[25] But then Buckingham was still gravely displeased at being denied command.

summer that he had only one life to lose. Now that the day was turning so heavily against him, and the last throw was failing, he might even have welcomed death. Both his brothers were safe in Europe. The succession would not end with him.

It was towards dusk, when over two thousand of his own men – compared to two hundred odd of the enemy – had been killed, that Charles at last consented to listen to the advice of those who wanted him to withdraw. The exact details of his escape from the town are obscure, partly because the King himself omitted them from the account of his flight which he gave to Pepys – no doubt they merged into the general confused horror of the day. We know that Charles left by St Martin's Gate, to the north of the city. Possibly he paid a last visit to his lodging before he went, leaving by the back door and narrowly missing the Parliamentary commander who was searching for him at the front. Such at any rate is the legend.

But if he had been prepared to lay down his life earlier in the struggle, Charles was now quite clear where the duty of a sovereign lay. He must escape. A dead king might be a martyr, a captive king would be a pawn.

Nine thousand of the Scots had already been taken. The rest of the roaming, hopeless men were easily harvested.

Worcester itself, like the surviving Royalists, had to wait for the Restoration for its reward, a Latin motto: *Civitas in Bello in Pace Fidelis* – A City Faithful in War and Peace. The petitions of those who had helped Charles on the day would also be numerous and poignant. (Although another point of view was put by an account at the Guildhall: 'Paid for pitch and resin to perfume the hall after the Scots – 2s'.)[28]

The Royalist cause was in ruins.

It remained only to scoop up the person of the fugitive King.

CHAPTER EIGHT

Heroical Figure

'King Charles the Second in the Oak near Boscobel, makes as Heroical Figure as in any Part of his Reign.'
John Oldmixon, *History of England*, 1731

After Worcester there seemed very little hope for the survival of Charles II as a free man. As one narrative ghoulishly described the situation, 'The ashamed sun had blushed in his setting and plunged his affrighted head into the depths of the luckless Severn, and the night, ready to stain and spot her guilty sables with loyal blood, was attiring herself for the tragedy.'[1] It seemed that the King's fortune was at its nadir. By our judgement, he was about to enter his finest hour.

To most people ever since, the amazing tale of his escape is one that does not diminish with time, nor with constant repetition – the only exceptions were the courtiers of Charles II who grew bored with the King's recital of his adventures. Nevertheless it *is* a truly extraordinary story; and the yawns of the complacent wits after the Restoration do them less honour than the King's conduct at the time did him. 'Read on and wonder,' wrote Thomas Blount in his introduction to *Boscobel*, published in 1660, one of the most accurate of the early accounts.*

* There have been many fictional versions of the escape, from Sir Walter Scott's *Woodstock* to Georgette Heyer's *Royal Escape*. None of them are more exciting than the true story.

It was only natural that the King himself should feel a nostalgic middle-aged affection for this 'History of Wonders'. He was aware that in the forty days following Worcester he had been stripped of the last vestiges of his kingly prerogatives. His character, not his office, was tested in the crucible. His first dictation of the story was to Pepys on board the royal yacht as it approached the shores of England on the eve of the miraculous Restoration; later he elaborated it, so that the version in which Pepys finally handed it down to us dates from a session at Newmarket races in 1680. He also commissioned one of his favourite artists, Robert Streater, to paint two of his obscure refuges as a practical record of his experiences.

There are of course many other sources for the order and detail of events – some of them slightly contradictory, as is ever the case with synoptic accounts, from the Gospels downwards.* But Pepys had preserved the King's own view of his tribulations. It gains importance as a unique piece of self-revelation coming from an otherwise secretive man.[2]

From the accounts of all the survivors, Charles emerges as a paladin. The combination of resource, intelligence and sheer courage which he showed fully justifies the verdict of John Oldmixon in his early eighteenth-century history of the Stuarts: 'King Charles the Second in the Oak near Boscobel, makes as Heroical Figure as in any Part of his Reign.'[3]

As the King vanished through the northern gate of Worcester, on that tragic night of 3 September, he was attended by only a few gentlemen. But they included some of the most notable figures in his entourage – the egregious Buckingham, the powerful Earl of Derby and the Scottish Lauderdale, less recognizable in England but an equally desirable prize for the Commonwealth to capture.

* There is a clear recent summary of the subject and the sources in Richard Ollard, *The Escape of Charles II*, 1966. The main sources are most accessibly printed in Allan Fea's two volumes, *The Flight of the King*, 1897, and *After Worcester Fight*, 1904. In *Charles II's Escape from Worcester: A Collection of Narratives Assembled by Samuel Pepys*, edited by William Matthews, 1966, Father Huddleston's original account – *A Brief Account of His Majestie's Escape from Worcester*, etc. – is printed for the first time.

In fact, the royal party soon found themselves quite lost in the darkness. They knew that they were somewhere north of Worcester – but that was about all, since the trooper who was supposed to know the district proved alarmingly ignorant. It was at this point that Lord Derby suggested that the King should continue to head north and try to hide out in the Brewood Forest. He also mentioned the name Boscobel – a name shortly to become associated above all others with the saga of the King's escape, but up till now the highly obscure possession of the moderately obscure family of Giffard. Derby was however in a position to recommend Boscobel, since he had hidden there himself after the disastrous rout at Wigan: he knew the people living there to be kind, hospitable and, above all, loyal.

They were also Catholics. The position of Catholics in England at this date was both melancholy and irksome. Officially, their religion was forbidden: those who did not attend Church of England services were termed recusants and heavily fined. Their priests in particular were in danger of death if apprehended. During the Civil War the Catholics had suffered from the assumption that they must inevitably be supporters of the King. Over sequestration, for example, a Catholic had to prove that he was not a monarchist; whereas an ordinary citizen had to have guilt proved against him. Yet, except where a magnate such as the Marquess of Winchester acted as a focus, the Catholics were more concerned to preserve the practice of their precious religion in private than to take any part whatsoever in organized resistance.[4] Bitter experience had taught them that they inevitably lost in such a situation.

Nevertheless, a sort of Catholic underground continued to exist, which handed the forbidden priests from hiding-place to hiding-place. It was an odd chance which brought King Charles II in touch with this underground while on the run himself. This secret world was so very different from the kind of Catholicism which Charles had known before – the foreign confessors of his mother, the French, Spanish and even Irish Catholics of the Continent. He discovered for himself that the English Catholics were then (as now) a very special breed in whom national loyalty was far from being extinct. In time he would wish to act upon this knowledge.

For the present however it was more a case of what the Catholics could do for their King. It transpired that Charles Giffard, the owner of the Boscobel estate, was actually amongst the little body of gentlemen still with the King. Giffard recommended not Boscobel itself (which was let to a Catholic family of yeoman farmers named Penderel) but another house close to it, Whiteladies, so-called because it was the site of a former Cistercian priory.* This safe house was reckoned to be about fifteen miles further. The decision was taken to press on there, and although the exact route taken is uncertain because of the general confusion of the journey, it is known that the royal party passed through Kidderminster. And they decided to speak French while passing Stourbridge, to avoid detection – a somewhat odd notion. For, if they had been overheard, the question of what a party of French soldiers were doing late at night in a remote corner of the West Midlands must inevitably have arisen.

The King reached Whiteladies at dawn. There is now little to be seen of the pleasant house of moderate size where he was welcomed except grass, ruins, and, appropriately enough, a few upturned Catholic gravestones. Even today it is difficult to find: in the seventeenth century Whiteladies was exceptionally isolated. That alone made it a welcome refuge for the exhausted Royalists. It had been a long – and appalling – twenty-four hours since the King saw the day break over Worcester.

Revived with some much-needed bread and cheese, the King quickly resolved that he needed to get rid of two things which were encumbering him. The first was his well-publicized clothing. He had taken off his George on first entering, and given it to a member of his party, Colonel Blague. (The George would enjoy adventures almost as strange as its owner's, being buried under

* One previous Giffard had played a part in Royal Stuart fortunes: a sixteenth-century scion of the family had acted as a double-agent in the sad story of the Babington Plot, resulting in the betrayal of Mary Queen of Scots. The seventeenth-century Giffards fully atoned for this blot on their history.

a heap of refuse, and finally smuggled out to France by the faithful Colonel.) Now the King emptied his pockets of gold and gave it to the servants. It was off with the buff coat and the red sash, in which he had vainly tried to rally the men at Worcester. The plan was for Charles to disguise himself in country clothes belonging to William Penderel, who was the tallest brother – a green jerkin, grey cloth breeches, leather doublet and greasy soft hat. 'And now his majesty was *à la mode* the woodman.'

The King's only remaining possessions were his socks, and those had their embroidered tops torn off. The trouble was that the new woodman – whose name was to be Will Jones – had enormous feet, to scale with his height, and even the pair of shoes found for him, torn in bits to give more room, chafed and rubbed his feet almost intolerably. On his subsequent journeys Charles' only real moment of despair came over the agonies of his footwear.* It was much less of a sacrifice to have his famous thick black love-locks shorn. Afterwards the King instructed that all his own clothes should be flung 'into a privy-house' to prevent the risk of discovery.

The second potentially dangerous encumbrance of which Charles decided to rid himself was his entourage. He must survive, and he would only survive alone. He was quite clear about this in his own account to Pepys. Nor would he consider trying to join Leslie and his men, rumoured to be close at hand and making for Scotland: 'which I thought was absolutely impossible, knowing very well that the country would all rise upon us, and that men who had deserted me when they were in good order, would never stand to me when they have been beaten'.

One of the King's attendants was Lord Wilmot, later created Earl of Rochester (and father of that dissolute Earl who would cut a swathe through the Restoration court). Wilmot was a man

* In exile the King became, no doubt as a result, a lavish orderer of shoes, which had to be specially made in Paris. He was also very careful about their fit. In July 1656 they were to be 'a little bigger than last time'. He remained aware of others' problems in that direction: in 1683 he commented on Sir John Reresby's thin shoes and told him to get a stronger pair so as not to catch cold.[5]

of considerable style – he refused to disguise himself during the escape, saying 'he should look frightfully in it', a point of view which compels one's admiration and irritation in equal parts. The only concession he eventually made was to wear a hawk on his wrist, a gentlemanly form of disguise.

Nevertheless, Wilmot, presumably because he was a much less conspicuous figure than the rest of the lords, was the only one entrusted with the King's secret decision. He would head for London, rather than the Welsh ports or Scotland; this would be all the safer for being unexpected.

The King agreed with Wilmot on an address where they might meet there. The secrecy was made easier by the fact that the other lords, far from pressing for information, begged *not* to be told, 'because they knew not what they might be forced to confess'. Indeed, very shortly afterwards nearly all the lords except Buckingham were captured. The Duke, born under a lucky star, made his way to France. But Derby was condemned to death, on the grounds that, being an Englishman, he had acted as a traitor by joining the Scots; Lauderdale, for being a foreigner and knowing no better, was let off with imprisonment.

Meanwhile the sun was up. The house was no longer safe from search. The King stole out of Whiteladies by the back door and took refuge in a nearby wood, the Spring Coppice. John Penderel went off to find a more secure hiding-place, depositing Lord Wilmot at Brinsford. Penderel's search was fruitless, but it was on the way back, by an extremely lucky chance, that he met someone whom he recognized as the chaplain in secret attendance on another local Catholic gentleman, Thomas Whitgreave of Moseley Old Hall. This was Father John Huddleston. Penderel tested the temperature of the water. Would Whitgreave be prepared to harbour the fugitive King? The answer was encouraging, although it is an indication of the isolation of this particular piece of country that Huddleston actually thought the King had gained the day at Worcester until Penderel disillusioned him.

The King's day in the Spring Coppice was far from tranquil. Accompanied only by Richard Penderel, he suffered from both hunger and thirst, and he also had the unpleasant experience of observing some troops on the road, evidently searching for fugitives. Only an unexpectedly heavy shower over the copse itself and nowhere else – which the King described as 'remarkable enough' – saved him from their attentions.

While in the wood however Charles changed his mind about heading for London. Penderel could think of no 'man of quality' to harbour him on the way there. Besides, Charles himself knew of several 'honest gentlemen' in Wales. So it would be the Welsh ports after all.

Under cover of darkness the King and Penderel left the wood, and, nourished only by some more bread and cheese taken at the door of another Penderel house, set off for the Severn. They encountered several more adventures, including a miller who chased them off, shouting 'Rogues, rogues!' – for the ironical reason that he was harbouring a number of fugitive Royalist soldiers. Indeed, the Midlands were still in a state of chaos, with roaming soldiers of both sides, one side gradually picking off the remnants of the other. But as yet no one was quite sure exactly what had happened at Worcester, still less what had happened to the King.

This confusion contributed materially to the King's preservation. His characteristic lolloping stride, for example, was not exactly that of a labourer. But it was not until 9 September, six days after the battle, that the first proclamation was put about seeking his capture. The day after that the reward was announced for laying hands on this 'malicious and dangerous traitor' – one thousand pounds, an absolutely vast sum by the standards of the time, and more than the average workman would earn in a lifetime, an unparalleled fortune to the humble people who were hiding the King. It is one of the heartening facts about the King's escape that, in spite of all the people in the secret – it has been calculated that they numbered over sixty and 'so many of them women!' as a contemporary wonderingly observed – no one ever did claim this reward.[6] Nevertheless, once the hunt was officially on for 'Charles Stuart, son of the late Tyrant', Charles' danger was obviously increased. Posters were put out by Parliament seeking 'a tall black man, over two yards high'.

In view of Charles' exceptional appearance it was lucky that so many of the English had not seen him in the flesh since boyhood, if at all.

The King spent the night of Friday, 5 September, in the barn of an old gentleman named Wolfe at Madeley, about seven miles from Whiteladies. It was then discovered that the plan of crossing the Severn was quite impractical, since a body of militia had installed themselves on the available bridges and were also guarding the boats. Mrs Wolfe's contribution was to stain the King's hands and face with walnut juice 'of a reeky [smoky] colour'. The only solution was to return to the Boscobel area. They had to ford a river on the way back: Charles was a strong swimmer – it was one of the many forms of physical exercise for which he had a passion – but Richard Penderel, who could not swim at all, pronounced it to be 'a scurvy river'. Charles remembered with pride that at least in this instance he was able to help Penderel by enabling him to cross the river safely.

They got to Boscobel at five o'clock in the morning. The house had taken its name from the Italian, *bosco bello*, 'beautiful wood', and it did indeed lie in a bosky setting, with the Forest of Brewood all about it, as early illustrations show: it had originally been built as a hunting lodge. Today the woods have receded, and the flat Midlands countryside gives a very different impression from that received by the King on the run. Boscobel's noble past is however omnipresent, from the white stones in the cobbled garden path, commemorating his visit in Latin, to the famous oak, now standing, looking rather lonely, surrounded by a fence in a field about five hundred yards away – its covering forest having vanished long ago.*

The first news which greeted the King at Boscobel was about Wilmot: he was safely stowed at Moseley Old Hall. He also

* The balance of the evidence suggests that this particular tree is actually a descendant of the royal oak, a successful sapling rather than the oak itself. Sightseers took their toll of the original tree, reported in 1660 as being of 'a firm sound trunk ... its deserved popular growth to outlast time itself'. A wall had to be built, later replaced by a palisade. Eighteenth-century accounts describe the growth of a sapling near by, as well as the dilapidation of the original tree. Later accounts describe two trees, then only one.[7]

learnt that a particularly gallant Royalist soldier, Major Carlis, who had stayed till the end at Worcester ('had seen the last man killed there'), was at this very moment concealed in the thick Boscobel Wood. The Major knew that his own home nearby would undoubtedly be searched. It was thus that Carlis – or Carlos, as he has gone down to history, having changed his name later to mark his association with his sovereign – found himself in the legendary royal oak, sharing it with King Charles II.

In those days the tree was a large and particularly bushy pollard oak. It still had some space round it, however, which the King decided would give them a good view. Here the pair remained all day, the King sleeping from time to time, with his head in Carlos' lap, on a cushion provided by the Penderels. As Charles told Pepys, 'We see the soldiers going up and down, in the thicket of the wood, searching for persons escaped, we seeing them now and then peeping out of the wood.' According to Hyde's *History*, the King also overheard the soldiers discussing what they would do with Charles Stuart when they found him.

It was not until the evening of what must have been another very long day that the King and Carlos dared to leave their home and venture back into the house. Afterwards the Royal Oak became a cult, a symbol of royalty and romance. Medallions issued abroad before the Restoration frequently showed the King's head on one side and the oak-tree on the obverse. After the Restoration, 29 May, Charles's birthday, was designated Oak-Apple Day; it remained a public holiday until the 1850s, and late into the nineteenth century was celebrated in parts of England with oak-leaves in the hat and oak boughs, sometimes gilded, over the door.*

The existence of a real Royal Oak has tended to obscure the fact that an oak had already long been considered to be a symbol of solid (non-revolutionary) government and establishment. It

* The author has traced several local continuances of this pleasant practice to the present time. The Royal Stuart Society also regularly celebrates 29 May with a dinner, and the various houses of the King's refuge hold ceremonies from time to time, associated with the descendants of his helpers. Founder's Day at the Royal Hospital, Chelsea, will be referred to later.

has been mentioned that in 1638, when Charles was made a Knight of the Garter, the medal struck to commemorate his installation depicted 'the Royal Oak under a Prince's Coronet'. A book published in 1649 (two years before the Boscobel escapade), *The History of Independency*, had an engraving as its preface, showing 'The Royal Oak of Britain', cut down by Cromwell. Another Royalist engraving of the same period shows the Royal Oak overturned, plus the prophecy 'that it will sprout again'. The happy coincidence of this symbol and the King's picturesque sojourn made it an easy step from here to the fertile quercine fancies of the post-Restoration years. The King prepared himself for them in exile by toying with the idea of an order of Knights of the Royal Oak.

It was at supper that night at Boscobel House that the King first heard from Humphrey Penderel of the price on his head – 'If it were one hundred thousand pounds, it were to no more purpose,' exclaimed the gallant Carlos instantly, and added that he would engage his soul for the reliability of all present. And it was on that same occasion that the King demonstrated how far he himself was out of touch with his putative subjects. Without thinking, he asked if he could have mutton for his supper. The Penderels had not actually tasted butcher's meat since the christening of their eldest child: it would have attracted far too much attention to have placed a sudden lavish order. So it was left to Carlos, who, with his usual resource, went out and stuck his own dagger into a neighbour's lamb. At least the King and Carlos both took a hand in cooking the collops: Charles ate heartily and asked 'merrily' afterwards who was the better cook, himself or his companion.

Yet the mutton incident was important. Like another monarch thrown out into the cold, King Lear, Charles was being forcibly exposed to 'what wretches feel'. He had not even been shaved by a barber before, as he told William Penderel when he cut his hair. Chafing shoes, the total inability to provide a food which he had taken utterly for granted (remember the meat provided for his coronation at Scone), had their lessons for him. He had no choice but to 'take physic, pomp'.

The night at Boscobel was spent in a priest's hiding-place at the top of the house. Still to be inspected, if not precisely in the same seventeenth-century form, the hole is sufficiently cramped for someone of normal stature to remind one vividly how Charles was being handicapped by his height. The following day, Sunday, 7 September, was pleasanter: the King spent some of it in the garden, reading in an arbour placed on a curious ancient mound there; but although he commented favourably on the house's 'retiredness', it was obviously impossible for him to rest there long. The risk of a house search only increased as the hours passed.

Charles was passed on to Moseley Old Hall, about five miles away. On his way he complained about the quality of his horse – another rude shock to one whose governor had been the great Lord Newcastle – calling it the 'heaviest dull jade' he had ever ridden on.

'My liege,' Humphrey Penderel exclaimed brightly, 'can you blame the horse to go heavily, when he has the weight of three kingdoms on his back?' There had been three Penderels with the King on this occasion; when the time came for them to separate, the Penderels' duty done, the King suddenly realized that in the general need for security he had omitted to thank them properly. He called them back and said graciously, 'My troubles make me forget myself; I thank you all.'

Once at Moseley, Charles was reunited with Wilmot, who was able to introduce him with a suitable flourish, greasy clothes notwithstanding, as 'your master, mine, and the master of us all'. Charles' 'exotic' dress had so 'metamorphasised' him that Wilmot would otherwise scarcely have known who he was. The King was fed. Whitgreave washed his cruelly blistered feet (Charles had stuffed the offending shoes with paper, which only made matters worse). A 'bloody clout' or handkerchief, with which he had staunched a nose-bleed, was carefully preserved by Father Huddleston as a relic, although Charles had made nothing of the bleeding at the time, describing such things as 'habitual to him'. After that, Charles was cheerful or gallant enough to announce that he was ready for another march, another fight.

But his fate was not to be so public. Moseley, built in about

1600, then lay amidst its own remote agricultural estate (the conurbation of Wolverhampton has since crept up, although Moseley is still an agreeable place of historical pilgrimage). Thomas Whitgreave was a lawyer, who had fought at Naseby; he was evidently a prudent fellow, for he instantly sent away all the non-Catholics from the house. At the Restoration, in her humble petition, one Elizabeth Smith, a Catholic, referred to herself as the only servant left in the house, who had in consequence looked after both the King's fire and his bed. And when Cromwell's soldiers were in the town, 'Your Majesty's petitioner rubbed softly Your Majesty upon the feet and legs, to wake Your Majesty and warn. . . .' She also reminded the King that she had put sweet herbs in his privy.[9]

The upstairs bedroom, where the King was installed, had its own convenient hiding-place nearby; it was rather better situated than most, between two rooms and having a false floor with an exit door to the brew-house chimney. 'The hole', as Blount calls it, contained a pallet. The usual incumbent of this nook, Father John Huddleston, now enters King Charles' story properly for the first time. Coming from a Lancashire family, and having served in the Royalist Army during the Civil War, Huddleston represented in his own person all that was best about that kind of patriotic English Catholicism which Charles was just discovering for himself.

Huddleston was outspoken, saying that the King now resembled him, being 'liable to dangers and perils'.[10] He had already shown Charles the secret chapel, 'little but neat and decent'. Charles looked on it, crucifix, candlesticks and all, respectfully. He then observed, according to Huddleston, 'If it please God, I come to my crown, both you and all of your persuasion shall have as much liberty as any of my subjects.' There is no reason to doubt Huddleston's story: Charles' generous intention to right a wrong was certainly always there once he had encountered the sufferings – and the loyalty – of the English Catholics.

Significant also was Charles' conversation with Huddleston on the subject of the Catholic Faith (as opposed to the problems of the recusants). Charles was encouraged to look at a Catholic catechism, probably Turbevill's Catechism printed at Douai, and a tract called 'A Short and Plain Way to the Faith and the Church' by Father Huddleston's uncle, a Benedictine monk. He described the catechism as a 'pretty book' and took it away with him. Of the tract, according to Huddleston, Charles spoke the memorable words: 'I have not seen anything more plain and clear upon this subject. The arguments here drawn from succession are so conclusive, I do not see how they can be denied.' This exchange has sometimes been cited as evidence of Charles' early conversion to Catholicism – ignoring the public stand he kept up against it in exile. In the context, it is more plausibly regarded as evidence of Charles' natural curiosity, coupled with politeness. He had certainly never studied the Catholic arguments before – why should he? Apart from his personal admiration for Huddleston, perhaps he was amazed to find the faith of his mother quite so reasonable.

No refuge, it was understood, would remain a safe house for very long. Besides, the net was closing in. On the Monday Boscobel was searched. The Penderels had their remaining provisions confiscated by the troops. At least Carlos escaped – it was he who would give Mary, the Princes of Orange, the first news of her brother's safety. The next day, 9 September, the date of the first government proclamation, Whiteladies was also searched. A cornet in Cheshire had given away the secret of the King's presence in the area. Giffard was badly man-handled, but kept his head admirably; he did not attempt to deny the visit of 'some unknown Cavaliers', but said that he had absolutely no idea whether the King had been amongst them.

That evening the danger was even more acute when a party of soldiers actually came to Moseley itself. The King was bundled into 'the hole'. But Whitgreave too showed aplomb. He convinced them that his own ill-health had prevented him being involved in any of the recent Royalist dramas at Worcester and elsewhere. And the soldiers went on their way.

The next day the King and Wilmot departed for Bentley Hall, the home of a Colonel Lane. The fugitives' desperate need was for some convincing cover story to explain their journeyings in a part of the world daily combed by inquisitive soldiery. It was discovered that Colonel Lane's daughter, Jane, was due to visit her sister, Mrs Norton, at Abbot's Leigh, for the birth of the latter's impending child. If Charles went in Jane Lane's company as a servant, he might conceivably get clean away.

Bentley lay three miles outside Walsall. Here Charles was transformed, from his somewhat improbable disguise as a woodman, up the social scale to being a servant. He was to be William Jackson, son of a neighbouring tenant, which was slightly more plausible than his previous manifestation – though only just, his gait and demeanour remaining unconvincing in either role. Besides, he did not even know how to ride on a double horse, as he was expected to do while in attendance on Jane Lane, let alone doff his hat with proper subservience.

But the little train duly clattered off on Wednesday morning (Charles used the wrong hand to hand Jane Lane up to her horse). It was on this occasion that Wilmot condescended to disguise himself with a hawk on his wrist. Otherwise they none of them presented a very romantic sight. Jane Lane's portrait shows her to have had a full figure and a plump face, comfortable English looks rather than glamorous ones. Like another Stuart saviour, Flora Macdonald, Jane Lane possessed character and intelligence rather than haunting beauty – preferable qualities under the circumstances, except for yearners after romantic fiction.

En route between Bentley and Abbot's Leigh, Jane Lane's horse lost a shoe* and it was Charles' duty to oversee its replacement. At this point the King discovered another fact for himself: the passionate loyalty of his Catholic adherents did not extend throughout England.

With characteristic bravado, Charles chatted freely to the smith as he worked, asking him, 'What news?'

'There is no news, except the good news of beating those rogues the Scots,' replied the smith. This gave Charles the irresistible opportunity of asking if 'that rogue Charles Stuart' had been captured, who deserved to be hanged more than all

* Probably not at Bromsgrove, as is generally stated, but at Longborough, according to the convincing recent research of Mr J. F. Downes in his unpublished manuscript *The Strawberry Roan*.

the Scots for bringing them in. 'Spoken like an honest man,' said the smith. This too was a salutary experience.

Somewhere near Stratford the party ran into a troop of horse. Charles was all for proceeding fearlessly, as being the best defence, but Jane Lane's brother-in-law had had previous experience of being beaten up by these roaming bands, and insisted on a detour. The King discovered how the spirits of his loyal subjects had been worn down.

At Long Marston, further on the road to Abbot's Leigh, Charles was set by the cook to wind up the jack for roasting the meat in the fireplace. He did it clumsily, but at least he demonstrated what he had learnt at the Penderels: he explained that, being a poor tenant's son, he seldom ate meat or used a jack.

Abbot's Leigh, which was reached on Friday, 12 September, lay three miles beyond Bristol, and the city had to be traversed to get there – a real hazard. Jane Lane decided not even to reveal Charles' true identity to the Nortons; she concocted a story about her servant recovering from fever and needing to be left to himself. Charles told Pepys that the tale gained plausibility from the fact that his various ordeals (including the lack of meat) had left him looking pale.

At Abbot's Leigh the mixture of farce and danger which characterized the King's escape continued. In the buttery Charles heard himself minutely described – except that the missing King was authoritatively pronounced to be 'three fingers' taller than the present Will Jackson. But when Charles discovered that one of the talkers had been in his regiment of guards, he beat a hasty retreat upstairs. He was infinitely more afraid of the fellow, now he knew him to be one of his own men, than when he had believed him to be an enemy.

Charles was correct. Later the butler of the house, one John Pope, who had been in King Charles I's household before the Civil War, confided his suspicions privately to Jane Lane. But it turned out to be a felicitous encounter: Pope swore loyalty to the King, an oath he would keep most strictly, proving himself a resourceful and loyal servant.

*

Once again the royal party was faced with the question: whither? Pope tried in vain to find a ship at Bristol. The government would be watching the Welsh ports. Better to strike southwards, where, it will be recalled, the Western Association provided one of the few genuine Royalist networks in England, other than the Catholic underground. One of the sleepy south Dorset ports would provide the kind of inconspicuous transport to the Continent which would suit the party's purposes. As their base, they would use Trent Manor in Somerset, home of Colonel Francis Wyndham, a founder of the Western Association and, as the brother of the former Governor of Bridgwater, a member of a family with long Royalist connections.

Of course, Jane Lane was still needed to cover the journey, and there was a distressing last-minute hitch when her sister gave birth to a still-born child; it seemed a heartless moment to be leaving her. In the end it was the King who devised the excuse: a fictitious letter from Colonel Lane, pleading illness and summoning his daughter back to his side. Wilmot wrote ahead to warn Wyndham: they all realized that he would know nothing of what had been going on ever since Worcester. It was now Tuesday, 16 September, the day on which the Council of State issued new instructions to the Committee of Examinations 'to use the best means they can for the discovery of Charles Stuart'. That vagueness of language showed that the government too were in the dark: this imprecision would pervade their announcements for a week or two.

And it was pure bad luck that, in the event, the King could not make his escape from the Dorset coast, for the planning was good, and the geographical area was far more promising than the perilous Midlands or the conspicuous Welsh Marches. The reason for the eventual failure was the coincidental Commonwealth campaign against Charles' old refuge, Jersey. As a result, the so-called sleepy ports of Dorset and Devon had been transformed, and there were a quite unaccustomed number of Commonwealth troops in the area.

At Trent Manor, however, lying in a lost village between high banks and steep lanes, they were not to know of this development. Trent was two or three miles north of Sherborne: it was (and is) in exceptionally deep country. You would have to know your way to find it. The manor was next to the village church: not a very fortunate locale. For when the bells began to peal unexpectedly, and Charles was sent to know the reason, he was told it was for the 'joyful news' of the King's death.

In happier days he might have observed, like Mark Twain, that the news was much exaggerated: the wit was quite in keeping with his own. In fact, all the King said at the time was, 'Alas, poor people!' It was a pleasanter moment when he greeted Colonel Wyndham on arrival: 'Frank, Frank, how dost thou do?' Frantic enquiries were immediately set in hand for a boat, for it was the same problem: how long could the King remain, without word of his whereabouts getting out? Charles divided his time between yet another hidey-hole (bequeathed by the Wyndham's Catholic ancestors, the Gerards) and the Colonel's mother's chamber, the most retired room in the house.

Lyme – the Regis came later, as a reward for its loyalty – was the obvious port for the getaway. It was small, but not too small, and there were plenty of boats sailing in and out of it, plying trade with the Continent. Henry Peters, the Colonel's valet, was entrusted with the commission, and he entered into negotiations with a Captain Ellesdon for getting away a mythical party of gentlemen, one of whom was said to be fleeing from his creditors.

Some confusion surrounds Ellesdon's subsequent behaviour: he found it necessary to rebut accusations of treachery after the Restoration. It was alleged that his wealthy Presbyterian wife had corrupted him. But Clarendon accepted Ellesdon's innocence.[11] He certainly showed every initial sign of trying to help the fugitives; and the strongest proof that he did not change his mind, on discovery of the King's identity, is the fact that Charles continued to elude capture. Ellesdon was assuredly in a position to put the finger on him most efficiently, had he wanted to do so.

Since there was a fair at Lyme, Charmouth, a nearby fishing village set in the wide bay which ends at Bridport, was selected. There, on Monday, 22 September, it was finally arranged that one Limbry, the master of a coasting vessel, would convey them to France for £60, although the tide would not let him sail until eleven o'clock that night. Peters, a practical man, immediately engaged a room in a Charmouth inn where the King and Wilmot could lurk; as a romantic, or at least a person of imagination, he explained the need for this limited late-night rendezvous by saying that he was assisting a runaway bridal couple from Devonshire.

Charles had said goodbye to Jane Lane. He arrived at Charmouth that night, riding double with another young lady, Juliana Coningsby, a Wyndham cousin. Her existence gave plausibility to the wedding story at the inn. Charles had already met Ellesdon at a lonely house in the hills behind Bridport which cut off the coastal strip. He gave him a gold coin through which he had personally bored a hole – one of the activities with which he whiled away the confined hours at Trent Manor.

With the King and Miss Coningsby in the inn at Charmouth, Wyndham, Peters and Wilmot went down to the shore and awaited the ship. Nothing happened. The tide came in, went out, and there was not a trace of Limbry. Cold, disconsolate and perplexed, they were forced in the end to return to the inn and confess failure. The reason for Limbry's non-appearance was in fact a quite ridiculous marital escapade: his wife, aware of the government's proclamation about Royalists, suspected Limbry as being up to no good with his nocturnal project (although she did not conceive it was the King he was helping). She followed him, and ended by locking him in his bedroom. In vain the captain raged. She would not budge.

In the absence of any explanation, however, the royal party were left with the problem of their next move. It was Charles, characteristically, who thought it the best course to head for Bridport, a much larger town, and stuffed with troops on their way to Jersey and Guernsey. There he could go 'blundering' among the soldiers and keep his rendezvous with Wilmot. Suiting the action to the word, he pushed his way through the concourse to the largest inn, with his horse, annoying the troops in the process. Bearing in mind that Charles had spent much time in the West Country only six years before, this must have been his moment of maximum danger, excepting only the session in the oak. He could not rely on the anonymity he had enjoyed in the Midlands. One ostler did remark that his face was strangely familiar. Charles kept cool, even when he discovered that the ostler had worked close to the house of a Mr Potter who had entertained the Royalists at Exeter during the Civil War.

'Friend,' he replied easily, 'you must certainly have seen me then at Mr Potter's for I served him above a year.' The two 'servants' parted with jolly vows to drink a pot of beer together at their next meeting. In spite of all this bravado, when Wilmot, based at another inn, joined Charles, they decided that the best course was to get back to Trent Manor. There in effect they would start all over again.

In the meantime the danger of discovery had not diminished. Another ostler, that of the Charmouth inn, had become very suspicious as he pondered on the horseshoes of the royal party, those luggage labels of the past. He recognized one as having been forged in Worcestershire. A servant who had been kissed by the King was told sardonically that she was now 'a maid of honour'. Luckily the ostler was a pious Presbyterian and took a long time at his prayers. By the time the hue and cry was raised, and the local magistrate had alerted the troops, the scent had gone cold. The soldiery set off in the direction of Dorchester – that is, to the east of Bridport.

But the King, Wyndham and Wilmot were by now about five miles north. As a matter of fact they were lost; Wyndham had to ask the name of the village where they decided to spend the night (it was Broadwindsor). Here, occupying upper rooms under false names, the King and his party got involved in a hilarious caper, since by complete coincidence a party of about forty soldiers on their way to Jersey also decided to put up in and around the same inn. One of their female followers gave birth to a baby during the night: the village was selfishly concerned that the baby should not be abandoned there, as a charge on the parish. In the hullabaloo which followed the presence of the King remained undetected.

By the next night, 24 September, the King was back at Trent Manor; here he was to remain for the next two weeks while deliberations were made for the next throw. Trent Manor was later described by Colonel Wyndham's wife Anne in her account of the King's escape as 'the Ark in which God shut him up when the floods of rebellion had covered the face of his dominions'.[12] His Ark certainly kept him safe enough. The odd rumour that there was an escaped Royalist staying there was scotched by Wilmot appearing at church with Wyndham; if there was any Royalist about, it was Wilmot. In between, Wilmot was busying himself about the Salisbury area, negotiating for a boat somewhere along the south coast.

In the end, it was found necessary to go as far as Sussex for the sake of safe embarkation, the Jersey campaign having ruled out Southampton. On Tuesday, 6 October, considerably rested, the King set out yet again with Juliana Coningsby on a double horse. He was heading for Heale House, near Amesbury, the home of Mrs Amphillis Hyde, 'a worthy discreet loyal lady' and the widow of a cousin of Edward Hyde, as the first step on his journey. For all her discretion, Mrs Hyde created a moment of tension at dinner by pressing her attentions on the King, which was extremely tactless in view of his deliberately dingy clothing. But there was a good day spent at Stonehenge: 'We stayed looking upon the stones for some time,' as the antiquarian Charles told Pepys, before the royal party doubled back to Heale House.

In all, Charles was there five days, using yet another hidey-hole: it was no wonder that the King, once restored, would be a prey to claustrophobia, and that sauntering in parks at his ease would be his idea of daily recreation.

It was not until 13 October that Charles was able to set out on his adventures once again with the hope of a Sussex boat. Wilmot had contacted a useful ally, Colonel Gunter of Racton, near Chichester, one who exclaimed, 'God be blessed!' when told that the King was well and safe. Charles spent the night on the way with Gunter's sister at Hambledon in Hampshire. Her husband, not being in the secret, became gravely worried by Charles' short hair, lest it denote 'a roundhead rogue'. On the next day Charles finally reached Brighthelmstone (as Brighton was then known) and was installed at the George Inn, on the site of the present King's Head in West Street.

Now everything seemed to be going smoothly. Gunter had fixed up a boat with a merchant named Francis Mansell, by the simple expedient of getting him drunk: the payment was to be sixty pieces of silver. Officially, his cargo was billed as a party of illegal duellists. The master of the promised brig, Captain Tattershall, also met the King. He recognized him immediately, perhaps because Charles' disguise had gone up in the world. From a servant he had turned into 'something like the meaner sort of gentleman'. The Captain held his peace until they were alone, and then fell to his knees and kissed the King's hand, declaring that he hoped to be a lord and his wife a lady when the great day came.

The rendezvous was for nearby Shoreham: Charles spent his last night in England at Bramber, a little village just to the north of it. Yet even at this stage there was danger: Charles narrowly escaped running into some Commonwealth soldiers in the area. But he did finally make the appointed hour at Shoreham harbour.*

And so at last it came about. On Wednesday, 15 October, at four o'clock in the morning, King Charles II finally departed England's shores. He had been on the run for six weeks; he had slept on pallet beds, slept in trees, crouched in innumerable hiding-places, his lanky frame doubled up in holes for recusant priests, his large body fed by the food of the poor. In all this time, his spirit never failed. Colonel Gunter, the last of his protectors, made the same point: he was amazed at the King's unwavering courage – that he never showed the slightest sign of apprehension. The Colonel compared the King to Elisha: his eyes must surely have been opened by God, to glimpse a heavenly host all around him. Moreover, more mundanely, they had got him away in the nick of time. Only two hours after Charles left, a very different boat was searching all around – for 'a tall black man, 6' 2" high'.

* This extended much further east from the present haven, making the Hove Basin his most probable point of embarkation.[13]

But by this time, by the mercy of Providence (and it is difficult to leave out the part of Providence in this extraordinary story of hair's-breadth escapes and near misses) the King was at sea. The brig was named *The Surprise*. She headed in the first instance for the Isle of Wight, on the excuse of selling coal along the south coast: she had originated at the coal port of Pittenweem, where it will be recalled that Charles had been lauded after his Scottish coronation – was it only six months before? His identity on board seems to have been an open secret. A sailor impudently blew the smoke of his pipe in Charles' face and, on being reproved, retorted that a cat might look at the King. Nevertheless, Tattershall was careful to cover his tracks – after all, he had a living to make under Commonwealth sway. Some of the sailors were bribed to persuade Tattershall to change his route so as to set down these so-called 'merchants' in France, and the Captain duly allowed himself to be publicly convinced.

The journey was a straightforward one. The wind blew from the north all night long, so that the brig merely had to run before it. Just before dawn the French coast came into sight. There was one more alarm – the look of a ship which might have been a privateer. The King and Wilmot were put into a cock-boat, manned by a Quaker named Carver, who was the brig's mate. It was Carver who finally carried Charles ashore on his back, at Fécamp, near Rouen.*

With many other good deeds, that of Carver would be remembered at the Restoration, along with the common sense and kindness of Jane Lane, the sterling worth of Huddleston and Wyndham, the enterprise of Gunter, the nobility of the Penderels, and on down the list of sixty people who knew something about the escape. Even Mansell, who had provided that Shoreham ship under the influence of alcohol, received a pension. *The Surprise* itself survived to be turned into a yacht

* In 1977, the Year of the Silver Jubilee of Queen Elizabeth II, a commemorative yacht race was organized between Brighton and Fécamp to celebrate the escape of King Charles II, sponsored by the Old Ship Hotel, Brighton, and the Sussex Yacht Club.

and renamed the *Royal Escape*. One list of people to be rewarded was drawn up in the King's own hand; it included 'the gentleman in whose house I was first received, whose name I have forgot' (Charles Giffard).[14] But the man himself was not forgotten, nor was the experience.

Gratitude would come like a golden shower. Jane Lane's benefits included a watch from the King himself, a jewel worth a thousand pounds (which was proposed during a debate in the House of Lords) and a yearly pension of a similar amount. The loyal Penderel brothers were introduced at Court after William had impetuously greeted the King in St James's Park; their children were assisted; they too received pensions, granted in perpetuity.

Opportunity for that gratitude lay far ahead.

One contemporary likened the escape of King Charles to the feat of David vanquishing the Goliath Cromwell.[15] The parallel was not exact. While the King had certainly escaped against enormous odds, England still lay in the grip of Goliath. But Charles could at least echo the words of David: 'Thou hast delivered me from the violent man; therefore I will sing praises to Thy name, O Lord.'

On the very day of his embarkation, the Earl of Derby, last seen before dawn at Whiteladies, was executed. Had he been captured, Charles Stuart the younger, a tall black man over two yards high, would likely have met the same fate.

CHAPTER NINE

A Difficult Game

'They, who will not believe anything to be reasonably designed, except it be successfully executed, had need of a less difficult game to play than mine is.'

Charles II, June 1653

The King who arrived back at the court of France at the end of October 1651 was so emaciated, and even dirty, that people generally failed to recognize him. In Rouen he had at first been taken for a vagrant. Then Dr Earle, his old tutor, who happened to be in the town, hurried to his hotel. Looking at Charles blankly, he asked to be conducted before the King. From his mother's favourite, Lord Jermyn, Charles received the first clean shirt to come his way since the garment given to him at Moseley by Father Huddleston.

After the first rapturous welcome, Charles was described as both 'sad and sombre'.[1] The cheerfulness which he assumed, against his inclinations, only lasted a few days. After that people noticed that he often fell very silent. There was indeed very little to comfort him at the French Court, to say nothing of his troubled thoughts wending backwards to those he had left behind in England. He could not even describe their courage in full for fear of endangering them further; it was not until after the Restoration that the full amazing story was told. Above all, he could not help them. As a result, the English government were slow to be convinced of the truth of his whereabouts – as late as 29 October the King was rumoured lost at sea. By November the official Commonwealth line, to explain away the unfortunate truth of his escape, was expressed in a sneering poster: this showed the King as 'a Fool on Horseback, riding backwards, turning his face every way in fears', weighed down by a full pouch of the Pope's money round his waist.

So much for the facts, which still impress us with their gallantry. Charles himself wrote gloomily to Jane Lane a year later (she had escaped to become lady-in-waiting to Charles' sister, the Princess of Orange). He deplored his inability to express his gratitude in some practical form, despite her need: 'I believe it troubles me more that I cannot do it yet, than it does you.'[2]

France herself was in the throes of the second civil war of the 'princely' Fronde, which had broken out in September. Basically, it was a struggle for power between Cardinal Mazarin and the superior nobility, led once again by the Prince de Condé. One such inconclusive struggle had already occupied most of 1650, following the earlier disturbance of the 'Parliamentary' Fronde. As a result, the French royal family was in a state of alarm and tension, which spread to all its dependents, including Queen Henrietta Maria. That in turn affected Charles. His mother's mood was grim. Since Charles had no alternative but to live off her charity, and she lived off the charity of the Cardinal de Retz, she made a note of exactly what his meals cost her: 'The very first night's supper which the King ate with the Queen began the account....'[3] The result was that, when Charles did eventually get a grant of sorts, he found that he owed much of it to his mother.

There was always the Grande Mademoiselle. Time had not treated her kindly – physically, at any rate – and Charles had grown up into a handsome, if penniless and homeless, man. This was no longer the uncouth boy who had been edged towards her by his mother, as Viola had been compelled to duel with Sir Andrew Aguecheek by Sir Toby Belch. His conversation was more beguiling too. Mademoiselle shuddered deliciously at Charles' tales of the uncouth life in Scotland, and how bored he had been by it all. Imagine an existence where to play the fiddle was a crime! And 'there was not a woman to be seen'. Under the circumstances, she was inclined to overlook his unfashionably cropped hair and 'a great deal of beard'.[4]

Mazarin continued to handle the situation adroitly, lest this wealthy French prize fall into the hands of the suppliant English. Whenever Mademoiselle grew too warm towards her cousin the English King, Mazarin was every ready to dangle the infinitely more magnificent prospect of her cousin the French king. Louis XIV had reached his thirteenth birthday – his majority – on 5 September 1651: he was thus in theory marriageable. But it was to be the war of the Fronde, not her romance with Charles, which proved the personal nemesis of Mademoiselle.

The arrival of the majority of Louis XIV also meant that both sides in this expensive and attritious French Civil War, Mazarin and Condé, could claim to act on his behalf. Charles II too was drawn into the struggle, although not precisely in the manner in which he would have desired. Unlike his younger brother, the Duke of York, there could be no question of the English King joining the army of the great Marshal Turenne and going into the field against Condé. Handsome, energetic James, tired of kicking his heels near his mother, applied for some active post. The courtiers were nervous whether his participation would further prejudice the position of the Stuarts – by identifying them in advance with one side or the other, when their one pathetic aim was to be on the winning side. In the end James was granted permission, on condition that it was a purely personal gesture.

James departed from Paris to serve in the French Army, having had to borrow money to buy his equipment, and embarked on what was probably the happiest adventure of his life – several years of active military service. He was a natural soldier, easy, practical and talented. One can understand how at this point Hyde regarded James as a more hopeful character than his elder brother, condemned to stay behind in Paris for an infinitely less agreeable life of poverty and negotiation. Charles' situation in the spring of 1652 was 'the most painful that can be imagined' – at least, that was how it would be described in James' memoirs.[5] The sufferings of mother and son at the Louvre were acute. They were not even receiving the French money on which they so much depended, and they had no-one else to approach. Meanwhile the ordinary people of

Paris surrounding them, who sympathized with the Condé faction rather than with that of the Cardinal, were openly indignant that the Duke of York was serving with the King's army under Turenne.

At the behest of the Duke of Lorraine, Charles undertook an unenviable task. This was to negotiate with the King of France. The Spanish had attempted to employ the changeable Duke against Turenne. Charles managed to bring the Duke of Lorraine to the French Court at Melun. There he secured the withdrawal of the Duke from the Spanish interest. But, having performed this service and returned to Paris, Charles found himself in the power of Condé, who had taken triumphant charge of the capital. Here, Charles' intervention made him extremely unpopular. Condé forthwith ordered Charles away and out of the city to Saint-Germain, and, having no funds whatever, he could not refuse. In this way Charles formed part of the French royal cortège, seated on a hill outside Paris, which witnessed the reduction of the city by Turenne on behalf of the young King Louis. Inside Paris poor Mademoiselle had seen her opportunity at last for achieving the *gloire* for which she had surely been born: dressed in a soldier's costume, heroic, splendidly cheerful, she whirled amongst Condé's troops, their Amazon and their inspiration. But none of this prevented Turenne from taking back the capital. Although it was Mademoiselle's personal intervention, as she proudly related, which saved Condé's life, her disgrace with the orthodox French Court was total. Louis XIV, a quiet boy rapidly turning into a man with a long memory, never forgave her.

By the autumn of 1652 the French Court was once more installed in Paris.

And now – at long last – would the French royal family redeem their promises and assist their poor English cousins? Regrettably, the answer was, as before, tangled in the webs of international diplomacy. Sir Edward Nicholas made a gloomy prognostication of the French King's intentions, 'notwithstanding all his fair words and kingly promises to our gallant Master'. Nicholas was to be proved right.[6]

*

It was a sad truth that the status of Charles II amidst the crowned heads and other leaders of Europe was declining all the time. The summer of 1652 had seen the outbreak of a war between the England of the Commonwealth and the Dutch. Naturally Charles tried to prise some advantage out of this, beginning with the suggestion that he might come on a personal mission to the United Provinces. But the Dutch, for all their problems with the Commonwealth, had reason to regard the Stuart connection warily.

One of the cruel blows of fate which had befallen the Stuart family shortly after the Scottish catastrophe of Dunbar was the death of Mary's husband William II. He died in November 1650, at the age of twenty-four. Six days later Mary gave birth to a son, another William, the heir to the House of Orange (and also of course within the Stuart succession). The guardianship of this baby produced an instant quarrel between the various interested parties in the United Provinces. As has been noted, the inheritance of the House of Orange was a complicated matter. The role of Stadtholder was not in theory hereditary, and thus evaporated on the death of William II. Yet the baby William inherited certain other specific rights and possessions, including a firm hold on the government of the province of Zeeland: this automatically made his guardianship of consequence in the politics of his country. The fact that these hereditary possessions of Orange were encumbered with debt did not rob them of their potential for the future.

In the prolonged squabble over the guardianship the Princess of Orange, Mary Stuart, and the Dowager Princess, Amalia von Solms, allowed themselves to be fatally divided by their own jealousies and rivalries. Wiser heads might have realized that it was imperative for the House of Orange to present a united front, if it was to preserve any kind of power in the United Provinces in the future, against the rising independence of the Estates. In the end Mary, the Dowager Princess Amalia and the Elector of Brandenburg (husband of Princess Louise Henrietta of Orange) were appointed co-guardians; but not before the Dowager Princess had carefully denigrated Mary by suggesting that she herself, not Mary, stood for the nationalist aspirations of the Dutch. It was a damaging charge to make at this juncture against a member of the vulnerable Stuart family.

In the summer of 1652, therefore, it is understandable that the Dutch were in no hurry to accept Charles' offer of assistance against the Commonwealth. What assistance, after all, could he provide? His few ships were away in the West Indies, under Prince Rupert, privateering with a view to filling his coffers if he could. He had neither money nor troops. None of Charles' increasingly desperate suggestions met with favour. Could he perhaps join the Dutch Navy, and help them to victory or 'perish in the attempt'?[7] Could he head a squadron of ships on their behalf? But it was made clear that his presence amidst the Dutch would be an embarrassment and there was no money to raise a squadron. The King of England was in the position of an extra chess-piece, superfluous to the requirements of the game; he could not even get onto the board.

Furthermore, Charles himself held no brief for the Dutch Calvinists. And it was a fact that the obvious spiritual links between the Dutch and the Commonwealth, like those between the Commonwealth and the Covenanters, would always work to his disadvantage, even without this personal disinclination. As it was, stories that he was approaching the Pope for aid did not help the Dutch to regard him with any greater favour.

Hyde, Acting Secretary of State since 1651, expressed an aspect of this unpalatable truth: he was not wise enough to judge which would be best for them, 'that the Dutch should beat the English or the English the Dutch'.[8] To look ahead, this natural accord of new Dutch leaders and new English ones reached its most cruel expression – for the Stuarts – when terms were finally discussed between the two countries at the beginning of 1654. The consequent peace was damaging enough from Charles' point of view. But one of the conditions was the 'seclusion' of the House of Orange from the government. This condition was originally imposed by Oliver Cromwell, Lord Protector of England since the previous December. But the Dutch, wishing to take very opportunity to humiliate the House of Orange, as one of their number told the French Ambassador, joined gladly in the scheme.[9] As a result, Mary Princess of

Orange, who had seemed back in the late forties the member of the Stuart family most likely to protect all the rest, was transformed into yet another distressed and protesting royal personage.

Of course, there remained Scotland. The price of Worcester – total defeat at the hands of the English – had been immediate occupation of the country. Legalization of this occupation followed, then union of the two countries, imposed from England. The situation was naturally inimical to many of the Scots, foremost amongst them the Highlanders, whose geographical situation enabled them to breathe defiance with virtual impunity if they so wished. There was however a considerable gap between Highland defiance and a royal triumph based on Highland action (as the past had already sufficiently demonstrated). A rising in the Highlands in the summer of 1652 proved once more abortive. The King wrote in disgust of the lethargy of the Highlanders, who, having promised to invade England, merely captured Inverness and then preferred to sleep in their own beds.

The real question about all these Scottish ventures was whether the leadership was to be local or imposed by the King from a distance; and, if the latter, a further question arose as to how local loyalties were to be stimulated, local feuds stifled. The appointment of John Middleton to the Highland command was along the right lines. Middleton had held command at Worcester and been imprisoned thereafter. He escaped from prison, wearing his wife's clothes, and rejoined the King. Middleton was an attractive character and a good commander. It was not his fault if the Highlanders failed to rise in abundant numbers.

The appointment of the Earl of Glencairn to a temporary overall command in the summer of 1653 was not such a wise move on the part of the King. He had once more straddled the Scots with a divided authority: the last thing they needed, in view of their own natural differences. Glencairn, unlike Middleton, was at the King's side. There was the renewed question of a Scottish expedition, to be sure, but with it the renewed problem – when should Glencairn sail, and, above all, when was the appropriate moment for the King himself to throw his weight into the fray?

In June 1653 Hyde was convinced that if 'no more probable adventure' offered itself, the King would go for Scotland.[10] Yet Charles did not set out. It is true that at this point Cardinal Mazarin still held Charles in a clamp; he would neither release him nor assist him. Nevertheless, the fact has to be faced that Charles was by now profoundly sceptical about the Scots, their capacity to implement their own promises, their ability to bring any kind of victory to his advantage out of their bleak and feudacious country. Therefore any possible Highland rising was born suffering from the disease of the King's secret disbelief – a condition which divided command did not help.

Nor can one criticize Charles for this conviction. As he had pointed out after Worcester, the Scots had not stuck by him in battle and were unlikely to do so when he was on the run; the same argument could be applied to a King in exile – the Scots were hardly likely to aid him whom they had failed to restore after his formal coronation at Scone. It was true that the English occupation, under the briskly iron rule of Colonel Robert, assisted the popularity of the absent Royalists. But there was no guarantee that this popularity would survive their actual appearance, since it had waned so many times before.

When this latest Highland rising did get under way, its progress confirmed these gloomy suppositions. There was a brief moment of glory when Middleton, the more experienced soldier, regained supreme command from Glencairn. But the treasured ability to form a proper Highland army and, having formed it, to lead it anywhere other than round and round the Highlands, was possessed by neither man. Help from abroad remained crucial. Might the Dutch come to the rescue? But by April 1654 the Dutch were no longer at war with the English Commonwealth. So hopes dwindled and ended with Middleton's defeat at Dalnaspidal in July 1654.

Meanwhile in England itself the elevation of Oliver Cromwell to the quasi-royal rank of Lord Protector was another blow to the prestige of the uncrowned King. The position of Protector was one which had its roots in English history – both Somerset and Hertford had occupied it. After Cromwell's assumption of the role, the Protectoral State replaced that of the

Commonwealth. It was a far more conventional concept. Negotiations between England and the various European powers were eased as a result.

France had indulged in a semi-official representation in England from late 1652 onwards in the shape of a clever, adaptable envoy, Antoine de Bordeaux. As the French Court settled back into its usual state of complacency, as the Cardinal resumed the reins of power twitched from his hands during the war of the Fronde, the melancholy observers of the exiled Royalist set began to suspect that yet another blow might be in store for them: the alliance of France and Commonwealth England. It would be the death-knell to Royalist hopes in France. Yet there was really nothing that King Charles, penniless, depressed and helpless, could do to avert it. He was thrust back on a series of diplomatic missions and enquiries – to the Danes, to Hamburg, Danzig, Poland, Queen Christina of Sweden, the German Diet and so forth – which, totted up, might win a prize for optimism and persistence, but achieved little positive result.

Money remained the key to absolutely everything, in the absence of the practical support of the great powers. Lack of money caused at least one mission to be withdrawn, since the emissary could not be supported. Already by 1652 the lack of money was chronic. The letters of the courtiers surrounding Charles began to be filled with the most poignant details of their penury. The childish jubilation of Richard Bellings on a mission to Ratisbon in April 1653, at having Christmas plum porridge, mince-pies, bakemeats and brawn, illustrates how low their expectations had become.[11]

It was not that the King was indifferent towards his friends' sufferings – far from it. But his official means of support were virtually non-existent. Jermyn had secured a nominal pension of £6,000 from the French government in February 1652 in order to end the King's maddening dependence on his mother. That sounded generous enough. But the pension was very seldom paid. Charles was thrust back on Loyalist contributions from England, a declining source of supply and surrounded by danger for those who tried to collect it. Privateers in the channel provided little joy: those from the Breton ports, while paying lip service to a tithe due to the English King, got away with what they could. The haven of Jersey had surrendered to the Commonwealth in December 1651. There was only the remote hope of rich privateering prizes to be provided by Prince Rupert from the West Indies.

It is against this background that the piteous pleas of the courtiers should be seen. And it would all get worse.

Under the circumstances, the propagandist charges that Charles was extravagant, wanton with money, make ironic reading. Had the King wished to outshine the sun itself in munificence, he would still have had absolutely no opportunity to do so. He was still living under his mother's roof at the Louvre. As he wrote to Rupert in the West Indies shortly before he left France, 'I am sure I am not only without money but have been compelled to borrow all that I have spent these three months'[12] – and these were necessary expenses of the sheer act of living.

Hyde laid his own charges that the young King, robbed of a sphere of proper action, became idle and pleasure-loving. How he nagged! The King did not write letters, the King did not attend to business, the King did this (bad) and did not do that (even worse). In short, he found that Charles' character had not been improved by adversity. 'God send us quickly from this place, for surely this lazy kind of life does nobody any good!' he exclaimed.[13] But it was not Paris and some fantasy existence of pleasure which was to blame, but an enforced life of disappointment.

Hyde's temperament was not improved by adversity either. He looked for some explanation of their continued trials – much as a Calvinist might have done – and found it in the King's lack of moral fibre, his inattention to the strict matter of the business. Charles was in effect the scapegoat. Hyde was in a more generous and a more accurate mood when he wrote, 'If you knew the miserable life the King leads, and how he is used, you would believe that he acts his own part not amiss; nor is it enough to say that it is his own fault....'[14]

It was no wonder that by the summer of 1653 Charles had fallen ill with a fever. Its exact nature was undiagnosed, except that he had to have blood let five times. But in view of the fact that contemporaries commented on his depression and withdrawal, one may suppose it to have been at least partly psychosomatic in origin, one of those fevers which the healthy Charles would have shrugged off without difficulty, but now laid him painfully low.

Relief, when it came, came in the form of change, rather than any true lightening of the situation. Nevertheless, to the King a change – any change – was obviously beneficial after the darkness into which he had been plunged at the French Court. As the steps of the diplomatic dance in which Protector and Cardinal were involved quickened, it suddenly suited the French to be rid of their dependent. Having been at times cozened by Mazarin, at times virtually imprisoned by him, Charles now found himself offered what his heart most desired – the full payment of his French pension – on condition that he left the country within ten days.

The gesture had very little grace about it: the French made it clear that the step was a necessary preparation for an English alliance. Nor was the departure of the King particularly ceremonious: he travelled on horseback, having put his coach-horses into 'a light cart' to convey his clothes and bedding. It was not quite the abject wretchedness of the post-Worcester period, but it was far from the state of a reigning monarch. Hyde wrote of his departure that 'the King is now as low as to human understanding as he can be'.[15] Yet at least Charles, literally putting the French Court, with its frustrations and chicaneries, behind him, had hope. And he was once more on his own, without his mother. As the years drew on and their differences increased, her presence aroused in him a combination of profound irritation and melancholy affection, which he was glad to avoid.

Indeed, first at Spa and then at Aachen for a month or two Charles actually found life rather fun. The decision to go to Spa was not of course taken from a very wide choice: Holland would not have him, and the various territories within and around the

Holy Roman Empire, on the borders of the Spanish Netherlands, offered the best alternative.

At Spa, the impoverished little band whistled to keep up their spirits, and, as descriptions of their life show, to a certain extent succeeded. It was high summer. All the afternoon the courtiers would dance, then take supper, then dance again in the evening light in the meadows: 'I think the air makes them indefatigable' was one comment.[16] The inclement weather, which was supposed to have affected the famous mineral waters of the Spa, obviously did not spoil this rustic fun. And the weather did not prevent salubrious bathing in Caesar's Bath.

One of the chief dancers was Theobald Lord Taaffe, an Anglo-Irish peer who had fought with Ormonde in the late 1640s. He had not done particularly well militarily, but he had later joined Charles in Paris, where, according to the Cardinal de Retz, he had become 'Great Chamberlain, Valet de Chambre, Clerk of the Kitchen, Cup Bearer and all' to the King – in short, that kind of necessary mixture of courtier, agent and boon companion of which all Kings stand in need, particularly those without proper courts. Taaffe had something else in common with his master – a relationship with Lucy Walter. He was probably the father of her second child, Mary Walter.[17] In Brussels Taaffe negotiated with the Duke of Lorraine, mortgaging the Fort of Duncannon to him on Charles' behalf for funds; there was also a proposal to marry James to one of the Duke of Lorraine's illegitimate children, and pop the pair of them on an independent throne in Ireland.

Apart from his usefulness as a confidant, Taaffe's chief value to the King was in his Catholicism. He could thus be used as an intermediary with the Pope or with the Catholic Count of Neuburg, without the potentate feeling insulted. Certainly Taaffe enjoyed a close and warm friendship with his sovereign throughout nearly all the years of exile (only clouded over towards the end, when Taaffe killed Sir William Keith in a duel over a tennis bet – for Charles maintained very strict anti-duelling rules). As much as anyone, Taaffe understood exactly what depressions, disappointments – and pleasures – marked the long exile of King Charles II.

As Taaffe danced, and on occasion waxed 'poetical', the more stable side of Charles' entourage was represented by the Marquess of Ormonde. And the mimic court was further gilded by the arrival of Mary Princess of Orange. Brother and sister occupied the two chief hotels at the Spa with their suites. Their mutual devotion was the subject of sentimental and approving comment, while Mary's widowed status involved her in various romantic rumours, including the notion that she might now marry her cousin Prince Rupert. There were other rumours too – that another eligible lady, the eccentric Queen Christina of Sweden, might join them. It was just as well the Royalists were unaware that the Swedish Queen was also somewhere in her strange heart sighing after Oliver Cromwell, professing herself '*vestra amica* Christina' and treasuring the Protector's portrait.

Brother and sister went to Aachen. On 7 September the King, all in black, with white silk stockings and the ever-present colour of the Garter, visited the Cathedral of Charlemagne at the invitation of the Canons. Mary kissed the skull and hand of the great Emperor, and Charles measured his sword against his own. There was plenty of mirth and dancing and drinking. It was all very jolly and apparently carefree and gracious at the same time. Charles was described as winning universal regard by his 'affable and free carriage'. It was left to an English spy to write a secret report to John Thurloe, Cromwell's Secretary of State and master of the Protectoral intelligence network: 'For all his dancing, I believe he [the King] has a heavy heart.'[18]

By the beginning of autumn that was undoubtedly true. The upsurge of optimism consequent on departure from France had waned. The courtiers' obsessional interest in their own poverty had taken over from their gaiety: Aachen was described as 'a most expenseful place', at five pence a night for a bed.[19] Their complaints about local prices and their own lack of cash remind one of the sufferings of British travellers denied foreign currency after the Second World War.

When the King and his sister decided to pass on to Cologne in early October it was because they hoped that this free archbishopric, owing no allegiance to the Emperor, would provide the right base for their next step – whatever that might be.

On the surface all went well. Mary discovered 'a very fair and curious house, full of decent rooms and pleasant gardens' for their lodging. The City Magistrates presented silver pots and wine to fill the pots. There were receptions for the royal brother and sister at the local Jesuit College, where young boys sang to them with great sweetness, and at convents round about. The natives being so friendly, and pressing them to stay, Charles graciously acceded to their invitation, and decided to take up residence in the city. The courtiers, ignoring the fact that very soon wages were owing to them all and there was little or no hope of payment, were once again resolutely cheerful: 'We are as brave and eat as well and are as jocund, as if we were in all plenty, so confident we are of God's continuance in his wonderful Providence towards us.'[20]

Charles himself also described an existence in Cologne which recalls that of the exiled Duke in *As You Like It*, fleeting the time carelessly in the Forest of Arden: 'Despite lack of money we dance and play as if we have taken the Plate-Fleet,' he wrote. As Charles told his aunt Elizabeth of Bohemia in one of his wry, joking letters, they had only two lacks: 'the one for want of fiddlers, the other for somebody both to teach and assist at dancing the new dances'. Otherwise all was perfection. Charles also ordered clothes, a sword, and a quantity of shoes (his obsession): three black and three coloured pairs from a Paris shoemaker, and six more from one in Flanders.[21]

But Sir Edward Nicholas' stoicism and the King's good cheer cannot conceal the fact that one of Charles' main reasons for picking on Cologne was its convenience as a collecting station for the money granted to him by the Imperial Diet. And that money proved as difficult to elicit as the French pension.... The Elector of Cologne only paid up 'his small quota', as Hyde described it, after an importunity 'unfit to have been pressed upon any other prince or gentleman'.[22] Furthermore, the Elector excused himself from paying an official call on Charles on the chilly grounds of 'ill-health'. The warmth of the City Magistrates was not paralleled by that of the Princes.

When the Count of Neuburg invited King Charles and Princess Mary to Düsseldorf, they accepted with alacrity. On 29 October they repaired there by water, floating down the Rhine in a kind of Siegfried idyll. At the end of the journey the Count and Countess awaited them, surrounded by a full assembly of their court with many an elaborate ceremony and repast to follow. For instance, twenty-two tables and sixty-eight dishes were designated for the evening banquet – one hopes that the starving English courtiers of Cologne revelled in the experience. There was music, new to their ears but delightful all the same, and the Count, who prided himself on his civilized way of life, did not even drink too much (unlike some other Germans of their experience).

It was unfortunate that the taste and elegance of the Count was not matched by that of his wife Elizabeth Amalia of Hesse Darmstadt: Charles had already declared himself against the notion of marrying a German wife – 'I hate Princesses of cold northern countries'[23] – and the Countess did little to dissuade him from his prejudice. Having no French, she decided to take no part in the festivities, but sat in an ungraciously lumpen manner throughout the banquet.

From Düsseldorf King Charles and Princess Mary ventured daringly a little way into the Spanish Netherlands, although Charles had no permission to do so. Then it was back to Cologne, where, after the Düsseldorf jaunt, the rest of the winter passed somewhat sadly and even sourly. The Elector still did not call. Charles studied French, studied Italian, hunted and – walked. He had no coach. He walked in the walled city. One of Thurloe's spies described him walking ceaselessly in the icy weather, bare-headed through this city which, originally a little paradise, had become an open prison. And of course the quarrels had broken out all over again among his advisers.

Under the circumstances, it was natural for all concerned with the royal fortunes to cast their eyes anew at England, since the near prospect was so unsatisfying. After only a few months Cologne was as stale as any other refuge. Temperamentally, Charles liked Germany no better than he liked the northern princesses. Years later, when the King was told that the widowed Duchesse de Châtillon, his lovely Bablon, was going to remarry and live in Germany, he observed with feeling, 'If she knew the country, that's to say, the way of living there and the people, so well as I do, she would suffer very much in France before she would change countries.'[24]

In England after 1653 some kind of revival of Royalist spirit had at last taken place. In November 1653 King Charles gave the first written credentials to an organization terming itself the Sealed Knot, as the official organ of Royalist conspiracy in England.[25] It had always been Hyde's contention that the King was not only most likely to be restored from within England, but also most beneficially – thus the stain of foreign aid would not be seen on his royal robe. But it was also part of Hyde's policy, with which the King heartily agreed, that the English rising, when it came, should be a co-ordinated once-and-for-all affair. The Sealed Knot was given its commission as much to hold in check other unplanned and thus doomed risings, as to set in motion its own.

The trouble was that the English conspirators were as disunited at home as the English Court abroad. The Sealed Knot could not prevent the eruption of two irresponsible plots in the summer of 1654, that of Gerard and the so-called Ship Tavern Plot.

When a splinter group, calling themselves the Action Party, decided to plan a major coup for the spring of 1655, the King found himself in a highly awkward and even embarrassing situation as regards the Sealed Knot. First, he was well aware that without the active participation of the Knot the rising was hardly likely to succeed. Secondly, the leading members of the Knot declined to take part, unless actually ordered to do so by the King. Thirdly, the Action Party made it clear that they intended to go ahead in any case, with or without the Knot.

This embarrassment culminated in the disastrous events of the spring of 1655. As the King paced round icy and far-off Cologne, he was compelled to receive the mission of an agitated member of the Action Party, Thomas Ross, who arrived at the end of January and implored him to give his group the royal support. This put Charles in a quandary. He outlined it succinctly to the Knot representatives. How could he order the Sealed Knot to go against its own military judgement? On the other hand, 'nor can it be reasonable for me to hinder them [i.e. the Action Party] from moving, who believe themselves ready for it. . . .' He concluded gloomily to the Knot members: 'And yet I cannot look for any great success, if whilst they stir, you sit still.'[26]

With hindsight it is easy to see that the King's eventual course of action did nothing to mitigate the conspirators' difficulties. He instructed Daniel O'Neill to negotiate between the two parties, to try and work out some agreement between themselves; he also despatched the new Lord Rochester (the former Lord Wilmot) to England. What Charles failed to do was provide some kind of firm authority which all sides would respect. Ormonde, who was at Antwerp, and sent emissaries from both conspiratorial factions, slightly favoured the Action Party, but was well aware of the need for a positive decision from the King, 'else it would be the certain loss of those that shall appear, and the very probable destruction of those that hold off'.[27]

Yet Charles' indecision – which is what it amounted to – reflected only too accurately his cut-off state, the impossibility of reaching any kind of major conclusion about a country of whose conditions he remained lamentably ignorant. In this sense, it is difficult to criticize the King too harshly. All one can do is note a creeping vacillation in the nature and policies of King Charles from 1655 onwards. Nicholas called this vacillation 'The fatal custom of his family'.[28] This is unjust. For the first twenty-four years of his life we have seen in King Charles a decisive, even heroically active, character: now this new strain of inaction develops to complicate what was originally a comparatively simple nature. Its genesis in the tense conditions of exile is easily understood. But it is a further ironic fact, as we shall see, that in exile the King did as well by inaction as by action – taking the long view.

However, that consoling notion was not available to the wretched conspirators of March 1655. Nothing happened at all in Leicestershire or Staffordshire (where plans collapsed). These conspirators were the lucky ones. In the North too nothing of any great consequence happened, except that Rochester arrived, and had to make yet another escape from the British Isles once it was realized that the government had the insurrection well in hand. The rising itself was officially postponed – except that the news did not reach the West.

There Colonel John Penruddock, a member of the Action Party, did enter Salisbury and seized the town on 12 March. The rumour – incorrect – of Leveller participation in the rising had the unfortunate effect of spurring on the government to vengeance without assisting the conspirators. This merely gave the Protectoral government an excellent excuse for repression via a much-increased militia, once they had put the rising down with comparative lack of effort. Indeed, the regime of the Major-Generals, a military rule by districts instituted in England shortly afterwards, was happily attributed by the government to the necessities imposed by the Penruddock Rising. Yet the Rising never posed the faintest danger to the established regime: what with the infiltration of the Sealed Knot organization by government spies and the quarrels of the English Court abroad, there was little to fear. The prejudices of the latter included the refusal to employ the Catholic Sir Marmaduke Langdale in Yorkshire, although he was a person of much influence there, and a noted soldier.

Naturally the King in Cologne knew nothing of this. He went as far as to move secretly to Middleburg in Zeeland, hoping from this convenient spot to be summoned to England. His host was a Dutchman named William Krimson, who had married a woman from the household of Charles' aunt Elizabeth of Bohemia; the secret of Charles' destination was only imparted to Hyde, Nicholas and two others. Letters were to be addressed to a Mr William Thomas at the Sign of the Town of Rouen, an inn in Flushing, and from there would be conveyed to Middleburg. Despite all these elaborate precautions, it was not so easy for Charles to elude the Protectoral spies in Cologne. Henry Manning, for example, furious at the King giving him the slip, tracked him to Flushing, where the presence of one of Charles' retainers gave away the secret. It is touching to find that Charles employed his old alias from Penderel days, Jackson, during his sojourn at Middleburg. And Ormonde reported that the presence of the daughter of the house, 'though little more than a girl', made 'Mr Jackson's' confinement more supportable.[29]

In every other way the episode was abortive and slightly ludicrous. Wild rumours reached the King that the whole of north Yorkshire had declared for him ... that towns as far apart as Exeter and Newcastle had risen up in his favour ... that Fairfax had five thousand men behind him and had declared for Charles ... that the Protector was dead ... all untrue.

On 9 April the King, disillusioned and despairing, went quietly back to Cologne. He maintained his spirit in his public verdict on the Penruddock rising when he criticized his critics: 'Those people, who take upon them to censure whatsoever I do ... They who will not believe anything to be reasonably designed, except it be successfully executed, had need of a less difficult game to play than mine is.' And he ended with a jocular boast: 'I shall live to bid you welcome to Whitehall.'[30]

But of that coming to pass, in the summer of 1655, there seemed but a slender chance.

CHAPTER TEN

The Courtesies and the Injuries

> 'You will do well to put him [Cardinal Mazarin] in mind that I am not yet so low, but that I may return both the courtesies and the injuries I have received.'
>
> King Charles II, October 1656

Hope was the necessary diet of all the exiled Royalists; above all, it was the food on which their King had to live. It was more through hope than conviction that King Charles now concentrated his ambitions on a Spanish treaty.

The failure of the Penruddock Rising made it abundantly clear that the English Royalists – from whom Hyde had persisted in expecting salvation – were good for nothing of consequence at the present time. That in itself was a considerable blow to Hyde's prestige, as several observers noted. To balance the decline of Hyde's pro-English policy came the rise of Protectoral aggression towards Spain. The summer of 1655 saw an expedition on behalf of Cromwell to the West Indies, whose most significant achievement was the capture of Spanish-held Jamaica. The King of Spain's beard was singed.

Optimists in Royalist circles thought that hostilities between Spain and England must soon follow – in fact, it was not until the spring of 1656 that war was actually declared. Pessimists paid more attention to the development of the alliance between Cardinal Mazarin and Oliver Cromwell, two men who had in common strength and initiative, the qualities of the self-made.

At the same time, there were startling whispers that Cromwell himself might take the crown. These insinuations had their own impact on the Royalist frame of mind. There was a divinity which hedged a king, a divinity which had so far hedged King Charles II in so far as it hedged anyone at all. The reasons given to Cromwell for taking one further step, and accepting the royal title, demonstrated that. The people of England knew their duty to a King and he to them, so ran one argument. Obviously what King Oliver I would gain, King Charles II must inevitably lose.

The Protector did not finally reject the notion of a royal crown until April 1657, and then only at the end of a period of agonized indecision. During this time a betting man would have gambled on his acceptance. For the next few years, the Protector's increasingly monarchical state presented to the European powers, including Spain, a continual reminder of the impotent situation of the theoretical monarch of the country. It was not a good augury for the Spanish negotiations.

There were rumours, as time went on, that one of Cromwell's pretty young daughters might provide a bride for the exiled King.[1] In this way, the Protectoral House of Cromwell and the Royal House of Stuart could be fused to the advantage of both: presumably the next step would have been the accession of King Charles and his Cromwellian Queen to an English throne left vacant by the death of Oliver. It is easy to despise the rumour as foolish; but in the slough following the Penruddock fiasco it was not such a ridiculous idea. The return of the royal family in modern Spain was accomplished when a dictator adopted a King to rule after his death. Monarchy can be restored in many different ways.

The 'dead calm' in England in the summer of 1655, and the renewed talk of 'making a king' (namely Cromwell), combined to render the state of the exiled Royalists particularly harsh.[2] Their brethren, who had trickled back to England and settled for the status quo, were well off by contrast. The shrill tune of poverty, which is the theme song of these bitter years, was chanted louder than ever by the exiles.

In July Charles was reported to be too poor to eat meat for ten days; in December a gift of a pack of hounds from England gave rise to dreadful embarrassment, since it cost a fortune to keep the hounds in food, and yet it was naturally out of the question to return them to their donor. The next year Dorothy Chiffinch could not even get together the money for the King's washing, and in September 1657 Hyde noted that everything, literally everything ('every bit of meat, every drop of drink, all the fire and all the candles') which had come the King's way had been acquired on credit. About the same date the King was said to have sunk so low that he had to manage with a single dish for his meals – just as well, perhaps, if nothing whatsoever had been paid for, but an extraordinary state of affairs by the standards of the time, when the meals of a king had a prestigious life of their own. By 1659 Hyde was writing of 'insupportable debts'.[3]

In the correspondence of the King's servants the phrases of want and desperation occur and recur. Sir Marmaduke Langdale described himself as being in such a 'mean condition' that he could not seek out the company of persons of quality. George Lane was in torment, trying to get money for his sick wife and child. A Scottish knight named Maxwell who quarrelled with his unpaid landlord was given this sapient advice by Ormonde: first of all to eat his words, and then (gratefully) his supper. Lord Norwich wrote of being dull, lame, cold, and totally out of money, to the extent that when his coat was badly singed he had to cut off the blackened area and continue to wear it as before, since he had no other. Even Thurloe's spies, set to watch the exiled court, were moved to pity. 'How they will all live God knows! I am sure I do not!' exclaimed one.[4]

As the year went by, many of the Royalists experienced those feelings so eloquently expressed by Lord Macaulay in 'A Jacobite's Epitaph'.*

> For him I threw lands, honour, wealth away,
> And one dear hope, that was more prized than they.
> For him I languished in a foreign clime,
> Grey-haired with sorrow in my manhood's prime....

* But written for another Charles Stuart who led his followers into exile, King Charles II's great-nephew, Bonnie Prince Charlie.

And some elected to make the sacrifice no longer.

To one prospective resettler in England, Hyde wrote anxiously, 'Ask yourself (for you must take a large prospect) … whether, if you were there, you would retain all your own zeal for your Master's interests.'[5] Hyde worried in particular that the creation of Cromwell the King would involve returning Royalists in an oath of loyalty to him – or at least an Oath of Abjuration from King Charles. But neither the neurosis of Hyde, nor the valiance of Charles, could prevent the gradual attrition of the royal cause within and without England.

In February 1655 the King had suggested to Anthony Ashley Cooper that his experience would tell him 'how unsettled all things must be, till I am restored to that which belongs to me, which would restore peace to the nation'. Ashley Cooper was an important West Country magnate who had elected to throw in his lot with the Protectoral regime by becoming a member of the Council of State. Unfortunately, his experience clearly told him the exact contrary. He never answered the letter.[6] He was typical of many who for the foreseeable future identified stability with Cromwell, not Charles.

It was in this context that the prospects of Spanish assistance were assessed with a mixture of hope and apprehension in the autumn of 1655. In the letters of Nicholas, for example, we find on the one hand confidence that the Spanish King will declare war on Cromwell for the rape of Jamaica: 'Which done, I doubt not but (for his own interest) he will find it most necessary to espouse the king's quarrel.' On the other hand, only a few weeks earlier Nicholas had summed up with far greater accuracy the complications inherent in any endorsement of Charles II: 'I do not think that the [Spanish] king will so suddenly and heartily embrace our Master's interests,' he wrote, 'having observed how slow his Majesty's party in England are to rise for him, how much he is entangled in the snares of France, and how many about him are suspected for their loyalty.'[7]

One step which the English King now felt it essential to take, if he was to make any progress at all with the Spanish, was to move nearer the centre of things. Besides, Cologne was beginning to pall. There was 'a jolly journey' – Hyde's words – to the

Frankfurt Fair in September, with Mary. In theory, brother and sister travelled incognito, but, as Charles wryly commented to his aunt Elizabeth of Bohemia, ''tis so great a secret that not above half the town of Cologne knows it.' He also told Elizabeth that he hoped to be furnished with 'some good stories' before the end of their journey. Which expectation was no doubt fulfilled, since at Frankfurt the King encountered the English actor-manager George Jolly, famous for employing 'skilful women' in his troupe, at a time when females on the stage were a distinct novelty. The King's patronage of Jolly was secured, and, in happier times back in England, would be amplified.[8]

Yet the King could not linger for ever in this outpost, making the occasional merry sortie to paper over the cracks in his confidence. His aim was to reach the Low Countries, preferably the Spanish Netherlands, where the presence of the influential governor, Don Juan (an illegitimate son of the Spanish King), would surely expedite a Spanish alliance. Finally, Charles secured permission to come to Brussels, the capital of the Spanish Netherlands, arriving there in March 1656. The crucial negotiations – from the English point of view – began.

The letters of the King back to his mentor Hyde on the subject make at times touching reading. The King showed a frantic desire to address Don Juan correctly, which was quite alien to his normal practice, and even regretted not having brought with him Hyde's guide to etiquette: 'your book of inscriptions, subscriptions and superscriptions'. In its absence, he had to copy the correct mode of address off another letter. The King's concern for proper communication extended to a desire to learn Spanish himself: he asked Ormonde to get him a Spanish New Testament, 'for I think we have much need of that language'.[9]

As for the negotiations, they were on the surface successful, or, as Charles himself told Hyde, 'At first I found them [the Spanish] dry ... yet at last they began to be very free with me.'[10] Projected clauses of the Spanish Treaty (which was not actually signed until 2 April 1658) included a monthly allowance of three thousand crowns for Charles himself and half that amount for James. The Spanish ports would in future welcome the English

Royalist privateers, while, most important of all, Spanish armed help was promised to place the King of England on his throne. In return, Charles promised the suspension, and if possible the Parliamentary revocation, of the penal laws against English Catholics once he had been restored; he also swore to maintain an alliance with the Irish Catholics. Lastly, the existing Royalist soldiers abroad, notably the fair number of Irish soldiers currently serving with France, were to be pressed into service with Spain – against France.

One may believe that Charles gave the promises concerning English Catholicism with a light heart, since he was evidently a very long way off being able to implement them. But the clause concerning the Royalist soldiers had the immediate effect of angering his brother James. The Duke of York had enjoyed service in the French Army; prospering, he had been offered a French command in Italy by Mazarin. Now he was expected to transfer his allegiance and also his fighting command to Spain. In an understandable huff at this high-handed disposal of himself, James declined to come to his brother's side but went instead to the United Provinces. It was left to Ormonde to act as peacemaker and conciliate James; in the meantime, Henry Duke of Gloucester served as a volunteer with the Spanish.

In Holland, too, Mary Princess of Orange was not best pleased by the Spanish alliance. Her beloved brother, the centre of her emotional life since the death of her husband – she would not live until she saw him again, she wrote of her departure from Düsseldorf – had joined with the hereditary enemy of the United Provinces. Mary's efforts to establish herself there as Princess of Orange and mother of William were not helped by her brother's action. For once Mary had something in common with her mother, since Henrietta Maria naturally abhorred the Spanish trend, which made her own position in France similarly awkward.

There was a period of coldness between Charles and Mary, the once devoted pair. Mary visited her mother in France at her own expense, to demonstrate her opinion of the Spanish alliance (although she may also have harboured a private ambition to marry her cousin Louis XIV, seven years her junior). Later

Charles came to criticize Mary for the lack of prudence in her behaviour. She quarrelled with Lord and Lady Balcarres, whom he had placed in her train, and he blamed her for her romance with the young Harry Jermyn, nephew of her mother's favourite. Mary pouted. In general, these were neither happy nor united times for the Stuart royal family, whose internal quarrels and dissension mirrored those of King Charles' advisers.

Of course, the bickering of brother and sister, brother and brother, was as nothing beside the fundamental division which did exist within the structure of the family. That lay between Queen Henrietta Maria on the one side, and King Charles on the other, and concerned the vital and by now highly political topic of religion. It sprang both from Henrietta Maria's missionary Catholicism, and from her son's rejection of it.

Much has been written on the subject of the religion of Charles II, about which only two things can be stated with absolute certainty: that he was born a member of the Church of England (like his father), and that he died fifty-five years later a member of the Roman Catholic Church (like his mother). The exact moment at which the change was made, first in his own heart, secondly in the form of an official conversion divulged to a Catholic priest, can only be suggested, not known. It is nevertheless important to point out the savagery with which Charles II denounced his mother's Catholic fervour in the 1650s, in order to refute firmly the proposition that this conversion took place in exile.

On the evidence, nothing was further from King Charles' mind. He was horribly aware that even a rumour of his conversion might fatally damage the prospects of his restoration to the English throne. At the same time, he was subject to constant surveillance from the spies and agents of the English government, who for their part were well aware of the propagandist value of such charges. The King's 'praying ministers', for example, were reported as wearing long black gowns, like those of Catholic priests, in Brussels; furthermore, they were actually said to have entered Catholic chapels in these vestments, causing scandal. Whenever the exiled King could, he issued denials of such tales.[11]

It would be wrong to claim for King Charles as a young man any excessive spirituality; and his interest in comparative religion, as seen in the dialogue with Father Huddleston, was more naively curious than deeply reflective. But he was extremely interested in the political effects of religious allegiance, as perforce the early experiences of his father, and his own dealings with the Scots and Irish, had trained him to be. When his grandfather, the great Henri, had changed religion, he had done it for a blatantly political reason. Now that Charles was dealing with the notoriously Catholic Spanish, he trod delicately to preserve the image of his own personal Protestantism; otherwise, he would not only be restored by the agency of an alien Catholic power, but in the guise of a Catholic alien himself.

This is not to exclude visits to Catholic churches and chapels, and even attendance at Mass. Ormonde was supposed to have seen the King at Mass.[12] There are sufficient travellers' tales and spies' reports of such incidents to make it perfectly plausible that the King in this way did join in the life of the countries where he found himself, during the long years of exile. But a strong distinction must be drawn between stories of attendance as Mass, when in a Catholic country, and conversion. A comparison can be made with Protestant or agnostic tourists today visiting Catholic countries such as Italy: it is as though every such attendance at a Mass in an Italian Catholic chapel was held to be evidence of a conversion. James Duke of York, who bore less responsibility, leant towards Rome sooner than his brother. The incidence of his visits to Catholic churches may also have increased the stories about the King, since it was easy for rumour to mistake one brother and another.

The single story of the King being seen to take the Sacrament of Communion is extremely dubious. It comes from the Commonplace Book of George Boddington, a clothworker of London, later a director of the Bank of England, and MP in 1702.[13] As a boy, Boddington went to watch Charles II ride through the streets of London on Restoration Day and was told on return by his angry father that the King he had watched was no true Protestant: he had seen him take the host at Antwerp, together with his brother the Duke of York. Such a second-hand tale is hardly enough to balance the weight of evidence the other way: that, as an English minister wrote, it was 'a thing so contrary to probability'. It is far more significant that Buckingham, whose intimacy with the King dated from childhood, certainly did not subscribe to the notion of his conversion in exile. He referred to him as having no religion at all except a kind of vague 'deism'.[14]

The crucial incident in all this is the attempt of Queen Henrietta Maria to convert Henry Duke of Gloucester to Catholicism in the autumn of 1654, when he was fifteen. First the King wrote 'Harry' a very strong letter on the subject, sufficiently vehement to dispose of any idea that he himself was contemplating such a step. Then he wrote to his mother in even plainer terms: if she was really determined to change Harry's religion, 'I cannot expect your Majesty does either believe or wish my return into England. For you will force me to do that which must disoblige all Catholics [that is, denounce the conversion] and on the other side all that I can say or do will never make my Protestant subjects believe but that it is done with my consent....' The King's analysis was incidentally perfectly correct. Even an English Catholic wrote of Harry's possible conversion that it would benefit the King, but only provided he was thought to have nothing to do with it, 'otherwise both His Majesty and we shall lose the fruits of it'.[15]

Plainest of all was the conclusion of Charles' letter to his mother: 'And remember the last words of my dead father (whose memory I doubt not will work upon you) which were to charge him – Harry – never to change his religion, whatsoever mischief shall fall either upon me or my affairs, hereafter.' Harry duly remained a Protestant and in September 1655 joined Mary at The Hague. The ghost of King Charles I, like Hamlet's murdered father, was quite enough to prevent his son from forgetting the Anglican cause for which he had died.

For two reasons then, political and emotional, the theory of Charles II's Catholic conversion in exile can be dismissed. For all the rumours, it is significant that nothing was ever proved in this respect. Yet, in the heady atmosphere immediately preceding the Restoration, there would be many who would have liked to have done so. A careful investigation of the subject, for example, by a minister of a Protestant church in Rouen, written to a friend in London and printed immediately after the Restoration, could confirm nothing. The sharp remark of Charles to Lord Bristol when the latter became converted to Catholicism – that his father had trained him to be a Protestant – was cited. The previous rumours concerning the King's religion, concluded the minister, 'came from hell'.[16]

They did not come from hell exactly, but from a more worldly source. As John Mordaunt pointed out in November 1659 of a current canard of Charles' Catholicism, he would be 'utterly ruined' if the story were true, and with *both* sides: ''tis his stability in that point that gains daily.' About the same period the King was taking enormous care to have a story that he had been seen at Mass at St Jean de Luz contradicted. He took it for a good omen that his enemies used such feeble 'bullrushes' to attack him, he wrote. As for parading this Catholicism – did they suppose he was 'in love with banishment'?[17]

Against this oft-repeated public constancy, the assertion of Bishop Burnet, written much later in his history, that King Charles was privately received while in exile by the Cardinal de Retz, with only his cousin Lord Aubigny in the secret, seems poor fodder indeed.[18] If it took place late in his exile, such a conversion would have been a most dangerous hostage to fortune, at a time when the King was desperately trying to assure the world of his Protestant 'stability'. If it took place earlier on, then, quite apart from the hypocrisy evinced in the correspondence about Harry, it is strange that the English King never chose to play this card in his dealings with the Catholic Spanish, and the militantly Catholic Don Juan.

Most difficult of all to explain, under these circumstances, would be the unsuccessful course of King Charles' negotiations with the Pope. Naturally, Charles was not averse to the notion of Papal support, along with any other form of European support available. This included money. The Pope was rich, the King was poor. As Charles told the Count of Neuburg in

January 1656, if the Pope's 'goodness' led him to 'make me some good present ... you know that I am not in the state to refuse'.[19] But the money did not come.

Hyde's attitude was slightly different. His eyes ever turned towards the English phoenix from whose ashes he expected restoration, Hyde was concerned that the King should preserve the allegiance of the English Catholics. King Charles, he wrote, was the sole ruler from whom they could hope for 'repeal or modification of the penal laws'.[20] But by the time Oliver Cromwell was well settled in his Protectoral role, that was no longer true. Cromwell, and the Protectoral government generally, showed considerable brilliance in the way they dangled before both Pope and Cardinal Mazarin the prospect of toleration for Catholics, without ever quite granting it officially. As a result, the condition of English Catholics did generally improve in the mid 1650s, before the demands of Cromwell's anti-Catholic Parliament of 1657 put a stop to the amelioration. In the meantime, Catholic records show an increase in conversions in England, and the attendance of the English at the Catholic Embassy chapels went up markedly.[21]

Against these practical improvements, King Charles had little to offer the Pope except the hope – or promise – of toleration when he recovered his throne. It was another bar to Papal support that he remained a Protestant. To Charles' indignation, he was never fully supported by the Pope. It is surely out of the question that something as favourable to his cause with the Pope as his own secret conversion would not have been mentioned had it taken place.

King Charles enjoyed Brussels after Cologne. But he was not allowed to remain there long by his new allies, the Spaniards. The so-called 'Spanish Method' of diplomacy was traditionally slow – very slow. Don Juan intended to take his time before implementing his promises to Charles. Meanwhile, it was thought better if the King of England removed himself and his little train from the capital of the Spanish Netherlands lest their mere presence enabled them to become too exigent. Charles took up his residence in the beautiful town of Bruges, a watery paradise of light and ancient buildings about nine miles from the North Sea; here rows of gabled houses were mirrored in the calm surface of the canals. It was a city redolent of the great days of Flanders and the Burgundian Dukes. Now however it was a backwater. Especially did it appear as such to Charles, anxious to prosecute his affairs at the centre. In the sixteenth century, when its trade declined, the town had been known as Bruges-la-Morte: Charles II agreed.

Nevertheless, it was here that the King was destined to spend a large part of the remainder of his exile. And gradually he established himself. He visited the enclosed English convent in the Rue des Carnes which had been founded in 1629; despite its enclosure, the King's rank gained him a collation from the Mother Prioress. His silver arrived from Cologne, together with a private cabinet for his papers – that seventeenth-century equivalent of the safe and an essential of the time for anyone as much immersed in secret correspondence as Charles II came to be. His household plate and linen however had to be left behind in Cologne until his debts were paid. At first, the King lived in the home of one of his Irish supporters, Thomas Preston, later Viscount Tara, at the back of the belfry. He recalled the episode with gratitude after the Restoration in a handwritten letter commending the return of their Irish estates to the Preston children; he even remembered to commend the maiden aunt – 'Miss Warren' – who had also formed part of the household.[22] Later Charles moved to the Rue Haute, where he occupied a pleasant house, with a garden at its back going down to the canal.

The burghers too treated him with great courtesy. The King was made patron of the Guilds of St George and St Sebastian – for crossbowmen and archers respectively. To these Guilds the English King promised certain monies after his death: it is good to relate that they were actually paid somewhat sooner – in 1662, two years after the Restoration. The Flemings, said Charles, were 'the most honest and true-hearted race of people he had met with'.

How debauched was this court at Bruges? It is necessary to ask this question, since rumours concerning the dissipation of the King's entourage, spread by English government propagandists, were on a level with the stories of his extravagance – and of course of his Catholicism. In December 1656, for instance, one of Thurloe's spies wrote with contempt of 'Charles Stuart's court' and how 'fornication, drunkenness and adultery' were esteemed 'no sin amongst them'. The spy went on to comfort himself with the reflection that God would certainly never 'prosper any of the attempts' of such people.[23]

As for the King himself, the same zealous vigilantes were anxious to discover fresh mistresses for him by every post. A bachelor prince is ever a target for such innuendoes: Charles II suffered even more than most because it suited his enemies to spread them. By the Restoration, Charles had been endowed with three more illegitimate children to follow James Crofts. Charlotte Jemima Henrietta Maria Fitzroy, born in 1651, was the daughter of Elizabeth Killigrew. Some eight years older than Charles and the sister of the Duke of York's chaplain, 'Betty' Killigrew had married Francis Boyle, later Viscount Shannon, shortly before the Civil War. Charles' principal mistress at Bruges, Catharine Pegge, the beautiful daughter of a Derbyshire squire, presented him with a son in 1657 and a daughter in 1658. The girl died, but the son, Charles Fitzcharles, survived to enjoy the patronage of his restored father: he was nicknamed Don Carlo, commemorating his 'Spanish' origins.

Charles had had another, older mistress in Paris, the twice-widowed Lady Byron, born Eleanor Needham, daughter of Viscount Kilmorey. She did not bear him a child, but did acquire some money from him: a tribute to her pertinacity, in view of the King's straitened circumstances (she did less well after 1660, having to make do with a pension of £500 a year, and the odd *ex gratia* payment). In the nine years between Worcester and the Restoration there were also encounters with pretty women who, like Charles himself, saw nothing wrong in such dalliance between consenting adults.

By the standards of the time none of this amounted to profligacy in a young unmarried monarch. As to the tell-tales, Charles dismissed them in a letter to Lord Taaffe as 'blind

Harpers', adding that he would never have had the time to enjoy half the ladies attributed to him.[24]

Despite these efforts, the watchers at Bruges and elsewhere were not particularly successful in making the charges of debauchery stick during the years of exile – in sharp contrast to post-Restoration times. Charles' habit of having French players to entertain him on the Sabbath caused quite as much scandal as anything else. He played cribbage and piquet with his courtiers: he won, he lost – that was the level of excitement. He sent for Italian books to pass the time – such as *Il Pastor Fido*, by Guarini – 'if nothing better could be found'. Certain of his followers in their 'right Highland apparel' did provide amazement, as they swaggered about the town.[25] But of outrageous sexual scandal there was little trace.

The truth is that King Charles II was at this time the reverse of high-spirited, and he did not try to cure his melancholia by debauchery. A portrait painted by a Spanish artist during the Bruges period shows rather a sad as well as a saturnine young man: it is a very different picture from those two traditionally associated with him, the brave young hero of Worcester – cheerful, even up his oak-tree – and the confident monarch of 1660 onwards – cynical, amused, above all in total command of himself and the situation. This is an introverted, even listless, figure.

For whatever the conditions of the latter years of exile offered, they certainly did not offer merriment. It was not so much the continuous demands of intelligence and counter-intelligence – at which Thurloe, having so much more money, would always win – as the debilitating mixture of depression and danger which these years provided. The King's life was popularly supposed to be in danger from assassination at the hands of the English government; one cannot totally dismiss the possibility (just as some of the Royalists aimed at the assassination of Cromwell). A story of Charles visiting Mary at The Hague in disguise, and being warned that he was in danger of his life by the Protectoral envoy there, Sir George Downing, is probably apocryphal.[26] Yet it illustrates the tensions and loyalties amidst which Charles lived.

Lucy Walter, mother of James Crofts, was the one who had gone from the King's embraces to lead a life of genuinely tragic dissipation. Taaffe having been amongst those who enjoyed her generous affections, that made him, in the King's opinion, the ideal person to deal with the problem which poor Lucy came to represent as the years went by. The royal connection was too well known. 'Advise her, both for her sake and mine, that she goes to some place more private than the Hague,' wrote Charles to Taaffe in May 1655, 'for her stay there is very prejudicial to us both.' Besides, there was the boy: 'every idle action of hers brings your majesty upon the stage,' wrote Charles' Groom of the Bedchamber, Daniel O'Neill, in February 1656.[27] Her alleged misdeeds included procuring the abortion of two further illegitimate children; she was also accused of murdering a maid – the charge was later dropped. In the summer of the same year Lucy thought up another 'idle' action: having shown the seven-year-old James to his father, she took herself off to England with James and his sister Mary, only to be arrested by Cromwell's emissaries and then put in prison. Here she was at one point described as 'the Wife or Mistress' of Charles Stuart, but the former title was obviously not believed, since she was easily able to persuade her captors to release her; a more accurate description was Charles Stuart's 'Lady of pleasure'.* Lucy made her way back to the Continent. Here her allowance, put in the hands of Taaffe, remained a vexed subject – vexed, that is, by the King's general inability to pay any allowance, be it honourable or otherwise, with regularity.

The next step was to remove her son from Lucy's care. It was not a pretty story. Repeated efforts were made – abduction, if not outright kidnapping, was planned in what the King called 'the matter of the child'.[29] By 1658 James had been successfully removed to the care of his grandmother, Henrietta Maria, in Paris. Yet in view of the fact that Lucy died shortly afterwards

* To prove that Charles married Lucy secretly, the point is sometimes made that Mary of Orange referred to her in letters as his 'wife'. But Mary also referred to Lucy's other admirers as 'husbands', e.g. 'her husband here', 'she thinks of another husband'. The allusions are clearly jocular. We should probably say 'sweetheart' today.[28]

of venereal disease, the removal, however callously performed, was clearly in the child's best interests.

Any emotion that the young Charles might have felt for the young Lucy back in those halcyon days before his father's death had certainly been exhausted many years back. But to the years of his exile does belong the story of one romance which clearly did mean something more to him than mere dalliance and desire. The extent of King Charles's feelings for the Princess Henrietta Catharine of Orange, daughter of the Dowager Princess and sister-in-law to Mary, has newly come to light. It is revealed in a series of letters written in Charles' own hand to his friend Lord Taaffe, to whom he confided his warm aspirations in this direction.[30]

Princess Henrietta Catharine, a Dutch Protestant (evidently not be confused with those despised Nordic princesses from cold countries), was a perfectly reputable match for Charles. It will be recalled that quite early on her elder sister Louise Henrietta, now the wife of the Elector of Brandenburg, had been suggested as a possible bride for him. Orange and Stuart were naturally drawn to each other in marriage, as representing two powerful Protestant houses. Two unions actually took place in the seventeenth century, but several more were plausibly suggested.

Nevertheless, it was as much Henrietta Catharine's character as her eligibility which attracted Charles. She was a girl of spirit: for example, she totally refused to marry the fiancé given her in infancy, a Friesian prince, on the grounds of her unconquerable aversion to his person. It was an unfashionable objection at the time, and cannot have been easy to sustain in the face of a determined mother like the Dowager Princess of Orange. Henrietta Catharine matched Charles' protestations with her own, as he related to Taaffe: 'The professions I receive from her every letter, are large and full as either you do or can say.'[31] The genuine passion in Charles' own utterances suggest that he was only too pleased to give himself up on this occasion to a courtship which was both materially suitable and romantically inspiring. Charles' gallantries were manifold. Six pairs of gloves were ordered for 'my friend' (at other times she became 'my best friend', and her code name was the 'infanta'. Charles himself used the pseudonym 'Don Lauren' or 'Loran'). The gloves arrived in the name of Taaffe because they were not up to Charles' own standards; he had ordered some like his sister's from Paris, but they would not arrive till Easter. On Shrove Tuesday he planned to eat pancakes and draw valentines with the women, while privately drinking the 'infanta's' health. 'For I cannot choose but say she is the worthiest to be lov'd of all the sex,' boasted Charles to Taaffe of his Princess.[32]

If love burgeoned in the King's heart at Bruges, to that town also fell a more surprising honour on the face of it: it could claim to be the founding place of a famous regiment, for it was here in 1656 that Charles formed his own King's Regiment of Guards, much later – after Waterloo – officially known as the Grenadiers. The reason for the formation was rooted in that clause of the Spanish treaty concerning Royalist troops which has already been mentioned.

It was not only a question of transferring Irish soldiers from the French Army: King Charles also undertook to raise some troops of his own. As a result, one regiment of English guards was placed under Rochester, a Scottish unit under Middleton and an Irish one under Ormonde. Early in 1657 three more regiments were added under the respective commands of the Duke of Gloucester, the Earl of Bristol (the former Lord Digby) and the Earl of Newburgh. Later the Duke of York was put in overall command, adding a small Life Guard under Berkeley. This international brigade went into service under the Spanish flag in June 1657. Later it would form the nucleus of the post-Restoration Army. At the time, its existence seemed to raise as many difficulties as it solved.

The names of the commanders have a solid and appropriate ring. It was the men serving in the regiments who presented the problems. Thurloe's spies were full of contempt for them. 'Of all the armies in Europe there is none wherein so much debauchery is to be seen as in these few forces which the said King hath gotten together,' wrote one of them, 'being so exceedingly profane from the highest to the lowest.' The Irish in particular were singled out as being 'better versed in the art of begging than fighting'. They were fierce enough to acquire financial contributions from whomsoever they accosted, 'whose fear makes him more liberal than his character'.[33]

It was indeed the perennial lack of money which was responsible for these troubles. The men, underpaid if paid at all, were ill-equipped and thus ill-disciplined. Hyde referred to these new regiments as 'naked soldiers' – a sad spectacle.[34] Such troops were hardly likely to provide patterns of martial behaviour. For the lamentable truth was that the fabulous Spanish gold had failed to materialize. In some ways, King Charles was even worse off than he had been before the move to the Low Countries: in Cologne he had lived off hope and the French pension. Now the latter source had, naturally, dried up. And as Charles found the Spanish 'Don Devil' as recalcitrant a banker as ever the French Cardinal had been, the fountain of hope began to drain away.

For all the bright horizons extended by the Spanish treaty, 1657 proved to be a year in which the English King touched the depths of depression. He had told Jermyn in the preceding October, *à propos* Mazarin's warmth towards Cromwell, 'You will do well to put him in mind that I am not yet so low, but that I may return both the courtesies and the injuries I have received.'[35] Yet as the months wore on, the King's ability either to reward or punish merely declined. In the summer campaign of Spanish against French, Don Juan would not allow Charles to the front, but insisted on him remaining passively at Bruges. It was a hard fate for a former commander-in-chief of a Scottish army, whose courage had never been called in question. The King's melancholia was once again the subject of comment. The fate of his younger brothers James and Harry, permitted to shine at the front, was enviable.

Refuge was taken in absurd schemes, and still more absurd rumours. Oliver Cromwell, for example, was said to have tried to lure Charles over to England in a single ship, accompanied by his two brothers, with a view to shooting all three of them out of hand on arrival. A glimpse of things as they really were was provided when Buckingham decided to desert; returning to

England, he married the heiress of Sir Thomas Fairfax. Although he ended up clapped into prison by the Protector for his pains, Buckingham had made it clear by his behaviour that he regarded the Royalist vessel as a sinking ship. In the autumn of 1657 Hyde summed up the mood of the Royalists at home as 'heartbroken': as a result, they looked for redress from 'some extraordinary act of providence' rather than from any endeavours of their own.[36]

Nor, by the autumn, had the Spaniards shown any sign of mounting that extraordinary force against England, based on Flanders, the promise of which had been the mainspring of the projected treaty. Out of England herself, those radicals discontented with the Protectoral regime, the Levellers, explored the possibilities of Spanish help via their agent Sexby. But the Spaniards, by no means convinced that the moment was ripe for any invading force, continued to indulge in that gentle art of procrastination, whose subtleties they understood so well.

In December it was the bright suggestion of Don Juan that some further light might be cast on the English situation if Ormonde reconnoitred it. If Ormonde was impressed by the state of readiness he found there, then it would still not be too late for a Spanish army to invade before the end of the winter season. So Ormonde set out at the turn of the year, dyeing his famous poll of fair hair black. Despite some nerve-racking experiences within London itself, which should have cautioned him concerning the strong grip of the Protectoral government, Ormonde returned a favourable report.

It was the final proof of the Protectoral government's confidence, of which Ormonde was unaware, that his escape was probably due to a decision by Cromwell to turn a blind eye.[37] The arrest of Ormonde in England, it was thought, would be politically embarrassing, and unnecessary as long as he quit the country.

Ormonde suggested that the King could land near Yarmouth with safety – a view for which there was no real justification. But Ormonde found himself coping with the renewed demands of the Action Party in England for the presence of their sovereign, to which once again they attributed miraculous powers of rallying otherwise reluctant insurgents. In the event, the petty risings of 1658 were easily, almost effortlessly, put down by the Protectoral government. That was not really so surprising in view of the fact that most of the Royalist organizations, including the Sealed Knot, were by now permeated with government spies. The Protectorate Navy was also now blockading the Spanish Netherlands, which ruled out any question of the despatch of the reluctant Spanish Armada.

King Charles now moved to Antwerp, a more convenient jumping-off ground for a projected invasion than Bruges-la-Morte. Here he gave in at last to the incessant clamour for honours with which the exiles were wont to greet his ears, as though peerages and decorations would at least stuff their starving mouths with glory. There is a particular despair shown in the decision to give the Garter, the sacred Garter, to a French Count not even of royal blood. Charles had already pawned his beloved George to pay for Ormonde's expedition.

At a ball given by the Countess of Newcastle, the intellectual wife of his former governor, a speech of the 'highest hyperbole' was made to the King by a Major Mohun, dressed in black velvet for the occasion and wearing a garland of bays. Major Mohun followed this success with another speech 'by way of prophecy of his Majesty's establishment' in England.[38] If there were any present who paid serious attention to the prophecy, by the spring of 1658 King Charles II was hardly likely to be amongst them.

The summer saw the climax of the seemingly endless war between Spain and France. The Spanish were defeated by the French and the English combined, at the mighty Battle of the Dunes; as a result, Dunkirk was given over to the England of the Protectorate. It was true that the Stuart brothers behaved valiantly throughout the campaign. James continued to add to his reputation as a soldier, and even Charles was allowed to lead one charge at Mardyke, which he did with his usual *éclat*. The arrival of an English Protectoral force in Flanders in support of France did at least provide some motive for Don Juan to employ the English King as a kind of counter-attraction. Yet the long war between Spain and France, from which Charles had tried so hard to extract some advantage, was drawing to its close. It was not a *dénouement* which favoured the Stuarts. If anything, the course of the war had assisted revolutionary England rather than the exiled Royalists. It ended altogether the following year.

The English King could think of no further expedient, apart from a personal appeal to the Spanish King. He was told that his presence in Spain would not be welcome.

Disconsolately, Charles set off on a hunting and hawking expedition from Antwerp. Even that seemed to suffer from a kind of doom. He found very few partridges and too much standing corn. He was actually at Hoogstraeten, on the borders of the Netherlands, and playing tennis – rapidly becoming his favourite game – when, on 10 September 1658, Sir Stephen Fox came and told him a remarkable piece of news. A week earlier, in the words of one of Hyde's correspondents, 'it had pleased God out of His infinite goodness to do that which He would not allow any man the honour of doing'.[39]

Oliver Cromwell had died of natural causes.

CHAPTER ELEVEN

At the Waterside

'The King of Scots hath an army at the waterside, drawn down towards the waterside, ready to be shipped for England. . . .'

Cromwell on Charles II, 1658

There was a short burst of wild but foolish rejoicing when the news of Cromwell's death on 3 September 1658 reached the Netherlands. Some people who should have known better danced in the streets. For one wonderful moment it did seem as though that 'extraordinary act of providence' referred to by Hyde had actually arrived to save them all. In France Cardinal Mazarin forgot himself sufficiently to refer to Cromwell as 'the dead monster'; he also hinted to Queen Henrietta Maria that the Anglo-French treaty might be running out.

This warmth proved ephemeral. An express letter from Bristol to Hyde, breaking the news, arrived marked 'cito, cito, cito': but there was in fact no hurry.[1] About the most significant effect of the Protector's sudden death – he died after a short period of illness, and the Royalists in Europe were taken unawares – was to forward the suit of King Charles to his 'best friend' Princess Henrietta Catharine. For a moment the Dowager Princess of Orange, like Cardinal Mazarin, seemed in danger of losing her head. She fondly imagined that from a penniless émigré her daughter's admirer had been transformed into a powerful monarch just about to embark for his kingdom.

King Charles himself did not let the opportunity slip. He

proposed immediately. Henrietta Catharine became ill with emotion. The news of the betrothal, as it was tacitly allowed to be, had the side-effect of infuriating Mary Princes of Orange. She was still smarting under Charles' denunciation of her romance with the young Harry Jermyn. Besides, it would have meant Mary yielding precedence to her sister-in-law as Queen of England, and the subject of precedence, as we have seen, always aroused a great deal of proprietorial anguish in Mary's breast.*

As it turned out, Mary had little need to worry. By November the Dowager Princess, in common with the rest of Europe (and Cardinal Mazarin), had realized her mistake: King Charles found coolness where once there had been ardour. Early next year, a 'new gallant' for Henrietta Catharine made his appearance: John George of Anhalt-Dessau. She subsequently married him, evidently finding no unconquerable aversion to this particular person. Towards her own behaviour, the King was philosophical as well as generous. He told Taaffe that his fondness for her inspired in him a real wish for her true happiness. He had convinced himself that Henrietta Catharine loved her prince, and would not interfere. Towards her mother he showed less tolerance, referring to her privately as 'an old strumpet' and suggesting in even cruder terms that the Dowager Princess had resented his lack of attentions to herself.[2]

The news of the Protector's death did not merely fail to crown Charles' efforts as a romantic lover, it also ushered in an even more extraordinary phase in a life already full of paradox. Nineteen months were to pass between the death of Oliver and the restoration of Charles. To those abroad, including the King, who had no means of knowing in advance at what hour the final curtain was destined to be rung down on revolutionary England, if at all, the last act seemed interminable.

The first figure to occupy the stage vacated by Oliver was his son Richard Cromwell. Theoretically chosen by his father's dying

* In view of Mary's concentration on the subject, it should be recorded that she never did have to yield her proud position as eldest daughter of the King of England to her brother's wife: by the time Charles II married, Mary was dead.

voice, Richard was immediately confirmed in his new position by the Council of State; Protector Richard was thus easily and uncontroversially substituted for Protector Oliver. Like the sons of Charlemagne, Richard Cromwell was a *fainéant*, a weak plant who had grown up thinly in the shadow of the strong stem of his father. He had taken refuge from the challenge of his father's personality early on in a kind of gentle wastrel's incompetence. Finance was never Richard's strong point: when the time came for him to step down from his Protectoral eminence, one of his chief reasons for not wishing to leave the precincts of the Palace of Whitehall was because they conferred immunity from arrest for debt.

But he was not a bad man, and therefore not a bad figurehead for the English state as it now stood. There were a number of dramas to be played out before any true desire for the return of the Stuarts could be anticipated. Shortly after the elder Protector's death, Nicholas wrote to King Charles that he was pleased to hear 'the rebels endeavour to set up Cromwell's son rather than a republic'.[3] That was a wise observation. The return of a republic would indeed have been a far more sinister development.

Yet at the time a pervasive hopelessness spread like a wide, calm surface of water over the shifting sands of the King's affairs. The death of Cromwell had broken this surface with a sudden sharp splash. Now even the ripples caused by it appeared to have died away. The real trouble was the strange tranquillity which settled over England, as Hyde put it: 'the same or a greater calm in the kingdom than had been before'.[4] This serenity was attested on all sides, both Royalist and Cromwellian.

Sir George Downing, the Ambassador at The Hague, thought that the death had come just too soon for the various foreign conspirators, perhaps two months too soon. But Thurloe, writing in England, used the same language as Hyde: 'There is not a dog that wags his tongue, so great a calm are we in.'[5] It was this public lethargy which was disastrous for the King's prospects in Europe. Now, if ever, was the psychological moment for Charles to prove to Spain that there existed a vast body of popular support to welcome him in England, should he reach its shores. But he could not point to any manifestations of unrest.

So Spain did not move. In one of his speeches to the Parliament of 1658, Cromwell had referred to a great army and navy of a foreign power, threatening them on behalf of the 'King of Scots ... drawn down towards the waterside, ready to be shipped for England'. But there the Spanish fleet in Flanders remained. There were vague discussions of help from minor powers, like the Elector of Brandenburg and the Duke of Saxe-Lauenberg; perhaps Dunkirk would declare for the King, and perhaps Marshal Turenne would head a force for the invasion of England. But in general, French, Spanish and German princes were not inclined to contemplate any form of Stuart crusade until their peace was established; the Treaty of the Pyrenees between France and Spain was not signed until May 1659. The gloom of the situation may be judged by the fact that Charles was even proposed for *Lambert*'s daughter – the Cromwell 'princesses' were by now both married.[6]

The next stirring came, as before, from within England herself. But it was not an 'extraordinary act of providence', as the death of Cromwell had been – merely an inevitable development of the *fainéant* Protectorate set up under Richard. By January 1659 a body of Army officers, including Lambert and Oliver Cromwell's son-in-law, Fleetwood, and his brother-in-law, Desborough, had come to feel in themselves rather than in Richard the source of the true power in England. Those opposed to them caused a Parliament to be summoned, sometimes known as Richard's Parliament. In this assembly, republicans, Presbyterians, and secret Royalists jostled with each other: from the other side of the water the King had at least managed to encourage some secret Royalists to put themselves up for election.

At the same time no one, certainly not King Charles nor the Royalist conspirators within England, dreamed that the time for military invasion had passed. In March of the same year John Mordaunt was given permission to form a new action group, to the annoyance of the Sealed Knot. Once again the King's presence in England, that magic talisman to which such powers were attributed, was being demanded. With quarrels between the rival conspirators, indecision from Charles, foreign missions, English intrigues, and a good deal of governmental counter-intelligence, it seemed that the whole dreary cycle was taking place all over again. And with the same lack of success.

The Protectoral Parliament was dissolved on 22 April. Protector Richard was transformed into Tumbledown Dick and slipped away to silence and exile in his turn. A Council of State became the new titular head of the government. A slightly desperate expedient, the return of the Rump Parliament – elected, in its original form, an unbelievable nineteen years previously – was employed. But desperation did not imply in any sense a return to monarchy. It is notable that at this critical juncture nobody suggested for a moment recourse to Charles Stuart, down by the waterside across the English channel. Yet exactly twelve months later he would be gladly, even ecstatically, summoned. So the dramatic story of the Restoration continued to unfold without forfeiting its surprise and tension.

The vital element in this summer's royal plans was deemed to be the army of King Charles, not the reappearance of the Rump. He now had as many as 2,500 men with him in the Low Countries, the effect of the new military organization following the Spanish treaty. Mordaunt paid the King a flying visit at Brussels in June. Unfortunately, it was clear that there was considerable opposition to Mordaunt within the Royalist ranks. Brodrick, who ran the so-called New Cavalier party, disliked Mordaunt; Mordaunt in return described Brodrick, no doubt accurately, as 'sadly given to drink'. Nevertheless, Mordaunt did succeed in his mission: he persuaded the King that things were sufficiently advanced in England. As a result, Charles assured Mordaunt on 24 June: 'I do therefore resolve that myself or one of my brothers, or both of us will (with God's blessing) be with you as soon as you shall desire.' He would sail on 11 July.[7]

At this point the question of the treachery of Sir William Willys, one of the founders of the Sealed Knot, and probably its secret betrayer ever since, reared its ugly head. Obviously Willys could not have acted as a double-agent for quite so long without suspicions being aroused. But the timing of the charges against him in July was particularly bad. An open placard on the subject in London caused every kind of dissension, accusation and counter-accusation to be aired. It was the very worst atmosphere in which to plan, let alone carry out, a complicated rising, depending on co-ordination throughout the country. The King suspended judgement while enquiries were made. The date for his arrival was postponed till August.

The motives of Willys, an ultra-ambivalent man in an ambivalent time, as well as the extent of his treachery, continue to baffle.[8] There was however much soundness in the argument which Willys used against this particular rising: it would unite the common people *against* the King, rather than causing them to rise on his behalf; especially since it was harvest time, and no sensible man would want to run the risk of starving in the winter, whoever was in power. But the eventual course of the rising showed that, like the Bourbons after the French Revolution, the Royalists in England had learnt nothing and forgotten nothing since their last disastrous concerted effort of 1655.

Once again the affair went off half-cock. It became popularly known by the name of Sir George Booth, because his force, easily put down by Lambert at Chester, was all that properly featured of the various para-military bodies promised. But Booth himself had not hitherto been a Royalist. Shades of 1655! This time King Charles took himself to Calais, for his impending departure. The Sealed Knot sulked. Rows, not only in England, but also with Hyde abroad, played their damaging role. By 9 September Jermyn was writing to Ormonde that the news from England was 'not only worse than we looked for, but even as ill as we could have imagined'. About the same date two other Royalists agreed that 'Hope cleaveth to the bottom of the box, and is not easily shaken out.'[9] The only good thing to be noted about the abortive Booth's rising was that, although the government speedily clapped the leaders in prison, they did not bother with the severe penalties of previous years.

To that extent, conditions in England were ameliorating. But of course lack of repression can signify lack of threat, as well as lack of confidence. It was a point not lost on contemporary observers.

*

King Charles, disillusioned yet again, resolved to seek his fortune in Spain herself. Perhaps he could galvanize that long-promised assistance by his presence. He was unaware that the single man who would play the most crucial part in his restoration had already come to a private conclusion which favoured the return of the monarchy.

George Monck was a professional soldier, who, being born in 1608, belonged more properly to the generation of King Charles I than to that of his son. Not only had the army been in a large measure his career, but he also took his high standards of order and efficiency from the conventional military ideals. In Scotland, where he not only held down but positively governed the Scots with his Cromwellian army, his rule was both wise and firm. He had not benefited personally from confiscated Royalist and church land in England and had thus no financial stake in the continuation of the Protectorate: Monck had been loyal to Oliver Cromwell. He would have been loyal to Richard too, had he considered that the younger Protector had any capacity for maintaining within England that law and order which he found so precious. As Monck expressed it, 'Richard forsook himself, else I had never failed my promise to his father or regard to his memory.' It is the contention of Monck's latest biographer that in August 1659 Monck had already reached a decision.[10] If England was not to dissolve into chaos once more (and Monck of course had both lived and fought through the Civil War), what he thought of as 'the old order' – that is, the King in Parliament – must be restored. It would be six months before Monck gave any public sign of this decision: yet in order to explain the suddenness of the events of 1660 one is forced to the conclusion that by the autumn of 1659 not only Monck but also some of the other leaders, and even more of the ordinary people, were in their heart of hearts beginning to explore this possibility.

For all his age, Monck represented a new type of man. Here was no regicide. Monck had played no part whatsoever in the death of King Charles I. He had not signed the warrant, nor been a member of the High Court of Justice which condemned Charles I. This was important. The feelings of Charles II on the subject of his father's murder had been passionate and were to remain so. As we shall see, he made no attempt to disguise the fact, and the penalties paid by the regicides after the Restoration were virtually the only area where the incoming King's vengeance went to work. Even in the dire straits of 1655 Charles refused to meet his cousin the Elector Palatine at Frankfurt, because the Elector had deserted his father. The incident occurred at the theatre, where the English royal party turned on their heels. Afterwards this was considered 'unnatural strangeness' on the part of Charles.[11] But it showed the depth of his obsession.

None of this mud could be attached to Monck. Recognizing his potential usefulness, the King had tried without success to make surreptitious contact with him in the summer of 1659 through his brother Nicholas Monck, a clergyman living in Cornwall. Even before Cromwell's death, Charles had been careful to distinguish Monck from some of his *confrères* in a memorandum drafted by Hyde, for a letter to be sent to the General: 'I am confident that George Monck can have no malice in his heart against me, nor hath he done anything against me which I cannot very easily pardon' – it was the latter sentiment which was important. Tentative offers of land, a title even, were made through various intermediaries, including Viscount Fauconberg, a Yorkshire magnate who had married Mary Cromwell, but possessed the diplomatic attribute of making himself indispensable to every regime. By 5 September Nicholas Monck believed that his brother would support a rising of the King's friends, if it occurred.[12]

A rising – that was not the way that George Monck's mind tended.

Under the circumstances, King Charles' foray to the Spanish borders at Fuenterrabia in the winter of 1659 proved unnecessary. At the time, the expedition annoyed and worried Hyde, since 1658 proud possessor of the Lord Chancellor's Seal. However, as the King more or less jumped on a ship and set sail down the French Atlantic coast, there was not much that Hyde could do about it, except fuss over the prospect of his being captured by an English vessel.

But this kind of spontaneous gesture of frustration was rare in Charles these days, as is shown by Hyde's comment that, in the forthcoming negotiations with Spain, he expected the King's chief assets to be his own 'dexterity and composedness'. There had been good reports recently of the royal character: people were beginning to be persuaded that the King could conduct his own affairs properly (although Hyde could not resist ending on a familiar note of chiding about his lack of 'industry').[13] All the same, Hyde put his finger on the King's problem, one common to heads of state in exile then and now: he had to show himself a potentially wise leader, so that all the advantages of statesmanship should not go to the other side. And he had to do so in a vacuum, or at his own mimic court. At the same time, the King had to keep up the pressures of opposition, acting as a partisan leader to his own followers.

As it turned out, events at Fuenterrabia were of no particular international significance either way, although the King's energy and intelligence continued to make a good impression. The Spaniards maintained their reluctance to provide armed support. By this time the news had spread that the English ice was thawing. This put the King's advisers in a panic. It was suddenly dangerous for the King to seem too dependent upon Spain.

But the expedition did have one consequence of great importance in the King's personal life. In December he rediscovered his youngest sister, Henriette-Anne. They had not met for over five years, since the involuntary retreat from France. Charles remembered Henriette-Anne (or Minette, as she was occasionally known)* as a thin little girl living in straitened circumstances with her mother. Henriette-Anne was still physically delicate. Louis XIV rudely described her as looking like the bones of the Holy Innocents when she married his brother. Her fragility was emphasized by the fact that she had one shoulder higher than

* This nickname, familiar to us from historical fiction, such as Margaret Irwin's *A Royal Cinderella*, survives in fact in a few letters from the King. Otherwise, Charles always referred to Henriette-Anne in letters as 'his dear sister' and even 'his dear dear sister'. It has been suggested that it was Charles' baby name for her, only recalled in his most affectionate moments.[14] To her mother Henrietta Maria she was always 'ma fille'. Later we shall know Henriette-Anne under her married title of Madame de France.

the other, the relic of her difficult birth during the siege of Exeter. In her youth she acted in a masque at the French Court, and brought tears to the eyes of the spectators with her verse:

> Mon jeune et royal aspect
> Inspire avec le respect
> La pitoyable tendresse.

For the rest of her short lift, Henriette-Anne never lost that capacity to inspire both pity and tenderness.

Yet in other ways she had changed and blossomed so much that the court women tricked the King agreeably by introducing the wrong young lady as his sister. It was her brilliant colouring, combined with her doll-like figure, which made Henriette-Anne so captivating. She had bright chestnut hair and eyes of a startling blue (the traditional colouring of the later Stuarts, Charles being the exception). Her teeth, unlike those of so many beauties of the time, were white and regular, and she had a smile of exceptional sweetness. As for her complexion, perhaps her best point, that was termed 'roses and jasmine' by a lyrical Madame de Motteville.[15]

But the real secret of the enchantment which Henriette-Anne undoubtedly exercised over her contemporaries was in her ability both to give and receive love. A childhood deprived of physical necessities had left her rich in love at least, from her widowed mother. As a result, as the Abbé de Choisy put it, one loved her without thinking one could do otherwise.

Naturally King Charles fell under her spell. They got on immediately, in spite of the long absence. As brothers and sisters with an enormous age gap (fourteen years in this case) sometimes do, they fell into a relationship which on his side was half-way between that of father and brother. Perhaps on Charles' side it was even a little lover-like, but all within the safe emotional degrees of the family circle. Their correspondence burst into flower immediately after they parted, proliferating with endearments and little tendernesses of every sort, as though to make up for the lost years. Early on, Charles asked Henriette-Anne not to put so many 'majesties' in her letters: 'for I do not wish that there should be anything between us but friendship'.[16]

By now the King's relationship with his mother was thoroughly soured. Mary in Holland had her own drawbacks of temperament. James had a restricting sense of his position as his brother's heir: besides, he tended to side with his mother. But with Charles' 'dear dear sister' all was pleasure and lightheartedness, the thrill of discovery and rediscovery. 'I am yours entirely,' he ended a letter dated 26 May 1660, written on board the boat which was taking him towards England.[17] Charles did not fail to think of Henriette-Anne even in the hour of his glory. It was a portent of the important role she would play as his ambassadress.

In the memoirs of James II (dealing with his campaigns as Duke of York) the beginning of 1660 was described as the 'lowest ebb' of Charles II's hopes, a time when all his optimism had left him. Yet, when only a few short months had passed, King Charles was to be restored 'without one drop of bloodshed, to the astonishment of all the Christian world'.[18] How did this seemingly amazing reversal come about, a revolution (in the strict seventeenth-century sense of the word, a turnabout) which on the surface astonished everyone by its dramatic arrival? As Samuel Pepys, an up-and-coming young civil servant, noted in the diary which he had only just begun to keep, 'Indeed it was past imagination both the greatness and the suddenness of it.'[19]

The first thing to be noted is that the Restoration of King Charles II was a strictly internal process. Charles was not restored by any of the efforts of the various foreigners whose aid he had sought down all the years of exile, not by the help of Spain, not by the encouragement of France, certainly not by the assistance of the Pope, nor by virtue of Scotland, nor the Scandinavian Kings and Queens, not by the German princes, bishops and Electors, nor the intricate politics of the Dutch. ... The manœuvres and prayers of Queen Henrietta Maria, the obstinate but clear principles of Edward Hyde had equally counted for nothing. Nor was that oft-predicted magnificent – and successful – Royalist rising ever destined to take place.

The final irony of the years of exile lay in the fact that King

Charles was in the end restored not for any efforts of his own, but just because the mighty tide of revolution had somehow exhausted itself quite early in the Protectorate. The vast waves of change which had crashed down on English shores had given way to gentler waters. Stability and order had become the concern of almost everyone in the state. That yearning for order had been satisfied by the old Protector, particularly as his successive disillusionments with his Parliaments had revealed him as an increasingly conservative figure. Ever since, a series of experiments had gradually led men of good sense (such as Monck) to think longingly of the old monarchy. None of these experiments had, mercifully, involved the King over the water. He was not contaminated. That was the King's strong – unconscious – appeal.

On 1 January 1660 Ormonde told Jermyn that 'the general disposition of the people ... seems to promise great advantages to the king; four parts of five of the whole people besides the nobility and gentry, being devoted to him'.[20] For an explanation of this seeming *volte face*, one cannot do better than quote Milton's sonorous outcry against the whole topic of restoration: 'For this extolled and magnified nation, regardless both of honour won, or deliverances vouchsafed from heaven, to fall back or rather *creep* back ... to their once abjured and detested thraldom of kingship!' It was true. England did fall back – or perhaps creep back is the more accurate term.

Did King Charles himself then play no part at all in these stirring events? Was he merely a royal puppet, twitched on a string held by mightier hands than his own – including the strongest hand of all, the hand of Fate? First it must be said that Charles, who had shown himself far from deficient in those qualities which compel admiration in a monarch such as courage, resilience and tenacity, was not directly invited back as a result of them. But this is not to deny the King participation in his own triumph. On the contrary, the character of the King was of extreme importance to the whole question of the Restoration. But it was of negative importance.

He did not scupper his own cause. And in this he did better than many a royal or political exile before or since.

Thomas Clifford, later the King's minister, noted in his commonplace book under the heading 'Reputation': 'The reputation of his Majesty was more instrumental for his restoration than an army.' Yet how many hidden rocks and shoals had existed in the years of exile on which King Charles II might well have wrecked both the reputation of the monarchy and his own! Foremost amongst these was certainly the charge of Catholicism. His strenuous efforts to maintain his Protestant reputation have been noted. It was King Charles' personal reward that, for example, in March 1660 the Puritan divine Richard Baxter was convinced of it: the King, having been born and duly educated in the true religion, had 'never departed from the public profession of it'. And this, after years in France and the Spanish Netherlands, gleefully described by the Commonwealth propagandist Marchamont Nedham as 'the most jesuited place in the world', was no mean feat.[21]

Had the charge been made to stick, it is possible that the claims of Henry Duke of Gloucester to the throne might have been considered (the Duke of York's religion was already in doubt). But that would have brought with it a number of consequences, including a rift in the Stuart royal family. Moreover, Henry would have ascended the throne, not as Charles did, free and unencumbered by promises, but already fettered – as a compromise candidate is always fettered. The whole character of the Restoration would have been altered.

Secondly, King Charles played the foreign hand as best he could, so that no positively disastrous charges of foreign intervention could be made against him. It is true that luck as well as judgement featured here. King Charles, as we have seen, was never averse to the assistance of either the French or the Spanish or the Dutch: but even in his lowest moments he was not prepared to make those sacrifices, such as a change in his religion, which could conceivably have swayed these powers. In this the influence of Hyde, ever aware of the dangers, was prominent. But that strange streak of vacillation, or masterly inaction, or sheer intrigue, depending on your point of view, which began to develop in an otherwise straightforward character in exile, also helped. It is a quality which will emerge more pronouncedly after the Restoration.

Thirdly, the King did not allow himself to be painted as either very debauched, or very extravagant, or very wild, or very inattentive to business, with impunity. Most of these charges were made at one time or another, mainly by government propagandists. But they could not be made to stick. It was possible to regard King Charles II, on 1 January 1660, as a decent, serious man. He was no saint certainly, as princes seldom were, but past his first youth, without too many peccadilloes to be overlooked, too much dissipation to be forgiven. He was after all in his thirtieth year. Yet once again, what opportunities of debauchery, founded on despair, an exile might have offered!

Fourthly, in public at least, King Charles II was never seen to commit the sin of despair. And that was his most important contribution to his own return.

Early in 1660 there were visible fissures in the surface of England. On 1 January Monck marched from Scotland, not only in search of pay for his woefully deprived men, but also with the avowed intention of restoring the sovereignty of Parliament. When he reached London, he forced the Rump Parliament to admit to its ranks a number of members hitherto excluded for political reasons. That was the first step. But in any form, however liberal, the hated Rump could not last long.

Pepys' reportage of the situation in February 1660 is as vivid as any: 'Boys do now cry "Kiss my Parliament" instead of "Kiss my arse" so great and general contempt is the Rump come to among all men, good and bad,' he wrote. A few days later there were thirty-one bonfires to be seen at one glance at the Strand bridge: and everywhere 'rumps' (of beef) were being roasted. One notes the progress in Pepys' *Diary*, from the man who showed him a clandestine Lion and Unicorn at the back of his chimney on 5 March, to the prevalent clamour on 16 March when people were beginning to 'talk loud of the king'.[22] It was on that date that the Rump finally dissolved itself, and a free election was announced – although a last-ditch attempt was unsuccessfully made to block the sons of former Royalists from standing. By the end of March, effigies of King Charles were being made.

Yet the continued uncertainty of the times is revealed in Hyde's correspondence. As late as 4 February he was worried over Monck's 'lewd carriage': if he continued to show himself so obstinate, they might still have to owe their recovery to a foreign army....[23] And Monck continued to play his cards close to his chest, denying publicly that he had any intention of acting for 'Charles Steward'. The fiction, as we must believe it to be, was to be preserved a little longer. A more revealing glimpse of the way things were blowing was given by the behaviour of Ashley Cooper. Despite the fact that he had been pursued ardently by the Royalists in tempting correspondence, Ashley Cooper had continued to reject their overtures. He appeared deaf to the personal appeals of the King. He had been elected to the Council of State by the Rump, although he was of the majority of the Council who refused to accept the additional clause renouncing Charles Stuart, proposed by Desborough. But it was not until February 1660 that he allowed himself to be drawn into correspondence with the exiled court, as we know from Hyde's complaints on the subject.

When on 24 February Lady Willoughby de Broke told Hyde that Ashley Cooper was 'his Majesty's fast friend', Hyde replied tartly that this was the first he had heard of it. Nearly twenty years later, when Ashley Cooper (transformed into the Earl of Shaftesbury) came to the conclusion that the monarchy had once more failed, he referred to his own feelings about the Restoration of 1660. He had discerned 'the hand of Providence' in the fact that there had been various forms of government, and several types of men in power, yet to none of them had Providence granted 'a heart to use it as they should'. For all Hyde's understandable fears and cautions, Providence was by now firmly pointing in the direction of Charles Stuart.

And that pejorative name itself was no longer heard. Hyde was assured that those formerly most against King Charles would now present themselves with halters round their necks and yield to his mercy. The cry was all: 'A King, a King!'[24]

At Brussels the King, now being acclaimed, continued to play the hand superbly – that is to say, with an air of universal friendliness. He told Mordaunt, for example, that the Royalists must take particular care not to 'discountenance anybody who may be made to do good service', for the sake of private jealousies or animosities amongst themselves. Of a warring pair, he observed, 'It may be they may both do me the more service even from ... their dislike of each other.' Yet, in common with the rest of the court at Brussels, he was of course following the English news with bated breath. On 24 March he told Lord Jermyn (now created Earl of St Albans for his faithful service to Queen Henrietta Maria) that a report had come via Calais of a vote being passed in Parliament for 'King, Lords and Commons'.[25] It was premature. Yet such rumours were easily spread in the atmosphere of rising excitement in which they were living.

On 27 March King Charles sent Monck a letter which was in itself a masterpiece of tact: it was certainly the kind of missive which his father had never learnt to write.[26] First he paid diplomatic tribute to Monck's demonstrably strong position in England: 'I know too well the power you have to do me good or harm, not to desire you should be my friend.' Then King Charles protested his own desire for peace and happiness – in words which do have a gleam of his characteristic humour: 'And whatever you have heard to the contrary, you will find to be as false as if you had been told that I have white hair and am crooked.' There is a blandness too about the King's phrase of desiring to secure 'all good men' in the possession of 'what belongs to them'. Who these good men might be, and in what those belongings might consist, was left charmingly vague: yet these would of course be two of the most vexed points concerning the Restoration settlement, as in the aftermath of any civil war.

King Charles ended on a note of enormous warmth: 'However I cannot but say, that I will take all the ways I can, to let the world see, and you and yours find, that I have an entire trust in you, and as much kindness for you, as can be expressed by Your affectionate friend. Charles R.' As a result Charles received from Monck at the end of March a piece of kindly advice in the form of a secret message: to remain at Brussels, under

Catholic sovereignty, when Spain and England were also officially at war, would be imprudent. As once before, the King retreated to the useful quasi-neutral town of Breda. He had absolutely no wish to show himself imprudent – now.

It was thus from Breda that on 4 April King Charles wrote formally to the Speaker of the House of Commons. On the same day he gave out the Declaration of Breda. The letter to the Speaker was a triumph of double-think, far in advance of his communication to Monck.[27] It referred constantly to the need for Parliaments, and how the presence of a monarch was justified by his role in preserving them. Ghosts must have danced – not only that of his father, but also of Strafford, and even of Oliver Cromwell. But King Charles II was able to observe unblushingly that their mutual liberties and authorities – King and Parliament – were 'best preserved by preserving the other'.

'We look on you,' wrote the King, 'as wise and dispassionate men and good patriots, who will raise up those banks and fences which have been cast down.' And he boasted of the Protestantism from which he had not swerved. There was only one drum-beat of revenge – his pointed allusion to his father's death. That 'crying sin' he believed that they would be quite as anxious to avenge as he was himself, being equally 'solicitous' to redeem the nation from 'that guilt and infamy'. Yet he ended on a note which still has the power to touch one, in view of the trials he had endured in the previous ten years: 'And we hope that we have made that right Christian use of our affliction, and that the observations and experience we have had in other countries hath been such as that we, and we hope all our subjects, shall be the better for what we have seen and suffered.'

The Declaration of Breda was largely the work of Hyde. Unlike the King's letter to Parliament, it was a deliberately bold document. First it granted a free and full pardon to anyone appealing to the King for his 'grace and favour' within forty days, with only a few exceptions to be decided by Parliament. The thought of the regicides continued to outrage the King. Otherwise no-one would be punished for their behaviour to either Charles I or Charles II; nor would their properties be touched.

Even more strikingly, the Declaration of Breda referred to the 'passion and uncharitableness of the times' which had resulted in many differences in religion. The King promised, via an Act of Parliament, 'a liberty to tender consciences'. No man was to be in future 'disquieted or called in question' for differences in religion, so long as these differences did not threaten the peace of the kingdom. Alas, for the Act of Parliament: it was not to be. Nevertheless, the intention at least in that brave happy April was there. Furthermore, it was for Parliament to deal with all the various transactions concerning property, inevitable after 'so many years, and so many and so great revolutions'. Last of all, the arrears of pay of the Army and its officers, under Monck, should be paid.

The Declaration of Breda was a remarkable piece of clemency combined with statecraft, the latter largely springing from the former. But these were remarkable times: King Charles II at Breda was living through a situation which even in his wildest fantasies of exile he cannot have envisaged. By mid-April in England it was reported by one of Hyde's young relations, an apprentice in the City, that 'those formerly called Cavaliers begin to appear in garbe fit for gentlemen, and their masters "*turn tide*" '. About the end of April there was actually a muster in Hyde Park, with trumpets sounding through the streets: the cry was heard loud and without fear that 'the King shall enjoy his own again'.[28] Through all this festivity, Lambert, the former darling general, whose daughter only a brief six months ago had been contemplated as a bride for the King, was brought as a prisoner. By the end of April too, Buckingham, a most reliable guide to the way the wind was blowing, was wearing his Garter in public.

It was on I May that Charles' letter and the Declaration of Breda were officially read out in the House of Commons. And on the same auspicious day – a day of national mirth and rejoicing which the Puritans had tried hard to obliterate – the House of Commons passed an official resolution to desire Charles to take the government of the kingdom upon his shoulders.

Most remarkable of all these remarkable events was the fact that not one single condition was suggested, let alone imposed upon the King. The storm of revolution had blown itself out so thoroughly that those Presbyterians reported by Pepys as wanting to bring back Charles tied by such conditions 'as if he had been in chains' could find not the slightest support. Instead, the scenes on May Day itself were so ecstatic as to turn Pepys' stomach. He witnessed people actually drinking the King's health on their knees in the streets, which he described as 'a little too much'.[29]

Well might King Charles be reminded of that lucky star which was said to have attended his birth. As the Estates of Zeeland put it, 'If Great Britain hath made bon-fires at the birth of your Majesty, what should it do now in this marvellous conjuncture?' He decided to move on from Breda to The Hague, in order the better to receive the delegation of Parliamentary Commissioners who were coming to offer him the government of his own kingdom.[30] The journey was made by water. Charles was offered the barge of the Dowager Princess of Orange for the occasion (*o tempora, o mores*, O Henrietta Catharine), but chose instead a larger vessel. It was in fact a *jaght schip* (hunt ship), a name anglicized as 'yacht'. He liked it so much that he decided to order one for himself, and was subsequently presented by the Estates with an identical copy named the *Mary*. Other members of the court and royal family also embarked in borrowed yachts.

James Duke of York was in charge of the whole expedition, and saw to it that there were sufficient kitchens in the floating cortège of thirteen yachts for meals of up to twenty dishes to be served aboard (O Cologne, O Bruges, O vanished austerity of yesteryear!). Unfortunately, Princess Mary, who had a capacity for untimely suffering, was badly sea-sick, which upset the journey. Nevertheless, when the royal party reached Delft, there was a vast crowd waiting to see 'this miraculous prince', despite the hour – it was dawn. The continuing volleys of the musketeers and the heavy explosions of the cannon became quite irritating to the royal ears: so quickly can a pleasure based on novelty pall.

Yet such petty complaints soon faded away in the bright stream of experiences, each one more wonderful than the next, which now came the King's way. It was a precious and solemn moment when Sir John Grenville asked to present the letters of the House of Commons, not least because he employed with veneration the sacred title of 'majesty', 'which not long since was the aversion of varlets and fanaticks'. The King, for his part, graciously *did* find his way to accepting the invitation to return.... In general, the Commissioners of Parliament satisfied everyone with their becoming reverence; it was agreed that the reference of Denzil Holles, that old parliamentary warhorse, to the twenty years' tyranny of Cromwell was most moving. It was touching too that amongst those who were received at this point were the master and captain of the ship which had transported the King to France after Worcester.

By the time the Speaker of the House of Commons received the royal acceptance, he was already dwelling in a capital where euphoria was breaking out on all sides. 'Our Bells and our Bonfires, and the report of our Artillery have already begun to proclaim the King and to publish our Joy,' observed the Speaker.

And at The Hague too these were never-to-be-forgotten days. The 'wonderful changes which were almost daily produced' in England had taken Europe by surprise. The Spaniards in particular, the King's laggard allies, found that 'His Majesty was almost in his own country' before they had taken in that there was 'any Revolution' towards it. They hastened to take advantage of his presence at The Hague before it was too late. All was sweetness and light – and honeyed invitation. There were rival French and Spanish dinner-parties to toast the future ruler. The Catholic-Irish clique joined with the Spanish-French clique in seeking promises of Catholic toleration for the future.

As for the petitions, the letters, the reminders of favours and loyalties past, the pleas for forgiveness of (regrettable but surely explicable) disloyalties – these all flowed in a happy, bubbling current towards the person of the twenty-nine-year-old King. Again, it was hardly surprising that amidst such amiable sycophancy Charles was in 'the best of humour that ever he was seen to be'. It would have been paradoxical indeed for the man who had kept such resolute public cheerfulness throughout the dark times of exile, to have turned the corners of his mouth down now.

King Charles on the contrary enjoyed himself to the full, his enjoyment only enhanced by a nice personal sense of the irony of things. He touched, constantly, for the King's evil, that strange mediaeval ritual which he had also performed in hiding at Moseley. Then the act had been a desperate confirmation that he was still King. Now it was an agreeable gesture to please others, not himself. He was pleased to receive from the States of Holland a magnificent bed which had been intended for his sister Mary's *accouchement*, but had been stored when the news came of her husband's death a few days before. And his nine-year-old nephew William of Orange, the baby deprived of the bed, rode wonderingly in the King's cortège as it passed through The Hague – although even now the States of Holland tried to avoid any diplomatic situation where William of Orange (Charles' nephew, but a prince in his own right) might rank behind James Duke of York and Henry Duke of Gloucester, the King's brothers. The complicated juxtaposition of Orange and Stuart remained to plague the new reign.

A happier omen, from Charles' point of view, could be discerned in the presence of a laughing young woman named Barbara. She had been born Barbara Villiers, a cousin of the Duke of Buckingham, and was married to a Catholic Royalist named Roger Palmer; but she was already in the months before the Restoration contributing in her own way to the King's royal good humour. Of less cheerful links with the past, poor Lucy Walter had died in Paris a year back. The King's son, James Crofts, now renamed Fitzroy, remained in the care of Queen Henrietta Maria. There, with his grandmother, the handsome, engaging young man had his head thoroughly turned. That too was an omen for the future.

Throughout all this period, the King and his train were wined and dined in a series of banquets whose gorgeous dishes were intended to indicate the exceptional warmth everyone had now discovered they felt for the English Court. Sauces steamed continuously by day and by night: pheasants were employed in one particular collation, with the lavishness of salt and pepper. In all this, stories of assassination plots and of the sabotage of the King's ship seemed to come out of a remote unpleasant past. They were correctly dismissed as malicious rumours.

The final banquet was given by the States of Holland. The King had his aunt Elizabeth of Bohemia on his right, his sister Mary on his left. Was he bored by the eternal junketings? One doubts it. A Danish observer noted that all through the courtyard and up the stairs of the house where Charles was now lodged, there were Englishmen kneeling to their king.[31] No one knew better than Charles II, for all his restlessness in the face of protocol, that the alternative to royal ceremony was very often royal flight. Hyde wrote in his *History* of this marvellous period, 'In this wonderful manner and with this miraculous expedition, did God put an end in one month ... to a rebellion that had raged near twenty years.' In May 1660 Charles was acutely aware that what had been built up in one little month, could be as easily and in as short a time destroyed again. So he sat through the endless ceremonies, and with good grace.

Now the good ship *Royal Charles* was riding at anchor and waiting to convey him towards England herself. (It had, as a matter of fact, only just stopped being the good ship *Naseby*.) A hundred pounds of roast beef had been put aboard, and silver plate to serve it on. Everything – at last – was to be fit for a king.

> Thus from the Belgick States delicious seat
> Triumphantly departed Charles the Great!

cried the poet William Lower, who was in attendance on the scene and noted every detail. That night of 23 May more than fifty thousand people went to watch the departure of the English King. But in fact there *was* no night; the torches and flares of the royal equipage illuminated the darkness. The drums beat a heavy and continuous assembly. Mary Princess of Orange broke down in tears and the tender-hearted Charles wept in sympathy.

The sea was calm, the heavens clear. Charles Stuart, the second, went up onto the poop of the ship to take a last look at Holland. It was also to be his last true sight of foreign parts. For the rest of his life he would not set foot outside England again. The King was coming into his own.

PART THREE

This Golden Age

Great Sir, the Star which at your happy Birth
Joy'd with his Beams (at Noon) the wandering earth;
Did with auspicious lustre then presage
The glittering plenty of this Golden age....

EVE OF CORONATION ADDRESS TO CHARLES II, 1661

CHAPTER TWELVE

Noah's Dove

'At which Time he prov'd himself the Noah's Dove, that finding no Rest anywhere, was receiv'd again into his own Ark, and brought a peaceable Olive-Leaf in his mouth.'

Aurelian Cook, *Titus Britannicus*

At Dover on 25 May 1660 the flags waved, the trumpets blew, and high above the heads of the crowd vast indications of new glories could be seen: the royal arms, publicly flaunted in joy.

On the sea voyage, however, the King himself deliberately turned his thoughts back to the past. He was, as usual, physically 'active and stirring', striding up and down the deck. But his conversation was of old times.[1] He talked, almost gossiped, of that flight after Worcester: it was a significant recitation. For the King was speaking not so much to Samuel Pepys, making notes at his side, as to himself. This King, who was about to be restored, never intended to let himself forget what he had endured – and might one day have to endure again. Thus he dwelt consciously on the nadir of his fortunes, where other men might have been puffed up with contemplation of the future.

Not that life on board was all retrospection. Before they sailed there had been pleasanter diversions, such as the renaming of the royal ships, to rescue them from their unpleasant Protectoral nomenclature. This probably took place on the quarter-deck table 'under the awning': thus the *Richard* (Cromwell) became the *James* (Duke of York), the *Speaker* (of the House of Commons) became the *Mary* (Princess of Orange) and the

Dunbar (oh hateful Scottish word!) the *Henry* (for the Duke of Gloucester). Pepys, like many of those suddenly enjoying intimate contact with royalty, allowed himself to be charmed by such evidence of the King's humanity as the fact that his dogs were busy making messes on the deck, just like any other dogs. Finally, at the King's suggestion, the three royal brothers, Charles, James and Henry, tucked into a seaman's breakfast of pork, pease and boiled beef.

The King was rowed ashore about three o'clock in the afternoon in the Admiral's barge: Pepys followed in a smaller boat which included one of Charles' errant dogs, escorted by a footman. Once on dry land, Charles, with his usual tactful sense of occasion, knelt down and thanked God for his safe arrival. And he continued to acknowledge the divine course of his salvation when the Mayor of Dover presented him with a rich Bible.

It was, said the King promptly, 'the thing he loved above all other things in the world'.

General Monck's claims to have assisted the Almighty in bringing out this happy state of affairs were not mentioned. But then they scarcely needed to be. Monck was the first to receive the King, with all obeisance and honour. And now it was time for the ordnance to speak. The thunder started with guns and cannons there in Dover, and spread all the way to Tower Hill in London, just as the bonfires sprang from hill to hill, from town to town, a sight commemorated by Abraham Cowley:

> All England but one Bonfire seems to be,
> One Aetna shooting flames into the sea.

But it was the ordnance which impressed the King. Indeed, so dominant did the sheer noise of his reception become that it would become the principal theme of the King's commentary upon it. As he told his sister Henriette-Anne in a letter the next day, 'My head is so prodigiously dazed by the acclamation of the people . . . that I know not whether I am writing sense or no.'[2]

From Dover Charles went on to Canterbury, and from thence

to Rochester. He took his time in treading the triumphal route, now lined by the local militia of Kent, as well as more gracefully strewn with herbs by Kentish maidens. The dalliance at Canterbury included Sunday service in the ancient cathedral, the first meeting of his new Privy Council and the presentation of the Garter to General Monck. All these events could as well have taken place in London. But the King's thirtieth birthday was imminent. It was part of the perfect timing of things, the way everything now fell into place with such marvellous felicity, that the King would be able to take possession of his capital on such an auspicious day.

At Rochester King Charles deserted his coach for horseback, and it was on horseback that he greeted the Army, drawn up for his benefit – or perhaps as a reminder of the source of his power – by Monck at Blackheath. It was on horseback too that he saluted the more pacific Morris dancers who gambolled on the heath. It was on horseback and bareheaded, riding between his two brothers, all three in silver doublets, that on Tuesday, 29 May, the King finally entered the capital. Met by the Lord Mayor at Deptford, he first rode through the borough of Southwark and then, preceded by the Mayor, crossed London Bridge. So clogged was the structure with wooden houses on both sides, that the royal party had to be content with a twelve-foot passage, while heralds and maids and other attendants milled about them. None of this diminished the general ecstasy. As John Evelyn, the Anglican and former exile, wrote in his *Diary* of the spectacle on Restoration Day, 'I stood in the Strand and beheld it and blessed God.'[3]

It was of course the King that the populace crowded to see. But the pomp of this first royal procession indicated that King Charles II did not intend to return as a suppliant exile – more as 'the Chiefest Ray of Lustre to all this Splendid Triumph'.[4] Not only a monarchy but a whole way of life was being restored. The cortège which reached London included three hundred gentlemen in doublets of cloth of silver, and an equivalent number in velvet coats, accompanied by footmen and lackeys in purple liveries and other uniforms of sea-green and silver. The buff coats of the soldiers evoked now no painful memories of the Civil War, adorned as they were with sleeves of cloth of silver, and other trimmings of silver lace. To this spectacle of affluence was joined that of the Sheriff's men in their red cloaks and still more silver lace, the gentlemen from the London companies, opulent in velvet coats and golden chains, the Aldermen of London in scarlet gowns also richly adorned.

The noise remained fulminating. It was a noise of guns and cannon, the bells which never stopped, the clattering of the soldiers and their horses, but above all the noise of the people – over twenty thousand of them, laughing, shouting and crying and jostling to see the King coming into his own. That day and night they were all Royalists. The streets literally flowed with wine: the Venetian Ambassador kept a perpetual supply on tap outside his house. It was seven o'clock in the evening before the King, surrounded by this happy tumult, reached Whitehall.

Here he was addressed by the Speakers of both Houses of Parliament. The Earl of Manchester, for the peers, began his address in a style which was almost ludicrously obsequious: 'Dread Sovereign!' he cried, 'I offer no flattering titles, but speak the words of Truth: you are the desire of three Kingdoms, the strength and stay of the Tribes of the People, for the moderating of Extremities, the reconciling of Differences, the satisfying of all Interests', and so forth and so on.[5] Yet it was true, as Manchester proceeded to point out, that the great magnates of the realm had found the destiny of the peerage had been peculiarly linked to the monarchy's own: the House of Lords had been abolished just after the execution of King Charles I, and, despite some Cromwellian experiments, had not really found its place again in the constitution in any proper form.

The King's 'Gracious answer', as it was afterwards described, was very short. To excuse its brevity, he said that he was disorientated by his journey and above all by the noise still sounding in his ears; but 'I confess [it] was pleasing to me, because it expressed the affections of my people,' the King quickly added.[6]

The oration of the Speaker of the House of Commons, delivered in the Banqueting Hall, took much longer. At the end of it the King was forced to acknowledge that he was so exhausted that he could hardly speak, but all the same wished the Speaker to know that 'whatsoever may concern the good of this people, I shall be as ready to grant as you shall be able to ask'. He was certainly too tired to attend a Thanksgiving service at Westminster Abbey, so that a shorter service was held in the Presence Chamber. At the end of it all the King still had to dine ceremoniously in public, showing himself to his people at his food, as his ancestors had always done.

Was the weary King solaced nonetheless by his mistress Barbara Palmer? Legend had it so. And for once, in view of the birth of Barbara's daughter Anne, almost exactly nine months later, on 25 February 1661, the legend seems perfectly plausible. It is true that Barbara's husband, Roger Palmer, did acknowledge Anne as his own at the actual time of her birth, either because he was hoodwinked by Barbara into doing so, or because he chose to turn a blind eye to an unpleasant situation in order to preserve his marriage. But as Anne grew up, her royal paternity became quite obvious. She was officially designated the King's daughter at the time of her marriage, created Countess of Sussex in her own right, and, with Charlotte Countess of Lichfield, Barbara's second daughter by the King, came to form an important part of his inner family circle.

To return to the legend, it would have been quite in character for the King to have relaxed in Barbara's arms after his triumphant if noisy processional: even if one cannot prove that he did so. Certainly he was in a high good humour at the time, giving vent to one of those wry, self-mocking observations at which he excelled. Turning to those about him with a smile, King Charles remarked that it was undoubtedly his own fault that he had been absent so long, since he had met no-one 'who did not protest that he had ever wished for his return'.

The man the crowds cheered through London on his thirtieth birthday was an engaging but not a merry monarch. This is confirmed by all contemporary accounts. For one thing, Charles II was no longer young by the standards of the time. (He was in fact over half-way through his own life, but of course the average life expectancy of the time was far less than sixty.) His appearance had much changed from those far-off days when Cromwell was wont to refer to him jocularly as 'the young man' and 'the young gentleman'. Sir Samuel Tuke, in a character of Charles II written to coincide with his Restoration, referred to the fact that his face, which had been 'very lovely' until he was twenty, had now become grave and even severe in repose, although much softened when he spoke. One witness of the royal procession commented on Charles II's new resemblance to his father, calling him 'black and very slender faced'.[7]

Undoubtedly his face was much leaner. The nose too had markedly lengthened. Already the characteristic deep lines which are seen in all the later portraits had formed from nostril to chin, curving round the wide mouth. They are already visible in a portrait painted towards the end of his exile, and praised by Pepys for being 'the most pleasant' and 'the most like him that I ever saw picture in my life',[8] as well as the many engravings commemorating the Restoration. Sometimes attributed to debauchery, these particular lines were more likely caused by the tribulations of exile.

In general, it was majesty, not youth, which supplied the charm of his appearance. 'You may read the King in every lineament' was the general verdict on his face. His tall figure, 'so exactly formed that the most curious eye cannot find any error in his shape', was as appropriate in a monarch as it had been inappropriate in a fugitive; its symmetry commanded universal admiration, as did his fine long legs and shapely hands.[9] Once again, there was favourable comment on his shining black hair, which had not yet started to go grey: surprisingly, for his father's black hair had silvered prematurely. The Plea Roll portrait of Michaelmas 1661 shows the curly black moustache which he preserved to the end of his life (Charles, unlike his father, was never bearded), the mass of black hair and heavy black brows which together gave a saturnine cast to his countenance – the exact word used by his contemporaries. However, even Charles was not to enjoy his thick black locks for long: three years later he went in his turn 'mighty grey' and adopted a periwig in consequence like everyone else.[10]

The King's other good feature, his 'quick and sparkling' eyes, attracted attention. But behind the sparkle, the expression remained watchful. And the King's habitual demeanour on his return was grave. As Pepys put it, 'The King seems to be a very sober man'; it was the fourteen-year-old George Boddington who ran back to his father after witnessing the procession and reported that the restored monarch was 'a black grim man'.[11]

And gravity, even temperance, was the keynote of the character now presented to his loyal subjects. An *Eikon Basilike* of Charles II (imitating the title of the famous book ascribed to his martyred father), published within a few months of his landing in England and probably written by Sir Richard Fanshawe, gives an interesting sidelight on the image of the new reigning monarch. Here Charles was inevitably credited with such sterling qualities as good judgement and apprehension, magnanimity and public-mindedness, as well as sheer goodness. (He was more good than great, as one phrase had it, contrasting Charles le Bon and Charlemagne: that recalled his father's last letter.) But the King was also presented as having 'sobriety and temperance': his diet spare, his attire plain, his recreations moderate, and his speech sober – a detail incidentally confirmed by Sir Samuel Tuke, who remarked how the King never swore.[12]*

It was hardly surprising if the new King was at heart sober, serious, even melancholy, rather than merry. Here was a man who had been undergoing harrowing experiences since boyhood: including his father's death, his family's poverty and his own humiliation. He had known, in Dante's words,

sì come sa di sale
Lo pane altrui, e com' è duro calle
Lo scendere e 'l salir per l' altrui scale

('the salt flavour of other's people's bread, the hard path up and down other people's stairs'). He had endured all this. He had

* The King's language remained moderate. 'Oddsfish' – his favourite expletive – was in fairly common use in the seventeenth century; it occurs in the work of Otway, Congreve and Vanbrugh. It was a corruption of God's Flesh, as the nineteenth-century 'Golly' stood for God.

never given up. Nevertheless, it is useless to pretend that this 'black grim man' was the same brave boy of Edgehill, or even the spirited general on the eve of Worcester fight. It was not that King Charles II never intended to feel again: as we shall see, he remained, admirably, a feeling man all his life, full of affectionate impulses, one of which (towards his wife) would bedevil the monarchy's future. But this was in private.

In public, he was determined never to be subjected again to the experience of humiliation, accompanied by helplessness. With this resolution went the presentation of a public mask of cynicism, gaiety, indifference – it could take many forms, according to the interpretation of the beholders. Behind the mask lay a melancholy which nothing, not all the fabled delights of the Restoration Court, quite dislodged.

But of course, this melancholy coexisted easily with an iron determination to preserve what was his, now wrested back from unlawful hands. Charles II believed passionately that monarchy was the rightful government of Britain: this conviction was built into his personal philosophy by his upbringing and had been welded there solidly by the death of his father. It was not a purely selfish view: of course he did not intend to go on his travels again, but he also, less personally and less selfishly, did not intend that his country should suffer again, as it had suffered so cruelly in the Civil War.

In the same way, an underlying melancholy was compatible with, and even inspired, a degree of doubt about the country which was now welcoming him with such rapture. He felt himself to be somewhat of an expert on the changeability of crowds. It was in keeping with the King's suspicions that he prided himself on being able to read people's characters from their faces, having studied the subject in a book – *Physonomia*, by G. B. della Porta.[13] As he searched the smiling visages of those surrounding him at this 'continuous Jubilee', he was aware of the darker passions which lay concealed – and which might return. It is tempting to suppose that King Charles enjoyed at least one day of unalloyed happiness as monarch – Restoration Day. But did he in fact do so? Is there not in all his remarks and behaviour on that auspicious occasion, including the quip that it was undoubtedly his own fault he had been away so long, a note of amiable but unmistakable caution?

As the bells rang out and finally died away, the myriad bonfires were reduced to ashes, the King remained wary. Outwardly, he could and would forgive the past – except for those directly involved in his father's murder. Even then he showed himself more merciful than those around him. The corpses of Cromwell, Ireton and Bradshaw (President of the court which tried Charles I) were exhumed and publicly hung at Tyburn, a gesture which did but little harm to the deceased. Of the forty-one surviving regicides, those who had signed the warrant and a few others closely associated with the King's death as well as the two (unidentified) executioners of Charles I, twelve died altogether. It was the King who prevented a further nineteen of their number, those who had given themselves up, from being pursued by the law; he told Hyde that while he could not pardon them, he was 'weary of hanging'.[14] He did not save Argyll in Scotland, but then Argyll was responsible for the death of Montrose; Sir Henry Vane, who also died, was charged with treason against Charles II rather than against Charles I.

The judicial process which brought the regicides to book was a great deal fairer than that allowed to King Charles I, since the prisoners were patiently heard in their own defence, and, in general, the rules of contemporary justice were observed. Charles was present at some of the executions, but John Evelyn put his attendance in the correct perspective. The executions were performed, he wrote, to avenge the murder of King Charles I and in the presence of 'the King his son, whom they also sought to kill'. Otherwise Charles II, never a personally vindictive man, proved himself 'no Orestes'.[15]

He preferred positive memorials to his father: as late as 1678 the House of Commons voted £70,000 for a funeral and a monument for the murdered King, a quite incredible sum. Perhaps it was too incredible: for the money never arrived, although Wren did produce a design for a monument.* But it

* But Le Sueur's equestrian statue of Charles I was re-erected on the site of the regicides' executions, with a pedestal designed by Wren, executed by Grinling

was the measure of the King's forgiveness that by a decade after his Restoration he was accepting hospitality from Henry Cromwell, second son of the late Protector, at his home near Newmarket.

Nevertheless, in Charles II a temperamental disinclination to vengeance was not at all the same thing as an inclination to forget the past. Revolution, and its possible consequences, was one spectre which stalked the corridors of the King's palace from the inception of his reign to its end (even though this spectre would take different guises in different decades). But at no point was the presence of such a threatening ghost felt more acutely than in the early 1660s. To understand this, one has to be wary of hindsight. Not to the monarch riding down towards Whitehall on 29 May was there granted the cheerful knowledge that he would die in his bed twenty-five years later. On the contrary, he arrived in a country in desperate need of settlement, coming from a Europe in which the tide of revolution, flowing strongly in 1648, was only just beginning to subside. Like his first cousin Louis XIV, Charles had been formed against a background of such experiences.

Thus one finds the implicit fear of another revolution expressed continuously and in all sorts of different ways in the early years of the reign. There were significant details such as the preference for Windsor Castle as a royal fortress, not simply because it was 'the most romantique castle that is in the world', but because it could be properly garrisoned.[16] There were broader policies, such as the concentration on forming a proper body of guards to surround the monarch. Richard Cromwell, exiled and debt-ridden, was clearly a burnt-out case: yet it was considered worth while reporting on his movements. A general jumpiness animated surveys of the careers of those with regicide connections.

Still more important is it to realize that in the early years plots were not only feared, but actually existed. Periodically substance was given to these apprehensions; otherwise they

---

Gibbons. It can still be seen at Charing Cross, and is regularly adorned with wreaths on 30 January, the anniversary of the death of Charles I.

might have dissolved in the growing stability of the Restoration state. In January 1661, for instance, the Fifth Monarchy men, members of a millenarian sect, ran amok under a Thomas Venner; the later plots of 1663 and 1664 led to the production of diligent if circumstantial reports on the subversive activities of republicans, Quakers, and other sectaries. The year 1663 also produced quite a serious republican plot in Ireland; similar disturbances in Scotland evoked from Pepys the nervous reaction that the Bishops' Wars might be happening all over again – tremors which demonstrate how finely balanced popular stability was considered to be in the early years of the reign. During the Dutch War there were genuine conspiracies in London, to give colour to royal and other fears.

The fatal years after 1640 had left their curse behind: never again could revolution be unimaginable. Not only had Charles himself suffered the strong marks of an impressionable child, but nearly all his current ministers had been sufficiently active to have retained potent memories of republicanism – from one angle or the other. One of the King's little jokes commemorated the fact, pleasantly but pointedly: he told the former Commonwealth commanders in his splendid new Navy that 'they all had had the plague but they were quite sound now and less accessible to the disease than others'.[17]

As to the absurdity of such fears – that the surviving regicides, aided by the soldiery, plus some new republicans, might overthrow the Crown once more – this was not so striking at the time. In May 1664 the French Ambassador, an intelligent observer, wrote that it did not seem impossible that the English would 'be tempted again to try and taste a Commonwealth', remembering their greatness under Cromwell.[18]

King Charles II made his own position on the subject clear in his speech to Parliament of February 1663. Referring to certain 'rogues' who had escaped punishment recently for want of legal evidence, including William Stockdale, MP, he said, 'But let him not believe it, although he creates just the same stirs as were prepared before the Long Parliament, that I, knowing the mischiefs then, will not prevent them now.' The King went on to say that 'justice I see must be done against such restless spirits, and let them not delude themselves into a belief to find me tame'.[19]

The glorious twenty-ninth of May, then, ushered in an age of anxiety as well as an age of rejoicing.

Yet with these twin provisos of watchfulness against the repetition of revolution and concern for justice to his father's memory, King Charles II arrived in a healing mood. 'At which Time he prov'd himself the Noah's Dove, that finding no Rest anywhere, was receiv'd again into his own Ark, and brought a peaceable Olive-Leaf in his mouth' – thus *Titus Britannicus*.[20] And the sentiments were not exaggerated. In his determined mercy, King Charles in 1660 did show himself indeed a veritable olive-branch-bearing dove. The only trouble was that to bear the olive-leaf involved another twin pair of considerations: conciliation and reward. One or the other he might have achieved: the conciliation of the Cromwellians, the reward of the exiled and wounded Royalists. To do both was likely to prove very difficult, if not impossible. Nevertheless, the King set out with the highest intentions.

Let us start with reward, the implementation of those hopes whose existence had been so vital to the maintenance of morale during the exile. The loyal petitions began to flood in at once: in fact, many of them had already been received before the King's arrival, and throughout May Hyde had been deluged with petitions for peerages, ecclesiastical preferments and the like. How many of these petitions related to Worcester! It was not only the King who looked back to that fearful time. One Mary Graves petitioned for having provided twelve steeds: one of these, she was reliably informed, had been shot down from beneath the King during the battle and 'the other I heard was that happy horse His Majesty got from Worcester upon. . . .' Less romantic were the drapers of Worcester who had been commanded to clothe the life guard in red cloth and had never been paid; they wanted £450.[21]

Sir Jonathan Wiseman of Glastonbury spoke for many when he wrote of himself in semi-biblical language: 'Your poor petitioner hath been tost and tumbled up and down and was hated of all men, and was tried eleven times for my life, and was imprisoned but still got away....' And then there were those, not a few, who had served Charles I, such as the poignant story of the dead King's cannoneer, who had lost both his eyes and his arms in service. In general, the Stuarts remembered their old servants. Poignant memories were aroused by some pensions granted. Four women cradle-rockers to 'our late dear sisters' the Princesses Elizabeth (dead at Carisbrooke) and Anne (dead as a baby) were rewarded, as well as those who had served Charles I and even James I.[22]

It was of course one of the penalties of the unopposed Restoration that very few names could legitimately be struck off the list. Sir William Killigrew, a royal servant who understood the ways of the world (he also wrote plays), had foreseen this in April: 'Suppose, Sir, that you were now called in without any restrictions. How impossible a work it would be to please all those that have really served your father, and yourself ... 'tis not your three kingdoms that will afford half enough places, or employments for them all.'[23]

There was another problem. Through all these petitions and the Restoration settlement itself, we can discern the obsession of the loyal not only that they should, understandably, be rewarded, but less attractively, that the disloyal should not. The point was made early on concerning the composition of the King's entourage: 'It is observed by your Majesty's said royal party, that all those who were the greatest actors both against your royal father and yourself are the only men who are preferred to the highest places of authority and trust about your Majesty,' ran one petition. Later Rochester the cynical put the same point as he sneered:

> His father's foes he does reward...
> Never was any King endued
> With so much grace and gratitude.

When Sir Richard Fanshawe, who had been promised by Charles a post as a Secretary of State, was passed over for Monck's protégé, William Morrice, he expostulated that he had been slighted in favour of 'one that never saw the King's face'.[24]

The Morrice incident summed up the King's difficulties in a nutshell. After the happy ending of the Restoration, he had to go forward and reconstruct the government of the country, and former foes were vitally important for the kind of healing settlement he had in mind. His attitude to the scientist Sir William Petty was characteristic. At the Restoration, Petty felt it necessary to explain that his involvement with the government of Ireland during the Commonwealth and Protectorate (including his celebrated survey of the country) had not been done out of any desire to harm the monarchy. 'But the King, seeing little to mind apologies, as needless, replied: "But, Doctor, why have you left off your inquiries into the mechanics of shipping?"' And the conversation quickly passed to such agreeable (to the King) topics as loadstones, guns, the feathering of arrows, the vegetation of plants and the history of trade.[25]

The first body of men who surrounded the King was indeed a combination of the old and the new (for all the complaints of the loyal petitioner quoted above). It was of course dominated by the trusted counsellor Hyde and the veteran Sir Edward Nicholas, who was given the other secretaryship of State. The Marquess of Ormonde was made Lord Steward of the Household to compensate for the fact that Parliament had appointed Monck Lord Lieutenant of Ireland – although the following year Ormonde was restored to the post for which, as a man who loved and cared for the country, he was so well equipped; he was also given a dukedom. But the Lord Treasurer was to be the Earl of Southampton, a magnate who, if he had had no truck with the Protectoral government, had not shared the exile either; and, even more significantly, his nephew, Anthony Ashley Cooper, who had been a member of the republican Council of State, was made Chancellor of the Exchequer. This group formed, in Hyde's words, 'a secret committee'.

Beyond them lay the Privy Council, numbering between forty and fifty. Beyond that lay Parliament, once again two-housed. What were its powers? For that matter, what was its relation to the monarchy? What indeed were the powers of the monarchy? It was one of the remarkable consequences of the King's unconditional Restoration that in spite of years of argument, civil war, discussion and experiment, no one in 1660 yet had a clear idea as to what the proper answers to these questions were.

In so far as an accepted *theory* existed, it gave the King wide powers. Although the whole Restoration was based on an optimistic feeling that the King and Parliament would in future amicably share power, there was absolutely no indication as to how this was to be worked out in practice. In the meantime, the King retained his prerogative untouched, and with it the right to prorogue or dissolve Parliaments at will, to control foreign policy and, when necessary, to wage war. As against this, Parliament, it was understood, would vote him the extra monies he might need for such matters, since he was no longer expected to 'live of his own' (and even the mediaeval Kings had sought money from Parliament to wage war). But the potential control of Parliament over the King inherent in this situation had no theoretical base to it. It was all very confusing.

In 1664 the French Ambassador commented disapprovingly of the English constitution that it had a monarchical appearance, as there was a king 'but at the bottom it is very far from being a monarchy'. He questioned whether this confusion was caused by 'the fundamental laws of the kingdom' or by the 'carelessness of the king'.[26] In fact, neither was responsible. The confusion developed out of the peculiar circumstances of the Restoration settlement, which presented the King with, on the one hand, very wide powers, and, on the other hand, equally wide problems, which he could not solve without the co-operation of almost everyone in the State.

It was a measure of the uncertainty of the times that the moment was not felt appropriate for a general election. Although the sitting House of Commons had not been elected legally (they lacked the King's writ), they were confirmed in their existence, and kept there till December to carry out all the vital post-Restoration legislation. This Convention Parliament thus passed a general Act of Indemnity and Oblivion, from which only fifty named individuals were excepted. The King put the argument for such a measure cogently: 'It will make them [the former rebels] good subjects to me and good friends and neighbours to you [the loyalists] and we shall have them all our end. . . ."[27]

Equally important was the settlement of the Army. A measure was passed to the effect that Commonwealth salaries need not be repaid – this reassured General Monck, amongst others – while of course the Act of Indemnity affected the soldiers as much as any section of the community. At the same time, King Charles took a prudent decision to alter the entire composition of the future Army.

Disbanding the old Cromwellian soldiers at considerable financial cost, he welded together by degrees a totally new kind of force out of his former Royalist regiments and whatever military elements in England were indubitably loyal. He retained, for example, the Coldstream Guards, who were a Cromwellian creation. It was, to be frank, the first English standing army – in the sense of a non-political military body in support of the civil power. But considerable effort was made to camouflage the fact: references were made to 'guards' and 'garrisons' rather than to the dreaded word 'army'. And the King's army was incidentally a convenient source of reward for that other army – of needy place-seekers.

Where the law was concerned, conciliation was more obvious, innovation less apparent. The vital principle was established that service during the Interregnum should be no disqualification: thus both Sir Matthew Hale and Edward Atkins, who had been esteemed judges under Cromwell, were reappointed, and as a result even Bishop Burnet credits Charles with good judges. Furthermore, the judges were for the most part appointed to the more liberal formula of *quamdiu se bene gesserit* – so long as they conducted themselves properly, rather than the more autocratic *durante bene placito* – so long as it pleased the King to appoint them.[28]

There was one area where public innovation simply could not be avoided, and yet conciliation of all parties was absolutely vital, and that was the vexed area of religion. The question of what sort of State church should exist in England after the Restoration was, like the constitution itself, left wide open at

Charles' return. The promises given at Breda had however been generous in scope. For the rest of 1660 the omens for some tolerant kind of establishment, allowing for both nonconformist and Catholic dissent, looked more hopeful than they would again for two centuries. The King was by temperament, conviction, and (by the implications of his word at Breda) personally inclined to toleration. As he had told Morrice from Breda, he was confident that he had 'offered nothing' in his Declaration and letters 'that I will not meet punctually and exactly perform'.[29] The Puritans who had recently ruled the State church knew that some severe alteration in their position was inevitable after his return. Nonconformists, like the Quakers, were petitioning for a situation by which they could rest within the State – peacefully rather than turbulently as hitherto.

On 25 October 1660 the King issued a declaration in favour of a modified episcopacy, which it was understood that the Presbyterians would also accept. Secretary Morrice offered that this declaration should be embodied in a bill, but this solution, most unfortunately, even tragically, was rejected by the Commons in November. A conference then met at the lodgings of the Bishop of London to work out the details of a compromise by which some Presbyterians could accept preferment.[30] It was a defeat, not only for moderation and toleration (leading the way to the much harsher Clarendon Code), but also for the King's own plan for the English Church. He had taken much interest in the conference, attending it personally. He listened while general concessions were discussed but finally abandoned because the Catholics might benefit. Throughout he held firmly to that view which he had never abandoned in exile, that the Anglican Church represented the right solution for England. He spoke movingly of the Book of Common Prayer: 'the best we have seen, and we believe that we have seen all that are extant and used in this part of the world....'[31]

Carlyle denounced the Restoration settlement in his usual fine splenetic style; he took the body of Oliver Cromwell hanging from Tyburn to be 'a fingerpost' into 'very strange country and far from the government of God. It called and thought itself a Settlement of brightest hope and fulfilment,' he wrote, 'bright as the blaze of universal tar-barrels and bonfires could make it: and we find it now, on looking back on it with the insight which trial has yielded, a Settlement as of despair.' But the despair did not come from the abandonment of Puritanism, as Carlyle fondly believed; it arose through the failure of the English Parliament in 1660 to follow their King's admirable lead in promoting an established Anglican Church, with the ability to tolerate other law-abiding sects in the wings of its many mansions.

The land settlement was in general more successful than the religious settlement, because here the status quo could be, and was, respected – except in the case of Crown and Church lands – even at the cost of the Royalists: it has been established that surprisingly little land actually changed hands at the Restoration. The Crown and Church lands were successfully restored, despite the conflict of interest with those who had acquired them, as a result of the successful manœuvres of Hyde and the King.[32] This was partly due to the fact that the sequestered Royalists had retained ownership of their forfeited lands more than was lawful by making it over to trustees or relatives; but it was also the innate wish of Parliament and King not to disturb England, as she was, more than was absolutely necessary to bring about justice. And in the view of some Royalists of course the justice brought about was rough indeed.

Where pomp was concerned, Charles II was outwardly traditional rather than innovatory. It was in keeping with this that the first year of his reign was always referred to as the twelfth – as though the eleven years' Interregnum since his father's death was of no account. And of course his display had a political purpose. He had after all been brought back to incarnate not a republican head of state, but the beloved old monarchy for which the people yearned.

Thus the immediate needs of a restored sovereign were felt to include tradespeople of all sorts, tinker and tailor, as well as soldier and sailor: an Arras worker, a bookbinder, a brewer, a coffee-maker, a fishmonger, mat-layer, milliner, fruiterer, saddler, milkman, woollen draper, clock-maker, comb-maker, corn-cutter (awarded a special scarlet livery, as was the royal rat-killer).[33] This list of positions was as endless as were the petitions to fill them: the equivalent to the royal warrants today, the coveted right to state 'By Appointment to . . .'.

On a grander level, the King needed, naturally, a Master of Tents, a Surveyor of Stables, Falconers, Cormorant Keepers. On the most important level of all, he needed to reorganize the entire paraphernalia of the royal existence, which had fallen into desuetude during the previous twenty years. Here the King's return was to take a palpable form, in terms of building and artistic commission, summed up by the great allegorical ceiling of the Restoration itself commissioned from Michael Wright and placed in the Banqueting Hall at Whitehall. His father's great art collection had been tragically sold after his death by the Commonwealth officials, and it was with a view to replacing it to some small degree that Charles had already acquired some paintings of his own while in the Netherlands.[34] The new collection was further augmented by twenty-seven old masters (including a famous Titian) hastily presented by the Dutch government, who hoped by this propitiatory gesture to atone for their previous slights to the English King.

The tastes of the new age dictated many of the earliest pieces of renovation: within the Whitehall complex the Cockpit Theatre was soon made ready. By June, over £1,200 had already been spent in furnishing the royal apartments. It would be two years before the King's bedroom, with its black and white marble paving and chimney-piece, its 'flying boys' holding the curtains of the bed alcove and its 'great eagles' over the bed itself, would be complete. Even then there was much mention of 'night work' – the seventeenth-century equivalent of overtime – needed to complete it.[35]

A sun-dial in the Privy Garden was however given priority, as was the 'King's Tube', or astronomical telescope. That was another indication of the way the new reign would go. The King's own natural bent for scientific discussion and discovery could now be given a free rein. Like the jackdaws who were his favourite birds, he was not only a great collector of curiosities, but inquisitive to boot. It was the kind of mind peculiarly suited to a monarch, who could engage his subjects in conversation as and when he pleased, on what topics had currently seized his fancy, without fear of seeming to bore them. It is true that Charles II felt fascination for practical results rather than investigation for its own sake. His was not the intellect of a Newton, as described by Wordsworth, 'Voyaging through strange seas of thought alone' (although Charles II patronized Newton). But then a practical turn of mind was a very useful thing for a sovereign in charge of the welfare of his people to possess.

Thus we find Charles happily discoursing with John Evelyn on the elimination of the 'wearisome' smoke from London (a problem which remained unsolved for three hundred years), as well as his more conspicuous interests, such as shipping and the improvement of gardens and buildings. Evelyn was privileged to hold the candle while the King was having his face crayonned by the great miniaturist Samuel Cooper, for the benefit of the new coinage: naturally, the King seized the opportunity to chat away about painting and engraving.[36]

He adored all clocks and watches. In the end there were no fewer than seven clocks in his bedroom (their ill-synchronized chiming drove his attendants mad), while another clock in the antechamber told not only the hour but also the direction of the wind. Hooke's balance-spring action was demonstrated in front of the King, while the royal accounts contain many items for the purchase of further clocks. The sun-dial referred to above had a particular function – for the King used to set his watch by it.

When the Royal Society came to be formed in November 1660 it was not mere flattery which caused the King to become its Fundator (or founder); he granted the Royal Charter on 15 July 1662. The man who was obsessed by the need to possess a lunar globe, with the hills, eminences and cavities of the moon's surfaces as well as the degree of whiteness solidly moulded, was well fitted to occupy the position. At the Society's inception it was reported that the King 'did well approve' of the new body and would be 'ready to give encouragement' to it.[37] Later he responded in style, presenting a mace to the Society and granting its arms.

The charm and catholicity of the early proceedings of the Society recall the King's own conversations.[38] Topics raised included oysters (at Colchester), ships in North America, the weather in Greenland and beer. The King's unsettling friend inspired a typically elusive entry in the Society's proceedings: 'The Duke of Buckingham promised to bring to the society a piece of an unicorn's horn.' It was a two-way process. The King made science fashionable by his own burning interest in the subject. At the same time, he was naturally drawn to those who shared it. While many of the founding members of the Society were, or had been, part of the Puritan establishment, others were former Royalists, the King's personal friends. Two of his doctors, his chaplain and his brother's secretary were amongst the founder members. Sir Robert Moray, who first told the King of the establishment of the Society, was a staunch Royalist, who had been Colonel of the Scots Guards in France and one of Charles II's intimates.

Now Moray, together with Sir Paul Neile, a Gentleman Usher to the King, was used as a conduit for the King's messages and enquiries to the Society.[39] It was Moray who reported Charles' earnest questions as to why sensitive plants contracted to the touch, why ants' eggs were sometimes larger than the insect itself. Moray produced a discourse on coffee written by Dr Goddard at the King's command; he also reported an experiment of the King's own, keeping a sturgeon in fresh water in St James' Park.

At first the King's interest in the Society was so zealous that, as reported by Moray, he wanted it to examine every philosophical or mechanical invention before the patent was passed. The King recommended to the Lord Lieutenant of Ireland that the officers and new settlers of that country (the Adventurers) should contribute to the Society. He made the Society gifts of curiosities. In later years the King's acute interest in the Society faded (although he continued to send venison for its anniversary dinners). But his interest in mathematics, navigation and his own laboratory experiments – his own and others' – did not. He was responsible for the foundation of the Mathematical School at Christ's Hospital in 1673 to instruct boys in navigation as well as mathematics; subsequently the King took an interest in the boys' apprenticeships. He was also responsible for the foundation of the Royal Observatory at Greenwich two years later. This was designed by Wren, as he himself confessed, 'for the Observator's habitation and a little for Pompe'.[40] Where science was concerned, Charles II made an excellent natural leader of post-Restoration society.

Only the chronic want of money hung over the new reign, a bad fairy at its christening, promising hardships ahead. In August 1660, a few months after his return, the King observed ruefully of his position: 'I must tell you, I am not richer, that is, I have not so much money in my purse as when I came to you.' A year later Pepys was describing how 'the want of money puts all things ... out of order'.[41] As a result the search for a bride for the King was much influenced by the question of her dowry; and once the lot had fallen upon the well-endowed Portuguese Infanta, it was a further sign of the King's financial straits that the dowry was already being pledged as a security for loans in September 1661, eight months before the bride herself actually landed in England. When she did arrive, the unhappy member of her entourage deputed to administer the dowry was Eduarte Da Silva, a New Christian (that is, a Jew converted to meet the requirements of the Inquisition). Da Silva had a spell in the Tower of London when the payments did not come quickly enough for the embarrassed King.[42]

How much was this situation of the King's own making? It was suggested by his enemies and critics at the time, and has been suggested by many critics ever since, that such qualities in the King as extravagance and mismanagement brought about the perpetual financial straits in which the Crown soon found itself. This view leaves out of account two important aspects of the Restoration. First, since Charles II had been brought back to personify royalty, that in itself necessitated all the traditional trappings of a king. Such things always had and always would cost a great deal of money, but to do otherwise would be to confound both popular and courtly expectations. Lord Halifax believed that the very reason that the English character was biased in favour of a monarchy was because of its childish taste for 'the bells and the tinsel, the outward pomp and gilding'. Secondly, the sum of money Charles II was originally voted by Parliament, although seemingly adequate, proved difficult to collect and in any case the yield had been over-estimated.

Immediately on his return, then, Charles II was torn between the fantasy of kingship and the reality of England's economic situation. Of course the very use of the latter term is anachronistic. To the contemporaries of Charles II, it was the kingship which represented reality, so that the conflict between the two was very imperfectly understood, if at all. In this way, from the very beginning, the Crown was immersed in a mire of debt from which it had little hope of escaping – by natural means. As we shall see, the King eventually resorted to unnatural means. But it was hardly his own fault that he found himself floundering in the first place.

The King's annual peacetime expenses were estimated by Parliament at £1,200,000; war was to be considered an extra, as had been customary in previous reigns. The sum itself was comparatively generous by the standards of the time – if not lavish – but the income which the King actually received was appreciably smaller. It has been estimated however that, on average over the entire course of his reign, the King received of those monies about £945,000 a year, increased to something under £980,000 by his private income.[43] Assuming he kept within his theoretical income, that in itself produced a gap between this annual income and his annual expenditure which Mr Micawber would have aptly summed up as 'result misery'. In fact, a paper on the state of the revenue shows that between Michaelmas 1661 and Michaelmas 1662 the King's expenditure was roughly £1,500,000, compared to the aforesaid official figure of £1,200,000. This was a state of affairs which would certainly have upset Mr Micawber still further.

But there were graver problems. With the Exchequer in control of agents for collection, rather than of the actual collection of revenues, administration of the Crown's finances was inefficient, corrupt and above all laggardly. Actual receipts were particularly low at the start of his reign, so that early on the King had to resort to the traditional monarchical expedient of high-interest loans in order to keep going at all. Prudent men like Sir George Downing were found advocating the punctual payment of the interest on the Treasury loans at least – in order to uphold the King's credit abroad.

Yet Charles II had little choice. Not only was austerity in a sovereign impossible to conceive in a body politic where rank was very much demonstrated by outward display – a fact amply borne out by the household accounts of the great magnates of the day, some of which vied with and even surpassed those of the King in generosity. But the very prestige of the nation seemed bound up with the appearance of the monarchy.

It was in keeping with his subjects' aspirations, therefore, as well as his own that the King now embarked on preparations for two ceremonies with their origins rooted deep in English history. He would hold a ceremony for the installation of the new Knights of the Garter – the first for twenty years. And after that, with even more magnificence, would follow the coronation, the joyous celebration of all that had happened over the last twelve months since that suppliant message had come from the House of Commons: that the King should come into his own again.

CHAPTER THIRTEEN

The Best of Queens

> The best of Queens, the most obedient wife...
> His life the theme of her eternal prayer–
>
> John Dryden on Catharine of Braganza

The Garter ceremony of April 1661 was a moving time for those who remembered the old order. The coronation of King Charles II, which took place immediately afterwards, on 23 April, was however more of a public demonstration of the strength of the new, as modern leaders parade their troops and armaments before the eyes of foreign ambassadors.

The Garter procession took place by ancient custom at Windsor on 15 April, but there was such a plethora of Knights to be installed that the ceremonies had to be staggered over three days.[1] Princes like James Duke of York and Rupert of the Rhine, for instance, had received the Garter from Charles I at Oxford in 1645, but sixteen years later had never been installed. The ceremony itself had not been held since Charles I left London on the eve of the war.

The new Knights' hatchments, and those of the Elector of Brandenburg and the late William of Orange, were now hung up for the first time. That loyal servant, the Duke of Ormonde, whose Garter was a fitting reward for all his efforts in exile, was there to swear his oath in person. It was however significant that the Knights' costumes had been redesigned along more elaborate lines. Possibly they were influenced by the French King's Knights of the Saint Esprit:[2] if so, it was part of the general new admiration of the English for French Court ceremonial.

The coronation began as a piece of panoply in which much attention was paid to the presumed wishes of the populace.[3] On the eve of his coronation, for example, the King took part in the traditional procession from the Tower of London to Whitehall, which was officially described as 'a spectacle so grateful [pleasing] to the people'. He trod the same route as the mediaeval kings such as Richard II.*

Like modern coronations, this procession demanded an early start; everyone had to be mustered on Tower Hill by eight o'clock in the morning. What was more, they had to take care that their mounts were not 'unruly or stinking'. As a result, John Evelyn felt able to comment favourably on the elegance of the prancing horses. Pepys, on the other hand, showed his particular interests by noting that the houses along the route had wealthy carpets and ladies (an interesting example of zeugma) hung out of their windows.[4]

Once again the conduits in the streets ran with wine, as on Restoration Day. But this time the streets were railed, and gravelled. As the foot guards of the King passed, their plumes of red and white feathers contrasting with the black and white of the Duke of York's guard, they represented the established order – and monarchical strength. The coronation medal bore the royal oak bursting into leaf and the appropriate motto *Iam Florescit* – now it flourishes. This was the Crown triumphant, come out of its hiding-place.

The symbolic references of the triumphal arches under which the King passed made the same point.[5] One arch supported a woman dressed as Rebellion, in a crimson robe crawling with snakes, a bloody sword in her hand. Her attendant, Confusion, was represented by a deformed shape, with the ruins of a castle on her head, a torn crown, and broken sceptres in each hand. At every turn it was heavily emphasized that the King himself stood, in contrast, for stability – for the whole social order. The

* Charles II was however the last English monarch to take part in this eve-of-ceremony procession.

dialogue between the figures of Rebellion and Monarchy, for example, went along simple lines, Rebellion beginning with 'I am Hell's daughter, Satan's eldest child', and Monarchy replying in valiant style, 'To Hell foul Fiend, shrink from this glorious light....' And so on and so on, for what to the King under his canopy must have surely seemed a very long time indeed, for all the impeccable nature of the sentiments.

The pleasantest arch to encounter was probably that supporting the woman Plenty, who addressed the King in the following glowing terms:

> Great Sir, the Star which at your happy Birth
> Joy'd with his Beams (at Noon) the wandering earth;
> Did with auspicious lustre then presage
> The glittering plenty of this Golden age....

Glittering plenty was exactly what the King needed.

A certain amount of it had already been expended on replacing the regalia essential to any decent coronation, most of which had disappeared or been melted down during the Interregnum. A committee had sat regularly to produce the requirements, retaining the 'old names, and fashion', and the total cost was over £30,000.[6] The figure however was not really surprising, considering the determination to crown the King in style and the elaborate paraphernalia needed, including two crowns (one of which was known as St Edward's crown, as before) and a quantity of ceremonial apparel for the King himself. The coronation ceremonial demanded, it seemed, an unceasing change of clothing for the monarch.[7] Most of it was made of cloth of gold or some equally costly substance, from the King's golden sandals with high heels (which must have made him tower over the assorted bishops and nobles around him) to his series of mantles of crimson velvet furred with ermine; even his under trousers, breeches and stockings were made of crimson satin. Rich golden tissue was also needed for the chairs of state. Then there was the horse of state, whose saddle was richly embroidered with pearls and gold, and although a large oriental ruby was donated by a jeweller named William Gomeldon, the further twelve thousand stones needed for the stirrups and bosses were only lent.

Scarlet cloth was used in abundance, including a false ceiling of red baize for St Edward's Chapel and red cloth to cover the benches in both Westminster Hall and the Abbey. More mundanely, blue cloth was used to line the way from the Hall steps to the choir in the Abbey. Everything contributed to the overall impression of magnificence, but everything – down to the silk towel held by the Bishops before Communion – had to be paid for.

Nevertheless, the impact on observers, both native and foreign, was all the King could have wished. As far as the former were concerned, it was not a complete coincidence that the coronation took place shortly before the elections to the new Parliament. Visitors from abroad were duly impressed to discover that England was not at all the barbaric place that they had imagined it to be, cut off for twenty years behind its own iron curtain of republicanism. Henry Fagel, a 'Foreigner at the Court of Charles II', describing a sight-seeing tour of England at the time of the coronation, was astonished at the splendour of palaces such as Windsor and Hampton Court, as an Englishman today might be amazed at the richness of the palaces preserved in Poland or some other Iron Curtain country. And he was particularly impressed by the spectacle of the coronation itself, which excelled in splendour anything he had conceivably expected.[8]

The culmination of the ancient and solemn service in Westminster Abbey was the moment when the King's crown was finally placed on his head by the Archbishop of Canterbury. 'A great shout' began.* Immediately afterwards the whole nobility swore fealty. Thus they 'firmly ascended the throne, and touched the King's Crown, promising by that Ceremony to be ever ready to support it, with all their Power'. It was no empty oath. Within their lifetime, it could be that they would be called upon

* Although Pepys, who had had to get up at four a.m. and had been for hours in the Abbey in his sumptuous velvet suit, needed to piss (as doubtless did some others).[9]

to implement it, as their fathers had. All this took place beneath the watchful eyes of the envoys who packed the gallery, from foreign powers as diverse as Spain and Sweden, Venice and Hamburg, as well as personal representatives of foreign dignitaries such as the Duc d'Orléans.

Even the weather (proverbially unkind to royal occasions in our own day) rallied to the King's support. It had been extremely rainy throughout the previous month, but the day of the coronation itself dawned dry or, as a rising poet, John Dryden, subsequently described it:

> Soft western winds waft o'er the gaudy spring
> And open'd Scenes of flow'rs and blossoms bring
> To grace this happy day, ...

The weather continued dry throughout the ceremonies. If it was not quite balmy enough to justify Dryden's ecstasy, a little over-enthusiasm can be forgiven on his part, in view of the fact that his last public work had been 'Heroical Stanzas' on Cromwell's death. However, in the evening a violent thunderstorm broke out just as the King was leaving Westminster Hall. This satisfied everyone. The superstitious were able to prognosticate a gloomy future for the realm or its King or both from the thunder and lightning; optimists pointed to the auspiciously sunny day.[10]

And still the ceremonies were not done. They were rounded off by an ostentatious post-coronation feast held in Westminster Hall. Here the chivalric ritual extended to the service of the food, with the Earl Marshal, Lord High Steward and Lord High Constable appearing in their coronets, riding richly caparisoned horses, to present the first course. Even the humble Clerks of the Kitchen, who brought up the vast procession of servers, wore black figured satin gowns and velvet caps.

The King's official champion, Sir Edward Dymoke, was there on his white charger, and made a grand entry preceded by trumpeters. Throwing down his gauntlet, he made the traditional challenge: 'If any person of what degree soever, high or low, shall deny, or gainsay our Sovereign Lord King Charles the

Second ... here is his champion, who saith that he lieth, and is a False Traitor.'

This was the very Hall in which twelve years earlier the King's father had been tried for his life. But the ghost of Cromwell did not answer.

At long last the King was able to wash his hands – in water ceremoniously brought to him by the Earl of Pembroke and a host of attendants – and, having done so, depart from Westminster as he had come, by barge along the river Thames.

But there was a fitting epilogue to all this parade of power and pomp 'deemed ... inferior in magnificence to none in Europe'.[11] The King and the Duke of York subsequently presented their coronation robes not to a museum for posterity – but to the theatre. They were used in a play by Sir William Davenant. And in *Henry V* in 1664 (a version by Orrery), Owen Tudor wore the coronation suit of King Charles II. For all the sacred ceremony at its heart, there had after all been a strong element of the charade about the King's gorgeous gold and scarlet crowning.

Henry Fagel had described the English ladies at the coronation with enthusiasm as 'everyone dressed as a Queen'.[12] But the position was in fact vacant; and Court and King alike stood in need of an incumbent. 'It is a truth universally acknowledged', wrote Jane Austen in the nineteenth century, 'that a single man in possession of a good fortune must be in want of a wife.' In the seventeenth century it was a universally acknowledged truth that a single King must be in want of a Queen – although he might expect to acquire the good fortune along with his bride. The concept of monarchy extended beyond the immediate person of the King, if only because the question of the succession could never be overlooked in this age of high and chancy mortality from every kind of disease.

This royal family had recently been depleted by two deaths, both by smallpox: Mary Princess of Orange at the age of twenty-nine, and Harry Duke of Gloucester at the age of twenty-one. The demise of this promising young man, described by Hyde as being 'in truth the finest youth and of the most manly understanding that I have ever known', ranks with the earlier death of his namesake Henry Prince of Wales as being one of the accidental tragedies of the house of Stuart. The death of the fabled Henry Prince of Wales left his younger brother to succeed as King Charles I, with dire results; the removal of the determinedly Protestant Duke of Gloucester from the royal succession (remember the steel with which he combated his mother's Catholicism) was equally fatal. As it was, the Duke of York remained in effect the *only* heir to King Charles II throughout his reign who was both male and legitimate – and wholly English.* But he was first a suspected, then an acknowledged Catholic. If the 'sweet Duke of Gloucester' had lived as an alternative Protestant heir, matters might have gone very differently.

The Duke of York's prestige and importance were inevitably increased by his brother's death. At the same time he had recently forfeited much of his previous popularity in Court circles, as well as his suitability to follow Charles II on the throne, if necessary, by what was generally regarded as a most unfortunate marriage. It was ironic that the lady in question was actually the daughter of Charles' faithful servant Sir Edward Hyde (he had been raised to the rank of Earl of Clarendon at the coronation, by which name he will in future be known). James had seduced Anne Hyde while she was acting as a Maid of Honour to his sister Mary; as a result she became pregnant. James then made a secret contract with Anne and was married to her privately by his chaplain on 3 September 1660.

Once the marriage had taken place, James had second thoughts. Now he behaved in the most ungentlemanly fashion; he ignored the contract and tried to wriggle out of the situation by suggesting that others than himself could have been the father of the child. He wished the marriage to be declared invalid. James' explanation in his Memoirs was that the contract

* There was of course the King's first cousin, Prince Rupert; if not wholly English, he had served the English Crown faithfully on land and at sea during the recent war and was a Protestant. But Rupert was by now over forty and hopes of his marriage – his own and other people's – died away after the Restoration.[13]

had been made 'in the first warmth of his youth' (he was twenty-six).[14] But he was unable to make the mud stick. On 22 October the child was born; it was a boy, who died. The marriage itself was generally known by the end of the year.

The irony lay in the fact that Clarendon himself was furious at the match. Marriage to his own daughter was no part of his elaborate web of marital plans, redolent of diplomatic alliances and wealthy dowries, for the two bachelor princes under his sway. At the same time, he incurred a great deal of odium for having apparently aimed to make his daughter Queen of England. It was unfair, but, given the relationship, natural. Really the only person who came out of the rather squalid incident of the York marriage at all well was King Charles. He refused to have the match declared invalid, which might have been politically wise, saying that it was unkind to Anne Hyde's reputation, to say nothing of her condition. And he ostentatiously visited her during her confinement, showing a lead which the Court reluctantly followed. As for the idea of having Parliament annul the marriage, he refused to allow Parliament to interfere with the succession – a stand for which James would one day be grateful.

Once the coarse jibes against Anne Duchess of York, based on her pregnancy but inspired by the Clarendon connection, had died away, she was able to establish herself as a considerable character at the Restoration Court. She was certainly no beauty: Pepys called her downright plain. But Anne was nevertheless both witty and intelligent, and the French Ambassador went so far as to describe her as having courage, cleverness and energy almost worthy of a king's blood.[15]

The untimely death of the Duke of Gloucester, the unsuitable marriage of the Duke of York: both of these increased the urgency to marry off the King. The eventual choice, the Infanta Catharine of Portugal, was no new candidate. Her father, King John IV, under whom Portugal had become liberated from Spain in 1640, had suggested it long ago when the bride and groom were respectively seven and fourteen. For sentimental reasons, it was pleasant to know that King Charles I had at the time favoured the match. But of course the point of the union to Portugal was very far from nostalgic. Put at its simplest, marriage into the Portuguese royal family brought England down firmly on the Portuguese side against Spain in the long-drawn-out struggle between the two Iberian countries. This contest was influenced by the fact that the young Portuguese King Alfonso was pretender to the Spanish throne through his grandmother the Duchess of Braganza; and his mother, the Queen-Regent of Portugal, was anxious to secure, by whatever means she could, the preservation of the relics of the Portuguese colonial empire (including of course Brazil).

Again, put simply, any support of Portugal was welcome to Spain's other neighbour, aggressive France. By the Peace of the Pyrenees with Spain in 1659, France had bound herself specifically not to aid Portugal; but already her resolute young King Louis XIV was casting ambitious eyes towards the Spanish Netherlands. If peace between Spain and France was not to be lasting, then it suited France to have Portugal, her natural ally against Spain, bolstered up by England. So that Charles' projected match could not only count on French support, but also, by implication, drew England within the French network of European alliances.

Republican England had of course been the official ally of France; in consequence, King Charles had been forced to throw himself on the mercies of Spain. Despite this disagreeable memory and the perfidy of his French relations, the King was by temperament far more in sympathy with the French than with the Spaniards. After his Restoration, he was prepared to let bygones by bygones. Forgiveness was made easier by the fact that the young King Louis XIV, now grasping the reins of power for the first time at roughly the same moment as Charles II was restored, had not been responsible for the French betrayal. The moment the Restoration was effected, the English royal family tilted back contentedly to their French-oriented sympathies. It was a fact underlined by the betrothal of Charles' surviving sister, the beguiling Henriette-Anne, to Louis XIV's brother, Philippe Duc d'Orléans (generally known as Monsieur, as she will now be known as Madame). The marriage took place shortly before the coronation.

Negotiations with the King of Portugal were known to be under way some time in late 1660, probably helped on by the presence of Queen Henrietta Maria, who approved of the match, in England. By February 1661 the Spanish Ambassador was energetically advocating the rival claims of the Hapsburg Princesses of Parma, who would be endowed by his master with a suitably large dowry for the occasion. (However, the Earl of Bristol gave left and right of disapprobation in his report on these young ladies: the elder, he said, was very ugly, and the younger monstrously big.)[16] Undaunted, the Spaniards continued to propose the claim of almost every princess in Europe, it seemed: a Danish Princess, a Princess of Saxe – anyone except the Portuguese Infanta.

King also protested to King. Philip IV of Spain expostulated that such a match cut across a previous Anglo-Spanish agreement. Charles II of England replied curtly that his marrying whomsoever he thought fit should not interrupt this friendship, much less cause 'everlasting war'. It is in this context, incidentally, that the spiteful remark of the Spanish Ambassador that the Infanta Catharine was barren should be seen. As it happened, he turned out to be right; but the prophecy was a brilliant piece of ill-wishing, rather than the product of any intimate medical knowledge, and should not be cited as any kind of evidence.

The Portuguese Ambassador was at least on the right track in emphasizing the dowry of his own candidate. From the first, the English showed themselves mesmerized by the enormous fortune offered with the hand of the Infanta. Augustin Coronel Chacon, known as 'the little Jew', who acted as consular and financial agent to the King in London, had outlined its glittering dimensions to General Monck before the King returned to England.[17] The actual implications of the match played a smaller part. It was as though the economic straits of the Crown had produced a kind of siege economy in which the first essential was to acquire money, any money; the diplomatic consequences could be sorted out later. So that although French support for the marriage was influential, it does not seem to have been crucial, as is sometimes suggested.

The Infanta's portion, dangled before English eyes, was to be two million crowns, or about £360,000 (then), the possession of Tangier on the Mediterranean coast, Bombay on that of

India. At the time, the King had to be shown where Tangier was on the map. It was more to the point that the dowry itself was to be paid in such diverse coins as sugar, Brazilian wood and cash itself; part on the day of the bride's embarkation, the rest in staggered payments. Clarendon swore to the Portuguese Ambassador that the principal inducement to the marriage was the 'piety, virtue and comeliness' of the Infanta: but then gave the game away by asking for Tangier to be handed over 'quickly' to reassure the English....[18]

A proxy courtship was carried out on the King's behalf in Portugal by the English Ambassador, Sir Richard Fanshawe. Charles himself was soon writing as flowery letters as could be managed, not only to the young lady herself but also to her powerful mother. He even made the effort to write in Spanish (the Portuguese Queen was Spanish-born), although he had to ask Clarendon to check his letters over for mistakes. To Catharine he referred to his sanguine feelings for the future; she responded in kind. By May 1661 the King and Clarendon were able to inform the English Parliament that negotiations were complete. Soon Charles in London was signing himself to Catharine in Lisbon: 'The very faithful husband of Your Majesty, whose hand he kisses.'

The odd thing was that no proxy marriage between the pair of royal correspondents, of the kind familiar to European royalties down the ages, had in fact taken place, although the King's language would seem to indicate that it had. Later congratulatory verses, part of a collection presented by Oxford University, made the same assumption, philosophizing thus on proxy marriage:

> Kings have ubiquity, while vulgar minds,
> Like bodies, Nature to one place confines....[19]

But since the Pope had refused to approve the independence of Portugal from Spain, his dispensation for such a ceremony was not asked, and this King at least was vulgarly confined to one place. Catharine was simply designated Queen of England, while remaining in Lisbon.

Nearly a year elapsed before she made the long and stormy sea journey to her new home, escorted by Lord Sandwich in the lucky ship which had restored her husband, the *Royal Charles*. Catharine arrived at Portsmouth on 13 May 1662. One of her first actions was to ask for a cup of tea. It was in its own way a milestone in our social history. It is true that tea-drinking had been known in England before this date but it was extremely rare. The national beverage was ale and that was what the Queen was offered. As no-one who wants a cup of tea has ever been satisfied with a glass of ale (and vice versa), it must have been a low moment. Subsequently Queen Catharine did a great deal to popularize the general drinking of tea; in 1680 Edmund Waller wrote a whimsical poem on the connection between the 'best of herbs' and the 'best of queens':

> Venus her myrtle, Phoebus has his bays,
> Tea both excels which she vouchsafes to praise. . . .

In the meantime, still for the time being tealess, the English worried over the delivery of the dowry, the garrisoning of Tangier and other practical considerations. Once the Queen's arrival was imminent, another practical arrangement preoccupied Clarendon and his master. Some sort of wedding had, finally, to take place. The Queen could not simply *assume* the married state. (Although it might have saved a lot of trouble in the long run if she had.) The question was, what sort of wedding?

Queen Catharine was of course a Catholic, like most of the royal princesses of Europe other than those cold northern ladies disdained by Charles. Her religion had already caused annoyance in those English quarters who disapproved of the Portuguese match in the first place. Yet a Catholic Queen, however irritating, could hardly be rated a cultural shock to seventeenth-century England. There were few alive in England who could remember a time when there had been a Protestant Queen, since James I's consort, Anne of Denmark, became a Catholic convert. A Catholic Queen might therefore be said to be the norm rather than otherwise, while the appurtenances of such a creature, chapels, the Mass, friars, confessors and the like, however distasteful to honest Protestant Englishmen, were at least very familiar to them. In any case, the Portuguese Ambassador had assured King Charles of his bride's docility on the subject: that it was 'true she was a Catholic, and would never depart from her religion; but was totally without that meddling and activity in her nature, which many times made those of that religion troublesome and restless when they came to another country.'[20] In short she was no Henrietta Maria.

In the Privy Council however Clarendon had written some of his masterful notes to King Charles on the subject of the wedding: he must have a Bishop with him when he arrived in Portsmouth, and he must have a Protestant ceremony for the sake of the legitimacy of the children. Queen Catharine, Clarendon had been assured, was prepared to submit to this. The King scribbled back, 'I hope she has consulted the Jesuits.'[21]

'She will do that [which] is necessary for herself and her children,' wrote Clarendon firmly.

And that proved to be the case. A brief and secret Catholic ceremony was held first in Catharine's own room, as a concession to her piety. The legal marriage took place on 21 May* in the Great Chamber of the house of the Governor of Portsmouth (his chapel was too small for the concourse). The King and Queen sat on two specially made thrones, behind a rail to keep off the press of spectators. Catharine wore rose colour, covered in lovers' knots of blue ribbons. Afterwards they were cut off, according to Portuguese tradition, at her request; everyone was given a piece. The lace of her veil was however covered with patriotic emblems of her new country, including Tudor roses.[22] The King presented the Governor's chapel with an altar cloth embroidered with a view of Lisbon, with reciprocal flattery.

After that, things did not go quite so swimmingly. The Queen's state of health did not permit the marriage to be consummated that night. The King jokingly reported to his sister Madame that he thought it was just as well that the long

* The date is wrongly given in the entry in the registry of St Thomas's Parish Church (made to comply with the Commonwealth Act of 1654), preserved today in Portsmouth Cathedral.

sea journey had upset her cycle, for he himself had had such a terrible journey down to Portsmouth that he was afraid that 'matters would have gone stupidly'. It seemed to be a family misfortune – Charles recalled his sister's own wedding night, where exactly the same state of affairs had occurred. Monsieur, to add to his other failings, or perhaps because of them – he was a homosexual who shortly after the wedding abandoned any pretence of being otherwise – had not been understanding about the situation. Added Charles of the eventual consummation, 'Yet I hope I shall entertain her [Catharine] at least better than he did you.'[23]

The one thing which had troubled no-one throughout all these prolonged negotiations towards matrimony – least of all the King – was the character of the bride herself. After doubts about her piety had been set at rest by the Portuguese Ambassador, he considered it enough to describe her, rather casually, as having an exceptionally good and modest nature, and having been brought up in a 'hugely retired' manner.[24]

Convent-bred – and certainly reared in a most secluded fashion, having made very few appearances in the outside world – Catharine of Braganza was already twenty-three years old, which one sour commentator said was like a woman of forty in English terms.* When she was told of her impending marriage, she made one of her rate sorties from the royal palace, to make a religious pilgrimage to some Saints' shrines in Lisbon: not perhaps the best preparation for marriage to King Charles II. The suite of over a hundred people that she brought to England sounded more like the cast of a grandiose opera than something suitable to the informal English way of life: it included numerous confessors, a deaf duena, a Jewish perfumer and a barber. Her ladies-in-waiting in particular – 'six frights', wrote the wicked Comte de Grammont – aroused English national

* She was born on 25 November, the Feast of St Catharine; it was an unfortunate coincidence that by English dating – ten days different – this was close to the Accession Day of Queen Elizabeth, an anniversary which later in the reign became an occasion for Pope-burnings and other manifestations of Protestant extremism.

prejudice, in their vast skirts, known as farthingales, or *gardas Infantas*, because no man could get near them.[25]

It was unkindly rumoured that the Queen herself clung obstinately to these Portuguese fashions, so unalluring to English eyes. In fact, she was on arrival pathetically anxious in all ways to do whatever might please the King, and first set foot on English soil wearing English clothes; it was the Duke of York, out of curiosity or a desire to put her at her ease, who desired her to change back into her own national dress. In *cuisine* Catharine was conservative: there are continual payments to 'Portugall cooks' in the royal accounts. But in costume at least she adapted quickly, showing a coquettish desire to wear man's clothing, which set off her pretty, neat legs and ankles; it was incidentally something she had in common with Nell Gwynn, who chose parts which enabled her to wear breeches on the stage for the same reason. Quite a fashion for a type of seventeenth-century trouser suit followed the Queen's lead – 'women like men' in velvet coats and caps with ribbons. Like many another grand lady, Catharine also enjoyed dressing up in general, as a village maiden, and so forth: the year after her marriage she was described by Pepys as looking 'mighty pretty' in a white-laced waistcoat and crimson short petticoat, her hair dressed *à la negligence*.[26]

Catharine of Braganza also came to enjoy such typically English preoccupations as fishing and picnics. For all her slight frame, she was not unathletic, particularly for one who had been nurtured in such a claustrophobic fashion. Catharine's skill at archery was noted; she was sufficiently interested in the whole sport to become patroness of the Honourable Fraternity of Bowmen. In 1676 its marshal was awarded a heavy silver badge engraved 'Reginae Catharinae Sagittarii' (the Queen was born under the sign of Sagittarius the Archer).

But that of course was once the Queen had learned to relax. The first impression given to the English was of a hieratic, almost doll-like, figure:

> See how unmov'd She views the Crowd and show
> As Stars above behold men's toils below,

wrote James Annesley, son of the Earl of Anglesey, in one of the Oxford University congratulatory verses. Catharine's tiny figure also militated against her at first sight (although she was taller than Queen Henrietta Maria). It is unlikely that King Charles exclaimed that they had brought him a bat, not a woman, when he first saw her: such an unchivalrous remark would have been quite out of character. But the malicious tale does reveal how Catharine must have appeared to the English: small and dark and very, very foreign. 'Swarthy,' wrote Evelyn, adding that she had sticking-out teeth. 'A long nose,' wrote another unsympathetic critic. She even made up or 'painted' in what was considered to be an un-English manner.[27]

As against this, the King himself, the person most intimately concerned, was charitable; 'her face is not so exact as to be called a beauty,' he told Clarendon, 'though her eyes are excellent good, and not anything in her face that in the least degree can shock one. On the contrary she has as much agreeableness in her looks altogether, as ever I saw.' Moreover, Catharine's character passed muster too (this type of analysis was after all the King's speciality). He went on, 'And if I have any skill in physiognomy, which I think I have, she must be as good a woman as ever was born.'[28] Finally, Charles described Catharine as having two other qualities pleasing in a woman, wit, and a most agreeable voice – a fact confirmed by the man appointed as her Chamberlain, Lord Chesterfield, who also called her voice very pleasing.

Yet the first crisis of Queen Catharine's married life nearly undid her.

At the court of King Charles II there was already an uncrowned queen in the shape of Barbara Palmer. Indeed, the Duchess of Richmond had already nicknamed her Jane Shore after the mistress of Edward IV, and hoped she would come to the same bad end (Richard III forced Jane Shore to do public penance as a harlot after Edward's death). Barbara, later Countess of Castlemaine and later still Duchess of Cleveland, has had a bad press from historians who have been only too well aware of her greed, extravagance and tempers and have been therefore inclined to agree with John Evelyn's verdict – 'the curse of the

Nation'. They have not had the opportunity to admire at first hand her sheer physical appeal, like that of a magnificent animal. Grammont described her as having 'the greatest reputation of the court beauties'; Sir John Reresby called her the finest woman of her age, while Bishop Burnet referred to her as 'a woman of great beauty' whose looks, even at the age of forty-two, were extraordinary.[29] Pepys made her out of all the royal mistresses his firm favourite: she was his 'lovely Lady Castlemaine'.

Pepys went as far as to buy a portrait of his pin-up, one of the many copies made by Sir Peter Lely for admirers of the great courtesan. Lely adored painting Barbara. With her heavy-lidded, slanting eyes and sensuous sulky mouth, it is Barbara of all the Restoration beauties who calls to mind those immortal lines of Pope:

> Lely on animated Canvas stole
> The sleepy Eye that spoke the melting soul...

The sight of her smocks and her pretty linen petticoats edged with lace drying in the Privy Garden affected Pepys so headily that even today his account of the sight retains the erotic thrill it gave the great diarist.[30] For all Lely's animated canvas, it is from this contemporary admiration, as from Homer's description of the old men turning their heads to watch Helen as she walked along the walls of Troy, that one learns more than from any portrait.

Barbara had great buoyancy of spirit: the sort of gusto which prompted her in later years to take as a lover not only the playwright Wycherley, but also Jacob the Rope-dancer; his gymnastics inspired in her an adventurous desire to know how he might be 'under his tumbling clothes'.[31] Another recipient of her favours was the actor Cardonnell Goodman, who would shout out 'Is my Duchess come?' before allowing the curtains to rise in the theatre. The act of love on which her fortunes were founded was certainly no chore to Barbara – later the satirists would even use the word insatiable. In youth however the impression is of enjoyment rather than of excess, and the kind of magnetism such unabashed hedonism always gives its possessor.

Perhaps her famous temper came from the same uncontrolled spirit. Certainly Barbara could be a termagant when aroused; the King, like many another man, quailed before her furies and gave in to them. He did not however find them particularly lovable, and as she grew older there was a law of diminishing returns in such things. Nevertheless, Barbara when young was clearly great fun. She kept a good table, as reported by the French Ambassador (a connoisseur).[32] She also showed heart as well as temper, being, for instance, the only Court lady to go to the assistance of a child hurt when a scaffold collapsed at the theatre.

Early reports coupled Barbara's name with that of Lord Chesterfield, and at one point she was said to have 'talked wantonly' (like many others) to the Duke of York. Her husband, Roger Palmer, to whom she was married at the age of eighteen, appears as a sensitive and somewhat gloomy figure, his depression hardly surprising in view of the outrageous cuckolding by his young wife. In the autumn of 1661 he accepted the title of Earl of Castlemaine, with the further humiliation that its inheritance was limited to 'heirs of his body gotten on Barbara Palmer his now wife' – making the source of the honour quite clear. Shortly after the birth of Barbara's second child by the King in June 1662, the new Earl separated from her, having first caused the boy to be baptized a Catholic. Barbara was to become a Catholic herself. But at the time she had the baby ostentatiously rechristened in the Anglican Church.

Some time in 1662 Barbara was accorded her own apartments within Whitehall. The accommodation included nurseries which proved most necessary since she bore a total of six children, all but the last acknowledged by the King. After her conversion to Catholicism in 1663 an oratory was provided. When quizzed on this *volte-face*, King Charles remarked with spirit that he never concerned himself with the souls of ladies, but with their bodies, in so far as they were gracious enough to allow him. The popular reaction – if the Catholic Church gained no more from her than

Janssens' painting *The Ball at the Hague* shows Charles II dancing with his sister Mary, Princess of Orange, on the eve of his Restoration.

Charles II being welcomed in triumph by the Dutch at Delft, before setting sail for England, from Lower's *Voyage of Charles II*, 1660.

Charles II depicted in an initial in a Plea Roll, 1661.

The coronation of Charles II in Westminster Abbey, 23 April 1661.

Catharine of Braganza, painted during her first years in England, by Lely.

Medallion celebrating Charles II's marriage to Catharine of Braganza, 21 May 1662, by George Bower.

King Charles and Queen Catharine arriving at Hampton Court after their marriage, by Dirck Stoop.

The marriage certificate of Charles II and Catharine of Braganza, now preserved in Portsmouth Cathedral (the date is wrongly given as 22 May).

Our Most Gracious Soveraigne Lord
Charles the Second by the Grace of God King of Great Brittaine France and Ireland Defender of the faith
And the most Illustrious Princesse Dona Catarina Infanta of Portugall daughter to the deceased Don Juan the Fourth and sister to the Present Don Alphonso King of Portugall were married at Portsmouth uppon thursday the two & twentieth day of May in the yeare of our Lord God 1662 being in the fourteenth yeare of his Maties reigne by the Right Reverend Father in God Gilbert Lord Bishop of London Deane of his Maties Chappel Royall in the presence of severall of the Nobility of his Maties Dominions & of Portugall
Anno Dni 1662

Mr Rose, the royal gardener, presenting Charles II with a pineapple probably in front of Dorney Court, Windsor. Painting by Thomas Danckerts.

The Royal Escape, as the ship in which Charles II left England in October 1651 was rechristened, painted by William van de Velde after the Restoration, at the request of the King.

'Madame' – Henriette-Anne, Duchesse d'Orléans, Charles II's favourite sister, by Samuel Cooper.

William III of Orange, nephew of Charles II, by Adriaen Hanneman; this painting and that of his mother, Princess Mary, hung in the King's Bedchamber at Whitehall.

James, Duke of York, and his first wife, Anne Hyde, daughter of the Earl of Clarendon, painted by Lely, probably soon after their secret marriage was made public in late 1660.

Charles II in his box at Windsor Races, 24 August 1684. Engraving by Francis Barlow, 1687.

A game of real tennis, a sport of which Charles II was a passionate exponent, by Comenius, 1659.

Playing the game of pall-mall, which became very popular in St James's Park, the course lying along the site of the present Mall.

the Church of England lost, 'the Matter is not Much' – displayed less charm.[33]

It was the coincidence of the Queen's arrival, Barbara's second pregnancy, and the resignation of Roger Castlemaine from his role as official husband, which brought about the unhappy 'Bedchamber Crisis' of the summer of 1662. After her marriage in Portsmouth, Catharine was welcomed to the capital with all the pomp due to a royal consort. John Evelyn called the floating procession which carried her from Hampton Court to Whitehall at the end of August the most magnificent ever seen on the Thames (although an eye-witness told Ormonde that the Queen, in the middle of it all, looked like a prisoner being carried in a Roman triumph).[34] But already at Hampton Court 'my lady Barbary' had exercised those powers she knew well that she possessed over the King.

On a petty level, she refused to light a fire outside her bedroom door to welcome the Queen – the only person not to do so. More flagrantly, Barbara insisted that her latest *accouchement* should take place at Hampton Court during what was in fact the royal honeymoon. Worse was to follow. The trouble was that Barbara at this stage understood perfectly how to manage Charles – she appealed on this occasion not so much to his lust, but to that other potent emotion he felt towards the female sex, a sense of guilt. Perhaps the feeling was rooted in a suppressed dislike and resentment of his own mother; perhaps, more simply, in the strength of his physical desires, which he knew to be unaccompanied by love. We shall certainly meet this sense of guilt later, in his treatment of his wife. Now it worked towards Barbara's, not Catharine's, advantage.

All his life, King Charles' method of dealing with a woman's complaints or tears was to attempt to cozen her with something to cheer her up, as a parent gives a lollipop to a child. Where Catharine was concerned, her piety gave him plenty of opportunities. Although normally a lazy correspondent, he was for ever sending off to his sister in France for little objects of devotion to please her. Catharine had such a passion for relics that she had brought them with her in a series of great coffers which had to be cloaked in red velvet cloths embroidered with the royal arms of England and Portugal. Barbara was made of sterner stuff. In a series of hideous scenes Barbara demanded, besought, and implored Charles to make her Lady of the Bedchamber to the new Queen. Eventually, out of pity for her abandoned, husbandless, pregnant condition (and worn out by the scenes), King Charles succumbed sufficiently to agree. He explained rather lamely that 'he had undone this lady and ruined her reputation, which had been fair and untainted till her friendship with him'.[35]

In doing so he risked an extraordinary insult to his wife. Catharine might have been brought up 'hugely retired', but she was not a fool, while the Portuguese Ambassador in London was an exceptionally well informed and worldly man, to whose machinations some critics ascribed the King's marriage. Catharine certainly recognized Barbara's name, having been doubtless warned of her existence in advance, and, on seeing it in the list of Ladies of the Bedchamber presented for her agreement, crossed it angrily out. However, when she was first presented with Barbara in person, she received her rival cordially, her poor understanding of English preventing her from realizing who Barbara was. The moment she discovered, Catharine's eyes filled with tears of rage; her nose began to bleed and she collapsed to the floor in hysterics.

King Charles shrugged his shoulders and sent Clarendon to reason with her. One dreads to think of the task of this elderly Anglican, left to explain to a devout Catholic princess exactly what she was going to have to tolerate in the name of marriage and concord. At first, Clarendon failed totally. He merely elicited further torrents of tears and threats to return to Portugal. The scandal reverberated. Madame in France was outspokenly shocked by her brother's behaviour to his wife. 'It is said here that she is grieved beyond measure,' she wrote, 'and to speak frankly I think it is with reason.'[36]

It took Queen Catharine a little time to discover that hysteria and threats were no way to play her cards where Charles was concerned – those were best left to Barbara, the mistress. In repose, Catharine discovered the strength of her own hand: not only was sheer goodness of character her strongest suit, but it was also as effective in its own way, where Charles was concerned, as sensuality and tantrums.

A year after the marriage, relations between the royal couple had settled down most amicably, thanks to Catharine's tact and restraint. Once she had actually supped in Barbara's apartments, the crisis was over – although to the end of her days as Queen of England, Catharine remained extremely touchy on the subject of royal protocol in so far as it concerned her own position. As late as 1684 tears stood in her eyes when she found the King's mistress, Louise Duchess of Portsmouth, waiting at dinner as Lady of the Bedchamber, 'contrary to custom', although in other ways she favoured Louise. More immediately, she formed a tactful friendship with Charles' bastard son James; but when he was created Duke of Monmouth, and had the baton sinister, which proclaimed his illegitimate birth, omitted from his coat of arms, Catharine felt it necessary to protest. (A second grant of arms included it.)[37]

It was of course far pleasanter for the Queen to join in the fun of the Court than to mope disapprovingly with her Portuguese ladies. Soon Charles was praising her 'simplicity, gentleness and prudence' to Catharine's mother – it was the third quality which had been lacking on her arrival. To Madame he spoke with a slightly stunned respect of her piety, how she would say the great office of the Breviary every day, as well as that of Our Lady, *and* go to chapel.[38] In the autumn of 1663 Catharine became violently ill, possibly with peritonitis: the King became quite frenzied with anxiety over her condition (although he still managed to sup nightly with Barbara).

She learnt to speak pretty, broken English, rather like that practised by another foreign princess, also a Katharine, prattling of her 'bilbo' to Henry v. It amused Charles to tease his Catharine by teaching her English swearwords without telling her what they meant, and then listening to her innocently repeating them. He also, like many unfaithful husbands, managed to work up a fit of illogical jealousy against Edward Montagu, the Queen's Master of the Horse, because he was thought to have squeezed her hand; Montagu was sacked. In time, Catharine was notably more spontaneous with Charles in public – grown quite 'debonair', as it was described; she even hugged him in public, something unthinkable to that grave Portuguese Infanta who had arrived at Portsmouth. There is also a pleasantly tart air about her exchange with Barbara, as reported by Pepys, in the summer of 1663. Barbara commented on the length of time the Queen had been under her dresser's hands: 'I wonder your Majesty can have the patience to sit so long a-dressing.' To which Catharine replied, 'I have so much reason to use patience that I can very well bear with it. . . .'[39] It was, in the contemporary slang, a considerable 'wipe' or put-down; in more ways than one the Queen was learning how to survive at her husband's Court.

Only one thing was lacking: an heir. It was not for lack of effort on the King's part. It was reported that he slept regularly with the Queen. (All contemporary evidence indicates that, while Charles kept many mistresses, he also made love to his own wife a great deal – no doubt this contributed to the marital *status quo*.) But royal brides were watched for signs of pregnancy virtually from their wedding night. Any failure to conceive immediately was converted into total barrenness by the unkind rumour-mongers within and without the Court. It was suggested that the Queen was barren as early as December 1662, surely a premature conclusion. Catharine had only been married a year when she was to be found taking the waters at Tunbridge Wells, as her mother-in-law had done a generation earlier. Catharine took the waters repeatedly that summer without success. Later she turned to the spa at Bath.

It was hardly surprising that, during her severe illness of the autumn of 1663, the delirious Queen raved of pregnancy and childbirth. To the King at her bedside, Catharine confided that she had been delivered of a 'very ugly' boy.

'No, it's a pretty boy,' Charles answered gently.

'If it be like you, it is a fine boy indeed,' whispered the Queen. There followed further rambling remarks on the same subject: at one time the Queen thought she had three children, including a girl who did look like the King.

'How do the children?' she enquired anxiously.[40]

The King might equip her chapel, redecorate her apartments,

employing Catharine's favourite greens and yellows, start to build her a new palace at Greenwich – none of this could bring the Queen true security or happiness without the longed-for heir. Yet for all the impatience of the Court gossips, there was a precedent. The example of Henrietta Maria was in itself encouraging – four years of marriage without conception, followed by a quiverful of healthy children. For the present, Catharine continued to justify Dryden's high praise of her and of her devotion to Charles:

> The best of Queens, the most obedient wife...
> His life the theme of her eternal prayer.

The Marvell who called her an 'Ill natured little goblin ... designed/For nothing but to dance and vex mankind' reflected his own dislike of the royal family, rather than the prevailing opinion of Catharine's character.

The day would come when Catharine's unarguable goodness would stand her in good stead. By the time of the Popish Plot, even the prickly, suspicious English had been so won to the side of their little foreign Catholic Queen that she was preserved from serious harm throughout this whole inflamed period. No-one could seriously believe ill of her. This was a major achievement in such an age, and can be compared with the very different treatment earned by the equally Catholic and foreign Henrietta Maria.

King Charles, in view of his preoccupation with the study of physiognomy, must have been delighted that his first impression of her character proved so accurate.

CHAPTER FOURTEEN

The Dutch Business

> 'All the news now is what will become of the Dutch business, whether war or peace. We all seem to desire it, as thinking ourselves to have advantages at present over them; but for my part I dread it.'
>
> Samuel Pepys, *Diary*, 30 April 1664

On 8 May 1661 King Charles II opened the newly elected Parliament: it was twenty years since a reigning English monarch had given the traditional speech from the throne. It was more than twenty years since there had been a legally elected Parliament. A comment was made on the youth of the members. 'I will keep them till their beards grow,' replied King Charles ominously.[1] And he was as good as his word. This body, known as the Cavalier Parliament, would yield little to its predecessor in longevity, for it was not to be dissolved until 1679.

Yet its first tasks were still redolent of the past. For all the valiant work of the Convention Parliament, there remained much to achieve in the nature of settlement for this new body, quite apart from confirming the acts of its predecessor. One outstanding question was of course religion. That wonderfully open, peaceful desire of Breda, that no-one should be 'disquieted or called in question' for their religious opinions, so long as they did not disturb the peace, still remained to be implemented after the fiasco of the previous autumn. What finally emerged as a religious settlement – the so-called Clarendon Code enacted between 1662 and 1665 – was however as far from the heady spirit of Breda as could be imagined. Only two-and-a-half years divided the Declaration of Breda from the first Act of the Clarendon Code, but it might have been an aeon.

The Clarendon Code was in fact a direct reversion to the harsh laws promulgated by the Puritans against the Church of England: such, sadly, was to be the Anglican revenge. It embraced a number of provisions. The Corporation Act, for example, excluded from municipal bodies all those who refused to take the sacrament according to the rites of the Church of England. These rites themselves were later defined by the Act of Uniformity to include not only episcopal government, but a standard liturgy: it was in essence a reinforcement of the Act of 1559, which had been generally enforced up till 1640. It was not even necessary to pass a new Act penalizing those who refused to adhere to the rites: the old Act of the reign of Queen Elizabeth I came happily to hand. The way was paved for the Conventicle Act; whereas the Act of Uniformity penalized those who did not attend Anglican services, the Conventicle Act penalized those who worshipped elsewhere. The subsequent Five Mile Act harried the nonconformist ministers by forbidding them to live in certain areas.

To understand this rigidity, one has to appreciate that it was certainly greater than Clarendon had contemplated, for all that the code bears his name. There is much argument over the exact nature of Clarendon's Anglicanism and how far he was genuinely prepared to exercise tolerance to dissenters.[2] What is however unarguable is the enormous decline of official toleration from the Breda high point to the Clarendon Code low, a decline to which Clarendon the man certainly acceded. We have also seen how staunchly he defended Anglicanism under attack during the Interregnum, how bitterly he resented the compromise with the Covenanters.

Breda itself had represented nonetheless a new deal. Yet almost immediately Clarendon found himself occupying that treacherous political territory, the middle ground. As plots and conspiracies, many of them found amongst the dissenters, darkened the political horizon, it was easy for Clarendon to revert to the exclusive Anglicanism which in his heart of hearts he had probably never really deserted.

For these measures King Charles himself held no brief at all. They represented if anything the exact reverse of what he conceived as the best religious settlement. Quickly he made his own position clear, by proposing a Declaration of Indulgence which would allow him to exempt certain individuals from the effects of the Act of Uniformity. To the fury of the Court and King (but not to that of Clarendon, who had thought it folly), the measure failed to pass through the Lords. 'That which shocks most people in it is the favourable mention of Roman Catholics,' wrote the King's rising new assistant, Henry Bennet.[3]

In August 1662 nearly a thousand nonconformist incumbents of livings had to vacate them or wrestle with their consciences for ever more. The Victorian division of 'church and chapel' was for the first time introduced into the fabric of English society, as nonconformity became a social force of its own, albeit a deprived one. And there was nothing whatsoever the King could do about it. William Denton, one of the King's physicians and a political writer, described a significant incident in that same August 1662. Some Presbyterian ministers visited Charles as 'humble suitors' for an indulgence against the laws. They ended up before some judges who declared that the King could not dispense with an Act of Parliament. 'So,' commented Denton, 'their cake is dough at present.'[4]

The King's cake was in an equivalent condition. The rejection of the sovereign's own measure, the Declaration of Indulgence, showed how ineffective the King was to control the Parliamentary will, once it ran contrary to his own.

Only one body of dissenters actually managed to derive benefit from the Clarendon Code. This was the Anglo-Jewish community.[5] A series of historical accidents, as well as the genial nature of Charles II, contributed to this. The Jews had been expelled from England at the end of the thirteenth century, but had nevertheless been resettling secretly in the country for many years until their lot publicly improved under the Commonwealth. Cromwell was philo-semitic for philosophical reasons; practically, he also employed Jews in his intelligence service. It was therefore on his 'nod', as Lord Protector, that the Jews' presence in England was once more tacitly acknowledged. However, a large proportion of the English merchant community remained resolutely anti-semitic from traditional motives of commercial rivalry: to the great distress of the Jews' leaders, they did not secure an official recognition of their position.

King Charles II was not particularly philosophically inclined towards – or against – the Jews: such was not the measure of the man. But he was kind and he was tolerant. He had another useful quality, gratitude, and, like Cromwell, he too was practical. In exile he had promised certain Royalist Jews in Amsterdam toleration in return for a loan: 'When God shall restore us ... we shall extend that protection to them which they can reasonably expect and abate that rigour of the Laws which is against them in our several dominions.' He may also have been aided by Augustin Coronel Chacon – 'the little Jew' – later agent to the King of Portugal in London. In the summer of 1660 the King's personal repute with the Jewish leaders was high. Conversations with the then powerful Monck produced this verdict: '*Segundo todos dizem he sua Benignidade tanta que nào se nesesitava de medianero algum.*' (According to what everyone says his good will is such that no intermediary is necessary).[6]

For all this, the atmosphere immediately after the Restoration was tense so far as the Anglo-Jewish community was concerned. For they were still without written permission to resettle. Although their synagogue in Cree Lane became one of the tourist sights of London (the ever-curious Pepys paid it two visits, and Gentile women made nuisances of themselves gaping) it was still theoretically possible to eject the Jews once more. The frowning rivalry of the English merchants remained a threat, and there were hostile references in the House of Commons. The Jews felt harassment to be on the increase. Then the Conventicle Act, that part of the Clarendon Code forbidding any religious assembly not in accordance with the laws of the Church of England, offered a chance to the Jews' enemies: no synagogue could possibly fit in with its provisions. First, Paul Ruycart threatened the Jewish leaders with removal under the new law. Then the Earl of Berkshire, son of the King's old governor, intervened in a manner which was hardly more attractive. He offered to intercede with the King on the Jews' behalf – but they would have to come to a speedy financial arrangement with him first, otherwise 'he will endeavour and prosecute the seizure of their estates'. In short, it was blackmail. Desperately, the Jewish leaders decided to go directly to the King. Their petition reminded him of their good behaviour and asked that they might remain 'under the like Protection with the rest of your Majesty's subjects'.

An unpublished Hebrew letter from Rabbi Jacob Sasportas to Rabbi Josiah Pardo of Rotterdam describes the incident: 'We live at a time in which God has seen fit greatly to ameliorate the condition of his people, bringing them forth from the general condition of serfdom into freedom, and to set them beneath the authority of one appropriate indeed to hold them in a subjection that is itself the essence of liberty [that is, Charles II]: specifically, in that we are free to practise our own true religion.... A further miracle has been vouchsafed us in these last days. Two nobles, being themselves in possession of access to the royal council, approached us purporting to have been given authority over our persons and property. We requested them to give us time, and we apprised the King, who chuckled and spat at the business; and a written statement was issued from him, duly signed, affirming that no untoward measures had been or would be initiated against us, and that "they [the Jews] should not look towards any protector other than his Majesty: during the continuance of whose lifetime they need feel no trepidation because of any sect that might oppose them, inasmuch as he himself would be their advocate and assist them with all his power." Blessed be the Lord....' So Charles II implemented that promise made in exile.

On 22 August 1664 the Jews trading in England received from the Privy Council the precious, long-sought document, an Order in Council, by which they might 'promise themselves the effects of the same favour as formerly they have had, so long as they demean themselves peaceably and quietly with due obedience to His Majestie's laws and without scandal to his Government'.[7] Charles II, as good as his word, continued to act generously towards the Jews, granting letters of endenization (that is, moderated naturalization) with an open hand, so that the Jewish community increased and flourished in his reign. Recognition of their religious status was further granted in 1673.

If only the King could have acted in a similar manner towards all those dissenters living 'peaceably and quietly' within his dominions! Such was certainly his inclination, and it was the good fortune of the Jews that they at least were able to benefit from it. Catholics, because held to be politically dangerous (which no one considered the Jews to be), were another matter.

Parliament was the bane. The basic trouble was with its composition. The newly elected body was subject almost immediately to an enormous turnover.[8] Part of this was due to natural (noble) wastage: a quantity of MPs who were eldest sons of peers replaced their fathers in the House of Lords between 1661 and 1667. Other MPs, of proven loyalty, were sent to the Lords as a reward. By 1664 forty-eight seats had changed their occupants and by the fall of Clarendon in 1667 well over a hundred. A body chosen in a moment of popular acclaim was subtly if unintentionally transformed. As a result, King Charles found himself reaping a bleak harvest. He could not in the end reconcile, in an age when the national divisions turned out to be great, and the art of parliamentary management was not yet understood.

On 30 January 1662, a day dedicated to the solemn commemoration of the murder of the late King, Pepys reported, 'All people discontented, some that the King doth not gratify them enough; and the others, Fanatiques of all sorts, that the King doth take away their liberty of conscience....' By April 1663 Parliament was capable of being described by the same source as being 'in a very angry pettish mood'.

It is true that 1664 saw the repeal of one Triennial Act and the introduction of a new one. It would prove a remarkably convenient victory for the Crown, even if the fact was not realized at the time. The Triennial Act of 1641 had laid down that a King should meet Parliament once every three years and its passing had been considered a notable concession by Charles I. The Act of 1664, however, referred to that of 1641 as 'in derogation of his Majesty's just rights and prerogative', as a result of which it might 'much endanger the peace and safety of his Majesty and all his liege people ...'. In the future, while it was regarded as right that no more than three years should elapse between Parliaments, it was left to the King to secure this happy state of affairs; no procedure was suggested for compelling him. This victory was the result of clever manœuvring on the part of the Crown, playing on those general fears regarding 'peace and safety' to which the Act alluded. Yet the Crown's tactics – proceedings were pushed ahead rapidly to avoid a full house – were aimed at this single success, rather than general Parliamentary management.[9]

The King's policy towards the House of Lords did nothing to reverse this effect created in the Commons.[10] It was Clarendon, not the King, who was eager to readmit the Anglican Bishops to the seats from which they had been expelled in 1641 – the King's Catholic friends, such as Lord Bristol, feared for their effect on Catholic toleration. And, unlike his father and his brother, Charles was not free with his new creations. After the first rewards for loyalty were over, creations only outweighed extinctions over his whole reign by nine; only ten peers were created between 1662 and 1670. As a result, the House of Lords during this period was once again by no means the docile Royalist body which might have been expected. Had not thirty of its members fought against Charles I? It would be a powerful hostile element in the fall of Clarendon. The fuss over the Irish Castle Bill, in which Buckingham kept the House of Lords talking till the candles ran out, was a typical example of the unruly paths down which these post-Restoration peers could stray.

There was then little appreciation of the importance of the composition of Parliament in the 1660s. This did not mean that no effort at all was made to carry through the royal policies. In Clarendon's efforts to form some kind of Court party in the Commons – rather than in later Whiggery – have been sought the origins of the English party system.[11] Through these manœuvres a new kind of man emerged to represent the King's interests in Parliament. Such a figure was Henry Bennet, created Baron Arlington in 1665 (by which name he will for simplicity's sake be known).

Arlington had little in common with the magisterial figures who had supported, advised and even overborne the young King in exile. Twelve years older than the King, ten years younger than Clarendon, he was in essence a civil servant. Clarendon wrote of him crossly that he 'could dictate; he could not lead'. But Arlington could also serve, and that was the type of man the King was beginning to need in an age where the theoretical rights of King and Parliament were amorphous, yet their practical relationship had to be hammered out day by day. Burnet noted that Arlington had the 'art of observing the King's temper, and managing it beyond all the men of that time', a quality he used to good effect once he had been given the Privy Purse; in October 1662 he replaced the ageing Nicholas as Secretary of State.

Arlington had a particular love of and interest in Spain, having begun his career on a diplomatic mission there in 1657. Soon the affairs of Spain, France, Portugal and Holland were channelled through him rather than the other Secretary of State, Sir William Morrice; Arlington taking advantage of his knowledge of languages, an attribute not shared by all his English contemporaries. With his rich dress, like that of a Spanish grandee, his air of formality described as 'his Castilian bearing', a strange piece of black sticking-plaster across his nose (the relic of a war wound), Arlington was something of an outward oddity at the Court of King Charles. But the intimacy he soon enjoyed with the King was based on usefulness: he was given a lodging from which he could easily reach the royal apartments by a private staircase. As time would show, it was the subservient Arlington, not the magisterial Clarendon, who represented the type of the King's advisers in the future.

For one thing, the King did not share Clarendon's great belief in the Privy Council as an instrument.[12] In Clarendon's declared opinion, this body was 'the most sacred, and hath the greatest authority in the government next the person of the King'. He envisaged a constitution in which the legislature consisted of the King in Parliament and the executive of the King in Council – with the two completely separate. Although we might be tempted to think that he occupied the role of Prime Minister,

Clarendon himself considered the idea of an official chief adviser highly un-English: it was exemplified by Richelieu and Mazarin across the Channel, as the French origin of the words *premier ministre* indicated.

To Clarendon it was Parliament which represented the danger, and the powerful aristocrats there who might try to exercise control over the King, as they had done in the previous reign. How much more desirable to Clarendon appeared a Privy Council (dominated of course by himself), which would withdraw from Parliament, for instance, control of the Treasury and the Navy. In Clarendon's view, Parliament was there to vote the money – but the Council was there to spend it.

But to King Charles II, aristocratic control via the Privy Council was scarcely more appealing than that by Parliament. When the King expatiated in 1664 on his affection for Parliaments, his honeyed words were not pure hypocrisy. 'I need not tell you how much I love Parliaments,' he declared. 'Never King was so much beholden to Parliaments as I have been. . . .' There was much truth in the sentiment. Officially, Monck's part in restoring him was now forgotten. He had been, if anything, restored by Parliament. He certainly preferred the concept of a Parliament to that of a Council, which, being closer to the person of the King, was potentially more disagreeable. When Queen Henrietta Maria complained of the Privy Council that it 'shadowed the King too much, and usurped too much of his authority and too often superseded his own commands', she was expressing a valid point from the monarchical point of view.[13]

So the relationship between the King and Clarendon was not entirely easy, for all the jocularity of their scribbled exchanges within the Privy Council itself:

Clarendon to the King on a prospective visit to Tunbridge: 'I suppose you will go with a light Train.'

King Charles: 'I intend to take nothing but my night bag.'

Clarendon: 'Yes, you will not go without forty or fifty horse.'

The King: 'I count that part of my night bag. . . .'

The religious settlement had aroused a passion, if a frustrated one, in the King. He showed a great deal less day-to-day interest in the settlement of those vast tracts of his kingdom, Ireland and Scotland. He had never visited Ireland, and it therefore exercised over him no powerful memories, good or bad. If anything, he was inclined to be favourable to those Catholic Irish who had supported his father, many of whom had served under him in the army of exile; in general, he had found them an agreeable lot, and in certain cases, such as Theobald Taaffe (now Lord Carlingford), real friendship had grown up.

The Duke of Ormonde, a man of great wisdom and equity, echoed this feeling for the loyalties and wrongs of the Catholic Irish – although himself a Protestant. He was determined to bring about a land settlement where the Catholic Irish, and those who had served in the Army in support of the late King in particular, would not find their claims ignored in favour of the Protestants, soldiers and adventurers who had merely supported the new King's restoration. In Ireland this aroused unhappy memories of Ormonde's Treaty of 1649, which had been surrounded by bitter controversy. In England Ormonde proved to be a lone voice amongst the King's other advisers, including Clarendon, who were happy with the status quo in Ireland – either because it suited them economically, or perhaps because it caused less trouble. For all Ormonde's efforts, justice was not done to the Catholic Irish. Even though Catholics were restored to trading privileges in 1661, the land settlement of Ireland remained very much as it had been in Cromwellian times: under the control of a Protestant ascendancy.

If Ireland to King Charles was a far-away country of which he knew nothing, Scotland was a country which he knew too well – and from which he hoped to remain as far away as possible. To Clarendon King Charles remarked carelessly in March 1662, 'For my part, rebel for rebel, I had rather trust a Papist rebel than a Presbyterian one.' The Lord Chancellor retorted, 'The difference is, that you have wiped out the memory of the rebellion of the one, whilst the other is liable to all the reproaches.' But in truth Charles had no memory of the Catholic rebellion. In his 'Gracious Message' to his Irish subjects, issued shortly before his Restoration, he assured them that their former treasons to King Charles I were washed away; he quoted the Biblical doctrine by which there was more rejoicing over one lost lamb than over all the other ninety-nine.[14] But Ireland was not Charles II's lost lamb. Scotland, if anything, could claim that honour. And nothing about Scotland, lost or found, caused him to rejoice. The subject of Presbyterianism still aroused sufficient ire in him after his Scottish experience, ten years back but never to be forgotten, for him to mask it in another of his characteristic pieces of mockery. Was it possible, he asked, for a man to be a Presbyterian and a gentleman? No doubt he carried Samuel Butler's satire on the Presbyterians, *Hudibras*, in his pocket (and protected its publication by royal warrant) out of the same teasing animosity.

As Ormonde was to Ireland, Lauderdale was to Scotland. But the two men were of very different calibre. Lauderdale, it is true, had force, an energy nearing on the manic, belied by his indolent appearance, coarse tongue and coarser habits; his period of imprisonment after Worcester had also been spent, rather surprisingly, in religious study and meditation. In his own way he was very much a Scot and later displayed a genuine concern for the future of his native land as a nation, not merely as an English appendage. But at the time of the Restoration, Lauderdale also believed in a healthy and curative measure of revenge. At all events, Argyll was publicly executed, which may have satisfied Lauderdale and at the bottom of his heart not displeased the King – who did not try to save him – but was scarcely a healing gesture. An Act Rescissory also swept away a number of liberties to which Scots had become accustomed.

However, Lauderdale's attitude to the Covenant in Scotland was at least healthily pragmatic. He suggested to the King that he should denounce it in public, but in private should leave matters very much as they were. This, one must believe, would have accorded with Charles' general dislike of any policy which involved him thinking about Scotland and the Scots for longer than was necessary. Unfortunately, both Middleton and Clarendon showed more idealism – and more obstinacy. Middleton was convinced that it was essential to restore episcopacy as soon as possible; a view to which it was easy to get Clarendon's agreement.

It was left to Lauderdale to watch like a vulture as Middleton tottered and finally fell; when Middleton introduced an unwise Act of Billeting, Lauderdale was able to present it as an attack on the King's prerogative. In the meantime, government policy on episcopacy foundered, as so often before, on the rock of the Scottish Covenant. Yet another reaction against episcopalian church rule – the Pentland Rising of 1666 – suggested that all the lessons concerning seventeenth-century Scotland had been learned in vain.

While the Catholic Irish people resigned themselves to an ominously unfair land settlement, and the Presbyterian Scots refused to resign themselves in the slightest bit to the bishops they so much disliked, King Charles himself won the hearts of his English people at least by concentration on the fourth quarter of his dominions – the sea. Here on one level there was splendid sport to be had. Charles, with his brother James, was responsible for introducing yachting to the English. It will be remembered how impressed the King had been with that Dutch craft (in fact a yacht) which had brought him from Breda to Delft, and how he had been presented with a replica – paid for by the Dutch East India Company. To this hundred-ton Dutch-built vessel, the *Mary*, falls the honour of founding the British yachting industry.[15] It was soon copied, virtually identically, by the King's shipbuilder Peter Pett, at a total cost of £1,335: although Pepys, who considered the *Mary* 'one of the finest things that ever I saw for neatness and room in so small a vessel', was sceptical whether Pett would succeed in his self-confessed aim 'to outdo this for the honour of his country'.

Soon yachts were all the rage. But these 'pleasure-boats', as they were alternatively called, still retained a distinctively warlike appearance, like the Dutch yachts of the time, with their eight guns and their crews of thirty men. Prince Rupert's yacht *Fanfan* even took part in an engagement during the Dutch War. This did not stop the Prince referring to the King's passion as part of the general levity of the new royal set: 'The King, with his characteristic frivolity, had a yacht moored opposite Whitehall in which he might fancy himself at sea. The childish hobby was appropriately called *The Folly*, and aboard this yacht was one of the many lounging places of the court.'[16] But age was making the former swash-buckling commander cantankerous.

To us today, these yachts would appear more like 'yachts of state', such as the modern royal yacht *Britannia*, rather than the pleasure craft at Cowes. Expenditure on them was considerable, even lavish. Some of their names – *Catharine*, *Henrietta* – gracefully echoed those of the royal ladies who were officially close to Charles' heart. The *Greyhound* evoked a tougher image. Later Charles descended *de haut en bas* with a yacht called the *Fubbs*: his pet name (based on the old English word for chubby) for Louise Duchess of Portsmouth. The household accounts are filled with entries for the various yachts' appurtenances: Holland quilts and pewter chamber-pots for the *Monmouth* in 1673; more luxuriously, a feather bed and crimson damask hangings for Queen Catharine's own ship. On the *Greyhound* yacht, the King himself indulged in crimson damask for bed and hangings, and gilt leather for the state room, while confining himself to 'a little bed' six feet long by three feet six inches broad.[17]

A little healthy sibling rivalry helped on the development of the yacht industry. Soon the brother ship-builders Peter and Christopher Pett were competing on behalf of the royal brothers Charles and James, the King himself visiting Deptford and pronouncing Christopher Pett's work (for his brother) 'very pretty'. Another yacht, the *Bezan*, was presented by the Dutch to swell this first British yacht squadron. By 1663 yacht-building was spreading downwards to the aristocracy, so much so that Christopher Pett demanded an extra gratuity for building pleasure-boats, because of all the people he had to entertain. Early owners included Sir William Batten, of the Admiralty office, whose wife (like Queen Catharine) was ungratefully seasick.

It was compared to the great square-rigged ocean-going ships that these new craft seemed so light and compact; contemporaries like Pepys always noted how small they were. They could certainly sail far closer to the wind, with their fore and aft rigs, and were thus much more suited to racing. The royal brothers took to matching their craft against each other with zest. Evelyn describes one such early yacht race: 'The King lost it going – the wind being contrary – but saved stakes in returning.' There was a race between the Dutch-built *Bezan* and the King's yacht *Jamie* (named for Monmouth), which the former easily won. Yacht-racing, and for that matter yacht-building, came to an inevitable halt at the time of the Dutch War, only to flourish again in the 1670s and 1680s.

Arlington, with more charity than Prince Rupert, summed up the King's enthusiasm in a memorable phrase when he said that twenty leagues at sea were more pleasing to him than two on land.[18] King Charles II was certainly not the first English monarch to find happiness on the ocean wave: but the coincidence of his personal passion and the age in which he lived was a fortunate one for his country. For it was not only yachting jaunts which commended themselves to the King. He was also deeply concerned with the Navy.

Here his intellectual curiosity married fruitfully with his own taste for adventure to provide an interest in navigation and astronomy, as well as in docks and ship-building. It amounted to an obsession. Fortifications and naval bases in particular fascinated him: he commissioned Danckerts to paint two views of Plymouth, a view of Falmouth Harbour, two views of Portsmouth and a view of his latest acquisition – the dowry of the Queen – Tangier. In danger of his life, escaping from England after Worcester aboard the *Surprise*, King Charles still managed to take an interest in the navigation of the boat. Renamed the *Royal Escape*, it was fitted up as a yacht after the Restoration and painted at the King's request by Van de Velde. It was also no coincidence that Charles had discoursed for hours to Sir William Petty on 'the philosophy of shipping'. In September 1662 the King launched a new type of ship with 'two bottoms', invented by Petty, which was aptly christened *The Experiment*. Later the King would tease Petty about his boat's odd appearance. In vain Petty offered to lay odds for his ship against 'the King's best boats': Charles refused to lay the bet and continued the teasing. Yet Petty, undiscouraged, built other double-bottomed boats, and made many further experiments in naval design.[19]

As for the sovereign himself, with his diligent visits to coastal fortifications, his inspection of naval plans, even his royal orders to commanders at sea – he would at times prove a mixed blessing to his underlings, teasing apart. Burnet typically extracted some snobbish criticism from the King's expertise. Charles, he wrote, 'understood navigation well: but above all he knew the architecture of ships so perfectly, that in that respect he was exact rather more than became a prince'.[20] Evelyn was right when he wrote of Charles II, quite simply, that he was a great 'lover of the sea'.

King Charles' concern with the sea had theoretical consequences as well. One incident gives a clue. In late 1661 King Charles waxed extremely indignant when the French King jibbed at the tradition by which 'ships belonging to the crown of England' (that is, men-of-war on the high seas) were formally saluted. He instructed his ships not to tolerate any diminution in the reverence which was their due, adding that he would be quite unworthy if he quitted a right, and went lower 'than ever any of my predecessors did'.[21]

Such a concern with symbolic ritual was uncharacteristic of Charles II. Except where the Navy was concerned, he made little of that concept of glory which both inspired and plagued his cousin Louis XIV of France and whose pursuit King Louis described as early as 1662 as 'the principal aim' of all his actions. Charles had spent too many years as a King with 'nothing but the name' to bother himself over an insubstantial notion such as glory. But the reality of power – the security presented by it – preoccupied him, if he only rarely dropped the mask sufficiently to display his feelings.

There was one area in which he deliberately emulated King Louis and that was in the establishment of regiments of Foot Guards, Life Guards and Royal Horse Guards (although he did not approach anything like King Louis' figure of sixteen thousand of such desirable bulwarks). In theory, these guards were to be used to police State ceremonies, but of course they also secured the person of the King against a possible coup. It was this aspect rather than the ceremonial side which interested King Charles. The Navy however was his *amant de cœur*, where the Army represented a reliable husband with a strong right arm. And he intended that the Navy he loved should bow to no-one. As King Charles wrote later, 'It is the custom of the English to have command at sea....'[22]

It was happy for him that the English ship-building industry itself made prodigious advances during his reign. At first, the industry was hard put to it to meet the rise in demand for vessels following the settled times of the Restoration, and there had to be large-scale buying of ships from abroad. However, two acts of Parliament put an end not only to foreign-owned ships carrying English trade (the familiar concept of the Cromwellian Navigation Acts), but also to the employment of foreign-built ships. The result was a speedy advance in native British ship-building. Even in wartime, British tonnage rose rather than fell, since the check to ship-building was more than balanced by the capture of foreign ships as prizes.[23]

King Charles' conception of England's maritime role was also central to his relations with the Dutch.

Charles II did not love the Dutch, or the 'Hollanders', as they were generally known by the English during this period. But he did not at first feel about them as he felt about the Scots, a visceral dislike based on personal ill-treatment. The Dutch had not treated him notably well during his exile, but then neither had France, Sweden nor Brandenburg, towards all of whom he was prepared to entertain friendly relations. Be it yachts or duck decoys, he was prepared to admire many things about their way of life and introduce them to his own country. If he was not prepared to dedicate himself to vengeance in England, he was still less inclined to the pursuit of old vendettas abroad.

At his Restoration, King Charles accepted the congratulations of Johann De Witt, who, as Pensionary (Minister of State) of the province of Holland, represented the effective power in the Netherlands. When Mary Princess of Orange continued to press her own claims as guardian of the boy Prince William – as well as William's possible rights as Stadtholder – she found her brother counselling moderation. At the start of his reign, King Charles certainly implied to De Witt that he was more interested in Dutch support for English policies than in his nephew's claims.[24]

Mary's premature death in December 1660 (while on a visit to England) upset this equilibrium. From the grave, Mary still emphasized that proud rank of a Stuart princess to which she had paid such marked attention in life. Her brother and mother were left as joint-guardians of the eleven-year-old William, with no mention at all of the States of Holland. It was hardly surprising that the States refused to confirm the guardianship of a foreign monarch, whatever his blood relationship.

Besides, there was still Mary's old enemy, her mother-in-law, to be reckoned with. By early 1663 the Dowager Princess, who possessed the enormous advantage of being actually resident in the Netherlands, had seen the wisdom of joining forces with De Witt rather than fighting him over the boy's future. She agreed to De Witt's conditions for William's education, and there was nothing the King and Council across the water in England could do about it.

King Charles' annoyance over the whole affair was in direct proportion to his rising anger with the Dutch on more fundamental matters. In this, as in his love of the sea, he echoed the prevailing emotion of his people.[25] With the exception of certain Protestant leaders, who found the theology of their Dutch counterparts sympathetic, the English as a whole in the middle of the seventeenth century glared across the Channel at their Dutch neighbours as a dog surveys a rival dog across the way. And, like quarrelling dogs, the two countries could not resist from time to time having a go at each other.

From the English point of view, this basic dislike made good commercial sense, since it was in commercial rivalry that it was rooted. The Dutch had in general the advantage of the English, being more adept at trade and having faster and cheaper ships: war offered the English an attractive alternative way of defeating them. For the Dutch cut across the English in certain vital areas: in Baltic trading, for example, and in distant lands, such as the West of Africa. Here a long-drawn-out struggle was already in progress for the possession of fortified trading-posts – the commodities traded to include of course slaves. ... Communications were extraordinarily slow between the mercantile capital London and the fever-ridden swamps of Guinea, where the English and Dutch agents vied with each other, but they did exist. Elsewhere, in Asia, the policy of the East India Company was to try and secure equal trading rights, as well as compensation for past wrongs, from the Dutch. As the Dutch were clearly stronger than the English in Indian waters, it was once again in the interests of the Company to have the Dutch defeated in a European war.

If it is an exaggeration to say that King Charles had at this stage a coherent economic policy, it is certainly an anachronism to say that he had a foreign one. Yet in so far as his instincts on the subject could be summed up in the early years of the reign, they were expressed by Thomas Mun in *England's Treasure by Foreign Trade*, written in the 1620s and reprinted in 1664. Mun fulminated on the subject of the Dutch: all over the world, by their trading 'they do hinder and destroy us in our lawful course of living, hereby taking bread out of our mouths'.[26] This was a point of view shared by many of the King's most vociferous subjects, for this was an area where courtiers and merchants alike were frequently joined in a would-be profitable commercial enterprise via a trading company.

As King Charles came to share these feelings, he was further weighted against the Dutch not only by their threat to his beloved shipping, but also by his own natural preference for the French. The use of Madame as a conduit for correspondence with Louis XIV – 'this private channel' – arose naturally enough in the first place out of her marriage to the French King's brother. Monsieur himself provided little competition for Charles as the central figure in his wife's existence. It was not purely a question of his homosexuality: many princesses in that age lived perfectly happily with husbands whose proclivities lay elsewhere. Monsieur fulfilled his duties as a husband sufficiently frequently for Madame to endure numerous pregnancies and miscarriages during her short life. But he was a spiteful creature, jealous of Madame's superior intelligence, her grace, and even the charm which otherwise enchanted the entire Court of Louis XIV. Burnet called him 'poor spirited and voluptuous' – a horrid combination.[27]

In face of such unhappiness within her marriage, like a sunflower Madame turned elsewhere. A brief period of romantic dalliance with her brother-in-law Louis XIV (the true extent of which can only be guessed) established a warm and loving trust between them. Nevertheless, Charles remained the lodestone of her life. A visit to London before her marriage had confirmed the intimacy of 1659. The King's love grew and deepened. As a result, Madame's sway over him in political and religious matters has been much stressed. The King himself added to the legend by stating that Madame was the only woman who had ever had any influence over him. Bishop Burnet chimed in by stating that Charles could deny her nothing. Yet the hard evidence points to the reverse: it was the King who influenced Madame rather than the other way round.

It is Madame whom we find in the Dutch War burning with English patriotism. 'It is only with impatience that I can endure to see you defied by a small handful of wretches,' she wrote to her brother. 'This is perhaps pushing glory a little too far, but I cannot help it, and everyone has his own humour, and mine is to be very keenly alive to all your interests.' An English observer in France thought Madame would literally have died at the news of an English reverse – all this from a Princess half-French by birth, brought up in France and married to a French prince. When Henriette-Anne visited England just after the Restoration with her mother, she had enchanted a deputation from the House of Commons with her tactful disposal of the fact that she could speak little of their allegedly common language. She had, she said, 'an English heart' if not 'an English tongue'.[28] One must believe that this violent partisanship sprang from her feelings for her brother.

Such English sympathies of course only increased Madame's value as an intermediary with Louis XIV. Gradually Charles' letters were transformed from mere repositories of cosy family news to business letters – which nevertheless concluded, 'I am entirely yours. C.' Certainly Madame was a far abler ambassadress for her native country than its official representative in Paris, the Presbyterian elder statesman, Lord Holles, who disliked the place. When Holles became involved in an absurd controversy over the precedence of his coach, Charles carefully upheld him in public for reasons of honour, but expected Madame to explain away his *bêtise* in private.

Following the Restoration the King had already made his choice of France over Spain according to his personal inclination. This orientation became more obvious after the Cromwellian acquisition Dunkirk, occupying a key position between France and the Spanish Netherlands, was sold to the former. It was true that financial necessity played some part in Charles' decision: quite apart from the high price paid by France (some £400,000), Dunkirk cost a fortune to maintain. But the drift of the English King's diplomatic desires was clear, even without his anti-Spanish Portuguese marriage, so gratifying to France. Into these dreams, the Franco-Dutch defensive treaty of 1662 came as an unpleasant reminder of the French King's priorities.

It was a question of the future ownership of the Spanish Netherlands, which in itself formed part of the general problem of the Spanish succession. In 1660 Louis XIV had married another farthingaled Infanta, Maria Teresa, daughter of Philip IV of Spain by his first marriage to Elisabeth of France. At that point the acknowledged heir to the vast Spanish dominions was Philip's only son Carlos, the fruit of his second marriage to an Austrian Hapsburg. Carlos was however congenitally retarded, probably as a result of too close intermarriage – his parents were first cousins. Such matches were not always disastrous – Maria Teresa and Louis XIV were first cousins, as were Madame and Monsieur. Both couples produced a line of descendants. But there was something unhealthy about the Hapsburg blood, which the luckier grandchildren of the vital Henri Quatre escaped. At any rate, it was always clear that Carlos would die childless, despite the fact that he was an unconscionable time doing so (in the phrase associated with Charles II): he survived until 1700.

It was much less clear who would succeed him. The Infanta Maria Teresa specifically renounced her own claim on her marriage: but at the death of her father in 1665 Louis found it easy to discover that the renunciation was void, since the other clauses of the marriage treaty had not been carried out. Even before this there was a continuing sense of crisis about the Spanish dominions, particularly ones so carefully designed, surely, to round off the French frontiers, so strategically placed for French invasion, as the Spanish Netherlands. As early as December 1661 letters from France were warning Clarendon, for example, that 'the King of France, when the King of Spain [Philip IV] dies, will send an army into Flanders to seize the country in the right of his wife'.[29]

Under the circumstances, Louis XIV looked on Holland less as England's commercial rival than as Flanders' potentially aggressive neighbour. King Charles was left to try and form a Northern league whereby the tiresome Hollanders would be confronted by a united Scandinavian phalanx. Sir Gilbert Talbot was sent on a mission to Copenhagen, but the project broke down on another traditional rivalry, that of Denmark and Sweden. This move, coupled with a partial (and unsuccessful) raid on the Dutch at Bergen, shows how far the King's anti-Dutch feelings were escalating.* He was probably speaking the truth when he told Madame in September 1664 that he did not desire war – 'almost the only man in his kingdom' who did not. He further described himself as lacking the 'brutal appetite' which induces rulers to break the peace.[31] That again had a recognizable ring. Brutal appetites in general had been eliminated by the claustrophobic years of exile, the perpetual need for self-control.

But lack of passion is in itself an ineffective weapon, particularly when confronted by zeal. Most of the Court and Parliament were full of contempt for the Hollanders – avid for personal gain – and were, in Pepys' phrase, 'mad for a Dutch war'.[32] If the King had been firmly convinced of the foolishness

* The Dutch were responsible for an outburst of unusually coarse language from the King to Madame. Told that a Dutchman had insulted him, he countered, 'You know the old saying in England, the more a T—— is stirred, the more it stinks, and I do not care a T—— for anything a Dutchman says of me.'[30] It was the language of exasperation.

of such an enterprise, he might have been able to combat the wave of nationalist feeling. As it was, it coincided with his own deep hopes for English maritime ascendancy. Moreover, Charles was still in the same cautious mood of his Restoration Day, aware how quickly fortunes could change. It was always easier to go with the crowd.

Besides, he trusted – no, he *believed* – the English would prove superior to the Hollanders. In this conviction, and in the subsequent débâcle, the role of the English envoy at The Hague, Sir George Downing, was crucial. Originally a Puritan businessman, Downing was one of those adept characters who had ridden the storm of the Restoration period, to glide smoothly from his position as envoy under Cromwell to that of the King's ambassador. In many ways he was worthy of the post, being highly intelligent and energetic – taking a lot of trouble, for instance, to acquire copies of letters from the Dutch archives.

But Downing had a failing. He was arrogant, and his arrogance took the form of such a low estimate of the Dutch national character that he ended by seriously misleading his own country. Again and again Downing reassured the King and Council that, whatever happened, the Dutch simply would not fight. 'Go on in Guinea,' he confidently advised. 'If you bang them there, they will be very tame.'[33]

Pepys showed infinitely more percipience than Downing, the man-on-the-spot, when he confided to his *Diary* at the end of April 1664, 'All the news now is what will become of the Dutch business, whether war or peace. We all seem to desire it, as thinking ourselves to have advantages at present over them; but for my part I dread it.'[34]

Downing's assurances were music to the pro-war party in England, who saw in a series of predatory raids on the passive Dutch in Africa the opportunity of still further gains at little cost to themselves. The war party included not only the East India Company lobby but the Duke of York, with his special interest in the Navy, Buckingham – possessed, as ever, of more personal influence than his character warranted – and Barbara Castlemaine, whose importance lay not so much in the influence she exerted over Charles, as in the influence she was presumed to exert by outsiders. From Africa House, the Admiralty and Navy offices there emitted powerful signals for war.

Fighting broke out during the winter of 1663–4, in Africa, where the English enjoyed success, and America, where the New Netherlands were seized. Nearer at hand in the Channel, the English fleet acquired a series of Dutch ships as prizes, victories which neatly combined prestige and profit. Downing's prognostications of glory appeared to be triumphantly justified.

In the autumn of 1664 the King still hesitated. Part of his vacillation was due to a laudable desire to be sure that the Navy was suitably prepared. The work of Sir William Coventry, Secretary to James and one of the Commissioners to the Navy, was however beaver-like in its application. On the eve of the war the two navies were at least comparable in strength.

The King's hesitancy was also in part a propaganda exercise. King Charles was understandably keen to woo King Louis away from the side of the Dutch, to whom the latter was only committed by a defensive, not an offensive, treaty. To achieve this it was necessary in propaganda terms to prove that the Dutch, not the English, were the assailants. King Charles sent to Madame a series of long letters hammering the point home from the summer of 1664 onwards: how the bellicosity of the Dutch was being – surely unintentionally – encouraged by the French King.

'For I assure you, they brag very much already of his friendship,' Charles told Madame in August; without Louis XIV's support, 'it may be they would not be so insolent as they are'. In September he wrote of the Dutch preparations, 'I am resolved they shall now send first, that all the world may see I do not desire to begin with them, and that if there comes any mischief by it, they have drawn it upon their own heads.' In October he described almost casually the capture of one Dutch possession on the East coast of America: 'A very good town, but we have got the better of it, and 'tis now called New York.' Even here he made it clear the town 'did belong to England heretofore'. In late December he was sending her a printed paper, 'which will clearly inform you of the state of the quarrel between me and Holland, by which you will see that they are the aggressors and the breakers of the peace, and not me'. He asked Madame to read it carefully, for he was sure that the Dutch Ambassador in Paris would use 'all sorts of arts' to 'make us seem the aggressors'.[35]

But King Louis did not budge.

Already by November the sheer aggression of ordinary Englishmen, and of Members of Parliament in particular, towards the Dutch was making it difficult for the King to continue his delaying tactics much longer. As he admitted to Madame in September, 'the truth is they [the Dutch] have not great need to provoke this nation, for except myself I believe there is scarce an Englishman that does not desire passionately a war with them'. On 24 November the King gave vent to a calculatedly patriotic speech to Parliament on the subject of his preparations for war: 'If I had proceeded more slowly, I should have exposed my own honour and the honour of the nation, and should have seemed not confident of your affections.'[36]

It was significant that the King also had to dismiss as 'a vile jealousy' the rumour that he might graciously accept the war subsidy now voted by Parliament, and then, having made a sudden peace, turn it to his own uses. War did pose an acute financial problem to a Crown already heavily embarrassed. It was true that the nationalistic optimism which pervaded the period, in the matter of this Dutch War, made light of such difficulties: Dutch prizes were expected to compensate for military costs. But so notoriously unstable were the King's finances by now, that he found the greatest difficulty in raising the actual cash needed in the first place. New remedies were desperately sought. Sir George Downing had always advocated the punctual payment of interest on Treasury loans to uphold the King's credit, but this had not always been done – because it had not always been possible to do it. This was the occasion of the issue of a government fiduciary currency; those who advanced the King money were for the first time enabled to obtain repayment 'in course', that is in rotation as funds reached the Exchequer.[37] Thus inevitably expenditure galloped ahead of revenue. Even so, people were reluctant to lend for the Dutch War – at eight or ten per cent interest. They might cheer the brave British sailors and shake their fists at the cowardly Dutch. But when it came to the deployment of funds, the government's finances were not such as to inspire any kind of confidence among the hard-headed.

It was better to concentrate on the magnificent possibilities of war. In December 1664 Captain Thomas Allin was ordered to attack the Dutch merchant fleet, homeward bound from Smyrna: in the event, the attack did not produce much effect. In February of the following year King Charles, tired of waiting for King Louis, declared war.*

There were wise heads who opposed the war. But they were overruled. Apart from these counsellors there were few in England who did not anticipate a glorious outcome of 'the Dutch business'. Dryden captured the heroic mood of patriotic anticipation on the eve of the Dutch War, when he wrote,

> Now, anchors weighed, the seamen shout so shrill
> That heaven, and earth, and the wide ocean rings....

* Historically, this is always known as the Second Dutch War, the First Dutch War having taken place under the Commonwealth, 1652–4. It is here referred to as 'the Dutch War' for the convenience of the narrative.

CHAPTER FIFTEEN

Black Day

Black Day accurs'd!...
When aged Thames was bound with Fetters base,
And Medway chaste ravish'd before his Face...
Andrew Marvell

The Dutch War brought in its train a series of damaging assaults on reputation. First, there were the Dutch victories, which, in view of English complacency beforehand, were difficult to assimilate psychologically. Then there was the attack on the credit of those who could be held officially responsible for the war – principally Clarendon. Thirdly, of most moment to the biographer of Charles II, there was the corrosion of the King's own royal image, like a bright statue tarnished by bad weather – the storms in this case being those of naval defeat.

It was ironic that King Charles had gone to war, in part at least, to satisfy that English appetite for martial success against their traditional seventeenth-century foes. The attitudes of a war lord were not even particularly agreeable to the King. Striking attitudes in general seemed to him to be a waste of enthusiasm. He had travelled far since those golden days at York on the eve of the Civil War, when, as a boy prince, he had vaulted onto his horse in full armour like Hotspur. The travels were as much of the spirit as of the body.

It was also ironic, as well as unfortunate, that such a militaristic conception of leadership had been incarnated quite recently – by the Protector Cromwell. The sour smell of national disgrace recalled sweeter perfumes. How different had been yesterday's battles! The shadows of the remembered Cromwellian triumphs lengthened and grew black across the reputation of the Stuart king. From memories they became myths, and no less menacing for that. As a legendary leader in the minds of his people, King Charles II had begun to fail.

There is a comparison to be made with the similar decline in the public esteem of King James I at the beginning of the century. On his accession, he had been greeted with delight, as a welcome respite from the cantankerous old woman Queen Elizabeth had become. A few years later such realities were quite forgotten in the shower of golden illusions which surrounded the name of 'the great Eliza'.

Pepys' later diary entries – towards the end of the sixties – are full of flattering references to 'Oliver'. In the early 1670s it was possible for Marvell to depict the two equestrian statues at Charing Cross arguing over the foreign policies of Cromwell and Charles II respectively. One horse declared himself firmly for Cromwell:

> Though his government did a tyrant resemble
> He made England great and his enemies tremble...

Even the French Ambassador was reported to have snubbed the English King with the remark that Cromwell had been a great man and made himself feared by land and by sea.

It was unfair perhaps to identify a monarch so closely with the fortunes of his country. But so long as national figureheads existed – and Charles II had been restored on that ticket – it was unavoidable. Besides, was not the ability to declare war – in short, the direction of foreign policy – one of the planks of the King's prerogative? The personalization of war remained a factor during this period. As the Lord Treasurer enquired plaintively of Charles' strenuous efforts to borrow money for the war from the City, 'Why will they not trust the King as well as Oliver?'[1] The perilous Commonwealth finances were apparently forgotten, as were Cromwell's own difficulties in securing money from the City.

To Charles in his innocence the prosecution of the Dutch War seemed at first a not unenjoyable occupation. Evelyn gives a delightful vignette of him stopping a chapel service to hear news of a battle, and then promptly turning the occasion into a thanksgiving.[2] It certainly gave him ample opportunities to pursue his naval interests: the inspection of coastal fortifications replaced visits to the yacht-builders' yards. At the beginning of the war the English had about 160 ships, with 5,000 guns and something over 25,000 men; the Dutch had fewer and smaller ships – but these were of course easier to manage in shallow waters; they also had more guns and more men. The English Navy was put under the command of the Duke of York, who had been confirmed in his boyhood title of Lord High Admiral at the Restoration. The appointment was not purely nepotistic; James, like his brother, was fascinated by the sea. He had already gained much popularity within the Admiralty Office for his serious approach to naval matters.

At the first proper engagement of the war, the Battle of Lowestoft on 13 June 1665, the Dutch were resoundingly defeated by the English under James' command. The element of personal involvement was carried further, the two flagships actually fighting each other, until the *Royal Charles* (carrying the duke of York) succeeded in sinking its opposite number, killing the Dutch commander in the process. But James' position as heir presumptive to the throne was a complication: an odd incident during the battle led to the *Royal Charles* eschewing the rest of the fighting; possibly secret orders had been given to preserve James' life from danger.[3] After the battle Charles certainly forbade James to risk it further by presence at the scene of action.

The veto did of course make sense, particularly in view of the lack of suitable heirs to the throne. It was pure chance which had saved James aboard the *Royal Charles*. No less than three of his friends had died as a result of a single gunshot. Standing amidst them, he had been drenched by their blood. Nevertheless, casting one's mind back to that episode in 1648, when Charles refused to let his brother go to sea, one cannot altogether acquit the King of rivalry. As a character, King

Charles was certainly not poisoned by jealousy, as the evidence of his private life will show; but, like most human beings, he knew the emotion. The prospect of James' direct participation in naval warfare (an area of such obsession to Charles) may well have aroused it.

It was the superiority of the English guns which carried the day at Lowestoft. They were loud enough to be heard, speaking 'thick like angry men' in the capital itself. Dryden gives an unforgettable picture of the reaction of those in London to the noise of the bombardment: 'Everyone went following the sound as his fancy led him; and, leaving the town almost empty, some took towards the Park, some across the River, others down it, all seeking the noise in the depth of silence.'[4]

Although the Dutch claimed Lowestoft as a victory (much as the Royalists had claimed that first Cromwellian success at Marston Moor), it was indubitably an English triumph. Less fortunate was the course of the war immediately afterwards. The daring Dutch Admiral de Ruyter – who had not been present at Lowestoft – captured a rich merchant fleet in northern waters. Furthermore, the English failed to recover it by a clumsy rescue attempt which depended on the connivance of the King of Denmark. In the end, the Danes even allied with the Dutch, although their participation remained nominal.

This England under stress of war was also beset by an enemy within. It was during the summer of 1665 that the ominous and disgusting signs of plague began to be found in London.[5] The first Bill of Mortality, giving it as the cause of death, occurred in the parish of St Giles in the Fields in early May. The June heatwave which followed – that same glorious weather which gave the English fleet off Lowestoft 'not a cloud in the sky, nor the least appearance of any alteration of wind or weather' – gave a fatal impetus to the spread of the disease. In one week alone at the end of June, one hundred plague deaths were registered. Soon the thin summer darkness was illuminated by the lights of innumerable night burials. Many unidentifiable corpses went to their resting-place under such pathetic labels as 'a child from Kingshead alley', 'a man from New Street', 'a maid from the Crown in Fleet Street'. On 10 August Pepys considered it time to draw up his own will – 'the town growing so unhealthy that a man cannot depend upon living two days to an end'. By the end of the month, burial in consecrated ground had been abandoned in favour of communal plague pits.

The King and Court remained in the capital till July and then headed for Oxford. Parliament was prorogued, and the Exchequer transferred to Nonsuch, a palace near Ewell. It was not a particularly convenient move, in view of the development of the Dutch War – not quite that easily terminated struggle which the English had anticipated. There would have to be a new campaign in the new year. Arlington commented in November on the difficulty of raising money at this distance (that is, from Nonsuch) 'towards our preparations for the next spring'.[6] It was also possible to criticize the Court for cowardice.

On one level, such a charge was obviously idle. It is true that the Court abandoned the sinking ship (leaving it in this case to the rats who brought the infection). But the plague was not a peril which could be fought manfully by a public example of courage – as King George VI was to expose himself to the London Blitz during World War II. Indeed, we shall discover King Charles II setting just such an example, in the following year of the Great Fire, when bravery and concern could have some effect on the capital's welfare. To have had the monarch die of the plague would have served no particular purpose, beyond upsetting the dearly won stability of England once more. The same excuse cannot be made for the flight of the President of the Royal College of Physicians, which was indeed culpable.

Yet it is true that the Court's departure did nothing to arrest the general breakdown of the central authority which aggravated the sufferings of those left behind. (While those who did stay, such as Lord Craven, earned the devotion of the people.) The Lord Mayor, for instance, had no control over the outer parishes; it was not until nine JPs were specifically appointed to deal with the problem that organization at least improved. The plague certainly became a hideous example of the sufferings of the poorer classes. The primitive Anti-Plague Laws of 1646, advocated by the College of Physicians, simply meant that the inhabitants of a plague-ridden building were immured behind a sealed door until they either died or recovered (generally the former). In the crowded tenements, as many as six families could be shut off – and die together.

The connection between infection and hygiene was not remotely appreciated. All sorts of customs entered our social life as methods of warding off the plague – including chewing tobacco, for the story was spread about that no tobacconist had ever died of the plague. The surviving fashion for blessing one who sneezes (a more spiritual preventive) has its origin in the days of the plague, since to sneeze was considered to be the first sign of an attack.

The whole period in London was, as one eighteenth-century historian would write, a 'prodigious mixture of Piety and Profaneness at the same time'. There were even comic moments (again, the comparison with the Blitz can be made) to relieve the popular horror: a drunkenly insensible bagpiper was carried away on the death-cart; when he awoke and proceeded to play his pipes, he was taken for the Devil himself. One house would bear the legend, 'Lord have mercy on us.' In the next there would be 'tippling and whoring', as the inhabitants chose a different way of passing the time till eternity.[7]

Yet those stricken households who chose the pious exhortation had good reason to cry out, in view of the semi-criminal nature of those left to tend the sick. These plague nurses were barely paid, and mainly illiterate: they supplemented their living by stealing from the dying bodies of those who should have been their patients and became their victims.* In the meantime, the restrictions were easily flouted by the upper classes, who either did not report the existence of the disease, or had themselves smuggled away from their sealed houses to the country.

By September the lack of traffic in the streets meant that the grass was beginning to grow in the main thoroughfare of

* The villainess of W. Harrison Ainsworth's memorable recreation of this grisly time, *Old St Paul's*, is one such plague nurse, a horrific fictional character perhaps, but no worse than the real-life nurses of the time.

Whitehall. And although the plague was found to have reached its peak during the week of 17 September, with a total of seven thousand deaths recorded, it was slow to die away. The official total of deaths exceeded sixty-eight thousand, but the true figure may have been something over one hundred thousand. There was general under-reporting, quite apart from the fact that certain sections of the community, such as Quakers, Anabaptists and Jews, were frequently not included in the church returns.

The King returned to Whitehall on 1 February 1666. He had got as far as Hampton Court by the end of January, despite rumours of the recurrence of the plague (which may in fact have been due to an outbreak of typhus). He told Madame that 'already the Plague is in effect nothing', but added, with a note of impatience, 'Our women are afraid of the name', and indeed Queen Catharine lingered at Oxford. By March Arlington, writing off to the envoy Carlingford abroad, was able to assure him that the disease really was declining, commenting that as a result 'the [funeral] bells are so silent'.[8]

But the fear naturally remained, since it was hardly to be foreseen that such a decimating disease would now die away. Parliament was again prorogued from mid-April to late September on the excuse of the plague, as it had been the previous year. The King personally may have acted with cunning rather than dread in order to get rid of a Parliament which was proving most irritating towards his plans, yet the excuse was held to be plausible. It would be a long time before the shadow of the disease which in a few months had claimed between a third and a quarter of the total population of the capital would lift altogether.

All this occurred at a moment when the honeymoon of the King and his people was, as has been noted, fast approaching its conclusion. A sick people, who are also at war, are hardly likely to love their monarch the more for such disasters. Nor had the events of the Great Plague increased the popularity of the Court, as may be imagined, particularly as news of their merry debaucheries and *dolce far niente* way of life was already beginning to spread downwards. At least one commentator put the Great Plague down to God's desire to punish these said debaucheries;[9] although, if this was indeed the Almighty's intention, he executed it but clumsily in sending a punishment which fell heavily on the poor, and was easily avoided by the rich.

At Oxford on 28 December 'my lady Castlemaine', as Barbara was now generally called, had given the King a very public Christmas present in the shape of a son, born at Merton College, where she was lodged. She was not otherwise having a very fruitful time in the university city, since a nasty libel had been pasted on her door: £1,000 was offered to discover the author, but in vain. Besides, the ties of affection, of not sensuality, which bound her to Charles were being alarmingly stretched.

It was not the little Portuguese Queen who was the danger, but a girl called Frances Stewart. Here was a most disquieting kind of rival. It could not be denied that Frances was elegantly dressed, with a sense of style which the French Ambassador complacently attributed to her education in his country – she had been at the court of Henrietta Maria and was now a maid of honour to Queen Catharine. Then her beauty was also without question, Madame describing her as 'the prettiest girl in the world and the most fitted to adorn a court'. Even Pepys, glimpsing her in black and white lace, head and shoulders adorned by diamonds, hailed her as 'a glorious sight', and later deserted his favourite Barbara to call Frances 'the beautifullest creature' he had ever seen.[10] Her lovely figure and long legs, much admired by the King, enabled her to wear the man's dress made fashionable by the Queen; Barbara, constantly pregnant, can hardly have shone in such garb, for all her voluptuousness. Frances was also eight years younger than Barbara, never the happiest of situations for the older rival in fear of being supplanted.

But Frances's youth was not the worst of it. Most dangerous of all, Frances Stewart was actually virtuous! In the summer of 1665, after several years at the English Court, Lely could paint her without irony as 'chaste Diana', a rare compliment. There was indeed something child-like, even childish, about Frances which accorded with her virginity and her determination to preserve it, Clarissa-like, against assault. She loved, for example, to play Blind Man's Buff, to build card castles, amusements which were harmless, if slightly frivolous. At the same time, she tantalized: as when she had an exciting dream that she was in bed with three French Ambassadors (what could the explanation for that be?) and told it to the Courts. The combination of provocation and virtue drove the King mad. He was discovering the fatal appeal of innocence, which allured and failed to satisfy all at the same frustrating moment. Charles, pursuing his suit with all the amorousness of Henry VIII, but without the cruelty, was heard to groan that he wished to see Frances become old and willing. . . .[11]

At first, Barbara attempted to deal with the situation in her own way. She set up some seemingly harmless diversions, with highly erotic overtones, featuring both herself and the younger girl. There was a mock marriage, featuring Barbara and Frances as 'bride' and 'groom', the couple being subsequently bedded in the traditional post-wedding ceremony. Barbara also made a point of inviting Frances to sleep with her. That in itself was not a particularly unusual gesture in an age of communal living and sleeping. But the manner in which Barbara followed it up smacked more of Laclos' eighteenth-century France than of Restoration England; for she then proceeded to tempt the King deliberately with the delicious sight of Frances asleep, Frances in bed. No doubt Barbara planned to make Frances the King's junior mistress, under her own control.

The plan failed, as did the King's own assaults, on the rock of Frances' virtue. As a result, the King's passion for this 'rising sun' only increased. He expressed it himself in a poem in which his unrequited desire took a graceful pastoral form, beginning,

> I pass all my hours in a shady old grove,
> But I live not the day when I see not my love;
> I survey every walk now my Phillis is gone,
> And sigh when I think we were there all alone;

and with the repeated refrain:

> O then, 'tis O then, that I think there's no hell
> Like loving, like loving too well.

There was a further complication, still less pleasing to Barbara's jealous ears. Despite what the French Ambassador called 'regular assiduity' on the King's part,[12] as well as those therapeutic visits to spas, Queen Catharine still had not succeeded in becoming pregnant.* Were the Queen to die – and she had been extremely ill in 1663 – the King would be free to marry again. There were plenty of precedents for Kings marrying British ladies not of royal birth *en deuxième noces* – even if the examples of Anne Boleyn and Elizabeth Woodville were not exactly quotable. Frances came of a good Scottish family. Her very virtue, her youth, her good spirits, all made her a not implausible candidate. It was happily appropriate that King Charles had her engraved with helmet and trident as Britannia, to preside over the British coinage for three centuries. She was a charming symbol of womanhood.

Then, in April 1667, Frances suddenly eloped with the Duke of Richmond. She did so exhausted by the pressures put upon her, and as if to prove once and for all that she valued a wedding-ring over the perquisites of a royal mistress. The King was appalled and then angry, although Frances' gesture, so much out of keeping with the age in which she lived, called forth poetic admiration from Edmund Waller. Frances carried the correctness of her behaviour to the extent of returning to the King the jewels he had given her. Charles in his turn carried his frustrated rage into his correspondence with Madame: 'You may think me ill-natured,' he wrote, 'but if you consider how hard a thing 'tis to swallow an injury done by a person I had so much tenderness for, you will in some degree [understand] the resentment I use towards her.' The next year, when Frances caught smallpox, the King gave way to *Schadenfreude*, 'fearing' she would be much marked. Fortunately his better nature returned when he heard that she was untouched: he told Madame that her affliction had brought him to overlook the past: when all was said and done, 'I cannot hinder myself from wishing her very well.'[13] But the uncommon exhibition of annoyance does

* The gynaecological history of Queen Catharine will be considered in its proper place (see pages 335–8).

bear witness to the degree of love the King had once felt; love no doubt spurred on by her rejection, yet love nonetheless. With Henrietta Catharine of Orange, Frances Stewart could claim to have possessed the heart, as opposed to that more frequently bestowed gift, the body of King Charles II. It was surely no coincidence that both were unconsummated passions.

There is a postscript to the story of Charles and Frances. Subsequently restored to favour, Frances and her husband were sent to Denmark, where the Duke was given the role of Ambassador. The Duke died prematurely, but Frances never remarried. She gave up her later years to cats and cards: at her death her cats were bequeathed to various female friends, with money for their upkeep. Since Frances also died childless, one can argue that she would not in the end have been a suitable bride for the King. Perhaps there was something externally girlish, frozen, even frigid about her, which fascinated but in the end would have disappointed the King. There was another hell, beyond 'loving ... loving too well', and that was the failure of desire. Both the King and Frances took care to guard themselves against that dismal fate.

In the spring of 1666 the King's campaign to gain allies against 'the Hollanders' was not much more successful than his pursuit of Frances Stewart. It was true that Louis XIV's support of them proved nominal and he did not, as Charles had feared at one point, send troops against England. But Charles still lacked help. In vain the previous summer Arlington had urged Lord Carlingford to secure the support of Bishops, Princes, Electors, but above all that of the Emperor; Carlingford's mission to Leopold I had been fruitless, as had been that of Sir Richard Fanshawe at the courts of Lisbon and Madrid. Carlingford's instructions cast some light on the complications of diplomatic life at the time: on the one hand, he was to allow no aspersions on his master's Protestantism, while, on the other, he was to take care not to discourage the Pope.[14]

In January 1666 Carlingford was deputed to tell the Emperor that the English King was by now inclined to peace with Holland – provided he could get good terms. The Emperor was not tempted by the prospect. Still these imperial dignitaries continued to play their own 'crafty games', as Arlington despairingly termed them, seeing no particularly good reason why they should not back France or Spain 'as it shall suit their occasions'. No one seemed prepared to sacrifice anything for the sake of England. By the end of April Arlington was deploring the treachery of the Bishop of Munster, whose support had been counted upon: 'God be thanked,' wrote Arlington. 'His Majesty hath a good fleet to supply the unfaithfulness of his friends and the fraudulent artifices of his enemies.'[15]

Soon Arlington's words would have an ironic ring.

The long hot summer of 1666 got off to a bad start. Charles wrote irritably to Madame in May, 'I can only now wish for peace and leave the rest to God.'[16] His subjects were beginning to feel the same way. The King's birthday had been since the Restoration an occasion of special rejoicing, directed towards the person of the monarch. On 29 May this year Pepys was moved to comment on the decline which six years' reign had shown in his popularity. Worse was to follow.

On 1 June commenced that prolonged naval engagement known as the Four Days' Battle, which resulted in a heavy defeat for the English at the hands of the Dutch and French. The vast casualties of the battle compel horror: the English lost six thousand men (many of them burnt to death when their ships caught fire) and suffered an incredible amount of wounded. According to the official account, eight English ships were sunk and nine captured. Against this, the Dutch lost two thousand men and seven ships. It was a bitter pill for the English to swallow: the superior Dutch guns, under their Admiral de Ruyter, were mainly responsible for this mayhem.

The natural English reaction was towards revenge. The King's new servant, Thomas Clifford, who shared his love of the sea, spoke defiantly of 'the Hollanders' brags', which, though set forth to the world in high measure, would soon 'vanish and turn to their disadvantage'. Described by Evelyn as 'a bold young man from Devon' (in fact, he was exactly the same age as Charles), Clifford had been appointed in 1664 Commissioner for the care of sick and wounded seamen, and later a sub-commissioner of naval prizes; he had gone on a mission to Copenhagen after the fatal Bergen raid, and in November 1666 would become Comptroller of the King's Household. Industry and loyalty were his two strong points, a useful combination at any court. Now he wrote feelingly of the magnificent spectacle of the fleet in July and the men's high morale, 'Even the common men cry out: If we do not beat them now, we shall never do it.' Clifford wished the King could have witnessed it. Arlington confirmed it to Carlingford: 'Our fleet is almost ready and the Dutch are expecting us.'[17]

By the end of July some kind of revenge was secured by these spirited men off the French coast, although the skilful Dutch seamanship enabled the enemy to withdraw in good order. Thus the episode did not amount to quite the crushing defeat which had been anticipated. It seemed that Hollanders and English were heading for a stalemate. As a result, Charles II, Louis XIV and Johann de Witt were now to be found arguing, proposing and counter-proposing over terms for peace. After eighteen months' war, all three of them had reason to desire it.

Charles' principal motive was lack of money. But if he believed in the fates, he had an additional reason to suspect that they had now turned against him after the smiling years. In September the Great Fire raged through the City, following the Great Plague – another cataclysmic blow, as it seemed at the time, although, unlike the plague, it was to have wondrous consequences. It was at least an episode from which King Charles emerged with the greatest personal credit, able to employ those qualities of courage and decision in action which had been too long dormant in civil (royal) life.

The fire began before dawn on Sunday 2 September, in Pudding Lane, not far from London Bridge.[18] A persistent east wind then drove the fire along the Thames and across the city. By Monday the flames had gained a front of half a mile. At the Palace of Whitehall, the bend in the river concealed the burning buildings, although later the glow of the fire at night, and the shooting flames, would be visible from the Palace windows. At any rate, the first the King knew of the crisis was the noise of

Londoners crying out on Sunday night, 'Fire, fire! God and the King save us.'

The fact was that fire in itself, and even a pall of smoke, was not unusual in the wooden-built capital. Because fire was unfortunately part of London's way of life, it was a favourite suspicion that conspirators would fire the city – which does something to explain the outrageous charges of incendiarism made after 1666. King Charles had always shown himself extremely concerned on the subject. In April, like Cassandra, he had written to the Lord Mayor, Recorder and Aldermen, warning them of the dangers of fire inherent in such narrow streets, overhung by wooden houses. They had his royal authority to pull such perilous excrescences down, and imprison those who contravened the Building Acts. Like Cassandra, he was not heeded.

The prevalence of the fire hazard may also explain the dilatoriness of the authorities in grappling with this particular outbreak. It was not until Monday that the extent of the emergency was grasped, by which time it was very difficult to establish a clear zone, to confine the flames. A special committee was set up by the Privy Council under the respected Yorkshire soldier and landowner Lord Belasyse, who years later would be denounced and even imprisoned by the wagging tongue of Titus Oates, simply because he was a Catholic. Now his efforts were Trojan, from the informal headquarters of Ely House in Holborn, where he was joined by Ashley Cooper (Lord Ashley since the Restoration), the Earl of Manchester and others, under the overall control of the Duke of York. Fire posts were established, with an official allowance of £5 per post for beer, cheese and bread. The rickety and inflammable wooden wharves of the Fleet River bank had to be cleared immediately, and the soldiers went to their work, aided by those passers-by who could be bribed to assist.

The King himself was also intimately concerned. When he first learned the news, he sent in his own Guards. In the afternoon, with the Duke of York, he was rowed down from Whitehall in the royal barge, and, from the roof of a tall building, watched the Waterman's Hall burning. He went as far as

Queenshithe, where he repeatedly urged the people to pull down the houses and strip the highly combustible market: he was afterwards said to have imperilled his life in his eagerness to give orders. On Tuesday the blaze spread hideously to engulf Blackfriars and the entire parish of St Bride's. Soon the fire 'rushed like a torrent down Ludgate Hill', as an onlooker described it. Worried for Whitehall, Charles had the buildings only recently erected by Denham at Scotland Yard unroofed and defaced so that the fire should not get a hold.

Very early on the Tuesday the King and the Duke of York arrived in the City on horseback and stayed there all day, riding from place to place, at times directing their Guards to fight the fire, and at times, accompanied by only a small escort, going to the very limits of the blaze, distributing water. From the first, the fire had been leaping great distances 'after a prodigious manner', as Evelyn put it.[19] Aware throughout of the vital need to demolish, if it was in any way to be held in check, the King moved about the City with a pouch containing one hundred golden guineas slung over his shoulder. These were to be handed out to the workmen at their destructive task *pour encourager*.

By the end of the day the King's clothes were soaking, his face black, his whole person muddy and dirty. But there were many testimonials to his bravery and resolution as he stood up to his ankles in the water, joining in the work with a will, wielding a bucket and spade with the rest, and encouraging the courtiers to do likewise. At Cripplegate, for example, he was known to have taken part in the extinction of the fire, as if he had been 'a poor labourer'; a foreigner living in London heard that the King had spent over thirty hours on horseback. He had shown 'singular care and pains' for the welfare of his people, and much real popularity was gained, or rather regained, as a result.

Nor did King Charles confine his activities to the showier pursuits of fire-fighting and water-dowsing. Throughout, he showed enormous concern for the plight of the many homeless, ordering the Victualler of the Navy to send bread to the poor at Moorfields (in the end biscuit from sea-stores was sent, but declined as inedible). The King also appointed a day of fasting and humiliation, to be accompanied by collections in aid of the suffering. He was experiencing that Lear-like identification with the wretched and needy which he had learnt after Worcester, not merely striking the public attitudes of a royal figure.

The Duke of York, a man whose courage in those days was never questioned (and rightly so – he was a brave soldier, a valiant admiral), showed himself equally to advantage. A younger scion of the royal family, the Duke of Monmouth, was also present: he formed part of the King's guard, which kept the people back from St Michael's church, whose mediaeval tower continued to stand, although its great bells fell clattering to the ground. It is a striking demonstration of the indifference to the truth which ambition breeds, that many years later Monmouth should dare to accuse James of starting the fire.

It was time for evacuation once more. The peregrinating Exchequer set off again for Nonsuch. Henrietta Maria was enjoying a serene old age improving her Somerset House residence, or, as a contemporary verse put it,

> The Peaceful Mother on mild Thames does build...[20]

Now she hastily took herself up river to Hampton Court. A Spanish Catholic in London gleefully reported the preservation of her chapel from the fire, while the Anglican St Paul's was destroyed. It was, he wrote, at the site of a holy house that 'the flaming tempest, which involved so many in disaster (and burnt 140 heretic churches) allowed itself to be subdued'.

But still the course of the fire was not stopped. Unlike the plague, it fell on rich and poor alike. Dorset House went up with the parish of St Bride's. The empty prison of Bridewell was made of sterner stuff and survived. But the royal apartments of this ancient palace burned, as did the City grain stored there. In Bridewell cemetery, overflowing from the plague, there was no peace for the dead: in their graves they burned again. During the four days' course of the fire* a light debris scattered a

* It is sometimes described as having lasted five days; but see W. G. Bell, *The Great Fire of London in 1666*, for the correction of this myth; he also corrects the legend that the fire ended at Pie Corner.

mantle of soot as far away as rural Kensington. Pieces of burnt paper and scorched silk sailed softly to the ground as far away as Windsor Great Park, Henley and Beaconsfield. The whole sky was of a fiery aspect for forty miles around, 'like the top of a burning oven', in Evelyn's phrase.

As for the experiences of those closer to the fire, a correspondent told Lord Conway that you would have thought it was Doomsday: 'and the fearful cries and howlings of undone people did much increase the resemblance'. While Dryden wrote movingly of the plight of the homeless,

> The most in fields like herded beasts lie down
> To dews obnoxious on the grassy floor,
> And while their babes in sleep their sorrows drown
> Sad parents watch the remnants of their store...

In all, the flames destroyed an oblong-shaped area about one-and-a-half miles long and a half a mile deep; or, as a preacher put it in terms of books, the City was reduced by fire from a large folio volume to a decimotertio. Most vivid of all was the comparison of a native of Westmorland, who wrote that the once great City had become 'just like our fells, for there is nothing to be seen but heaps of stones'. After four days of holocaust, dead calm came. On Sunday the first rains fell. But there were periodic alarms for weeks after that, and the smouldering amidst the ruins continued, with occasional outbreaks of minor fires, until a vast downpour of rain in October put an end to it altogether.

A pamphlet published in Holland (by the Dutch) put the whole fire down to the will of God, who was visiting his vengeance on the English for burning the Dutch ships: "Therefore not for long did they triumph and glory in this proud and self-satisfied City.... And now comes the Almighty and just God ... and sends this wind, His strong wind. And He with His wind threw down all the remaining buildings, beautiful palaces and shops of the rich merchants which were swallowed up and destroyed by an unquenchable fire."[21] Oddly enough, the official report of the Privy Council, asked to investigate the causes of the blaze, agreed in principle with the Dutch, and differed only in interpretation. They wrote that 'Nothing had been found to argue the Fire in London to have been caused by other than the hand of God, a great wind and a very dry season.'[22]

It may seem strange to our ears that any other explanation was sought than the three (or even latter two) suggested by the Privy Council, in a rickety wooden city where fire was generally acknowledged to be a common hazard. On 6 September the King addressed all the homeless Londoners assembled at Moorfields. It was a macabre scene. The grass was littered with rescued belongings, interspersed with ashes. The ruins of St Paul's provided a sombre background. Wisps of smoke were rising from the stones of the once 'proud and self-satisfied City'. The King came on horseback, attended by only a few gentlemen. As he addressed the people before him, his first care was to state with all the firmness at his command: *there had been no plot.* The Fire was due to the hand of God.

He spoke in vain, except to the rational. From the first, the Catholics were prime suspects for firing the City, with the Anabaptists second in line. The Catholics themselves were inclined to believe, like the Dutch, in the theory of God's vengeance; the Quakers too worked it out that God was punishing the City of London for persecuting *them.* But in the minds of the populace, and of many who should have known better, purulent suspicious against the Catholics formed. The fact that the Post Office had burnt down early on meant that reliable news was hard to come by – and gave a field day to the rumour-mongers. As fear of revolution was to some (like King Charles), fear of the Catholics was to others: irrational, but a fact of the age. Hidden from outward eyes, the infection festered and waited for the next outbreak of strident anti-Popery.

In his Moorfields speech of 6 September the King had vowed, by the grace of God, to take particular care of all Londoners. The manner in which he intended to implement this promise was an exciting one. He intended to build on the ruins of London. Only ten days after the start of the fire he was prophesying a thrilling development for 'this our native city' – a judicious reminder that London was his birthplace. But it was to be a Phoenix of brick and stone, not inflammable wood, which was to rise from the ashes.

The replanning of London was of course a long-held aim. The King had a strong streak of the town-planner in his nature, be it palaces or parks, streets, squares or gardens. He had been disappointed at the Restoration that funds had not permitted him much expression of it. He had wished, for example, to sweep away the whole complicated, unaesthetic Whitehall complex (with the exception of the Banqueting Hall). Since this could not be afforded, he had turned his energies towards constructing a new palace at Greenwich, sending for designs and designers and taking much personal interest in progress. Building was begun there in 1661. To the extent that everyone was quoting the mysterious ways of God as an explanation of the fire, it must have seemed to Charles another – far pleasanter – example of the workings of Providence that he should now be compelled to rebuild London.

Providence might perhaps receive another credit: for having produced at this crucial moment in the history of London an architect of the genius of Christopher Wren. Nevertheless, King Charles II was not without credit himself for having perceived the quality of the man he was offered. From the first, King Charles had attempted to employ Wren's manifold talents, vainly seeking to persuade him to supervise the fortification in Tangier in 1661; Wren was content with the Savilian Chair of Astronomy at Oxford. When Wren became the Deputy Surveyor of Works to John Denham, it was said by Denham to be 'by the King's desire', and in the official terms of the appointment 'according to our [that is, the King's] particular direction and recommendation'. In 1669, when Wren became the actual Surveyor of the Works, it was to open the longest reign in the history of the office – lasting nearly fifty years. He would serve under six monarchs and twenty-four Lord Treasurers.[23]

At the vital moment of inception, the work most popularly associated with Wren's name, the rebuilding of London, owed much to the energy of King Charles, and his proclamations.

Without the King's zestful patronage, Wren might have struggled in vain with London's narrow, devastated streets, and with its scarred stones like Westmorland's fells. As it was, the King was the prime motor, setting up a Committee of Lords in the Council, under the Lord Chancellor, to discuss rebuilding with the City's representatives, as soon as the fires were properly extinguished.

By 10 September Wren, as Deputy Surveyor, had already submitted a plan to the King and Council. A few days later the King issued a royal proclamation, remitting for seven years the Hearth Tax of two shillings per annum on new buildings, by which it had been hoped to keep the spread of London under control. He went further in practical steps. After the Act of Parliament was passed for the rebuilding, he not only promised further help to the Lord Mayor and Alderman 'to the beauty, ornament and convenience of the City', but took an energetic interest in the details of the reconstruction.[24]

There should, for example, be sufficient open markets to make the clogging street markets unnecessary. The halls of the lesser companies might be erected along the Thames Quay, to add to the charm of the river frontage. Where the buildings of lesser streets abutted on the main thoroughfares, they should range with the high buildings in height, for the look of the thing. In the following February King Charles sent for the Acts of the Common Council and a map; then with his finger he proceeded to trace the vital proposals for straightening the chief streets, such as Fleet Street. Wren's vision had included a straight view from Ludgate Circus to St Paul's, then on to the Royal Exchange: alas, it was never carried through, any more than was the concept of one large thoroughfare from Smithfield to the river. The City rulers objected that the new Act gave them no powers for sufficiently compensating the owners of the required land. Had such a vision come to pass, the seventeenth-century London of King Charles and Wren would vie with the nineteenth-century Paris of the Emperor Napoleon and Haussmann.

As it was, the King's patronage was freely acknowledged by the City, at least for the next fifteen years. On 23 October 1667 he travelled to the City in state, attended by kettle-drums and trumpets, and laid the first stone of the first pillar of the new Royal Exchange. Seven years later this patronage was acknowledged when he received the freedom of the City from the Lord Mayor, Sir Robert Viner – the only reigning Sovereign to have done so.* The scroll was presented in a massive gold box, its seal enclosed in another one 'beautifully enriched with diamonds'. At the same time the King also paid the City the 'unparalleled favour and honour' of dining at a Mayoral banquet[26] – a favour, unlike the freedom itself, which has since been paralleled by many reigning monarchs.

'Eheu fugaces' ... In 1681 the City authorities would put up, of their own accord, a Fire Monument attributing the great conflagration to 'the treachery and malice of the popish faction'.[27] And Marvell did not fail to satirize that golden casket, presented

> Whilst their churches unbuilt, and their houses undwelt
> And their orphans want bread to feed 'em.

Nevertheless, the King's prompt and determined action with regard to the reconstruction of London immediately after the fire was laudable at the time, and remains something for which later generations should call him blessed.

It was good that he actively enjoyed the process. For there was little else for his comfort in that discontented autumn of 1666. When the year ended – one which had included the disappointments of the Dutch War as well as the biblical ordeals of fire and flood – Pepys described it as one of 'public wonder and mischief to this nation – and therefore generally wished by all people to have an end'. Dryden in his poem *Annus Mirabilis* (Year of Wonders) used the same word. A correspondent wrote to Ralph Verney even more passionately: 'Let not '66 come these hundred years again.'[28]

As for the King himself, the insufficiency of his received income was beginning to bite and accumulate in a particularly horrid kind of compound interest. The House of Commons

* There are several instances of the Sovereign receiving the freedom *before* accession; but the Sovereign is normally considered to be the fount of all honours.[25]

was at best unsympathetic. Andrew Marvell, MP for Hull, described the situation in November 1666 to a correspondent:

> Foreign excise, home excise, a Poll Bill, subsidies at the improved value of at six pence per pound, Privy Seals, Sealed Paper, a land tax have been all more or less disputed with different approbation but where we shall pitch I am not wise enough to tell you. For indeed as the urgency of His Majesty's affairs exacts the money so the sense of the nation's extreme necessity makes us exceedingly tender whereupon to fasten our resolutions. . . .[29]

'The urgency of His Majesty's affairs' was an apt phrase. For the previous few years, the annual deficit had been running at some £400,000. One effect of the fire was to cripple the yield of the taxes. Then there was the question of the King's debts and those of his father, which Parliament had promised to redeem, though it had not done so. By July 1667 Clifford, who was one of the five Commissioners appointed to act as Lord Treasurer after the death of Southampton, estimated the general debts at £2,500,000 – with one million owing for the Navy. Retrenchment was the order of the day and a committee of the Privy Council was set up with that in mind.

But still the war, the greatest cause of poverty, dragged on. Dutch, French and English seemed unable to agree on terms. The resistance of both the English and the Dutch was being whittled away. It was against this seemingly dreary background of diplomatic negotiation and royal manoeuvre and counter-manoeuvre that the Dutch carried out their daring raid on the Medway in June 1667. De Witt was determined to strengthen the Dutch hand materially in the peace proposals. An attack on 'London's river', as De Witt termed it, had been planned as early as the Four Days' Battle, but the Dutch had been too cautious to carry it out. This time they were given explicit instructions 'to deliberate and to proceed with vigour and rather to take a risk than return without some notable accomplishment'. The playwright Aphra Behn, who played a resourceful role in English intelligence at the time, warned the government in advance of what was intended. As she wrote in her memoirs, her news might have 'sav'd the nation of a great deal of money and disgrace had credit been given to it'. But her warning was disregarded.[30]

With the aid, it is distressing to relate, of two renegade English pilots, the fort of Sheerness was captured, the boom at Chatham broken and, worst of all, the English fleet – in Evelyn's words – 'A dreadful spectacle as ever Englishmen saw and a dishonour never to be wiped off!'[31]

The result exceeded De Witt's wildest expectations. There was panic in the capital, ruled over by a shaky King and government. One rumour suggested that the King had abdicated and escaped. While there were those who suggested that Charles would now refuse to make peace until he had avenged this blow, the King was in fact in no position to meditate retribution. Clarendon referred to peace as an offer that the English would find it difficult to refuse. 'Although peace can be bought at too high a price, it would suit us highly in the circumstances and we are not in a position to decline. Peace is needed to calm people's minds, and would free the king from a burden which he is finding hard to bear.' Thus the Peace of Breda between the two countries was officially brought about at the end of July. The Dutch were conceded their demands in West Africa, the island of Pulo Run and Surinam.

At the same time, England was confirmed in the tenure of the former Dutch possessions of New York, New Jersey and New Delaware, as well as sundry other benefits. It could not be said therefore that the country itself had bought peace at too high a price, since its need for rest and recovery was so manifest. Yet the humiliation symbolized by that 'black day accurs'd', as Marvell called it,

> When aged Thames was bound with Fetters base,
> And Medway chaste ravish'd before his Face

could not be easily expunged from the national consciousness.

The price had to be paid – by someone.

CHAPTER SIXTEEN

This Revolution

> 'Many particulars . . . have inclined me to this revolution, which already seems to be well liked in the world and to have given a real and visible amendment to may affairs.'
>
> Charles II to Ormonde, on the fall of Clarendon

For a long time Charles II's relationship with the Earl of Clarendon had been permeated by resentment. Some of this was personal. It was not pleasant to be treated as a lazy schoolboy, as the King approached his fortieth year. Whether King Charles was laggard in his transactions of business or not, Clarendon should perhaps have put his knowledge of history to work on the subject of monarchs and their former bear-leaders – the early intimacy generally making tact more important rather than less. The notes passed between Charles and Clarendon in the Privy Council, despite the humorous exchanges, illustrate how firmly the elder man considered himself in control.

But there was more to the fall of Clarendon from Charles' favour than mere annoyance at an irksome manner: that, the King could have easily pretended to tolerate, if it had suited his book to do so. Had he not cultivated in exile an unusual ability to mask his feelings? The fact was that the King was by now evolving his own theories on how the country should be governed, along pragmatic lines. It has already been noted that he did not favour Clarendon's emphasis on the Privy Council, whose domination seemed to him scarcely preferable to that of Parliament. He would have liked to free the Privy Purse, the source of his personal expenditure, from the overlordship of the Exchequer, and equally to place the Irish Seal above the Great Seal so that Irish affairs (and money) could be handled by him directly when necessary. He had also suffered acutely in recent years from Clarendon's failure to control the House of Commons (he did not appreciate the real need for able speakers on the Court side), or for that matter the Lords.[1] As a result, its 'angry pettish' members had in his opinion kept him woefully short of funds. Nor had Clarendon produced the French alliance of his dreams, which would have made the whole Dutch business so much easier to pursue.

Affluent, pompous, by his very virtues reminding everyone uncomfortably of an earlier age, Clarendon had no widespread popularity to counteract the loss of the royal favour. Two marriages were further held against him – the alien Portuguese match to Catharine was laid as his door; while the fact that his own daughter was likely to be Queen, if Charles died without issue, only increased Clarendon's unpopularity, exacerbated by the failure of the Dutch War.

In the meantime, the King was discovering for himself the advantages of younger, more accommodating servants. Besides Arlington, now married to a rich Dutchwoman, and Thomas Clifford, there was Buckingham's Yorkshire protégé Thomas Osborne, two years younger than the King. Osborne was a handsome fellow who probably joined the anti-Clarendon group when Clarendon slighted him over the profitable Yorkshire Excise. The King himself understood his worth: for example, Osborne's name was inserted in the King's own handwriting into the list of commissioners appointed to examine the Irish accounts.[2]

One mark of Buckingham's Yorkshire-based group, in Clarendon's prejudiced opinion, was exhibitionism. They were, he wrote, 'all bold speakers, and meant to make themselves considerable by saying upon all occasions what wiser men would not, whatever they thought'.[3] As a matter of fact, Osborne had diligence as well as boldness, as his subsequent career in the King's service would demonstrate. Nevertheless, the sport of Chancellor-baiting was an easy one for these younger men to propose in the embittered atmosphere of that autumn of 1667.

There was a temporary reverse in Buckingham's fortunes in the summer, a silly matter of the King's horoscope being cast. By September however the ebullient Duke, his good looks becoming puffy with age, but his spirits in no way weighted down, was back in favour. Nor was Buckingham the only one to see in the fall of Clarendon a convenient solution to the expensive fiasco of the Dutch War. Arlington was joined with Buckingham in the cause. Barbara Castlemaine, who hated Clarendon – the feeling was mutual – joined with her cousin Buckingham and exerted what was literally petticoat influence: after Clarendon's disgrace she was spotted in her aviary at Whitehall, wearing a smock and 'joying herself at the old man's going away'.[4]

Under different circumstances, Clarendon might have survived these animosities. In the spring of 1667 he wrote to his old friend Nicholas that he intended to lodge peaceably in his own (newly built and magnificent) house and enjoy his sustained good health, 'which is worth a great deal of money'.[5] But the violent Parliamentary attacks coincided with the King's own feeling that the Chancellor had outlasted his usefulness, and that he needed to evolve a different method of handling the government, if the monarchical role was to be played as he wished. New advisers raised in him hopes of new and better parliamentary management.

The public move against Clarendon came from Arlington and Sir William Coventry combined. Coventry, another of the new men who was roughly the same age as the King, was an attractive character, possessing both wit and courage, as his career in the Civil War as a very young soldier had demonstrated; his work at the Admiralty, under the Duke of York, was devoted and intelligent, and in the summer of 1667 he was made a Joint Commissioner of the Treasury. Now Coventry turned to the attack on Clarendon with zest.

Parliament bayed for blood. The Chancellor's windows in Piccadilly were broken; it was the fate of another old servant of the State, the Duke of Wellington, whose windows at Apsley House were broken two centuries later by the mob. At some point, flight was suggested to the elderly Chancellor to avoid the penalties of impeachment. Lady Clarendon in her anguish was 'given over for dead'. The Chancellor duly went, his departure witnessed by Arlington, amongst others, 'with great gaiety and triumph' from Barbara's windows. Clarendon looked up. 'Pray remember that, if you live, you will grow old,' he said to the radiant favourite.[6]

So the ageing Earl of Clarendon took up his residence at Montpellier, to enjoy the health of which he had boasted only six months before to Nicholas. Only he employed it not to contemplate the aggregate of his worldly possessions with serenity, his pastures, his mansions and his apple-trees, but to write, with measured anger but also with sonorous recall, the history of his own times.

Most likely it was the King who suggested his flight, promising in return that his estates and honours would be safe. It was no part of his plan that Clarendon should have an opportunity to justify himself against the accusations of his enemies. The general charge of high treason brought against Clarendon would never have been made to stick; but the episode might have had unpleasant ramifications. Besides, Charles avoided confrontations, by temperament, whenever possible. The King did not attempt to conceal that Clarendon's disappearance from the political scene was a profound relief to him personally. He regretted of course that Clarendon would not allow the dismissal to be handled 'privately' – he had asked James to get his father-in-law to resign. Beyond that, 'the truth is, his behaviour and humour was grown so insupportable to myself, and to all the world also, that I could not longer endure it'. But the nub of the matter came in the next sentiment: 'It was impossible for me to live with it,' wrote Charles to Ormonde, 'and do those things with Parliament that must be done or the government will be lost.'[7]

Long, long ago Charles II had decided to run before the storm, whenever that storm, if faced, was likely to buffet the royal vessel beyond repair. The decision was not therefore the product of weakness, still less of cowardice: rather of his own particular brand of strength; one might even term it ruthlessness.

The point has been made that the members of Parliament – like intelligent, trained animals – learned a new trick from the Clarendon affair, which they subsequently turned against their master. The impeachment of the King's minister could be the first road to office. The control of patronage rather than the mere removal of an unpopular minister was the ultimate result. Thus Arlington's adherents would drive out Buckingham; Shaftesbury would drive out Danby.... It was in this sense that James long after referred to the impeachment as 'the most fatal blow the King gave himself to his power and prerogative'.[8] The remark illustrates a profound difference of character between the two brothers. James saw the royal prerogative as something which had to be seen to be wielded; Charles merely wished to wield it when absolutely necessary. In 1667 he saw his problem quite correctly as ruling *with* Parliament – his policies, their supplies – and this Clarendon had not enabled him to do. The King hoped to do better in the future. Referring to the recent 'revolution' – the common seventeenth-century word to denote a change-round in affairs – Charles showed himself confident that it would bring about 'a real and visible amendment' to his affairs. Already it seemed to him 'well liked in the world'.[9] Indeed, in view of Clarendon's failures, and the demands of Parliament, it is difficult to see that the King was politically wrong. The spectacle of a sovereign 'dropping the pilot' – the phrase applied to the dismissal of Bismarck by the Kaiser – is never an attractive one. But from 1660 onwards King Charles II was not in business to charm by his actions. To rule, if possible with the approval of Parliament, struck him as being the first duty of the King.

Who now gained political power? Certainly the Buckingham faction benefited from Clarendon's fall. Osborne became a Joint Treasurer of the Navy. Other supporters of Buckingham were preferred. But it was not simply a case of the rise of the Cabal – that acronym which, as every schoolboy knows (or tries desperately to remember), conveniently covers the names of Clifford, Arlington, Buckingham, Ashley and Lauderdale. For one thing, the Cabal was not nearly as united as the acronym suggests, particularly in the late 1660s, and it would be several years before anything like a Cabal policy could be discerned. Nor did Buckingham assume that total leadership which Clarendon had once enjoyed. Arlington was popularly regarded as his rival for the King's favour in the group.[10]

The most striking immediate effect of Clarendon's fall was to divide the King and the Duke of York. The closeness which had existed between them earlier in the reign gave way to a 'kind of inward distance', in Pepys' phrase.[11] This change was in part engineered by Buckingham. With hindsight, we know that Clarendon was not to emerge from his exile (he died in 1674) and that Montpellier proved no Colombey-les-deux-Eglises. But Buckingham and his supporters lived in terror that matters might be suddenly reversed. And the Duke of York, as Clarendon's son-in-law, they conceived would be the principal agent in such a reversal.

At this point it is worth taking a cool look both at the position and the character of the Duke of York towards the end of the first decade of Charles' reign. For one thing, it is not conceivable that the seeds of discord could have been sown between the two brothers if Charles' attitude towards James had not already been slightly ambiguous. On the surface, there was genuine camaraderie – not only the jolly, competitive yacht races, but also brother advancing brother, as Charles promoted James' interests at the Admiralty. But Charles' complicated feelings towards the presence of James at sea have also been noted. James had grown up to be an interesting character: he was brave, genuinely so, and not unintelligent. But he had a rigidity which sometimes goes with courage. Charles, on the other hand, had decided early on to bend, not break. This makes the political contrast between the two remaining brothers of the Stuart family peculiarly intriguing. Their experiences – many of them shared – had pointed them in totally different directions.

The same contrast can be discerned in their respective attitudes towards the Catholic religion. Unlike Charles, James had shown a propensity towards it during the later years of exile, as though its certainties appealed to that streak of the martinet in his own nature. At the Restoration he was described as 'a professed friend to the Catholics'. The inclinations of his first wife played their part. Anne Duchess of York died as a Catholic in March 1671, having leant in that direction for several years. James was increasingly unfaithful to her throughout their marriage: but, as a woman of strong character (and strong build – for she took refuge in eating), Anne continued to influence the more serious side of his life.[12] The precise date of his own conversion is not known – it is given as 1669 in his Memoirs and it was probably at about that time, or slightly earlier, that he became convinced of Catholic truths. By July 1671 James was telling the French Ambassador that he felt extremely pressed by his conscience to declare himself publicly; he had not taken Communion at Easter that year. It seems that he was officially received into the Catholic Church early in 1672. However, he continued to attend Anglican services until 1676. After that his conversion was an open secret, although, at his brother's request, he never declared it publicly. This proved a tactical advantage at the time of the Exclusion debates, when it was argued by some that it was not yet 'legally' certain that James was a Catholic.[13]

With Charles the whole process was very different. It was not that he had any temperamental aversion to changing his religion: many of his forebears had done so. The religion of princes – and people – was changeable for reasons of expediency in the seventeenth century to an extent that it is sometimes difficult for the twentieth century to conceive. But Charles drew a sharp distinction between a political standpoint and a private faith.* With regard to the former, his fierce declarations of Protestantism in exile and at the Restoration gradually gave way to a more relaxed attitude. Then the notion of his own conversion, leading on to that of England herself, began to serve as a useful card in the tortuous negotiations with the Catholic King Louis XIV. Later still, the *furore* of the Popish Plot made royal Cath-

* A more modern parallel may be drawn between the Catholicism of King Charles II and that of the first Catholic President of the United States, John F. Kennedy. He made it clear that he drew a distinction between his role as President and as a private member of the Catholic Church; as the former, for example, he was not subject to the authority of the Papacy.

olicism once again dangerous. All this remained in the domain of politics.

Where the King's private faith was concerned, the most revealing description was that given by Bishop Burnet, who wrote in 1683 that the King had formed 'rather an odd idea' of the goodness of God in his mind. He thought that 'to be wicked and to design mischief, is the only thing God hates . . .'. As a result, the King felt free to gratify his appetites if they did no harm.[14] It was – and is – an attractive philosophy, if not precisely orthodox. Time and his own tastes, including, we must assume, that philosophy, led Charles inexorably towards Catholicism, a religion where the frailty of the flesh has always been understood. At all events, his devout proclivities grew with age, a development not confined to kings. A number of other factors were at work, including the docility of the English Catholics, the intolerance of the Anglicans, the Catholic timbre of his Court, even the Queen's pious sweetness. At last, on his death-bed, the King allowed himself to be received. By then it was too late for any declaration to damage the position of the monarchy. The need for a political standpoint was over. He went to his royal grave a Catholic, and at peace.

Yet it is a wood so large that it has sometimes obscured the trees – the fact that Charles never did declare himself to be a Catholic during his active life. Not only did he tell Madame (in 1670) that he was not yet satisfied with the Catholic truth: in November of the same year he received a visit from the Papal Nuncio at which the subject of his hypothetical conversion was not mentioned – odd indeed if this tumultuous change had recently taken place. As late as 1675 he told the French Ambassador Barrillon that his brother James' Catholicism endangered the throne – which was of course true. Even at the King's death-bed, Louise Duchess of Portsmouth, the mistress who shared the intimacy of his later years and probably knew more of his private inclinations than anyone else, herself an ardent (if not pious) Catholic, could not say more to Barrillon than that the King had always been a Catholic at heart.[15] It was a strange remark, if the King had been converted many years earlier.

Most cogent of all is the testimony of Father Huddleston,

the priest who finally received the King. Charles II, in his general confession, declared himself heartily sorry 'for that he had deferr'd his Reconciliation [to the Catholic Church] so long'.[16] That again was a strange statement for a man to make on the eve of his death, if it was not true; and a strange statement for Father Huddleston to publish afterwards if it was demonstrably false.

It is true that one account exists by which the King, in an affecting scene, proclaimed 'his mind in regard to religion' on 25 January 1669. He was said to have shed 'tears of joy at the thought of the revival of the Romish religion in England' in front of an audience consisting of James himself, Lord Arundel (a Catholic), Arlington (a Catholic sympathizer) and Clifford (a future Catholic). But the provenance of the story makes it suspicious. The authority is found in the so-called Memoirs of James II – in fact, a document compiled by other hands to supplement James' own notes.[17] It was edited and printed in the early nineteenth century: most of the original has since disappeared and cannot be compared with the text. One cannot therefore regard these memoirs as a first-hand or even reliable source on such an important topic. This is not to say that the story was invented, only that the details were coloured up in the light of the King's death-bed conversion. Probably Charles made one of his welcoming speeches on the subject of Catholicism – to be compared with his warm words to Father Huddleston after Worcester. But his indubitably secretive behaviour on the subject of religion was not altered.

At the same time, Charles the pragmatist was not without a reluctant admiration for James the man of principle, where religion as well as politics were concerned. It was as though he was fascinated by James' intransigence, that very quality he had dismissed for himself as being disastrous in a king. He never, for example, wished James to suffer for his religious principles, and even, incredibly, did not forbid James' second Catholic marriage – a manifest political disaster. Then there was the whole question of the succession. That too was crucial to the relationship between the two brothers. Like the religion of Charles II, it was not at all a straightforward matter.

James' position as heir presumptive went through several phases during the 1660s, first weakened by the King's marriage, then strengthened by the Queen's apparent infertility. For as the years went by Catharine still did not succeed in conceiving.* It was not until 7 May 1668 that the King wrote to his sister that his wife had miscarried that morning. On the same date Pepys reported that the Queen had miscarried 'of a perfect child' about ten weeks old. Charles was more cautious: 'And though I am troubled', he wrote, 'yet I am glad that 'tis evident she was with child, which I will not deny to you till now I did fear she was not capable of.'[19] Poor Catharine had already endured the primitive suffering of a barren wife for six long years of marriage. Not only was her fertility the subject of constant speculation, but Barbara's growing brood constituted a perpetual reminder that the fault lay with her and not her husband. Now her hopes were once more dashed.

By this time several of the notorious ways of dealing with a barren wife had already been publicly mentioned. At the time of Charles' unrequited romance with Frances, the notion of his remarriage – perhaps on the Queen's death, perhaps on divorce – had been vaguely mooted in gossip, if nowhere more substantial. By May 1668 the rumours had grown. Meanwhile, the ground swell of suggestion that Monmouth was actually legitimate, or would be now legitimized, grew.

In the spring of 1669 there were two further developments. First, Lord Roos, suffering from a wanton wife and separated from her in the spiritual courts, decided to take his case to the House of Lords in order to secure a civil divorce as well. He wished to remarry, and a special Act of Parliament was his only possible recourse at this date. The Roos case was followed with

* This deliberately sets aside two contemporary references to a pregnancy in early 1666, one from Pepys, who heard that the Queen had miscarried, and one in the Hatton Correspondence. But Clarendon, who mentioned the 1666 miscarriage in the *Continuation* of his *History*, stressed the King's belief that it had 'been a false conception'.[18] The King made no reference to this pregnancy or miscarriage in his correspondence with his sister, where such matters were always much to the fore. His testimony – the testimony of the husband – that the 1668 pregnancy was the first, clinches the matter.

extreme interest by all parties who felt themselves concerned with the question of the succession. No such extreme step had been taken before. The case was widely regarded as a kite flown to test the wind in that direction for the King himself, should he wish to divorce Catharine. Not only was it advocated by Buckingham and Bristol, his confidants, but the King made a point of attending the debates, commenting gaily that the action was as good as a play. James and his faction were not unnaturally most hostile to the Bill.

Then in May, exactly a year after her first conception, the Queen was pronounced – possibly – pregnant again by the King. 'My wife has been a little indisposed for some days,' he told Madame, 'and there is hope that it will prove a disease not displeasing to me. I should not have been so forward in saying this much without more certainty, but that I believe others will write it to Paris and say more than there is.' As if in confirmation of this, Pepys wrote in his *Diary* a few days later that everyone at the Court concluded that the Queen was far gone with child! A week later the diarist himself saw the Queen in a white pinner and apron, the maternity dress of the time.[20]

Madame of course was overcome with excitement and agitation, and demanded full details. She was rewarded with a letter full of medical exposition on 24 May. The relevant passage reads:

> She missed *those* [that is, her period] almost, if not altogether, twice, about this time she ought to have them, and she had a kind of colic the day before yesterday which pressed downwards and made her apprehend she would miscarry, but today she is so well she does not keep her bed. The midwives who have searched her say that her matrix is very close, though it be a little low; she has now and then some little shows of *them*, but in so little quantity as it only confirms the most knowing women here that there is a fair conception.[21]

Alas for these expectations. On 7 June the King wrote again to his sister informing her that a miscarriage had taken place 'after all our hopes' and 'without any visible accident' (although one story has it the misadventure was caused by the Queen's pet fox). The King reported the doctors as being still divided 'whether it had been on a false conception or a good one'; nevertheless it seems likely on the evidence that the wretched woman had indeed conceived twice.* If Burnet is to be believed, then Dr Willis, the celebrated physician, told Dr Lloyd (who told Burnet) that the Queen miscarried so late on an unspecified occasion that the sex of the child could have been identified.[22] What is quite certain is that Catharine never conceived again. Even more to the point, she was not expected to do so. The King, who had, on his own admission, been doubtful of her capability in 1668, definitely gave up hope after the fiasco of 1669, which in any case had been antedated by the appearance of the Roos case.

The clear loser from any royal divorce was James. For it might soon endow his brother with a new and fertile wife, a quiverful of children. It is no coincidence therefore that this period, in which Charles tentatively, even whimsically, played with the notion of divorcing Catharine, was also a period of coolness between the royal brothers. It was not such an absolutely shocking suggestion. As the King himself was supposed to have observed about this time, if a man could be divorced for impotency, he did not see why a woman should not be divorced for barrenness.

The divorce of a Queen who failed to provide an heir was hardly without precedent: by the laws of the Catholic church, barrenness constituted one clear ground for annulment. Matters would be made easier if Catharine herself agreed to retire into a nunnery, thus acknowledging her own fault. Buckingham was rumoured to have suggested kidnapping her, if she would not agree to this comforting solution. Marvell heard that Madame

* The author is grateful to Sir John Dewhurst, President of the Royal College of Obstetricians and Gynaecologists, for his consideration of the medical evidence concerning the pregnancies of Catharine of Braganza, which supports this view. The sweeping theory of C. MacLaurin in *Mere Mortals* (New York, 1925) that the Queen's major illness of November 1663 was pelvic peritonitis, which left her sterile after an inflammation of the Fallopian tubes, takes no account of these later conceptions and is not otherwise supported by evidence.

would arrange for a marriage with a Frenchwoman, or alternatively a sister of the King of Denmark or even 'a good virtuous Protestant here at home'.[23]

Many rumours do not necessarily add up to one hard fact, particularly if unsupported by firm evidence of the King's own commitment. Charles' public interest in the Roos Bill does seem to provide this evidence. John Wilkins, Bishop of Chester, who was its chief intellectual promoter, referred significantly to the fact that 'divorce might be not only in case of adultery but also of the immundicity of the womb, which is given forth to [be] the queen's condition'.[24]

The Roos case was decided in the husband's favour but the King did not take advantage of the decision. There is a sharp distinction to be drawn between the King's flirtation – it may have been no more than that – with the idea of a divorce, and the parallel rumours concerning the legitimization of Monmouth. This move would have been of course even more unwelcome to James. A new Queen (who might prove barren in her turn) had to be accepted; at least her offspring would stand quite indubitably ahead of him in the succession. The legitimization of Monmouth was quite another matter, constituting a lethal snub to James. And although rumours continued to fly about on the subject, it has to be faced that the King never at any time gave them countenance.

The favourite canard was that Charles would declare himself to have legally married Lucy Walter (who had died a few years before he married Catharine, so that the validity of this second ceremony would not be affected). As has been pointed out, the idea of this marriage was a fantasy, the King having been very much otherwise engaged at the time, unlikely to contemplate any wife except a rich and powerful princess. There is no solid evidence to suggest that Charles ever contemplated dispossessing James by a piece of calculated deception concerning Monmouth's birth. On the other hand, it may easily have crossed his mind to divorce Catharine, and thus by implication dispossess James – but that move would incidentally have been in direct contradiction to the policy of legitimizing Monmouth.

The Monmouth *coterie*, like Monmouth himself, were the prey of their own optimistic visions: how the King would like to 'own' Monmouth but did not know how to do so. But the King did nothing. Catharine remained undivorced, Monmouth unacknowledged. Meanwhile, this temporary ruffle between King and York became gradually smoothed. A better relationship was established. James' stature as heir presumptive was undiminished.

The King's true preoccupation from the fall of Clarendon onwards was not his own successor but his serpentine discussions with France. He may even have been cynically pleased that the hue and cry over Queen, Duke and Monmouth diverted the loud mouths of the Commons and Court from a secret wooing which was taking place between the two kings, Charles II and Louis XIV. For Charles, described so often by his contemporaries as being lazy at business, was not showing himself lazy where foreign policy was concerned. Quite as much as his subjects, he was humiliated and furious at the memory of that 'Black Day accurs'd' when the Dutch had ravished the chaste Medway. By the end of 1668 he had secured a remarkable diplomatic triumph from this degrading position. After the Peace of Breda, a Triple Alliance was constructed between England, Holland and Sweden. Newly vulnerable, France immediately concluded the Peace of Aix-la-Chapelle with Spain, and an ostensible tranquillity prevailed across the map of Europe.

It is probably correct to regard this apparent turnabout in alliances – two of the three powers concerned had recently been fighting each other in a nasty and quite prolonged war – as mere shadow-boxing. There is no evidence that Charles II's competitive aversion to the Dutch had abated. But he hoped that the Triple Alliance might prove an efficient way of dealing with his growing domestic problems. These included a bankrupt Treasury and a highly restive House of Commons, many of whose members were beginning to voice anti-French – and anti-Catholic – sentiments. The Triple Alliance had a nice Protestant sound to it; more money might be forthcoming from Parliament as a result. It is significant that Clifford, ever representing the naval point of view, disliked the Alliance. At the same time, of course, Charles had effectively prevented Holland from ganging up with France against England once more.

Across the straits of the North Sea, Johann De Witt was animated by a similar consideration, to keep England from the arms of France. Indeed, the first move towards the alliance came from De Witt.[25] The notion was delicately conveyed to Charles' Ambassador in Holland, Sir William Temple, in the autumn of 1667. Temple was instructed to explore the possibility. From the first it was an unnatural alliance, much less sweet to Charles than the ultimate prospect of 'revenge on Holland'. Nevertheless there was certain unfinished business between the Dutch and English rulers which these negotiations might assist. This was the position of Charles' nephew, William III of Orange.*

At the end of the war, De Witt considered it prudent to have the seventeen-year-old boy admitted to the Council of State; but at the same time the Stadtholdership of Holland was abolished (although not hereditary it might have been granted to William as Prince of Orange). William however showed some sign of that implacable political quality which would one day both chill and dazzle Europe. He went before the States of Zeeland and pleaded successfully to be admitted as first noble, by right of his inherited position as Margrave of Flushing and Vere. On his eighteenth birthday, 14 November 1668, he was declared to have come of age.

There was also the question of the considerable sums of money Charles had borrowed from the private coffers of the House of Orange, while in exile. These monies had never been returned and even the late Princess Mary's dowry had never been paid in full: the total was nearly a quarter of a million pounds. William paid a four-month visit to England in 1670 to try to secure them – an optimistic foray in view of his uncle's financial position. However recourse was had to one of the King's chief financial agents, Edward Backwell. He had already

* His correct title: he succeeded his father, William II of Orange. He subsequently became William III of *England*. To avoid confusion, in this narrative he will henceforward be known as William of Orange.

burnt his fingers over the Queen's dowry by advancing money to the King before the Portuguese paid up (a slow business as it proved and never satisfactorily completed). Even so, valuing the royal connection, Backwell took on the task of paying off William over a period of four years on the security of orders on the Customs' receipts.[26]

More immediately William was given the due precedence of his blood royal, out-ranking, for example, his cousin Prince Rupert (also the son of a Stuart princess) in an age when such things were marked. For Charles, whatever cozening noises he made towards his nephew's Dutch hopes, continued to view him as a Stuart dependent who was conveniently placed in the enemy's camp.

A portrait of William as a boy, by Adriaen Hanneman, together with a portrait of his dead mother Mary, hung in the King's bedchamber at Whitehall: unconsciously Charles may still have thought of him as that child. The King's attitude to the young man was both patronizing and critical. The French Ambassador reported that King Charles found Prince William too passionate a Hollander, too much a Protestant.[27] The King's surprise that this should be so, in view of William's upbringing (did he expect a Catholic-oriented Frenchman?), betrays a certain naïveté. Given their respective tastes and characters, it was perhaps not to be expected that Charles II and the future William III would fall into each other's arms. Nevertheless, the stance adopted by the uncle towards his nephew did nothing to increase the prospect. As it was, Charles, who expected both to help William by the alliance and be helped by him, was disappointed.

The Dutch involvement was popular with the English Parliament because it aimed at France. Nor did all Charles' ministers disapprove of it as Clifford did: Arlington, for example, the Spanish sympathizer, with a Dutch heiress for a wife – '*Espagnol par lui-même et Hollandais par sa femme*', as Ruvigny termed him – loved the concept. 'God be thanked it is done,' he exclaimed.[28] Determined to fan some financial warmth out of the Members of Parliament with his new bellows, the King spoke eloquently in February 1668 of his renewed need for money: 'I lie under great debts contracted in the last war; but now the posture of our neighbours abroad, and the consequence of the new alliance will oblige me, for our security, to set out a considerable fleet to sea this summer.' Fortifications had to be repaired and 'besides, I must build more great ships'.[29]

The King's financial situation at the time is best summed up by the later witticism, 'desperate but not serious'. A committee was set up for retrenchment; pensions were cut, or stopped, without being cancelled, by the simple expedient of not paying them. Ambassadorial expenses were severely checked and plate, often regarded as a perquisite of office, was demanded back after use. When Lord Sandwich asked for £5,000 for his mission to Spain, he was asked to be more specific about his needs.[30]

Nor did the influence of Buckingham introduce any kind of order into the chaos. Buckingham, as has been observed, devoted his elastic energies to the demolition of the York party, in the process of which he chose to bring about the fall of Sir William Coventry. It was comparatively easy to lay the blame for the naval failures at the Admiralty's door. In October 1668 Pepys described Buckingham as 'all in all' and determined to 'ruin Coventry if he can'.[31] Despite the fact that Coventry had joined in the hue and cry against Clarendon, he was attacked in his turn, and attacked successfully. A brief spell of imprisonment in the Tower in the spring of 1669 followed an imbroglio with Buckingham over a satirical play; later Coventry retired altogether from politics.

Far more serious was Buckingham's freakish vengeance on the Duke of Ormonde, which resulted in the fall of that genuinely great man. Buckingham had the frivolous energy of a born intriguer, which from small beginnings will often secure calamitously great results. Ormonde's removal from the Lord Lieutenancy was brought about in February 1669. Probably there were some instances during his period of office which justified impeachment, or at least did not bear close inspection. Ormonde would have been unique in his period to have headed an administration in Ireland without stain. Yet in another way Ormonde *was* unique: in his appreciation of the native quality of Ireland. He had, for example, influenced the foundation of the Irish College of Physicians, and prohibited the import of Scottish linen in revenge for the iniquitous Bill (Buckingham's delight) prohibiting the import of Irish cattle into England. Ormonde's removal, followed by the appointment of the ineffective Lord Robartes, demonstrated once again how adversely the feuding of English internal politics seemed to affect Ireland's internal destiny.

If Buckingham, and for that matter Osborne, had pursued some constructive policy of their own, their destructive efforts in other directions might not have proved so catastrophic. As it was, they were more obsessed with building up and maintaining their own power base without in fact offering the King, within Parliament, a particularly solid structure.[32] It was true that there were numerous Court officials. Also, Buckingham could muster his own body of MPs, the Duke of York (once reconciled to his brother) and his friends, another body. Counting those MPs who had demonstrated a willingness to support the Crown on various occasions, there was in theory a substantial conglomerate at the King's disposal.

Reality was very different. Between the pro-Dutch sympathies of Arlington, for example, and the pro-French leanings of Buckingham there was an obvious and unbridgeable gulf. Other pettier divisions existed. In the late 1660s nothing like a homogeneous Court party was in fact at the command of Charles II. His groans to Madame over his constant financial troubles amply illustrate one side of this, as do his reiterated pleas to Parliament itself on the subject of money. Charles expressed it to Parliament, called again in October 1669 after an eighteen months' gap for this precise purpose, thus: 'I desire that you will now take my debts effectually into your consideration.' The House of Commons remained more interested in its internal disputes, arguments over the relative powers of the House of Lords. In February of the following year the King was reduced to begging that their squabbles should cease, while asking for money 'with greater instance'.[33]

This irksome impotence was the background not only to the King's crucial initiative in foreign policy in the direction of

France, but also to the efforts of Lauderdale to bring about a proper union between England and Scotland. In 1667 Lauderdale had acquired at last the position he coveted, as Lord High Commissioner for Scotland. His protégé Lord Rothes was further installed as Chancellor. Lauderdale played some part in the fall of Clarendon, and subsequently developed that influence over Charles which had begun as far back as 1648, when Lauderdale turned out to be the one Scot Charles really liked. He paid his first visit to Edinburgh in his splendid new vice-regal role in October 1669. Neither Lauderdale himself nor his termagant red-haired wife, the former Bess Countess of Dysart, allowed any tinge of austerity to touch their conception of their Scottish court. Bribery, nepotism, corruption, *louche* – and lavish - spending: these would be amongst the charges whispered and shouted against the Lauderdales. For all that, Lauderdale was no Buckingham in his lack of a proper policy to pursue.

The coarseness of the man, the extravagance of his entourage (he was said to cost the King £18,000 a year in Scotland), should not blind one to the fact that Lauderdale was intent on offering something positive to his sovereign in the shape of a Scottish policy. To him the country he referred to as 'poor old Scotland' could nevertheless be turned into 'a citadel for his Majesty's service'.[34] To be frank, it was about the one proposition for Scotland's future which was likely to sound musically in Charles' ears. If Scotland could genuinely be transformed into a monarchical citadel, how much more fortunate might Charles II prove than Charles I, for whom Scotland had been a quagmire rather than a bastion?

It was Lauderdale's conviction that Scotland's internal government – and problems – should be her own, while the strong central administration which he expected to set up would ensure her a place in the British monarchical scheme of things. To draw a line between Lauderdale's instinct for self-aggrandizement in all this, and his genuine desire to discover some solution for a strong Scotland, is probably impossible: like many men of force, Lauderdale was inclined to equate his own best interests with his country's. Yet in the sense that Lauderdale did intend to right the many grievances of the Scots – suffering as second-class citizens – by an Act of Union, he did display both understanding and patriotism. He showed an unfortunate impatience towards his Presbyterian opponents, characteristic of one side of him; yet even in the opinion of Robert Law, a Covenanting minister, he was 'a man very national'.[35]

To many Lauderdale was quite simply 'the Hector of State,/The rascal we hate' as in the rude rhyme of the Earl of Aboyne. Yet he reacted with genuine indignation to the Navigation Acts, whose careless neglect of the very existence of Scottish trade caused the country much unplanned suffering. Ever since the reign of James VI and I, indeed, the Scots had been penalized over their trading, whether with the colonies or the Dutch. The fact that this sprang more from lordly English indifference to Scottish interests than deliberate victimization still did not endear the process to the Scots. Lauderdale demanded that Scottish trade conditions should revert to the situation as it was before the punitive Navigation Acts. He considered it intolerable, for example, that the Scots should have to pay duties on English imports.

To Lauderdale the Union offered the Scots the opportunity to flourish equally with England. In his rough and wily way (the two adjectives were compatible where Lauderdale was concerned) he was a patriot. By offering brilliantly to Charles a 'citadel' where his prerogative would be respected and enforced, he hoped to overcome those coldly negative feelings which the King had long entertained, in so far as he entertained any feelings at all, towards Scotland. In return, the King would ameliorate the conditions of Scottish trade.

By October 1669 Lauderdale had worked on Charles sufficiently to win him to the idea of a Union. The King recommended the idea to his Parliament. Unfortunately, by exaggerating the nature of the support the King would find there he also laid up further political troubles along the way. There was a question of a body of 24,000 men: the King believed in its existence, taking Rothes' word for it, and the opposition fulminated at the idea. Yet all along this force was more of a phantom army than a power base.

The Union of 1670 failed however not so much on this

aspect as through English xenophobia. Another Union had failed in the same way, that finely conceived Union proposed by King James I in 1606 (which, if accepted, might have altered the entire internal history of the two countries). King James had spoken of 'a perpetual marriage', suggesting eloquently that two nations 'under one roof or rather in one Bed' ought to have economic integration. But the House of Commons merely expressed disgust at granting parity to the carpet-bagging Scots. The Parliament of Charles II had similar doubts. Nor were the Scots for their part accommodating, after sixty years of maltreatment, including the Cromwellian occupation. They claimed – without success – equal representation in the united Parliament.

In the House of Commons Andrew Marvell symbolized the angry English reaction to these proposals: when Lauderdale was given the Garter, Marvell declared he actually deserved a halter. The King himself was not prepared to transform cautious approval of the Union into anything much warmer. In November 1670, he told the commissioners appointed to look into the whole matter that they must meet later: union was not at present feasible. Thus the Union of 1670 joined the ranks of Anglo-Scottish unions – and Anglo-Scottish opportunities – lost. King James' two nations in one bed would continue to toss and turn restlessly, without the perpetual marriage of his dreams, for another thirty-seven years.

CHAPTER SEVENTEEN

A Very Near Alliance

'I do believe we are not so tied, as if we received satisfaction over the principal matter of the sea, there is scope sufficient for a very near alliance.'

Charles II to Madame in 1668, on the subject of France

At some point late in 1668 King Charles decided formally to pursue an alliance with his cousin Louis XIV by any means that might prove useful (not necessarily of the most honourable or open). As has been mentioned, Charles II had veered towards France since the beginning of his reign, just as he had backed away from the Dutch. He had hoped for French neutrality during the Dutch War. But this decision represented something new.

His cynicism towards his own Parliament was growing, and the French initiative cannot altogether be separated from it. The secret feelings of such a wary character as Charles II must always be analysed with care; nevertheless, the distinct impression is gained that he saw in the French alliance, from the first, one solution to his domestic insecurity. Charles the politician was taking unto himself the maxim of Machiavelli: 'Every government, whether it be republican or of the princely type, should consider beforehand what adverse times may befall and on what people it may have to rely in times of adversity....' It was a precept which King Charles I, unassisted in his hour of tribulation by any major power, should have heeded. His son intended to be warier.

The character of Louis XIV also exercised a baleful fascination over Charles II – as indeed it did over the whole of Europe. The two monarchs, who had of course known each other in youth, were not destined to meet after that abortive encounter at Fuenterrabia in 1659. Yet the personality and reputation of Louis XIV represented the living challenge to Charles II, much as that of Oliver Cromwell represented the dead. Critics detecting weakness in Charles were quick to point out strength in Louis – Buckingham was a notable example. Pepys reports a conversation round the dinner table in November 1668 in which 'the greatness of the King of France' was the subject of much favourable comment: 'his being fallen into the right way of making that Kingdom great, which none of his Ancestors did before'.[1] There is evidence that King Charles did not care for this atmosphere of odious comparison.

Rationally he was aware that his cousin of France enjoyed the perquisites of absolute monarchy, while he himself had to jog along with something the French Ambassador had critically described in 1664 as 'at the bottom ... very far from being a monarchy'. Charles II would have been less than human not to have resented the contemporary admiration for Louis XIV in view of his considerable efforts to make his own kingdom great. The incident of the Persian Vest, which shows up King Charles for once in a slightly foolish light, is only explicable in terms of his obsession with King Louis.[2]

Fashion as such never much interested Charles II after 1660. In exile he showed a taste for ordering beaver hats and swords from Paris, and at the moment of restoration a wardrobe of summer clothes from the great Parisian tailor Sourceau, trimmings to be chosen by his mother, was deemed appropriate. These were the predilections of enforced idleness. Afterwards the wardrobe accounts reveal the occasional order for six yards of lace, forty yards of linen – fitting for a King – as special adornment for his birthday; but there is a more characteristic glimpse of him taking off his wig in order to inspect Chatham dockyard in comfort.[3] Casualness, even carelessness, rather than magnificence, was the keynote of Charles' appearance in the eyes of his contemporaries.

The Persian Vest incident was however an example of an

early kind of Buy British campaign. Following the great depredations on trade made by the Fire of London, the King ordered French fashions to be abandoned. Instead he donned a loose surcoat, resembling fashions seen in Persian miniatures of the time. 'Nothing like it since William the Conqueror,' commented a newsletter. It was John Evelyn, seeing this strange new garb for the first time in October 1666, who compared it to 'the comeliness and usefulness of Persian clothing'.[4] At the Court ball for the birthday of Queen Catharine in November there were one hundred of such vests to be seen, each costing one hundred pounds to make; the King's was of suitably rich material, with a silver lining.

Unfortunately the Sun King of France, a sartorial connoisseur where his cousin was not, found the opportunity irresistible. He took to dressing his footmen and servants in a parody of the new English fashion. The mockery was reported back across the Channel. King Charles attempted to brazen out his newfangled elegance. The personality of King Louis was too strong. By the early 1670s the English had surrendered and returned to the French fashion.

The English king's obsession was however more compounded of admiration than annoyance. And his letters reveal also a true desire for intimacy with King Louis especially remarkable in one who was on his own confession a laggard correspondent. King Charles was in the habit of keeping King Louis in touch with all his family news: when the little Duke of Cambridge, son of the Duke and Duchess of York, died, Charles did not doubt that Louis would be as concerned as usual over everything to do with 'ma maison' – that is, the House of Stuart. In May 1669 we find King Charles appealing in a handwritten letter to King Louis, his *bon frère*, to use his authority to intervene in a dispute between Prince Rupert and one of his brothers.[5]

Religion – or 'the design about R.', as Madame coyly termed it – does not seem to have played any part at all in Charles' calculations at this point. Aiming at greatness abroad, security at home, and having lassoed for the time being the horns of the Dutch, Charles prepared to stalk the bigger game of Louis XIV. He was not ashamed to admit to Madame that the Triple

Alliance had its genesis in his disappointment with France. She might be 'a little surprised' by the treaty he had concluded with the Dutch, he wrote airily in January 1668, but she should not be. 'Finding my propositions to France receive so cold an answer, which in effect was as good as a refusal, I thought I had no other way but this to secure myself.'[6]

Louis XIV was intended to take the point and did. In May Charles was observing to the French Ambassador, Ruvigny, that he saw no reason why the two kings should not talk to each other 'de gentilhomme à gentilhomme' (although neither Charles II nor Louis XIV, in their diplomatic dealings, quite justify the use of the word). In August Louis despatched Colbert de Croissy to replace Ruvigny, with specific instructions to break up the Triple Alliance. Among methods recommended was the bribing of the pro-Dutch Arlington. In September Charles allowed himself a crack at Louis XIV's own support of the Dutch in the past war; in a letter to Madame, mentioning his own new Dutch commitment, he wrote that Louis XIV had recently given him an example of being 'a martyr to his word' in that respect. Nevertheless, 'when I have said this, I do believe we are not so tied, as if we received satisfaction over the principal matter of the sea, there is scope sufficient for a very near alliance'.[7]

Charles repeated the same sentiment in January of the following year: 'The only thing which can give any impediment to what we both desire is the matter of the sea, which is so essential point to us here as an union upon any other security can never be lasting.' By this time cautious negotiations were in fact proceeding. Madame, for example, had planned a visit to England in December. Her arrival had to be postponed owing to her pregnancy; Monsieur insisted on his marital rights, with the precise object of spoiling her plans. Yet the visit had obviously been intended to forward discussions between the two kings.

So the scene was set for Madame's embassy, the zenith of her life. It was also the most vital period so far (if more commonly rated the nadir than the zenith) in the reign of Charles II. For so, surely, the months between the signature of the Triple Alliance and the signature of the Secret Treaty of Dover in May 1670 must be regarded. Madame was given a special cipher for the purpose by her brother. Nevertheless, she remained the ambassadress of England rather than of France. Nothing emerges more clearly from Madame's letters to her brother than the continuance of her English as opposed to her French sympathies. As she told Arlington in a personal letter, she was concerned to bring about King Charles' advantage 'jusque au plus petite chose' – down to the slightest detail. The death of Henrietta Maria on French soil provided a striking demonstration of this. The Dowager Queen had survived the husband she adored by twenty years. She was only sixty-one; yet she reminded everyone of old, unhappy, far-off things, and her passing was not much regretted. Monsieur wanted to take the opportunity offered by French law to grab all her belongings and jewels for his wife, the only child actually resident in France. But Madame strenuously resisted the process. She insisted on returning to the Crown of England what was due to it.[8]

Secret but exhilarating negotiations continued throughout the spring and summer of 1669. Madame even described it as 'perilous' to confide the design to the Pope, since he would have no part in its execution. Everything was still publicly seen in terms of English victory over Holland. 'Your glory and profit will coincide in this design,' wrote Madame on 27 September. 'Indeed what is there more glorious and more profitable than to extend the confines of your kingdom beyond the sea and to become supreme in commerce, which is what your people most passionately desire and what will probably never occur so long as the Republic of Holland exists.'[9]

So Madame exulted, and so the prospect of 'the very near alliance' grew excitingly nearer to the royal conspirators.

In the spring of 1670 it was the opinion of Andrew Marvell that no king since the Conquest had been so 'absolutely powerful' as Charles II. Certainly the King opened the 1670 session of Parliament in state for the first time, a practice which stirred uncomfortable memories of the past for some; to others it was equally disquieting mimicry of the absolute state of Louis XIV across the water. Marvell noted another development which he described as sinister: the King taking his seat in the House of Lords. 'It is now so old, that it is new,' he wrote, 'and so disliked that at any other but so bewitched a time as this it would have been looked on as a high Usurpation, the Breach of Privilege.'[10]

That was how the royal position appeared from the angle of a critical MP. What was the King's own attitude to Parliament? Parliament was not yet quite disillusioned with Charles II. But he was certainly, by 1670, disillusioned with it. He was already using the prorogation of Parliament with quite new dexterity throughout 1668 and 1669 as an instrument of strategy; as a result, many fewer Acts were passed.[11] It is an inescapable fact that in early 1670, at the very moment Charles was negotiating with France, he played on the hatred of the House of Commons for the French by asking for money to fight them.... The conclusion of the King's contempt for his Commons is unavoidable.

If one may contrast Charles with Cromwell (a comparison the King would not have appreciated personally), Cromwell continually and rather pathetically believed in the theory of Parliaments. He would summon them, find himself angrily horrified by their selfish behaviour in practice and dismiss them. Charles II duly noted the self-seeking behaviour of the Parliaments in the first decade of his reign, shrugged his shoulders over the theory of the thing and decided to try and manipulate Parliament before it could manipulate him.

What inspired him? It was most emphatically not the vision of an autocratic monarchy: for that would have been once more theory rather than practice. But there was a vision all the same. It was the vision of an England strong abroad and at home, her fleet triumphant, superior to the Dutch, supported and abetted by her natural friend France. In January 1670 Charles II made this quite clear in an important personal memorandum beginning, 'As a war against Holland would in all respects suit with the interests of England and be very advantageous to it if the King of Great Britain had force ready to be master of the seas: so on the other hand if the Hollanders should be strongest at sea nothing in the world could be so pernicious to England as that war' – for then English trade would be at the mercy of the Dutch.[12]

By May 1670 the negotiations with France were sufficiently

advanced for Madame to pay her long-deferred, long-desired visit. Monsieur's permission had of course to be sought – and he gave it with a bad grace. He also attempted to stop Madame's journey by pregnancy as he had done before, his excuse being that he needed an heir (their only son had died as a baby). Failing, Monsieur granted the minimum period of absence consonant with etiquette. All the same, Madame was at last free to go. She arrived off Dover on 16 May. Unbelievably, it was close on ten years since they had met face to face, for Henriette-Anne had last visited England that winter of 1660 before her marriage. Yet the intimacy was as close as ever.

It was true that the girl Charles held in his arms at their ecstatic reunion aboard the flagship was more exquistely fragile and pale than ever (we now know that she was already seriously ill). But her spirit was as great as before. And the King found in her even greater enchantment. Only the English weather failed to respond to the challenge of Madame's visit. It poured with rain – cold English spring rain. Surely it never rained at the perfectly arranged Court of Louis XIV? But once the secret dealings were completed, as many royal junketings took place as could be fitted into the short span allowed to Madame. Louis XIV – not Monsieur – had granted her a few extra days. This satisfaction, Charles wrote back in a personal letter, 'm'oblige si sensiblement'.[13] Charles II's fortieth birthday happily fell within the period.

Notwithstanding the weather, there were parties at sea. Madame showed herself a worthy sister to the sea-loving King, for she was as 'fearless and bold' as though she were on dry land, walking along 'the edges of the ships'.[14] There was an inland trip as far as Canterbury, where Madame watched a comedy given by the Duke of York's troupe. She also attended her favourite ballet (it was not the King's favourite ballet: something about the art irritated him, and a few years later he would become publicly restless at an Italian ballet performed in honour of another birthday). Throughout Madame's stay, Charles loaded her with presents. He also gave her two thousand gold crowns to build a chapel at Chaillot in memory of their mother. However, when he tried lightly to obtain one little jewel in exchange – his sister's lady-in-waiting Louise de Kéroüalle, with her 'childish simple and baby face' – Madame firmly refused on the grounds that she was responsible to the young lady's parents in France. The inception of this royal relationship had to wait for another occasion.

In time came the dreaded hour of Madame's departure for France. Charles and James, overcome with grief, accompanied her on board the ship that would carry her away. Charles in particular could hardly tear himself away. Three times he said goodbye, only to return and embrace her. It was as though he had a presentiment that they would not meet again. The French Ambassador, Colbert de Croissy, wrote that until he witnessed the King's tears at this farewell he had not realized that Charles II – the cool-hearted monarch – was capable of feeling and expressing so much affection for anyone.[15]

One can make a case for saying that in her own way the poor, doomed Henriette-Anne was indeed the great love of Charles II's life. He had experienced other passions, including two unrequited loves for the eligible Henrietta Catharine and the unattainable Frances Stewart. He came to feel genuine admiration for his wife Catharine's character. He undoubtedly felt sexual passion for Barbara, later for Nell Gwynn and Hortense Mancini. For Louise de Kéroüalle, the mistress of his declining years, as we shall see, his feelings were slightly more complicated. It would be wrong to suggest that love was absent. But Henriette-Anne, with her charm, her affection, her loyalty, not forgetting her intelligence, could possess his whole heart. And sexuality, except in the most unconscious way, was not involved. Madame was that most seductive of things to a man sometimes wearied by the demands of his own sensuality: a ravishingly pretty sister.

Alas for King Charles: Madame, his delight, had only a few days of life left to her on her return to France. On 27 June she wrote a touching letter from Paris to Thomas Clifford in England: 'This is the ferste letter I have ever write in inglis. you will eselay see it bi the stile and the ortografe . . . i expose miself to be thought a foulle in looking to make you know how much I am your frind.'[16] The first English letter of this expatriate

Stuart princess was to be her last. She fell ill on 29 June and died the next day, after convulsions and other agonizing sufferings which appalled all those who attended her death-bed. It has been established that she died of acute peritonitis, following the perforation of a duodenal ulcer (hence the sickness which had ravaged her before she left France for England).[17] At the time, of course, the suddenness of her end and the public venom of her husband and of his favourite the Chevalier de Lorraine meant that the inevitable accusations of poisoning were raised. But no poison was in fact needed to finish off poor delicate Madame. She was just twenty-six years old at the time of her death.*

It was the famous Abbé Bossuet, himself amongst those present at Madame's death-bed, who preached her funeral sermon in language which Lytton Strachey, in a critical essay, compared to a stream of molten lava: 'O nuit désastreuse! O nuit effroyable! où retentit tout à coup, comme un éclat de tonnerre, cette étonnante nouvelle: Madame se meurt! Madame est morte!' It was Bossuet who had asked her as she was dying, 'Do you believe in God?' Madame replied, 'With all my heart.' But according to Ralph Montagu, the English envoy, Madame's last whisper was of her brother: 'I have loved him better than life itself and now my only regret in dying is to be leaving him.'[18]

When Charles was brought the desperate news by a courier coming post-haste from France, he collapsed with grief. The rumours of poison hardly helped him to endure the blow. The King did not appear outside his bedroom, where he lay prostrate with grief, for days – the only recorded occasion of a physical collapse in this almost unnaturally self-disciplined monarch, who had hitherto borne the plenitude of crises in his life without giving way to any of them.

* She died without presenting Monsieur with that male heir he so much desired. But Madame did leave two daughters; from Anne-Marie, who married a Duke of Savoy, the present (Catholic) Wittelsbach claimant to the English throne descends. The claim is based on the fact that the descendants of Henriette-Anne, daughter of Charles I, should have precedence over the present royal family, the descendants of Elizabeth of Bohemia, daughter of James I. But this of course ignores the fact that a Catholic is disqualified by Act of Parliament from occupying the throne of Great Britain.

It was Lord Rochester who had the last word on Madame. She had died, he said, the most lamented person in both France and England. 'Since which time dying has been the fashion.'

King Charles II was left to implement the consequences of that treaty which Madame had worked so hard to bring about. It was as though she had died in giving birth to it: the King, the bereaved survivor, now had to raise the infant.

There were in fact two separate treaties. The first treaty, which was kept secret, was signed by the English, including Clifford and Arlington, on 22 May 1670.[19] Not only was it secret, but it was also a strange and slippery document, reminding one in its various twists and turns of that legendary wrestler Proteus. King Charles was to support the claims of King Louis to the Spanish monarchical possessions (pursuing his wife's alleged rights), as and when they should be made; in return, England would receive certain South American territories. But a further clause stipulated that King Louis would not break the Treaty of Aix-la-Chapelle recently concluded with Spain; that again enabled King Charles to remain, theoretically at least, faithful to the Triple Alliance.

Together the two kings intended to wage a war against the United Provinces, and the military and naval arrangements for such a war were laid down: this might seem clear enough, albeit aggressive. But this clause was linked to another, often regarded as the crucial text in the so-called Secret Treaty. This described the English King as 'being convinced of the truth of the Catholic religion and resolved to declare it and reconcile himself with the Church of Rome as soon as the welfare of his kingdom will permit'. In order to carry out this declaration (for which no date was given other than the vague phrase, quoted above, concerning the 'welfare of his kingdom'), Charles II was promised money from the French King, half of it in advance, and troops as well, if necessary. The Anglo-French assault on the Dutch was scheduled to follow rather than precede the undated declaration.

The second treaty was signed by the five members of the Cabal – Clifford, Arlington, Buckingham, Ashley and Lauderdale – on 21 December 1670. It was in effect a cover-up. For those ministers not in the know, a phoney treaty with France was worked out, including details of future Anglo-French action against the Dutch, down to the troop movements. Charles was to supply fifty ships and six thousand soldiers, Louis thirty ships and the rest of the soldiery. The conduct of the naval war was to be left to the English, who were to receive Walcheren, Cadzand and Sluys at the mouth of the Scheldt as their share of the territory about to be conquered. But the 'Catholic' clause of the original Secret Treaty of the summer was veiled from the prying eyes of the unsympathetic ministers. Thus no string was attached to the timing of the Anglo-French initiative.

It must be obvious that the strength of this famous – or notorious – Catholic clause was in consequence much diluted. For better or for worse, the way was left open for a combined operation to be mounted against the Dutch, *without* the King of England declaring himself a Catholic – as indeed happened. There is another significant point to be made about the Catholic clause, one which is sometimes missed by the more prejudiced critics of King Charles II. It was not suggested in the text of the Secret Treaty that Charles was going to change the religion of England as a whole – merely his own. Under the circumstances, the equivocal nature of this clause, dependent upon the 'welfare of the kingdom', hardly needs stressing further.

It was the signature of the first treaty which mattered most to Charles II. He had acquired at long last the French support which he conceived as being paramount to his purposes. It is true that by this treaty he also secured a financial subsidy. But it is important to note that the sum involved was by no means exorbitant: modern scholarship has disposed of the notion that vast sums of French gold were laid out. Louis' official subsidy was intended to be three million *livres* Tournois a year: in fact, Charles received from France, throughout his reign, a *total* of nine million nine hundred and fifty thousand *livres*, amounting to £746,000 (then). Eight million of this came from the Secret Treaty. Money values of times gone by are notoriously difficult to translate into our own terms.* It is more helpful to quote

* Besides which, the rapid rate of modern inflation often makes the comparison out of date a few years after it is made.

the recent estimate of Dr C. D. Chandaman that this was the equivalent of less than one year of the King's ordinary income.[20] Thus the financial value of the French subsidy is placed in perspective: in the eyes of Charles II, its psychological value was what counted.

This 'very near alliance' of France and England, signed by the ministers of the Cabal, was not made public. As for details of the Secret Treaty of Dover, these were not in fact generally known until 1830, when the historian Lingard printed the text. At the time knowledge was restricted to a magic circle. The joyful ambassadress Madame knew everything, of course. Thomas Clifford was also fully involved, and as late as the 1930s the Clifford papers revealed hitherto unknown details of the transactions leading up to the treaty. Of the Cabal, Buckingham, who, although pro-French in foreign policy, was in religious terms pro-Puritan, did not know. Nor did Lauderdale. Arlington knew.[21] He disapproved, but, as a professional servant of a royal master and a man ambitious to rise, he bowed to the treaty. Ashley (created Earl of Shaftesbury two years later) did not know at the time, and despite rumours to the contrary, it is unlikely that he ever did. Outside the Cabal, Osborne, just conceivably, knew.[22] But the Secret Treaty was in essence the King's measure, carried out by his sister and most intimate servants to service his private, if nationalistic, policy.

For this treaty Charles II has been harshly judged. He has been condemned for two reasons: first, for the acceptance of French money. Yet this was an age when foreign subsidy was by no means the shocking fact which might be supposed from the disgusted reactions of some of the King's Whig critics. Richard Cromwell asked for a £50,000 subsidy from Cardinal Mazarin immediately after the death of his father. Poverty-stricken rulers were not alone in their blithe attempts to get the wealthy to support them. Later we shall find not only the Dutch gold of William III, but also the French gold of Louis XIV, finding its way to certain English Whig MPs – opponents of the government. They saw nothing wrong in allowing themselves to be 'subsidized' in their opposition by a foreign power. The passionate statement of Sir John Dalrymple is often quoted.

Writing in 1771 of his feelings when he discovered from the French despatches that Lord Russell was intriguing with the French Court and Algernon Sidney receiving money from it he declared, 'I felt very near the same shock as if I had seen a son turn his back in the day of battle.'[23] Thus the eighteenth century flinched from the seventeenth.

Where the French subsidy was concerned, Charles II was in the position of the apocryphal judge, who took bribes – but only when the judgement desired coincided with the judgement he had intended to make in the first place.

It was certainly not a particularly scrupulous attitude. Yet in terms of Charles II's vivid wish to maintain maritime supremacy and extinguish Holland, it was a perfectly intelligible one. One should bear in mind that seven-eighths of the first French payment went directly towards the Navy. As Dr Johnson, as ever a mine of common-sense, exclaimed, 'If licentious in practice, Charles never failed to reverence the good. Even if he did take money from France, what of that? Never did he betray those over whom he ruled, nor would he ever suffer the French fleet to betray ours.' Dr Johnson might have added that in the seventeenth century, as in the age that followed it, rulers were expected to be not so much scrupulous (except by their opponents) as successful.

It is the second salvo fired against Charles II which has been most properly responsible for the smoke of treachery surrounding his name. This is the charge that he intended to subvert England to a Roman Catholicism it had rejected, becoming, in the words of Lord Macaulay, the 'Slave of France' if not its 'Dupe'. It has been postulated in the previous chapter that King Charles II was not, by 1670, the convinced Catholic of some imaginings; definitely not the proselyte who would engage himself to such a cause for sheer religious ardour. Supposing, then, this charge to be unjust, it must immediately be granted that a certain mystery surrounds the religious clause of the treaty. What then was its purpose, and indeed its motivation?

One possibility would be that the religious clause – the 'design about R.' – was inserted to please Madame. There is nothing in the King's correspondence to contradict such a view: indeed, there is evidence of Madame's growing preoccupation with religion, her own, her brother's and that of her native country. Madame may well have believed that she inclined Charles towards its insertion, just as she inclined him towards a French alliance.... In both cases however it is doubtful whether Charles would have allowed himself to go with her tide, had it not suited him in the first place. It is necessary to seek a less charming and more cynical explanation.

The religious clause set the seal, in the King's view, on that security which he expected to enjoy from the support of Louis XIV. It was not so much a question of Charles II's religious proclivities as those of Louis XIV: the English King, in signing such a clause, which committed him to a personal declaration with no time schedule whatsoever, expected to bind the French King to him further. In politics, it cannot be denied that the end very often does justify the means. By 1670 Charles II had decided to make this truth – regrettable or otherwise – the principle of his actions both at home and abroad. One may nevertheless agree with Cicero that certain political actions are objectively bad. It is still difficult to apply that judgement to Charles II at this juncture in his career. The maintenance of the Navy, the expansion of empire, the 'making that Kingdom great' – these had been the classic preoccupations of those English idols (in their different ways), Queen Elizabeth I and Oliver Cromwell. By means of a French alliance, Charles II intended to pursue these policies, without being tumbled from his throne, as had Charles I.

CHAPTER EIGHTEEN

Virtues and Imperfections

'A Prince of many virtues, and many great imperfections'

John Evelyn on Charles II

The summer of 1670 – when Charles II reached his fortieth birthday – represented a turning-point. To a far greater extent than such anniversaries generally do, it marked his emergence not only as a fully fledged governor of his own kingdom but also as a mature man set in his ways. The years of youthful exile, while they had developed in him abnormal courage and resilience, had also artificially held him back as a ruler. Such development had to take place in his thirties, and was further retarded by the presence of Clarendon until 1667. After the great manager's departure, King Charles was left to discover certain facts about himself, his views and intentions for the first time. By the summer of 1670 these facts were fully known to him.

On 29 May 1660 the crowds cheering the restored monarch had been greeted by an evidently wary, if affable, man. By 29 March 1670 the reserve had become so deep as to be impenetrable. The affability was virtually impenetrable too. A man of political strength, cunning and purpose, he was prepared to show himself at all times gracious to his people. The hope of Henrietta Maria that the son would not repeat the clumsy, shy discourtesies of the father had borne fruit. As a monarch, Charles II was renowned for his friendliness, the ease of access which he offered to his subjects, to include not only the poorest amongst them but also a traditionally less welcome category for kings – his critics.

There was however one aspect of his public face in which his subjects might feel that ease had gone altogether too far. It was after the fall of Clarendon that the Court of King Charles II began to enjoy that reputation for debauchery which has surrounded it in the popular imagination ever since. Gone was the attractive picture of a temperate king painted by Sir Richard Fanshawe in 1660 – or at any rate swallowed up in a series of vignettes of Court life depicted in far more lurid colours. Clarendon had been an imposing figurehead, who might not be revered but whose name was certainly never synonymous with debauchery. Buckingham offered a very different image.

A duel in which the husband of his mistress, Anna Maria Countess of Shrewsbury, was mortally wounded caused scandal, and a temporary fall from grace for Buckingham himself. The King, although he subsequently pardoned those involved, showed himself extremely stern on the subject of duelling, which he wished to stamp out. But, *autre temps autre mœurs*, the gesture which provoked the most genuine horror, even among the charitable, was Buckingham's decision to have his illegitimate son by Lady Shrewsbury christened in Westminster Abbey. A duel was a duel, an unhappy feature of the times, but such a baptism offended against the established order of society.

Sir Charles Sedley and Charles Sackville, Lord Buckhurst (later Earl of Dorset), two culpable rakes in Pepys' view, were involved in an inglorious drunken orgy at a Fleet Street tavern which brought them before the magistrates. The mutilation of Sir John Coventry was another highly discreditable incident. When Sir John Berkenhead tried to avert the imposition of a tax on the playhouses on the grounds that they had been of much service to the King, Sir John Coventry enquired cheekily whether he meant the men or women players ...? After which the troopers of the Duke of Monmouth waylaid Coventry and all but cut off the wretched man's nose.

Of the Cabal, not only Buckingham gave offence. The Duke of Lauderdale was in private life a gross figure and his wife

Bess a legendary amorist who even claimed to have dangled Cromwell's scalp at her belt. The story was certainly not true – there are always ladies to claim the favours of great men – but Bess, holding her court at Ham House, made characteristically bold play with it. As against that, it should in fairness be pointed out that Clifford's Devonshire-based life was a pattern of domesticity; Arlington's private life was impeccable, as might be expected from such a 'Castilian' figure; Shaftesbury's interests lay in political controversy rather than in private indulgence, and an open verdict has been returned by his biographer on the various theatrical references to his 'lechery'.[1]

Can it then be argued that this reputation for debauchery in 'Good King Charles' Golden Days' has been much exaggerated? That a few vicious shooting stars have distracted attention from a host of lesser lights, who shone, in so far as they shone at all, with virtue? This view would of course discount not only the legends which have followed the reign – ever a necessary process – but the manifest criticisms and exclamations on the subject of the King's contemporaries. The clue is to concentrate not so much on the question of debauchery but on the true keynote of the King's Court after 1667: and that was laxity.

Much of the colourful aura which surrounds the Restoration Court in the popular imagination is derived from the behaviour of 'the Wits', rather than of the more powerful ministers. This little group, which flourished for about fifteen years after 1665, included John Wilmot, the second Earl of Rochester, Henry Jermyn, Lord Buckhurst, John Sheffield, Earl of Mulgrave, Henry Killigrew, Sir Charles Sedley, and the playwrights Wycherley and Etherege, as well as Buckingham (who straddled both circles). The first point to be made about the Wits, with regard to Charles II, was that they were in the main much younger than the King. Their characters had not been honed like his by fighting in the Civil War: they had grown up in the post-war years, when the atmosphere was very different. (Buckingham, as usual, was the exception.) Rochester, for example, was seventeen years younger than Charles, born only a few years before his father shared the King's escape from Worcester; Mulgrave was younger still.

Rochester's portrait shows a young man of almost insolent sensuality, wide lips curling with devilment, but with 'something of the Angel yet undefac'd in him', as was said of Etherege's cynical rake based on Rochester, Dorimant, in *The Man of Mode*. To his own gaping generation Rochester was 'so idle a rogue' – Pepys was in a tizzy at the idea of Charles making him his constant companion[2] – a virtual alcoholic as well as a brilliant and therefore hurtful satirist. To ours he has become the poet who, for all his obscenity, understands the sad side of passion.

The King enjoyed the outrageous side of his company and, where possible, shrugged off his excesses. There are many anecdotes of Rochester's wildness. One of the most characteristic has Rochester wandering drunkenly in the Privy Garden at Whitehall; on spying the King's favourite sun-dial, one of the rarest in Europe, he flung his arms around it and, quoting Shirley's famous lines,

> Sceptre and crown
> Must tumble down,

he added, 'And so must thou!' Whereupon he hurled it to the ground.[3] That kind of zany dash and style had always fascinated the more cautious house of Stuart: one is reminded of the madcap pranks of the elder Buckingham, catching the eye of James I. In Rochester's case the style included a genuine love of literature in many different forms.

These high-spirited gentlemen – the 'merry gang', as Marvell called them – diverted themselves at times with poetry, plays and literature in general, at times with sardonic comment on everything about them, couched, very often, in scabrous language. Their tendency to the latter has become more famous than their patronage of the former: yet it was to the Wits that much of the abundance of Restoration drama was owed, a more important achievement than their unprintable rhymes about the King's mistresses. It did not harm the theatre that play-writing became a fashionable occupation, practised by aristocrats, aspired to by gentlemen. At least one play, Wycherley's *The Plain Dealer*, was saved by the applause of the Wits, as theatre-goers hesitated, uncertain of their own taste.[4] Rochester was the friend of Aphra Behn and the model for Willmore, *The Rover*, in her play of that name. Buckingham himself wrote a play, *The Rehearsal*: an attack, full of humorous ingenuity, on Dryden and heroic drama in general. Its fame crossed the Channel: Louis XIV twitted his own prime minister on not being able to write a successful farce, as his cousin's had done. It is still occasionally performed, if better known as the work from which Sheridan took his own play, *The Critic*.

Buckhurst loved drunken frolics, but his lyric on the eve of a naval battle against the Dutch in 1665, 'To all you ladies now at land ...', represents courtly elegance; later in life he gave himself over to literary patronage. The notorious Sedley was also a great lover of the arts. Known to his contemporaries as 'Apollo's Viceroy', he was the author of several plays as well as lyrics set exquisitely to music by Purcell. Baptist ('Bab') May, who became Keeper of the Privy Purse to the King, was a *bon viveur* whose appetite for life was matched by his appreciation of the arts. The brother of Hugh May, the architect who worked on the renovation of Windsor Castle, Bab May made a valuable collection of pictures in his own right.

In the eighteenth century the reputation of the Wits became further exaggerated, and Rochester in particular was the subject of gloating, frequently inaccurate, biographies.

While the King indulged himself with the company of these boon companions as a form of relaxation, he is definitely not to be identified with them. Far from being a 'Wit' himself, he could even be called their victim – along with anything else even remotely established which came within their sights. From time to time he issued reprimands: Grammont describes Rochester as having been sent away from Court at least once a year;[5] the 'profane' Earl even had a spell in the Tower after eloping with an heiress, although he was subsequently forgiven. One suspects that the 'merry gang' had something in common with the lovely ladies of the Court: their irreverent company helped to dispel the unspoken melancholy lying within the King's nature.

This was above all a liberal or, as we should now say, a

permissive era. People of rank took their pleasures as they found them and made no secret of their practices because they saw no harm in them. 'Is it not a frank age?' asked the young blade Sparkish in Wycherley's *The Country Wife*. 'And I am a frank person.' If it is accepted that the level of 'sin' remains roughly constant in human behaviour, then the difference between the age of Charles II and that preceding it – the so-called Puritan age of Cromwell – was this: after 1660 it was not considered necessary to hide these things. Naturally not everything which crept in under this permissive umbrella was equally desirable. Laxity towards moral behaviour at Court, in contrast to the rigidity of the Commonwealth period, meant that vice was able to take its chance with virtue and frequently – but not always – won.

In terms of the age itself, it was even more important that obvious laxity in high places – coupled with conspicuous extravagance at a time of national financial stress – antagonized, as it generally does, those in low places who were unable to share in it. Yet, pleasure-loving, easy-going as the Court of Charles II was, it was not a bad and certainly not an evil place.

It is hardly necessary to go as far as the classical comparison with ancient Rome. Let us take the Court of Louis XIV just across the water. It is not only that, mistress for mistress, Louis XIV matched his cousin. His Court was also marked by practices which would have been inconceivable at the Court of Charles II, including black magic and the celebration of the Black Mass for the King's favour, degenerating into the widespread use of poison – horrific events which involved the King's most flamboyant mistress, Madame de Montespan. Nevertheless, the grandiose formality so dear to the heart of Louis XIV has ensured that the Court of Versailles is not famous for such things. In the same way, the English Court takes its reputation from the easy-going nature of its own sovereign.

As a matter of fact, where Charles himself is concerned, his personal 'debauchery', as opposed to sheer love of women, does not appear to have been very great. In 1667 Pepys repeated a rumour that the King had expressed a wish to join with Barbara and Lord Jermyn in troilism; later Rochester spread rumours of his sovereign's impotence, saying that only two ladies at a time could take care of this state – but impotence was a subject which obsessed Rochester, and the story probably tells us more about him than about the King.[6] In an age beset by dirty rumours and innuendoes about the sex life of all and sundry, Charles emerged pre-eminently as a man of great physical energy who quite simply loved women.

He had after all ample opportunity to do so. Charles II had three great advantages where women were concerned. First, he was a king. And if he had little money himself, he was in a position to grant money, rank and other *douceurs* to his favourites: even Halifax admitted that 'sauntering' was a greater temptation to princes than to other people. Nor were such escapades held against them.

> May not a man then trifle out an hour
> With a kind woman and not wrong his calling?

exclaimed Jaffeir in Otway's play, *Venice Preserv'd.* In the seventeenth century – and for many generations to follow – the answer was generally speaking 'Yes', when the man's calling was that of King. It was a point of view expressed by the King himself in conversation with Burnet. God, he was convinced, would never damn a man 'for allowing himself a little pleasure...'.[7]

Secondly, Charles II was extremely sexually attractive, or, as he put it more modestly to Sir John Reresby, 'because that his Complexion was of an amorous sort' women often offered themselves to his embraces. To the objection that the second advantage really sprang from the first – women were the aggressors, for mercenary reasons – it can be answered that there is plenty of evidence of this attraction. Barbara Castlemaine – who certainly knew what she was talking about – confided to a friend that the King was exceptionally well endowed physically to make love.[8]*

* A fact expressed by Rochester in these lines:

> Nor are his high desires above his strength,
> His sceptre and his — are of a length.

Thirdly, Charles II actually liked women. He enjoyed their company, not only for the purposes of making love to them, but to talk to them, to have supper with them, to be entertained by and to entertain them. He did not snub them or bully them, unlike many of his companions. He allowed them to have brains and talk politics – as a result of which he was of course criticized for subjecting himself to petticoat influence; nevertheless, to our ears such an attitude makes a refreshing change from the English masculine tradition of boredom in female company.

There is indeed something very modern in this appreciation on the part of Charles, this capacity of the King to turn his mistresses into friends. Even if it is again objected that this process comes easier to kings than to other people – since the aforesaid mistresses have much to gain from remaining at Court – it is still much to Charles' credit that he wanted to do so.

Above all, he knew himself and was not hypocritical where women and his desires were concerned. His witty – but courteous – refusal to interfere with Barbara's 'soul' has already been cited. There is another characteristic tale of this tolerant and humorous attitude to his own reputation. Passing through the Palace of Whitehall, Charles overheard a young lady singing a satirical ballad in her room, based on his prowess as a 'stallion' – 'Old Rowley the King'. Instantly the King knocked on her door. When she asked who was there, he replied with a flourish, 'Old Rowley himself, Madam.'[9]

If a great lover is one who shows certain essential qualities of tenderness and appreciation for the opposite sex, rather than a sheer sexual athlete, then Charles can lay claim to the title. One may cite Louis XIV once more, who showed nothing like the same emotional generosity to his former mistresses. The incident at the French Court, where the Princesse de Monaco more or less had to retire because the key to her room was *not* found outside her door by the King (it had been confiscated by another admirer), could not have happened in England: Charles' very public pursuit of Frances and his equally public rejection, while they caused him anguish and even rage, ended with her installed as a grand and respected duchess.

It can even be argued that in the first seven or eight years of his reign Charles was something of a 'one-woman man'. Pepys, in conversation with Evelyn in that period, accepted that the King never kept two mistresses at the same time.[10] Obviously this paradoxical fidelity, in which 'a faith unfaithful kept him falsely true', as Tennyson wrote of Lancelot, did not last for ever. The seventies were a different matter.

Louise Duchess of Portsmouth and Nell Gwynn unquestionably shared his official favours in the early years of the decade. There were shorter-lived parallel romances. Not only was there the affair with Moll Davis, but there was also a fling with one of the Queen's Maids of Honour, Winifred Wells, whose attractions included the 'carriage of a goddess and the physiognomy of a dreamy sheep' (but Barbara compared her to a goose), and Mrs Jane Roberts, daughter of a clergyman, who died young 'with a great sense of her former ill life'. The singer Mrs Knight, whose angelic voice Evelyn and others so much admired, figures in the royal accounts; as does another Killigrew, Mary, the widowed Countess of Falmouth, who subsequently married Lord Buckhurst, and Elizabeth Countess of Kildare. Then there were the nocturnal visitors introduced up the Privy Stairs by William Chiffinch, the King's confidential servant, and Page, Keeper of the Privy Closet. Their numbers, like their identities, remain unknown to history.*

Nevertheless, Pepys' conversation with Evelyn should not be totally dismissed. For one thing, Pepys was an acute observer of sexual matters in general, because he was so interested in them. Then Evelyn was a reliable source on the subject of the King in particular because he had close contact with him over so many years. Pepys' Diary entry pointed to an important strand in the King's character: Charles was not by conviction promiscuous, whatever the temptations offered to a king in a permissive age.

* The *louche* William Chiffinch succeeded his brother Thomas in 1666. But it should be noted that Chiffinch too was a lover of the arts of painting and music – as well as of the arts of love.

He did not share the attitude made fashionable by his friend Rochester:

> If I, by miracle, can be
> This live-long minute true to thee
> 'Tis all that Heaven allows.

He liked settled relationships. He believed in them.

Frances had declined the honourable post of King's official mistress with what Barbara ungratefully described as 'the new-fashioned chastity of the inhuman Stewart': as a result, Barbara's own star remained artificially in the ascendant until the late 1660s. This was a remarkable achievement when women were said to be 'at their prime at twenty, decayed at four and twenty, old and insupportable at thirty', in the words of Etherege's Dorimant. Barbara tended to agree with Rochester on the subject of fidelity (although violently denying it). When she was accused of intriguing with Harry Jermyn in July 1667 – that same Jermyn who had caused a flutter in the breast of Mary of Orange – the King was deeply upset. Jermyn was obliged to leave the Court for six months. As late as 1668 (when Barbara was nearly thirty), the Crown Jewels were said to have been taken from the Tower to adorn her for an amateur performance of Katherine Philips' version of *Horace* at court. The public opinion of her reign, somewhat less glamorous, was expressed in the infamous fictional 'Whores' Petition' of March 1668. Some London apprentices, in a fit of morality or malevolence, had pulled down certain brothels in the Moorfields area. Both the 'Whores' Petition' and Barbara's alleged reply to 'the rest of the suffering sisterhood' were highly scurrilous, not to say disgusting, in content.[11] The most interesting references are those to her Catholicism (she had recently been converted): these display another even stronger popular prejudice.

Then the appearance of a pert young professional actress named Nell Gwynn signalled that Barbara's era was over. Barbara was asked to remove herself from her convenient Whitehall apartments. It was true that in August 1670 she was created Duchess of Cleveland, Countess of Southampton and Baroness

Nonsuch; all this was however in the nature of a golden handshake. About the same time, at least in Marvell's version, the King had a ballad sung under her window beginning, 'Alinda's growing old ...'. Marvell himself contributed his own drop of vinegar:

> Paint Castlemaine in colours that will hold
> Her, not her picture, for She now grows old...

Barbara's own version of the King's dismissal of her, quoted back to him afterwards without contradiction, was less crude if equally wounding. The King said, 'Madam, all that I ask of you for your own sake is, live so for the future as to make the least noise you can, and I care not who you love."[12]

Two years later Charles pointedly refused to acknowledge Barbara's sixth child, a daughter. The baby began life as Barbara Fitzroy, the surname borne by her five quasi-royal brothers and sisters. Then she was consigned the simpler patronymic of Barbara Palmer, a name to which, like her mother, she brought some colour; for she entered a convent and then left it to bear an illegitimate child.

Duchess Barbara's latest career was not so happy. Having lost her youthful bloom, she did not lose her rapacity: there was an ugly incident when the Viceroy of Ireland, the Earl of Essex, had to defend Phoenix Park, Dublin, against her covetousness. Nor indeed did Barbara lose her equally demanding sensuality. Quite possibly she owed her latest daughter to the attentions of her young lover John Churchill, the future warrior Duke of Marlborough. In 1676, after the Test Act had forced this Catholic Magdalen to renounce her position as Lady of the Bedchamber, she flounced off to Paris. She returned three years later, but at this point she passes out of the romantic history of Charles II.

The King's new mistress was familiarly known as Nelly Gwynn. On the subject of her official nomenclature, the various royal accounts suffered from some confusion, calling her variously Mrs Hellen Gwynn, Mrs Ellen Gwynn and Mrs Elinor Gwyn, 'spinster'. She was known as Madam Ellen on play bills after she received the King's favour. Nell was virtually illiterate.

Appointing an attorney for herself in 1680, Nell managed a very large and childish EG: so that obviously some version of Eleanor was correct; other receipts for payments for herself and her son were also signed with an ill-formed EG.[13]

Nell was introduced to the King by Buckingham some time before January 1668. She remained on fond terms with the Duke, visiting him in the Tower during one of the periods of his disgrace. Nell was not the only actress to entrance her sovereign. Moll Davis also succeeded in doing so by singing a particular song, 'My lodging is on the Cauld ground ...', after which, as John Downes commented, her lodging was in the royal bed. Castigated by Mrs Pepys as 'the most impertinent slut in the world', Moll Davis was praised by other kindlier tongues for the especial grace of her dancing. Pepys thought her a better actress than Nell Gwynn. Richard Flecknoe was moved to address to her the following lines, which breathe sincerity if not poesy:

> Dear Miss, delight of all the nobler sort,
> Pride of the stage and darling of the court...

Moll Davis was a member of Sir William Davenant's troupe at Lincoln's Inn. In return for the King's presents, said to include a ring worth £600, a house and even a pension, Moll presented him with a daughter, known as Mary Tudor.

But the relationship was not enduring. Whether or not the evil tale is true which has Nell Gwynn lacing Moll's sweetmeats with julap (a purgative) when she was due to sup with the King, Moll fell from favour comparatively soon.[14] She took refuge in another less lucrative passion – for cards and high play.

Nell Gwynn was made of sterner stuff, as was her connection with the King; one way and another, it would only end with his death some seventeen years later. Nell was of Welsh extraction. One story connects her birth with Hereford, a place with a great acting tradition. It is more certain that she spent her early years working in the London establishment of her mother, old Madam Gwynn; this, if not precisely a brothel or 'bawdy-house', was something pretty close to it: Nell served drinks – 'strong waters to gentlemen' – there, and later graduated to being an orange girl in the theatre, another profession which existed in the exciting, nebulous territory just outside acknowledged prostitution.

The first reference to her as an actress in the King's Players occurs in 1664 (when she would have been fourteen). Her early lovers included the actor Charles Hart, Charles, Lord Buckhurst,* and the playwright Thomas Otway, who would remain a true friend through life; he was given power of attorney in her business affairs twenty years later. By 1670 Nell had achieved that guarantee of an establishment, pregnancy by the monarch; she gave birth to the first of her two sons and was set up in consequence in a little house at the east end of Pall Mall, later closer to Whitehall. Throughout 1670 and most of 1671 she reigned supreme.

Physically, Nell was tiny, with, it was said, the littlest foot in England as well as perfect legs. The King, who had a *penchant* for good legs, indulged his passion to the extent of paying for some of her theatrical costumes, including some 'Rhinegraves' – shirt, wide, divided skirts, guaranteed to fly up provocatively as the wearer danced. Nell certainly did not have the classical looks admired at the time: her nose turned up, unlike the aquiline noses of the conventional Stuart beauties. But everything about her was charmingly rounded, including her plump cheeks, where two dimples appeared when she smiled. As for her full lower lip, it aroused this tribute from a contemporary admirer: 'An out-mouth that makes mine water at it.'[15] It was no wonder that the King, at the height of his desire, paid frequent visits to Lely's studio, where he was painting Nelly naked.

Like Charles himself, Nell had natural wit, although hers was the wit nurtured in Madam Gwynn's bawdy-house rather than the courts of Europe. Her surviving letters, dictated to others as they may be, show a sparkle nonetheless. Evelyn describes her taking part in some jolly backchat over her garden wall with the King, out on one of his saunters. On another occasion she

* The repetition of the Christian name is supposed to have led Nell to refer to her lovers as Charles I, II and III.

told Charles smartly how to deal with his finances: 'Send the French into France again, set me on the stage again, and lock up your codpiece.'[16] Nell's rivalry with Louise de Kéroüalle, who prided herself on coming of a good French family, was enlivened when Louise went into mourning for the death of some professedly grand relation; Nell proceeded to dress *herself* in mourning for the Great Cham of Tartary. And Nell is of course famous for her riposte, at the time of the Popish Plot, to the angry crowd who mistook her for the Catholic Louise. Poking her head out of her carriage, Nell cried, 'Good people, this is the Protestant whore!'

But if she justified her reputation in one respect as 'pretty witty Nell' or 'Mrs Nelly the impudent comedian', as Pepys called her, Nell Gwynn was in other ways not quite the golden-hearted prostitute of popular imagination. Or rather, she may have had a heart of gold, but she also liked the stuff for its own sake. The records show that, like all Charles' mistresses, she was extremely mercenary and demanding. By the end of 1674 she had acquired at least eight servants, a French coach needing six horses, satin window curtains, sky-blue shoes, other shoes of silver, green, gold and scarlet, all as befitted the grand lady she sought to be. Nell also coveted some kind of rank, to acknowledge her position. It seemed odious and unfair to her that she should not be rewarded on the same handsome scale as the other ladies, simply because she was an actress – considering she performed the same services. In 1675, for example, about the time that Madame de Sévigné at least believed that Charles was dividing his favours equally between the two, Nell received £1,000 from the Secret Service account, but Louise received £2,000 in the same period.[17]

Nell's mockery of Louise, her insistence that she, Nell, was not ashamed of her profession, while Louise gave herself unjustified airs, begins to have a slightly sour note as the seventies wear on. 'As for me, it's my trade, I don't set myself up as anything better!' cried Nell. And she lifted up her petticoats to Courtin, the French Ambassador, to emphasize how magnificent – and how clean – they were, after boasting that the King slept with her constantly in preference to Louise.[18]

One feels that the lady – if one may so call her – protests her own frankness about her profession slightly too much.

And the sad truth was that for all her loud complaints Nell never did carry her democratic point of equality with the other favourites. It was Burnet who put it most cruelly: Nell was not treated with the decencies of a mistress, but rather with the lewdness of a prostitute.[19] It is said that she secured the vacant Burford title for her surviving son Charles by calling him 'You little bastard!' in front of the King, and then blandly enquiring how else she should address him, since he had no other name.* Just as Nell was about to be created Countess of Greenwich – the other 'ladies' were all made Duchesses – the King died. To commentators, up to the King's last hours, she remained 'Nelly', where Louise was 'Portsmouth' and Barbara 'Cleveland'. And thus she has gone down to history.

It is sometimes overlooked that the private tastes of Charles II ran as much to conventional as to unconventional sports. Viewing his obsession with physical exercise of all sorts, including tennis, swimming, walking and riding, it is tempting to suggest that his legendary 'amorous complexion' was merely an extension of this natural bent. He once referred to his daily tennis game, to Clarendon, as his 'usual physic'; perhaps making love came into the same category. The Wardrobe accounts certainly provide as ample expression of his interest in tennis – real tennis as we should term it, played in an indoor court – as in women, ornamental beds and rich carriages for mistresses jostling there with the day-beds, linen, towels, curtains and so forth needed for the royal tennis-courts.

The tennis 'sheets' (that is, towels) were specially made by Dorothy Chiffinch (wife of the respectable Thomas, not the disreputable William), a lady so accustomed to looking after the King's linen that she had done so as long ago as that disastrous expedition to Scotland in 1649. These 'sheets' cost ten shillings

* An alternative story has Nell Gwynn threatening to drop the child out of the window of a house just as the King was passing, unless he granted the boy a title. The site of the house varies. The drama of the tale does not.

a pair. One day-bed on which the King could recline after a hard game cost £38.[20] The Hampton Court establishment in general cost about £200 a year to run, including not only the quilted nets, but also the hire of boatmen to take the King up-river to his sport. The renovation of the court there had been considered one of the prime needs at the Restoration. In 1662 a new court was built at Whitehall on the Hampton Court model, and a further one at Windsor, for which nets, cords and lines had to be provided.

Earlier royalties had enjoyed the game of tennis:[21] Henry VIII had been an *aficionado*. It was also very much part of the Stuart family tradition: Charles I had played, and so did his nephew Rupert. In exile, Harry Duke of Gloucester had become so expert that he was rumoured to be contemplating earning a living at the game when times were hard.

Tennis, as practised by Charles II, satisfied the same kind of need in his life as squash might satisfy in the life of a busy, would-be fit man today. It was Charles' custom to play early in the morning, six a.m. being a favourite time. And he played on into his fifties, challenging much younger men, like John Churchill. He also derived considerable satisfaction from the sauna-like qualities of a game played very fast on wood in an indoor court: he once weighed himself before and after playing and found that he had lost four-and-a-half-pounds.

Charles II also adored swimming. As Richard Penderel had discovered to his advantage after Worcester, Charles was an exceptionally strong and fearless swimmer. On occasion he was found plunging happily into the freezing waters of the Thames, while his courtiers shivered on the bank. His swimming too was apt to take place early in the morning. He would rise at five, go boating and swim, often with his brother James at Battersea, Putney or Five Elms.

The life of the Thames, river life in general, appealed to him: he was an enthusiastic fisherman. (One of Rochester's more printable nicknames for his sovereign was Flatfoot the Gudgeon-taker – Flatfoot being a horse at Newmarket.) It was a taste Queen Catharine – tactfully – came to share. We hear of the King getting up at five a.m. to join her at Hampton Court to go fishing, 'a recreation in which she takes much pleasure'. The King also spent much time on the Thames at Datchet when he was in residence at Windsor. There the royal cormorant-keeper received a special allowance in the household accounts. As a result, Henry Sidney complained in his diary of 1679 that the King at Windsor did nothing all day *but* fish. The following year the King's serious illness was attributed to him going fishing in the kind of weather 'when a dog would not be abroad'.[22]

Fishing at least was a sedentary occupation, one of the few that the King practised. In general, his extreme physical restlessness was an attribute to which all contemporary observers drew attention. His famous walking, for example, went on at a horrendous pace. The courtiers panted to keep up with him. When Prince George of Denmark was brought before the King as the putative spouse of his niece Princess Anne of York, Charles advised him merrily on his future course of action at the English Court: 'Walk with me, hunt with my brother and do justice to my niece.' Leaving aside the second and third of these precepts it is doubtful that the stolid Prince was up to carrying out the first.

At least this love of walking dovetailed with the King's passion for dogs. Wherever he went he moved with a little train of spaniels scampering and barking – or yapping as their detractors had it. He did not actually introduce his favourite breed of spaniel, whose particular appearance can best be gauged from the contemporary portraits, to England. Some form of these engaging dogs had in fact been known here, petted by royalty, for at least a hundred years. Mary Tudor, Queen Elizabeth, Charles I, and later Louis XIV, Prince Rupert and Madame are amongst those known to have enjoyed these 'comforters'. But such was King Charles' enthusiasm for them that they have become identified with his name.* As a result a tradition has arisen that a law was passed in his time giving these dogs free travel anywhere within the realm; it is, alas, unsubstantiated.[23]

Trifling with his spaniels was Charles' habitual way of whiling

* The King Charles breed of spaniel was registered at the formation of the Kennel Club in 1873 and the Cavalier King Charles breed in 1926.

away the time during government business: hence that charming link-with-history anecdote which involves a very old man remembering as a very young boy seeing the King playing with his dogs in the Palace of Whitehall.* The royal pets, in the opinion of courtiers, were better outside than in. Obviously the King's commitments would not allow him to cope with their exercise single-handed. Dog-walkers were essential, and well rewarded. In 1662 George Russell, serjeant of hawks, was paid twenty pence a day for taking out the King's spaniels: he also obtained £7 a year for a suitable livery.[24]

Pepys had waxed sentimental over the spectacle of the King's dogs misbehaving themselves on the yacht bearing Charles to his Restoration. Evelyn was more caustic on the subject. Sumptuous cushions were ordered for them, according to the royal accounts. But the undisciplined spaniels would creep into the royal bedchamber and even the royal bed; here the bitches whelped and suckled their young. A loyal gentleman, being bitten, exclaimed: 'God bless your Majesty! but God damn your dogs!'[25] King Charles' own affection for his pets remained sublimely above these annoyances: they could do no wrong.

Horses had of course been an early love which the presence of an equestrian expert as his tutor only encouraged. By the age of ten Charles had been riding 'leaping horses', often controlling those who had managed to throw more experienced horsemen. His subsequent prowess was of infinite satisfaction to Newcastle (created a Duke after the Restoration). He wrote: 'No man makes a horse go better than I have seen some go under His Majesty the first time ever he came upon their backs, which is the quintessence of the art.'[26] The household bills include details of bits with silver and gilt bosses, hunting saddles of coloured velvet, crimson silk reins for the new travelling coach. At the royal mews at one time there were forty-three coursers, stallions

* There are several versions of it. One of the most plausible involves Oxford. Dr Martin Routh, President of Magdalen College, who died in 1854 in his hundredth year, used to say that, when young, he had known an old lady who as a little girl saw King Charles walking with his spaniels in Oxford. (The author, who lived in Oxford as a child in the 1930s, likes to think she might have known someone old enough to have met Dr Routh.)

and colts, sixty hunters, numerous grooms and a gentleman saddler. In 1668 horses, including not only these but also coach horses, chariot horses, rack horses and stool horses, were costing the King over £1,000 a year in hay, and over £700 in straw. In 1680 the King's serjeant farrier, Andrew Snape (whose family had been farriers to the Crown for two hundred years), wrote a book on *Anatomy of an Horse*. It was appropriate that he should dedicate it to his royal master.[27]

Charles II grew up with a taste for hunting, including deer, stag and otter (fox hunting in general belongs to a later period, when the shortage of deer could no longer be remedied). This was once again part of the Stuart family tradition. Even his otherwise unathletic grandfather, James I, had such a mania for the chase that his subjects complained of neglect on that score: similarly Charles II used the fact that he had got into 'such a vein of hunting' as an excuse for lagging behind in his correspondence with Madame.[28]

At the Restoration the parks and forests had to be filled again with deer, poached unmercifully throughout the Commonwealth period. Thus the New Forest and Sherwood Forest were restocked. The King's House at Lyndhurst in Hampshire, built by Charles I in 1635 (now offices for the Forestry Commission), was used as a hunting lodge for the New Forest. Charles II spent £4,000 enlarging it and building new stables. An edict of 1662 concerning Sherwood Forest forbade anyone there to kill a deer without a warrant from the King, unless Charles himself or the Master of the Buckhounds was actually present.[29] The Duke of Oldenburg sent over a freight of stags from the Continent to help with its replenishment. The King's deer were kept in Windsor Forest, Waltham Forest, Enfield Chase and Hunsdon Park. Richmond Park, once royal property, had been confiscated during the Commonwealth. It was typical of the King's tact that he consented to receive it back from the Corporation of London, who had acquired it 'not of restoration but of a free gift'.[30]

One Simon Smith petitioned at the Restoration to become Master of the Otter Hounds. He had actually hoped to become Master of the Tennis Play, and, with this in mind, he had not only taken the precaution of marrying the widow of the previous Master, but had also improved a court at his own expense.[31] This new petition acknowledged the link which joined all the King's pleasures: they provided useful remunerative posts for loyal subjects. The Master of the Privy Buckhounds, in charge of organizing one branch of venery for the King, had an average of thirty-four servants beneath him.

Yet as the King grew older, the enthusiasm for hunting gave way to a passionate involvement in racing: it was the Duke of York who was left as the chief upholder of hunting in the royal family, as Charles' teasing remark to George of Denmark indicates. Charles II concentrated on what has become known appropriately enough as the Sport of Kings. The value of his patronage to British racing can hardly be over-estimated: at the beginning of his reign, race meetings were still suffering from the blight put upon them during the Protectorate, when they were banned as being opportunities for the seditious to meet (the first meeting of the monarchist Western Association had actually taken place at Salisbury races). By 1685 racing was thoroughly established as an integral part of British social and sporting life.

The King probably first went racing at Epsom Downs in 1661: but it was Newmarket in particular which owed so much to his prolonged personal patronage.[32] The Duke of Tuscany, who paid the town a visit, drew attention to 'the almost level territory which lies in every direction around it' and commented, 'It has, in the present day, been brought into repute by the king....' This was true. The royal stables there were referred to as 'ruinous' in 1661. John Baypole, Surveyor of the Royal Stables, was granted £800 for immediate work, and though restoration proceeded slowly, since the money, in its usual fashion, trickled through slower than had been anticipated, enough was found to breed there twelve choice horses a year. The King also came to maintain four jockeys-in-ordinary.

There were races at Newmarket by March 1663. In 1666 Charles II paid his first visit to the spring meeting; thereafter he went two or three times a year for visits lasting several weeks. Although tents and pavilions formed part of the royal baggage, the King himself stayed at Audley End with the Earl of Suffolk, and used the Earl of Thomond's town residence. Gradually the King found Audley End so convenient for his racing life that in 1669 he bought it for £50,000. His enthusiasm continued to grow: in March that year he left London before three a.m. in order to reach Newmarket in good time, only to be rewarded – or punished – for his early rise by having his coach overturn at King's Gate, Holborn. 'The King all dirty but no hurt,' wrote Pepys philosophically.[33]

There was an acute lack of money at the time (this was the period of so-called retrenchment) and the price of Audley End was never paid in full. In any case, £10,000 had to be spent on it straight away for essential improvements. Buildings inside Newmarket also began to be made more 'commodious', in the Duke of Tuscany's phrase, as the visits of the *noblesse* proliferated. The King himself decided to build a palace in the town and commissioned Wren to draw up plans, the old palace having been knocked down under the Commonwealth.* Evelyn however found it a very odd sort of palace, which lay 'in a dirty street ... without any court or avenue'. And even Charles had some complaints about the low ceilings of Wren's rooms. Wren, who was a short man, assured the King that they were quite high enough.

'Aye, Sir Christopher,' replied the King, squatting down from his great height, 'I think they are....'[34]

The King's involvement in racing embraced every aspect of this rich and many-sided sport, including, on occasion, dining with the jockeys. He instituted four-mile heats at twelve stone for a Plate 'for ever' – the precursor of all the subsequent royal Plate races at Newmarket. The idea of these heats over such a long distance – by modern standards – was to develop the breeding of 'big stout horses'. What was more, the Plate race had something generally lacking in races at the time, a set of formal rules. Otherwise informality was so great that the King

* Today the north part of the site is occupied by the International Stores, and the south-east block is part of a nineteenth-century building called Palace House Mansions; the latter name at least recalls its occupation by Charles II.

was sometimes used as an adjudicator. On one famous occasion, in April 1682, he was called in to decide the rights and wrongs of a race between Sir Robert Kerr's horse and a gelding belonging to Sir Robert Geeres.

The King would get up early to watch the training gallops, either installed in his 'Chair', a small pavilion on top of the hill, or riding on his own hack. His overflowing energy prevented him from being a mere spectator whenever there was an alternative. The Duke of Tuscany described how the King would watch the races on horseback with his friends, riding parallel with the runners as they approached the finish, until the roll of drums and the blare of trumpets signalled the winner. Finally he rode in a number of races himself. In 1671 he rode the winner of the Plate – 'a flagon of £32 price' – beating, amongst others, the Duke of Monmouth. In 1675, when he was in his mid-forties, the King rode in three heats, a course and the Plate, all being 'hard and near run races'; he won the Plate by what Sir Robert Kerr assured a correspondent was sheer 'good horsemanship'.[35]

Today the Rowley mile at Newmarket still commemorates Charles II in its own fashion: it was named after that famous stallion of the day, sire of a vast progeny – and, as has been mentioned, Charles himself was nicknamed Old Rowley in honour of his own similarly prolific powers. As for Newmarket itself, Alexander Pope wrote angrily in the next century,

> In Days of Ease, when now the weary Sword
> Was sheath'd, and Luxury with Charles restor'd...
> The Peers grew proud in Horsemanship t'excel,
> Newmarket's Glory rose, as Britain's fell...

Today, as British horse-racing and breeding flourish, following the lead of Charles II, many would think that, on the contrary, Newmarket's glory had contributed to that of Britain.

There was a bucolic side to the life centred there. One is reminded of the lush pastoral backgrounds to some of Lely's portraits. One incident, inspired by Queen Catharine's wish to go to a fair incognito, has overtones of another country-minded

Queen, Marie Antoinette. Catharine set off for the fair on the back of a cart-horse ridden by a courtier, in what she fondly imagined to be true country style. Unfortunately, both Queen and courtiers, including Frances, now Duchess of Richmond, and the Duchess of Buckingham, 'had all over-done it in their disguise'. In their red petticoats and waistcoats, they looked more like 'Antiques than Country folk'. Catharine continued for a while innocently to enjoy herself. At a booth she bought a pair of yellow stockings 'for her sweetheart'. But of course, quite apart from her 'antique' clothes, her heavy foreign accent – what a witness unkindly called her 'gibberish' – could not help drawing attention. Soon a crowd gathered to gape at these strange birds in their even stranger plumage, and eventually mobbed the Queen.[36]

There was another rather different natural extension to the King's love of physical exercise – his addiction to garden and park planning. A work on gardening printed in 1670, *Le Jardin de Plaisir*, by André Mollet, which was dedicated to Charles, suggested with true nationalistic fervour that his good taste in gardens must derive from his French blood. Perhaps there was something in it; although those years of French environment probably played quite as much part as his French heredity in influencing the King. At all events, it was after consulting the French master Le Nôtre that he reafforested Greenwich. Avenues of Spanish chestnuts were planted and over six thousand elms, as well as small coppices of birch, hawthorn, ash and privet, Greenwich today still being remarkable for its luxuriant hawthorn. At Hampton Court the King planted what Evelyn approvingly described as 'sweet rows of lime trees'. Botany also caught his scientific fancy: a famous picture shows King Charles II, before the façade of Ham House, being shown the first pineapple cultivated in England.

Not every British sovereign has had a genuine love of London. Charles II felt this passion for the city of his birth. St James's Park was his *chef d'œuvre*. Here he loved to walk on his fast daily round or 'saunter' from the adjacent Palace of Whitehall, accompanied by his dogs: one charming tradition associates this saunter, or morning 'constitutional', with the naming of

Constitution Hill, which today runs up beside Buckingham Palace to Hyde Park Corner.* St James's Park indeed benefited as much from the King's patronage as Newmarket, although, as with Windsor Castle, the fact has been obscured by its later history (in both cases George IV swept away many of the improvements of Charles II in favour of further improvements of his own: today we see a park 'anglicized' by John Nash). The area had originally taken its name from a thirteenth-century hospital for female lepers, called St James in the Fields; in the seventeenth century it came to have more pleasurable connotations. The marshy area was drained. Then Charles completely transformed the layout into something very much in the French manner. Water was an integral part of the vision. Once again influenced by Le Nôtre, he had a formal pattern of ornamental water and avenues designed, which recalled the Versailles of Louis XIV. There was a further foreign influence: from Venice the Doge despatched two gondolas – 'very rich and fine' – to ride on the new canal.[38]

The King's gesture in throwing open the park to the public was however genuinely English. As were the games which he either introduced or extended in their range. Croquet and bowls, both of which the King enjoyed, were played in the park. For the game variously called pêle-mêle or pall-mall, a form of croquet using a wooden ring suspended above the ground, a fine new mall or alley, nearly fifteen hundred feet long, was laid out on the site of the present-day Mall. It was surfaced with fine cockleshells under the supervision of yet another official on royal pleasure bent – the King's Cockle-strewer. The King was an expert at the sport: in Waller's phrase (not too sycophantic, one hopes),

> He does but touch the flying ball
> And 'tis already more than half the Mall. . . †

* Although authorities are doubtful that this road was named Constitution Hill as early as the reign of Charles II, the true origin of the name remains mysterious;[37] so that one can still speculate happily on the connection with the King's morning saunter.

† The recent transformation of the Mall to a pedestrian precinct on Sundays gives it an air of popular recreation again.

Miniature of Charles II in 1665, at the age of 35, by Samuel Cooper (another version of this miniature was given by the King to his mistress Louise, Duchess of Portsmouth).

Medallion commemorating Charles II's foundation of the Mathematical and Nautical School in Christ's Hospital, by John Poettier, 1673. The reverse (*right*) depicts a Bluecoat boy being encouraged by figures representing Arithmetic, Astronomy, Mathematics and Mercury.

The King's Ladies

Opposite below: Barbara Villiers, Countess of Castlemaine and Duchess of Cleveland, about the age of thirty, by Lely.

Left: Frances Stewart, Duchess of Richmond, by Lely.

Opposite: Hortense Mancini, Duchesse de Mazarin, by Mignard.

Below: Nell Gwynn, engraving by V. Green.

Louise de Kéroüalle, Duchess of Portsmouth, described as 'the most absolute of the King's mistresses'; by Henri Gascar.

'Don Carlo' – Charles, Earl of Plymouth, the King's son by Catharine Pegge, who died at Tangier in 1680; from the mezzotint by J. Savage.

Charles, Duke of Richmond and Lennox, only child of Charles II by Louise, Duchess of Portsmouth, by Henri Gascar.

Charlotte, Countess of Lichfield, Charles II's favourite daughter and one of his five children by Barbara, Duchess of Cleveland, by Lely.

Opposite left: Henry Purcell, 1695, by or after Closterman.

John Wilmot, 2nd Earl of Rochester, *c.* 1665, after Huysmans.

The Empress of Morocco by Elkanah Settle at the Dorset Garden Theatre, 1673.

Below: Isometric view of St Paul's Cathedral, London.

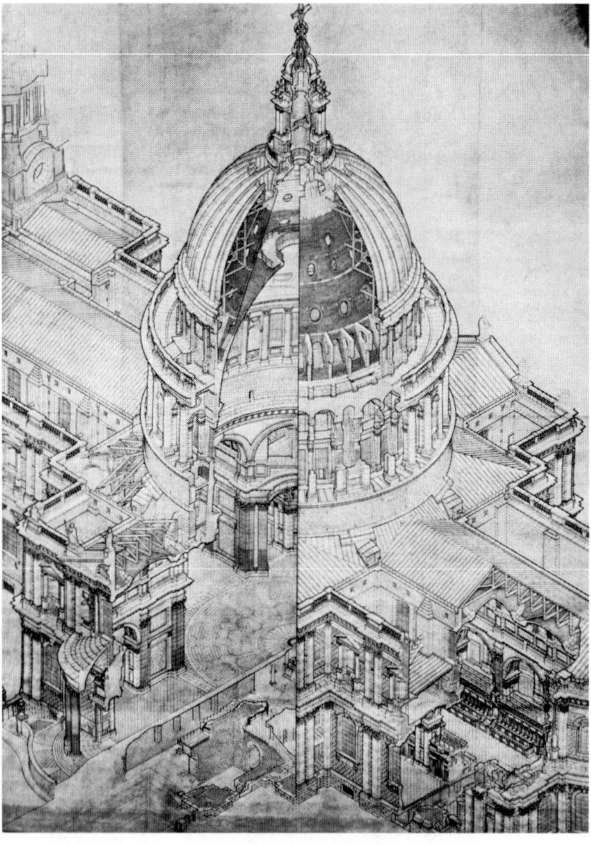

John Evelyn by Nanteuil, 1650.

John Dryden, the Poet Laureate, by Keneller, 1693.

There was also wrestling in the park. Evelyn attended one match, held in the presence of 'a vast assemblage of Lords and other spectators'; the prize was £1,000, and the 'Western men' wrested it from the 'Northern men'.[39]

The King's new rectangular lake (or canal), for all its formality, was another new source of popular pleasure. Although only the King swam in it, winter was different. That of 1662 was one of the harsh seasons common at the time. The Dutch practice of 'sliding', as it was known (although we should now call it skating), was quickly introduced. Pepys, much taken with the spectacle of the 'sliders', with their skates, in the park, described it as being 'a very pretty art', the Duke of York being a particularly skilful slider. Evelyn was equally impressed by the dexterity of the practitioners, who would swoop to a graceful stop exactly in front of the King and Queen.

Summer brought its own delights. It was fashionable to drink warm milk, freshly drawn from the herd of cows placidly grazing in the parks, at a kind of early milk bar provided for the purpose. The women in attendance advertised their wares: 'A can of milk, ladies, a can of red cow's milk, sir!' In adjacent Green Park the King had a 'snow-house' and an 'ice-house' constructed on the site of the former duelling-ground, in order to 'cool wines and other drinks for the summer season'; it was another taste he had acquired in France.[40]

Much as he enjoyed catering to his subjects' tastes – and his own – King Charles' real excitement within the confines of the park consisted in the various species of bird which he introduced, both in his specially built aviary and on the 'Duck Island' in the middle of the lake.[41] It was true that exotic livestock had been seen in St James's Park before: James I, another connoisseur of wild life, had introduced two young crocodiles as well as duck and pheasants. Charles II was able to make the more picturesque, less predatory addition of a pair of pelicans from Astrakhan, a present from the Russian Ambassador. Evelyn, who was fascinated by the pelican's appearance, as well as the way it played with fish before devouring them, described it as 'a fowl between a Stork and a Swan' and otherwise, more imaginatively, as 'a Melancholy Water Fowl'. Once again the King's interest in rare birds is remembered in the name of Birdcage Walk, just beside Buckingham Palace, and Storey's Gate, called after his aviary keeper.

Less exotic fowl also flourished. A duck decoy was created on the Dutch model – despite the King's feelings about the Dutch, he was not above introducing those original aspects of their way of life which appealed to him, including yacht-racing and flower cultivation. A chain of pools, fed by a subterranean passage to the Thames at high tide, kept the duck happy, and they bred abundantly; while the household accounts also reveal expenditure on hemp-seed for their delectation. On the site of the present Marlborough House a pheasantry was established.

It is necessary to stress the outdoor character of many of the sports and amusements which marked the reign of Charles II since, in contrast to the so-called debauchery of the Court, they united him with, rather than divided him from, his humbler subjects. It is less necessary to stress his well advertised love of the theatre. It has been mentioned how many of his friends were patrons of playwrights. So, for that matter, were many of his mistresses, including Barbara, Nell Gwynn and Louise. Writers as a whole amused Charles II. He enjoyed the vicarious sport of suggesting subjects to them. We hear of the King walking with Dryden in the Mall and confiding to him the subject for a poem which he would write himself 'if I was a poet and I think I am poor enough to be one ...'. Dryden took the hint, wrote the poem along the lines suggested by the King, and became a little less poor himself as a result.[42]

When John Crowne was suffering from that familiar complaint, playwright's block, the King presented him with a ready-made plot to encourage him – in the shape of a Spanish play to adapt. Crowne subsequently scored great success with the result, *Sir Courtly Nice or It Cannot Be*.[43]* To Thomas Otway the King is said to have suggested the character of Antonio (based on that of Shaftesbury) in *Venice Preserv'd.*

As for attending performances, obviously a man who chose

* But Charles himself never saw it, for he died on the first day of rehearsal.

at least two of his best known mistresses from amongst the celebrated actresses of the day had a strong motive to do so. This was, after all, the period in which women first flourished on the public stage. But Charles' enthusiasm extended beyond merely casing the joint for the latest pretty face. The King would almost as soon see a new play, wrote one wag, as have a new mistress (at times of course he was able to combine the two experiences). It was in keeping with his general desire to cry 'Hence, loathéd Melancholy' that he preferred comedy to tragedy. One can imagine that the King felt that he had had enough of tragedies in his own life not to want to see them re-enacted upon the stage as an evening's entertainment. John Lacy, a comic actor, was a special favourite with the King. Lacy's *forte* was dialect: in 1663, for example, Pepys described his playing of an Irish footman in Sir Robert Howard's *The Committee* as 'beyond imagination'. The King commissioned his portrait from Michael Wright and hung it at Windsor Castle in a passage on the way to his withdrawing room (it is still in the royal collection). 'The greatest pleasure he had from the stage was in comedy,' wrote Crowne, 'and he often commanded me to write it.'[44] One way and another, the King visited the theatre regularly and with pleasure – almost daily, while the Court was in London, in his younger years.

If the allure of the theatre remains constant, its hours have changed considerably. It is interesting to reflect that performances in the Restoration period were held in the early afternoon, taking advantage of the natural light, with the addition of chandeliers over the actors' heads and footlights (double burners) in front of the stage. They were thus in effect matinées, bywords for respectability today, but the perfect occasion for saucy rendezvous then. The King would dine beforehand and take his place in the royal box – 'the King's box' – at the Dorset Garden Theatre. Heavily adorned with gilt and decorated with the royal arms, a gilded figure of Apollo towered over it. Dryden, criticizing Settle's play *The Empress of Morocco*, said that, if Settle convinced him of its absurd message, he would be 'as great an Apollo as he over the Kinge's Boxe ...'.[45]

Gallants were everywhere, including in the 'tiring-rooms' of the actresses. Gentry who preferred it went and sat downstairs amongst the 'naughty women', whom, in the words of Mr Pinchwife in *The Country Wife*, they 'toused and moused'. Ladies of higher social strata, offering themselves for similar experiences, went masked. But that, as Mr Pinchwife observed, 'like a covered dish', gave a man 'appetite'. Masks or no masks, 'ogling' went on without cease, despite the fact that the smell was horrific – a fact generally acknowledged at the time, when the exact recipe for a protective nosegay was discussed with as much seriousness as a cooking recipe today. The King however kept his tousing and mousing for supper after the play.

In contrast to the pit, magnificence was the keynote of what actually transpired on the stage. Indeed, at first sight those heavily bewigged figures, waddling about in their bepadded and bepuffed clothes, would hardly strike us as symbols of libertarianism. For it is important to realize that throughout the Restoration age there was a feeling that a politer – not a bawdier – form of art was being introduced and performed. It is also worth noting that, while the language used on stage was certainly extremely 'frank', in Sparkish's phrase, and sex the theme of many of the plays, the action itself was not overtly sexual.

The first plays put on after the Restoration tended to be revivals, Beaumont and Fletcher being especially popular. Then there was a tiresome wave of plays whose subject-matter was intended as a kind of loyal rebuttal of the recent Protectoral regime: a typical title was *The Usurper*. After that the great orchard of Restoration drama was planted, and began to flower with all its multitudinous fruit-trees. But some of the old plays, notably a coarse piece called *Hamlet*, caused disgust to 'this refined age', whose elegant taste had been formed by the King's long absence abroad. They were often performed in bastard or adapted versions.

Shakespeare's language continued to be criticized for its (unnecessary) bawdiness throughout the Restoration period, while those very plays were being freely performed which we today consider almost synonymous with bawdiness, whatever their other merits. About 1680 Nicholas Clément, the French royal librarian, made a note in his catalogue on the subject, in which he expressed the opinion that, although the playwright's thoughts were natural, his words ingeniously chosen, and he showed 'a somewhat fine imagination', nevertheless 'these happy qualities' were obscured by 'the dirt' Shakespeare persisted in introducing into his plays.[46]

As the theatres proliferated, so did the theatrical companies. The King's first troop had been formed a year after his own birth – 'Prince Charles' Players'. Only three months after the Restoration he issued patents to Thomas Killigrew and Sir William Davenant to form two licensed theatre companies – the King's Players and the Duke's Players respectively. It was a speedy return to normal after the long interval in which Puritan forces had waged war on the theatre as an immoral influence (although the new-fangled opera had crept in under their guard). The King's Players eventually came to rest at the new Theatre Royal, Drury Lane, in May 1663; the Duke's Players' best-known theatre was at Dorset Garden, designed by Wren, which opened in 1671. In 1682 the two licensed companies, under the sons of Killigrew and Davenant respectively, amalgamated and inhabited the Dorset Garden Theatre. As a sign of the way things were going, the Duke of Monmouth's Servants were licensed in 1669, and the Duchess of Portsmouth's (Louise de Kéroüalle) Servants licensed in about 1673. In 1671 King Charles was keeping eleven 'Women Comedians' and sixteen Men, who were allowed 'several' yards of scarlet cloth and crimson velvet every second year; Queen Catharine also had her Comedians.[47]

This is not the place for a history of the Restoration theatre. Suffice it to note that King Charles II, in his genuine passion for the art, was once again united with rather than divided from his subjects. The gentry – and the orange-girls – who saw him at ease at the play did not love him the less for sharing in their own pleasures. As for the advancement of at least one former orange-girl – Nell Gwynn – that, like the story of Cinderella or the boss who marries the secretary, gave encouragement to all the rest.

Lord Halifax, summing up the character of King Charles II, presented him as not altogether a common type of man. The age over which Charles II presided was not altogether a common one either. Perhaps it was not quite the golden age of glittering plenty predicted in that eve-of-coronation address of 1661. Yet if the plenty is forgotten, that other phrase, 'In Good King Charles' Golden Days', is still appropriate. John Evelyn, more simply than Halifax, wrote of Charles II as 'a Prince of many virtues, and many great imperfections', who brought in 'a politer way of living' – even if he turned later to luxury and expense.[48] A kind of freedom existed in the first decade of the King's reign, not only for hedonism but also for enquiry and experiment. That freedom took its cue from the free, enquiring and of course hedonistic spirit of the King himself.

PART FOUR

The Monarchy in Danger

'The Monarchy itself is in great Danger, as well as His Majesty's person....'
JAMES DUKE OF YORK to William of Orange, 1679

CHAPTER NINETEEN

Subsisting Together?

> 'Affairs are at present here in such a state as to make one believe that a King and a Parliament can no longer subsist together; that they [the King and the Duke of York] must now think only of the war against the Dutch, using the means which they now have, without further recourse to Parliament.'
>
> James Duke of York, July 1671

The position of Charles II in the two years following the Secret Treaty of Dover of 1670 would have struck any cognizant observer as ironical, even humorous. On the one hand, the English King was committed by the treaty to a war against Holland as soon as was convenient – and the French King was committed to participate in the action. For such a war Charles II would need an ample additional 'supply' from his Parliament. Quite apart from the troops promised, this was especially true if his beloved Navy was to acquit itself with glory. The new French subsidy was nothing like sufficient for a land and sea campaign.

On the other hand, the very existence of this treaty was unknown to the English Parliament as a whole: of those ministers who were in the secret, only the most intimate knew the whole truth. In the next few years many members of both Houses would begin to guess from the pro-French drift of the King's actions that something of the sort had taken place. But the ability to make foreign treaties, like that to make peace and war, remained within the most closely guarded enclave of the royal prerogative.

One result of this secrecy was that Members of Parliament remained extremely suspicious about the use the King might make of the supplies they voted. Just as the King feared in the recesses of his mind the return of revolution, or something approaching it, Parliament feared the arrival of absolutism. In February 1673, after the start of the Third Dutch War, Charles II castigated Parliament for 'a jealousy ... that is maliciously spread abroad', so weak and frivolous that he would not have mentioned it, but for the fact that it had gained ground with some 'well-minded people': and that is, 'that the forces I have raised in this war were designed to control law and property'.[1]

But the fact was that the King's growing disgust with Parliament, the cynical if understandable determination he showed to circumvent it where possible, contributed to this paranoia on its part. Equally, the King's own wariness about the attacks on his prerogative – where would it all end? With another 1642? With another 1649? – was fed by the obstreperous nature of Parliament from 1671 onwards. Neither side trusted the other. And there was a good deal to be said for both points of view.

The behaviour of the Parliament called by the King in February 1671 did nothing to smooth the situation. Back in the early 1660s, how lovingly the King had spoken of Parliaments: with genuine emotion he had declared that neither King nor Parliament could function without the other. By July 1671, in contrast, the Duke of York was doubting whether Parliament could contribute anything at all to the current royal project. 'Affairs are at present here in such a state,' he wrote, 'as to make one believe that a King and a Parliament can no longer subsist together; that they [that is, the King and the Duke of York] must now think only of the war against the Dutch, using the means which they now have, without further recourse to Parliament."[2]

This session of Parliament ended in April, when the King prorogued it once more; Parliament did not meet again till February 1673. The most significant effect of this session was to demonstrate the new amity of the royal brothers. The Roos divorce case had come and gone. A precedent had been set up that a man could gain a divorce by Act of Parliament. The King had not availed himself of it. Succession-watchers – who comprised most members of the Court and many Members of

Parliament – considered that the Duke of York's position was in consequence much strengthened.

The trouble was that the King still needed money to make his promised war, and his finances were in their familiar critical state. By adjourning Parliament, he had forfeited certain valuable revenues not yet voted to him. This was the background to the desperate new remedy proposed – probably by Clifford – known as the Stop of the Exchequer. This measure put a violent end to the system started in 1667 by which direct assignments of revenue were issued by the Treasury in return for loans to the government. These paper orders or tallies were registered in the Treasury Book in order to be paid off in order of issue by funds on their way to the Exchequer. Now the King announced that in future monies would go directly to the Exchequer, regardless of these tallies.

Much later the King would say of the Stop to Lord Bruce: 'It was a false step.' It was certainly a colossal psychological mistake. Marvell expressed the national mood of indignation when he called it 'the Robbery at the Exchequer'. Many of those ruined were the weak, those traditionally at the mercy of the mighty. There was another side to it, equally psychologically damaging, the destruction of the strong. Evelyn referred to the Stop in poignant and angry terms as 'an action which not only lost the hearts of his subjects, and ruined many widows and orphans, whose stocks were lent him, but the reputation of his Exchequer forever'. Two banking businesses never recovered. Edward Backwell, for example, he who had persistently put his trust in a prince's credit, held nearly three hundred thousand pounds' worth of paper orders, many incurred in the interests of paying off William of Orange, and as a result he could never lend on a large scale again.[3] The fatal impression was created that it was too dangerous to lend money to the English monarchy.

While it is not possible to quarrel with the King's own estimate of the Stop – it was a false step – one can also sympathize with the circumstances which drove him to it. The goldsmiths were reluctant to lend: the interest they charged – between eight and ten per cent – was not inordinate in an age when fifteen, even twenty per cent was known and they themselves were probably having to pay six per cent. Loans were difficult to obtain.[4] The real culprit was the current English banking system, or rather the lack of it. The problems were not properly solved before the reign of William III, when not only was the Bank of England founded (the happy Dutch already had a national bank), but the concept of a 'perpetual fund' was developed; while William's Parliament – unlike that of Charles II – was willing to underwrite the debts of the State.

The unpopularity and distrust incurred over the Stop did not assist the King in the promulgation of his next measure, done without the support of Parliament. This was the Declaration of Indulgence, given out by the King on 15 March 1672.[5] Its terms made it quite clear that it rested solely upon the powers of the King. Charles II had long wished to do something for both types of religious extremist contained within his kingdom, dissenters and Catholics. It will be remembered that back in 1662 he had issued a declaration granting toleration to both sets of believers.

Then he attempted – in vain – to get the declaration ratified by the authority of Parliament. Now he made no such attempt. The King himself in the new Declaration referred bitterly to the 'sad experience' of the past twelve years and how there was 'very little fruit' from it. Now therefore he felt himself obliged to make use of 'that supreme power in ecclesiastical matters which is not only inherent in us, but hath been declared and recognized to be so by several statutes and Acts of Parliament . . .'. Resting on this power, he proposed to suspend all the penal laws against nonconformists and Catholics. Nonconformists should further be allowed public places of worship by licence; the Catholics would be allowed to worship in their own way privately in their homes.

The words were bold, the sentiments admirable. The measure was taken 'for the quieting the minds of our good subjects . . . for inviting strangers in this conjuncture to come and live under us' – the language being reminiscent of that of another exponent of toleration, Oliver Cromwell, who declared himself as 'loving strangers', hoping that they would live in England's midst. Like

Cromwell, Charles II was to be unsuccessful in swaying the spirit of the times.

The trouble was that it was by no means generally agreed that the King possessed any such 'supreme power in ecclesiastical matters'. The attempt of Charles II to exercise such a power without seeking Parliamentary ratification, while Parliament was not even in session, provoked several types of fear. The Stop of the Exchequer had scarcely prepared the way for the popularity of the King's personal policies. Now the Declaration of Indulgence, by appearing to favour Catholics (for so it was inevitably interpreted by the anti-Popish lobby), confirmed suspicions already aroused by the rumoured conversion of the Duke of York.

Even so, the King might have spiritedly carried through the Declaration of Indulgence, were it not for the demands of the Dutch War. Without money voted by Parliament, he would not be able to carry out that provision of the Secret Treaty of Dover most precious to him. Seen from that angle, the timing of the Declaration of Indulgence, a few days off from another declaration – that of war against Holland – was too spirited altogether. There was a rancorous outcry, not only from Westminster but from far beyond its purlieus. 'It is incredible how much excitement the measure causes all over the country,' wrote the Venetian Ambassador. Neither all the criticism, nor all the support, came from predictable quarters. The judges, for instance, disapproved of the measure because they considered the King was claiming powers he did not possess – this despite the fact that since 1668 they had generally held their offices *durante bene placito* (at the King's good pleasure) rather than *quamdiu se bene gesserit* (so long as they behaved themselves).[6] Lord Ashley, on the other hand, approved of it because he believed that it was widening the basis of the Church of England.[7] Shortly afterwards he was created Earl of Shaftesbury, as part of a general distribution of honours to members of the Cabal on the eve of the war, by which name he will in future be known. Arlington also received an earldom, Clifford a barony, and Lauderdale a dukedom.

There was another crucial element in the treatment of the

Declaration within Parliament. And that was the ability of the King's ministers to provide some sort of Court bloc. Lately Clifford's and Arlington's right-hand man, Sir Joseph Williamson, had apparently been more successful in this respect, although the fact that by February 1671 well over two hundred seats had changed hands since the original election of the Cavalier Parliament in 1661 meant that the composition of the body was more mysterious than the Court managers supposed.

Williamson, another government official of the King's own generation, had begun his career in the office of Sir Edward Nicholas. He transferred to the service of Arlington when the latter succeeded Nicholas as Secretary of State. Williamson entered Parliament himself in 1669, after various attempts; in 1672 he became Clerk of the Council, and was knighted. Possessing exceptional diligence, he also acted as editor of the *London Gazette*, the official publication of the government, which had grown out of a news-sheet disseminated in Oxford at the time of the Court's residence there in 1665. He was, then, like Arlington, an able and devoted servant of the Crown.

But the abortive affair of the Declaration of Indulgence would demonstrate that, for all the work of Williamson, Arlington and Clifford, the King might have his way in small things, but he still could not push through any measure to which Parliament was opposed. His 'supreme power in ecclesiastical matters' was a hollow boast.

There were a series of ostensible excuses for making war on Holland. The official line was given by Charles II in March 1672, when he wrote of England (to his brother) as 'having received many wrongs and indignities from the States General of the United Provinces'. Wrongs were suffered in Surinam, over the East India trade and the English fisheries; indignities were also suffered by the King's Majesty in a series of Dutch satirical pamphlets and medallions. English tactics leading up to the war were however more frankly summed up by Arlington: 'Our business is to break with them and yet to lay the breach at their door.'[8]

Charles' unwavering personal view was given by the Venetian

Ambassador: 'The King is convinced that the hatred of the Dutch for England is hereditary, that it increased because of trade and became implacable owing to the pretensions of the United Provinces.' As to the place of France in the awkward triangle which had existed for the last five years between the three countries, the King told the Council, 'The French will have us or Holland always with them and if we take them not, Holland will have them.'[9]

These were familiar arguments: later Shaftesbury would cry out for the destruction of the Dutch, quoting the famous phrase of the Roman senator, on another hereditary feud between two peoples: '*Delenda est Carthago*'. With more convictions than Shaftesbury, because he had held the view much longer, Charles II believed in the need to crush, or at any rate curb, the United Provinces at sea, in the various corners of the growing English empire and wherever else their 'pretensions' might prickle the English. This, plus a French alliance, was the foreign policy he had worked out for himself. Under the circumstances, a dreadful insult endured by the English yacht *Merlin* at the hands of the Dutch was largely irrelevant – and almost wholly manufactured. All the same, the mixture was not quite as before. On the Dutch side, there was a new and explosive element present. This was their recently appointed General, William of Orange.

It is time to return to this solemn youth, last heard of visiting England in 1670 and attempting to get his engaging uncle to pay his debts to the House of Orange. William too was busy working out the proper direction of his foreign policy. In February 1672 he was made Captain General and Admiral General of the Dutch forces in the field. But, faced as he was with the hordes of France only an inadequate land-mass away, he could hardly afford the luxury of treating England as a foe. Besides, the natural link between England and Holland, from the Orangists' point of view, was one of warm family alliance rather than enmity.

The Orangists naively believed that William's new office would sway his uncle of England in his approach to Holland. They could not understand that Charles' debonair approach to William concealed a genuine inability to understand his nephew's point of view. The insensitivity which Charles continued to show in his letters to William throughout 1672 is striking in such a normally diplomatic man. In April Charles suggested that although 'our interests seem to be a little differing at this present' – a blithe way of alluding to a state of war between their respective countries – he had still done William a considerable service; for had war not broken out, William would never have become General of the Dutch forces!

In July Charles was confident that if William would only follow his advice, 'I make little doubt by the blessing of God of establishing you in the power there [that is, in Holland] which your forefathers always aimed at.' Charles was presumably taking the line to himself that the terms of the Secret Treaty of Dover stood to carve a hereditary principality out of the United Provinces for his nephew. Equally obtuse were Charles' attempts later in the year to make a humiliating peace with Holland via William: 'Such a one as in the bad condition of your affairs will be much better for you and that poor people than any war can be....'[10] To Charles II's amazement, William did not answer.

This insensitivity is striking. It is also surprising. One is obliged to conclude that it sprang from Charles II's own peculiar and deep-seated attitude to family relationships. Towards the end of the seventies these relationships – with his brother, his wife – were tested in a crucible and survived. In the mean time, because Charles II felt warmly towards his family, he obviously expected his relatives to feel the same. In the case of his sister Mary, his expectations had been fulfilled. In the case of her son William, they were to be grievously disappointed.

As William told Buckingham and Arlington, on a joint mission to Holland in 1673 in search of a satisfactory peace – satisfactory to England, that is – 'he liked better the condition of Stadtholder they [the Dutch] had given him ... he believed himself obliged in conscience and honour not to prefer his interest before his obligation.'[11] For the next few years William, all unaware of the Secret Treaty of Dover, would see his obligation as the task of detaching England from France. First however he had to win his spurs in his own country, by saving it from extinction.

When war was declared on 17 March, the total forces of

French and English far outnumbered those of the Dutch, both by land and by sea. Only in naval guns – 4,500 to the allies' 6,000 – did the Dutch approach any kind of equality. Charles II was confident that the spoils of war would include not only those Dutch territories specified in the Secret Treaty, but also some rich naval prizes calculated to swell his depleted Treasury. Since the conduct of the war at sea was left to the English, Charles construed it as his 'obligation', as William would have put it, to interfere himself whenever possible. He paid two visits to the Nore off Chatham, where the Duke of York was once more installed in charge of the fleet; at the end of June he was accompanied by Queen Catharine and Shaftesbury, as Lord Chancellor; at the start of September he took Prince Rupert, Shaftesbury and other members of the Council.

At the beginning of May Charles also wrote James a long letter in his own handwriting, beginning, 'I was this day in our meeting for the business of the fleet, and amongst other things I thought it not amiss to give you this hint....'[12] The hint was the inadvisability of fighting with the Dutch alone: the Duke ought to wait until he had joined up with the French squadron. But at the first proper battle of the war, neither French nor English – nor, by implication, the English commander the Duke of York – covered themselves with glory.

On 7 June, lying in Southwold Bay, off the East Anglian coast between Yarmouth and Lowestoft, the combined squadrons were surprised by the great Dutch Admiral De Ruyter. In the ensuing action both sides endured vast losses. On the English side, the Duke of York had to abandon two successive flagships, the *Prince* and *St Michael.* Lord Sandwich was killed; his body, drifting anonymously in the sea, was only recognized by the George it still wore, the insignia of the Garter. De Ruyter was now limited by lack of funds to using guerrilla tactics. Yet this he did brilliantly, using his superior knowledge of the shoals and islands off the Dutch coast to pounce and harass, then disappear.

It was on land that the Dutch situation seemed most desperate. How could the unfortunate Dutch hope to hold off the great swoop of the French forces through the southern and eastern provinces? The answer was the dramatic and totally unexpected response of a small nation to the aggression of a great power. The Dutch opened their dykes, flooding the land in the face of the oncoming invader. Shortly afterwards William received supreme civilian as well as military command.

The French had been held off, but that was all: the crisis remained. There was no prophet to foresee that 8 July 1672, the date on which William III became Stadholder, had ushered in a new era in Europe.

In August Johann De Witt and his brother were murdered by 'the people' – as Charles II described the killers in one of his missives to William – for being 'the authors and occasion of the war'. William kept himself coldly aloof from the crime. It is extremely unlikely that he participated, as his enemies suggested.[13] Nevertheless, the assassins went unpunished, and later he paid one of them a pension. Admittedly, it was granted for quite a different reason, but the implication that William was not sorry to see Johann De Witt out of the way was easily drawn.

In England, in contrast to fierce and fighting Holland, reactions to the war were desultory. By June, many of the English were talking openly of peace. Even her forces were not immune from this general malaise. In August Sir Charles Lyttelton wrote back from his ship, 'I never saw people so intolerably weary as they are all of being at sea, not only land men and volunteers, but the seamen themselves.'[14] In general, the autumn of 1672 was not a golden time for good King Charles. William, as we have seen, did not acknowledge his uncle's vulpine overtures for peace. Then Charles had a growing problem with the Catholicism of the Duke of York: much publicity was given to the fact that the Duke had not taken Anglican Communion at Easter. A smashing naval victory under the Duke's command might have given him some further mileage in the popular esteem; instead, he was faced with the responsibility for Southwold Bay.

The Duke of York was not the only prominent Catholic who had newly swum into the public gaze. The King's latest mistress, that well-born French girl who had caught his eye in his sister's train at Dover, Louise de Kéroüalle, was also a Catholic. Out of the Queen's discreetly conducted but acknowledged Catholicism, the conversion of Barbara Duchess of Cleveland, the suspected Catholicism of Clifford and even Arlington, it was possible for the imaginative to weave a positive web of Popery around the King.

Under the circumstances, it cannot be denied that the choice of a new Catholic mistress was unfortunate – assuming that any political criterion at all was to be used in such matters. It was additionally unfortunate that Louise was French. Thus in her beguiling person she managed to combine the two attributes most likely to worry the English paranoiacs.

On the surface, there was some substance to these fears. There is evidence that Louis XIV did indeed view Louise as his secret French weapon. Madame cannot be accused of forwarding the plot, having frowned on her brother's proposed abduction of Louise at Dover. But her death freed the girl to accept an invitation probably phrased in the first instance by Buckingham.[15] But, as ever, the wayward Duke showed a reluctance to carry through his own settled plans. He allowed Louise to wait in vain at a French port for his yacht to convey her across the Channel. It was an unwise piece of neglect. As a result of her suffering, Louise arrived in England the friend of Arlington, who treated her with greater courtesy; it was not until later that the firm alliance of Buckingham and Louise became a feature of the scene at Court.

Louise arrived at Court a virgin. Such was her mixture of romance, propriety and ambition, that she may actually have convinced herself that the King intended to marry her before she allowed him to seduce her. She certainly spoke of the Queen's health to the Ambassador, Colbert de Croissy, as though it was likely to deteriorate violently at any moment; then she would marry the King. With similar wishful thinking, Louise later reckoned on making her son, the little Duke of Richmond, the King's heir at a time when the prospect of a half-French, wholly Catholic bastard succeeding was remote indeed. Where marriage was concerned, Louise never even enjoyed the putative chance of Frances Stewart. If Queen Catharine had died in the 1670s, the King would surely have headed for some rich princess, with a European alliance as an additional dowry. Louise, while retaining the pretensions of a lady, as Nelly angrily protested, suffered the vicissitudes of an older profession: she is reported to have caught the pox from the King, who gave her a pearl necklace to make her better.[16]

In other ways Louise did not suffer quite so much. Her baby face, with the fat cheeks that led the King to nickname her Fubbs (for chubby), stares innocently out of her lovely portrait by Gascar, surrounded by a halo of dark curls. One small round breast is revealed: altogether, she resembles a fat little pigeon, or the soft white dove beneath her hand. Though she was described by a contemporary as 'wondrous handsome', we should probably term her merely pretty – and wondrous appealing.[17]

There is no trace in the portraits of Louise's slight cast, which caused Nelly to christen her 'Squintabella' at first sight; so perhaps jealous Nell exaggerated. But there is shrewdness in the expression of her almond-shaped eyes, dark and watchful in the childish face. Louise was nearly twenty-one when she caught the King's eye in Madame's train; it was surprising that such a beautiful girl remained unmarried: 'la Belle Bretonne' she was called at the French Court, where the manners were politer than Nell Gwynn's. The explanation lay in her parents' poverty: Louise had no dowry. As a result, she imported into her role as *maitresse en titre* a nice sense of the importance of money. It was respectable French Louise who saw to it that her pension was tied to the profitable wine excise, where reckless English Barbara settled for a much less stable source of income.[18] When the dukedoms were being handed out to the royal bastards, Louise saw to it that her son gained precedence over Barbara's by the stratagem of getting Danby to sign the relevant document at midnight on the given date.

Tears and hysterics, as well as respectability, were part of Louise's stock-in-trade; it was not for nothing that Nelly chose to nickname her the 'weeping willow' when bored by 'Squintabella'. Louise had correctly summed up Charles as a man who would be made uncomfortable, then guilty, by such things. Later she would swoon and threaten suicide in order to avoid losing his favour. In one sense she overplayed her hand. The Duchess of Monmouth relates the story of the King being told – not for the first time – that Louise was dying: 'God's fish!' he answered. 'I don't believe a word of all this; she's better than you or I are, and she wants something that makes her play her pranks over this. She has served me so often so, that I am as sure of what I say as if I was part of her.'[19] Yet he never did quite get rid of her.... Louise would survive the determined broadsides of that magnificent fighting ship, Hortense Mancini, Duchess of Mazarin, and come to safe harbour as the resident mistress at the time of Charles' death.

Sir John Reresby, a vigilant observer of such matters, described Louise as 'the most absolute of all the King's mistresses'. She was certainly the most disliked by the populace. None of the ballads of the time were particularly tasteful – Barbara was generally depicted as insatiable in her sexual appetites – but the language addressed to Louise was notably intemperate:

> Portsmouth, the incestuous Punk,*
> Made our most gracious Sovereign drunk,
> And drunk she made him give that Buss
> That all the Kingdom's bound to curse...

So ran a fragrant piece, of 1673, entitled 'The Royal Buss Rock'. The most playful piece of satire – if such an innocent adjective may be used – was that dialogue which, taking advantage of the King's notorious weakness for his dogs, made Louise and Nelly into two pampered pets, named Snappy and Tutty. Even so, there was a social sneer: Snappy (Louise) was made to criticize Tutty (Nell) for her low breeding and suggest that she return to her 'dunghill'.[20]

Louise's rise was rapid. Her seduction by the King – if one may use the word for an event so obviously planned on both sides – seems to have taken place in October 1671 at Euston

* In its original sense of harlot; the secondary meaning of rotten, revived in the present day, came later.

Hall, Arlington's splendid new county house near Newmarket. The scene, as reported, had dramatic overtones which must have pleased Louise's histrionic nature, while its erotic ones pleased everyone else. For there was a 'mock marriage', at which 'the Fair Lady Whore' (Evelyn's phrase for Louise) 'was bedded one of these nights and the stocking flung, after the manner of a married bride'. By July 1672 her ascendancy was great enough for a large new coach for 'Madame Carwell', as her incomprehensible Breton name was anglicized, to feature in the royal expenses.[21] In the same year, roughly nine months after the 'marriage' at Euston Hall, she gave birth to her only child; this boy was, incidentally, to be the last of the acknowledged royal bastards. In February 1673 Louise was created Duchess of Portsmouth, Countess of Fareham and Lady Petersfield – while Nelly still languished as Mrs Gwynn.

As befitted her position as she interpreted it, the new Duchess kept increasing state in the large area over which she held sway in Whitehall – she finally acquired a total of twenty-four rooms and sixteen garrets. Evelyn described her appartments as having 'ten times the richness and the glory' of the Queen's.[22] He also paints an inviting picture of Louise having her hair combed by her maids in bed, while the King and his gallants stood around. Three times her rooms were redecorated (amazing luxury). Her acquisitions included French tapestries specially woven at her command, such diversities as Japanese cabinets, clocks, silver, great vases of wrought plate and ornamental screens, as well as paintings originally belonging to the Queen.

'What contentment can there be in the riches and splendour of this world, purchased with vice and dishonour?' enquired Evelyn in elegant disgust. The answer was that Louise Duchess of Portsmouth found a great deal of contentment in such things; riches and splendour, after all, were visible to the naked eye, which was more than could be said for vice and dishonour.

For all this, Louis XIV did not really succeed in planting a Trojan horse in the person of the desirable Duchess. The reason for the failure lay in the character of Charles II. The varied intrigues which led to the establishment of Louise, the whole process of dangling this nubile beauty before a famously susceptible King, all presupposed that Charles' political sympathies followed his amorous inclinations. In the cool light of history, one cannot view the King in quite such a romantic light. As with Madame, so with Louise: it seems more likely that the reverse was true. Charles chose a confidante whose views or tastes accorded with his own, rather, than tailoring his to fit those of the lady.

Oddly enough, Louise's strongest card with the King appears to have been the aura of charming domesticity which she cast around her. In the end, it was this traditional attribute of a French mistress down the ages which delighted Charles II: the ability to provide agreeable surroundings and good food (Louise was famous for her table) as much as her physical appeal. Mercenary as she may have been, haughty to her social inferiors, at times tiresomely hysterical, Louise possessed an excellent instinct where men were concerned. She was clever enough to spot that Charles II was reaching an age where a settled and comfortable salon possessed at least as much attraction as a voluptuous bedroom. It was in this manner that Louise's French blood won Charles II, rather than in any more Machiavellian sense of political alignment.

Nevertheless, the murmurs against Popery in high places grew from the spring of 1672 onwards. Charles might in fact be immune from petticoat persuasion; but it was too much to expect his raucous popular critics to believe such a paradoxical fact about a King of such evident 'amorous complexion'. The rise of Louise, for all the private ease it granted, coincidental with the conversion of the Duke of York, and the disappointing course of the war, increased the problems the King had to face by the autumn of 1672.

To the north, the outlook was not much brighter. Lauderdale had promised his sovereign a citadel in Scotland. But in June 1672 the Scottish Parliament demonstrated that its sympathies lay – perhaps not surprisingly – with the Protestant Dutch, with whom the Scots did a great deal of trade, rather than with the Catholic French. Lauderdale's appeal to this body for much-needed money to prosecute the Dutch War was therefore not a success. Moreover, the coarse and tactless streak in the man had been enhanced with age: Lauderdale no longer managed his Scottish opponents with the same wiliness that he had displayed in the 1660s, while his foul-mouthed manner gained him additional enemies.

Nevertheless, the old warhorse remained sufficiently canny to see the most obvious dangers of his situation. In England, Shaftesbury was his particular enemy. In Scotland, the Duke of Hamilton led a rising faction against his policies. Lauderdale could see for himself that the patronage of the King was vital to his survival. Therefore his management of Scotland was dedicated to giving Charles II what he wanted.

At least the King was quite clear what that was. He continued to regard Scotland as a useful reservoir of money and men, and that was about all. His letter to Lauderdale of August 1672, which he himself admitted to be both overdue and over-brief, concentrated on the needs for an invasion of the United Provinces. If the first attempt of the English to land were to succeed, he would want additional troops at hand to back them up: 'therefore if it were possible to have two thousand men ready in Scotland upon such an occasion ...'.[23] In the event, there was no invasion, so that the crisis was not reached. All the same, the tide of revolt against Lauderdale's vice-regal rule was rising in Scotland, with the King quite unaware of the danger.

It was as well for Charles II, concentrating on the needs of an 'important necessary and expensive war', as he would later call it to Parliament, that Ireland was in one of her rare periods of quiescence. The Irish Army was, like the country, poor, and not much reliance could be placed on reinforcements from that source.* Sir William Petty analysed the situation in the island in 1672: 800,000 Papists, 200,000 English and 100,000 Scots. It was not a prescription for future happiness. Yet after the horrors of Cromwell's campaign and the subsequent wave of settlement

* Although in some respects it was in advance of the English Army. Kilmainham Hospital provided the model for Chelsea Hospital for veteran and wounded soldiers.

(following on so many waves of settlement), Ireland in the 1670s temporarily resembled Gibbon's description of Abyssinia: 'the world forgetting by the world forgot' – even if it would hardly be allowed to sleep for a thousand years. In November 1670 the *Dublin Gazette* actually ceased to appear on the wonderful – for Ireland – grounds that 'there was no news'.[24]

The country's condition was ameliorated still further when the Earl of Essex succeeded the corrupt Lords Berkeley and Robartes as Lord Lieutenant in 1672. Essex was much esteemed by his contemporaries for his upright character as well as his love of learning, and of libraries in particular. He was the son of a war hero – always a passport to respect. His father Arthur Capel, who had been in Cornwall with Charles II (when Prince of Wales), was executed in 1649 shortly after Charles I. Charles II, having the death of a beloved father in common, paid young Capel special attention; he was created Earl of Essex at the Restoration.

In Ireland, Essex's determination to stamp out English corruption was symbolized by his fight against the rapacity of Barbara Duchess of Cleveland. Barbara may well have received £10,000 from Berkeley as the price of his office. She was certainly granted Phoenix Park in Dublin, as well as some deliciously fertile lands round it, by the King. He showed by the gift his total lack of knowledge of the geography of the town as well as his indifference to Irish affairs. Essex was furious. 'I will not have the least concurrence with it,' he announced.[25] He was undeniably influenced by the fact that Phoenix Park was the only place where the Lord Lieutenant could walk or ride in comfort, Dublin Castle being hideously uncomfortable. Yet by Essex's action Phoenix Park was saved for future generations (remaining to this day one of the largest public parks in the world).

The cancellation of the Declaration of Indulgence was a blow to Irish Catholics, as it had been to English: Essex was instructed to 'suppress the insolency of the Irish Papists', this insolency having among its component parts 'convents, seminaries, friaries, nunneries and Popish schools'. But Essex, like all the wisest rulers of Ireland during this period (and like Charles II himself), distinguished between Catholic gentlemen and Catholic rebels. He pointed out that there were several hundred thousand Catholics in the country and that to 'suppress' them – the word was frequently used – he would need an army of over fifteen thousand, regularly paid. . . .[26] As it was, not all the titular Catholic bishops left the country according to the new proclamation; the lesser clergy were often left in peace.

The existence of the ordinary people as a whole was not enviable; but the harsh choice of the next centuries, emigration or misery at home, had not yet reached them. Catholic laymen, although virtually excluded from Parliament, were able to practise most other professions. Essex's main domestic problem was one he shared with the Irish people as a whole – the failure of law and order (the rise of those brigands known locally as Tories brought the word into the vocabulary of the English people).

Charles II, however, unfussed by Irish Tories, continued to regard Ireland as a fertile pasture to be milked. Now that his original generous desire to establish a state of indemnity in Ireland had lapsed with time and fierce pressures at home, revenues were treated as rewards (Barbara's grant came into that category). His personal participation was limited to the odd occasions when he intervened over harsh treatment to an individual with regard to land.

If Ireland gave out little hard news, by the end of 1672 there was plenty of news in London. The *London Gazette* would shortly be reporting the recall of Parliament. Failing to secure his peace with William of Orange, Charles II was left with the impossibility of sailing his fleet the following spring without money to hand. The royal expenses display the nature of the preparations. Hay, two whole loads of it, was ordered for stuffing the seats, sacks and benches in the Parliamentary chambers. Two pairs of tongs – 'handsome and serviceable' – were acquired, as was a pillow of down for the Lord Chancellor. Candlesticks had to be got and that ever-present expense of the time, close-stools (nine of them). Green baize was to be employed in quantity, so that the seats in the House of Commons could be 'new repaired'. More green baize was to be used for window curtains for 'H.M.'s service'.[27]

The fact was that this session of February 1673 contained a crucial appeal by the King for money for his 'important, necessary and expensive war', and an equally crucial rejection of that appeal by both Commons and Lords. Where Charles spoke emotionally of his ships, and the contest into which he dared to say that he had been 'forced', the Commons clamoured furiously to have the Declaration of Indulgence of the previous year withdrawn. Only Parliament, they reiterated, could suspend the penal laws. The King first prevaricated; then equivocated. Referring to 'his power in ecclesiastics', he assured the Commons that he never had any thoughts of using it otherwise than as it had been 'entrusted' to him, for the peace and establishment of the Church of England, and 'the ease of all his subjects in general'. He had no thought, he declared, of 'avoiding or precluding the advice of Parliament'.[28]

Wriggle as the King might, he could not avoid the tight hold of the Parliamentary pincers in which the demands of his war had placed him. He tried in vain to appeal to the House of Lords, whose relations with the Commons were at the time sufficiently acrimonious for him to hope for better things from their assembly. He continued to put the most comforting gloss on what he had done: 'My Lords and Gentlemen: if there be any scruple remaining with you concerning the suspension of penal laws, I here faithfully promise you that what hath been done in that particular shall not for the future be drawn either into consequence or example.' But the Lords would not support him. In the end the King was obliged to withdraw the Declaration in return for an assessment of £70,000 a month for three years.

It was a galling defeat.

There was worse to come. Immediately after their triumph the Commons pressed through a Test Act. This measure was as divisive as Charles' Declaration of Indulgence had been potentially healing. Every holder of office had to take public communion in the Church of England. Furthermore, various oaths of allegiance were framed, as well as a declaration concerning the doctrine of transubstantiation; together they formed a test, in the truest sense of the word, which it was impossible for an sincere Catholic to pass. Once again, the King found himself in no position to combat the challenge.

Bowing his head before the storm, a familiar posture, he gave his assent to the Test Act on 29 March. The consequences were felt at once. The Duke of York and Thomas Clifford both failed to take Anglican communion at Easter. The Duke laid down his post as Lord High Admiral in June. Clifford also resigned as Lord Treasurer – to die shortly afterwards. The King took refuge in one of those pieces of 'raillery'. He was heard to say that he would purge his Court of all Catholics except his barber 'whom he meant to keep in despite of all their bills, for he was so well accustomed to his hand'. The joke was a pointed one: if a Catholic could be trusted with a razor so near the royal person, his co-religionists could hardly be the cut-throats of popular imagination.[29]

How prescient had proved the words of the Duke of York two years before! In the summer of 1673 it was even more difficult to see how a King and a Parliament could 'subsist together' for very long. Inevitably, the King prorogued Parliament once more. He was alleged to have observed that he would rather be a poor King than no King. . . .[30] But the long war of attrition between King and Parliament was in fact gathering new momentum.

CHAPTER TWENTY

The Knot in the Comb

'This knot will again return to the teeth of the comb and never disentangle itself unless the King take courage to combat the licence of Parliament.'

The Venetian Ambassador, 1674

It was the presumed connection of Catholicism with royal absolutism which dominated the politics of the next few years. The installation of a young French Catholic mistress might be shrugged off with a worldly air, although the rumour that Charles II and Louise were secretly married by a Catholic rite showed how far suspicion could desert sense – a Catholic rite was the last thing which could have united the King and his mistress during the lifetime of Catharine of Braganza. The genuine marriage plans of the Duke of York to a Catholic princess were quite a different matter. Anne Duchess of York died in March 1671 and thereafter James looked around for a new wife. These plans followed a joint venture with the French of increasing unpopularity. Meanwhile the absolutist French government across the water aroused fears that the King himself might be contemplating something similar.

Charles II strenuously denied the connection of Catholicism and absolutism, for the good reason that the two were not connected in his own mind. The rise of Catholicism in England was in fact a chimera. Like many popular scares, statistics show that it had no foundation. The numbers of Catholics in the country were actually declining, as they had been declining throughout the century and would continue to do.* They were a persecuted and depressed body, given an artificial appearance of strength and spirit by three factors. First, like immigrants in our own day, they tended to group together, so that they could share a priest without too much loss of security. Wolverhampton, for example, was termed 'a little Rome'. Secondly, there was a link in the popular imagination between Catholicism and the Army. This had some basis in the original Royalist armies, where Catholics from Ireland and elsewhere found employment. And Catholics continued to serve in the Army (although officers were excluded by the Test Act), particularly in campaigns and outposts abroad. The standing army of Charles II was always subject to keen and worried scrutiny: the association of the Catholics and the Army made for a vicious circle of apprehension.[2]

Thirdly, as has been stressed, the characters boldly lit up on the public stage of the Court were beginning to have a Catholic air. Or, as Evelyn put it, the 'fopperies of the Papists' were now coming out in the open.[3] To the suspicious country, the Court appeared to be going rapidly Catholic – a disastrous state of affairs.

The King continued to view these matters from quite a different angle. Since Worcester, he had seen the poorer Catholics in their true light as essentially loyal, if unhappy, creatures. It was a point of view he had twice tried to impose on the law of the land by repealing the penal laws, without success. When he drew up the Army at Blackheath in the autumn of 1673, it was a gesture widely interpreted as menacing towards the capital. But no evidence has ever been found that Charles II intended to parody in such a way the actions (and mistakes) of his predecessor Cromwell – let alone use his standing army as a Popish instrument.[4] He made nothing of the Catholic air of the Court: he breathed it with enjoyment, but to him it did not reek of absolutism. Because this connection between Catholicism and

* Obviously the numbers of members of a proscribed religion are hard to estimate: they have been put as low as sixty thousand – just over one per cent of the population.[1]

absolutism did not exist, he seemed unable to grasp that it played a part in the suspicions of Parliament. To the extent that he was unwilling to check his brother's Catholic marriage plans, Charles set up an intricate tangle for himself in the autumn of 1673.

The political scene was further complicated by the mounting intrigues of William of Orange, to bring about that separate peace with England, cutting off France, on which he had set his heart. His plan was to concentrate on the manifestly weak link in the chain of the King's pro-French foreign policy – the House of Commons. Various agents were employed, principal amongst them Peter Du Moulin. A code language evolved in which, for example, the King was known as 'Mr Young', the Duke of York 'Mr Cook' and the Catholics 'the Stone-Chandlers'. It was Du Moulin, a man of devious yet lucid intelligence, who had first pointed out to the Dutch prince that England was setting her compass in the direction of France. In his report on the subject, he had underestimated the personal control of Charles II over the nation's affairs. Nevertheless, his original plan of sowing dissension amongst the various members of the Cabal, while at the same time emphasizing the threat of France to the House of Commons, could hardly be said to have failed.[5]

Even if he had misunderstood the wide powers remaining with the King – and who did understand the disposition of power between King and Parliament at this point? – it was perfectly true that by the summer of 1673 the King's ministers were in demonstrable disarray. Dutch money was also dispensed with a generosity not usually associated with a country described by an English statesman later as 'offering too little and taking too much'. Perhaps most of it was spent on satirical pamphlets and other pieces of sordid but carefully aimed abuse, rather than on paying the English MPs on a large scale. Nevertheless, the presence of Dutch *largesse* on any scale provides a sardonic counterpart to the King's own reception of French subsidies. It was an age when political purses somehow existed on a very different level from political principles.

The Catholic marriage project of the Duke of York was an open invitation to the Dutch-inspired satirists to spread their calculated venom. In his search for a bride, one of the Duke's aims was to provide himself with a male heir whose claims to the succession would supersede those of his two surviving daughters Mary and Anne, now eleven and eight respectively. But the Duke, who was showing himself almost as convincing a womanizer as his brother, also paid a particular attention to his future wife's appearance: as he approached forty, his taste ran to young and beautiful girls.

It was ironic that James's first choice, the widowed Susan Lady Belasyse, was actually a Protestant: and he selected her for the good reason that he was much in love with her. Charles made short work of the project. James, he said, had made a fool of himself once and was not to be allowed to do so again. He had in mind a foreign princess who would bring some prestige and power in her train, even some money, rather than a mere Englishwoman. As for love, it was Charles who dismissed the whole notion of marrying with that in mind – one could get used to anyone's face in a week, he remarked.[6] Charles' witticism that his brother's mistresses were so plain that they must have been imposed on him by his confessors as a penance is sometimes quoted as evidence of James' general boorishness – there is something very unattractive about having a positive taste for plain women. Anne Hyde was undoubtedly plain, but perhaps this early experience gave James a good fright. For Lely made of James' post-Restoration mistress Lady Chesterfield a doe-like creature with nothing plain about her. The evidence of this quest for a bride is also very much to the contrary: it is Charles who concentrates on the worldly position of the lady, James who anxiously queries her physical attributes.[7]

A taste for pretty girls was really James' only vice: unless you took into account that sinister rigidity, increasing with the years, remarked on earlier. Gradually the brave, bluff Duke of York was being moulded by circumstances and age into the future James II. His appearance had altered markedly from the slender, thoughtful youth he was in exile. By the mid-1660s he had become 'all fat and ruddy and lusty' from the sun and air aboard ship.[8] James' character had also expanded, strengthened and hardened. His courage was turned in another direction. Buckingham's clever saying of the King and the Duke, that Charles could see things if he would and James would see things if he could, contained a kernel of truth, as such aphorisms often do, albeit simplified. The trouble was that the things James *did* see were the need for 'Papistry' and 'arbitrary government' – matters with which most English people were quite out of sympathy.

Having adopted his Catholicism 'with full deliberation', he could not imagine himself abandoning it, 'though I were sure it would restore me into the good opinion and esteem of the nation which I once had', as he told Laurence Hyde (Clarendon's son) in 1681. His great-grandmother, Mary Queen of Scots, had made the same kind of proud declaration when urged to embrace the Protestant religion to please Queen Elizabeth: 'Constancy becometh all folks well, and none better than princes, ... and specially in matters of religion.'[9] However admirable, it was a very different spirit from that of Henri Quatre – and Charles II.

His religion was only one aspect of his development. James had also acquired a youthful conviction of the rightness of absolutist government from his years in the French Army – here, if anywhere, was the connection of Catholicism and absolutism feared by his brother's Parliamentary critics. It is sometimes forgotten, in stressing French influences of all sorts on Charles II, from the political to the literary, that he was expelled from the country in 1654. In no sense did he return from *France* to England in 1660. James, on the other hand, both spent more of his exile in direct touch with French influences and had happier memories of the experience.

The Duke of York was also, understandably, a stern advocate of the legitimate succession. In 1675 he made a significant remark to the French Ambassador: Queen Elizabeth, he said, had been as much of a usurper as Cromwell. This alluded to Elizabeth's birth, which by Catholic standards was illegitimate, and left Mary Queen of Scots as the proper sovereign of England by her legitimate Tudor descent. The Duke of York clearly intended the same standards to prevail a hundred years later. On another occasion Admiral Tromp told him not to worry about his lack of a son, since England had been well ruled by women. James replied tartly that the reign of Queen Elizabeth had been 'the worst reign since the Conquest'.[10] He referred here as much to the growth of Parliamentary liberty as to her bastard birth. As the Duke of York fired off on the subject of Elizabeth the disaster, the English people were busy celebrating her Accession Day with increasing Protestant fervour. It was a symbolic contrast.

Over his impending marriage, the Duke of York certainly displayed all the resolution for which one alternately admires and condemns him. The King's choice had been an Austrian archduchess; but she was wrested from James' grasp when the Emperor, finding himself unexpectedly a widower, promptly made the archduchess his own. The plain Princess of Neuburg was banned by James – to Charles' amazement – and Charles himself banned a Princess of Württemberg, either because he continued to dislike princesses of 'cold Northern countries' or for the more rational reason that she had a trouble-making mother.

There was a certain haste over the enquiries, because James at least was determined to marry before the autumn, when Parliament was due to reconvene. He was under no illusion as to what their reactions would be to the kind of Catholic match he now had in mind. When word came of the availability of *two* Princesses of Modena, the fifteen-year-old Mary Beatrice and her thirty-year-old aunt, James' marital pulse raced – particularly when he learnt that these pious Catholic ladies would be backed up by substantial payments from Louis XIV. For Modena lay within the French interest: Mary Beatrice's mother had been a niece of Cardinal Mazarin. In the end, reports of Mary Beatrice's beauty – 'her hair black as jet' and her graceful figure – as well as her tender age, inclined the Duke of York towards her. The proxy marriage was performed on 20 September with Lord Peterborough acting the part of the groom.[11]

When the news was made public, the uproar was immense. It became the violent concern of Parliament to fend off this marriage with 'the daughter of the Pope', as Mary Beatrice was unkindly termed, before it could actually be consummated.

Shaftesbury in particular was vociferous in his opposition. In any case, this strange, warped and talented politician was veering towards more public opposition to the King, and his days as Lord Chancellor were clearly numbered. Admittedly, he had voted for the Declaration of Indulgence, but he had also, like Arlington, voted for the Test Act. Like Arlington, he was on increasingly hostile terms with the Duke of York as a result, and by the autumn was reported to be unable to sit at the same Council Table with him. At the same time, the balance of power in the King's inner councils altered.

In June 1673 Thomas Osborne was made Lord High Treasurer: he was also created Lord Latimer, and the next year Earl of Danby (by which name he will in future be designated). Danby's contemporaries did not bother their heads with jealousy, cynically supposing that in view of the state of the economy the post of Lord High Treasurer was calculated to ruin anyone.[12] But the rise of Danby, a firm Anglican, a supporter of the Triple Alliance, and a man obstinately determined to put the King's finances on a better footing, was in fact the most hopeful thing which had happened to Charles II, domestically, for several years, although its full effects would not be felt immediately.

The angry chaos provoked by the news of the Duke of York's match remained. Charles, as so often before when under pressure, took refuge in delay. On the one hand, he withdrew his offer of the public chapel of St James to Mary Beatrice: she would have to make do with a private one. The Queen was made to claim the St James' chapel in order to gloss over the affront. On the other hand, Charles put off the summoning of Parliament for a crucial week, hoping that in the meantime Mary Beatrice would arrive in the country and the marriage would be duly consummated before any further protests could be heard.

London was already awash with ugly rumours. The notion that the King might divorce the Queen – and thus at a stroke defeat the Duke of York's Popish plans – was once more publicly discussed.[13] More talk was heard on the subject of the King's favourite son, the Duke of Monmouth. The 'Revolting Darling', as a popular ballad described him – flattery was intended – was now twenty-three; his marriage to Anne, the heiress of Buccleuch, had presented him with a solid base of money and estates. The Catholicism of his youth (he had been educated at one point at the Oratory in Paris at the orders of Henrietta Maria) was a thing of the past; Monmouth had been quick to see the advantages of a Protestant position.

Delay for Charles II did not mean irresolution, nor the desertion of the Duke of York. It was Parliament the King hoped to outwit, not his brother. Shaftesbury in particular was showing his hand in a way which was ominous in such an adroit politician. He was sympathetic to the Dutch, rather than actually working with them. But his marked hostility to the Duke of York made it unlikely that the King could preserve both men within the same regime, even if he wanted to. Shaftesbury showed his hand even more publicly when he suggested in Council that the King should divorce Catharine and marry a Protestant. In addition, Charles suspected Shaftesbury of stirring up trouble for Lauderdale in Scotland. He was probably wrong. But even if this particular charge was unjust, Charles had had enough of Shaftesbury.

To know Shaftesbury and his 'slippery humour' was not necessarily to love him. He has been immortalized as Dryden's Achitophel:

> Restless, unfixed in principles and place,
> In power unpleas'd, impatient of disgrace....

While Charles II did not match Dryden in venom, he did not subscribe to the view that Shaftesbury's various changes in 'principles and place' sprang from a deep concern for the common weal. As Clarendon expressed it, 'Few men knew Lord Ashley [Shaftesbury] better than the King himself did, and had a worse opinion of his integrity.' Charles for once did not trouble to hide his opinion. On one occasion at the theatre, observing the swarthy appearance of the Murderers in *Macbeth*, he enquired rhetorically, 'Pray, what is the meaning that we never see a Rogue in a Play, but, Godsfish! they always clap him on a black Periwig? When, it is well known one of the greatest Rogues in England always wears a fair one ...' – an allusion to Shaftesbury's florid looks, as well as, no doubt, to the King's own dark ones.[14]

In general, the estimates of Shaftesbury's own contemporaries are much less favourable than those of a later age, influenced by the success of his principles – or at least some of them. The younger Whigs came to consider him a dangerous opportunist.[15] King Charles II was to be counted amongst those who had reason to remember his conduct under the Commonwealth and on the eve of the Restoration. As men today cannot altogether elude the stigma of a bad war record, Shaftesbury's 'integrity' was suspect in his own day for historical reasons.

It was a nerve-racking time for the King. Outwardly, he remained steady. But for once his inner confidence seems to have been shaken, since he took the unusual step of consulting the eminent astrologer, Elias Ashmole, on the subject of the House of Commons. Very likely the step was taken at the suggestion of Clifford, who was interested in astrology and in touch with Ashmole. Nevertheless, King Charles in better days showed praiseworthy disregard for the superstition which obsessed so many of his contemporaries. In exile he had joked about Lord Bristol: he hoped 'the stars' would permit Bristol to stay in Brussels till he got there; and then, if 'Taurus be as successful to him as Aries has been ... I hope he will think a little more of terrestrial things.' He made the point that a comet visible in 1664 interested him for scientific reasons and not for its 'prophecies' (although, if it portended anything, he joked, he hoped it might be an English victory). When a 'prophet' or fortune-teller came to the Court, Charles told Madame that he gave little credit to 'such kind of cattle'. He added even more definitely, 'The less you do it the better, for if they could tell anything 'tis inconvenient to know one's fortune beforehand, whether good or bad.'[16]

It is a valuable indication of the atmosphere of tension in late October 1673 that Charles II should have gone against his own instincts to the extent of letting Ashmole set up a chart. In so doing, Ashmole combined the time of the King's address to the House of Commons following the short prorogation with that of his nativity. The ensuing predictions should justly have sent the King back to his original sceptical position. Ashmole was infinitely calming, as prophets are wont to be with princes, even those as merciful as Charles II. He foresaw 'a notable harmony and unity between the King and Parliament' within a few days; that the King would be able to dispose of and control the House of Commons, which 'in all things, shall please him'.[17]

In fact, Parliament when it did meet proved itself horribly vociferous on the subject of Popery, royal absolutism and royal money. The King saw no other course but to prorogue it once more till after Christmas.*

It was in November that the King finally got rid of Shaftesbury. Although he continued to sit on one council, that of Trade and Plantations, till the following March, he was dismissed as Chancellor. When Mary Beatrice finally arrived at Dover towards the end of the month, the atmosphere was still so strained that hardly anyone dared make the ride out to meet her. Yet Charles II had in the end demonstrably preferred the interests of his brother's marriage to those of 'harmony and unity', in Ashmole's optimistic phrase, with Parliament. The politicians, including Shaftesbury, who would stir up the powerful movement to exclude James from the succession five years later, should perhaps have remembered the fact.

January 1674 inexorably brought another session of Parliament. Its inception, as usual, was due to the acute royal need for money, and in an effort to secure it, Charles now found it in himself to give Parliament a personal assurance: 'There is no other treaty with France, either before or since, not already printed, which shall not be made known.' It is true that he fumbled with his notes as he spoke; but that was probably due to nervousness not shame: he remained a diffident speaker, probably the effect of the lurking family stammer not otherwise evident in his speech.[19] The straight lie did not however save him. Both Houses of Parliament voted for a separate peace with the Dutch, a culmination, amongst other things, of the secret intrigues of William of Orange.

* Ashmole was consulted once more, in January 1674; he also continued to follow the King's astrological progress in the future, although there is no proof that he did so with the King's approval other than the fact that it was in theory treason to cast the sovereign's horoscope without authorization.[18]

Once more Charles II took cover. Abandoning the policy which had secretly obsessed him for the last five years, he gave Parliament another assurance on 11 February: he hoped for 'a speedy, honourable, and I hope, lasting peace with the Dutch'.[20] And his ally, Louis XIV, still bent on securing those lowland dominions on which he had set his heart? The Treaty of Westminster with the Dutch was such a clear public repudiation of the Treaty of Dover that one might imagine Charles II would have had some difficulty in justifying it to the betrayed French King. But Charles, that redoubtable diplomat, who had concluded the Triple Alliance while secretly negotiating with France, was equal to the task. He convinced Louis XIV that he was obliged to adopt this course by lack of money. A year later he would be able to form another secret alliance with Louis XIV, seamed together by further French subsidies.

Yet the interests of the two Kings had diverged. While Louis XIV was determined to make his life 'a battle and a march', in the words of Schiller's Wallenstein, Charles II had perceived at last the impossibility of combining an aggressive foreign policy and a docile Parliament. That did not however leave him without a European role. Between William of Orange and Louis XIV it was surely practical for a man who was the uncle of one and the first cousin of the other to act as mediator. For the next few years Charles would confine his foreign relationships, perforce, to compromise and negotiation. And since Louis XIV remained rich, while Charles remained poor, his role might bring him financial benefits.

At home, the King speedily prorogued Parliament once more. The seats of the MPs, covered in their new green baize and stuffed with their newly bought hay, were emptied once again. Before this could happen however Parliament also witnessed the final disintegration of the Cabal. Buckingham overreached himself in his criticism of the royal policies. Rash as ever, he appealed in person to the House of Commons, without seeking the permission of the King, or indeed that of the body to which he himself belonged, the House of Lords. He was stripped of his offices, the ultimate humiliation occurring when he was made to surrender his patent as Master of the Horse to that popinjay

Monmouth (but the King had to pay Buckingham compensation).

With Shaftesbury and Buckingham out of the way, only Lauderdale and Arlington remained of the original five who had formed the acronym of the Cabal, and Arlington's star had been eclipsed by that of Danby. Lauderdale was fully occupied trying to hold down Scotland to the royal will – as interpreted by himself. The fact that Shaftesbury would now go to all intents and purposes into opposition (to use the modern phrase), forming the nucleus of the future Whig party, showed how shallow had been the surface unity of the Cabal. Only the common aim of carrying through the King's policies had brought them together. Now this task was left to Danby alone.

The Venetian Ambassador gives an interesting portrait of Charles as he appeared to a foreign observer in 1674. 'The King lives from day to day,' he wrote disapprovingly, but 'This knot will again return to the teeth of the comb and never disentangle itself unless the King takes courage to combat the licence of Parliament.' Unfortunately, he was not likely to do so. The Ambassador continued, 'The King is intent on enjoying life, has no heirs and always hesitates to raise a finger for fear of a relapse into the miseries and perplexities of youth.'[21]

The last part of this analysis certainly rings true: a relapse – not only for himself but for the monarchy as a whole – into the aptly termed 'miseries and perplexities' of his youth was exactly what Charles II did fear. Whether he enjoyed life in this confused period may be doubted. Still more it may be doubted whether his best course was to tug valiantly at the Knot in the Comb represented by the licence of Parliament. Courage was one thing, cunning another. Courage would lead to a confrontation which he might well lose. Cunning suggested skirting round the whole subject of the licence of Parliament, until Danby had established the monarchy on a more solid basis, both economically and politically.

In the economic sphere at least, Danby scored an early success. He raised the royal revenues considerably, an increase which joined with a natural upswing in trade in the early seventies to provide new affluence. Danby also took retrenchment extremely seriously and, under his guidance, some kind of austerity was once more introduced into the conduct of the royal household and finances. He aimed at disbanding the new regiments of the Army, for instance, and ended by saving £97,000 by cutting the Army to its normal peacetime complement of six thousand men. The Navy alone was costing £1,500 a *day* at the date when Danby became Lord Treasurer: this kind of disbursement Danby realized was simply not within the King's power to keep up, if he was to be left with any resources of his own.[22]

Some of Danby's expedients have an odd air to modern economists. For example, he added to the annual rent received from the farming of the Excise the sum which farmers would have normally dispensed in pensions, and undertook that the King would pay them himself, where they were justified. The idea, a laudable one, was to increase the King's cash flow. The result was to add a whole new list of financial dependents to the monarchy, already cursed with far too many. But in an age when the practice of economics was barely understood – remember that desperate, unhappy measure the Stop and the equally desperate situation it sought to cure – Danby passed for a genius because he actually brought about a positive improvement. Expenditure on the Household, Wardrobe, Chamber and Privy Purse, which had risen to over £250,000 a year, from an average of £185,000 between 1660 and 1669, was brought down sharply in 1675.[23]

The trouble was that it was impossible to divorce the economics of the period from the politics – and the Court intrigues. Unquestionably the King's expenditure on his mistresses, not perceptibly extravagant by the standards of the time in the 1660s, had moved into a more lavish sphere. And it would expand still further as the 1670s wore on. Where women were concerned, the King was weak, not only in the bed-chamber, at the sight of their tears, but in the counting-house. Louise Duchess of Portsmouth, as has been seen, regarded a large income as one of the unalterable prerequisites of a royal mistress; Nelly Gwynn was equally mercenary, if not equally successful; Barbara Duchess of Cleveland – mother of five children by the

King – was still on his payroll; Hortense Duchesse de Mazarin would prove another expensive luxury.

The economic demands of Louise Duchess of Portsmouth – what has been aptly termed 'harem finance' – did the King far more real damage than her alleged Catholic influence. For Danby, good husbandman as he might be, flinched from quarrelling with the reigning mistress. The result was that the annual household expenditure rose once again after 1675 to £210,000. There were other 'extraordinary' expenses for the ladies – of vast, if ultimately unknowable, proportions, since much of this was found from French money: the Secret Service account. Where knowable expenditure is concerned, it has been pointed out that the Treasury records in the 1670s show *permanent* grants of more than £45,000 a year to Barbara, Louise and their children alone.[24]

The controversy concerning the extravagance of Charles II persists – did he contribute to his own problems or was he kept permanently short by Parliament? Whatever the force of the latter view, it is surely impossible to acquit the King altogether of extravagance, or rather weakness, where his mistresses were concerned, in the last ten years of his reign. A King must keep state, ceremonies are demanded by the populace which then criticizes the cost of them, and so forth – all these arguments have been advanced in Chapter 12, discussing his Restoration. In those days Goethe might have been quoted on the subject: '*Ein Mächtiger, der für die Seinen nicht/Zu sorgen weiss, wird von dem Volke selbst/Getadelt*' ('A man of power, who cannot look after the interests of his own favourites, will be blamed even by the people'). The mood changed as the reign progressed. Such a saying would not have been applied to the immoral panoply of Charles II's later Court by a nation grown less joyous. It was a difference in degree, but it was a significant difference.

The spending on the royal bastards should not have appeared so irksome: it has been correctly pointed out that the monies laid out on the various dukelings and little ladies was a tithe of what a proper legitimate royal brood would have consumed.[25] The King himself was not personally extravagant. He was not lavish over matters like dress; where food and drink were concerned he was positively abstemious. But the planting of trees round his palaces, afforestation generally, was an expensive pastime. The renovation of Windsor, begun in 1674, also cost a pretty penny. The concentration on Windsor – it was the only palace easy to fortify – symbolized the new type of monarchy evolving in the last decade of the King's reign: embattled but at the same time loftier and more magnificent than the institution restored in 1660. It is here that one can imagine the King as described by Thomas Otway in a long memorial poem: 'Windsor Castle is a Monument to our Late Sovereign King Charles II':

> Then in his Mind the beauteous Model laid,
> Of that Majestic pile, where oft, his Care
> A while forgot, he might for Ease repair:
> A Seat for sweet Retirement, Health, and Love....

But Windsor was also

> Britain's Olympus, where, like awful Jove
> He pleas'd could sit, and his Regards bestow
> On the vain, busy, swarming World below.

In 1675 commenced the building of St Paul's, another Olympus, another symbolic act, since the great new cathedral would come to embrace the ceremonies of state under its powerful dome.

This same summer of 1674 two pathetic little skeletons, believed not implausibly to be those of the vanished 'striplings' Edward V and the Duke of York, were turned up by workmen at the Tower of London. The point is debatable and, as with all evidence pertaining to the controversial life of Richard III, keenly debated. Here we are only concerned with the reaction of Charles II. The find was reported to him by Sir Thomas Chicheley, Master of the Ordnance. The King's immediate instinct was to command a more reverent burial for these pathetic relics: they were transferred to Westminster Abbey and Sir Christopher Wren was ordered to design a marble urn to encase them. Admittedly, the Royal Warrant, signed by Arlington the following February, hedged its bets by referring to 'a white

Marble Coffin for the supposed bodies of the two Princes ...'. Nevertheless, here, in the Abbey, they lie to this day, with a Latin inscription commemorating the action of the *Rex Clementissimus* – the most merciful King Charles the Second. Moreover, the English inscription beneath declares, in bolder terms than the Royal Warrant, that the bones 'were deposited here by command of King Charles II, in the firm belief that they were the Bones of King Edward V and Richard Duke of York'.[26]

Whatever the rights and wrongs of the boys' death, it was a gesture towards the concept of legitimate monarchy – as represented by the youthful Edward V, in contrast to his usurping uncle *Richardus Perfidus*, as the Latin inscription had it. The same instinct led to the glorification of the tomb of Charles I at about the same time, another monarch whose life was brought to an unnatural end. Less sceptical perhaps than his minister Arlington in his attitude to the 'supposed' remains, Charles II was reaching down for his royal roots.

For the first time, in 1674 the Court spent four months at Windsor during the summer. Within the picturesque fortress both King and Queen had new apartments created by Hugh May. Grinling Gibbons and Antonio Verrio were employed by May to adorn them; May was inspired by the patronage of the King. Charles showed throughout his life a love of the arts quite natural in a boy educated at that legendary, cultured Court of the 1630s who could remember going by barge with his father to visit the studio of Van Dyck. His predilection has however been understandably overshadowed by the supreme artistic taste of King Charles I. Charles II did all that he could to reacquire his father's great art collection (it has been mentioned that he secured some pictures from the Dutch on the eve of his Restoration) although some masterpieces proved irrecoverable. Of his cabinet of treasures and curiosities, he spoke wistfully that it was not to be compared with his father's, thirty years before. Charles II may well have been responsible for the collection of drawings by Leonardo da Vinci at Windsor, either by purchase, or by receiving them as gifts.[27]

As he enjoyed the company of writers, so Charles II appreciated that of artists generally; he sent for a doctor from Paris to treat the history painter, Robert Streater, for the stone. Gibbons' work was originally shown to the King by John Evelyn: as a reward for the recommendation before which, in Evelyn's words, 'he was scarce known', Gibbons presented Evelyn with a walnut table 'incomparable carved'. Charles was so enthusiastic at what he saw that he rushed out of the room to show it to the Queen – who was less so. Later Charles, supported by Lely and Bab May, had his way. At Windsor, Gibbons, who also ornamented other royal dwellings, was allowed £100 a year. Verrio subsequently came to occupy the post of Chief Painter set up for Sir Peter Lely, at a salary of £200 a year. At the time of the Popish Plot the Catholic Verrio, and some other Catholic stonecarvers, assistants to Gibbons, were protected from the consequences of their religion.[28]

As is the way of the world, not all the payments went directly to artists. The Dutch dealer Gerrit Uylenbergh, a cousin of Rembrandt's wife Saskia, got into trouble when the pictures he was trying to sell the Elector of Brandenburg were denounced as fakes. Reaching England a poor man, he quickly fell on his feet, painted some backgrounds for Lely, and joined the King's service as Purveyor and Keeper of his pictures. Uylenbergh helped to select and arrange the pictures for the private apartments of the King and Queen at Windsor; he was paid £50 for his 'Extraordinary Care and Pains ... and for Several Journeys'. Two young French painters, Nicolas de Largillierre and Philip Dolesam, also set to with their brushes, and, where necessary, fitted the King's pictures into their new frames, carved by Gibbons. The King was particularly delighted with Largillierre's partial repainting of Caracciolo's *Cupid Sleeping.*[29]

At Windsor the only remaining rooms of Edward III were gutted, although many of the old walls remained embedded in the structure. Some of the modernization however brought unexpected problems, as when a series of tanners' skins were found in the water supply. Water was once again used for embellishment at Windsor, on the French model. Charles II was fortunate to be able to enjoy the fruits of the ingenuity of Sir

Samuel Morland, appointed his *magister mechanicorum.* A special feat of Morland's in 1681 caused water to be pumped from the Thames to the top of the castle, and thence in a great jet sixty feet high, which, mingled with red wine, was clearly and splendidly visible.[30]

Today the Windsor revivified by Charles II is best pictured from the Queen's Presence Chamber, with its swirling Verrio ceiling; otherwise, the elegant hand of George IV has once more been at work, sweeping away the older embellishments with the new.[31] In this Presence Chamber the King was wont to dine in public, that strangely intimate glimpse of the monarch traditionally granted to his subjects since mediaeval times. Elsewhere the spirit of Verrio was much in evidence. The new royal apartments were decorated with splendid allegorical paintings in which fantasy brought a comfort denied by reality. Queen Catharine was at last depicted as Britannia – a role for which she had been passed over in favour of Frances Stewart when the new coinage was designed, as being too small. There was more reality in the fact that the Duchess of Portsmouth and her son were granted their own apartments. When four continents were seen bringing Charles II their riches, the King seated on a convenient cloud, then fantasy was certainly rampant.

Yet compared to the extravagance of his father, or for that matter of Louis XIV, Charles II had modest tastes. His own subject the mighty Duke of Beaufort, who with his wife struck terror into the hearts of servants and neighbours alike, kept as much princely state. The Duchess made a daily tour of her domains, instantly sacking any servant not about his or her lawful occasions. The Duke's neighbours planted trees 'to humour his vistas' and 'arranged Hills free of charge'.[32] Queen Catharine made no such tour; the King planted his own trees.

There were also rural pursuits to be enjoyed at Windsor, even if some of them – those of Catharine rather than Charles – smacked a little of the Petit Trianon. The King could fish. The Queen could go on picnics. On one such outing each of the Queen's attendants brought one dish: 'Lady Bath's dish was a chine of beef, Mrs Wyndham's a venison pastry ...', and so on.

Catharine sat under a tree and was 'wonderfully pleased and merry'.[33]

The King's cousin, Prince Rupert, had been made Governor and Constable of the Castle in 1668. The old warrior enjoyed his fortress-residence and made it his permanent home. He was thus able to oversee the King's numerous refurbishments. At the same time he reminded himself of the less pacific past by ornamenting his own rooms with a collection of arms, which made the post-war generation open their eyes wide when they visited him.

Music was another example of Charles II's feeling for culture rather than for formality. He loved music more for its own sake than for the splendour surrounding the performance. In the mid-seventies expenses in the royal accounts for dresses – shepherds, satyrs and the like – for masques recall but do not emulate the great masque world of Inigo Jones in the previous reign. In 1674 Queen Catharine suggested a masque, *Calisto*, to John Crowne. The intention was quite plain: to provide a starring vehicle for the two young Princesses of York, Mary and Anne.* It was only a moderate success. The story of Calisto, in Crowne's own words, posed the problem of writing 'a clean, decent and inoffensive play' on the subject of rape – featuring two girls aged twelve and nine. Neither Crowne nor his leading ladies were equal to the challenge. The masque was dull. The amateurs' voices had to be supplemented by those of two graceful professionals, Moll Davies and Mrs Knight. As both ladies were suspected – with good reason – of unprofessional relationships with the King, this led to considerable tension during rehearsals where the Queen was concerned.[34]

The King's personal preference was for the French instrumental music he had grown to love in exile; Pelham Humfrey was sent to France to learn it, that the English Court might be graced with the innovation. By Humfrey's death in 1674 this

* More often known as the Lady Mary and the Lady Anne, according to the convention of the time, which was less lavish with the term 'princess' than our own: Mary and Elizabeth Tudor, for example, were generally termed the Ladies Mary and Elizabeth, despite the fact that they were the daughters of a reigning monarch, Henry VIII.

new type of music was prospering. Violins were introduced into church music at the King's request. As for the royal bills for violinists' costumes – 'Indian' gowns trimmed with tinsel – and garlands for their violins (cost £6),[35] these would have seemed mere trifles, albeit agreeable trifles, to a Louis XIV. One of the beneficiaries of this new style in music was Henry Purcell. Taught by Humfrey, among others, Purcell sprang from a family closely connected with the Chapel Royal. Purcell himself – 'so arch especial a spirit', as Gerard Manley Hopkins described him two hundred yeas later – was a Child of the Chapel Royal. (He features by name in the Wardrobe accounts from time to time for two suits, a bed and so forth.)[36] As such, he was inevitably much in contact with the King. The 1670s saw the metamorphosis of Purcell from a chorister to a composer, but the royal connection was maintained. Two welcome songs to the King and Duke of York respectively brought him into prominence.[37] Many of his early odes hymned such court events as the King's return from Newmarket, his return from Windsor, his reappearance at Whitehall after a summer outing. Later it seems that Charles introduced Purcell to the delights of Italian music as well as French. Purcell's *Sonatas in Three Parts*, dedicated to the King, make some allusion to the introduction.

Queen Catharine enjoyed Italian opera and Italian songs generally (if less so when sung by Mrs Knight). Charles was fond enough of Italian songs – and expert enough in the language – to hold a part himself from time to time at Windsor. He had a great 'thorough-bass' voice. A duet by Carisimi, Charles' favourite composer, exists written out in Purcell's handwriting. Purcell became successively organist at Westminster Abbey in 1679 (John Blow, who probably taught him composition, resigned in his favour) and Composer in Ordinary in 1682.

It was helpful that Charles II had a predilection for experiment, be it scientific or musical: under his influence music was also introduced into the English theatre, on the French model. The French musician Louis Grabu came to England and was appointed 'composer to His Majesty's Musique' in 1665. The appointment of a Frenchman caused some raised eyebrows.[38]

Nevertheless, Grabu was made Master of the English Chamber Musick in ordinary, following the death of Nicholas Lanier. The first public concert in England was also given in the reign of Charles II. It was organized by the violinist John Banister, for a while leader of the King's Band, and held in a large room in Whitefriars in 1672.

Nevertheless, in seventeenth-century England all this kind of expenditure – on music, on art, on building and redecoration – was understood and appreciated; whereas the vast sums visibly deployed on the foreign Popish mistresses were seen as a sign of weakness in the bedroom. Might the King, under such dangerous influences, be equally weak in the council chamber? The question remained. A witticism went the rounds to explain why the Accession Day of Queen Elizabeth I was being celebrated with such warmth: 'Because she being a woman chose men for her counsellors and men when they reign usually choose women.' It was an unfair barb. Women were not the King's counsellors but his concubines – and his companions. But the extravagance which he permitted on their behalf invited it.

In the short term – but only in the short term – the political methods of Danby looked like being as successful as his economic policies. Stoutly Protestant himself, Danby aimed at a political alliance in Parliament which would comprise Anglicans, and other confirmed Royalists, against those whom he conceived of as being the King's enemies. These were the Catholics, the nonconformists, and the opponents of the royal prerogative. It will be appreciated that the latter group included many whom Charles II had sought persistently to conciliate by toleration. Nor did Danby, in his concentration on the alliance of the monarchy and Anglicanism, allow for the special position of the Duke of York in the King's favours.

James was not unnaturally offended and alarmed by Danby's Anglican policies. The shifting nature of political alliances in this period was once more underlined when the Duke of York moved away from Danby's so-called Court party towards the arms of the Protestants Buckingham and Shaftesbury.

All the same, Danby laboured hard at building up his

Parliamentary base: a conglomerate of well disposed MPs has been traced, based on his home ground of the West Riding of Yorkshire.[39] The lop-sided representation of certain areas in Parliament also helped because in general it favoured the Royalist cause. There was another theoretical advantage accruing to the King: the appointment of the Lords Lieutenant, who in turn were responsible for local patronage (although this had to be used with care). Then there was that method of building up a Court party, or any other party for that matter – bribery. Accusations of bribery against Danby were part of the stock-in-trade of his opponents. In fact, some of Danby's payments were disbursements to genuine office-holders. Where did these legitimate payments end and bribery begin? In a situation where office-holding was much complicated by the relics of the pre-war structure on which the post-Restoration structure had been imposed, this is difficult to establish. The important point was that Danby earnestly strove to put together governmental support. It was not easy in an age when party politics as such, to say nothing of the parties themselves, were still in an embryonic state.

The third plank in Danby's platform, after pursuing economic and political solidity, was the strengthening of ties with the Dutch. It was essential to this particular policy that the King should secure sufficient supplies from Parliament to uphold his beloved Navy. Otherwise it was easy to see that the King would have little motive to wrench himself from the lucrative embrace of Louis XIV. When Parliament met again in April 1675 for Danby to secure supplies, the King was all honey to its members. He told them that he wanted to have a better understanding with them and 'to know what you think may yet be wanting to the securing of religion and property'. This was a far cry from his claims of 'supreme power' in ecclesiastical matters. But he did not fail to dwell on the theme of the Navy. 'I must needs recommend to you the condition of the Fleet,' he said, 'which I am not able to put into that state it ought to be, and which will require so much time to repair and build, that I should be sorry to see this summer (and consequently a whole year) lost without providing for it.'[40]

It was all the more important that Danby should succeed in managing Parliament to good financial effect, since his policy of positive Anglicanism went against the King's natural inclinations as well. On 1 May the King signed a declaration expelling Jesuits and other 'Romish priests' from the realm. Already in February, an Order in Council had been made for the strict enforcement of the penal laws against the Catholics, and for the restricting of Catholic chapels to those of the Queen and the ambassadors.

But this session of Parliament proved to be a contest between two equally handicapped opponents. The Commons continued to cry out against the French involvement, demanding that the English troops which had been sent to back up Louis XIV should now be withdrawn under the terms of the Treaty of Westminster. The King promised that further recruitment would be forbidden (in fact, he turned a blind eye to its continuance), but declined to withdraw troops already serving under Louis before the Treaty. The Commons responded by showing intractability over the supplies he wanted for the Navy. They linked them to the Excise – a source of supply he already possessed.

There was even a move to impeach Danby, as the King's minister, for his pro-French attitudes – which would have been a wry turn of events, considering Danby's own attitude to France. Luckily the impulse behind it was feeble and the motion easily defeated. Besides, Danby had his own notion of dealing with possible Parliamentary opposition, by introducing a new type of Test Act promoting 'Non-Resistance'. All office-holders were supposed to take a new oath declaring that resistance to the King was unlawful, and promising to abstain from all efforts to alter the constitution of the Church and State.

The bill had a long and wearisome passage in the House of Lords; at one point the King himself stayed till midnight, following the proceedings. Nevertheless, it might well have become law had not a quite unrelated quarrel broken out at this point between the two Houses of Parliament. The case of Shirley *v.* Fagg rested on the right of the House of Lords to hear appeals from the Court of Chancery, when one of the appellants was a member of the Commons. The Commons considered that by summoning Sir John Fagg, an MP, the Lords had acted in breach of their privileges. The quarrel grew. All parliamentary business was suspended.

The King was aware that at the bottom of 'this most malicious design', as he called the fomented row, was the intention to procure a dissolution of Parliament. Whereas a mere prorogation helped the King, it was the increasing conviction of certain MPs that a dissolution – followed by a fresh election – would produce a House of Commons more favourable to their cause. The King saw through this ploy. And he said so. He appealed to the disputants to patch up their differences and not allow a body of 'ill [that is, wicked] men' to sway them. He also observed, 'But I must let you know, that whilst you are in debate about your privileges, I will not suffer my own to be invaded....'[41]

The disputants were however obdurate. On 9 June the King saw no alternative but wearily to prorogue Parliament. The 'unhappy differences' between the two Houses were, he said, too great. And he spoke bitterly of 'the ill designs of our enemies [that] have been too prevalent against those good ones I proposed to myself in behalf of my people'.[42]

The King and Court went to his delightful new abode at Windsor. When Parliament met again in the autumn, Danby returned with new vigour to the task of carrying through the government's policies. Nor had he wasted his time in the intervening months. Over a hundred MPs had been lobbied by the Secretaries of State, to ensure their attendance. The number of Excise pensioners was increased. Despite these sanguine, if not salutary, precautions, Danby found himself once more desperately bogged down. The *cause célèbre* of Shirley *v.* Fagg still dominated relations between the two Houses; and Danby found himself quite unable to secure the King's financial needs, while the demand for the dissolution of Parliament grew.

The irony of this demand – and irony is never far away from the politics of this period – was that Charles II himself was more or less committed to dissolving Parliament, but in secret, and in his latest negotiations with Louis XIV. It was proposed that Charles should dissolve the English Parliament if its attitude towards France grew too aggressive, or if it failed to vote the King the supplies he needed. In return, Louis XIV would give

Charles II a yearly subsidy of something like £100,000. Did Danby know of the bargain? It seems that he did. Even so, he still pressed on, doggedly trying to secure money for the King via Parliament, for much more than £100,000 was needed to float the Navy.[43]

When Danby failed, it was still open to Charles to dissolve Parliament – as Shaftesbury and his faction so much desired – and call on the French subsidy. Even the Duke of York now supported a dissolution, believing for his part that a new Parliament would not be so rabidly anti-Catholic. But Danby, by pulling out all the stops of his own organization, managed to defeat the motion in the House of Lords. And Charles deftly but determinedly proceeded to prorogue Parliament yet again.

What was more, by taking advantage of France's military embroilment, he managed to secure the French subsidy all the same, while he had not satisfied its condition. The newest secret treaty with Louis XIV, that of February 1676, provided for an annual subsidy, payable in quarters. In vain Danby begged his master to commit himself to the Dutch – the old principle of the Triple Alliance. Charles II once more pursued his own bent, albeit secretly, and signed on with France again for a three-year period. Danby was aware of its existence, but only Lauderdale, 'never more high in His Majesty's favour', and the Duke of York were privy to the actual treaty.

The winter of 1675/6 might be regarded as one of general discontent in England, both in and out of Parliament. The MPs were furious that their fox had eluded them; in addition, the hunt was postponed for an unprecedentedly long period (the prorogation was to last fifteen months). Danby's Protestantism in foreign affairs was not prevailing. Only Charles II himself had managed to survive without any major defeat, 'living from day to day', in the words of the Venetian Ambassador. As for the knot in the comb, he had not forgotten it. But he was not yet ready to try and disentangle it.

CHAPTER TWENTY-ONE

Peace For His Own Time

'For he was not an active, busy or ambitious Prince ... he seemed to be chiefly desirous of "Peace and Quiet for his own Time".'

Sir John Reresby, *Memoirs*

By 1676 it was the opinion of Sir John Reresby that King Charles II was 'chiefly desirous of "Peace and Quiet for his own Time"'. But this was not necessarily the unambitious lethargy outlined by Reresby. 'Peace and Quiet' still had a wonderful resonance to those who remembered the troubles of the previous generation. It is notable that when Lord Halifax in his *Character of a Trimmer* wanted to sum up the effects of the two political extremes, Absolute Monarchy and Commonwealth, he conceded the ferment created by the latter: '[Absolute] Monarchy, a thing that leaveth men no liberty, and a Commonwealth, such a one as alloweth them no Quiet.'[1] The views of Charles II on the monarchy remained at this point as amorphous as those of most of his contemporaries; but he would have profoundly agreed with Halifax on the subject of Commonwealths.

'Peace and Quiet for his own Time' had for him no ring of appeasement. It was a thoroughly laudable aim. Oddly enough, for a brief period between the prorogation of Parliament in the autumn of 1675 and its reconvening in 1677, it seemed possible that he might achieve it without a struggle.

It was true that a 'Country' – as opposed to 'Court' – opposition was being developed by the coalition of Shaftesbury and Buckingham. Increasingly this group had to be reckoned with. Although we shall hear more of the Green Ribbon Club towards the end of the decade, its constitution was in existence by 1676, even if its meetings were not yet recorded. The Green Ribbon Club provided an important rallying point for those discontented with the government – particularly when Parliament was not sitting. '*Les mal intentionnés*' was how Charles had described them to the French Ambassador when they persisted in voting against him. The King's Head Tavern, at the junction of Fleet Street and Chancery Lane, proved a convenient rendezvous. For all the efforts of government spies to permeate the meetings, the Green Ribbon Club succeeded in linking together the various disparate elements – former Puritans, merchants, lawyers and so forth – which would go to make the future 'Whig' party. The first of the long line of English political clubs, it performed a function which even the most capacious private house could not fulfil.[2]

From another angle, the Green Ribbon Club also survived the clampdown on the coffee-houses because it was a private association. It is interesting to consider that beverages like coffee, chocolate and even sherbert, seemingly innocuous to us (because they are non-alcoholic), began life in England as dangerous, expensive and exciting symbols of dissidence. At the new meeting-places, the eternal beer of the English was replaced by a heady combination of coffee – and political sympathy. As a result, the government came to identify the places with the politics. An Order was given in December 1675 to suppress the coffee-houses as once race meetings had been suppressed under the Protectorate.

All the same, the appearance of peace was maintained. And the upswing in the royal and the national finances increased the illusion of a widespread, placid prosperity. As late as June 1677 the King told the French Ambassador that England enjoyed 'a profound tranquillity'. She successfully enriched herself, while other nations were drained or ruined by war. The English would one day thank him, he observed, for having kept them by prudence in 'so happy a state and so advantageous for their commerce'.[3]

In fact, the trade boom broke early in 1676.[4] And as the seventies wore on, the image of a liberal and healing King was being succeeded by something rather different. It is true that towards individuals the King had lost none of his humorous affability. It was a quality which he would retain till his dying hour. He was still the bonhomous monarch who supped with jockeys when at Newmarket. There are several well-known stories which illustrate his particular kind of ironic benevolence. One has the King watching a man who boasted of having invented a new process by which he could stand on the point of a steeple for an unprecedented length of time. At the end of the display Charles announced himself to be duly impressed and said that he would buy the patent of the process – to prevent any of his other subjects using it. Another described him dining with Sir Robert Viner in the City. Viner, overcome with the honour, became hopelessly drunk towards the evening and tried to stop the King from departing. 'Sir, you shall stay and take the other bottle!' cried Viner. Where other European monarchs might have resorted to a ferocious frown, Charles II merely smiled and quoted a popular song: 'He that's drunk is as great as a King.' Then he allowed himself to be led back.

When William Penn, as a Quaker, insisted on remaining covered in the King's presence – an extraordinary piece of *lèse-majesté* for those days – Charles took off his own hat.

'Friend Charles,' Penn is supposed to have asked, 'why dost thou not keep on thy hat?'

'It is the custom of this place that only one man should remain uncovered at a time,' replied the unruffled King.[5]

He remained a most accessible sovereign, in the modern phrase. It was Charles II who set the style by which the royal withdrawing-room, hitherto a select preserve, was open to any 'Person of Quality as well as our servants and others who come to wait on us'. The King would emerge from time to time to discourse with these Persons of Quality: and so the style was set for the official court 'Drawing Rooms' of later centuries. Even his bedchamber, dominated by the great bed, railed in in the French manner, was not particularly intimate. Its door was left open. Here he would receive ministers and favoured individuals; he would also use it to eat in slightly more privacy than the stately public meals allowed. True privacy, in so far as a seventeenth-century prince enjoyed it, was enjoyed in his closet (where he kept the scientific rarities and little treasures described by Evelyn), although even here he would receive certain advisers.[6]

Charles II fell back on another form of privacy. The long legs which had carried him successfully away from Worcester now served increasingly to carry him away from the pleas and complaints of his subjects. As the King grew older, his daily walk in St James's Park was taken at a faster and faster pace, the sovereign considering it enough to scatter random 'God bless yous' about him as he strode, like jesting Pilate, not stopping for an answer. Indoors he took to taking out his watch (wise men made themselves scarce at this signal) and falling asleep after meals, another cunning way of resisting importunities.

Part of this change of image was due to the inevitable erosion of time. The thick black periwig which he now habitually wore recalled in memory, no more, the black love-locks of yesteryear, for the King, having gone grey, was now almost entirely bald. As he was obviously no longer young, he was also no longer debonair. The melancholy which, as we have seen, lay at the core of his being often overlaid the engaging gaiety he had chosen to manifest in the sixties, in public. His face was already lined at the Restoration and adversity was the cause. The later portraits – that of 1675 by Lely onwards – display with relentless truth the deep lines which time had laid on his face; cynicism and an inner weariness at the folly of men – and women – were responsible.

Besides, a new generation was growing up who did not remember the Restoration or those happy years when an invited monarch came from overseas to heal and to forgive. A young man of twenty in 1676 would barely recollect that inauguration of a golden age – as it had seemed to so many – let alone the perils of Commonwealth and Civil War from which the restored monarch had rescued his country.

While the King retained his popular touch with individuals, many of his policies – such as the Stop of the Exchequer –

presented him in a much less attractive light. Then there was the question of his honour. Naturally the full extent of the deceit which he had employed in foreign policy – and was still employing while he received French money – was known to very few. But a feeling that the King's word, like the King's financial bond, was to be regarded with caution, began to pervade Court and political circles, nonetheless. And from there the malaise had the chance of spreading outwards. This is not to suggest that Boy Scout ethics either were or should be expected in a seventeenth-century monarch. But Lord Halifax probably got it about right when he wrote of dissimulation in a ruler, that it was a defect not to practise it at all, and a fault to practise it too much: 'It is necessary and yet it is dangerous too.'[7]

The King's persistent poverty contributed to his practice of deception. Charles II was no exception to the rule that debtors are often liars for the sake of survival, where rich men can afford the luxury of honesty. An anonymous burlesque of 1670 summed up the connection which was felt to exist between the King's lack of money (through extravagance) and the King's lack of truth; Charles was portrayed addressing Parliament as follows: 'You may perhaps think it dangerous to make me too rich, but do not fear it, I promise you faithfully whatever you give me, I will always still want: though in many other things my word may be thought but slender security, yet in this you may rely upon me....'[8]

The sardonic epigram ascribed to Lord Rochester on his master also comes to mind:

> We have a pritty witty King
> Whose word no man relies on,
> Who never said a foolish thing
> Nor ever did a wise one.*

* There are many versions of this epigram, which has been transformed into an epitaph in the best known version of all, beginning 'Here lies our Sovereign Lord the King ...'. But since Rochester predeceased Charles II, it could hardly have originated in this form. The epigram does not appear in the early editions of Rochester's works. The version above, with the circumstances which led up to it,

Admittedly Rochester was supposed to have first produced the verse in the following fashion: the King, in his easy way, told his courtiers that 'he would leave everyone to his liberty in talking when Himself was in company, and would not take what was said at all amiss'. At which Rochester saw his opportunity and lunged. Perhaps the King was not totally enchanted by the sally of his friend. For he responded with a thrust of his own blade: his words were his own, he retorted, but his deeds were his ministers'. But, like all slurs with a taste of truth in them, Rochester's wicked little rhyme has survived the test of time, where the King's equally quick riposte is often forgotten.

Even more fatally, Charles II ignored the force of popular prejudice with regard to Catholicism, France, and their hated bedfellow, arbitrary government. That twenty-year-old man alluded to above would contemplate a Catholic Court or, what was almost worse, a French-dominated one, for the links with France were increasingly resented on almost every level. Yet in his youth Charles had shown extraordinary determination in avoiding the Catholic taint while in exile, lest his chances of restoration perish. This degeneration of his sensitivities had come with age. Half of him was aware that the price of 'Peace and Quiet for his own Time' was eternal vigilance where Parliament and the nascent Whigs were concerned, plus a willingness to bow to the strong feelings of the majority of his subjects, however prejudiced and distasteful. The other half relaxed, and hoped that by successful juggling of French money, Parliamentary supplies, and those forces represented by Danby, Shaftesbury and even Buckingham, the same result could be achieved. He would shortly receive a terrible lesson.

Before that happened, Charles II was subjected to an assault of a rather pleasanter nature: from a beautiful woman. The rise – and fall – of Hortense Mancini, Duchesse de Mazarin, demonstrated two things. First, that those closest to the King continued to believe tenderly that he could be influenced by a woman. Second, that the King's sexuality was not yet extinct.

---

was first given by Thomas Hearne in his *Remarks and Collections* (notes for his historical works) in his entry for 17 November 1706.

The affair with Hortense would be his last very public throw in that direction. But Hortense, unlike Louise, was not of the material of which successful mistresses are made. She was an attractive, self-destructive creature whose wanton disregard for her own best interests (in the worldly sense) seduces from afar, even if it drove her promoters mad.

Once upon a time Hortense could have had the impecunious and throneless King as a husband; as the niece of Cardinal Mazarin, she would have been a useful wife for Charles in the late 1650s. In the intervening years Hortense as well as Charles had seen some revolutionary changes in her state. Her first husband, created Duc de Mazarin in her honour, proved to have a touch of religious mania. The unappreciative Hortense fled to Savoy, a decision which had caused Charles to quip to Madame at the time, 'I see wives do not love devout husbands. . . .'[9] In Savoy an episode with the Duke led to her expulsion from the country after his premature death. But on leaving Savoy, Hortense was noted to be gaily 'bewigged and befeathered' at the head of a train of twenty men, as though nothing particularly humiliating had happened. Accompanied by her black page, Mustapha, she now turned to England to try her fortunes there.[10]

Despite her mature age – she was about thirty – there was something unalterably splendid about Hortense's appearance, in which her Italian inheritance predominated. She was 'one of those lofty Roman beauties', said a French admirer, 'in no way like our Baby-visaged and Puppet-like Faces of France'; Edmund Waller in a poem similarly termed her the 'Roman eagle'. She was blessed with a mass of black waving hair, and eyes said to be of three colours – combining the sweetness of the blue, the Irishness of the grey and the fire of the black. Ruvigny, a Protestant, sniffed that she was not really so beautiful: which, he added as a Frenchman, did not stop her being more beautiful than anyone else in England.[11]

Hortense also had an avidity for life which recalls that of Barbara in her prime. Indeed, in many ways the reign of Hortense represents a short-lived reversion of the King to the type of mistress of his younger days, high-spirited and reckless, as opposed to the domestic docility offered by Louise. In

Hortense's amatory exploits there were hints of sexual ambiguity: as Saint Evremond, commenting on the triumph of this new siren ('Fair beauties of Whitehall give way/Hortensia does her charms display'), saw fit to remark, 'Each sex provides its lovers for Hortense'. Certainly most aspects of pleasure lured her. She was a compulsive gambler, a lover of good food, adored dogs – three favourites were named Boy, Little Rogue and Chop – as well as cats, monkeys and birds which included a white sparrow, a canary, a starling called Jacob, and a parrot called Pretty. She was an excellent shot who could bring down quail. She too, like Charles, loved to swim, if she was not quite so adept at it: we hear of the faithful Mustapha (who luckily swam like a fish) dragging her about in the water on her front and her back. Hortense, wrote a contemporary, thought of nothing but enjoying herself: she triumphed over everything by an excess of folly. These were surely delightful attributes in a lover, if Hortense lacked the fundamental application for such a serious role (as Louise would have had it) as that of royal mistress.

Hortense's ostensible reason for arriving in England in the winter of 1675 was her cousinship to Mary Beatrice, Duchess of York. But her conquest of the King (on whom Louise's domesticated charms were perhaps temporarily palling) was rapid. By the summer of 1676 it was being said that the only time Hortense was *not* at the King's side was when he was bathing. Courtin told Louis XIV in another piece of Gallic chauvinism, 'It is the only decency which they observe in this country. There is a great deal of laxness in the rest of their conduct.'[12] By August Louise was in floods of tears – and Hortense was in Barbara's old apartments.

Naturally the rise of a new mistress caused a flurry of wings in the political dovecots. Arlington, who had attempted unsuccessfully to pursue his early alliance with Louise, now turned to Hortense, hoping to put down Danby. In consequence, Hortense was rumoured to be pro-Dutch. There seems no real proof that Hortense was anything quite so solid-sounding. Besides, Danby quickly adapted to her friendship. But Hortense did create a great deal of trouble by intriguing in a more intimate sphere. For she developed a passionate friendship with Anne

Countess of Sussex, one of the King's two daughters by Barbara. The Earl of Sussex, previously Lord Dacre, had been given the superior title on his marriage to Anne in 1674. The wedding, at Hampton Court, had been a glittering affair, attended by royalties on both sides of the blanket, including Prince Rupert, the Duke of York and the Duke of Monmouth. Anne received a £20,000 dowry from the King, who also played the father's role at the wedding; the bridegroom got a £2,000 a year pension. Despite this *largesse*, the new Lord Sussex intended to be master in his own house.*

He disapproved of the connection with Hortense. Nevertheless, Anne, who had some of her mother's obstinate temperament, persisted in it. The two ladies took fencing lessons together, proceeding to St James's Park for the purpose on one occasion, with drawn swords beneath their nightgowns. The crisis came when Anne announced her intention of sharing a balcony in Cheapside with Hortense at the Lord Mayor's Show in November. Barbara, like many another mother with a purple past, found it in her to write an extremely priggish letter to her daughter from France, advising 'wifely obedience'.[13] Eventually Lord Sussex took his wayward spouse in high dudgeon to the country. But he should have been warned. His troubles with her were not over – nor, for that matter, were Barbara's.

Returning to Hortense and her brief but victorious sway over the King, this was still sufficiently marked in February 1677 for her to be quoted by the French ambassador as being 'in a very prominent position raised above all the other ladies' at the opening of Parliament.[14] By the summer however the eternal Eve in Hortense had reasserted itself. She indulged in a prolonged and public flirtation with the Prince de Monaco. Hortense was dismissed. Louise dried her tears. The King settled back with a shrug into her waiting arms. Since Hortense had not presented the King with a child, alone among his mistresses-in-chief to

* The King, as usual, was more generous on paper than in fact. He was a long time paying the various bills, including that of Anne's wedding dress; but this was due to financial necessity. The ceremony, and the King's official acknowledgement of Anne's paternity, certainly made it improbable that she was actually Roger Palmer's child (see page 235).

fail to do so, the main residue of her reign was the unfortunate political impression she created. Marvell expressed the general indignation

> That the King should send for another French whore
> When one already hath made him so poor.

Charles II had not sent for Hortense. But the smear remained.

William of Orange, with the necessary tenacity of the ruler of a small country, had forgotten nothing of his plan for wresting England away from France. Nor after the Treaty of Westminster was he in any position to rest on his laurels. The military campaigns of Louis XIV proceeded apace. The year 1677 would see spectacular advances by the French. Before that date William had already put out feelers concerning marriage with his first cousin Mary, Protestant daughter of the Duke of York.[15] He found a receptive audience in the English Ambassador, the erudite and agreeable Sir William Temple.

Temple had viewed with deprecation England's entanglement with France. He was now in a much stronger position to exert pressure to end it. Having been withdrawn from the Netherlands in 1671 when his pro-Dutch views were clearly incompatible with the pro-French ones of the English government, he was recalled to government service over the negotiation of the Treaty of Westminster. Shortly afterwards, declining both the Embassy at Madrid and a Secretaryship of State (leaving it scornfully to Sir Joseph Williamson), Temple took up residence at The Hague.

The spring of 1677 brought a wave of victories for Louis XIV. 'I have loved war too much,' declared the French King on his death-bed. But his triumphant campaign brought him at the time not only his own heart's desire but also his country's. In the United Provinces William girded himself for another span of heroic defence. Much depended yet again on the attitude of England. Charles II had shown himself able and willing to act as a mediator in the past, once the forced Treaty of Westminster had put an end to his more ambitious plans. Louis XIV, who was paying good money over to his cousin, naturally hoped for

Charles' French sympathies to be exhibited in a more positive manner: neutrality would however be better than nothing. The pro-Dutch party in England, on the other hand, keenly desired England to come to the rescue of that poor beleaguered country.

This projected marriage of the Prince of Orange and the niece of Charles II was one subterranean manoeuvre. Having been backed by Temple in Holland, it was taken up by Danby at home. However, early in 1677 there was a renewed opportunity for Parliamentary interference on the subject of foreign policy. It was time for Parliament to reconvene after its prorogation – high time, in the opinion of such leading members as Buckingham. Indeed, so long had been the gap (fifteen months) that a new and wily argument was developed by Shaftesbury and others for the necessity of a general election. The King had prorogued Parliament beyond the legal limits, so ran the proposition, and thus automatically ensured a dissolution.

It was nonsense, of course. Buckingham addressed the House of Lords on the subject in February. The great Duke had lost his sense of personal magnificence – or did not care. By 1679 not only was he wearing false teeth, but Nell Gwynn, who remained his friend, begged him at least to wear new shoes and a new periwig when he knocked at her door, so as not to stink the place out.[16] Was this the son of the gorgeous George Villiers, whose sheer physical beauty had fascinated two generations? To the King he may have seemed like a curio, preserved for the sake of ancient loyalties from youth and childhood, where a Henry VIII might have employed the purgative axe. Buckingham, no longer the peacock he had once been, was in fact more like a wasp, an angry wasp at that, determined not to recognize the end of his own personal summer; like a wasp, he retained his sting, as the King and Danby would soon discover.

In the House of Lords he certainly made a bold show, attended by a host of followers 'in great bravery in liveries of blue'.[17] The argument was nonetheless rejected by both Houses. The King was furious. He was also deeply worried by the implications of the incident. Was this perhaps that first rumbling of the revolution he had long, consciously or unconsciously, dreaded? Danby pounced forthwith on the four principal peers involved. At the orders of the House of Lords Buckingham was imprisoned in the Tower, as were Shaftesbury, Salisbury and Wharton. It was held at the time to be an over-reaction. Later, when Danby too found himself in the same ominous prison, Bishop Burnet at least thought it a 'just retaliation' for the 'violence' of this incident.[18] But if Danby was the public instrument, there is no doubt that the King approved of the gesture.

Latterly the officials of the law in general were being subjected to his critical scrutiny. There were complaints that the quality of the King's judges was declining. Following the departure of Matthew Hale as Lord Chief Justice in 1676, tenure itself was insecure. In June Sir William Ellis was dismissed from the Court of Common Pleas on the advice of Danby. His substitute, William Scroggs, a sinister if clever fellow described by Roger North as 'a great Voluptuary' whose debaucheries were 'egregious', was, in addition to all this, very much a royal nominee. In 1678 the process continued, Chief Justice Ramsford departing in May and Twisden in December, their respective ages of seventy-three and seventy six being given as an excuse (although even today these ages do not debar incumbents from such positions).[19]

Obviously such a campaign did not pass without remark. Marvell chose to comment on it in his trumpet blast, published in 1677, *Account of the Growth of Popery and Arbitrary Government in England*: 'What French counsel, what standing forces, what parliamentary bribes, what national oaths, and all the other machinations of wicked men have not yet been able to effect,' he cried, 'may be more compendiously acted by twelve judges in scarlet.' He saw it as part of the general decline in English life, set off by the noxious spread of Catholicism; on which topic itself he exploded with eloquent bigotry: 'Were it either open Judaism, or plain Turkery, or honest Paganism, there is yet a certain bona fides in the most extravagant belief ... but this [Popery] is a compound of all the three.'

The meeting of Parliament itself was dominated by the needs of the Navy. The continuation of the quarrel between the two Houses over the issue raised by the Shirley *v.* Fagg case helped

Danby to maintain some kind of control. A stirring speech by Samuel Pepys secured a supply of £600,000 for the ships. So far, so good, even if Danby was probably over-confident in those MPs he listed as supporting the Crown – because such type of prognostication was still in its infancy.

In addition, Danby's strategy was leading him into some strange paths. He may not have fully thought out the significance of what he preached when he urged the King to declare the war in April – against France – on the grounds that *then* Parliament would have to grant him a fully paid-up Army and a Navy, and *then* he would be independent of them....[20] The first implication of this was that the King might well use these forces for a purpose other than that for which they were voted by Parliament. That was not only outside his powers as generally understood at the time, but was also of course the development that many Members of Parliament had been ostentatiously dreading over the years. Had Charles II not constantly denied such suggestions as 'malicious' and 'jealousies'? The second implication, more serious still, was that he might use the Army and Navy to suborn the rule of Parliament.

But the King declined to declare war, either at the instance of Danby or of the House of Commons. The Dutch partisans there continued to agitate for some show of help for Holland, in face of the sweeping French victories. On 23 May the Commons asked in plain terms for an offensive and defensive alliance with Holland. This was quite beyond their rights: public interference with foreign policy undeniably invaded the royal prerogative and the King said so sharply. To mark his displeasure and his determination to preserve his prerogative, he prorogued Parliament until 16 July.

There was an uncomfortable feeling of stalemate by the summer of 1677. Parliament would not vote all the money needed for a war until the King declared that war. The King naturally would not declare war without money. Nor was the opposition quashed. Buckingham emerged from the Tower in July. Marvell believed it to be at the instance of the King's boon companions: 'This was by Nelly, Middlesex, Rochester and the merry gang....'[21] He had already been allowed out for two days in June to oversee the building of his grand new palace at Cliveden – a sign of the King's indulgence or Buckingham's priorities. Shaftesbury attempted in vain to secure his own release by appealing to the King's Bench for a writ of *Habeas Corpus*. He lingered there for the next six months. But his confinement was now much less severe; and, as he was able to receive visits from his colleagues, he was by no means cut off from the opposition's continuing intrigues.

Still without proper funds from Parliament, Charles II signed his third secret agreement with Louis XIV, by which Charles was to hold off his anti-French Parliament until the following May, and in return Louis was as usual to pay up. At the same time Danby was making progress in the negotiations for the Dutch marriage: in this area the King wished to accommodate his minister. It was as though the King were astride a giant see-saw, with William and Danby on one side, Louis XIV on the other, and Parliament determined to upset the whole structure. Rather than let that happen, Charles determined to shift his weight dexterously now to one side, now to the other, rather than lose his balance.

Danby therefore was able to derive comfort from the success of the Dutch marriage project. Temple's mission to tie up the details of the marriage between William and Mary was accomplished. William had characteristically made enquiries about the girl's disposition. Fortunately, Lady Temple was a close friend of the Princess' governess, so that William could satisfy himself on this score: the link with England was evidently not his sole consideration. To Sir William Temple he observed prosaically, if sensibly, on the whole subject 'that if he should meet with one to give him trouble at home, it was what he should not be able to bear, who was like to have enough abroad in the course of his life'.[22] The only unhappy principal in the whole affair was the fifteen-year-old Princess. She wept 'grievously' when she heard the news. She saw herself being exiled for political reasons to an unappealing country, on the arm of an equally unappealing bridegroom: William was several inches shorter than she – to her hysterical eye, virtually a dwarf.

Queen Catharine, ever kind-hearted, tried to make things

better by pointing out: 'Child, when I came to England I had not even seen the King.'

'Madam, you came into England!' exclaimed Mary with the despair and cruelty of youth, 'But I am going out of England.'[23] Shades of earlier Stuart princesses who had made suitable Protestant matches abroad – her great-aunt Elizabeth of Bohemia and her aunt Mary Princess of Orange. The odd thing was that the marriage of this Mary, begun in tears, was to turn out the most successful of them all in a worldly sense. Not for this Mary the years of impecunious exile endured by her great-aunt, the premature widowhood of her aunt. Not only would she occupy the throne of England, but, probably even more to her satisfaction – for she had an essentially shy nature – her marriage of convenience turned into a love affair on her side. She loved her William devotedly and dutifully, becoming a true Dutchwoman in the way her proud aunt had never condescended to do.

It may seem surprising that Charles II should welcome or even tolerate a public event calculated to outrage the susceptibilities of Louis XIV. It is true that Danby pressed the match with great firmness, so that in a sense Charles was able to plead political pressure with perfect accuracy. But Charles, now that he was in his balancing mood, could see another advantage to it. Mary was the heiress presumptive to the throne in the younger generation, or, as it was put at the time of her wedding, 'the Eldest Daughter of the Crown', who was now happily sleeping in 'Protestant Arms'. In his speech to Parliament the following January, Charles referred pointedly to the fact that he had done all he could 'to remove all sorts of jealousies, I have given my niece to the Prince of Orange; by which I hope I have given full assurance that I shall never suffer his interest to be ruined'.[24]

The King trusted that the nuptial arrangements of Mary, deposited in Protestant arms, would distract attention from the fact that her father, who was even closer to the succession, was sleeping in Catholic ones. What was more, Mary Beatrice was pregnant; this always aroused the fear that she might give birth to a son to be brought up a Catholic (she had already borne two daughters). In fact, the baby, born just three days later, was a boy. But the public, who received the news coldly, might have spared their disapproval: by December, this latest Duke of Cambridge had perished like his half-brothers, who had in turn borne the unlucky title.*

But the pregnancy had at least played its part in persuading James to agree to Mary's match, which was otherwise most distasteful to him. Nor, on the occasion of the marriage, could there be any doubts where the popular sympathies lay. According to Pepys, nobody had been pleased at Mary's birth: a disappointing girl and Clarendon's grand-daughter at that. Now, in contrast, such 'bells and bonfires' and general rejoicing had not been seen since the Restoration, wrote Sir Charles Lyttelton.[25] Edmund Waller, the Court poet, represented it as a romantic union of a soldier king and a beautiful princess:

> Nor all the force he leads by land
> Could guard him from her conqu'ring eyes...

It was a measure of the general satisfaction at the Protestant combination that it should be rumoured – quite falsely – that Mary had been adopted as the King's own daughter.

All that Charles II actually did at the ceremony in November 1677 was to play the part of a jolly, slightly bawdy uncle. He told the groom to remember 'Love and War do not agree very well together'. When William put down the traditional handful of gold on the prayer book (symbol of all his worldly goods), Charles said briskly to his niece, 'Take it up, take it up. It's all clear gain to you.' And he urged on the prim William on his wedding night, 'Hey nephew, to your work! Hey, St George for England!'

It was left to Louis XIV to exclaim with predictable disgust and horror at the consummation of his worst fears. His reported reactions ranged from the disagreeable ('two beggars were well-

* The other children of James and Mary Beatrice – all daughters – died young during the reign of Charles II. It was the birth of a son in June 1688 then called James Edward, known to history as the Old Pretender, which provoked the crisis which led to the departure of James II from the throne.

matched in public') to the histrionic: he behaved as if he had just lost an army when he heard the news, and told the Duke of York, 'You have given your daughter to my mortal enemy.'[26] More to the point, Louis XIV stopped payment of the latest subsidy to Charles II. He also attempted to prick the King's exposed flank by its own Machiavellian means. An obvious weakness of Charles II's position was the dislike of the opposition for Danby – an emotion only sharpened by his imprisonment of Buckingham and Shaftesbury. From the point of view of the French King, Danby's resolute pro-Dutch stance could therefore be circumvented by the time-honoured expedient of pressing money into the palms of his political enemies.

Thus men like Lord Russell and Algernon Sidney – later advertised as champions of liberty – as well as Buckingham were in correspondence with Barrillon, the representative of Versailles (a home of Catholic absolutism, if ever there was one), and, what was more, were receiving funds from that tainted source. At the time, the intrigue was not exactly shocking: it was merely one more manoeuvre in the endlessly complicated wheeling and dealing which went on in Europe at the time, before Louis XIV would and the Dutch could make peace.

Charles II retaliated against Louis XIV's blocking of the subsidy by summoning Parliament for early February – not May, as proposed; he then brought it forward another ten days. By this time he had already allowed Laurence Hyde to sign a defensive alliance with the Dutch on 10 January. Yet the Dutch never ratified the treaty, and the English never went to war as promised; this treaty should be seen as yet another manoeuvre.

Charles' speech at the opening of Parliament on 28 January had a noble ring. He recalled his own efforts at mediation, by which he had hoped to procure 'an honourable and safe peace for Christendom'. It was not his fault, he said, if he now came before them seeking supplies for the Navy and Ordnance, finding that peace was 'no longer to be hoped for by fair means' and that which 'be not obtained by force … cannot be had otherwise'.[27] But the King's inner hope was not for war. He trusted that Louis would accede to this form of blackmail and negotiate a peace all the same, along lines acceptable to Charles and his nephew William.

The fall of Ghent to Louis XIV on 27 February made the possibility of a compromise peace more remote. At the same time it increased the demands for a positive Dutch alliance in Parliament. In general, the mood there was obstreperous, even ugly, especially on the subject of supplies. William Sacheverell, the rising orator, declared on 4 February that he knew 'what mind the country are of. They will not be pleased if we thrust a sum of money blindly into those hands that have so ill managed affairs.'[28]

Shaftesbury was finally released from the Tower on 26 February. Halifax had presented his first petition a fortnight earlier; but it was not until Shaftesbury had fully and publicly recognized his error, both in demanding a dissolution and in appealing to the King's Bench thereafter, that he was allowed to go free. It all had the air of an abject apology. But wise observers like the French ambassador saw in Shaftesbury's reappearance 'a great mortification' for Danby. Shaftesbury after all understood only too well the art of *reculer pour mieux sauter*. And he was probably aware in advance of Louis XIV's negotiations, since Lord Russell had been a frequent visitor to the Tower. Buckingham, who, like Rochester, had the knack of hitting on the unpleasant truth about his contemporaries (hence his demolition of Dryden in *The Rehearsal*), compared Shaftesbury to a Will-o'-the-Wisp 'that uses to lead men out of the way, then leads them at last in a ditch and darkness and nimbly retreats for self-security'.[29]

All the same, neither side had yet devised a way out of the familiar stalemate – a policy of If No War, Then No Money on Parliament's side; If No Money, Then No War on the King's. Charles II made an equally familiar move on 25 March when he wrote privately to Louis XIV. He suggested that in return for a subsidy of six million livres annually for the next three years, he would secure a proper peace in Europe, along conciliatory lines. But his winning streak had not left King Louis in the mood for territorial compromise: for the time being, he rejected both terms and subsidy.

King Charles was left with the elaborate Parliamentary game of cat and mouse which was being played at home over the question of supplies: with Parliament as the cat and the King for once in the position of the mouse. Later it was claimed in the memoirs of James II that at this point the House of Commons was in reality far more jealous of the King's power than of that of France.[30] Certainly their behaviour lent plausibility to the theory. The opposition bore every sign of being terrified that the King would escape their financial clutches. Although they were armed with their own private subsidies from France, they set up a continual caterwaul that help should be given to the Dutch; yet when money was finally voted which would enable the King to declare war on France (should he so wish), Parliament immediately followed this up by an embargo on French imports. Since the only effective way of raising money quickly was to use the Excise, and since the French imports provided by far the largest share of this, it will be seen that the second action effectively nullified the first.... The result was, as before, a stalemate.

The absolute monarch, Louis XIV, Charles was beginning to find, was easier to cope with than his own elected Parliament. A deft piece of diplomatic blackmail from the English king – the threat of an alliance with Holland, Spain and Austria – did produce the first promised payment of six million livres from the French King in May.

In the meantime, Charles II was not the only one at home who was beginning to think back edgily to the events of 1641 and 1642. So traumatic had been the experience of those days on two generations – the men in their prime and the young who also suffered the consequences – that the survivors tended to see fearful parallels when certain circumstances prevailed. Trouble with the Scots, especially on religious matters, was always held to be a bad omen, so that when an English Parliamentary attack was mounted on the King's regent in Scotland, the Duke of Lauderdale, in May, that too seemed all of a piece. Charles II suspected that the English opposition had been stirring up Lauderdale's new enemies, the Scottish supporters of 'Conventicles', as had previously suspected Shaftesbury of being in touch with the Hamiltonians.

'Conventicles' were a form of independent religious gathering unlawful under the new regime, and a series of moves of increasing severity were made against those taking part in them from 1669 onwards. In fact, the rise of this new type of Covenanter was a manifestation of the Scottish national character which Lauderdale, and by implication Charles II, should have taken more seriously. Originally, they had been animated not so much by political motives as by a sincere desire to practise their religion in their own fashion. It was really impossible to cut out the truly Presbyterian heart of the Scots, as successive rulers had found to their cost.

It was made incumbent upon local magnates to put down Conventicles held upon their land. Yet as the Covenanters were driven towards more violent resistance, it was virtually out of the question for the landowners to carry out this provision without force. And force, military force, should surely be provided by the central government. Furthermore, if it was to be a question of a military crusade against the Covenanters, that raised the second question of who was going to pay for it. In July 1678 the Scottish Parliament voted an extremely large sum – £1,800,000 – for the suppression of the Conventicles. It was quite clear that the raising of this money would be enormously resented by those who did not wish the Conventicles suppressed in the first place. No, the auguries in Scotland were definitely not encouraging.

In England, the address against Lauderdale was carried through the Commons, for all Danby's sedulous efforts to prevent it. Charles, although it was in his nature, as his brother James said, 'to keep measures with everybody', was obviously furious at the impertinence of the Commons. Saying icily that he preferred not to answer the address, he adjourned Parliament for ten days.

In Europe a further impetus towards peace was given by the exhaustion of the Dutch. And Louis XIV, already worried by Charles II's little gambit of proposing a quadruple alliance excluding France, was not averse to being involved in further negotiations. Even so, he retained a very hard-headed notion of the value of his own conquests: the peace negotiations underwent one further check, until Charles II, either in genuine disgust or more probably to bring about the conference he desired, proposed sending some English troops to Flanders to assist the Dutch. The way was finally cleared for the negotiations which led to the Peace of Nymegen on 10 August. By this, France was left with a good deal of the conquered Flemish territory, if not all she had desired; she also secured a workable boundary with the Spanish Netherlands.

The Dutch got the respite that they, rather than William, wanted. William had been reluctant to see his 'mortal enemy' confirmed in so much new ground; nevertheless, he too was able to use the temporary lull of the next few years to build up himself and his country against the final assault. Sir William Temple hailed the role of Charles II in all of this grandiloquently: the King, he declared, was once more 'at the head of the affairs of Christendom'.[31] This was the reassurance the King wanted since the waning of his European prestige after 1673.

The same happy claim could not be made for the King's affairs at home. So ragged had relations between Parliament and King become by the summer of 1678 that it has been suggested that Danby at least was considering the maintenance of the King's authority by use of the Army internally. It has also been proposed that the King himself might have contemplated such action.[32] But there is no proof that Charles II ever contemplated what would have been – by his standards – a disastrous course. Mending and patching, ironing over, smoothing down, these were the natural instincts of Charles II. So deeply were they ingrained that even an outbreak of passion, as over the Lauderdale incident or the Commons' open interference with foreign policy the previous year, was generally followed by a show of regained composure. And there were two good reasons to dissuade him.

First, there was a practical point. He had no money in hand with which to pay the soldiers on any grand scale. It is true that the Commons had voted supplies for the 'disbandment' of the Army on 30 May, the King having told them a week earlier that the issue of peace or war would depend upon their supplies: 'I leave it to you to consider whether to provide for their [the Army's] subsistence so long or for their disbanding sooner.' The Commons opted for the latter course on the grounds that the King was obviously determined not to fight France: peace would leave him in control of just that kind of force the Commons dreaded, unless something was done about it. When the King asked for – and was refused – an extra £300,000 a year on 18 June to ensure peace, the Commons were even more suspicious. The King was, however, left with the 'disbandment' supplies, which he proceeded to use for the Army's maintenance. But this sum alone would not take him very far.

One lesson taught by the Commonwealth was that unpaid soldiers sought new masters. It was true Charles II had emerged from the Restoration with full powers as Commander-in-Chief of the Army. As Sir Joseph Williamson pointed out in 1678, 'I know of nothing that can hinder the King from raising what forces he pleases, if he pays for them himself.'[33] But there was no way that a king hamstrung financially could possibly have financed such an arbitrary force in such a way as to maintain power by it for any effective period.

The second reason, which was psychological, was even more important. Charles II had witnessed at first hand the fatal – because it was unsuccessful – use of the Army by his own father. He had himself been restored by the Commonwealth Army, but in their good time, not his own; his Army in exile had proved useless in recapturing the throne. He loved the new English Army which he had constructed since 1661, devoting much time to details of its welfare. Yet an interest in the special red and black uniforms of his hundred Yeomen of the Guard – 'a livery coat of fine red cloth guarded with black velvet with Rose and Crown, his Majesty's motto and Scroll C R, back and breast, embroidered with silver and gilt spangles. Similar breeches' – should not be equated with a manic wish to take away the Parliamentary bauble by military means, as Oliver Cromwell had once done.[34]

Charles was perfectly prepared to sacrifice a number of things in the good cause of the peace of his kingdom – ranging from the abstract, such as the truth, to the concrete, such as his financial independence; but he was not prepared to sacrifice that peace itself. The use of the Army would have been another 'false Step', like the Stop on the Exchequer; this one might have disrupted the careful structure of the kingdom altogether.

It was easier to prorogue Parliament yet again. Charles II's so-called Long Parliament was adjourned on 15 July. Perhaps peace in Europe would after all be matched by the return of 'tranquillity' at home.

CHAPTER TWENTY-TWO

Against Exclusion

'On the other hand, some argued against the exclusion that it was unlawful in itself, and against the unalterable law of succession (which came to be the common phrase).'

Bishop Burnet on Parliament, 1679

The August of 1678 was fiercely hot: a surprise which even the English summer can sometimes spring. Charles II, revelling in all the varied enchantments of Windsor, went fishing and tried to let his cares run softly by the waters of the sweet Thames.

One of his minor cares was the danger of assassination. It was a seventeenth- as well as a sixteenth-century weapon (the first Duke of Buckingham had fallen to an assassin's dagger; the Royalist conspirators had aimed frequently, if unsuccessfully, at the death of Cromwell). There had been various plots against Charles' own life, from the Fifth Monarchists of 1661 onwards. Given the King's temperament, both courageous and fatalistic, it is unlikely that it represented more than just that – a minor care. A man who had the habit of an early morning walk represented an easy target; a man who regularly promenaded among his subjects in St James's Park obviously counted on his popularity rather than his guards to protect him.

Nevertheless, having survived so far, Charles II did not intend to fall victim either to clamorous opposition in Parliament or to armed attack elsewhere. As a plotter himself, he believed in keeping a casual eye on such tendencies in others. He also appreciated instinctively, better than we can today, just what his contemporaries might hope to achieve by the death of a king. He had seen the devastation brought upon the monarchy by the execution of his father. The substitution of one monarch for another, be that monarch any one of his assorted relatives, might be plausibly expected to bring about a great alteration in affairs: religious, political, or both.

Shortly before the King left London, a man named Christopher Kirkby warned him about a plot against his life. Kirkby was known to the King because he shared his interest in chemical experiments.[1] With some difficulty Kirkby managed to deliver the first part of his warning just as Charles was entering St James's Park on his morning saunter. Although Kirkby suggested that the assassination might be carried out imminently in the park itself, the King still proceeded on his way. It was only in the evening, still unassassinated, that he hearkened further to Kirkby's dramatic tale. This story was subsequently supported by one Israel Tonge, a slightly dotty Anglican clergyman who had allegedly uncovered the plot.

The plot's substance was however quite incredible: it involved the Catholics in England, notably the Jesuits, and Louis XIV ganging up together to kill the King; then they would all take up arms together to prevent the accession of the Duke of York; the end result would be the conquest of England for France. The assassination complex of the time had taken Charles as far as listening to Kirkby and Tonge – at his leisure – but it could take him no further, given the ludicrous nature of their revelations. It was therefore probably because the accused Catholics included a member of the Queen's household, Sir George Wakeman, that Charles handed the matter over to Danby.[2] Then he went to Windsor.

In Danby, Tonge found a more susceptible audience. Danby did not love France, to put it mildly, and had a prejudiced Anglican view of the Papists. Besides, it was Danby's duty to ensure the safety of the King. Tonge produced papers which Danby found sufficiently convincing to proceed to a further examination of the subject. It was in this way that another character was summoned onto the stage, one whose sheer roguery should, if there had been any justice, have shown it up at once and for ever for what it was. This was a man named Titus Oates.

Titus Oates had been born in the year of the execution of Charles I and was thus nearly thirty at the time of the egregious events for which he was later remembered. Westminster School and Merchant Taylor's, Gonville and Caius College and St John's: all these could claim the honour of his education. Despite these advantages, up till 1678 Oates had had a generally disreputable career. Betrayal was its keynote. He was himself a practising homosexual but had chosen to bring this charge against another man (it was dismissed). From being in Anglican Orders, Oates was converted to Catholicism; instructed as a Jesuit, he abandoned his new faith in 1677. His *curriculum vitae* was certainly not one which should have inspired any confidence in his testimony.

Contemporary descriptions of Titus Oates are almost universally unfavourable. His low forehead, little nose, tiny deep-set eyes, fat cheeks and vast wobbling chins make him sound more like a pig than a man. Once he had achieved fame, or infamy, Oates also showed a taste for playing the dandy which must have made him still more grotesque. But such descriptions also dwell on his voice. It was the 'speech of the gutter' wrote a Jesuit historian: in a tone both 'strident and sing-song' he 'wailed rather than spoke'.[3] One suspects that, like many others whose true impact has perished with them, including Rasputin, Oates was a bit of a mesmerist. Otherwise he could hardly have maintained his remarkable career, even allowing for anti-Popery, over three reigns.

First examined by the Council, at Tonge's suggestion, on 28 September, Oates produced a fusillade of fantastic accusations. Some of his rounds were fired across the water at the Catholic Archbishop of Dublin, Peter Talbot, amongst others. Most of his charges constituted a tarradiddle of lies, easily contradicted. It was only when Oates pointed his weapon wildly but enthusiastically in the direction of the personal servants of the royal family that he met with a piece of undeserved luck. Oates named Sir George Wakeman, Queen Catharine's physician, and Edward Coleman, secretary to the Duchess of York.[4] Using Wakeman's medical expertise, they were supposed to have plotted the death of the King by poison. And very soon the Council did bring to light some highly unwise correspondence between Coleman and the confessor to Louis XIV.

The trouble was that these royal Catholic households presented a sitting target for the charges of the malicious, such as Oates, and had done so since the days of Henrietta Maria. At best, they were tolerated, their existence guaranteed in theory by a marriage treaty, but their numbers were heavily circumscribed and subjected to disgruntled questioning from time to time by the House of Commons. At worst, they were harried and suspected. At all times such Papist enclaves were highly unpopular. As a result, these worlds within a world were Byzantine in character. The men concerned were often cut off from the ordinary life of England for years, even if they had been born there; they were thus quite ignorant of it. And where Catharine of Braganza and Mary Beatrice of Modena were modest, pious, charming women, their servants did not always have the same standards of behaviour. Coleman, the son of an Anglican clergyman, was full of the traditional zeal of the convert. No doubt, on his arrival in the household of the Duke of York in 1675, he did see intriguing with France as part of the work he should do to restore the true Faith to England (although that of course was a far cry from planning the assassination of Charles II). The King had several times asked his brother to dismiss Coleman (but that again hardly gave Coleman a motive for a daring murder).

Coleman's indiscreet and of course treacherous correspondence had consequences beyond its own intrinsic importance. For, using guilt by association, it enabled a finger to be pointed at the Queen's household. Sir George Wakeman firmly rebutted the charges against him, which were more than usually ridiculous. He was a highly respected physician, a former Royalist and a devoted servant of the Stuarts restored: the death of Charles II by poison would have broken not only his Hippocratic oath but also his oath of loyalty to his sovereign. As John Evelyn, who was 'well acquainted' with him, commented, he was 'a worthy gentleman' and one who would have totally abhorred such a deed as the assassination.[5] Yet the discovery of Coleman's correspondence provided the necessary fire to make the smoke go whirling round Wakeman's head. And these clouds of smoke might spread to envelop the Queen.

The relationship of Charles II and Catharine of Braganza had changed since those rather pathetic days when Catharine first came to England. How could it not? Marriage is no exception to the rule that time transforms all alliances. Charles and Catharine had now been married for over sixteen years, almost as long as Charles' parents, before the Civil War separated them. The King, with his ready sense of guilt and tenderness where the fair sex was concerned, now felt quite different emotions towards the woman who had been at his side longer than any of his mistresses – except Barbara, now dismissed.

Besides, the Queen herself had changed. She no longer resembled Princess Katharine of France: there was no more talk of 'bilbo', no oaths sworn by mistake. Like many good women, Queen Catharine had gained support from her virtue over a long period and had emerged as a character of remarkable fortitude. (In this heredity was on her side: both her mother and grandmother had been women of strong character.)

Dryden's play about Antony and Cleopatra, *All for Love*, was first performed in 1677 and dedicated to Danby. Dryden in his own preface purported to 'imitate the divine Shakespeare'. But there is an interesting variation from Shakespeare's construction when Antony's rejected wife Octavia confronts Cleopatra and, from a position of wifely dignity, has the better of the exchange. As Cleopatra angrily exclaims,

> You bear the specious title of a wife,
> To gild your cause, and draw the pitying world
> To favour it...

There is emphasis in general on the respect due to a royal consort – 'Justice and pity both plead for Octavia. For Cleopatra neither,' says Ventidius – and the triumph of goodness – 'My wife has brought me, with her prayers and tears ...,' cries Antony. Both had their echoes in the situation at the English

Court, where Dryden had been Poet Laureate since 1670.

It was not only a case of the King's esteem and that of the Court. Where the English public were concerned, Catharine's dignity and goodness were just the sort of qualities to appeal to them in their Queen over a long period. It was significant that Catharine's servants had been excepted from the ill effects of the Test Act in 1673.

In contrast to the royal mistresses, Catharine displayed no taste for impertinent show. At the same time, she made it clear that she enjoyed the life and pleasures of her adopted country – a feat which may have cost her more pain than she admitted in public, judging from her sad little remark to Princess Mary. The House of Lords in debate positively 'went upon the virtues of the Queen'. When it was all over, the King was able to write with satisfaction to Catharine's brother in Portugal concerning the accusations: 'Such of them as took but time to deliberate how the Queen hath lived found motives to reject the complaint ... instead time was spent magnifying her virtues.'[6] It had taken another foreign Catholic princess, Henrietta Maria, ten years to gain the opprobrium of such as Prynne, who termed her the dancing goblin. Catharine, in a far more anti-Catholic period, spent ten years building up a solid reputation. In public, the Queen also maintained a regal serenity as her husband dallied with a succession of mistresses. She continued to do so until his death: there were to be no more scenes such as had sullied the early months of her marriage – at any rate, in the mind of the King. Like Queen Alexandra, consort of the equally errant Edward VII, she saw that supreme dignity – and love – lay in tolerance.

As yet, the Queen's relationship with her husband had not quite attained that halcyon quality on which observers were to comment in the following eighteen months. A year later Lady Sutherland would cry out that the Queen was 'now a mistress, the passion her spouse has for her is so great'.[7] She was not alone in the view. It had taken the shenanigans of the Popish Plot and the Queen's own behaviour to achieve this 'extraordinary favour'.

In 1678 Charles II, out of neurotic guilt, could not take it for granted that his wife's virtue would protect her. Supposing Wakeman as well as Coleman had been indiscreet, who knew what might be charged against her, however unfairly? In the ensuing proceedings of the Council there is no doubt that the King displayed extreme jumpiness on anything which pertained to the Queen's household, or might prove to do so. Otherwise it is not possible to understand how this sensible and indeed cynical man allowed the fabrications of Oates and his accomplices to have any official credence at all.

Even without the investigations of the Council, the autumn of 1678 bid fair to be a time of unusual tension. A new session of Parliament had been promised by the King, which prospect enchanted no-one but excited not a few. Then in early October an event took place which transformed the whole situation from one of measured enquiry and political anticipation into – strident panic. This was the death of a Protestant magistrate, named Sir Edmund Berry Godfrey, which took place some time between the evening of 12 October, when he left his house to go out to dinner, and 17 October, when his battered corpse was discovered on Primrose Hill. Much later Lord Halifax would sapiently observe, concerning the Popish Plot, that 'the angry buzz of a multitude is one of the bloodiest noises in the world'. The news of the murder (for so it was naturally assumed to be) of Godfrey had a cataclysmic effect on London society. As Serjeant Maynard later declared to the House of Commons, 'The world was awakened.'[8] From now on the angry buzz of the multitude would sound in everybody's ears – King, courtiers, opposition members, Catholic priests, Anglicans, foreign envoys alike – and drown the sweeter strains of reason and common-sense.

The death of Sir Edmund Berry Godfrey has still not been satisfactorily explained three hundred years later. When Godfrey's bruised body was discovered, he had been dead for some days. Murder was the obvious plausible explanation, either by random muggers taking advantage of Godfrey's night walk, or by any one of the enemies a magistrate can acquire in the exercise of his profession. One of these was the drunken Earl of Pembroke, known for his maniacal assaults. But the injuries on Godfrey's body were mysterious; although he seemed at first sight to have been killed by his own sword, the autopsy showed that this wound had actually been inflicted after death.

So another more complicated theory has arisen that Godfrey, who suffered from melancholia, committed suicide; his body was then treated so as to make the cause of death look like murder. There could be two reasons for this: either to avoid the penal laws applied to the estate of a suicide, or, more melodramatically, to throw the responsibility for the crime onto someone else – or onto some persons else, the Papists. But this would have been an elaborate, even over-elaborate, way of going about things. There is no proof that such a concealment ever took place, while random mugging in the seventeenth century was at least a common phenomenon.

As in another classical mystery, the Gowrie House Plot, no one theory of the death of Sir Edmund Berry Godfrey seems able to explain all the known facts. For all the optimism of researchers in the field of historical crime, perhaps the whole truth never will be known.* From the point of view of the biographer of Charles II, the true explanation of Godfrey's death is of secondary importance compared to the furore its discovery caused at the time. It was most unfortunate, with the nerves of London society already on the edge, that Godfrey had recently taken Oates' deposition on oath and was reputed to have given Coleman an informal warning. He was a personal friend of Danby and Bishop Burnet (as well as of Samuel Pepys). Popular imagination suffered from no difficulties in unravelling the cause of Godfrey's death, and at once. It was quite clearly the wicked Jesuits at work. Godfrey had been killed because he knew too much. On 21 October, only a few days after the discovery of Godfrey's corpse, Parliament was recalled. The King still hoped that this assembly could be held to the purpose for which it was intended: to reimburse him for the cost of the army still in Flanders. Anticipating criticism, he explained that although he

* J. P. Kenyon, *The Popish Plot*, London, 1972, contains an excellent summary of the various theories in the light of recent research (Appendix A, 'The Murder of Sir Edmund Berry Godfrey').

had not disbanded the army as promised, at least his forces were being employed in ensuring a peaceful situation in Europe. As to the alleged conspirators, he was careful to begin his speech with a firm disassociation from them: he would take as much care as he could 'to prevent all manners of practices by that sort of men, and others too, who have been tampering ... and contriving how to introduce Popery amongst us'.[9]

The King would willingly have kept his eyes fixed on the European horizon, where his own interests lay. But in London the chase was on. Oates' accusations and Godfrey's death represented an opportunity for harrying the 'Catholic' Court which an experienced politician like Shaftesbury was hardly likely to neglect. As Shaftesbury observed, memorably and no doubt truthfully, on the subject of the Popish Plot, 'I will not say who started the Game, but I am sure I had the full hunting of it.'[10] Oates, for example, was in touch with that focus of the opposition, the Green Ribbon Club. Although John Evelyn wrote from the point of view of the Court that the testimony of such a 'profligate wretch' should not be taken 'against the life of a dog', the members of the Green Ribbon Club saw Oates in quite a different light: as a most apposite swallow on the eve of the assembly of Parliament.[11]

London was in ferment. So profound was the atmosphere of fear and agitation that fashionable ladies took to going about with precautionary pistols in their muffs. Indeed, the rumours which now abounded concerning the presence of priests everywhere can best be compared to the fear of German parachutists landing disguised in Britain during World War II. But the search for weapons, supposedly concealed by the rabid Catholics in preparation for their insurrection, produced a singularly unheroic armoury – 'from the Widow Platt, one old gun', and so on. Nevertheless, so fierce was the fervour that another Catholic widow was advised by a JP to marry a Protestant to cover herself; while Christopher Wren, as royal Surveyor, duly searched the cellar of the House of Commons for a latter-day Guy Fawkes, and was ordered to put padlocks on the communicating doors of the Spanish Ambassador's house, to fence in this notorious Papist.[12]

Shortly after the recall of Parliament, Oates had some further resounding revelations to make. He charged five Catholic peers – Lords Arundell of Wardour, Powis, Petre, Stafford and Belasye – with plotting to kill the King. These were honourable men who had on the whole led slightly obscurer lives than their position in society warranted – for the sake of practising their proscribed religion in peace. They had a great deal to lose by involving themselves in any plot, nor was there a shred of evidence against them. The King burst into laughter at the idea of the aged Lord Arundell as commander of the insurgent forces. Lord Powis was a man of over sixty, liberal-minded enough to have helped the Quakers in their own religious troubles on occasion. William Howard, Lord Stafford was a Fellow of the Royal Society. A devout Catholic, he was also, like many of his co-religionists, a loyal adherent of the established order. Nevertheless the five Catholic peers were arrested on the orders of the House of Commons. Their vast combined ages made them a touching group of dignity at bay, reminiscent of those long-bearded Roman senators who decided to await the barbarian hordes in silence, motionless within the Capitol.

On 2 November Shaftesbury judged the time ripe to demand the exclusion of the Duke of York from the Privy Council, in a speech quite as dramatic in its effect as his famous cry over Holland: '*Delenda est Carthago!*' A Bill was introduced into both Houses to debar Catholics from sitting – a far stronger measure than the Test Act of 1673, which had only been concerned with the actual office-holders. The royal households were also attacked, but the servants of the Queen were once more excepted – an even greater tribute to her prudence than that of 1673. The King appeared to bow. He persuaded the Duke of York that it would be unwise to attend the Privy Council, and, as to the Catholics, he told both Houses that 'he was ready to join with them in all the ways and means that might establish a firm security for the Protestant religion'.[13]

Although the measure was passed, Danby fought a brilliant rearguard action which was to prove the last triumph of the parliamentary organization he had sought so hard to establish. James was excluded from the Act. The measure had thus netted the mice but lost the lion, since one Catholic heir presumptive, still legally at liberty to sit, was worth a clutch of Catholic MPs and peers excluded. Nor was the King himself quite so meek as he pretended. As the dirty tide of prejudice swilled through Whitehall, leaving behind its debris of false accusation, the King did not lose his own balance. William of Orange had on occasion complained of the English Court, how it blew hot and cold, and how his uncle should pay heed to the words of a pilot he had heard at the helm of a ship during a storm: Steady, steady, steady. Charles II's conduct at this juncture showed steadiness. He refused to allow his old friend Father Huddleston to be included in the general proclamations against the Catholic priests. But he tried and failed to protect his armed forces, and disbandment was once more pressed to the clamour of MPs determined to prove a Catholic connection with the Army.[14]

November was ever a notorious season for anti-Popish demonstration. There was a new venom in the celebration of Guy Fawkes Day in 1678. Pope-burnings had been on the increase recently: one such conflagration had been provoked by the arrival of Mary of Modena as a bride in November 1673; in 1677 a figure of the Pope was burnt in the streets of London and the presence of some yowling cats imprisoned inside the effigy was generally held to add to the artistic effect. In 1678 there were several effigies to be seen.[15]

Further west in the city, at the beleaguered Palace of Whitehall, the Court attempted to put on an equally bold, if less outrageous, show. This was for the birthday of Queen Catharine, which by an unlucky coincidence fell about the same time. She was forty. 'I never saw the Court more brave,' wrote John Evelyn on 15 November. But the flickering of the anti-Popish bonfires and the cries of the rabble made a coarse accompaniment to celebrations in aid of a gentle Queen. Besides, the King was more occupied in fighting off the attacks on his wife than in dancing attendance on her birthday. On 24 November, at the second of his two meetings with Oates during that month, the King listened to accusations coupling Queen Catharine with Wakeman in trying to poison him.

Oates had now been joined by a worthy accomplice, 'Captain'

William Bedloe (he had no right to the military title but had found it useful in his early career as a confidence trickster). Like Oates, Bedloe knew the Jesuit organization from the inside, having been employed by them on sundry missions, and was able to profit from his knowledge to make some lethal accusations against the priests in the royal household. Bedloe was now a member of the criminal underworld.[16] Attaching himself to Oates' soaring coat-tails, he offered evidence on the Godfrey murder which was, despite his scandalous past, received with joyous credulity. The importance of Bedloe was that, having joined in the anti-Popish hue and cry, he was prepared to perjure himself without hesitation. He could thus provide the essential 'first-hand' witness to these rumoured misdeeds which would be required by a judge at a proper trial. He could 'corroborate' Oates. Or he could himself be 'corroborated' by much vaguer witnesses.

Not for one instant could the King credit that his wife had conspired to poison him. Throughout the examination of Oates, the King had represented the voice of common-sense, pointing out for example that Oates had called the Spanish Prince Don Juan, an alleged conspirator, tall and dark, whereas he was actually short with red hair. When Oates in his new testimony mentioned the Queen's apartments where the plotting was supposed to have taken place (he could not even describe them), the King reacted swiftly. He confined Oates to his rooms in Whitehall under guard; there the perjurer remained briefly until the Council had him released.

At the end of November, Coleman, a less innocent figure, was tried for high treason. The presiding judge, William Scroggs, spoke of him being condemned by 'his own papers', which had been seized; they were in fact ruled treasonable by the judges before the trial. (The testimony of Oates and Bedloe proved dangerously lame on examination and was quickly glossed over at the end of the trial.) It was thus for the treason of his papers that Coleman was condemned to death and executed on 3 December.

How different were the fates of Oates and Bedloe: despite this demonstration of the perjured nature of their evidence, both received State apartments in Whitehall; Bedloe was granted a modest allowance at the request of the House of Commons. Oates' state was more splendid: with his allowance of £1,200 a year, he might have been a national hero – Admiral Nelson himself.

In view of the King's instantaneous strong defence of the Queen, and in view of their success in other areas, it can be argued that Oates and Bedloe made a psychological error in trying to implicate Catharine in the first place. Charles blamed Shaftesbury, the fair-haired villain, at the time.[17] But Shaftesbury, with his superior intelligence (and superior knowledge of the King's mind), had not attempted to attack the Queen. Of course the element of calculation in Oates' behaviour, once he had tasted the heady wine of popular approval, should not be exaggerated; it would have been an elementary precaution to have ascertained the nature of the Queen's apartments, for example. Yet Oates, in concentrating on the Queen, had touched on one of the King's few genuinely sensitive spots: he might let Clarendon go without too much regret, and sacrifice Danby perforce; but, as he had already shown over the prospect of a divorce, Catharine was another matter.

He told Burnet, *à propos* the Queen, that 'considering his faultiness to her in other matters, it would be a terrible thing to abandon her now'. He went on to say that he knew that he had led a bad life ('of which he spoke with some sense'), but he was breaking himself of all his faults and he would never again do a base and wicked thing. And more strongly than that: 'They think I have a mind to a new wife; but for all that I will not see an innocent woman abused.' Queen Catharine wrote a most moving letter to her brother the King of Portugal on 'the care which he [Charles II] takes to defend my innocence and truth. Every day he shows more clearly his purpose and goodwill towards me, and thus baffles the hate of my enemies.... I cannot cease telling you what I owe to his benevolence, of which each day he gives better proofs, either from generosity or compassion.'[18] The result naturally was to draw the royal couple still closer together. By acting as knight errant to his Queen in distress, Charles had at last found a way of atoning to Catharine for all the pain he had caused her.

None of this however enabled him to dismiss Oates' allegations. He was obliged rather to rebut them and to strike back. In another sense therefore Oates' attack on the Queen was a brilliant (if unintentional) coup. By involving the King so personally, Oates ensured that the whole matter of the Popish Plot was given a gravity it lacked in essence. Meanwhile Shaftesbury whipped up his pack, ready for the full hunting of the game so conveniently started for the opposition.

At the end of November the House of Commons presented the King with a Bill for placing the Militia under the control of Parliament. This, the very measure which had precipitated the Civil War, was a sign of hostility to the prerogatives of the Crown which Charles II was hardly likely to miss. For the first time in his reign the King employed his veto to put an end to the Bill.

So far he was holding his own. But the King had an Achilles heel in politics as well as in private life. This was the position of Danby. September had seemed to mark splendid new advancement in Danby's success, when he married his daughter Bridget Osborne to the King's illegitimate son by Catharine Pegge, 'Don Carlo', the Earl of Plymouth. Then there was his coup in carrying the amendment concerning the Duke of York's position through Parliament. But Danby was a marked man where the opposition was concerned. When an opportunity came to hunt him down in his turn, it was likely to be taken with gusto. Less important to the King emotionally than the attack on his wife, the crisis over Danby represented a far more critical assault on the position of the monarchy.

The occasion of the attack was provided by yet another unsavoury character, if not in the same class as Titus Oates either by birth or behaviour: Ralph Montagu, the English Ambassador to the Court of France. Women brought luck to Montagu. He married an heiress. Before he was appointed to the Court of France as Ambassador Extraordinary at the time of the Secret Treaty of Dover, he had worked his way up the Stuart household ladder; he was successively Master of the

Horse to Anne Duchess of York and Queen Catharine. It was he who attended and reported the piteous death-bed of Madame in France. As a ladies' man, Grammont described him as one to be feared more on account of his assiduity than his appearance – the most dangerous sort of gallant.[19]

Returned to the Court of France as full Ambassador, Montagu became the lover of that full-blown expatriate beauty, Barbara Duchess of Cleveland; but he also allowed himself the luxury of trifling with the affections of her daughter, Anne Countess of Sussex. This promising *Liaisons Dangereuses* situation was spoilt by Barbara's unpredictable temper; she incarcerated her wayward daughter in a convent. But Anne, lured by Montagu, bounced out again. Barbara peppered Charles II with letters of outraged complaint. Montagu was now 'the most abominable man'; Anne had been 'up with Montagu till 5 a.m.', sending her servants away. Like many another ageing courtesan, Barbara clearly found herself gravely shocked by the morals of the younger generation. 'I am so afflicted that I can hardly write this for crying,' she exclaimed.[20] In revenge, Barbara revealed some of Montagu's intrigues with Danby (he was a great intriguer, as well as a ladies' man). Montagu returned to England to defend himself and was sacked for making the journey without permission.

The motto of all this might appear to be that Hell hath no fury like a mother scorned in favour of her daughter. But as a matter of fact Montagu, an Ambassador scorned, now ran Barbara close. And, in sheer damage done around him, he far outstripped her. In view of the prolonged secret relationship of Charles II and Louis XIV and his own position as intermediary, Montagu obviously had some powerful weapons at his command. He also had an ally in the French Ambassador in London, Barrillon, no friend to Danby and the pro-Dutch policy he represented.

Buoyed up with French money and French promises, Montagu now stood for Parliament himself – nor could Danby's much-vaunted organization prevent him from being elected, an eloquent commentary on its growing failure in these late days of 1678. Montagu's intention was to gain immunity for his attack on Danby.

In vain Danby tried to seize Montagu's papers. Two crucial letters eluded the snatch. Supported by Barrillon, Montagu revealed their contents to the House of Commons. They were lethal. Here was Danby undeniably proposing to Louis XIV that England would settle the war in return for a substantial whack of cash. It would have taken much less than that to bring the gleeful cry of 'Impeachment!' to the eager lips of the members of the House of Commons.

For all his charms and intrigues, Montagu was not an adept politician. He was not, for example, in the same class as Charles II, whom he had dismissed airily but inaccurately as 'a governable fool'. Montagu's declared intention was to secure the acknowledgement of Monmouth as Prince of Wales, and he took strength from the fact that Louis XIV seemed not averse to such a prospect. But the French King's real interest was in the promising confusion which a disputed succession would bring about in English affairs. Barrillon, echoing his master in wiliness, never paid Montagu all the money he had been assured. And Charles II, recognizing danger when he saw it, employed that potent weapon which remained quite unblunted in his hand – the termination of Parliament at the sovereign's will.

In a sense, the attack on Danby was a familiar crisis: Charles II had grown up against a background of impeachment, or threatened impeachment, of a minister, ever since that day when, as a child prince, he had pleaded with Parliament for Strafford's life. But in another sense the move against Danby was part of the grave new threat to the position of the monarchy. The fact was that Montagu's former position – he may even have known the full truth of the Secret Treaty of Dover – made him peculiarly dangerous. The King acted with swiftness and decision. At Danby's suggestion, he wrote, 'I approve of this letter C.R.' on the drafts of Danby's letters produced in Parliament to protect him.[21] And to protect himself he then got rid of Parliament on 30 December by dissolving it.

Shaftesbury and the Whigs had nevertheless scented blood. The smell encouraged them wonderfully. Their noses were firmly pointed towards the man at the King's side, the man described by Montagu as a 'wilful fool', as opposed to his 'governable fool' of a brother: James Duke of York. For it was a fact that James' position as heir presumptive remained as yet officially untouched, despite all the attacks upon it – just as the Crown's ability to control the timing of Parliament was also untouched. It was time, felt Shaftesbury and his associates, to remedy that disagreeable state of affairs.

The General Election of February 1679 was the first to be held for eighteen years. Not only was the experience therefore novel to the country as a whole, but that country was also in a continuing bubbling state of ferment, attendant on the 'Popish' revelations of the previous autumn. In the quick-heating capital, there were many unpleasant manifestations of the unpopularity of the Court. Louise Duchess of Portsmouth continued to embody that kind of alien immorality which even the greatest English sinners saw it as their duty to resent. Lady Gerard, who was taken for 'the French whore', found her chair surrounded by a hostile mob (as a respectable woman, she did not have the wit or the opportunity to deal with the situation as Nelly did). At the Duke's Theatre the real-life duchess was booed and the theatre closed in consequence.[22]

Louise's loss was Nell's gain. For Nell was now the recipient of new praise. Aphra Behn, for example, that ornament to Nell's sex and the playwright's profession, dedicated a play, *The Feign'd Curtezans*, to her in 1679 (in this war of the dedication, Louise would score three years later with *Venice Preserv'd*, from Thomas Otway). There was a swings-and-roundabouts element about it all. *Janna Divorum*, a study of gods and goddesses by Robert Whitcomb, referred to Nell as possessing the primitive wisdom of Apollo, the pristine wit of Mercury, the greatness of mind of Juno, the delicate beauty of Venus, and the God-like courage and brave spirit of Hercules. With such high-flown praise sounding in her ears, Nell could afford to ignore those critics who described her somewhat less pleasingly as 'puddle Nell', the 'hare-brained Whore', and the 'darling Strumpet of the Crowd'.[23]

The Court wits continued to snarl out their smutty jokes. They exhibited nothing but derision for Charles II at this juncture. Rochester, for instance, took pleasure in hammering home the message that the King cared for nothing but sex. In 'The Royal Angler' he alluded crudely to the 'fatal bait' which Rowley would always greedily swallow:

> And howe'er so weak and slender be the string,
> Bait it with Whore, and it will hold a King.

Buckingham with equal rudeness referred to the monarch as one who could sail a yacht, trim a barge and loved ducks, tarts and 'buttered buns'.[24]

But the King's comrades did not necessarily see behind the mask of indifference he wore. And perhaps he chose them for that very reason. No doubt Charles II would far rather not have dealt with a major political crisis in the nineteenth year of his restored reign. As we have seen, he had originally tried to coast through his political difficulties, 'living from day to day'. But given the challenge of the Popish Plot and Montagu's machinations, leading to the Whig attack headed by Shaftesbury, the King responded to it.

In the spring of 1679 he took a solemn decision concerning the future of his brother. His contemporaries, fooled by the mask, did not immediately appreciate that it had been made. There were also interested parties, like Shaftesbury and Monmouth, who either believed or wished to believe themselves that the King favoured Exclusion – and certainly wanted to convince those around them that he did. As Henry Sidney wrote in his diary later in the summer, they did great harm in that respect, bringing MPs to quite the wrong conclusion concerning the King and Exclusion – 'Which everybody knows he is utterly against'.[25] Indeed, for the next six years, Charles II was steadfast, even obstinate, in support of James' claims to succeed, as he had been over very few things in his essentially flexible life.

On the surface, the King appeared to be pliant in the face of necessity, as so often before. In February he told the Duke of York that he must leave England for the time being. The King's letter to his brother was couched in gracious terms: 'You may easily believe that it is not without a great deal of pain I write you this, being more touched with the constant friendship you have had for me than with anything else in the world...'[26] Nevertheless, this was no more than a characteristic allusion to shared family loyalties in the days of yore.

The crucial observation was that made by the King to Parliament at the end of April. As the new session was ending, he volunteered to accept any law whatsoever that the House of Commons could devise 'that may preserve your Religion' – provided that there was no interference with 'the Descent of the Crown in the right Line' – that is, the legitimate succession. There is no clearer statement of the conviction Charles II had reached with regard to the future of the monarchy. The Lord Chancellor's long explanatory statement reiterated the point at the end: 'If anything else can occur to the Wisdom of the Parliament, which may further secure Religion and Liberty against a Popish Successor, without defeating the Right of Succession itself, his Majesty will most readily consent to it.'[27]

Why had he reached this conviction? First of all, he was not fighting for an absolutist role for his brother; he would subsequently show himself willing to accept various kinds of compromise concerning James' actual position, including the humiliating concept of a guardianship of James by his own children. When it was all over and Exclusion defeated, the King even told Barrillon that he might have agreed to it if Parliament had offered more money and they had not attacked his prerogative at the same time – particularly as it would not have stopped James succeeding all the same!

Nor did Charles II reach this conviction out of an increased opinion of his brother as a potential ruler. James was no Hamlet, 'like to prove most royal'. While Charles continued to respect James' bull-necked strength of character, he also continued to deplore the lack of tact which went with it. To the last years of the reign of Charles II belong his various unflattering references to James, featuring '*la sottise de mon frère*'. When James remonstrated with Charles for his famous habit of walking in St James's Park, frequently unattended, Charles is supposed to have replied lightly, 'I am sure no man in England will take away my life to make you King.'[28]

Most famous of all is that remark made to William of Orange, when Charles observed that Exclusion would make little difference in the end, since if James succeeded to the throne, with his 'turbulent and excessive temperament' he would not stay on it four years.[29] This judgement has gained prominence for the wrong reason. Because it proved uncannily correct as a prophecy, it is generally held to be illuminating about the character of James II. But its real importance lies in the light it casts on Charles II. Here was a king who had decided, *faute de mieux*, that he must uphold the principle of the legitimate monarchy; in his usual clear-sighted, if cynical, way, Charles recognized the material he had to deal with in implementing his decision.

The conviction of Charles II concerning the need for 'the descent in the right line' was based on the present danger to his own monarchy rather than on any future dangers to the monarchy as a whole. He identified attacks on the legitimate succession as part of a campaign which would turn on the royal prerogative, decimate the other wide powers of the Crown, and in general transform the face of English politics. From there, the slippery slope led downwards all the way, via political strife in Parliament to the dreaded abyss of civil war and revolution. Thus 'descent in the right line' became closely, almost mystically, linked in the King's mind with that beneficent order he sought to preserve in his kingdom.

The temperament of Charles II as he approached fifty was turning to pessimism. The steel of his youth, that essential quality of public hope which had carried him from Worcester to exile and back to England again, was no longer necessary. Charles II's famous remark about his brother and the future sprang from his own deep-seated conviction of the essential melancholy of human affairs.

The Duke of York, accompanied by Mary Beatrice, sailed for the Netherlands on 3 March. The ostensible reason for his journey was to visit his son-in-law and daughter, William and Mary of Orange.

He left behind him a political scene unpleasantly transformed by the recent General Election. This, which has been described as the first English General Election fought along 'distinctively party lines',[30] resulted in a happy triumph for that Country group increasingly identified as the Whigs over those of the Court nicknamed Tories.* It was also incidentally marked by such heavy drinking on all sides that 'Sober Societies' were later formed in towns – an interesting example of locking the stable door after the horse had fully refreshed itself. Far from gaining new adherents, the government did not gain more than thirty seats, against 150 to their opponents. The Crown had miscalculated.

The men who now mustered at Westminster were later described in James' memoirs as being like 'so many young Spaniels that run and bark at every lark that springs'. But they were not wholly without a sense of purpose. Quite apart from the subject of Exclusion, there remained the unsettling matter of Danby. The King probably hoped that Danby might be allowed to settle his affairs – and the King's – and then depart with something like dignity. Danby probably hoped, with Charles' support, to be able to ride the storm and survive afloat.[31] But the 'young Spaniels', organized by Shaftesbury, were not content with such a tame solution. The Commons requested Danby's arrest and the Lords agreed. This of course posed a threat to Danby's actual safety as well as his ministerial position.

Danby, reluctantly, offered his resignation. On 25 March the King, after assuring the House of Lords that he had authorized the Montagu letters, accepted it. Afterwards Danby blamed the King's decision on a new man in his counsels: Robert Spencer, Earl of Sunderland. Originally designated as Montagu's successor in Paris, Sunderland belonged to the rising generation (he was in his thirties) which would increasingly dominate political events in the last years of the King's reign. But Sunderland was merely echoing the general feeling of the Court party that Danby had to go.[32] Besides, Charles himself could propose no better solution to save Danby than to pardon him for all the offences he had committed up till 27 February.

* As the Tories took – or rather received – their name from Irish brigands, the Whigs were dubbed after the Whiggamores, Scottish Presbyterian rebels. (The word was originally spelt 'Whigg'.)

Even this caused fearful trouble with the House of Commons. As William Sacheverell, the fiery Whig MP, put it, 'If they confirmed this pardon to Lord Danby, they made the King absolute.... What difference was there between that and arbitrary power?'[33] The King insisted. The House of Commons did not budge. In the end, Danby was imprisoned in the Tower. It was now that his treatment of Buckingham the previous year came home to roost. Danby was not even allowed to visit his wife, who was believed to be on her death-bed. Buckingham and his friends had vindictive memories.

The introduction of the First Exclusion Bill was in the King's opinion a further manifestation of the general attack on his position. When one considers Sacheverell's sentiments yet again, it is difficult to think the King was wrong. Sacheverell did not take his stand on the need for a Protestant king. 'Let the King and the Council be as Popish as they will,' he cried. He took his stand on the far more dangerous point that it did not matter if the King was Popish – so long as 'we can wind the King to a good will and liking of what we shall do'. In short, 'The foundation of Government is in the People's hearts, and upon the same foundation the King came in at his Return....'[34] This cut at the very root of the royal position. More to the point, it cut at the root of the practices of a Charles II. If the foundation of government was in the people's hearts, then clearly the monarchy was not the strongest force in the country, for it lay below that of the people, as expressed by Parliament. The appearance of such radical arguments goes far to explain the personal horror Charles II felt for Exclusion, over and beyond its consequences in banning his brother from the succession.

For the time being however the Exclusionists were weakened by their own internal disagreements. Exclusion was a comparatively new concept. Essentially it was personal to James: the First Exclusion Bill sought to exclude the Duke of York in particular from 'the imperial crown of England' – not any unnamed Catholic successor. But no-one had quite decided how the hand should be played. If James were debarred from succeeding, the main contenders for the throne were his two daughters: Mary, married to William of Orange, and Anne, as yet unmarried (she was only just thirteen). Then there was 'the Protestant Duke' – James Duke of Monmouth, still the crowd's darling, still unlegitimized. All sorts of combinations of these figures would be suggested in months to come; but immediately there was no obvious winning card. Anne's youth obviously ruled her out, but at this point Mary's marriage made her equally suspect. For it is important to realize that the Whig attitude to William of Orange in 1679 was quite different from what it subsequently became. By no means did he represent a kind of dream candidate. William was at this point regarded pre-eminently as a Stuart, and as such an authoritarian figure.

Monmouth too was an uncertain quantity. 'Young Jemmy was a fine lad' – so ran a popular song. But was he? Sir John Reresby described him as having a fine exterior but not being all of a piece inside, which was probably an accurate assessment. In appearances he had markedly Stuart looks, with that slight heaviness of chin and sensuality of mouth with which many of the members of his family were endowed. But he was undeniably handsome. In character he lacked weight. He could not, for example, conceive of a course of action or an opinion without wishing to give it immediate expression. He had none of the secrecy and substance of his father, the constancy of his uncle the Duke of York. One remembers Evelyn's charge against his mother, Lucy Walter, that although beautiful she was 'insipid': perhaps it was from her that Monmouth derived his own fatal lightness. Or perhaps, more simply, Monmouth was spoiled. 'So pretty a child', he had been indulged but not properly educated by his grandmother, Henrietta Maria; that was a dangerous combination.[35]

Like many exhibitionists, Monmouth was also quite ignorant of other people's feelings. As Buckingham wrote, he lived 'as if the world were made only for him'. It was typical of Monmouth that he described his mistress, Henrietta Wentworth, as his wife on the grounds that he had been too young to know what he was doing when he married Anne, the heiress of Buccleuch. As a contemporary wrote, it is 'a pretence, very airy and absurd'.[36]

Nell Gwynn, in her witty way, hit off Monmouth's mixture of royalty and impudence when she christened him Prince Perkin, a nickname which somehow fits him better than the languishing lines of Dryden on the subject of Charles' children:

> Of all this numerous progeny was none
> So beautiful, so brave as Absalom.

The King of course loved him – and also spoiled him. But where Charles was concerned, that did not necessarily mean blind, uncritical appreciation. Charles was on the contrary well aware of Monmouth's instability. As a father, he may have loved him all the more for frailty; as a monarch, he could not help seeing in Monmouth's flawed character, in particular his lack of judgement and his choice of 'knaves and flatterers' as counsellors, another of his own problems.

Monmouth's sponsors were not put off by his flawed character – nor, for that matter, by what was described as his 'flawed title'. There was even an argument in favour of choosing a prince thus handicapped: he would take care to govern well, as Lord Howard put it, because he could not dispense with popular support. It was basically Monmouth's Protestantism which made him attractive to backers in the succession stakes. In the November of 1678, as anti-Catholic prejudice mounted, toasts were drunk to Monmouth, the first real indication of his candidature.[37] Even so, in the spring of 1679, his genuine backers were not really very numerous. Shaftesbury, for example, still harped on the idea of the King divorcing the Queen (which, with its implied consequence of a new wife and a new family, was the very reverse of supporting Monmouth).

This was where Monmouth's lack of acumen hampered him. As he swaggered on the political stage, he could not perceive the obvious fact that his cousins, Mary and Anne, and least of all William of Orange, were hardly likely to support his pretensions. Their reasons were straightforward ones of self-interest. William told Monmouth quite frankly that 'if he aimed at the crown he could not be his friend, but in all things else he would'.[38] The King never supported Monmouth's pretensions publicly for a moment.* Of course, daydreams could and would be spun concerning Charles' secret intentions. Yet to secure the succession, with so many disadvantages and opponents, Monmouth needed to work like a mole underground. He was however one of nature's roosters and could not emulate a mole to save his life (as events in the reign of James II would show).

Returning to the supporters of Exclusion, it will be seen that their campaign, like Monmouth's title, was flawed: it had no positive objective as yet, only the negative one of keeping out the Duke of York. Against Exclusion, not only the King but many within Parliament were prepared to argue, as Burnet put it, that 'it was unlawful in itself, and against the unalterable law of succession (which came to be the common phrase)'.[40] Yet even without unity on the part of the Exclusionists, the situation was quite ugly enough for the King. In Parliament he was being pressed on all sides, not simply for or against his brother's cause. In particular, his faithful servant Lauderdale was being attacked: like the assault on the Duke of York, the campaign smacked of insult to the monarchy.

Lauderdale's situation, both in England and in Scotland, was acute. In Scotland there had been the predictable outburst after the imposition of taxes for a 'Highland Host' to suppress supporters of the Conventicles. Three thousand Lowlanders and six thousand Highlanders neither managed to suppress these spirited Covenanters nor to ensure peace in the troubled land. In England Shaftesbury chose the spring of 1679 to mount a violent attack on Lauderdale's Scottish regime in the House of Lords. He took it to symbolize the way things were going generally – downhill towards absolutism. On 25 March he described Scotland as 'the little sister' of England. The only difference was that in Scotland slavery was to come first, then Popery; in England it was to be the other way round.[41]

Charles II stuck by Lauderdale. He reckoned to be able to protect him, where the discovery of his 'treasonable' correspondence had made it impossible to save Danby. In any case,

* According to Evelyn, Monmouth admitted on the scaffold that Charles II had 'indeed told him he was but his base [illegitimate] son'.[39]

of the two men, the King felt infinitely more bound to Lauderdale, for reasons of long association and political sympathy.

In Ireland the Test Act had been strictly enforced: Catholics who had crept into the corporations had been hastily eliminated from them and priests proscribed. In Ireland too there was rising tension. Inevitably, Ireland felt the effects of the Popish Plot: where Catholicism was concerned, it was a case of England sneezing and Ireland catching cold.

In 1677 the Duke of Ormonde, Ireland's best friend where stability and mercy were concerned, was once more put in charge of the country. Despite his disgrace at the hands of the intriguing Buckingham, Ormonde had been kept in touch with Irish affairs by the former Lord Lieutenant, Essex – another example of the latter's good sense. Ormonde had not achieved the post without a struggle. The nature of it reveals once again the selfish indifference of the English Court – including its King – towards any interests in Ireland other than its own aggrandizement. For there was an opposition manoeuvre to make Monmouth Lord Lieutenant, a post he would however continue to occupy in the salubrious atmosphere of London, while Lord Conway, as Deputy, did the dirty work on the spot. Although this scheme had the support of both Danby and the Duchess of Portsmouth, for internal reasons to do with their own English-based intrigues, Ormonde emerged triumphant.[42]

He now tried to sort out what was undoubtedly the curse of Ireland at the time: the incredibly complicated situation with regard to land titles. This was the product of forty years of settlement and counter-settlement, larded over with unfortunate grants made by the English Crown, often quite ignorantly. Clare and Connaught were in a particular state of chaos. After all, if Charles II placated his suitors with grants of land which actually had lawful occupants already, he was not likely to feel the consequences personally. It was not incidentally that Charles acted more selfishly towards Ireland than the rest of his contemporaries. Like Cromwell in the previous generation, with his ferocious genocidal victories, Charles merely personified the English attitude of his time. But the result was 'a mere scramble'.[43]

A second problem facing Ormonde was that of law and order. The brigands – the original Tories – continued to multiply. Characteristically, Ormonde tackled both the land question and the rising anarchy with measures designed to cast a mantle of forgiveness over the past. The legislation he proposed included a Bill of Oblivion. There was considerable opposition to Ormonde's plans, some of it comprehensible, since obviously some interlopers might find themselves confirmed in their titles.

It was in this sense that the Popish Plot, naming the Catholic Archbishop of Dublin, Peter Talbot, and potentially smearing all Catholics, came at an awkward time. Shaftesbury was only too easily able to play on folk memories of the 'massacre' of 1641 by suggesting that there would be another Irish insurrection. It is hardly likely that the Irish off-shoot plot for a French invasion ever existed, any more than the alleged conspiracies of the English Catholic Lords; it was correctly described later by Oliver Plunkett, Archbishop of Armagh, as being 'all plain Romance'. Nevertheless, as in England there were casualties. Archbishop Talbot died in prison in Dublin late in 1678, and about the same time Plunkett was arrested. Plunkett was a man of the greatest probity, of whom nothing worse could be said than that he had not left Ireland when the Catholic hierarchy was officially banished: yet a charge of high treason was later fabricated against him. Since it proved impossible to find an Irish jury to convict him, two years later this particular witch-hunt was destined to move to England – the land of more amenable jurymen, where a Catholic prelate was concerned – with scandalous results.

Meanwhile, in England the summer of 1679 seemed unlikely to provide a happy resolution from the King's point of view. Danby was gone, leaving no obvious successor. The trial of Sir George Wakeman, with possible injury to the Queen, was pending. Parliament was sitting and about to debate the Exclusion Bill. The King as usual lacked money. Popular prejudice had, if anything, heightened since the previous autumn. It is true that Catholics were not actually being torn to pieces by the mob – a negative achievement – but the atmosphere of hysteria was such that no-one, whatever their allegiance, could be confident such a thing would not happen. A satire on 'Affairs of State' demanded:

> Would you send Kate to Portugall
> Great James to be a Cardinall . . .?
> This is your Time.
> Would you send confessors to tell
> Powis, Stafford and Arundell,
> they must prepare their souls for hell?
> This is your Time.[44]

It was certainly the time of Titus Oates. In April he was able to postulate publicly such extraordinary fantasies as the fact that James I had been murdered, that the Great Rebellion and the death of Charles I were due to the Jesuits, and that the Duke of York had started the Great Fire! Useless to suggest that no sane person could believe such mad perversions of reason and common-sense – when popular prejudice is aflame, the very madness of such tales brings with it an orgiastic release to hearers: the greater the madness, the greater the satisfaction.

A famous pamphlet of the time – a best-seller – is a classic illustration of this. Protestant citizens were adjured to go to the top of the Monument in the City and imagine the consequences of Popish rule:

> the whole town in flames, and amongst the distracted crowd, troops of Papists ravishing their [the Protestants'] wives and daughters, dashing out the brains of their little children against the walls, plundering their houses and cutting their throats in the name of [being] heretic dogs. And, tied to a stake in the midst of the flames, they were to picture themselves their fathers or their mothers screaming out to God with hands and eyes uplifted to heaven.[45]

What chance did the real Catholics – obscure, oppressed people – stand against this dramatic image?

In its deliberate excitation of the most basic fears in every human breast, this is the language of the rabble-rouser down the ages. Sir John Reresby wrote afterwards of 'the Torrent of the Times' that no one who had not actually witnessed them could conceive 'what a Ferment that raised among all Ranks and Degrees'.[46] But those who have lived through similar periods of irrational persecution, that of the 'Reds' in Macarthyite America, for example, can imagine them quite well.

Related afterwards, the actual events which took place might not amount to much in terms of massacre or the kind of mayhem which chills the blood centuries later. If the innocent died, they died after due – if not fair – trial. But it was an atmosphere in which rational decision and steady action were, if not impossible, exceptionally difficult. No-one knew what the next day would bring, whether they were a Catholic fearing slaughter, or a righteous Englishman fearing the assassination of the ruler, followed by armed insurrection. The predatory Shaftesbury, blowing his hunting-horn to encourage the Whigs, added both to the excitement and to the confusion.

Charles II maintained his balance by firm adherence to twin principles – for the Queen and against Exclusion.

CHAPTER TWENTY-THREE

A King at Chess

So I have seen a King at Chess
(His Queens and Bishops in distress)
Shifting about, growing less and less
With here and there a pawn.

Charles Sackville, Earl of Dorset, 1680

An unacknowledged deadlock existed between Charles II and his Parliament after the fall of Danby in March 1679. There was no obvious candidate to replace Danby as chief minister, one who would both be acceptable to the King and succeed in managing Parliament. The King listened to the advice of Sir William Temple. It might be that the time had come for a political experiment. He now instituted a new type of Council, consisting of thirty members, half of whom were to be ministers and half without office (Temple himself was a member).

It was an intelligent move. Such a choice had the desirable effect – from the King's point of view – of promoting discord between those who were selected and those who were not.[1] At the same time, it was the intention of this Council to transform poachers, such as Shaftesbury and Lord Halifax, into gamekeepers. The distinction between these two professions was not necessarily so rigid: unlike most poachers, Shaftesbury and Halifax had been gamekeepers once upon a time. Halifax, member of a great Yorkshire family and endowed with even greater brilliance of intellect, had been made a Privy Councillor in 1672; he had supported the Test Act. Although Halifax accepted the authenticity of the Popish Plot, where James was concerned he did not take a hard line. Halifax stood more for the limitation of James' powers than for his total Exclusion.

The other members of this Council, trainee gamekeepers, included Sunderland and Laurence Hyde – 'Lory'. Like Sunderland, he was in his thirty-ninth year, eleven years younger than his master. He had been a diplomat (accredited to The Hague) as well as an MP; he was made one of the new Lords of the Treasury in March 1679, when Danby fell. Hyde had inherited from his father, the once mighty Clarendon, a certain arrogance. But he had also inherited Clarendon's great loyalty towards the monarchy. Hyde was considered personally close to the Duke of York and, although he regretted James' Catholicism, was against Exclusion.

Then there was Sidney Godolphin, in his early thirties, another Lord of the Treasury appointed in March. Since 1668 he had been an MP, first for Helston and later for St Mawes, and he had included a variety of royal appointments in his career: page of honour (when Charles described him as never *in* the way and never *out* of it), groom of the bedchamber and finally in 1678, Master of the Robes.[2] But he also had close Dutch contacts and disliked the Duke of York. The junior member of the group was the Earl of Mulgrave, barely thirty. One of the Wits and Dryden's noble patron, Mulgrave had also been a naval commander; he was now colonel of the 'Old Holland' regiment of foot. Mulgrave preferred the Duke of York to Monmouth, for whom he had felt a military jealousy.

From their youth, these men were to be known as 'the Chits'. A mark of this generation in 1679 was a capacity to remain on friendly terms with Shaftesbury and his associates, as well as with the Court, where their natural interests lay, unless there was some specific and dangerous issue. Indeed, there is a fluidity about the stance of men like Sunderland and Godolphin which echoes the generally confused political alliances of this period.

The new Treasury commission after Danby's fall was however headed by a figure of greater maturity: the Earl of Essex, recently returned from his spell as Lord Lieutenant of Ireland. At the new Treasury it was felt that Essex's 'clear, though slow sense' would make him 'very acceptable to the King'.[3] Indeed, Essex's instinctive moderation was illustrated only a few months later, when he advised the King to disband his newly raised Guards, as being unnecessarily provocative.

Later Essex favoured Exclusion. And even the wise Essex would lose his head, believing in such a far-fetched notion as the guilt of the aged Lord Stafford, and involving himself in the Rye House Plot. But at the time when the King's experimental Council was formed, the employment of a man like Essex, coupled with Shaftesbury, Halifax and the younger men, represented a positive decision to try and break the deadlock which existed between King and Parliament: a deadlock which had virtually brought government to a halt. The plan was that this Council should transact all business, and for reasons of convenience it was therefore divided into committees for Intelligence, Ireland, Tangier and Trade and Plantations.

It is true that as this perturbed spring turned into a still more hectic summer, the King tended to lean more and more on those members of this Council who were sound on the subject of the royal prerogative. But this was inevitable, given that the prerogative was under renewed attack, and given the King's anxieties on the subject. The rise of the influence of Essex, Hyde and Godolphin was not implicit in the constitution of the Council when it was first formed; nor is it necessary to suppose that Charles II formed the Council in a derisive mood, as a kind of blind to his real activities. The formation of the Council was an intelligent move in its own right, because it stood to bring strident members of the opposition within the nullifying orbit of the government. As a pragmatic operator, the King would have been perfectly content had the Council succeeded. In any case, the burning issue of Exclusion, filling Parliament with both smoke and fire, was occupying all his positive energies.

On 29 April, as an effort against Exclusion, the King agreed to considerable limitations on the powers of any 'Popish' successor. These included lack of control over judicial or ecclesiastical appointments (a limitation which would put this Popish sovereign in a very weak position indeed, compared with his predecessors). Parliament was also to assemble immediately on the death of the sovereign, as of right – another important sacrifice of the royal prerogative. It was not enough. Shaftesbury and his clique continued to demand the sacrifice of James. Thus the Exclusion Bill was given its first reading and carried.

On 21 May it was also carried on the second of its three necessary readings, before going to the Lords. The majority was large, without being overwhelming (207 to 128, and there were over 170 people who did not vote). The Commons was not however likely to be in great haste to accord the Bill its third reading, since relations with the House of Lords were still in that state of nagging discord which is an important political feature of this period. Once they had passed the Bill finally, the Lords would probably reject it. The King therefore, as an experienced general, fell back on the tried weapon of prorogation. On 27 May he prorogued Parliament until 14 August.

Parliament was not the only front where the royal authority was directly threatened. In Scotland, the murder of Archbishop Sharp on 13 May meant that the precarious peace there could no longer be maintained. Archbishop Sharp had gratuitously attacked the Covenanters for what were undoubtedly sincere religious beliefs, but, as with all acts of terrorism, the shocking nature of the deed shifted the balance: the Archbishop was dragged from his coach and hacked to pieces in front of his daughter's eyes. In June the government's forces, under John Graham of Claverhouse, were defeated by the Covenanters, and had the rebels now not indulged in the eternal sport of Scottish dissidents, internal bickering, their cause might well have flourished outwardly, as it did in the hearts of the Scottish people. As it was, the main outcome of the Scottish insurrection, from the English point of view, was a change in the position of Monmouth.

The dashing young 'Protestant Duke' was presented with a nice opportunity to shine when he was despatched north to command the loyal militia. He was appointed Captain General. It was Monmouth's finest hour. Not only was he officially responsible for the government's triumph at Bothwell Brig on 22 June, but he also issued instructions for mercy thereafter, understanding the essentially harmless nature of most Conventiclers. As the 'clement victor' in Scotland, Monmouth acquired a *kudos* which his actions at the English Court had not brought him.

Meanwhile, the English Parliament had passed one Act which should have been enough to immortalize it – had anyone at the time realized the consequences of what they were doing.[4] This was the Act since known as Habeas Corpus, and widely regarded as one of the cornerstones of English civil liberty. At the time it was loosely known as 'Shaftesbury's Act', but that did not mean that Shaftesbury alone understood what was involved: the Act caused little stir with anyone at the time when it was passed, slipping on to the Statute Book, rather than marching on to it in glory.

Previously, a writ of Habeas Corpus, as the Latin indicates, had required the body of a person to be brought by his jailer before a judge or into court; its advantage lay in the fact that, once the aforesaid person was produced, the nature of his custody – lawful or otherwise – could be investigated. So far, so good. But recently there had been extraordinary difficulties made over the granting of writs. Once granted, the difficulties were not over: as many as three writs had on occasion been needed for the prisoner to be produced. Nor was bail necessarily granted thereafter. Political detainees were not the only ones to suffer: those on criminal charges were subject to the same ordeal.

One of the questions asked was whether any court other than the Court of the King's Bench had the right to issue such a writ. Then there was the whole issue of imprisonment at the King's command – that is, by royal warrant. To suggest the abolition of this was a clear attack on one aspect of the royal prerogative. But by the end of the debate MPs were merely demanding the abolition of various abuses to do with this type of imprisonment. Equally, the Act of 1679 simply specified that there were to be no delays in granting the writ, without touching on the question of the courts involved. In effect, all parties had shied away from the issue of the royal warrant, which was really at the centre of the abuse.

It showed how little the significance of the Act was understood that the King himself was mildly favourable towards it. He saw it as a useful means of protecting Danby and the imprisoned

Catholic lords – the latter, at least, the victims of a tyrannical incarceration quite as arbitrary as anything a Stuart monarch could provide. There is also a persistent story that the Act only passed through the House of Lords as a result of a piece of impudence on the part of the teller, who boldly counted one exceptionally stout peer as ten. Be that as it may, *31 Chas II* was duly entered on the Statute Book.

Then Parliament was duly prorogued. The King was under no illusions on the subject of Exclusion. He was aware that the reassembly of Parliament would be rapidly followed by a return – probably successful – to the painful subject of the Bill. Having granted himself a breathing-space, he cast his thoughts, as before, towards means of ruling without this tiresome assembly.

Renewed negotiations – or intrigues, as the opposition would have termed them – with France was one answer. Charles II had never yet turned to Louis XIV totally in vain. The reopening of discussions on the subject of a French subsidy was planned in the summer. Throughout the autumn these deliberations with the French Ambassador, Barrillon, would continue.

There was another possibility – that expedient contemplated, if only for a moment, by Danby twelve months previously: the use of the King's standing army to solder together the worn surface of his personal power. There were of course plenty of commentators who discerned this intention in the King's slightest move. In particular, the raising of new royal guards in July (that measure condemned by the sensible Essex as being provocative) aroused the familiar suspicion that 'governing by an army' was on its way. The King however scoffed at the criticisms and raised his guards all the same. As far as he was concerned, all the reasons which had militated against a military solution in 1678 still obtained.

In June five Jesuit priests had been put to death. The King had no means of knowing that the impending Wakeman trial would represent the turning of the tide where reason and justice were concerned in London. The Scottish situation was hardly encouraging, and Monmouth's success brought its own problems where Exclusion was concerned. The so-called Triumvirate of chief ministers in the King's Council – Essex, Halifax and

Sunderland – were now convinced that a proper dissolution of Parliament was essential. They feared that otherwise, when Parliament returned, Shaftesbury would introduce a newly triumphant Monmouth as his Exclusion candidate. It has been established that the Triumvirate were mistaken, and that Shaftesbury had no intention of supporting Monmouth at this juncture: but this is hindsight.[5] On 3 July the King raised the question of dissolution in his Council, and after discussion it appeared that the majority were against it.

A week passed. Then, on 10 July, the King dissolved Parliament all the same. The thoughts of Charles II at this critical period can only be divined. He was careful to avoid committing them to paper. The written word had proved a dangerous medium where Danby was concerned and he had never much favoured it in the first place, either out of laziness or some profound need for self-concealment. The move to dissolution was the effective termination of his experiment with a new type of Council: he had ignored its decision. But then the Council's decision would have interfered with his royal prerogative to prorogue or dissolve Parliament at will. Charles had not anticipated this particular confrontation when he set up the new Council. But where the prerogative was concerned, he knew where the royal interests lay.

A further week later, on 18 July, Wakeman, the Queen's physician, was acquitted by a jury presided over by the Lord Chief Justice William Scroggs. At the time it was widely believed that Scroggs had been got at – bribed, for example, by the Portuguese Ambassador. Certainly he met a fair reward at the Court for presiding over such a welcome verdict: at Windsor thereafter it was noted that 'the favourites of both sexes rejoiced', and the soft white hands of the Duchess of Portsmouth were supposed to have patted the unwieldy form of the Lord Chief Justice in gratitude.[6] But this was after the event. It has been pointed out by legal historians that Scroggs' conduct of the case cannot be faulted by the conventions of his own age. He cast well-founded doubts on the testimony of Oates and Bedloe. Scroggs' own language to the jury was also more impressive than the contemporary reaction might indicate. He told them,

'Never care what the world says, follow your consciences.' And of his own participation, Scroggs observed, 'I would be loath to keep out popery by that way they would bring it in, that is, by blood and violence. I would fain have all things very fair.'[7]

There is in fact no evidence that Scroggs was influenced. Given that Wakeman was innocent, and given that his defence (unlike that of the Jesuits) was efficiently organized by some person of authority whose identity is unknown, Scroggs simply allowed justice to take its course.[8] Afterwards a dead dog was thrown at his coach. The Popish issue was not yet equally dead – the trial of the Catholic lords was to come – but at least some progress had been made in killing it off.

The acquittal of Wakeman on the one hand, and the possibility of renewed Anglo-French manoeuvres on the other, meant that by August 1679 the King could at last hope for the ease which had been denied to him during the last horrendous twelve months. Virtually everything he held dear, both of a private and a public nature, had been under attack. But the essential sea wall had not yet been breached. It was at this point, by one of those strange flukes of personal misadventure from which the course of history is never wholly free, that the King fell violently ill.

This dramatic twist to events – occurring at a moment of maximum uncertainty concerning the succession – was all the more startling because it was so unexpected. The King was famous for his superb health. Like many men who consider physical exercise the best panacea, he had a cheerful disregard for the medical profession, 'ever laughing at physicians', and 'would not come under their hands'.[9] No one at Court was foolish enough to suppose that their King, who had survived so much, would actually elude the ordinary laws of mortality as well. Charles II was now in his fiftieth year. The constant fuss over the succession, the care taken to guard the King's person against assassination: all this illustrates a general preoccupation with the future. But his *imminent* death had never been contemplated.

It is relevant to Shaftesbury's tortuous policies over Exclusion, for example, that he was working towards a future he never expected to see. Nearly ten years older than the King, with a sickly and twisted body, Shaftesbury could not legitimately hope to outlive the vigorous, athletic monarch. The Duke of York himself was only three years younger than his brother and Charles was always reckoned to be the healthier of the two. James thought it worth recording in his memoirs that he too had not expected to outlive Charles II.[10]

Now, from one moment to the next, all that was changed.

On 22 August at Windsor the King was struck down. He was seized with an acute fever, probably of the malarial origin which was so common in seventeenth-century Europe, since he was cured by 'the Jesuit's powder', actually an early form of quinine imported from the South American bark *cinchona*. Appropriately enough, the King owed his cure to his own zest for scientific knowledge.[11] Although the bark had been known in England since the time of Cromwell, the dosage was not yet fully understood and the established doctors regarded the new cure with baffled suspicion. But Charles, being 'the most inquisitive King in the whole world who is also the greatest patron of empirics', had looked favourably upon one Robert Talbor, an early expert on the subject. He had joined with him in experiments using the new powder, and chided the physicians for their lack of interest. Even so, they might have denied the King his own cure in 1679 had they been able to think up anything else to administer. Evelyn tells the story of Dr Lower's continued childish reluctance to admit its efficacy; eventually, faced with the King's undoubted recovery, he fell back on the formula that it was 'a Remedy fit only for Kings'! The King, more gratefully, knighted Talbor and granted him a pension.

Returning to the royal sick-room at Windsor, here no such happy outcome was predicted at the time of the King's collapse. According to the prevalent insanitary custom (when infection was not understood), the poor King had his chamber crowded with his councillors – anxious as much for themselves and their future as for his. The councillors, standing on their own right to be present, warded off still greater crowds, but the spectacle of their grim and enquiring visages looming over him can only have added to the King's fevered dreams. One unresolved question faced them. What was to be done about the Duke of York, lurking in unofficial exile at Brussels?

James' legal position as heir presumptive was quite unaltered. Councillors could foresee an ugly situation arising if the King died, the Duke of York took over the throne which was his by right – and they had somehow neglected to acknowledge this fact. On the other hand, it was equally possible that the Duke of York, being absent, would fail to secure the throne: Monmouth, dominated by Shaftesbury and bolstered by his position as Captain General, might grab it; that spelt catastrophe for his former opponents. Presence often constituted right in a doubtful succession, as the weak Richard Cromwell gained over his stronger brother Henry, at the time of Oliver's death, simply because Henry was absent in Ireland.

On 24 August Sunderland, faced with this dilemma, sent word to James that the King was ill. A day passed and it was suggested he should return. On 2 September James arrived back in England.

It was a decisive moment. Admittedly, by this date the King himself was recovering; he exchanged water-gruels and potions for the more robust fare of mutton and partridges. Soon he was demanding to go to Newmarket – no doubt to escape the claustrophobia of his closely watched sickroom. The doctors forbade it on the grounds that the season was too advanced and, as a result, 'the Air too serene' (meaning not so much calm as liable to a noxious twilight dew, from the Latin *serus*, 'evening'). All the same, it was a decisive moment because James made it so. Such an ambiguous situation brought out the best in the military-trained Duke, accustomed to a lifetime of decision and command in the field and at sea. Suddenly his stalwart figure appeared as a bastion against contention and the worse evil of civil strife.

The Duke of York went back to the Continent three weeks later, but not before he had been assured that, had the King died, the Lord Mayor of London would have proclaimed James as his successor. The point was taken by courtiers and politicians alike that, were a similar crisis to arise, the Duke of York would be the gainer. The King's health could never again be taken for granted: it was about this time that a 'sleeping chair' was ordered for the King's progresses, symbolic of a general easing up in his restlessness.[12] In the following May he was ill again (with twice-daily bulletins on his progress). Thus the whole episode secured an ascendancy for the established candidate, in which the pretender Monmouth was the inevitable loser. Monmouth still had much to prove, and he did not help matters by his own behaviour.

It was in vain that Monmouth had attempted to prevent the return of the Duke of York. His own welcome from Scotland as the 'clement victor' was now eclipsed. Charles II preferred the interests of his brother – representing the 'descent in the right line' – over those of his son (although Monmouth and his backers seemed unable to take in the point). It was Monmouth who was deprived of his general's commission and, like the Duke of York, was asked by the King to absent himself from the felicity of the royal circle for a while.

The people had rejoiced to see Monmouth. Bonfires in abundance were lit in the streets on his behalf. But mob appeal, which Monmouth clearly possessed, was no substitute for his father's *imprimatur*. There were those at Court who wondered whether the King's attitude was 'but a feint'; wiser heads decided that he was 'in good earnest'.[13] Monmouth, unconvinced, lingered for a while disconsolately. Then he headed for The Hague. There he managed to cause the King even more annoyance by striking up an unholy alliance with William of Orange: something which Charles, in a sharp autumnal mood, believed was directed against his own French interests.

The ascendancy of the Duke of York was not achieved without sacrifice. Charles was prepared to protect his brother's right to the succession, but no more than that. In return for the dismissal of Monmouth as Captain General, James was obliged to agree to leave the centre of things himself. He was appointed as yet to no official position in Scotland; it was a year later that Lauderdale resigned 'for your own solid and wise reasons', as the King put it. Nevertheless on 27 October 1679 James and his family, whom he had collected from Brussels, set off north.

It was significant of what had passed that it was something in the nature of a royal progress. Gentlemen took care to greet the heir presumptive to the throne on his way. It was an expression of that law described by Halifax: 'Men's thoughts are naturally apt to ramble beyond what is present; they love to work at a distance . . .',[14] and put even more poetically by the great Queen Elizabeth: 'Men ever seek to worship the rising sun. . . .'

At the centre of things, Charles II was left to cope with what was present. There was a trail of damage left by his illness and the behaviour of his brother and son. Meanwhile, the General Election of the summer had given him another House of Commons. The bitterness of the anti-Popish mood of the capital persisted. The popular celebrations in November reached a new pitch not only of hysterical malevolence, but also of organization. What was more, the date was shifted from 5 November – Guy Fawkes Day – to 17 November – the Accession Day of Queen Elizabeth. The shift was deliberate. The famous Queen's image was menacingly paraded, with its implied reproach to a lesser sovereign. As Marvell's satiric 'Dialogue between the Two Horses' had it:

> A Tudor! A Tudor! We've had Stuarts enough,
> None ever reigned like old Bess in a ruff. . . .

In the organization, the Green Ribbon Club took a hand. Buckingham also put his knowledge of the theatre to brilliant, if Luciferian, use. The result was a show at once spectacular and inflammatory. So dazzling was it to the eye that even the poor Catholics it was directed against could not resist watching it, as the Jews might have watched the great military rallies pass in Nazi Germany. So rousing was the show to the spirits of the rabble that many felt compelled to express the anti-Popish fire within by lighting real bonfires in the streets.

One of the newspapers supporting Oates, *Domestick Intelligence*, gave a gleeful report of it all. The centre-piece of the show was still the Pope himself. His figure cost £40 in wax alone: indeed, the total cost of the whole show, including claret for spectators, was nearly £2,500, a colossal sum for the times. Figures of devils attended the Pope – 'Hail Holy Father' – but more ominous to the Court were his other attendants: nuns – 'the Pope's Whores' – labelled 'Courtesans in Ordinary'. Another typical placard showed a Jesuit with a bloody sword and pistol and the legend: 'Our Religion is Murder, Rapine and Rebellion.' The spectre of Sir Edmund Berry Godfrey demanded vengeance.[15] Finally, as Dryden put it, 'the mitred poppet [doll] from his chair they drew', and the Pope was duly consigned to the fierce bonfire which, it was hoped, symbolized his ultimate destination.

In such an atmosphere, it was hardly surprising that when a new Plot was put forward for popular inspection by one Thomas Dangerfield, it was not found wanting. Dangerfield, a scurrilous rascal, belonged to the tradition of Oates and Bedloe as a witness; his novel invention consisted of uncovering a plot involving the Whig leaders, including Shaftesbury. When that failed, he turned the plot on its head and vowed that a Popish conspiracy, centring on the death of the King, lay at the heart of it after all. This new farrago was nicknamed the Meal Tub Plot, after the hiding-place where a Catholic midwife was supposed to have concealed incriminating papers. The King, commenting that 'he loved to discover Plots, but not to create any', made it clear that he regarded it all, Whig coup d'état and Popish assassination, midwife and meal tub, as dangerous nonsense.[16] But there was no doubt that the absence of a clamorous House of Commons assisted him in maintaining this firm view. The whole parading mob, with their lighted torches, were not half as threatening to him as a few vocal Members of Parliament.

Under the circumstances, animated also by the renewal of the French negotiations, the King decided not to meet his new Parliament. At this point, Shaftesbury went too far for the second time. Just as he had infuriated the King in the autumn of 1673 by his open attack on the Duke of York, which then seemed *lèse-majesté*, he now called a meeting of the Privy Council to discuss James' projected departure for Scotland. He suggested the matter should have been discussed in the Council first (he pretended to believe the journey was being made without the royal assent).

The King dismissed Shaftesbury instantly, and the next day drove the message home by telling the Council that he did not propose to allow Parliament to meet until the following January. The 'Chits' were appointed with Laurence Hyde replacing Essex as First Lord of the Treasury. On 10 December the King let it be known that he had thought better of that date too, and, still further buoyed up by the progress of matters with France, indicated that Parliament would not actually meet again until November 1680. By December 1679 the irrepressible Monmouth had still further blotted his copybook by returning from the Netherlands against the King's specific orders. Monmouth's – and his backers' – reasoning was that the absence of the Duke of York in Scotland provided a heaven-sent opportunity. Monmouth could build up just that kind of solid support which he needed to press his own claims and, thinking ahead, secure the King's acknowledgement of them. There were many fingers in this Protestant pie, some of them the pretty, meddling fingers of the royal mistresses. Nell Gwynn, for example, justified her popular reputation as a staunch protagonist of that religion by supporting Monmouth; later even Louise Duchess of Portsmouth, her Catholic counterpart, took part in an intrigue to get the King to name his own successor.

But it was unwise to count on the susceptibility of Charles II to petticoat government. The King was plainly furious with Monmouth; Nelly's poignant descriptions of the wan looks of Charles' once-beloved son, his Absalom, did nothing to allay his fury. They might cry 'God bless Monmouth' in the playhouses, but at Court the young Duke was ostentatiously stripped of his various civil and military positions. In February the Duke of York was permitted to return from Scotland. In the absence of a Parliamentary session, an angry war of pamphleteering concerning the claims of the rival dukes (and not ignoring those of the two Protestant princesses) broke out in the late summer.

In particular, the legend of the King's marriage to Monmouth's mother, watered by the hopes of the opposition, grew apace. The campaign of rumour had begun in the late summer. All sorts of stories were given credence, generally on the sanguine principle that two improbabilities added together make a possibility, and four improbabilities a certainty. It was pointed out gleefully that James had once tried to deny his marriage to Anne Hyde; another comparison was made to Edward IV's refutation of Lady Eleanor Talbot in order to marry Elizabeth Woodville. The fact that James had been contracted to Anne Hyde, and the supposition that Edward IV had been contracted to Eleanor Talbot, were given as proofs that Charles' refutation of Lucy Walter was also false: it was smear by analogy.[17] Even details of the supposed marriage were now given: solemnized by the late Bishop of Lincoln (who was of course dead) in the house of an innkeeper at Liège, and witnessed by certain lords. The marriage certificate was said to be preserved in an exciting 'Black Box', one of those objects of which it could be said that everyone knew of someone else who had definitely seen it.[18]

The trouble was that a putative marriage was by far the most convenient way of establishing Monmouth's claim: it hurt no one (except the Papist Duke of York, and who cared about that?) and provided a neat solution to the problem of the succession – so at least ran the argument of Monmouth's sponsors. Thus the rumours nagged and badgered the King and would not go away.

The total lack of substance in these rumours need not be reiterated. By the spring of 1680 Charles was beginning to feel rather the same way. For a long time his instinct had been to ignore the matter as being too ridiculous to dignify with official discussion. Early in 1679 however he had made, with some reluctance, a declaration to four of his councillors, including the Archbishop of Canterbury. Two months later he repeated this declaration to the Council as a whole, and also committed it to paper, 'it being all written and signed in his Majestie's own hand'. This he judged to be the best way to kill this particular snake.

The document, dated partially according to the old style by which the year began on 25 March, is worth quoting in full:

> For the voiding of any dispute which may happen in time to come concerning the succession to the Crown, I do here declare in the presence of Almighty God, that I never gave

nor made any contract of marriage, nor was married to any woman whatsoever, but to my present wife Queen Catharine ['Queene Catarine' in the original] now living. Whitehall the 3rd day of March 1678/9. Charles R.

The impatience can be seen in the handwriting, the words 'Almighty God' being the only ones written with any care at all. This document was ordered to be kept in the Council Chest.*[19]

But the snake was scotched, not killed.

In the summer of 1680, driven beyond endurance on the subject, the King decided to put an end to these rumours once and for all. The *London Gazette* of 8 June, the official government organ, gave a prolonged recitation of the steps leading up to this decision, with the preamble: 'We cannot but take notice of the great Industry and Malice wherewith some men of a Seditious and Restless Spirit, do spread abroad a most false and scandalous Report of a Marriage or Contract of Marriage....'

In particular, care was taken to nail the story that there was 'a Writing yet Extant' – that is, a marriage certificate; it was pointed out that the very lords said to have been present at the marriage had been examined and had denied the allegation. Then the *London Gazette* printed the King's own declaration to his Council in full.

'Though I am confident that this Idle Story cannot have any effect in this Age ...', wrote the King. But the idle story persisted simply because it suited men's purposes at the time. It would haunt the first year of James II's reign for the same reason, and bring the wretched Monmouth to his death.

In general, the spring of 1680 was a period redolent of anger and disgust on all sides. Halifax wrote frankly in January that it would be pleasanter in a wasps' nest than in London at the present time.[20] In January also seven Catholic priests were tried merely on grounds of their ministry (although it was stated that they were not on trial for their lives, unlike those priests already

* It is now in the Pierpont Morgan Collection, New York, having been purchased from an unknown source in the present century.

executed in the provinces). Lack of cash meant that even members of the royal household were clamouring for their salaries. The King, encouraged by Sunderland, took refuge in the hope that foreign policy would once more rescue him from his bonds.

Sunderland's strategy was based on the notion of a series of treaties bringing in Spain, the Austrian Empire and even the United Provinces.[21] It was of course the reloading of the see-saw. France was not likely to view this new weighting with approval. Charles II acknowledged the change by making no official gesture at the time of the wedding of Louis XIV's son. The secret talks with Barrillon were however not excluded, as they had not been excluded during the sway of the pro-Dutch Danby. Sunderland, like Danby, simply occupied one end of the see-saw. The Austrian Emperor, however, a vital character in the proposed new alliance, declined to commit himself. In common with the rest of Europe's happily absolute monarchs, he was anxious to see how the King of England would deal with this obstreperous Parliament of his. Thus the foreign policy of Charles II, which he trusted to free him from Parliament by the manipulation of foreign powers, remained uncomfortably dependent upon it.

Many in England at the time believed that the Crown itself was threatened. James Duke of York had written to William of Orange the previous year that 'the monarchy itself is in great danger as well as his Majesty's person ...'. To a certain extent the King himself shared this view. There had been a rumour at the time of his illness in August that a Commonwealth would be set up if he died. At all events, he was quite prepared to take a series of steps to ensure that the country did not become further inflamed. Essentially he saw himself as forced to take these steps. They were produced out of a situation which was not of his own making, a situation which might otherwise lead to revolution. That was the King's angle. Seen from another angle these steps represented quite simply the beginnings of tighter, even absolutist, control. In May, for example, the judges (now far more the King's men than before, thanks to the new policy towards judicial appointments) gave a unanimous opinion to the Council that the King might prohibit all unlicensed newsbooks and pamphlets in the interests of good order. The King had another asset in the crucial royal warrant by which municipal corporations were granted their charters. It was in essence a question of control over the composition of the House of Commons. Four-fifths of the MPs at that time were city or borough members, and, by packing the governing body of a corporation in charge of their election – or in fact selection – attractive results could in theory be gained. The technique was to recall the charter of a given corporation on the excuse of a misdemeanour, using a *Quo Warranto*, if it was not surrendered voluntarily. This was not a new issue, nor were the steps which the King now began to take new:[22] it was the confidence he showed in his attack which was new.

Back in the 1630s his father had struggled with the City of London over its charter; Cromwell, following the Stuart trend in power, had fought with the City of Colchester. It has been pointed out that there is evidence of Crown efforts in the 1660s to impose some kind of control by using the uncertain position, after the Restoration, of many corporations whose charters had been granted by Cromwell. These early manoeuvres, in which the Duke of York seems to have played a part, came to an end not so much out of fear of the corporations, as out of fear of the House of Commons defending their own privileges in this respect.

By 1680 there was no question of the King avoiding a clash with the House of Commons: as he saw it, the Whigs were snapping at his privileges. Moreover, his dissolutions of Parliament had been disastrous: he found himself with a more Whiggish body each time. By calling in the charters, he might provide a more satisfactory selection of Parliamentary candidates. Once again he saw himself combating a trend; others might view the situation differently.

It was true that the summer of 1680 also saw the beginnings of the inevitable blacklash which violent happenings – and the possibility of violent change – bring. This backlash worked naturally to the advantage of the monarchy. Francis North, in his judicial progresses at the time, witnessed 'some dawnings of loyalty to the Crown'. The reprinting of the works of Sir Robert Filmer (begun in 1679) was another notable manifestation of Tory resurgence: he was the only theoretician in the 1630s who had actually supported Divine Right. The lapsing of the government order against unlicensed printings meant that the summer was loud with a cacophony of propaganda, Tory as well as Whig. Roger L'Estrange, an able and vituperative Tory journalist, conducted a pamphlet war against the Whigs in general and Titus Oates in particular.[23]

In Scotland the latest anti-government revolt, in June, brought to prominence the Cameronians – named for one of their leaders, Richard Cameron. These rebels styled themselves as standing for the 'anti-popish, anti-prelatic, anti-erastian, anti-sectarian, true Presbyterian church of Scotland' and, not surprisingly with such a sweeping ideal, forswore allegiance to the King of England. They also believed in preventive murder – in other words, terrorism. The Cameronians were however easily defeated and their leaders killed. Scotland under the Duke of York (who returned there in October) was to enjoy at least a stability of administration which was to his credit. Although his reputation was blackened later, the suppression of terrorism was at the time seen as essential, and James' methods no more severe than those generally sanctioned at the time in Scotland. To many of the nobility and gentry, the presence of the King's brother was welcome, while he himself became 'highly esteemed'.[24]

Meanwhile, back in England, there was a meeting of ministers in June, known as the Althorp conference, which included Halifax, as well as Sunderland, Hyde and Godolphin. It was agreed that these ministers should labour to produce a more amenable Parliament. The King promised in return not to ask Parliament for money unless his foreign alliances necessitated it; and he gave securities against Popery (but not against the succession of James). Halifax pronounced himself satisfied with such a position. The Althorp conference was an earnest of the kind of reasonable accommodation the King might be able to achieve in the future.

As a portent however it was far outclassed by certain outrageous public events which promised a very different outcome of the King's struggles. Most notable of these was the attempt by Shaftesbury to indict the Duke of York as a Catholic recusant and Louise Duchess of Portsmouth as a common prostitute before a Whig Jury in Middlesex. The penalty for the latter crime was unthinkable for the royal mistress (Louise stood to be incarcerated in the stocks, amongst other painful humiliations). The penalty for the former was purely financial. Nevertheless the joint attack was a calculated piece of provocation on the part of the Exclusionists. In the event, Lord Chief Justice Scroggs had the jury discharged. And so the matter ended; although it had the effect of sending the terrified duchess scurrying over to the Exclusionists, hoping to save herself by abandoning the cause of James. The King's mood became ever blacker and more withdrawn.

'Our most solitary sovereign,' Thomas Bruce called him. A rhyme by Lord Dorset, circulated that autumn, compared him to a King at chess, who has already lost his rooks and knights:

> (His Queens and Bishops in distress)
> Shifting about, growing less and less
> With here and there a pawn.

One effect of this withdrawal was to make him increasingly inscrutable. As Barrillon wrote back to France, 'His conduct is so secret and impenetrable, that even the most skilful observers are misled. The King has secret dealings and contacts with all the factions and those who are most opposed to his interests flatter themselves that they will win him over to their side.'[25] It had never been particularly easy to gauge the secret emotions of Charles II, since his youth had trained him to hold his feelings, like playing-cards, close to his chest. Charles had, on the other hand, prided himself on being able to gauge the emotions of others – which gave him a double advantage. Now, in the momentous autumn of 1680, this inscrutability was to be a prime factor in the ultimate fate of the Second Exclusion Bill.

For there is no doubt that a large proportion of those who voted in favour of it genuinely believed that the King was prepared to ditch his brother. As Halifax reported, by October 1680 half the world was absolutely confident that the King would quit the Duke of York and the other half absolutely confident that he would not.[26] Yet, as has been expressed, the King had in fact no intention of doing so: so that one-half of the world was (as often happens) confident but absolutely wrong. Baffled by the King's prudent secretiveness, the Exclusionists allowed optimism about his intentions to sway their judgement. They expected support from him and none came.

Admittedly, the opponents of the Bill gained no great royal support either. The King had called Parliament for quite another purpose. Tangier, the Queen's dowry, was in danger as an outpost, being beset by the Moors. Only vast injections of cash to raise more troops could be expected to save it from falling into their hands. The French discussions were still covertly proceeding, but, as Louis XIV appreciated, 'He [Charles II] only treats with me to derive an advantage in his future negotiations with his subjects.'[27] Under these circumstances, King Louis was in no hurry to conclude yet another secret agreement which might bolster up King Charles, but leave England officially no better disposed towards France than she had been before.

Charles II therefore opened Parliament in October strongly on the theme of Tangier and its desperate plight. In the summer its defender, the Earl of Ossory, Ormonde's son, had been killed. Charles had written a personal letter to his parents concerning the great loss, in which 'I take myself to be an equal sharer with you both'.[28] Without new fortifications – which had to be paid for – Tangier was lost: 'Therefore I lay the matter plainly before you, and desire your advice and assistance.' Throwing in assurances about the maintenance of Protestantism at home the while, the King pleaded for money which would provide 'greater strength and reputation both at home and abroad'. He would also bring King and Parliament together. For above all he desired 'a perfect union among ourselves'.[29]

The answer of the House of Commons to this powerful pleading was to introduce the Second Exclusion Bill. The so-called Tangier Parliament did not share the King's concern at the fate of this outpost – quite ignoring its strategic position on the Mediterranean; later one member of Parliament would refer to the King's preoccupation with Tangier as being like Nero's decision 'when Rome was on fire, to fiddle'. The first reading of that Bill which the Commons considered so much more important took place on 2 November; the Bill was carried.[30]

On 6 November the House of Commons moved that Exclusion did not apply to the children of the Duke of York; their title would be unimpaired. But the next day the King sent a message to the Commons, offering once again to agree to any securities with regard to the maintenance of Protestantism, provided the 'descent in the right line' was not touched. The day after that the House of Commons, ignoring the King's suggestion, moved that Mary, James' elder daughter, should inherit the throne (as would have happened if her father had been dead).

At this point Sunderland moved over to the Exclusionist cause, to the indignation of the King. Sunderland's point was that Exclusion represented the only viable alternative to a French involvement. He also dreaded dissolution and the prospect of yet another unsatisfactory Parliament. And he threw in for good measure that it safeguarded the King's own life. But Charles, intent on his own steady course, referred to Sunderland's behaviour, in an audible aside, as 'the kiss of Judas'.[31]

The meetings of the Commons also took place against a dramatic background of movement on the part of the rival claimants. The Duke of York, who had returned from Scotland in February, was despatched thither again by the King in October. Monmouth, who had still not learnt his lesson about the limits of the King's indulgence, set off on a series of progresses around the country which aroused a satisfying loyal chorus of support from those who witnessed them. It is possible that Monmouth was encouraged in this unlicensed display of strength by Shaftesbury. If so, Shaftesbury also had not yet understood the King's capacity for sharp action when tried too far; the lesson would shortly be rammed home for him.

The Commons, having passed the Bill on the third reading, with the question of James' descendants left open, passed it on to the Lords. And at this point the Lords, seeing an opportunity to avenge themselves for the various insults and insolences dealt them by the Commons during this period of warfare between the two chambers, joined battle.

In 1678, for example, the House of Lords' right of originating Bills of Supply (that is, money bills) had been attacked by the Commons. The latter claimed that 'all aids and supplies ... are the sole gift of the Commons'. Later the Lords counter-attacked on this particular subject; but in the autumn of 1680 the defeat of the Exclusion Bill offered the possibility of revenge in a different area.

The King himself paid the debate in the House of Lords the closest attention; a practice he had begun in the days of the Roos Divorce Bill, another measure which had seemed likely to affect the fortunes of his family. On occasion he threw in a word himself, and was formally thanked by the House. The King's posture in the House of Lords was characteristic: he began by sitting on the throne, then moved to the fire, where he felt more comfortable, and finally went round like 'a common solicitor', as Burnet vividly expressed it, lobbying on behalf of his own interests.[32]

Many of the speeches – so far as can be judged from the existing texts since the debate has only come down to us in fragmentary note form – expressed a reassuring conservatism. The contribution of old Lord Ailesbury was one such example.[33] Ailesbury was certainly over-optimistic when he suggested that James might turn Protestant, as Henri IV had turned Catholic (how that celebrated conversion continued to haunt the descendants of Henri Quatre!). But when he spoke along these lines, 'If the right heir should be thrown out may we not be subject to invasions abroad or Wars at Home. More insecurity from Wars than to suffer him to Reign', he was striking exactly the note of alarm which had long sounded in the King's ears. Lauderdale prayed that 'We must not do Evil that good may come of it' and reminded the House – another significant touch – that the Duke of York was 'Son to Charles the First of Blessed Memory' as well as 'only brother to King Charles 2d'.

But the key speech came from Halifax. Only details of Halifax's superb and successful effort remain:[34] but from these it is clear that he dwelt firmly on the possibilities of revolution – or at least an armed rising under James – which the passing of the Bill might offer. These references to the power of the Duke of York in Scotland, Ireland and elsewhere 'with the Fleet', caused fury when they were reported to the Lower House. One MP exclaimed angrily that Halifax should be told, 'If the Duke had such power, it was time to take it out of his hands.' But Halifax remained steady. The Catholic succession, if it occurred, could be dealt with by other means, such as limitations. To throw out the Duke of York's claim by means of a Bill was to provoke exactly the kind of trouble they all wished to avoid.

It is clear from the reports of contemporaries that Halifax's decision to oppose Exclusion proved crucial. Only Halifax had the trenchant style necessary to cut down Shaftesbury, capable of demonic leadership in such a cause. There was one particularly telling exchange. Shaftesbury suggested sarcastically that Halifax could not really believe the Duke to be a Catholic, since he 'combated with such warmth' their own reasonable precautions against the Duke's Catholicism. To this Halifax riposted that of course he knew the Duke to be a Catholic. Since he feared the consequences of the Duke's Catholicism, he had opposed the Declaration of Indulgence (which Shaftesbury had supported) and worked for the Triple Alliance (which Shaftesbury had worked against). At this Shaftesbury was 'much disconcerted'.

Dryden afterwards paid tribute to Halifax's influence: his

> piercing wit and pregnant thought
> Endued by nature and by learning taught
> To move assemblies...
> So much the weight of one brave man can do.

During the ten-hour debate Shaftesbury never got up to speak without Halifax answering him. The final verdict was that Halifax's rapier was 'too hard' for Shaftesbury.

At the end of the day the Second Exclusion Bill was defeated by sixty-three votes to thirty. And so the issue of the succession was, unexpectedly to many, disastrously to not a few, settled for the time being in favour of the Catholic Duke, who represented the old order as well as descent in the right line. As for Exclusion, another satiric couplet summed up its dismissal in lines not quite up to the level of Dryden, but pithy nonetheless:

> Our Renowned Peerage will not have it so,
> The Demi-Gods and Heroes thunder, No.[35]

PART FIVE

His Autumnal Fortune

'In his autumnal fortune ... yet there remaineth still a stock of warmth in men's hearts for him.'
LORD HALIFAX, *Character of King Charles II*

CHAPTER TWENTY-FOUR

Bolder and Older

> 'Men ordinarily become more timid as they grow old; as for me, I shall be, on the contrary, bolder and firmer and I will not stain my life and reputation in the little time that perhaps remains for me to live.'
>
> Charles II, March 1681

With the defeat of the Second Exclusion Bill, it might appear that Charles II, that expert on the subject of survival, had survived yet again. To Sir John Reresby, on the eve of Christmas 1680, the King had never seemed more at his ease, his sang-froid never more marked. At his *couchée*, that semi-official gathering of an evening, Charles weighed in a humorous vein against the fallacy and emptiness of those who pretended to a greater degree of sanctity than their neighbours: they were most of them 'Abominable Hypocrites'. Above all, as the King had told Reresby the previous month, he was aware of the need of sticking by his old friends, otherwise 'I shall have no Body to stick by me.'[1]

Much of this must be regarded as whistling to keep the royal spirits up – as well as the spirits of those surrounding the royal person. The King's real mood was better expressed a few months later at that classic confrontation, the Oxford Parliament, when he observed something along these lines: 'Men ordinarily become more timid as they grow old; as for me, I shall be, on the contrary, bolder and firmer and I will not stain my life and reputation in the little time that perhaps remains for me to live.'[2] The deaths resulting from the Popish Plot, the persistent chicaneries (as he saw them) of the Whig opposition, the attacks on his wife, mistress and ministers, had produced a new 'Severity in his Disposition'.

James Welwood attributed this directly to the Catholic executions: and Welwood, although writing some time after the event, at the request of Mary of Orange (he was her physician), knew the Court gossip.[3] It is also possible that such severity had always been latent beneath the courageous forgiveness which Charles II displayed at the Restoration. But a more plausible case can be made for the fact that all the Stuarts became more conservative as they became older – those that survived to do so. James I, who died in his late fifties, certainly developed a kind of obstinacy very different from the dexterity he displayed as monarch of Scotland. It scarcely needs stressing that Charles I, who was executed at the age of forty-seven, had shown these tendencies; James Duke of York had been marked for his rigidity since his thirties. Charles II, a far more flexible character in every way, who had learnt in a hard school the value of pliancy, was nevertheless not quite immune from the same tendency.

The next few months constituted the greatest challenge yet to the King's nerve. He discovered in the course of them that this new boldness, the boldness brought by age, led to triumph, not disaster. This result did not encourage the King to revert to his previous easy-going stance. The concept of 'peace for his own time' was abandoned since, like so many other attitudes of appeasement, it had manifestly failed.

The day after the defeat of the Exclusion Bill, Shaftesbury struck again. He still did not reckon himself to be totally overborne on the subject of the King's successor. 'Sick in health', he was 'yet in action nimble and busy as a body louse'.[4] If Monmouth's chances had temporarily vanished beneath a hail of mockery from Halifax, then the other expedient (of divorce) could be resurrected. In the House of Lords the next day, Shaftesbury outlined another project 'as the sole remaining chance of liberty, security and religion'. This was designed to separate the King from his existing Queen, and provide him with an opportunity for 'a Protestant consort', and thus leave the Crown to his legitimate issue.

This gained little support in the Lords. It also offered the King an opportunity to demonstrate his loyalty to his wife publicly. That night he ostentatiously supped with the Queen, when he had been in the habit of supping with the Duchess of Portsmouth. And, even more ostentatiously, he took his post-prandial nap in the Queen's chamber. It was a signal rebuke to Shaftesbury's plans. Queen Catharine had been ill that autumn, her fragility producing the usual unattractive speculation about her possible successors, including some cold 'northern princesses' and the daughter of the Earl of Manchester. Now the King had made it clearer than ever that she could not be attacked with impunity.

His speech to Parliament on 15 December was one of bitterness and disappointment. He had not succeeded in obtaining those funds which would enable Tangier to be made secure; as he saw it, Parliament had preferred to concentrate on this perpetual bickering over his successor, while forgetting the wider issue. He had hoped for a united front; they had responded with dissension. He had given them assurances concerning religion and they had not responded with any kind of financial backing. 'I should be glad to know from you,' exclaimed the King, 'as soon as may be, how far I shall be assisted by you, and what it is you desire from me.'[5]

One further piece of Parliamentary presumption he ignored. During the autumn session the House of Commons had reacted to the King's new treatment of the judiciary by asking for a change in the tenure of the judges – or else for some limitation to their powers. The King made no reference to this request. All the same, the mantle of royal protection could not be flung out much further than the King's own circle. In January the House of Commons made a move towards the impeachment of Lord Chief Justice Scroggs (in the event, the House of Lords refused to take him into custody and then Parliament was prorogued). More serious was the move of the House of Commons against Lord Stafford.

The five Catholic lords were still languishing in the Tower of London, to which they had been committed two years before. Although various Catholic priests, mainly Jesuits, had been put to death, and others condemned, no trial had yet taken place of these far more prominent victims. Scaffolding had been erected in May with a view to preparing Westminster Hall for such a magnificent public event. The mob, with its taste for gloating rhyme, had sung of the preparations beneath the windows of the imprisoned peers.

The death of one of the chief movers of the plot, Bedloe, in the summer of 1680, was a blow to the prosecution: it was not until the autumn of 1680 that it was decided by the House of Commons to move against Lord Stafford.

This particular peer was chosen because the witnesses against him had the greatest air of plausibility.[6] Thus the verdict of guilty which was given against him was in a sense justified by the evidence produced – except that it happened to be perjured evidence. Witnesses happily swore that Lord Stafford had bribed them to kill the King, that Oates had delivered to him a commission to act as Paymaster-General for the Pope's Army, and so on and so forth.

The condemnation of this decent and harmless old man was a blot on the age in which he lived. Already the ridiculous 'Pumpkin Plot', as it would be described satirically two years later in Otway's masterpiece *Venice Preserv'd*, was beginning to be revealed for what it was: 'It is indeed a Pumpkin-plot, which, just as it was mellow, we have gathered, and now we have gathered it, prepared it and dressed it, shall we throw it like a pickled cucumber out of the window?' But in his prologue Otway spoke more soberly of the period of suspicion through which he had lived:

> In these distracted times, when each man dreads
> The bloody stratagems of busy heads;
> When we have feared three years we know not what,
> Till witnesses begin to die o' the rot.

It was thanks to the 'bloody stratagems of busy heads' that, while the pampered Protestant ladies shivered in their coaches, Lord Stafford was executed on 29 December.*

* The attainder on the Stafford title remained in force until 1824. The original Bill of May 1685, to reverse the attainder, was dropped at the outbreak of Monmouth's rebellion.

His fellow lords remained in prison for the next five years, with the exception of Lord Petre, who was released earlier by death. But there were no cheers from the crowd when Lord Stafford's head was held up by his executioner. The publication of his affecting last speech, the 'Brief and Impartial Account' (which was, unusually, not forbidden), brought further waves of uneasy sympathy. 'My good Child,' so Lord Stafford addressed his daughter Delphina, 'this is the last time I shall write unto you, I pray God bless you. Your poor old Father hath this Comfort, that he is totally innocent of what he is accused of, and confident of God's mercy....'[7]

Charles II told Thomas Bruce that Lord Stafford's blood was on the heads of those who had brought about his murder – 'I sign with tears in my eyes'; and he made clear his anger and disgust at those peers who had voted guilty, especially those whom he considered to be supporters of the Court.[8] But he did not reprieve Stafford, as he would later fail to reprieve Oliver Plunkett. He could only remit the more extreme penalties for treason, including the traditional and disgusting mutilation – and even this merciful remission was criticized by the House of Commons, who wondered whether the sovereign had the right to grant it.

Then, on 18 January, the King dissolved Parliament and announced that the next Parliament would meet in March – and in Oxford.

It was an audacious move. It indicated that the King was at last prepared to take the initiative. Even before this, the Crown was at last mounting some kind of propaganda campaign, equivalent to the agile manoeuvres of Shaftesbury and his associates.* The anti-Tory Green Ribbon Club had after all proved itself to be a more dangerous enemy than the anti-Popish mob. Noise merely

* For example, one of Nahum Tate's pedestrian reworkings of Shakespeare, *The History of King Richard the Second*, which opened at the Theatre Royal, Drury Lane, on 11 December 1680, was taken off after three days: the government hastily assumed that the plot must elevate the nobility (that is, the Whigs) at the expense of the King. In fact, the play had no such message, as Tate himself indignantly protested in his Preface to the printed text.[9]

battered the ears; propaganda wooed them. The point was there to be taken. There were the efforts of Roger L'Estrange in particular. Certainly the new Parliament turned out to be no *more* Whig in complexion than the previous one, and possibly slightly less – a notable improvement on the record of the previous two years, when each successive Parliament had marked a further setback for the King's party. Against this background, the choice of Oxford, whose University was a secure Royalist nursery, was inspired. Here was no London mob, hostile to so many of the King's entourage. Perhaps the setting was the suggestion of Danby, for although still immured in the Tower, he was now able to receive visits and thus proffer advice. Eighteen months before he had proposed: 'Parliament to be called to some other place; the King to reside out of London', in a memorandum.[10]

The removal of Parliament from the seething capital did not merely recognize the dangers threatening the monarchy; it also took advantage of the very wide powers remaining with the King. It is true that he had not felt himself able to save Lord Stafford, but a man who could choose the *venue* of Parliament without contradiction was still in a very strong position. There was much aggressive talk in the capital in February. One of the City MPs, Sir Thomas Player, a notorious anti-Papist, answered boldly when questioned at dinner as to why Parliament would not raise money to preserve Tangier and pay His Majesty's debts.

'Hang Tangier!' he replied. 'We resolve to raise no money to pay the whores at Whitehall and arbitrary government. And, as the King has called us to Oxford, we know the next will be to York, but for all that we will give him no money.' Sir Thomas went on to say that the disposing of the Crown was in the Commons and as alterable as the exchanging of pipes between men, 'and taking up pipes in his hand [he ex-]changed them'.[11] For all this kind of public boasting, the Commons had not the ability to deny the King his choice. To Oxford, then, reluctantly but without the ability to resist, came the Whig leaders.

The King and Court did not come there directly, but took in the spring race meeting at Burford, twenty miles away in the stony, beautiful Cotswolds. It was a meeting at which the King's twelve-stone heats for the royal Plate were due to be run. However, on this occasion Burford was transformed into something of a political Ascot; the Duke of Monmouth was amongst those who contested and there was a quality of nervous display about the whole occasion. Only the King himself kept up that appearance of relaxation which subsequently trapped his enemies and destroyed them. He hawked across the nearby fields and dined with Sir John Lenthall, son of the celebrated, if acquisitive, speaker of the Commonwealth House of Commons.

Once the Court reached Oxford, the scene was a curious mixture of the significant and the profane. Of course the Court was not unknown to the university city. Nor for that matter was Parliament. The King had been careful to reassure himself on that front, in an age when precedents, however dubious, were held to cover a multitude of sins. There were one or two (including Charles himself) who could remember Oxford as the seat of his father's government nearly forty years ago; but it was only fifteen years since not only the whole Court but also Parliament had merrily romped off to Oxford to be out of danger at the time of the Plague. It was then that Barbara had given the King her Christmas present of a son, born at Merton College. Now both the Duchess of Portsmouth and Nell Gwynn were in attendance, as was the Queen; but the atmosphere was more political than lascivious, and there were to be no presents of such an exciting nature. Once again Merton was a Royalist stronghold, as were Christ Church and Corpus Christi. The Whigs concentrated on Balliol: Shaftesbury directed that 'the younger sort of students' should retire to make room for the elderly politicians.

There remained that concomitant of courtly pleasure, the theatre; while that concomitant of the theatre, a good row, was also to be found. The King's Players petitioned furiously to be admitted, despite the claims of the Irish Company, which were supported by the Duke of Ormonde as Chancellor of Oxford University. The Irish were 'a barbarous Mass', said the King's Players, and in the end this xenophobic view prevailed. More satisfactory than this squabble was the actual performance attended by the King on 19 March: *Tamerlane the Great*, by Charles Saunders, with an Epilogue by Dryden to make the message even more acceptable.[12]

Troops of soldiers as well as actors were present. Even more than the players they set the scene. It seems that their total did not exceed five hundred.[13] Yet since they lined the roads on the way to Oxford, and lounged in the streets of the city itself, the impression of a trial of strength was there. The Whigs arrived at Oxford marked out by the bows of satin in their hats, blue and with the words 'No Popery! No Slavery!' woven into the material at a cost of two shillings a yard (these impudent bows were afterwards used to arraign Shaftesbury).* But the Whigs, like the King, were armed with something more serious than satin bows. They brought their own troops with them, if they did not have the possibility of a full standing army to back them. At St Mary's, that same church where the young Charles had shocked his governor by laughing and eyeing the ladies in the congregation, the rival parties now carefully took their places according to political allegiance and eyed each other across the church.

And of course the Press was there. A flurry of news-writers gave the scene at Oxford something of the air of a modern party conference – except that on this occasion both parties were present. Cartoons played their part. So did lampoons. The Whigs made as much use as possible of the weapon of satire, some of it gross, in order to portray the King's choice of Oxford as an act of absolutism. 'The Raree Show' depicted him as a man with a travelling peep-show, a pack of Parliamentary motions on his back, and the 'Saints' pulling him into the mire. The Duke of York was shown, more venomously, as a figure half-Jesuit and half-devil, setting fire to London.

Halloo! The Hunt's begun,
Like Father, Like Son...

* Blue, now the colour of the (Tory) Right in contrast to the red of the (Socialist) Left, was then adopted in opposition to the traditional scarlet of royalty; the Covenanters also wore blue, based on a Biblical text which adjured the children of Israel to put on 'a ribband of blue', and Presbyterian preachers threw blue aprons over their preaching-tubs.

so ran the verse (before proceeding with considerable indecency). It was a gloomy and, as it turned out, inaccurate prediction. A loyal poem of the time, occasioned by seeing the ageing King walking near the river, was nearer the mark when it adjured him:

> Go on, blest Prince! the power of years defy...[14]

The King's opening speech to his new Parliament on 21 March was however placatory rather than defiant. It is true that there was a warning contained in the phrase, 'I, who will never use arbitrary government myself, am resolved not to suffer it in others' (the classic anti-Whig position). But at the time it seemed more important that the King stressed his continued affection for his dissident Lords and Commons: 'No irregularities in parliaments shall make me out of love with them.' It was a gruesome echo of those words uttered by the King shortly after his Restoration: 'I need not tell you how much I love Parliaments. ... Never King was so much beholden to Parliaments as I have been.' Then the King had felt quite a measure of love for the body which had shown the good taste to restore him; how, seventeen years later, love had well and truly grown cold, but the question remained how the King was to deal with his inconvenient old flame.

On the subject of religion and the succession, the King went out of his way to emphasize that he wanted 'to remove all reasonable fears that may arise from the possibility of a Popish successor's coming to the Crown' and was therefore ready 'to hearken to any such expedient, by which the religion might be preserved, and the monarchy not destroyed'. Was the King contemplating imposing some form of regency upon James, to be undertaken by William and Mary jointly, under the influence of Halifax? The words were at least capable of that construction and gave hope to the 'moderate' Exclusionists in the Commons, who believed that the King was to be counted amongst their number. But the rest rated this a 'subtle and crafty' speech, 'so unexpected that they should be put upon taking new measures'.[15]

Shaftesbury, in the makeshift House of Lords sited in the

Oxford Geometry School, wasted no time in returning to the attack. He demanded the consideration of a Bill, already passed by both Houses, which would give relief to nonconformists but not to Catholics. The House of Commons, in cramped quarters which gave rise to complaint, reverted to their favourite subject of Exclusion. Fatally – from their own point of view – the Commons felt no particular urgency. The debate was postponed until the following Saturday, 26 March, so that there might be an opportunity for compromise, possibly along the lines touched on in the King's speech.

During the next few days the King, brilliantly, paid out the rope for the Whigs. Shaftesbury, for example, was encouraged to come right out with his own solution. This was the legitimization of Monmouth by a Parliamentary Bill. But of course this had the effect of dividing the opposition. Many Whigs quite sensibly preferred Mary of Orange (who was generally understood to represent rule by William) to Monmouth. Here was descent in the right line of a sort, since Mary, as James' heiress, would receive the Crown one day in any case; while to know the wayward Monmouth was not necessarily to trust him in a position of authority. Time was rectifying the Whig distrust of William's 'Stuart' authoritarianism; whatever the nature of the animal was, William clearly did not resemble his uncle the Duke of York, nor for that matter his grandfather, Charles I.

The House of Commons in the meantime concentrated on the fortunes of yet another Pumpkin Plotter, one Edward Fitzharris. In an age when plots were endemic, as poison to the age of the Borgias, Fitzharris does not shine out as a particularly fascinating figure. It remains obscure where his allegiances lay and as a plotter he lacked the baroque, if horrifying, imagination of Titus Oates. Nevertheless, Fitzharris was to have a significance beyond the revelations he proffered. In themselves, these were contradictory; on the one hand, Fitzharris knew of a plot whereby the Duke of York would kill the King; on the other hand, he possessed the draft of a pamphlet in which the King was accused of being a Papist like his brother. The Commons at Oxford decided that these matters were best dealt with by impeachment for high treason in the House of Lords, instead of by a straightforward trial.

The Lords declined to impeach Fitzharris. All the old antagonism between the two Houses – from which the King had already profited – was aroused all over again, and at the very moment when the latest Exclusion Bill was to be read in the Commons: Charles himself, advised by Halifax, even went so far as to suggest a regency of the Princess Mary. It was probably a gambit, for it was however about this time that Charles II made those remarks, quoted at the beginning of the chapter, on the subject of boldness and age, which concluded, 'I do not fear the dangers and calamities which people try to frighten me with. I have the law and reason on my side.' Under the circumstances, it seems more likely that the King was still paying out the rope for the Whigs to hang themselves than that he was actively contemplating such a regency. James, as he well knew, would never agree to such a humiliating proposition. To agree to it was tantamount to condemning the country to civil strife on his death – the one course he was determined to avoid.

This debate in the Commons took place on the Saturday, 26 March. Taking advantage of the Commons' complaints of their uncomfortable accommodation, the King pleasantly suggested that they should meet the following Monday in the Sheldonian Theatre.

The Sunday was passed by the King in secret conference at Merton College.

On Monday the King took his place in the House of Lords, now set in the Hall of Christ Church. There was nothing out of the ordinary about his costume. But Thomas Lord Bruce, who knew him well, received 'a most gracious smile' and noted his exceptional bonhomie.[16] As for the peers, they too were in ordinary dress, having been given no notice to put on their robes. Very few present were aware that the King's own robes and crown, those trappings essential to a dismissal of Parliament, had been secretly smuggled into the building.

The King proceeded to send for the House of Commons, who were engaged in discussing the various precedents over Exclusions from the throne. Indeed, one of the members was in the very act of complaining at the isolation of Oxford in that respect: 'Amongst our misfortunes in being called to this place, we are far remote from Records and Books.' He went on, 'I have heard of Record 4.E.3 where when the Earl of March—' At that moment the official, Black Rod, arrived, to command the Commons' attendance at the House of Lords.[17] So off the Commons trooped, and the member's clinching comparison with the past was never completed. The Commons however trooped off not so much disconsolately as eagerly, expecting some new offer or concession.

The entrance to the Hall was narrow, down a little flight of steps. There was a crush as the Commons pressed through it. The sight which met their eyes – the monarch attired in full robes and crown – was both unexpected and for one moment inexplicable. The Lords themselves had barely taken in the sudden transformation. There was a babble of voices, and in the confusion the Serjeant at Arms had to call for silence three times before the noise died away. Then the King in a single sentence ordered the Lord Chancellor to dissolve Parliament: 'All the world may see to what a point we are come, that we are not like to have a good end when the divisions at the beginning are such.'[18]

Finch carried out the King's command. Charles promptly left the Hall. He had wasted neither time nor breath. These, the last words he would ever speak in Parliament, were brusque to the point of incivility. They came from a man otherwise famed for the graciousness of his manner. They represented the end of a downhill road and a long-declining relationship.

Afterwards, however, the King displayed 'a most pleasing and cheerful countenance' as he took off those smuggled robes. It was the MPs who greeted the news with 'dreadful faces' and 'loud sighs'. The King, good humour fully restored, observed to Bruce, 'I am now a better man than you were a quarter of an hour since; you had better have one King than five hundred.'[19]

Charles then dined in public, as was his custom; but he did so with exceptional rapidity. Then it was down the backstairs and into Sir Edward Seymour's coach, standing ready. The King

Charles II in 1684 (the last year of his life) by Laroon; the portrait was commissioned by Christ's Hospital and shows the King as Founder of the Royal Society.

Right: Thomas Osborne, Earl of Danby.
Opposite page: George Villiers, 2nd Duke of Buckingham, painted in about 1675, when he was forty-seven, by Lely.

Below: Henry Bennet, Earl of Arlington, after Lely; the wound on his nose, covered by a black plaster, was received in the Civil War.

Thomas, 1st Lord Clifford of Chudleigh, after Lely.

GEORGE VILLERS DUKE OF BUCKINGHAM.

John Maitland, Earl and later Duke of Lauderdale, with his formidable Duchess, Bess, Countess of Dysart in her own right, by Lely.

James Butler, Marquess and later Duke of Ormonde, *c.* 1665, after Lely.

Anthony Ashley Cooper, 1st Earl of Shaftesbury, *c.* 1672, after J. Greenhill.

Medallion commemorating Shaftesbury's acquittal in 1681, by George Bower. The reverse depicts a view of London with the Latin motto *Laetamur* – Let us rejoice.

Broadsheet concerning the Rye House Plot against Charles II and the Duke of York in 1683.

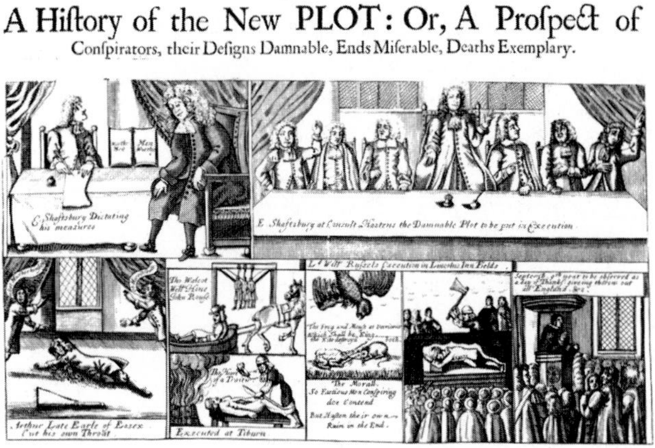

James, Duke of Monmouth, *c.* 1683, after Wissing.

Charles II's declaration, in his own handwriting, later printed in the *London Gazette*, contradicting the rumour that he had been married to Monmouth's mother.

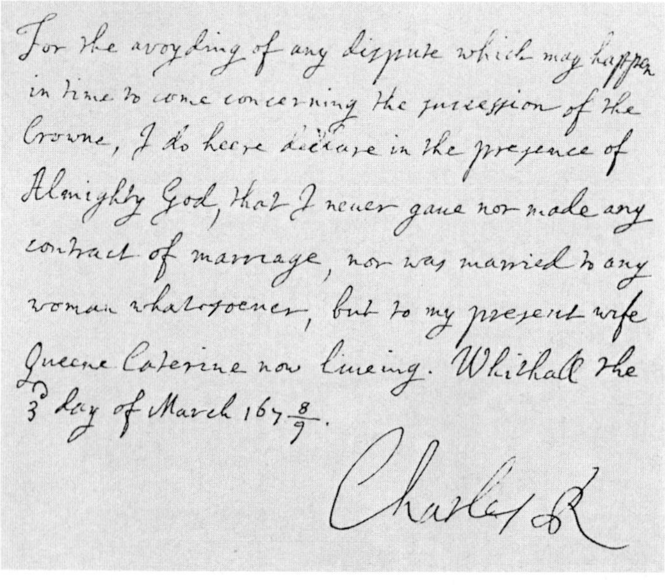

For the avoyding of any dispute which may happen in time to come concerning the succession of the Crowne, I do heere declare in the presence of Almighty God, that I neuer gaue nor made any contract of marriage, nor was married to any woman whatsoeuer, but to my present wife Queene Caterine now liueing. Whitehall the 3d day of March 167 8/9.

Charles R

Dutch medal celebrating the marriage of William of Orange and Mary, daughter of the Duke of York, November 1677.

Mary of Modena, second wife of James, Duke of York, *c.* 1685, by Wissing.

Louis XIV, 1680.

The effigy of Charles II in his Garter robes, made immediately after his death, still to be seen in the Crypt of Westminster Abbey.

joined his own coach at the next stage, to which he had prudently sent it in advance. And so he went on to Windsor, along a route discreetly guarded – another precaution. The King's Oxford troops clattered away unused. The Whigs, baffled and outpointed, had no choice but to leave as well, taking their own unused troops with them. Many of them had furnished their Oxford lodgings for a long stay – the measure of their astonishment.

Gradually Oxford became quiet again. Parliament never met again during the lifetime of King Charles II.

It is logical to suppose that the King arrived in Oxford with a rough plan of action already in his head. It was time to take on the Whigs. Given that he was prepared to act with decision, it was in fact an uneven match – not so much because the King was inordinately strong as because the Whigs were extremely weak. Nothing so far had gone right for them. In the House of Commons they had not succeeded in acquiring control of the Militia, for example, but had both alarmed and alerted the King by demanding it. Their battles with the House of Lords, also not yet conclusively won, occupied much of their attention, and had distracted them at several crucial moments. In terms of Whig policy, they concentrated their minds wonderfully on the question of the King's Papist successor; yet the King was not a Papist himself and no one (*pace* Fitzharris) seriously supposed that he was.

All this loaded the dice in favour of a sovereign with very wide theoretical powers at his command, who was also able to demonstrate the sheer intransigence of the Whigs by appearing to offer compromise. Above all, the Whigs had not made up their minds about the practical possibilities of resistance to the Crown, if any. It was scarcely likely that they would succeed against the sovereign until they did.

Nevertheless, the nerve demanded from the King by the dissolution was considerable. There were troops present – on both sides. Armed clashes in the streets of Oxford, and the further nightmare of civil strife, were to be dreaded, whatever their outcome. Oxford University was Royalist, but the city itself was known to be Whig. The feeling that revolution – some new violent turnabout – was pending was not confined to the King. Men could read the signs, or thought they could. A correspondent wrote to Pepys in January, 'I cannot but pray God to preserve us from the tumults, confusions and rebellions of 1641 and 1642, which seem to threaten us on one hand as much as Popery on the other.'[20] No-one wanted a return to unsettled times; the man who risked plunging his country once more into such 'tumults, confusions and rebellions' bore a heavy responsibility if his plan went awry. It was therefore relevant that on 8 April, the day on which a long Declaration from the King on the subject of the recent Parliament was ordered to be read throughout the country, he also received the first payment of a new subsidy from Louis XIV. The two events were closely connected.

This fresh agreement had been negotiated by word of mouth between Barrillon and Laurence Hyde. About the same time Hyde also spoke comfortingly to Barrillon on the subject of England's tiresome involvement with Spain, that treaty negotiated by Sunderland a year back: Charles II would gradually divest himself of this obligation, which of course cut quite across French interests. Hyde, shortly to become Viscount Hyde and then Earl of Rochester after the death of Charles II's sardonic friend, certainly deserved Dryden's sobriquet of Hushai: 'the friend of David in distress'. For without this agreement, it is doubtful that the English King – in the character of David – could have grappled so successfully with his 'Goliath' of a Parliament.

The confidence that Charles II needed to organize his abrupt dissolution came from France. Even though the Whigs had not made up their minds to anything except to press raucously and childishly for the Exclusion of the Duke of York, this mental disarray might not prevail for ever. It was not even a question of the money which Charles II would now receive from Louis XIV – about 4,300,000 *livres* or over £300,000 spread over the next four years; although it was true that that would enable the King to jog along comfortably without Parliament for the time being.* Once more, as in the 1660s, Charles II drew strength

* The actual agreement with Louis XIV was for more; five million *livres* for a three-year suspension of Parliament.

from the notion that Louis XIV was on his side and would help him, if need be, to uphold his 'legitimate authority'.[21]

Armed with this knowledge, the English King was able to display those qualities of attack and surprise which constituted one side of his nature; the other side, which craved ease and knew that delay often brings its own solution to difficulties, had enjoyed a long run. Fortune, which traditionally favours the bold, smiled upon the new determination of Charles II.

The Declaration on the subject of the recent Parliament, ordered to be read aloud in all churches on 8 April, was as long as the message of dissolution had been short.[22] It was also hypocritical. No-one should be persuaded that he was not going to use Parliament in the future, declared the King: this was merely 'the restless malice of ill men who are labouring to poison our people, some out of fondness for their old beloved Commonwealth principles, and some out of anger at being disappointed in their own ambitions'. He repeated his familiar theme: no 'irregularities' would make him out of love with Parliaments. The King showed more of himself in disdaining responsibility for what had happened: 'Having done our part ... it cannot be justly imputed to us that the success hath not answered our expectations.'

Charles II had done with dealing with five hundred Kings. In future he would deal with one French King and rest master of his own fate.

The summer of 1681 bore a very different air from that of the previous year. Then there had been some dawnings of loyalty to the Crown visible to a discerning eye. Now the reactionary sun's rays could be felt in a variety of ways. 13 April 1681 saw the first issue of Roger L'Estrange's newspaper *The Observator*. Nahum Tate wrote of L'Estrange's energies in attacking the Whigs, playing on his paper's name: 'He with watchfull eye/Observes and shoots their treasons as they fly....' When the King and Queen went to dine at the Guildhall, the people's rejoicing as they entered and left the City was considered to be in marked contrast to the coolness of previous years. As Henry Sidney wrote in his *Diary* at the end of June, 'But which is most extraordinary is the favour the Queen is in."[23] She had emerged unscathed from the crucible of the bad years. It would take further time for the Duke of York (still in Scotland) to recover his lost popular prestige: nevertheless, the rehabilitation of the Catholics was part of the overall popular shift away from Whig influences.

It was true that the summer of 1681 witnessed the dissection of yet another Pumpkin Plot at the trial of Edward Fitzharris. But Charles II's cool and vigorous attitude towards this episode demonstrated as much as anything else how far he had moved from the worried stance of 1678. Optimists among plot-watchers expected, as usual, great things from Fitzharris' revelations, and a connection with the household of the Duchess of Portsmouth was deemed encouraging.[24] In the event, the King made it quite clear that he expected to see this petty informer condemned and executed. And executed he duly was, on 1 July. Justice was certainly done, since Fitzharris had sought to bring about the execution of a great many more. All the same, it was a public blow to the repute of the Whigs, notably Shaftesbury; it demonstrated how far their vicious control of these events had slipped. The condemnation and execution of another informer, an anti-Papist joiner named Stephen College (amongst whose alleged crimes was the singing of the gross ballad 'The Raree Show' at Oxford),[25] continued the trend.

About the same time quite a different trial, that of Oliver Plunkett, Archbishop of Armagh, showed up both English justice and the royal character in a less attractive light. Plunkett's trial on a charge of high treason was a travesty. Dragged to England and kept in prolonged imprisonment there, he was unable to secure satisfactory Irish witnesses because of the expense and difficulty of travel. Those that did manage to arrive presented an alien spectacle, with their thick, often incomprehensible Irish accents, and were correspondingly badly treated in court. The witnesses produced on the other side, for this conspiracy that never was, puffed up with their own perjury, received a gentler welcome.

Thus Oliver Plunkett was found guilty and on 1 July went

presumably to his heavenly reward.* As Sir Charles Lyttleton wrote, he was 'generally pitied and believed to die very innocent of what he was condemned'.[26] Yet no one cared to save him, not the Earl of Essex, who, as former Lord Lieutenant, knowing the Irish scene, might have protested effectively against his condemnation – nor, for that matter, the King. Charles II could see the significance of condemning Fitzharris, but, in common with most Englishmen, no matter how liberal, could not see that there was much to be gained from saving this Irish archbishop.

The royal eye was fixed elsewhere. The newly piercing glance of the King was focused on Shaftesbury. On 2 July, the day after the executions, Shaftesbury was arrested. The King's move was not unexpected. Shaftesbury had wagered his strength against the King's in a series of provocative actions, including the attacks on Louise and James as prostitute and recusant, as well as the sallies at Oxford. Shaftesbury was also on excellent terms with those the King considered his enemies, such as the arch-informer Titus Oates, still at large, if not quite the popular hero of yester-year.

The charge against Shaftesbury was frankly weak, as weak as some of the charges against the Catholic priests who had died (the fact has to be faced that Charles II did not regard the course of justice as imperturbable, any more than the Whigs had done). Shaftesbury was accused of treason because he had conspired to levy war against the King at Oxford; but the most cogent piece of evidence against him was a Bill of Association, a list of people who were to be invited to protect the King and prevent the Catholic succession.

The truth was that Shaftesbury's arrest was an aggressive action which Charles II now felt himself strong enough to make. He was also animated by his strong personal dislike of the fair-haired villain. This dislike, like his rare outbursts of jealousy, stood out in contrast to his generally mild attitude to politicians. On the whole, Charles was content to be guided by their

* Later his heavenly status was confirmed. He was beatified in 1920 and canonized in 1975.

usefulness. In this way he amiably agreed to a reconciliation with the 'Judas' Sunderland in the following summer after some pleading from Louise, Sunderland's long-term ally.[27] But Shaftesbury was different. He was the burr under the saddle of the King, as Charles' obstinate pursuit of his trial and conviction this autumn proceeded to demonstrate.

It would have been wiser to have let Shaftesbury depart for the Carolinas, as he himself wished.[28] Shaftesbury had business interests there. An absent Shaftesbury was all the King really required in terms of safety. Instead, carried away one must believe by an animosity founded on fear, the King demanded a trial. He was punished for deserting his own former policies of forgiveness and flexibility. The new Lord Chief Justice, Pemberton, made strenuous efforts to secure Shaftesbury's condemnation. He quoted the Act of 1661 by which it was treasonable to try and interfere with the King's liberty. This, it was claimed, Shaftesbury had done at Oxford, supported by the presence of armed men. The famous blue silk bows in their hats were quoted in evidence against him. But on 24 November a Grand Jury composed of resolute Whigs returned a verdict of *Ignoramus* and Shaftesbury went free.

In short, the King had struck too far too soon. He should have been more wary of the deeply Whig sympathies of the City: at the Lord Mayor's Banquet a few weeks earlier 'every little fellow' was said to have censured both the King and 'his proceedings at that time'.[29] The acquittal of Shaftesbury was a personal blow. The Lord Mayor himself, on the King's instructions, refused to allow the bonfires or rejoicing which the Whigs wished to mount. But neither King nor Lord Mayor could prevent the striking of a celebratory medal in honour of the event, adorned with the humiliating motto *Laetamur* – 'Let us rejoice'. The obverse showed the sun emerging radiant from clouds over the Tower of London. *Laetamur*! No, the King did not rejoice.

There were however other causes of rejoicing. There is an interesting juxtaposition between public and private happiness in the lives of famous men. The presence of private happiness can always atone for the lack of public fulfilment, if the man himself will suffer it to be so. The personal life of Charles II during the last years of his life was extremely happy, even serene. Queen Catharine, comforted by his championship, had settled into a role which suited her and did not conflict with the King's other pleasures. She had, for example, protected Catholic Louise from the consequences of the Test Act of 1678 by including her name in the list of her own ladies who were not to be expelled. In explanation Catharine said that Louise had always behaved 'decently' towards her, unlike Barbara, who had been 'cruel'.[30] By now, the King's mistresses resembled the great ships he also loved, floating grandly on the tide of the royal favour, their hulls weighed down with jewels and other riches. They flew their ducal titles like pennants, their ennobled offspring following in their wake like flotillas of lesser boats. Emotionally however the King had reverted to the 'monogamy' of the first decade of his reign, on which Pepys had commented.

While Nell Gwynn retained what Aphra Behn called her 'eternal sweetness', the solace of the King's later years, Madame de Maintenon to his Louis XIV, was Louise. Relaxation, not religion, was however what Louise offered. Just as the King's accord with his wife and her own popularity were the subject of comment, the domestic ascendancy of Louise was also remarked. She had grown plumper, more 'fubbsy' than ever, as her later portraits show; it only increased her air of luxurious cosiness.

Absence was one test of the King's affections. With her son, Louise paid a visit to France in the autumn of 1684; she secured the settlement of the Aubigny estates and dukedom upon the boy as a result of Charles' intercession with Louis XIV. The King's delight at her return was unqualified. He also passed that other test of love, the appearance of a rival. When stories were circulated of Louise's dalliance with Philippe de Vendôme, nephew of Hortense de Mazarin, Charles had the presumptuous swain thrown out of the country. To celebrate her ascendancy, Louise had her own medal struck, embellished with a Cupid and bearing the legend: *Omnia Vincit* – it was a more flirtatious form of insolence than Shaftesbury's.

It is impossible to be certain when – if ever – the sexual bond between King and Duchess ceased. In January 1682 there were rumours that the King had not slept with the Duchess for four months. Bruce's testimony that the King supped with Louise 'without intent' is to be taken more seriously because of Bruce's intimate position in the King's household.[31] Yet no outsider can pronounce with complete confidence on such matters. Given the continued healthy vigour of the King, absolute cease seems unlikely. What is much more certain is that the domestic bond increased. In principle, King Charles, Queen Catharine and Duchess Louise created a master triangle in which all parties, for the first time in their lives, were roughly content with the status quo.

The King does not appear to have practised any form of birth control – there are no references to the topic by any of the interested parties. He also derived a great deal of happiness from his children. As far as one can keep track of them, the total of those that survived long enough to feature in the royal records was a round dozen. As Buckingham brightly observed, a King is supposed to be the Father of his People, and Charles II was certainly the father of a good many of them. These twelve known bastards were born from seven women: Lucy Walter, Elizabeth Killigrew, Catharine Pegge, Barbara Villiers (mother of five), Nell Gwynn (mother of two), Moll Davis and Louise de Kéroüalle. The King certainly did not suffer from that complex characteristic of some Casanovas who must claim the paternity of every child conceived within their orbit: to be cynical, he could scarcely afford to do so, since paternity for a sovereign was a serious (financial) business. At the same time he honoured his genuine paternal obligations with a mixture of love and liberality.

The royal accounts include payments which have a distinctly nursery flavour – rattles, cradles and so forth. As the children grew older, more substantial sums were disbursed. In April 1684 Lady Mary Tudor, daughter of Moll Davis, received a suite of tapestry hangings, a looking-glass, a little crimson damask bed for country use, a bed of druggett for her gentlewoman, and for her chambermaid, laundry-maid, page and footman 150 ells of Holland to make six pairs of sheets. There were wedding expenses, which any father might expect to pay (the King's heart was in the right place: as we have seen over the wedding of Anne Fitzroy, he accepted the responsibility, even if payment came at a characteristically slow pace). There were dowries and allowances. As late as 1693 Charles Duke of Southampton was still being allotted an allowance of £6,000 a year.[32]

Where the emotions were concerned, so affectionate were the relations of Charles II with his illegitimate children that it was all the more regrettable that he should lack legitimate heirs. The next century would see disputes between royal father and son become the norm, not the exception. Since children tend to reproduce the family pattern they have experienced, a terrible chain reaction was set up. King and Prince of Wales were in constant conflict. The boy dreamt of by Queen Catharine in her delirium would have had a happier fate, since Charles II had always enjoyed delightful relations with Charles I. For that matter, Charles I had been greatly loved by his own father. The Stuarts, for all their weaknesses in other respects, made good parents; unlike the Hanoverians, they were characterized by warm family relationships. Charles II would have been an excellent father – within the marriage bond.

As it was, he did make an excellent father – but outside it. His blood courses down through the veins of the English aristocracy into the body of English life. His descendants, if not quite as numerous as the sands of the sea, are at any rate numerous enough for the line to be unlikely to die out. 'Six bastard Dukes survive his luscious Reign': so Defoe summed up the King's achievement; and it is a point often made today in attacks on the hereditary House of Lords that so many dukedoms derive from the *amours* of King Charles II.* Such critics would undoubtedly approve the contemporary satire of Marvell on the subject:

* But since the dukedoms were originally introduced into England and Scotland only for the King's sons, not for ordinary peers, Charles II was, in fact, behaving in an enlightened manner by not penalizing his sons for their illegitimate birth.

The misses take place, each advanced to be duchess
With pomp great as queens in their coach and six horses,
Their bastards make dukes, earls, viscounts and lords,
With all the title that honour affords...

In fact, six of the King's sons received nine dukedoms: Monmouth and Buccleuch for Lucy Walter's son; Southampton, Northumberland and Grafton and Cleveland, on her death, for Barbara's three boys; St Albans for Nelly's surviving son; Richmond and Lennox (joined together) for Louise's only child.* Monmouth's marriage to Anne Duchess of Buccleuch in her own right, led to the pair being created Duke and Duchess of Buccleuch in England jointly. After his death, Duchess Anne was allowed to retain her own Scottish Buccleuch title, although that of Monmouth was swallowed up in her husband's disgrace.

But Charles' daughters were not forgotten. Some were married off to lordlings, who were then further ennobled. Mary Tudor was granted the rank and precedence of a Duke's daughter at the same time as her step-brothers gained their coveted dukedoms. Two of the King's sons made political alliances – Henry Duke of Grafton married Arlington's daughter, and Charles Earl of Plymouth married the daughter of Danby.

Taken all in all, they were an agreeable bunch, with no real black sheep amongst them – unless one counts Monmouth. Out of a dozen children, that was not a bad record. It is true that none of them showed the exceptional calibre of their father, and what one must suppose to have been the exceptional talents of their mother in one direction at least. But then exceptional parents rarely breed exceptional children. Charles II's extraordinary qualities had been largely forged by adversity: these children enjoyed quite a different upbringing.

Nor can it be argued that the children of Charles II were noted for their waywardness. Charles Duke of Southampton and later Duke of Cleveland on his mother, Barbara's, death,

* Today four of these dukedoms still represent the quasi-royal line: Buccleuch (although Monmouth's own dukedom of Buccleuch is still under attainder), Grafton, St Albans, and Richmond and Lennox.

was described by her in one of her accesses of maternal disgust as a 'kockish idle boy' while at Oxford; and she sent for the Dean of Christ Church to tell him so.[33] But such undergraduate behaviour must be regarded as the rule, not the exception. Some of the girls were flighty: not only Anne Countess of Sussex but Mary Tudor, who married the Earl of Derwentwater, caused her husband distress. Yet such infidelities were hardly above the average for well-born ladies during this period. As for the King's favourite, the solace of his later years, Charlotte Countess of Lichfield, her sweetness and impeccable virtue bore out a pleasanter axiom: that an amoral mother will often produce a paragon of a daughter – for she was the offspring of the hot-tempered Barbara Duchess of Cleveland.

Charlotte Countess of Lichfield is one of those characters whose goodness survives differences of style and period to charm us still. Her appearance was appealing rather than beautiful: her mouth (like her father's) was too large and so were her eyes; her face and chin were too small. It was her personality rather than her looks which won hearts. Whether bearing and rearing her enormous family (at the age of nineteen she had four children and gave birth to a total of twenty), playing basset, crimp or billiards, going riding, adorning her houses, her attitude to life recalls that of Queen Charlotte a hundred years later: she wanted each day to bring its own pleasure.

She was married off in 1677 at the age of twelve, her husband being rewarded with the Lichfield title. The new Earl also received the more spiritual reward of great happiness. Together the Lichfields enjoyed a married life of forty-two years. Their shared monument in Spelsbury Church commemorates the fact that 'at their marriage they were the most grateful bridegroom and the most beautiful bride and that till death they remained the most constant husband and wife'.

To King Charles II, in a series of fond if scribbled notes often enclosing money, she was his 'dear Charlotte', as once Madame had been his 'dear sister'.[34] He was her 'loving' and at other times her 'kind' father. There is a vignette of Charlotte tickling the King's bald pate as he took his post-prandial nap. Other glimpses of family intimacy include fatherly advice on

Charlotte's building plans for a new house, which should not disturb those of her sister Anne, but 'I think it a very reasonable thing that other houses should not look into your house without your permission.' When Charlotte is pregnant, the King is delighted and hopes to see the child ere long; when they are apart, he is sorry he will be so long deprived of seeing his 'dear Charlotte'.

As for the boys, the King was proud of his fine brood of dukelings: Evelyn's wry pen gives a portrait of him receiving communion at Easter 1684 with Richmond, Northumberland and St Albans, 'sons of Portsmouth, Cleveland and Nelly', three boys on his right hand – and three bishops on his left. Barbara's second son, Henry – 'Harry' – Duke of Grafton, was rated the handsomest; he also pursued a career as a sailor. These two attributes were sometimes in conflict. 'Your brother Harry is now here and will go in a few days to Holland,' wrote the King to Charlotte. 'By the time he returns, he will have worn out in some measure the redness of his face, so as not to fright the most part of our ladies here.' Charles Earl of Plymouth – 'Don Carlo' – much resembled his father. Said to be 'a fine youth', he was authorized to raise Plymouth's Foot for Tangier; he died there in October 1680 before his promise could be fulfilled (he also left a mass of debts including tailors' bills, so his promise was not entirely military). But the Duke of Northumberland, Barbara's third son, he who had been born so festively at Merton College, Oxford, was generally considered to be the most like Charles – at eighteen he was 'a tall black man like his father the King'. Because he was also 'well-bred, civil and modest', Evelyn rated Northumberland the 'most accomplished and worth the owning' of Charles' children.[35]

Nelly's sons, one of whom died at the age of nine, and Louise's boy, belonged to a later period. They were duly ennobled after the frantic efforts of their mothers – Louise's son was only three when he was raised to the peerage – but were still only in their early teens at the time of their father's death.

In general, all the bastards were easily and unselfconsciously treated by their legitimate relatives, whether they pursued the Whig connection of William and Mary or the Jacobite one of

James. Their Stuart Christian names emphasized rather than diminished the connection: no fewer than four of the King's sons were named Charles, two of them James, and Barbara's third son, like the third son of King Charles I, was christened Henry and nicknamed Harry. The girls were Charlotte, a name otherwise hardly known in England at that date,* or Anne or Mary, the names of Stuart princesses. The King's daughter by Elizabeth Killigrew was named Charlotte Jemima (for James) Henrietta Maria, a Stuart mouthful. Surnames employed were unashamedly royal: Fitzcharles, Fitzroy, Tudor. The name of Crofts, taken from his guardian, was only used for Monmouth in the desperate days of exile, when a royal connection was not necessarily blazoned. (On his marriage to an heiress, Monmouth took his wife's surname of Scott.)

The Duke of York was particularly devoted to his niece, Charlotte Lichfield, and corresponded with her while he was in Scotland;[37] he also favoured Harry Duke of Grafton. Charlotte Jemima Henrietta Maria Fitzroy had a daughter by her first marriage, Stuarta Howard, who became a lady-in-waiting to Mary of Modena. Mary Tudor was the mother of the two Jacobite Earls of Derwentwater, who died respectively in 1715 and 1745 in the cause of their Stuart relations; they had been brought up as companions to James Edward, the so-called Old Pretender. Harry Duke of Grafton, on the other hand, supported William of Orange and was rewarded by being integrated into the Whig establishment; he died as a soldier under Marlborough's command in 1690.

The King was also extremely fond of Charles, Earl of Burford and then Duke of St Albans, surviving son of Nelly. He too was 'very pretty' in youth. There is evidence that Charles worried over Burford's education more than that of his other children: as though Louise, the *bien née*, could be trusted with that of her son (in fact she gave him the playwright Wycherley, Barbara's former lover, as a tutor), but Nelly, the girl of the people, could

* When the King was godfather to Sir George Carteret's daughter in Jersey the diarist Chevalier was at some pains to explain the derivation of the name Charlotte as being somewhat eccentric.[36]

not. In 1682 George Legge, the King's intimate, commented on the King's fondness for the boy: now he was of an age 'to be bred into the world', he was to be trusted to Lord Preston in France. Here the King wished him to study mathematics and the art of fortification (two of his own preoccupations), as well as observing the progress of Louis XIV (another of them). Nelly herself was torn between coveting this glorious future for her boy, and not wanting him to leave England before 'some settlement' had been made upon him.[38] Later Burford justified his father's faith by fighting the Turks in Hungary – his colonelcy was not to be regarded as a sinecure – and his mother's by marrying an heiress.

If the whole effect of the Popish Plot and its aftermath on Charles II was to bring about 'a severity in his disposition', this was the public monarch. Halifax later commented on this new sharpness, which we may suppose to be the outward sign of the inward decision to be yet bolder and firmer. He developed, says Halifax, 'a very peevish memory': in his anger, scarcely a blot escaped him.[39] In private the King's life was marked by new contentment as he grew older, and, in terms of good relations with his growing children, he led a life of richness which many men of his age might have envied.

CHAPTER TWENTY-FIVE

Another Way of Ruling

'I learnt from a Great Man, that we were in no Way of having a Parliament, there being some near the King, who advised him to another way of ruling the Kingdom.'

Sir John Reresby, *Memoirs*

Charles II spoke directly on the subject of government to Lord Bruce some time after the Oxford Parliament. He confided to him, 'I will have no more Parliaments unless it be for some necessary acts to be passed that are temporary only as to make new ones for the good of the nation, for,' he added, 'God be praised, my affairs are in so good a posture that I have no occasion to ask for supplies.'[1] In the winter of 1684 Sir John Reresby was informed by a certain 'Great Man' that there was no question of a Parliament, since those near the King had 'advised him to another way of ruling the Kingdom'.

Certainly in the last years of the life of Charles II another way of ruling was tried out. It was found highly satisfactory – from the King's point of view. The nation as a whole also enjoyed that happiness ordinary people are often content to desire, knowing too well the hideous possibilities of disruption which change brings in the lives of the lowly. The connection between prosperity and happiness being ever strong, it was relevant that England enjoyed a trade boom in the early 1680s. This boom, which has been traced in the customs figures, happily transformed the receipts from this source.[2]

Unaware of these blessings about to flow, Charles II took a firm line about his own finances. The French subsidies could be counted on to settle outstanding military needs. Where Court and personal expenditure was concerned, the value of economy – an unpleasant prospect, but anything to avoid having to call a Parliament – was recognized. Retrenchment in general was noted at the Court in the spring of 1682: the King was cutting down at his own table and that of everyone else, 'except that of the Maids of Honour to the Queen'. More painful to him must have been retrenchment in the number of his horses. The Queen herself played her part and remitted to him her marriage settlement for one year, 'so that his Majesty seems to have taken serious thoughts of endeavouring to live without subsidies from his Parliament', as an observer (correctly) commented.[3] It is true that the essential needs of a sovereign could not be transformed overnight; bills for beds, one of crimson and orange velvet and silver tissue, costing nearly a thousand pounds, continued to disfigure the accounts. There were new lodgings in Whitehall and a twelve-oared barge for the Queen in 1683.[4] This period also included a major building programme for a new royal palace. But that, as we shall see, was envisaged by the King more as a political move than as an architectural foray. The point remained that the King was by now taking the business of ruling without Parliament more seriously than ever before, even if it meant cutting down on the courses at his own table, the horses in his stable.

These were negative gestures. More positive and more practical were those measures taken to consolidate the political base of the monarchy. That these measures were deliberate is generally agreed. A rhyme of April 1684 summed up the angry astonishment in certain quarters at the turn-round in the royal fortunes:

> Who could have thought in '78 that we
> So much enslaved by '84 should be.[5]

The extent to which the King himself took an active interest in extending his own powers is more difficult to assess. This royal leopard did not choose to change his protective spots of apparent laziness and even indifference. Under the circumstances, it is certainly possible to make a case for the Duke of York as the master-mind of this absolutist trend.[6] James returned from Scotland for good in June 1682. He had made a brief return in March, but headed north again to fetch his Duchess. It was a disastrous expedition. On the way back James and his entire party was shipwrecked off Yarmouth with much loss of life, although as James himself rather callously remarked, no one 'of quality' was drowned. The opportunity was given to his enemies to spread the canard by which James had thought only of saving his strongbox, his priests and his dogs. James himself was in fact more guilty of an obstinate and characteristic refusal to abandon ship in face of danger. It was his entourage who beat off the desperate 'lesser' passengers with their swords.[7]

In Scotland James had conducted affairs justly enough by the standards of a troubled time. His administration brought about calm in the Highlands – no mean achievement – and he also coped competently with the Scottish militia and all the problems of Scottish finance. A new Oath of Allegiance imposed upon all officials the necessity of upholding the Protestant religion (from London the King approved it). That hit the extreme Covenanters. But the Catholic minority – who were not officials in the first place – were able to live in unofficial peace. James also approved of much in the Scottish spirit and law, including the fact that the death penalty was imposed for perjury. As he told his niece Charlotte Lichfield grimly: 'If it had been so in England so many innocent people had not suffered.'[8] The only exception to the orderly quality of his rule was his clumsy attempt to eliminate the Earl of Argyll. This ended with the Earl's escape and the Duke's red face.

In England James was not without natural sympathizers. He had for example employed the powers of patronage he possessed in the Army both widely and wisely. Many of the bright sparks of the day owed their advancement to the Duke of York, including John Churchill, George Legge, Sir Charles Lyttleton and Henry Jermyn. His native honesty and courage won respect, as they had done throughout his career (although his father's 'peremptoriness', so different from the affability of Charles II, was detected in his manner).

James' climb back to favour and power is one of the features of the reign's end. By the beginning of 1684 Sir John Reresby commented that the Duke 'did now chiefly manage affairs', adding another dig at his 'haughtiness'. By the end of that year, James' 'indefatigability' at the King's side was generally remarked. James had certainly always possessed more obvious indefatigability that his brother, who took care to show as little as possible of this worrisome quality. From there it was a short step to assuming that James was actually deciding on the direction government should take.

But the case for James as master-mind is not proved. The fact was that James' ideas and policies were now convenient to the King. James, for example, approved in his memoirs that campaign for calling in corporations' charters begun in 1680 and shortly to be stepped up: 'His Majesty had at last taken those vigorous counsels, and resolute methods the Duke had so long pressed him to.'[9] James had been keen on such measures in the sixties – without success. That still did not mean he was responsible for the new initiative. It was Charles who decided when the time was ripe. The indefatigable James was allowed his hand on the tiller just because he was guaranteed to steer the ship in the direction his brother now approved. It was in this way that the royal brothers drew closer and closer together, just as they had grown apart when James had shown himself a liability to Charles. Charles respected his brother but he did not fear him. He had been the senior partner all their lives; he did not desert that position now.

If James' 'absolutism' is rejected, there is an alternative explanation of the events of the King's later years: that Charles sank into happy cynicism, now that things were going well in the short term, leaving all to his younger ministers. It is an attitude summed up not so much by the prophecy of Louis XV – '*Après moi le déluge*' – as a more devil-may-care '*Après moi je m'en fou* . . .'. Neither attitude – reliance on James or indifference – seems however to accord psychologically with the decisive, vigorous and above all cheerful King who dismissed the Oxford Parliament; nor with the wily sovereign who would play a subtle hand at foreign policy during the next few years.

Implicitly Charles II agreed with the doctrine of Sir Robert Filmer, posthumously published in the 1680s, that a king was a father of his people.[10] Even Charles I had not adhered to Filmer's extreme doctrines concerning Divine Right; and, where Divine Right was concerned, Charles II certainly did not. But when Filmer wrote that 'anarchy is nothing else than a broken monarchy, where every man is his own monarch or governor', his words found an echo in the breast of Charles II. They also of course found an echo in the hearts of the people. The King instinctively appealed to those sentiments aptly phrased by Oliver Goldsmith eighty years later. Goldsmith denigrated the great Whig leaders who

> blockade the throne,
> Contracting regal power to stretch their own...
> When I behold a factious band agree
> To call it freedom when themselves are free...
> I fly from petty tyrants to the throne.

As a father, Charles II had not yet abdicated his responsibilities.

In May 1682 the King endured another bout of illness, but, as in previous years, he gave the appearance of a complete recovery. Once restored to health, the pattern of exercise was unabated, including such famous killers of the middle-aged as tennis games with much younger men. He rode and hawked as before. Buck-hunting remained a passion: in the course of his sport he was able to introduce his Italian sister-in-law, Mary of Modena, to the English countryside, including Dorset and one of its jewels, the hunting retreat at Cranborne.[11] Physically, this was not a monarch in decline: whatever sharp warnings of the future were being administered in the shape of these attacks, they were intermittent signals delivered to a still active man. There is no reason to suppose that, mentally, the King was in decline either.

People saw what they wanted to see. Where Reresby witnessed the Duke's indefatigability at the expense of his brother's indolence, Roger North, writing the life of his brother Lord Keeper Guilford, described quite a different phenomenon: how the King, after his various illnesses at Windsor, 'appeared to be more considerative, and grew more sensible of the niceties of State Government, than he had been before, especially relating to the Treasury'. Charles' words to Burnet – spoken with regard to his championship of Catharine – will be recalled; in the autumn of 1678 he described himself as having led a bad life which he now wished to amend. He was 'breaking himself of all his faults'.[12] Among those faults it is plausible to suppose that he listed a lack of interest in the *minutiae* of government. 'Another way of ruling' represented his own attempt to redirect his energies. And in so far as the Duke of York and ministers gave to outsiders the air of being in control, it was because their thoughts and policies coincided with those of the King.

The attempt to secure a friendly judiciary was an essential part of 'another way of ruling'. For all the indignation of the Whigs, the calibre of the new men was not low.[13] Thomas Raymond, Edmund Saunders, Robert Atkins and Francis Pemberton, Evelyn's 'very learnedest of the judges', were all estimable appointments. What they did share however, and share with the Crown, was the view that their tenure sprang from that Crown and depended upon it. Once again the King was taking advantage of tradition, the judiciary merely failing to flout it. (It is however that kind of flouting which leads to progress.)

Most significant of all was the appointment of the Chief Justice, Francis North, as Lord Keeper in succession to Lord Nottingham in December 1682 (North was created Lord Guilford the following year). North was a good man and a distinguished judge: the manner in which he swayed the trial of Stephen College to secure the desired guilty verdict in August 1681 was probably the only blot on his career. But he was famous for his loyalty to the royal prerogative. It was his declared opinion that 'a Man could not be a good lawyer and honest, but he must be a Prerogative Man. So Plain were the Law Books in these cases.'[14]

In 1683 Jeffreys, not such an agreeable man, succeeded as Chief Justice on the death of Sir Edmund Saunders. Under his presidency, the King's Bench began to produce the pro-governmental verdicts for which the King and his *coterie* hoped.[15] By the end of 1683 eleven judges had been removed – at the King's wish – and a new model judiciary had come into being. It is true that the difficulty the King experienced in getting Danby released would show that this new model was not totally subservient. But as Guilford's words on the prerogative amply demonstrated, their hearts – and their judgements – were in the right place.

The other angle to any verdict was provided by the jury. It was here that the great weakness of the King's flank had been demonstrated in his attack on Shaftesbury: the City of London continued to throw up Whig juries, because juries were 'pricked' or chosen by the sheriffs and the London sheriffs were Whigs. At midsummer 1682 Tory sheriffs were duly elected, although the skulduggery of the manoeuvres involved did not bear inspection.

More charters of corporations were called in, along the lines referred to earlier in chapter 23, whenever some light excuse of misdemeanour could be found to justify it. The excuse given for calling in the charter of York had at least a nice period touch to it. The Lord Mayor was said to have refused a mountebank permission to erect a stage, although the fellow had been recommended by the King himself.[16]

In the last year of the King's life, towns in the four corners of England were included in those who lost their original charters. Colchester, Swansea, Lyme Regis and Wigan ... east and west and south and north the King's messengers, like those of Lars Porsena, went forth. On occasion the arrival of the new charter was greeted with loyal demonstrations which underlined the popularity of the settled regime, or at least of a skilful Royalist mayor; at seaside Lyme there were all-night bonfires and great shouts of 'God save the King and the Royal family.' Elsewhere, at Berwick and at Malmesbury, for example, there was a disturbing air of resentment.[17]

The varied popular reaction was less important than the fact that the warrants on the new charters all contained the vital clause which gave the King a veto over the election of the officers. Suitable Tory figures locally would see to it that equally suitable Tory figures were returned to Westminster – if the occasion ever arose.

The apex of this campaign was the great struggle to secure the charter of the City of London. It was said that the Common Council there had imposed an illegal tax at the time of the rebuilding of London after the Great Fire; and, furthermore, the Council had sent in a disrespectful petition in 1680. In June 1683 the Court of the King's Bench voted that, consequent upon these heinous acts, the charter should be put in the King's hands. At last, as Jeffreys put it, 'the King of England is likewise King of London'. By 1684 the charters of the Livery Companies in the City of London, including the Plumbers, Goldsmiths, Grocers and Apothecaries, were being surrendered with petitions for their renewal.[18]

About the same time as the collapse of the City's independence, the Convocation of Oxford University passed a decree condemning 'certain pernicious books and damnable doctrines, destructive to the sacred person of princes, their state and government, and of all human society'. The decree only survived until 1688.[19] Since it explicitly denied that there was any compact between a prince and the people, that a prince forfeited his right to rule through misgovernment, and that civil authority itself was in any way derived from the people, it represented a highwater mark of Royalist theory.

In the country the Crown's approaches, if more subtly deployed, were twofold. Authority over the country magistrates was built up, and so long as care was exercised not to infuriate the local magnates, the King was able to re-emphasize his right to appoint and dismiss Lords Lieutenant.

A Commission for Ecclesiastical Preferments was set up in 1681 to review appointments. These were monitored carefully, both by William Sancroft, Archbishop of Canterbury, and by the King's minister Rochester. Their conservative (as opposed to Catholic) tenor was illustrated by the fact that many of them had connections with the Duke of York. Francis Turner, Bishop of Ely, had been his personal chaplain, as had William Thomas at Worcester; Thomas White, Bishop of Peterborough, had been chaplain to Anne Duchess of York. For the Duke of York, as a political figure, continued to represent a kind of solid conservatism at variance with his actual religious beliefs.

In the last year of his life the King even revoked this commission. He resumed a free hand in the election of bishops, and as there were a notable amount of sees falling vacant, received an ideal opportunity to strengthen the number of his personal nominees (such as Thomas Ken, his chaplain, and Thomas Sprat, Dean of Westminster) in bishoprics.

The printed word continued to be regarded as the dragon's teeth. Francis Smith was put in the pillory in June 1684 for disseminating that famous and gross libel, 'The Raree Show'. Savage penalties were extended to James Holloway in April of the same year for that astonished rhyme on the change-round in the royal fortunes already quoted. On 17 December 1684 Sunderland, on behalf of the King, granted to Roger L'Estrange, as Surveyor or Overseer of the stationers, the power to stop 'these intolerable liberties of the press', with the right to search and seize.[20] Yet it should be pointed out that the mere existence of such blanket ordinances and their reiteration showed that censorship – like the control of the judiciary – was far from complete.

Nor was England subjected to more restrictions than the rest of Europe in this respect and at this date. As with all other aspects of an absolute rule, she still lagged behind.

The first real effects of these policies were felt in the King's handling of the so-called Rye House Plot of the spring of 1683. The Whigs as a whole were quiescent after the disbanding of the Oxford Parliament – it is notable that only a few ardent members of the Green Ribbon Club played any part in events after 1681. The autumn of 1682 went without the flickering fires and raucous cries of the great Pope-burnings of recent years: such political conflagrations were now banned. The streets were patrolled to make the ban effective.[21]

The Whig leaders however could not bring themselves to regard the question of the succession as solved. In the late July of 1681 William of Orange had paid a visit to London. But the Whigs as a whole were still not converted to the concept of

William as sole candidate for the Protestant succession. For his part, the King deliberately contributed to the confusion. He prevented William from dining with the Whig faction in the City by the simple means of inviting him to dinner at Windsor on the same date.

The increased cordiality between the King of England and the Prince of Orange was gloomily noted by the Whigs; nor was William's attitude to his uncle of York sufficiently hostile to be satisfactory. Thus the taint of Stuart authoritarianism had not been removed from William in the Whig view. William, for his part, was not in a mood to be particularly accommodating. He calculated that a man who stood to become an English King one day (through his wife) had no motive for becoming a Whig pawn in advance.

So the most active Whigs continued to concentrate on Monmouth, fearing the painted devil of William. This support, in particular the growing embroilment of Shaftesbury, took place despite ominous signs of the King's official disfavour towards his son. These only thickened between the summer of 1681 and the spring of 1683.

The dashing Duke – he could no longer truly be counted as young, being now older than his father had been at his Restoration – had not ceased to trail his coat in the last few years; he had learned nothing from his father's public fury. When Monmouth ostentatiously stood bail for Shaftesbury, that increased the King's ire to the point where, with equal ostentation, he gave offices previously occupied by Monmouth to his half-brothers Richmond and Grafton. Then there was the matter of the Chancellorship of Cambridge University. Monmouth was removed from this in April 1682, by royal injunction, and his portrait burnt.

Yet throughout 1682 Monmouth continued to fly high. He tried, for example, to eliminate Halifax from his father's counsels by accusing him of prejudice against him, and, failing in that, challenged Halifax to a duel. The King coldly sided with Halifax. Monmouth was treated as a pariah by the Court. Then Monmouth resorted to his previous habit of making a progress in the country, with all the panache of the true-born prince he believed himself to be. The progress turned out no better than the challenge to Halifax, for on 20 September Monmouth was arrested at Stafford, allegedly disturbing the public peace, and brought to London. He was then banned altogether from appearing at Court.

It was some time in the summer of 1682 that the Rye House Plot was hatched. A certain confusion of aim existed from the first, and persisted in the matured plot. There were those, like Shaftesbury, who believed in a series of risings in the country – as did Monmouth. But there were also those who were republicans, like Algernon Sidney – as Monmouth was of course not. The matter of assassination was particularly clouded in mystery. Afterwards Monmouth swore that he had never agreed to any plot which necessitated the killing of his father – 'I wish I may die this moment I am writing if ever it entered into my head' – he had on the contrary worked to distract the conspirators from this heinous course by concentrating on the possibility of risings.[22] It seems only fair to accept Monmouth's word: he was weak and vain but not without affection for the father who had done much for him.

On 28 September the fateful election of Tory sheriffs in the City of London convinced Shaftesbury that he was once more in serious danger from the King, and this time he might find it more difficult to wriggle out of a tight corner. It was a development which had been predicted in advance of the election in 'Advice to the City', a famous burlesque by Thomas D'Urfey, set to music by Signor Opidar. Its Tory sentiments so enchanted the King that he sang it with D'Urfey himself at Windsor, leaning familiarly on his shoulder and holding a corner of the paper. The opening lines were enough to commend themselves:

> Remember ye Whiggs what was formerly done,
> Remember your mischiefs in forty and one [1641]...
> When cap was aloft and low was the crown
> The rabble got up and nobles went down....

The chorus was equally rousing:

Then London be wise and baffle their power
And let them play the old game no more.
Hang, hang up the sheriffs, those barons in power,
Those popular thieves, those rats of the tower....

As for 'Tony' – Anthony Lord Shaftesbury – the rabbles' 'speaker', the song went on: 'He knows if we prosper that he must run....'[23] And so it proved. 'Tony' did run. He went into hiding for a few weeks and then fled to convenient Holland. In Holland the sickness which had so long threatened but not sweetened Shaftesbury at last overcame him: he died in January 1683. If he had personally advocated a rising in England, he certainly left it without making any practical plans concerning troops and money.

Shaftesbury had a notion of the after-life which is uncharacteristically romantic to our ears: he believed that the souls of men entered stars after death and animated them. If so, then the star animated by the soul of Shaftesbury was sure to be brilliant; one feels that it might also cause trouble in the galaxy. In England, the tangled webs left behind by Shaftesbury found public expression in the Rye House Plot.

The Plot took its name from the Hoddesdon, Hertfordshire home of one Richard Rumbold, who long before had acted as a guard at the execution of Charles I. The Rye House (its previous owner, whose widow Rumbold married, had been a maltster) was conveniently sited from an assassin's point of view, for it lay at a peculiarly narrow point on the Newmarket road. The bones of this particular plot seem to have consisted of a plan to 'lop' both King and Duke of York on their way to or from their sporting retreat. It went wrong, as such brilliant ideas often do, as a result of a fortuitous accident: a fire made the royal brothers leave Newmarket early.[24] The alleged plot, having been put off, was then betrayed.

So far there might seem nothing earth-shaking in an unsuccessful move towards a double assassination – for, as we have seen, the King's life was regarded as generally under threat, like that of any modern head of state, and the Catholic Duke of York was certainly not without enemies. The importance of the

Rye House Plot derived from the involvement of the Whig leaders. That gave an extra nightmare quality to the violent daydreams of certain old Cromwellians.

Both Lord Russell and Algernon Sidney were arrested; Lord Grey of Werke escaped. The latter was a zealous Exclusionist and an avowed supporter of Monmouth. His private life was as colourful as that of some of the Wits: he had eloped with his sister-in-law and was tried for the offence. William Russell, the Whig aristocrat who intrigued with the Catholic Louis XIV as and when it suited his own best interests, had seconded the Exclusion Bill in March 1681. Algernon Sidney, the proud self-confessed republican or 'Commonwealthsman', as he significantly termed himself, had only narrowly escaped condemnation as a regicide in 1660. After wanderings abroad he had just returned to England in time to plague the King with his joyous support of Exclusion in 1677.

A colleague whose implication in the plot deeply distressed the King was Essex, once his serious and respected minister. Essex committed suicide. The King exclaimed that he would not have demanded his death when he heard the news.

'I owed him a life!' he said, referring to the execution of Essex's father, the Royalist hero Arthur Capel, thirty years before.[25]

The existence of the plot was only discovered officially at the beginning of June. It was convenient timing. As with the alleged plots against the life of Queen Elizabeth, so deftly handled by Walsingham, the sovereign's life was wonderfully preserved without having been actually endangered. Popular sympathy was however in proportion to the peril averted rather than the ordeal endured. From Holland, William of Orange hastened to send his own favourite, Bentinck, with a message of congratulations to his uncles on their joint escape. It is highly unlikely that he had been implicated in the plot himself;[26] but he was personally embarrassed by the presence of certain of the escaped conspirators in Holland, and wished to make the point of his continued Stuart loyalties.

Of those actively participating, Monmouth assuredly fared the best. The King himself took the line that Monmouth's involvement was, like his personality, showy without being deep. In July a Grand Jury found against Monmouth and a reward was offered for his capture. However, nothing too energetic was done to secure this. Monmouth was allowed to skulk in hiding at the home of his mistress Henrietta Wentworth (she to whom he considered himself married in the eyes of God), while the other conspirators were subjected to trial. At the instigation of Halifax, the King was soon prepared to stretch out his arms to his errant son once more. Monmouth's wife, Duchess Anne, also wrote piteously in his favour: 'So I hope your Majesty will not refuse to accept any of that entire submission and great penitence from him, which your goodness would not perhaps deny to another man."[27] In view of Monmouth's behaviour as a husband, it was indeed gracious behaviour on her part.

At first the King received Monmouth with displeasure: but to observers it was 'the displeasure of a parent who seeks the reformation of his child'. The trouble was that Monmouth did not give much genuine proof of this reformation. Although he wrote two penitent letters (probably drawn up by Halifax), he jibbed at any further confession concerning his associates.[28] Monmouth was also determined that his recantation should not be made public. The King however was disgusted that his generosity should be met by quibbling. Monmouth was not allowed to get away with his partial submission. Eventually he flounced off to the Continent, where William of Orange took the opportunity to stir the pot – and stir up family trouble – by entertaining him.

This new toughness towards Monmouth has been ascribed to the Duke of York.[29] Yet as indulged children learn to their cost, even the mildest parent may reach a turning-point. In his heart of hearts the King probably loved his spoiled son as much as ever. In 1682 a play by Nathaniel Lee, *The Duke of Guise*, had been banned because it was rated an attack on Monmouth: it was remarked at the time that 'though his Majesty's pleasure is to be dissatisfied and angry with the Duke of Monmouth yet he is not willing that others should abuse him out of natural affection for him'. Nevertheless, the King had been cut to the quick by Monmouth's defiant action in going bail for his avowed enemy Shaftesbury. Immediately afterwards, at the launching of a ship at Deptford, he was seen to be 'very serious and more concerned than the greatest business did usually make him'.[30]

By 1683 Charles II, sadly profiting by experience, had decided that there was no peace while Monmouth was around. That progress the previous year would have been interpreted as a rebellion in a jumpier age; the Tudors, for example, would have made short work of a claimant to the throne who gallivanted around the country accompanied by an armed retinue, showing himself gorgeously to the people. Money, the parent's panacea, was not withheld for ever. The next year Monmouth was granted an annuity of £6,000 a year. But a lawful return from the Continent was denied to him.

The truth was that both Monmouth's personality and his position were against him. One of James' biographers has suggested that he might have quoted to his brother about this time the words of Prince Hal to Henry IV:[31]

> My due from thee is this imperial crown,
> Which, as immediate from thy place and blood,
> Derives itself to me...

Had James done so, Charles II would have respected the sentiment. So long as Monmouth was allowed to parade or intrigue in England, he ever served as a magnet to draw towards him the forces of dissent; and he lacked within himself the strength to resist such temptations.

As it was, Monmouth left behind him an uncle triumphant in the shape of the Duke of York. For James himself was now popularly felt to be a wronged man: he stood for the old values of monarchy and strength. When some Scholars of St Paul's School (headed by Lord Dartmouth's son) thanked the Duke of York for getting them a 'Play Day' (by Colet's statutes only to be granted by the sovereign or an ecclesiastic), James genially told their 'very Master to be careful to teach them their duty to the Church and Crown'. The very existence of the Rye House conspirators proved these bulwarks were under attack.

The glory of the British line
Old Jimmy's come again!

So ran a song of the time. Burnet commented angrily on the 'indecent courting and magnifying' of the Duke of York which took place.[32] Demonstrations of joy began to greet his appearances, similar to those which greeted Monmouth, but in direct opposition to them.

The King seized the hour: 'It is plain that an Handle was taken from that Discovery – i.e., of the Plot, to let in the Duke of York,' wrote a contemporary.[33] A declaration of 28 July 1683 gave the King's official view of the recent plot and his escape: 'Divine Providence which hath preserved us through the whole course of our life, hath at this time, in an extraordinary manner, showed itself in the wonderful and gracious deliverance of us, and our dearest brother, and all our loyal subjects, from this horrid and damnable conspiracy.' On 9 September a public Thanksgiving Day was held for the King's lucky escape. But Divine Providence had done even better than the King admitted. Once the uncovering of plots had cast the English nation into a state of neurotic panic on the subject of Popery. Now, as the State Papers plenteously reveal, plots were used to justify measures of repression. Monmouth may have been treated with mercy: Lord Russell and Algernon Sidney were not.

It is doubtful whether these conspirators had actually done much more than talk among themselves – albeit treasonable talk. Both Russell and Sidney admitted that they had declared it was lawful to resist the King on occasion, while denying they had converted words into deeds. But in their different ways they represented the elements most resented by the King in the Whig faction.

Russell's trial in July, presided over by Pemberton, did at least conform to the rules of justice at the time: Roger North in his autobiography cited it as an example of the fairness then to be found in English courts. Russell was executed, despite the intercession of his family and Louise Duchess of Portsmouth (who was paid to do so); pleas were even addressed to Louis XIV, via Barrillon, to save him – but in vain. When George

Legge gave a list of reasons for leniency, the King replied tersely: 'All that is true, but it is as true that if I do not take his life he will soon have mine.' The King was also said to have cast 'a sarcastical eye' towards the trial of Lord Stafford when Russell was condemned to a simple beheading; far more barbarous penalties had been demanded for Stafford and only commuted on the King's edict. Charles listened to Bishop Burnet's account of Russell's death in silence.[34]

The same fairness was not exhibited towards Sidney in November. In the interval between the two trials Saunders had been replaced by Jeffreys as Chief Justice of the King's Bench, as part of the reorganization of the judiciary. (Jeffreys had merely prosecuted Russell, not presided.) Jeffreys interrupted Sidney in a shocking manner; while his loaded summing-up brought no credit either to him or the royal system which had introduced him to the office. Sidney died on 7 December; according to the Duke of York, he met his end 'very stoutly and like a true republican' – the ungrudging admiration of one iron man for another.[35] Sidney protested the illegality of his trial, but declared that all the same he was prepared to die for the 'old cause' – the Commonwealth – fighting for which he had spent his youth.

The situation in Europe did not remain as stable as the English, otherwise engaged, might have hoped. Charles II had more than ever a strong motive for desiring European peace. The aggressive martial policies of Louis XIV continued to threaten the United Provinces – that he could bear; but the potential threat to his own French set-up was another matter. If Louis showed himself all-invading, there would be demands for military action on the part of England which Charles might find it very difficult to refuse. At the same time such military action (which no French subsidy could cover) would necessitate the recall of Parliament.

That was not a consummation to be wished by Charles II, nor for that matter by Louis XIV. But at least the French King's known distaste for an English Parliament and English military action offered the English King a possible way out of his predicament. Charles II could hold Louis XIV's advances in check by the threat of calling a Parliament. The English King was back in the world of the diplomatic see-saw on which he had balanced so successfully in the 1670s; in both cases the existence of a secret French subsidy added to the complexity of the situation.

The blockade of Luxembourg by Louis XIV in late 1681 provided an instance of Charles II's poise. Charles spoke firmly to Barrillon. He would be most reluctant to call a Parliament – 'they are devils who want my ruin' – but might yet be obliged to do so, 'if an expedient is not found over the Luxembourg affair'. 'Please tell the king my brother,' he begged Barrillon, 'to relieve me of my embarrassment.'[36]

It is doubtful whether Charles would in fact have called a Parliament. Too many things militated against it. Yet by the spring of 1682 Louis XIV had lifted the blockade of Luxembourg and was requesting Charles II to arbitrate between the various warring nations. It is true that Spain (England's ally, according to the most recent treaty negotiated by Sunderland) refused to accept Charles' arbitration. He was obliged to draw back. Still, Charles had not lost his balance on the European see-saw. Neither one King – Louis XIV – nor five hundred – the English Parliament – had managed to upset it.

What would now be termed the life-style of King Louis XIV continued to impress Charles II, as it impressed all Europe. We have seen how Charles' royal guards were an imitation of his cousin's. The King had laid out his parks and gardens in the grand French manner displayed by Le Nôtre. Now, on 23 March 1683, the foundation stone for a new royal palace was laid in England.

Nothing on a similar scale had been planned for years: the work at Greenwich begun at the start of the reign had never been completed and life at Newmarket had been conducted on altogether a more modest scale. The palace at Winchester owed its origin directly to Charles II's admiration for splendiferous Versailles and in design it resembled the work of Le Vaux there.[37] Its geographical site in southern England also fitted in with the concept 'of another way of ruling'.

The love affair with Newmarket, begun in the halcyon sixties, had faded. The trouble was that Newmarket lay in an area already dotted with the great palaces of the Whig lords. There was no way that the King could cut a more imposing figure than his own nobility, since all the available land had already been commandeered. The fire in his Newmarket lodgings which had enabled him to elude the Rye House assassination gave him an excuse to look elsewhere; the connection of this conspiracy and the Newmarket route was in any case an uncomfortable one. The King's eye fell on Winchester, which lay in the balmy south in Hampshire: an area where – on the whole – men and magnates were Royalists. More romantically, Winchester was on the way to that coast and those coastal towns, including Portsmouth, which nursed the Navy. Like many an enthusiast since, the King could go yachting off the Isle of Wight. The King expected to be able to see the fleet at Spithead from his projected palace; what fairer prospect?

The dwelling, designed by Sir Christopher Wren, was to be surrounded by a park and connected to the town's historic cathedral by a 'stately street'. It would lie east and west. There were to be 160 rooms, surmounted by a lofty cupola which would be visible from the sea. The grand staircase was to be ornamented with marble columns, a gift to the King from the Duke of Tuscany. Then there were to be a central portico and two wings, as well as a raised terrace all the way round, such as dignified Windsor Castle. As for the park, here a thirty-foot cascade was proposed; the King hoped to repeat his success with ornamental water in St James's Park. A river through the park was intended to be navigable by small vessels. The park itself, an eight-mile circuit, would open into the forest, suitable for stag-hunting. Back at the palace, stables, kennels and mews would house the equipment of the chase.[38]

In September 1682 Evelyn described the King as 'mightily pleased' by his plans; building began the following May. He intended Winchester, wrote Evelyn, to be the seat of 'autumnal field diversions' (as Newmarket had once been).[39] Long before the structure became habitable, the Court flocked down to the grave and charming cathedral town. They devoured it for lodgings, as once they had raided Oxford, producing an atmosphere of revelry reminiscent of Comus' rout. The houses of the

Cathedral clergy were not immune. During the King's early visits he lodged with the Bishop of the town, to the extent that a polite enquiry was made whether he intended to make the Bishop's house his inn.

A King was one thing but a mistress was another. When a new Bishop was needed for Winchester, it was made clear to the incoming incumbent that his duties included lodging his sovereign. But Thomas Ken was furious at the sacrilege of being asked to house Nell Gwynn. He considered it sacrilege on the not unreasonable grounds that 'a woman of ill-repute ought not to be endured in the house of a clergyman,' adding, 'least of all that of the King's chaplain'. Ken's fervour did him no harm. Later, when the bishopric of Bath and Wells fell empty, Charles recalled the incident – 'God's fish! the little black fellow who would not give poor Nelly a night's lodging' – and laughingly approved Ken's appointment. As for Nell Gwynn, she found a niche at the deanery, overruling further protests.[40]

In the last year of the King's life virtually the whole of September was spent at Winchester. Considerable expenses were also run up for furniture for the future for both King and Queen; for example, green damask chairs and stools embroidered in gold and white silk were ordered for Catharine, green remaining a favourite colour. The main expense was of course the structure itself. Only a shell had been completed when the King died – outside walls and a roof – but various payments had been authorized, although, in the general fashion of the time, not necessarily paid. The £90,000 found in the King's strong-box after his death was probably intended for this purpose. It was indeed expense rather than distaste for the new palace which caused James to halt building immediately on his brother's death. He probably intended to return to it at a leisure moment in his reign: but such a moment never arrived.

So Winchester Palace lingered on, the subject of vague royal plans from time to time. Queen Anne contemplated it as a residence for her consort Prince George of Denmark; in the end the financial demands of her foreign wars took precedence. French prisoners-of-war were incarcerated there in the middle of the eighteenth century, and in the Napoleonic wars the quondam palace was used as a barracks. At the end of the nineteenth century it finally burnt down. It was a melancholy end for a project which had once been intended to rival Versailles; at least the Versailles imitation of Ludwig of Bavaria, Herrenchiemsee, survives on its island, more substantial if equally melancholy.

The true memorial to Winchester Palace lies in the eager conversation of Charles II with Lord Bruce on one of the last evenings of his life. The King spoke with enthusiasm of the 'favourite castle' he was building, and how he would arrange for Bruce to be in waiting there. 'I shall be so happy this week as to have my house covered with lead,' he exclaimed.[41] As the King's body was wrapped in its lead coffin within the week, it was a prophecy – of the ambiguous sort beloved of the Greek oracle – that came grimly true.

In the last years of Charles II, his restless mind did not cease to turn over new schemes, explore new horizons. Less power-obsessed, more fruitful than Winchester Palace was another foundation – that of the Royal Hospital, Chelsea, in 1682.[42] This home for veteran soldiers, or for those incapacitated by wounds, was created directly on the model of the Kilmainham Hospital, Dublin, recommended by Sir Stephen Fox to the King. The site of Chelsea College, which had been founded by James I for controversialists against Catholicism and had then been granted to the Royal Society, was purchased for £1,300. Fox put up the money. Yet even here the influence of Louis XIV was felt: Monmouth, describing to his father the Hôtel des Invalides, a similar form of hostel built in 1670 in Paris, had also ignited his imagination.[43] In-Pensioners, as the residents were termed, were to be organized on military lines, and occupy a single quadrangle known as Figure Court. (The Royal Hospital today is considerably expanded, although Figure Court still exists.)

The Royal Hospital was not opened until 1692, by which date Charles II had been seven years in his house of lead. It fell into the kind of financial difficulties which might be expected and the money granted in maintenance proved hard to come by. Nevertheless, Founder's Day was regularly celebrated on 29

May – Oak Apple Day and the King's Birthday – in honourable acknowledgement of his part in it all.*

Not only the welfare of his Army and the well-being of his fleet were dear to the King's heart. He had other far-flung interests. In general, the reign of Charles II saw a remarkable accession of distant lands to the English flag. The great Hudson's Bay Company was founded in 1670. Not only in North America, but in the West Indies and West Africa, this was an age of territorial expansion and, above all, commercial energy. Along with his concern for soldiers and sailors, this nascent feeling for 'empire' was something which Charles II had in common with his great predecessor Cromwell. So unalike in so many ways, the two men shared a vague missionary feeling for the benefits of British rule extended, which was in its own fashion a kind of patriotism. In the case of Charles II, his curiosity drove him on, even if he did not understand the economic implications of colonial aggrandizement.

In India, for example, it was the great trading companies which were the sovereigns, not Charles II. The latter was quite content to hand over Queen Catharine's dowry of Bombay, which it had taken several years to possess owing to local opposition, to the East India Company. In April 1681 Charles II granted a vast tract of land, now Pennsylvania, to William Penn the Quaker – no doubt a far more congenial activity than his disbanding of the Oxford Parliament, which took place about the same time, particularly as it was in discharge of a Crown debt. He liked to hear details of life in the Carolinas, where busy colonists were enjoying a more fruitful kind of exile than he had known. Life in Tangier, because of its military importance, was something he could probably understand more readily; he took the eventual evacuation of the fortress hard.

At home in July 1683 there took place a royal event which might even, had Providence decreed, have granted one final

* The actual date changed; first it was too close to the birthday of George III on 4 June; then, in the 1920s, it was too close to the Chelsea Flower Show, celebrated in its grounds. Founder's Day and its Parade is now held on the Thursday of the first week in June.

satisfaction: a peaceful future for the monarchy. This was the marriage of James' daughter Anne to Prince George of Denmark. In this same year Bishop Burnet had made 'a melancholy speculation' on the withering of the Protestant succession in 'this family that [once] put forth so fair and promising a blossom'.[44] It was true that at the time of Anne's marriage the legitimate succession, Protestant or Catholic, was problematic. As had happened once before to the royal family of Stuart in Scotland, the harvest of descendants of James I had suddenly become a very meagre one; this despite the fruitful marriages of Charles I and Elizabeth of Bohemia, with six and thirteen surviving children respectively.

The two Catholic daughters of Madame were as yet childless: Marie Louise was married without children and Anne Marie, from whom Madame's line descends, did not marry until the following year. The Catholic Mary Beatrice Duchess of York had not yet succeeded in producing offspring who survived childhood. As for the Protestants, Mary of Orange had been married for six years and showed no signs of producing any heirs. The vast family of Elizabeth of Bohemia had proved itself as yet astonishingly infertile: the Elector Palatine was childless, while one sister had succeeded Madame as the next Duchesse d'Orléans, which put her within the unsuitable French Catholic orbit. Prince Rupert had died a bachelor at the end of the previous year.

The hand of the eligible Anne had been sought within England itself, notably by the Earl of Mulgrave. The King angrily snubbed his pretensions. An outside claimant was the Prince of Hanover, the son of Anne's youngest Palatine cousin the Electress Sophia (from his line, ironically enough, was to spring Anne's own successor). George of Denmark was widely rated to be a French-inspired choice, because the King of Denmark fell within the diplomatic network controlled by Louis XIV. In the Cambridge University *epithalamiun* celebrating the match, Matthew Prior referred to it gloriously as the mating of Venus and Mars. Given the protagonists, that was perhaps going a little far.

Nevertheless, very soon this amiable Protestant pair did

produce a child. Little significance was attached to the fact that this first baby died: it was merely one of the commonplace griefs of the time. The important point was that Princess Anne had proved herself fertile. Other children would surely follow. No one could foresee that the unfortunate woman would be condemned to bear seventeen children, not one of whom survived childhood.

As the last year of the life of King Charles II dawned, from the point of view of the monarchy there was no longer any reason to fear and much reason to hope.

CHAPTER TWENTY-SIX

The Dregs of Life

No one would live past years again,
Yet all hope pleasure in what yet remains,
And from the dregs of life think to receive
What the first spritely running could not give....

John Dryden

The last year of the King's life was exteriorly a tranquil one. His country was at peace and he took care that it should remain so. A soft sunlight of prosperity illumined the perilous landscape of his finances: however transient these shafts, they were enough to light him to the end of his reign. No major domestic embroilment ruffled the calm of these autumnal days – neither the angry debates of a Parliament nor the demands of a Pumpkin Plot nor official cries of anguish on the subject of the succession.

The French subsidy, which had been phased over three years, came to an end in theory (although the money had not yet been paid in full).[1] In any case the King remained openly, even gaily pro-French. He sent a message of congratulation to Louis XIV on his acquisition of Luxembourg. The Truce of Ratisbon in the summer of 1684 confirmed the French monarch not only in that precious possession but also Strasbourg. Without English help, there was no way that the United Provinces could play an aggressive part in keeping the French wolf at bay: the checking of this all-conquering animal would have to wait for another day, another reign.

The foreign policy of Charles II gave him no trouble at all during the last year of his life because, while it was emotionally pro-French, that meant being practically neutral.

Two matters could however have plagued him, had he allowed them to do so. One was the continued incarceration of Danby in the Tower of London, five years after he had been consigned there (without a formal trial). The other was the return of Parliament, which had now been dissolved for over three years; this was a significant period, although the Act of 1664 left it conveniently to the King to decide to call Parliament; there was no machinery to compel him to do so. One matter bothered the King, the other his opponents. As it fell out, one was resolved successfully, the other not. In both cases the result was only to further the King's mastery over the political scene.

The freeing of Danby on bail was not quite such a simple matter as the alterations in the character of the judiciary, stressed earlier, might have promised. Indeed, the anxiety of the judges concerned not to act in any way outside their own consciences illustrates an important point about them. Merely believing in the sanctity of the royal prerogative did not make the judges corrupt: it was a question of political conviction leading (generally) to docility, rather than a built-in pliability.

Danby in the Tower became quite desperate early in 1684, when there was a change of judges on the Court of the King's Bench. Holloway and Wallcott, the newcomers, asked for a longer time to consider the matter of giving Danby his freedom. On learning from his daughter-in-law, Lady Scroop, that the King had 'good intentions' towards him, Danby wrote back to Charles in alarm, 'But I would find that was not sufficient....' As to the new judges' plea for more time: 'If your Majesty will please yourself to let these two Judges know your mind and not let them be left to be informed by others I shall have relief this term.' Otherwise Danby feared to wait for the next legal term, and then any judge would once again ask for more time and so forth and so on. 'The way to my liberty is very obvious,' cried Danby.[2] He meant through the exercise of the royal will.

The judges did free Danby. The supposition is that the King had a private word in the ear of Holloway and Wallcott. Certainly Charles swore to Danby's son, as the latter duly reported back to his father, 'If the judges would not bail you ... by god he would free you himself.'[3] But it did not come to that. The judges, including Jeffreys, satisfied their consciences and Danby was bailed against an enormous surety of £20,000 to appear in the House of Lords in the next session to answer the charges against him. Four peers put up £5,000 each. The very day of his release Danby appeared before the King and, on kissing hands, bewailed his long imprisonment. The King shrugged off the complaint: he replied that it was against his will and left it at that. At least Danby was free to commence his ascent back into public service and would, it seems, have formed part of a new administration in 1685 had not such a development been cut off by the King's death.[4]

The question of Parliament was equally resolved, but negatively. Within the King's own councils, Halifax at least believed that the spirit of the Triennial Act should be respected. But in March the King told Barrillon that he had 'no thought' of summoning a Parliament. In case the point should be missed by those further from the centre of power than the Byzantine Barrillon, Sunderland sent a circular letter on the King's behalf to the Lords Lieutenant and others. There were rumours that there was to be a new Parliament: but his subjects were to be disabused immediately of the notion, 'he [the King] having as yet no such intention'. As to the idea that there were or might be tumultuous petitions from the country for a Parliament (remember those odious Whiggish petitions which had made the time of the Popish Plot additionally uncomfortable): the King 'cannot but utterly dislike and condemn any such attempt'. He regarded such petitions as 'seditious practices inconsistent with the peace and quiet of the kingdom'.[5]

By October, as a result, the Whigs were reported to be quite cowed: 'I never knew the Whigs in London so wary of managing their discourse and of their company. If three or four be together on the Exchange talking of news or what each has to communicate, if two or more of their own party join them, part of the rest walk away....'[6]

In May 1684 the Duke of York took his place in the Privy Council once more. It was the final step in his restoration. He had been absent for eleven years. Now the King was confident enough to introduce him without fear of trouble. At about the same time Titus Oates was arrested at a coffee-house in London on a charge of *scandalum magnatum* against the Duke of York for calling him a traitor. Tried briefly by Jeffreys, he was sentenced to a token fine of £100,000 – token because of course there was no question of his paying it; thus Oates was consigned to prison and irons were put upon him. This preliminary fall of Oates (far worse things were to happen to him once James ascended the throne) marked a reaction against him which had begun just about the time that James' own star began to rise. From 1681 onwards Oates was no longer the secure and boastful rascal he had once been; in August 1682 he had lost his government pension.

James, triumphant, was restored to his former post as Lord High Admiral in all but name: the King continued to sign documents since the provisions of the Test Act were still officially in force, but the moving spirit was that of James.

It was a fortunate restoration for the Navy itself. The Navy, once a favourite child, had suffered signally not only from the departure of James in 1673 but also from that of Samuel Pepys in 1679. Pepys, that mastermind of creative organization, had acted as secretary to the Lord Commissioners after the fall of James, when the Admiralty was put to commission. He was driven from office and into the Tower of London – repository for the unlucky as well as the damned in this period – by intrigues based on his connection with the Catholic Duke of York.

Thereafter the King had been both too poor and too busy to remedy the situation. Those sums of money which were voted by Parliament were inefficiently administered. Matters drifted downwards until only twenty-four ships were actually at sea, and some of the new ships had never managed to leave the harbour.[7] Now the brothers were united to invigorate the Navy as it deserved: and Pepys, rescued, drew up a scheme for its reformation (put into commission in 1685 and finished in 1688).

Appropriately enough, to the last year of Charles' reign also belongs his support of Captain Grenville Collins, the royal hydrographer. A survey of the coasts of Great Britain was to be undertaken, for which the King recommended subscriptions and practical help, especially from naval officers and traders. The result, which the King predicted correctly would be 'of great use for the safety of navigation', was printed in 1693, and emerged as Collins' *Great Britain's Coasting Pilot.*[8] It was good that, where the Navy and navigation were concerned, the reign ended as it had begun, on a high note of investment for the future.

The rebirth of the Duke of York as a public (as opposed to private) figure of influence was also at the bottom of the government changes which occurred in August 1684. Slightly mysterious because their effects were so soon blighted by the King's death, these changes were clear in one thing: they worked to James' advantage by diminishing the power of Rochester and enhancing that of James' ally Sunderland.[9]

Having left Scotland with some feeling of accomplishment, James now turned his attention to Ireland. The plain truth was that Ireland had prospered under Charles II – if only its riches had not been drained out of the country to meet the needs of the King and Court. Some of its riches, although siphoned off, had not even got that far. Lord Ranelagh, the Lord Treasurer, was finally dismissed for peculation and the collection of taxes handed over to Revenue Commissioners under Lord Longford, a talented financier. James' aim, a laudable one by the standards of Ireland today, if not of England then, was to introduce more Catholics into the administration there.

The palace revolution at Whitehall could be made to fit into the overall Irish plan. Rochester was kicked upstairs, losing his post as First Lord of the Treasury for that of the Lord President of the Council. 'The King hath given me a great deal of ease and a great deal of honour,' commented Rochester wryly. Charles himself was careful to note that 'he did not make these Alterations out of any Dissatisfaction'.[10] But the hand of Rochester's open critic, Halifax, can be detected. Halifax, while his attitude to such major topics as Parliament and foreign policy was ignored, could still be made useful. It was however Sunderland, not Halifax, who ultimately benefited. The coveted post at the Treasury went to Sunderland's ally Godolphin.

Rochester was also promised a more lucrative position, that of the Lord Lieutenancy of Ireland, occupied over a long period of time, if intermittently, by the great Ormonde. There Rochester had the prospect of making himself both rich and secure. Once again Sunderland stepped in, and, acting in alliance with the Duke of York, saw to it that Rochester would not enjoy the independent viceregal style of an Ormonde. As Ormonde's son reported, matters were to be very differently organized in Ireland and therefore Rochester, 'who fears no odium', had been selected for that purpose. Ormonde himself had no great regrets at losing the Lord Lieutenancy under the new deal: for now the power of making army appointments was to be stripped away from the Lord Lieutenant. All such decisions and appointments were to be made in London. 'From this difficulty, I thank God and the King I am delivered,' commented Ormonde vigorously.[11]

Rochester never took up his emasculated appointment, the King's death bringing about yet another revolution in the political situation. But the whole handling of affairs both in London and Dublin demonstrated the new control of the York–Sunderland axis. It is unlikely that Halifax himself would have survived long at the centre and the King's reign been further extended.[12]

Where the succession was concerned, neither Monmouth nor William of Orange had now the muscle to bar the smooth ascent of the Duke of York towards his legitimate goal. In the autumn the King felt particular indignation all over again at the news of William's 'extraordinary caressing' of Monmouth in Holland. Charles forbade his own envoy to visit William for the time being; furthermore, the royal anger was to be conveyed both to the Dutch States and to William's ministers. In vain William's own ambassador in London protested his master's innocence of any conspiracy. The King's response was forthright.

'It is as if a man going to a brothel should ask me to believe and accept the excuse that he had done no wrong because he had only gone in to convert people ...,' exclaimed Charles in derision. The Ambassador was left rather feebly responding that although anyone entering a brothel must be 'suspect', yet his general character should also be taken into account, and if he was a man of 'probity and honour', the King should be prepared to listen to his explanation.[13] The Ambassador should perhaps have realized that where the English succession and the Whig opposition were concerned, Charles considered neither his nephew nor his son men of probity or honour.

There was a wistful notion entertained by Monmouth's admirers after the King's death – still occasionally resurrected even now – that some time during the last autumn Monmouth was actually promised the succession.[14] Monmouth himself spoke wildly on the subject after his father's death, when there was no-one to contradict him. It is true that the forbidden favourite did slip into England from Holland at the end of November. He was accompanied by Henrietta Wentworth. The Duke of York, for one, when he got wind of the foray, comforted himself with the thought that Monmouth was after a settlement of his mistress's estates upon himself. As for a reconciliation, 'there is no real danger of it,' James wrote firmly up to Scotland, 'H.M. having no inclination to receive his [Monmouth's] deceiving submissions again. . . .'[15]

In one sense, the Duke of York was wrong. There was probably some kind of limited reconciliation, although the King in his secretive way left no record of the encounter and did not even confirm to his brother that it had taken place. An enthusiastic letter written to Monmouth from Halifax on 3 February spoke of his 'business', which he had heard was 'almost as well as done' but must be 'so sudden as not to leave room for 39 [code for the Duke of York]'s party to counterplot'.[16]

Yet given the King's knowledge of Monmouth's character and given what had only just transpired in Holland, it is unlikely that this reconciliation amounted to more than the mere prospect of Monmouth returning to England. The conditions would probably have been stringent and, as after the Rye House Plot, humiliating. The Duke of York was therefore right in his further assumption that no 'real danger' to his own cause was presented by Monmouth's clandestine journey. Had the reconciliation genuinely produced a violent change in the King's feelings he would hardly have kept his mouth shut on the subject. As we shall see, he maintained this silence even on his death-bed. Once again in his enthusiasm Monmouth was the victim of his own over-optimistic and self-deceiving nature. The tranquillity of the King's public life was not disturbed at last by the maverick sortie of his erstwhile favourite son.

So far as we can tell, the interior man was tranquil too. Of all people in the world, King Charles II was in a position to test the truth of Dryden's dictum on the subject of old age:

> No one would live past years again,
> Yet all hope pleasure in what yet remains,
> And from the dregs of life think to receive
> What the first spritely running could not give....

Much of Charles' 'spritely running' had been spent literally eluding his own and his father's enemies in the crippling period of exile: no one could have wished to relive those bitter years again. The more recent past, including the long war of attrition with Parliament, brought its own memories of danger and suffering. Yet from the 'dregs' of his own life it was true that there were pleasures still to be tasted.

This was no Henry VIII, a monstrous figure bloated with disease. The King's upright appearance impressed observers. A portrait of him as Founder of the Royal Society, commissioned by Christ's Hospital, was painted by M. Laroon in 1684. With a background of ships, and an appropriate foreground of a globe and other aids to navigation, it shows a strong man unbowed. His energy continued to startle and confound even those who had known it to their cost for years. It is true that he was having trouble with a sore on his leg as well as painful gout; the long walks were reluctantly cut down. His keenness was now channelled into his laboratory, where he would devote himself to his experiments for hours at a time in the same obsessional manner. Besides, the King believed the delay in the walks was only temporary. Soon he would be striding out once more, outdistancing courtiers and subjects alike, pausing only for the demands of the ducks. In the last winter of his life, he was described by Bishop Burnet as looking 'better than he had done for many years'.[17]

Unlike that of Henry VIII, the character of Charles II was not permanently marred by savagery, even if he had displayed something verging on it, in recent years. One effect of England's public calm was to enable Charles II to regain that unruffled air with which he preferred to confront the world at large. The plotting was over; the trials were through; Shaftesbury was dead; the Whigs were cowed. His ministers were there to conduct the country along the guide-lines he had evolved; his brother was there to provide the vim and vigour of the policy and if necessary to take the brunt of the unpopularity. A typical anecdote was related by the playwright John Crowne, who was in negotiation with the King over that adaptation of a Spanish play referred to in Chapter 18. Crowne swore that he overheard the King say to the Duke of York, 'Brother, you may travel, if you will, I am resolved to make myself easy for the rest of my life.' There are other variants of the same story: we must accept that the King harped upon the theme as his life drew to its close. To Sir Richard Bulstrode, the English Resident in Brussels, he spoke warmly of the people of Flanders, but as for himself: 'I am weary of travelling, and am resolved to go abroad no more. But when I am dead and gone, I know what my brother may do: I am much afraid that when he comes to wear the crown he will be obliged to travel again. And yet I will take care to leave my kingdoms to him in peace....'[18] Part of the King's 'easiness' consisted in radiating a fatherly benevolence, now that he had brought about peace at home by defeating those who had sought to defeat him.

The winter of 1683 was one of the most severe ever recorded; the King, who had himself known vividly what it was like to be cold and hungry, gave particular orders for the relief of the poor. His subjects' welfare in distress was indeed an interest he maintained throughout his reign. His efforts after the Fire of London have been remarked; in 1675 he gave the town of Northampton, badly damaged by its own Great Fire, one thousand tons of wood from his estates – thirty-six years later the Mayor and Corporation showed their appreciation by erecting a statue to him, still to be seen today, above the portico of All Saints' Church.

In 1683 there was at least one benefit to be derived from the ice and snow. The new sport of skating flourished. Nahum Tate wrote of the popular enthusiasm in his elaborate way:

> Ourselves without the aid of Tide or Gale
> On Keels of polish't steel securely sail....

Yes, the King too was securely sailing. And the ice beneath his feet was no longer thin and cracking. The vast statue erected to him at the Royal Exchange was one symbol of the powerful stability of the monarchy. Less tangible but equally real was the affection felt for the sovereign by his subjects. Halifax, weighing up his last period from a critical standpoint, had to admit that 'in his autumnal fortune' there still remained 'a stock of warmth in men's hearts for him'.[19] This warmth was reciprocated.

King Charles II, wrote Bishop Burnet, was the greatest instance in history of the various revolutions of which any one man was capable. His deathbed, fittingly, was to be the scene of yet one more. Played out over nearly a week, a fugue for alternating voices of hope and despair, it also involved his secret conversion to a proscribed Faith.[20]

The drama began quite suddenly on a Sunday night. It was 1 February 1685. The day itself had passed placidly enough. The King's leg still bothered him. He told Sir Richard Mason that he did not feel well, but believed that it would pass. He could not take his favourite constitutional; instead, he went for a drive with his attendant Thomas Lord Bruce, whose period of waiting had begun the previous Monday and was due to end on the morrow. It is thus to Bruce that we owe many of the most affecting details of his master's last days, still vivid in his memory when he wrote his memoirs many years later.* At supper the

* These and various other sources for the King's death-bed are considered and collated in Raymond Crawfurd, *The Last Days of Charles II*, 1909. But Crawfurd's list of sources is not exhaustive: amongst others an interesting account by Anne Margaret, wife of Sir Richard Mason, second Clerk Comptroller of the Household, printed in *Household Words*, 9 (1854), as by 'a wife of a person about the Court at Whitehall', is omitted by Crawfurd.

King ate his customary hearty meal, but it included something out of the ordinary, a couple of goose eggs. Afterwards Bruce sought both natural and supernatural explanations of the King's collapse. On the one hand, he blamed the eggs, on the other hand, he divined in the sudden extinction of a vast wax candle held by a page, 'where no wind was to be found', a fearful omen of what followed.

At the time the King merely carried out his usual practice after supper and loped off to the apartments of Louise to see who might have been supping there. These were the rooms whose indiscreet opulence both enchanted and shocked John Evelyn. Here Louise held her own not-so-mimic court. More rounded than ever, the King's 'Fubbs' was also more cherished since an illness in November which had held the Court in a state of well publicized public distress. On this occasion a high game of basset was being played, which also shocked Evelyn. His eyes widened at the sight of £2,000 in gold on the table, with about twenty courtiers and 'other dissolute persons' surrounding it – all this on a Sunday to boot! For Evelyn the tale lost no moral in the telling: 'Six days after was all in the dust,' he wrote with doleful glee.[21]

It seems more relevant to the life of King Charles II that he spent the last active night of his life in his own version of peaceful domesticity. Evelyn also professed himself appalled to see the King 'toying' with 'Cleveland' and 'Mazarin' (Barbara and Hortense respectively, both returned to England and restored to friendly favour), as well as his hostess 'Portsmouth'. A French boy was singing love songs in the background. These songs may have been recent imports from the Court of France, but as for the great ladies they, if anything, represented love's old sweet song. Not one of them could be remotely considered young and between them one way and another they could number nearly fifty years in the King's service. The evening was therefore marked as much by the King's fidelity to old friends as by profligacy.

Afterwards there were plenty of people to bear witness that they had never seen the King in a better mood. Bruce duly conducted his master to bed: it was at this point that the wax candle was so ominously extinguished (although it is surely straining credulity to suggest that *no* draught could be responsible in a corridor in February – in the seventeenth century). The King put on his nightgown. Bruce, as Gentleman-in-waiting, and Harry Killigrew, as Groom of the Bedchamber, were to share his room according to custom. The King lay down to sleep.

That night the vast, sprawling Palace of Whitehall was restless. There were the endless striking clocks, none of which kept time with each other, chiming through the small hours. There was the flickering, shooting light of the Scotch coal in the enormous grate, lighting up rich tapestries and dusty corners. There were the King's indulged dogs, a whole pack of them in the very bedroom and even in the bed, the bitches and their whelps whimpering and shifting. Bruce, the Lord-in-waiting, could not sleep. None of these sounds, however disturbing, was unusual. Besides, Bruce was going off duty the next day – he could sleep then.

What was both unusual and disquieting was the fact that the King himself tossed and turned. Normally he was a very heavy sleeper when he finally got to bed (worn out no doubt by his various versions of physical exercise). He even muttered occasionally in his sleep, as Calpurnia cried out before the death of Caesar, something Lord Bruce had never known him do before. Robert Howard, another Groom, hearing of this, commented, 'Lord! that is an ill mark, and contrary to his custom.'

When the King did awake, he looked quite different. His normally olive complexion was 'pale as ashes'. He went immediately, still earing only his nightgown, into his Privy Closet just off the bedroom. When Howard went to join him, he found the King completely silent. Buckling on his garters, Howard took a worried look at his face and exclaimed, 'Sir, how do you do?' The King merely blew out his cheeks and 'puffed' as he did when he was vexed.

In the meantime, the royal doctors were actually waiting in the antechamber to the bedroom to dress the tiresome sore on his leg. As time passed and still the King did not emerge from his closet, the worried Bruce searched for William Chiffinch, the King's Keeper of the Closet (and confidant), to take his master something thicker to wear than a mere nightgown. Etiquette forbade anyone other than Chiffinch to enter the closet unbidden. In the end it was Chiffinch, who had carried out so many more cheerful errands in the past, who conducted the King out of the closet back into the bedroom.

The King's speech was obviously by this time seriously impaired, if not worse. The Earl of Craven, proffering him a paper on which were written the passwords (for the guards) for the new month, could get no response. The King could only occasionally manage a few disjointed words, such as 'All-All' when trying to discuss the death of Lord Allington.[22] At one point he began to mutter in French: in what shadows of the past was his mind lurking?

But the King did manage a little sherry and China Orange. And because no one dared to take it upon themselves to interrupt his routine – although it must have been obvious that he was dangerously sick – his barber Follier now proceeded to shave his master as usual.

The King was sitting as was his wont, with his knees against the window, and Follier was just fixing the linen round his neck, when the King gave vent to the most extraordinary and piercing noise. Afterwards described by one as 'the dreadfullest shriek' and by another as an 'exclamation as one that dies suddenly', it was clearly audible outside the chamber.[23] Then the King sank back into Bruce's arms, unconscious. It was exactly eight o'clock in the morning. It could no longer be denied that something was horribly, even catastrophically, wrong.

The responsibility for making the first decision about treatment fell upon Bruce, the senior gentleman present. By this time one of the doctors, Sir Edmund King, had arrived in the bed-chamber and had witnessed the incident. Bleeding was the obvious remedy of the time. And bleed the King this doctor now proceeded to do in style, while a panic-stricken message was sent off to the Duke of York and the rest of the Privy Council were summoned as hastily as possible. By the time a Privy Council of sorts had gathered together in the outer room at midday, Charles had had sixteen ounces of blood removed via a vein in his arm, a task for which the doctor was afterwards paid £1,000.[24]

Soon other doctors came flocking in as the news of the King's collapse reached them. A series of remedies were frantically applied. The King's head was shorn. Cantharides was used as a blistering agent. A further eight ounces of blood was removed. And as a result of these steps – or despite them – the King did actually recover. Two hours later his speech had come back.

He found the Duke of York beside him. The Duke was once more in command of the situation, as he had been in 1679, but it was a token of the general disarray that he had forgotten to put on both his shoes and was still wearing one slipper. One of the first things the King did, with his speech returned, was to ask for the Queen. He also explained what had happened to him earlier: how he had felt ghastly on rising and had immediately gone to his closet to take some of the so-called King's Drops, made up in his own laboratory out of extract of bone after a formula of Dr Jonathan Goddard. Leaving his closet, the last thing he could remember was feeling intensely giddy. The King was now laid on his bed.

All round the relief was incredible. The official newsletter of the day, referring to 'the fit' which had seized the King, was also able to pronounce him out of danger. It was to be, surely, a repetition of those illnesses of 1679 onwards – sharp but short-lived.

Immediate precautions had been taken following the King's seizure. Horse guards and foot guards were posted everywhere in Whitehall. Sentries were reinforced. Above all, the ports were stopped. No passengers or ships were allowed in or out. Even in his agony – and he wept unashamedly beside his brother – the Duke of York was quite clear that for the time being no message should reach the Duke of Monmouth, or for that matter the Prince of Orange, lest they try to turn the situation to their advantage. A few days later outgoing traffic was allowed to continue, but incoming was still banned. Only Barrillon, as usual receiving most favoured treatment, was allowed to transmit a solitary letter to Louis XIV. Similar precautions had followed the death of Oliver Cromwell (in order that Charles Stuart should not seize the day).

In the country the Lords Lieutenant were asked to keep themselves in readiness against a crisis. The Lord Mayor and other dignitaries of the now docile City of London were quick to show where *their* sympathies lay by sending a message of loyalty to the Duke of York. As for the common people, those whose affections the King had never lost throughout his autumnal fortune, they too demonstrated their sympathies by grieving openly: 'They cried as they walked the streets, and great sadness in all faces, and great crowds at all the gates.'[25]

In the general relief, the doctors at least did not let up on the application of their remedies. It was actually in the presence of his physicians – twelve of them by this time – that next morning, Tuesday, 3 February, the King was seized with another 'fit' or convulsion. Immediately and with renewed frenzy the remedies were stepped up and new ones were imported.

Lord Macaulay described Charles II on his death-bed as being tortured like an Indian at the stake. The comparison is apt, except that one doubts whether any tormentor of Indians ever had quite such a battery of instruments at his command as the seventeenth-century royal doctors. It has been estimated that a total of fifty-eight drugs were administered over five days, many of whose names are as exotic to us as their effects were painful to the King.

There was white hellebore root (a sneezing powder to clear his nose) and plasters of combined spurge and Burgundy pitch (these were applied to his feet), as well as plasters of cantharides on his head. The ingredients of the enemas which were applied frequently were rock salt and syrup of buckthorn. As an emetic, an orange infusion of metals, made in white wine, was employed. White vitriol was dissolved in paeony water; other remedies varied from the homely, such as the distillation of cowslip flowers, to the more striking spirit of sal ammoniac. An anti-spasmodic julep of black cherry water, oriental bezoar stone from the stomach of an East goat and spirits of human skull were amongst other cures named.

The poor King's body was purged and bled and cauterized

and clystered and blistered. Red-hot irons were put to his shaven skull and his naked feet. His urine became scalding through the lavish use of cantharides. Cupping-glasses and all the many weird resources of medicine at the time were applied. They all had one thing in common: they were extremely painful to the patient.

These prodigious efforts were much admired at the time. Colonel Thomas Fairfax, an Irish officer visiting London, hastened to write to Dublin of the employment of 'all the means that the art of man thought proper for the King's distemper'.[26] The doctor's report afterwards spoke of 'every kind of treatment attempted by Physicians of the greatest loyalty and skill'. The doctors did not exaggerate the universality of their treatments; their loyalty was doubtless incomparable; but they did somewhat gloss over their own incompetence. The King's mouth and tongue became 'much inflamed' with scalding medicines and where his teeth had been forced apart during convulsions. Not all the doctors were as skilled at blooding as Edmund King. James Pearse, Charles' Surgeon in Ordinary, and Surgeon General to the Navy and Land forces, could not find the jugular vein successfully, a desperate experience for the patient. Another doctor, Thomas Hobbs, who lived in nearby Fleet Street and was Surgeon to the Household and the King's troops of the Horse Guards, had to finish the job: for the efficiency he was later rewarded by inclusion in Dryden's poem on the King's death, 'Threnodia Augustalis'.[27]

The need to keep up the patient's strength through all this was however fully recognized: from time to time the King was given draughts of emulsion, light broth and liquid posset. At the same time the purges and emetics continued remorselessly to drain his resistance from him. Once again the comparison with torture arises, as when the tormenters are determined that their victim shall not finally elude them through death, and therefore fortify them.

Once again the King rallied. By the Wednesday morning he was distinctly better. He was however forbidden to speak. With a gleam of the old wit he observed that the edict would have killed Harry Killigrew, a notorious chatterbox, but 'he would obey it'. Dryden celebrated the wave of relief in the world at large:

> Friends to congratulate their friends made haste;
> And long inveterate foes saluted as they passed....

As usual with illnesses which may prove fatal, people behaved both well and badly. Burnet afterwards tried to create scandal by suggesting that Louise took care of Charles throughout as 'a wife of a husband'. In fact, the reverse was true. The ladies of the Court reacted entirely according to type. Louise, the ready weeper, swooned and had to be carried out for air. Nelly 'roared to a disturbance and was led out and lay roaring behind the door'.[28]

The Queen was overcome with pure grief and had to be carried back to her apartments in a state of collapse, or, as the poet more picturesquely put it,

> Which was nearest the Grave could scarce be seen
> The dying Monarch, or the living Queen....

But Princess Anne, who was pregnant again, was not allowed into her uncle's chamber because he looked so dreadful, with his eyeballs rolled back, that it was feared a miscarriage might ensue.[29]

Louise, once she recovered her energies, showed that practical streak in her nature of which she was never long devoid. According to Lady Mason's story, she sent her boxes of goods packing to the French Ambassador's house, where they would be safely stowed if things looked ugly. It was a wise precaution for a Catholic foreigner who had once been in danger of being arraigned as a common prostitute (and who, furthermore, had a lot of worldly goods to lose). Less appealing is the second half of the story that has Louise drawing off two great diamond rings from the King's fingers. Interrupted by the Duke of York, she is supposed to have blushed. At which James begged her courteously to proceed: 'No, Madam, they are as safe in your hands as mine. I will not take them till I see how they go.'

But the rings, according to Lady Mason's account, vanished from view for ever.[30] It is however unlikely that this ghoulish incident ever took place (although one can believe that Duchess Louise packed her bags) for sheer lack of opportunity.

In truth, one of the main features of the death-bed of King Charles II was its total lack of privacy. When a rather more serious matter was at stake than the future of a couple of rings – the future of the King's immortal soul – it would prove extraordinarily difficult to secure a moment's relief from the throng surrounding him. Just as the number of medicines proliferated, so did the interested observers. When the room came to be cleared on Thursday, it contained seventy-five assorted lords and Privy Councillors, surgeons and servants. By this time the company also included no fewer than five bishops.

Thomas Ken, the King's former chaplain, now Bishop of Bath and Wells, was the first of these to arrive. He appeared on the Wednesday morning, when the King was thought to be rallying. He was present on the Wednesday afternoon, when the King suffered another major convulsion and the hopes aroused by each small recovery were finally dashed. From the first, 'little Ken', as the King had familiarly termed him in the past, made his presence felt; the man who had refused Nelly her place at Winchester was not likely to flinch now from his duty. Ken had last administered Communion to the King at Christmas. He now pressed the King to receive it again. Charles however steadfastly declined to do so, giving two contradictory reasons: first, there was no particular hurry, and secondly, he was too feeble to receive it. He was silent too when Ken asked him to declare himself a member of the Church of England, either because his voice was weak or because some deeper emotion was already stirring within his failing body.

Towards the evening of Wednesday the King's condition worsened. He broke out in a cold sweat. He also suffered from intermittent bouts of fever. That night six of the chorus of physicians watched by his bed as well as Lord Chesterfield, Lord Keeper Guilford and two others deputed by the Privy Council. The bulletin issued on Thursday morning was sanguine: the Privy Council 'conceive His Majesty to be in a condition of safety, and that he will in a few days be freed from his distemper'. But this of course referred to the apparent progress of Wednesday. The church bells began to ring, bonfires were readied, when the dramatic news began to leak out that the King was sinking. Silence stole over the city as vigils of continuous prayer in the royal chapels replaced the joyful cacophony of the bells.

Exactly what was wrong with the King? At four o'clock on Thursday afternoon, in the language of the doctors, there was 'some exacerbation or paroxysmal increase'. In other words, the convulsions were mounting. Great bouts of fever were shaking his body. Ironically enough, the same doctors who were so busy at the cure were still very much in the dark as to what they were curing. Their energies were great; but then so was their ignorance. Guilford angrily pointed out that, when finally taxed on the nature of the King's illness, they behaved in the Spanish way over difficult cases: '*Hazer il bove*, that is stared and said nothing.'

After the King's death the official verdict was apoplexy. It would be translated today more familiarly as a stroke. Apoplexy was a portmanteau word, much used in the seventeenth century and not necessarily narrowly defined: Lord Chesterfield called it 'a sort of apoplexy'. It is easy to believe that the King, like many middle-aged men, was suffering from high blood-pressure, followed by a stroke, brain damage and finally cardiac arrest. However, that verdict presents certain difficulties.

If the King had a stroke, then it is remarkable that he was never paralysed – paralysis down one side would have been expected. He also recovered his speech totally, while he never lost his reason. This point is not a purely academic one: for if the King had had a stroke, it could be argued that he was incapable of making a positive decision in favour of the Catholic faith. Yet it is clear from the account of Father Huddleston and others that his mind was quite clear, if his body was weak. The intermittent fevers or 'fits of ague' to which the doctors bear witness are equally puzzling if the King had had a stroke.

We may discount the usual titillating rumours of poison which surrounded the death-bed of Charles II, as with most other notable characters in the seventeenth century, including his grandfather and Oliver Cromwell. Monmouth, predictably, later accused the Duke of York of poisoning his brother. Other popular scapegoats were the servants of the Duchess of Portsmouth (presumably because they were Catholics and foreigners). One rumour had the King being killed by inhaling poisoned snuff. James Welwood, ardently advancing this view in the memoirs written later at the command of Queen Mary, had to admit, as a physician himself, that there were no outward signs of poisoning. But he sidestepped this neatly, in a manner worthy of twentieth-century spy fiction: 'It must be acknowledged that there are poisons ... of so subtle a nature that they leave no concluding marks upon the bodies of those they kill.'[31]

The fact that Peruvian bark of *cinchona* (the so-called Jesuit's powder) was now once again, as in 1679, used to treat the King's fever excited another suggestion in the nineteenth century. The Principal of the Calcutta Medical College formed the opinion that the King died of malaria, from his habit of feeding the ducks in St James's Park.* But the malaria *P. (plasmodium) vivax*, from which a great many people suffered in Europe in the seventeenth century, was not a lethal disease and should not be confused with the malaria *P. falciparum*, which swept away so many Europeans in India in the nineteenth.[32] One is glad to acquit the ducks and St James's Park.

Another enterprising theory has been recently advanced that the King poisoned himself slowly through his constant experiments, trying a process for the fixing of mercury; gradually he developed erethisma. Uraemia attendant on kidney failure is one of the common sequents of mercury poisoning. Thus the massive blood-letting caused a temporary recovery by removing the circulating toxins from the King's system: the nephritic damage was however irreparable. It is a tempting thesis, but further exploration is needed, since it is outlined in a very short article, in which the medical and historical evidence cited is far from exhaustive. As the authors themselves conclude, 'Further work

* See Norman Chevers, M.D., *An Enquiry into the Circumstances of the Death of King Charles the Second of England*, Calcutta 1861 (not mentioned in Crawfurd).

will no doubt be necessary....'* For example, the King's increased irritability as time went on is given as one proof of mercury poisoning: but that could be attributed to a number of causes, including quite simply advancing years.

At the present time the theory of Raymond Crawfurd, elaborately set out in 1909, still seems the most plausible: the King was suffering from chronic granular kidney disease (a form of Bright's disease) with uraemic convulsions. During the winter he had been plagued by gout. The fatal use of cantharides, to promote blistering on the first night of his illness, must have done much to rob the King's kidneys of their vestige of functional activity. The autopsy fitted exactly with what would now be expected of 'gouty kidney' coupled with uraemia. It would nevertheless not be fair to describe King Charles, as Macaulay did, as the victim of his doctors. The physicians did substantially increase his sufferings, while failing to alleviate the cause. But they did not kill him. The disease would have done so in any case.

In the end however most medical historical investigation, however fascinating, has a double disadvantage. First, there is never a body, let alone a patient, and the bones of Charles II have never, rightly, been troubled. Secondly, the medical language of the time, on which reliance has to be placed, is not precise by our standards. There can be no certainties. King Charles II was ageing and had endured some recent severe attacks of illness. Perhaps in the end the best verdict on the King's death was given in a poem by Abraham Cowley, addressed to his leading doctor, Sir Charles Scarburgh:

> Let Nature and Art do what they please,
> When all is done, Life's an Incurable Disease.

* See M. L. Wolbarsht, Naval Medical Research Institute, Bethesda, Maryland, and D. S. Sax, Psychiatric Institute, University Hospital, Baltimore, Maryland: 'Charles II, A Royal Martyr', in *Notes and Records of the Royal Society of London*, vol. 16, no. 2, November 1961. As they themselves point out in an Appendix to the article, Pascal's death 'was almost certainly not due' to mercury poisoning; as for Faraday's death, 'it would be difficult to say mercury was the specific cause....' Yet both Pascal and Faraday's experiments far outstripped those of Charles II.

The men of science proving useless, the men of God were given their turn. The Archbishop of Canterbury and the Bishops of London, Durham and Ely were now ranked round the King's bed, joining Bishop Ken. The King however paid no attention to these princes of the Church, perhaps because their nebulous and rather unattractive voices did not reach him. Ken, who had a voice 'like to a nightingale for the sweetness of it', fared better. He read the Prayers for the Sick out of the Book of Common Prayer.

In the meantime, a dangerous and different drama was being played out behind the scenes. It is not clear who made the original suggestion that the King should receive a Catholic priest. One obvious candidate was the Queen. As early as Monday Catharine had said to the Catholic Duchess of York: 'Sister, I beg you to tell the Duke that he, who knows as well as I do the King's convictions about the Catholic religion, should do what he can to take advantage of any opportunity that offers.' Mary Beatrice went to her husband. The Duke of York replied, 'I know, and I am thinking of nothing else.' But he took no action.[33]

The Duke's cautious attitude illustrates the extreme delicacy of the situation. The fact was that the King could well recover (and indeed subsequently did so, albeit temporarily). Then, although the Queen referred to the King's 'convictions' about the Catholic religion, a sentiment echoed by Louise, who described him as a Catholic 'at the bottom of his heart', neither lady pretended that these convictions had as yet been given public expression. Indeed, the nervousness of the King's intimate circle is yet another argument against the proposition that the King was already an established Catholic. It has been postulated throughout this book that the King never at any point underwent an official conversion – neither in his youth in exile, nor in 1669, nor in 1684 when he was rumoured at the French Court to have become a Catholic, nor at any other date. This whole death-bed episode, attested by so many witnesses, makes little sense if such a conversion had already taken place.

All the Catholics surrounding the King – all in their way branded by their religion – were well aware of the care with which he himself had avoided suffering similar damage. Catharine was in a particularly difficult position: a woman who had valued discretion throughout her time in England, she well knew that she was closely watched. The King had not asked for a Catholic priest. Catholicism was a proscribed religion; not only were its priests under heavy sentence, but many of them had recently been executed. Were his family now to involve Charles in something desperate and ruinous, for which a convalescent King would castigate them?*

Nevertheless, the question remained: given that the King intended to live as a 'public' Protestant, did he intend to die as a private one? The fateful move to introduce a Catholic priest was only made when the King was clearly dying, and then in fear and trembling. Catharine was not involved: her approach to Mary Beatrice on Monday, passing the responsibility to the Duke of York, was as far as she dared go.

The two people who did finally broach the matter were both in their different ways more reckless. Louise Duchess of Portsmouth received a visit from Barrillon in her apartments. He found her in the midst of her general grief, extremely agitated on the subject of the King's religion. She bewailed the fact that he was surrounded by Protestant bishops since, in her precisely limited observation, 'at the bottom of his heart the King is a Catholic'. Was there any possibility of a priest being produced? She herself could no longer enter his room 'with any decency' since the Queen was nearly always present. Barrillon, with his usual freedom of movement, could go to the Duke of York.

* There is of course the mysterious matter of the two papers 'containing about a quarter of a sheet on both sides' shown by James, then King, to Pepys about six months after his brother's death. These papers gave arguments in support of the Church of Rome. But it is not clear if they were in Charles II's own handwriting, annotated by him, or merely copies certified by James. Nor is it clear if these arguments were supposed to be Charles II's own composition or the arguments of others proposed by him. Most of the evidence concerning these papers is second if not third hand. (Pepys never wrote about the matter himself but reported it to Evelyn. Burnet heard about it from Thomas Tenison, but his account differs from that of Evelyn. Halifax would say no more than that the King 'might do it'.)[34] All one can reliably conclude is that Charles II continued to show an interest in the tenets of Catholicism.

The Queen being absent – she was being 'blooded' herself to alleviate her distressed condition – Barrillon delivered Louise's message.

A Capuchin monk, Padre Mansueti, one of the chaplains to the Duchess of York who came over to England with her, was also prompted to go to the Duke of York with the same message. He had been entertaining a Benedictine monk, Dom Gibbon, at dinner, when the news came that the King was sinking; Gibbon spurred on Mansueti to act.*

To Barrillon, James was said to have responded immediately with a characteristic declaration: 'I would rather risk everything than not do my duty on this occasion.' He told Barrillon he was aware that there was no time to lose. To Mansueti he was said to have been equally accommodating. It may be questioned whether these pleas were necessary: whether James the straightforward believer would really have let his brother die as a Protestant. The answer seems to be that it was not until he knew his brother to be dying that he dared countermand his known policy, and then only when encouraged by Barrillon and, on another level, one of his priestly entourage. So close and secret had Charles kept his inner soul.

The introduction of a Catholic priest into the royal chamber remained a challenging task. For one thing, there were the Protestant bishops, innocent vultures unaware of the embarrassment their presence was causing: how could they be politely ejected? Even if that were accomplished, the problem of discovering a Catholic priest at short notice and smuggling him into Whitehall was even more horrendous in the fierce light of publicity which shone down upon the whole palace.

First of all, the King's consent still had to be gained. Only the Duke of York had the opportunity to do so. As discreetly as possible he bent down and whispered in his brother's ear. The King answered. From time to time James had to repeat his words, so low did he speak. The King himself was barely audible,

* See *A True Relation of the late King's Death*, by P. M. Dated early march 1685. Printed in full in J. G. Muddiman, 'The Death of Charles II', *The Month*, 1932. (Not mentioned in Crawfurd, cited above.)

except to those closest to him, who included Barrillon. But the King's basic answer remained the same: 'Yes, with all my heart.'

The King had agreed.

On Barrillon now devolved the duty of actually finding a priest. All parties concerned agreed that time was short. But there was an absurd complication. Those priests most readily available were the Queen's chaplains; for they were in a room divided from the King's only by the entrance to the Privy Stairs, used by Chiffinch and others to conduct visitors discreetly to him. The Queen's priests were not in on the secret – there seems to have been a general, if unacknowledged, conspiracy to keep the Queen's household clear of it for her own sake as well as the King's. That was less serious than the fact that they only spoke Portuguese, a language the King had never mastered.

The chaplains of the Duchess of York, on the other hand, spoke Italian, a language in which he was comparatively fluent. But these priests were both well known and extremely unpopular: they would be immediately recognized for what they were if they attempted to enter the King's chamber, with fatal results. And the Duke of York's apartments lay on the wrong side of the King's: entry from one to the other could be vetted by the watchful.

It was the Portuguese Count of Castelmelhor who pointed out the language barrier of the Queen's household. Barrillon and James between them therefore decided to tackle the house of the Venetian Resident, where they would find an Italian priest. Before they set off, Castelmelhor did look into the Queen's room. And there, by a merciful dispensation, he discovered Father Huddleston.

It had been a long road from Worcester for both parties. Mary Beatrice afterwards described Father Huddleston to the nuns at Chaillot as '*un homme très simple*'. She even regretted that a more suitable 'subject' could not have been found 'to help this great Prince make a good death'. She had presumably managed to avoid taking in (language barrier again) her brother-in-law's tales of escape and derring-do, which involved the good priest. Otherwise she must surely have realized that no more appropriate missionary could have been discovered.

Besides, if Father Huddleston had preserved a certain simplicity in the quarter of a century which had passed since Worcester, it was appropriate holy simplicity rather than something more rustic. Rewarded by the gratitude of the King after the Restoration, he had formed part of the household of two Queens, Henrietta Maria and Catharine; he was thus hardly a stranger to Court circles.

Disguised in a wig and a cassock, Father Huddleston was led from the Queen's suite of rooms to a closet just off the King's chamber which had a private communicating door. Here he waited. There was a further problem. Father Huddleston had not been bearing the Blessed Sacrament with him on his visit to the Queen's rooms (although he did have a viaticum of holy oil). So one of the Portuguese priests, Father Bento de Lemoz, had to be despatched outside the palace on the vital mission to secure a Host. In the meantime, the Duke of York cleared the King's room in soldierly fashion by simply announcing in a loud voice, 'Gentlemen, the King wishes everybody to retire except the Earls of Bath and Feversham.' The former, a fervent Royalist, was the Groom of the Stole; the latter, a Frenchman naturalized English, the Queen's chamberlain. But both gentlemen were Protestants, which helped to pacify the Bishops. Their continued attendance, which was contrary to the King's own wishes, was also due to James' concern that his dying brother's conversion should be seen to be voluntary; he did not want to be the sole witness to such a momentous event. When the room was ready, Chiffinch, who had brought so many clandestine night visitors to his master in the past, brought in one more, a man of God.

Charles II cried out with pleasure at the sight of Huddleston. The various accounts of the conversion scene vary in detail, but the King's general reaction to Huddleston was clear: 'You that saved my body are now come to save my soul.' He was certainly well aware of the providential element in the presence so close at hand of 'this good father, whom, I see, O good Lord, that Thou hast created for my good'.

Father Huddleston put a series of questions to the King. Did he wish to die in the Faith and the Communion of the Holy Roman Catholic Church? Did he wish to make a full confession of all his sins? To all these questions, Charles answered firmly, in a low but distinct voice. His resolution was clear. Then he made his general confession. Amongst the things for which he declared himself 'most heartily sorry' was the fact that 'he had deferr'd his Reconciliation so long' – these words on the lips of a dying man, reported by Father Huddleston without contradiction, being yet another proof, if proof were needed, that the King was not already a secret Catholic.* The King's confession ended in an act of contrition: 'Into Thy Hands, Sweet Jesus, I commend my soul. Mercy, Sweet Jesus, Mercy.' The priest gave him absolution.

Huddleston's last question concerned the Blessed Sacrament: 'Will you receive it?'

The King replied, 'If I were worthy of it, Amen.'

But since the Host had not yet arrived, Father Huddleston asked the King's leave to anoint him with the holy oil, in the Sacrament of Extreme Unction. To which the King agreed 'with all my heart'. When the Portuguese priest returned with the Host – probably from the chapel at Somerset House – Huddleston went to the side door and received it. The King, with a touching flash of the old spirit, tried to rise. As he struggled, he said, 'At least let me meet my heavenly Lord in a better posture than in my bed.' Father Huddleston calmed him: Almighty God, who saw into his heart, would accept his good intention.

So the King received the Catholic Communion and afterwards Huddleston sat quietly by him, reading the Catholic prayers for the dying in a low voice. It was by Charles' own request that Huddleston recited once again the Act of Contrition, ending 'Mercy, Sweet Jesus, Mercy.' Then the priest put a crucifix into the King's hands, saying that it only remained to him to meditate on the death and passion of 'Our dear Saviour Jesus Christ'. Father Huddleston recited more prayers as the King held the crucifix: 'Beseech Him with all humility, that His most precious

* Barrillon was told by the Duke of York afterwards that Father Huddleston 'made the King formally promise to declare himself openly a Catholic if he recovered his health'. But Father Huddleston does not mention this in his own detailed account.[35]

Blood may not be shed in vain for you ... and when it shall please Him to take you out of this transitory world, to grant you a joyful resurrection, and an eternal crown of glory in the next.'

Then Father Huddleston left as he had come, through the secret door. The whole momentous episode had lasted three-quarters of an hour.

The King's progress out of the transitory world, although sure, was slow. The stubborn way his body clung to life even gave hope to those Catholics in the know that his conversion might have wrought a miraculous cure. The King himself summed it up with his ineffable politeness: he told the gentlemen surrounding his bed that he was sorry to trouble them by taking so long a-dying, and he asked their pardon.[36]*

Throughout the long night of Thursday, 5 February, Charles remained conscious. The physicians, allowed back into the torture-chamber, set to work with their remedies again with even greater energy. At one point the King referred to his continuing ordeal. He told his attendants, 'I have suffered very much and more than any of you can imagine.' Once, listening to those innumerable palace clocks striking, he asked the time. They told him and he said, 'My business will shortly be done.' But his stoicism continued to excite the admiration of all those about him. It was an exemplary death-bed, as might have been expected of one who had learnt early to confront the unknown with courage and hope.

There were a series of farewells. Catharine came. Charles greeted her lovingly. But her distress, both at the King's tenderness and at his suffering, was too great. Tears overcame her. She was carried back to her own apartments, half-fainting. She sent back a message to her husband to beg his pardon if she had ever offended him.

'Alas! poor woman,' said the King. 'She beg my pardon! I beg hers with all my heart.'

* A saying given its unforgettable expression in Macaulay's *History of England*: 'He had been, he said, a most unconscionable time dying; but he hoped they would excuse it.'[37] But the word 'unconscionable' is not in the original source.

To James too, linked to him by every shared memory of boyhood and now at last by Faith, the King showed much tenderness. James, kneeling, could not hold back his own tears. Charles begged his pardon too, for the hardships which he had inflicted upon him from time to time. At some point in the long midnight hours he handed him the keys of his cabinet and begged God to give him a prosperous reign. The Duchess of York remained openly weeping at her husband's side.

The King also spoke of his children. He recommended his little family most touchingly to his brother, naming each one meticulously. When he stumbled on the name Burford – as Nelly's handsome, spirited boy was still known, despite his new dukedom of St Albans – the King put the boy 'into his [James'] hand'. He asked James to take particular care of Burford's education, 'for he will be spoiled else'.

But the King did not name Monmouth. And James, repeating the list back to him, did not mention the forbidden name either.

The ladies, those other members of his extended family circle, were not forgotten. In a phrase sometimes supposed to be apocryphal but in fact attested by three sources, the King adjured the Duke of York 'to be well to Portsmouth' and 'not let poor Nelly starve' – even in his last hours the vital social distinction between the two ladies was preserved.[38]

One by one his children came and knelt down by the King's bed and received his blessing. At which the throng of people once more surrounding the royal bed, and crowding into the chamber, cried out that the King was their common father. So all present in fact knelt down for his blessing. It was of course an Anglican blessing. But when Bishop Ken repeatedly urged the King to take the Sacrament, Charles declined it. He would only say that he had thought of his approaching end, and hoped that he had made his peace with God. Ken was unaware what this characteristically courteous evasion meant.

At six o'clock in the morning the King asked for the curtains to be drawn back. He wanted, he said, to watch the dawn for the last time. He was still conscious enough to ask that the eight-day clock in his room should be wound up, because it was the appointed day. An hour later he became breathless and struggled to sit up. Once again the doctors bled him, taking twelve ounces, and gave him heart tonics. At half-past eight his speech began to fail once more. This time it did not return. By ten o'clock he was in a coma.

The rising sun over the Thames was probably the last sight he took in. It was an appropriate one for this man who had so loved the early morning on its misty waters.

King Charles II died at noon. It was now high water on the river and the time of the full moon. The day was Friday, 6 February 1685, and he was in his fifty-fifth year.

CHAPTER TWENTY-SEVEN

His Royal Ashes

'Let his royal ashes then lie soft upon him, and cover him from harsh and unkind censures.'

Halifax, *Character of King Charles II*

After the death of King Charles II the ordinary people walked about 'like ghosts'. Roger North wrote that 'almost every living soul cried before and at his Decease, as for the loss of the best Friend in the World'.[1] Others felt that they had lost a father, that feeling spontaneously expressed at the King's death-bed when all present, not only his children, had knelt for his paternal blessing.

The universal application was given its first expression when the King's body lay in state in the Painted Chamber at Whitehall for several days. As was the custom of the time, his wax effigy, standing upright over the catafalque, dominated the scene. It was dressed in robes of crimson velvet trimmed with ermine, and surmounted with an imperial crown of tin gilt, all specially ordered for the occasion by the Lord Chamberlain. Such effigies, taken from the death-mask, often have a haunted look: the lines on the face of Charles II are deep, the face is slightly twisted, the expression very sad. Still to be seen exhibited in the precincts of Westminster Abbey, it commemorates the cruel sufferings of his death-bed.

Queen Catharine, as befitted a devout woman who had once been a Portuguese Infanta, understood how to conduct her official position as widow with stately grief. She received the

Ambassadors and other great persons who came to offer their condolences on a vast black bed of mourning. Her whole chamber, from the ceiling to the floor, was hung with black, and lit by innumerable tapers. The callers came thronging and their sympathy was not purely formal: no-one doubted the sincerity of the Queen's own passion for the King, and besides, she had won universal respect.

One does however detect a firm, even righteous hand, in the way the funeral and other mourning arrangements kept the mistresses at last in their place. The royal concubines were allowed to wear black themselves in their official capacity as ladies-in-waiting, but could not put their households into mourning, a privilege reserved for royal persons. There were other nice distinctions preserved, such as that between the cambric doled out to the Queen's entourage, while the rest made do with mere muslin. It was not for nothing that the Lord Chamberlain commanded from the Treasury yards of black and white satin for eight escutcheons showing the royal arms of England and Portugal.[2]

The funeral itself took place on the night of 14 February. The King's body was enclosed in a lead coffin – that 'house of lead' which had been prophesied – bearing a solid silver plate with an inscription which began: '*Depositum Augustissimi et Serenissimi Principis Caroli Secundi. . .*' In its last line, '*Regnique sui tricesimo septimo*' ('in the thirty-seventh year of his reign'), the inscription dated the King's accession once again from his father's execution.

Then the body of Charles II was laid to rest in a vault beneath the Henry VII Chapel in Westminster Abbey. There it remains to this day.* Many of the King's natural children were later buried near him: Charles Earl of Plymouth had already been placed there in his early grave.

Careful provision was made for discreet display – banners of

* According to Dean Stanley, that great Victorian guardian of the Abbey, the vault was accidentally disclosed in 1867 in the process of laying down the apparatus for warming the Chapel. The lead coffin was very much corroded and had collapsed; the King's remains were visible. In 1977, when the vault was again opened, the remains, as described by Dean Stanley, were still visible.[3]

black taffeta with strings and tassels of black silk – and appropriate sad sound – black-coated trumpeters, kettle-drummers, and a fife. Despite this care, despite the fact that the body was carried under a velvet canopy from the Painted Chamber to Westminster Abbey in a procession headed by the Archbishop of Canterbury and Norroy, King of Arms, and attended by James II, Mary of Modena, various other royalties, nobles and their servants, the rumour has arisen that, in the words of John Evelyn, 'the King was very obscurely buried'.[4]

This has sometimes been ascribed to the religious embarrassment caused by the King's last-minute conversion. The new monarch, it is suggested, did not wish his brother's body to be buried according to the Anglican rite and did not dare employ the Catholic one. This is also the explanation sometimes given for the fact that James himself stayed away from the burial. The truth is rather less dramatic. Royal interments at the time were traditionally held privately at night, as for example that of the Duke of Gloucester in 1660 and of Prince Rupert in 1682. It was according to custom that the nearest relative stayed away, the role of Chief Mourner devolving upon an officially designated person: in the case of Charles II it fell upon the stalwart shoulders of his nephew-in-law, Prince George of Denmark. He was 'supported' by the Dukes of Somerset and Beaufort, and 'assisted' by sixteen earls – hardly a meagre representation.[5]

An exception was the state funeral of Cromwell, the Lord Protector, in 1658. Like a coronation, this august ceremony had its own rhythm: it took place three months after his death (both impressing and disgusting Evelyn). The actual burial might even be separate from the State ceremony: Cromwell's corpse was secretly interred about a fortnight before this took place, because the embalming had failed. Such a magnificent piece of pageantry was mounted with the explicit intention of demonstrating the strength of the regime – in the case of the Cromwellian Protectorate, to bolster its prestige abroad against a young man then known as Charles Stuart. The money spent was crippling: not much less than £50,000.[6]

Where the late King Charles II was concerned, no such demonstration was felt to be necessary. A staid succession was, surely, to be followed by a steady reign. Above all, there was the question of paying for such pageantry: the monies voted by Parliament for the late King all came to an end with his death, while Charles himself had left large debts. James II, faced with a financial crisis and the daunting prospect of a Parliament to solve it, was in no mood for unnecessarily lavish expenditure. The shade of Charles II, no stranger to State penury and its ramifications, would certainly have agreed.

The outbreak of verse on the King's death (including an ode by the Quaker Penn, a tribute to the King's tolerant spirit, and Otway's long poem on Windsor Castle, a tribute to his artistic enthusiasm) showed a genuine spirit of lamentation.

> Sad was the morn, the Sadder Week began...

was Aphra Behn's contribution. Two other slightly bathetic starts were as follows:

> No more, he's gone, with Angel's wings he fled...

and:

> O God! Some pity, and I am turned to stone...

All however stressed the state of serenity in which King Charles left his realm. One, by Edmund Arwaker, will serve for many:

> The best of Christians as the best of Kings:
> By him such Blessings to his Realms were given;
> He seemed created for his People's good...[7]

So, in a mellow atmosphere of regret the King was buried. It seemed that the peace which he so much desired for his country had fallen upon it, even as he himself was laid to peace in his grave.

It was not to be. Only a few months later those characters dismissed from the stage by the final curtain of one play, found themselves engaged in quite a different drama. There was to be no happy ending to the reign of King James II.

Monmouth died at the executioner's axe after his foolish and bloody rebellion, only a few months after his father's death. Three years later James himself was fighting off the political onslaught of William of Orange and his own daughter Mary; the birth of the long-dreaded Catholic Prince to Mary Beatrice in June 1688 had brought disaster in its wake. By 1689 Titus Oates, savagely whipped after trial for perjury in May 1685, was being received by William, now King of England: Oates remained a weather-vane for the direction of the English political wind. As a counter-poise it is good to relate that Father Huddleston lived on to the ripe old age of ninety – protected in the household of Queen Catharine at Somerset House.

Another mercurial figure, whose story had been even more closely entwined with that of Charles II, did not survive to see the new Protestant reign. Buckingham had divided himself from the opposition in the King's last years, unable to remain in accord with Shaftesbury, and had thus been received back into Charles' favour. On the accession of James, he retired to his great Yorkshire estates, which his friend Etherege complained was like the hero leaving the play at the beginning of the fourth act. But Buckingham's health was failing, through prolonged dissipation, as it was generally thought. He died two years after his master and childhood friend; but it was somehow characteristic of the man that his burial at least – like that of Charles himself in the Henry VII chapel at Westminster Abbey – was a most splendid affair. As for the younger politicians, Sunderland, Rochester, Godolphin and the like, for the most part they stepped willingly onto the new stage to act out all the intricate if not heroic dramas of politics in the ages of William and Mary, and Anne.

The mistresses did not fare so well. Most of their latter ends would have satisfied a Puritan moralist. Nell Gwynn died – of a stroke – two years after her royal Charles. She was only thirty-five. The King's death had plucked from her at the last minute the coveted title of Countess of Greenwich. She also endured the common struggle of the late King's pensionaries to secure those payments she had been promised. At one point she addressed James in language strangely reminiscent of another ill-treated royal servant, Cardinal Wolsey, a character with whom she cannot otherwise be said to have had much in common (perhaps one may attribute the Shakespearean echo to Nelly's theatrical education): 'Had I suffered for my God as I have done for your brother and you, I should not have needed either of your kindness or justice to me,' she told the new King.

In general, James did his best by the mistresses and their children, hampered in his turn by lack of money, but recognizing the duty of their upkeep. He did make the point very firmly to Louise Duchess of Portsmouth that her debts must be paid: but the ladies, like their late protector, remained a byword for negligence. To quote Nelly once more: 'The King's Mistresses are accounted ill Paymasters. . . .'[8]

Barbara Duchess of Cleveland was made of more lasting stuff. She may have lived to regret her own durability. For at the age of sixty-five she married a much younger man, a notorious rake known as Beau Fielding, who treated her abominably; what was more, the marriage itself proved to be bigamous. As for Louise, she survived (in France) to the then remarkable age of eighty-five – the yacht *Fubbs* named in her honour lasted even longer: it was not broken up until 1770.[9] She died, wrote Saint Simon, 'very old, very penitent and very poor'. The Louise who held luxurious court at Whitehall beneath Evelyn's fascinated gaze would have deplored all three states, but particularly the last.

Catharine of Braganza survived too. It was characteristic of her tenderness that she pleaded with James II for the life of Monmouth, who was certainly too desperate to appreciate the irony of his supplication to the childless Queen: 'Being in this unfortunate condition, and having none left but your Majesty that I think may have some compassion for me; and that, for the last King's sake . . .' In her first widowhood Catharine withdrew to Hammersmith and spent her time amongst the nuns in a convent she had founded there. Later she moved to Somerset House, the palace which belonged by right to a Queen Dowager (Henrietta Maria had also occupied it). She was present at the controversial birth of James II's son, the so-called

Warming-pan Baby, and acted as the child's godmother; she subsequently bore witness that no act of substitution had taken place. Catharine was still in England at the Revolution of 1688, her return to Portugal having been delayed by a lawsuit against her former Chamberlain. She finally sailed back to Portugal in March 1692, after thirty years spent in England, during which, as Evelyn said: 'She deported herself so decently upon all occasions ... which made her universally beloved.'[10]

Even then her public life was not over. Catharine's last years were spent acting as Regent of Portugal for her sick brother Pedro. Her efforts were rewarded in at least one direction: in 1703 she was able to see an alliance with England, the so-called Methuen Treaty, which she advocated, carried through. Catharine of Braganza died at the end of 1705, twenty years after the husband she had loved, served, and in all but one vital respect over which she had no control, satisfied. In her case a magnificent state funeral in Portugal testified to the general esteem in which this practical and pious lady was held.

King Charles II had inherited a country war-torn and poor, divided, restless and suspicious. He left behind him a country outwardly at harmony. He was personally beloved from his early days, when the crowds saluted their Black Boy come again, to those last years, when he still basked in national affection. One mourning sermon of the time – 'A Loyal Tear Dropt on the Vault of the High and Mighty Prince Charles II', dedicated to the Bishop of Winton, Prelate of the Garter, by a Hampshire vicar – referred repeatedly and with evident sincerity to the late King's 'Clemency and Tenderness'. These were enduring – and endearing – qualities. When Evelyn wrote of his sovereign as having 'many Virtues and many great Imperfections' he did not specify the contents of either category. The balance of the character of Charles II, where vice and virtue are concerned, was in fact a very human one which could not fail to appeal to many of his subjects and fellow-sinners. Here was a man who knew all about Sloth and Lust, but was singularly free from Pride, Greed, Avarice, Anger and Envy. As for the Virtues, he was touched in some measure by them all, from Charity downwards, including Temperance while in exile, and Prudence at home.

The admonition of Halifax at the very end of his *Character of King Charles II* (written some time after 1688) expresses the final mood of that time: 'Let his royal ashes then lie soft upon him, and cover him from harsh and unkind censures; which though they should not be unjust can never clear themselves of being indecent.' For all Halifax's criticisms of his master, Halifax and his contemporaries understood that they had good reason to be grateful to him.

But his royal ashes have not in fact lain particularly softly upon the King. History is inevitably a long avenue of hindsight: and the basic law by which men are judged according to what follows after them, whereas they act in accordance with what has come before, is illustrated to the full in the life of Charles II. The 'Glorious' Revolution of 1688 casts its shadow backwards without difficulty across his career, whereas the obscurities and murkiness left behind by the English Civil War are too often ignored.

The historiography of his reign, a fascinating subject in its own right, is however not the concern of the present volume.* Here it is more appropriate to judge the character of King Charles II in the light of those challenges he actually faced. The first of these – and indeed the key challenge throughout most of his career – was the challenge to the position of the monarchy. Where Charles was concerned, it proved a triple contest.

First, as Prince of Wales, he had to endure the strange and unexpected ordeal of civil unrest, followed by war. If Charles was by nature a straightforward, affectionate, essentially normal creature, his early upbringing confirmed that tendency. Loved by his parents, endowed with a happy family life, and many brothers and sisters, he found it natural to display exactly that kind of open and gracious character most suited to his position. He made the transition to a martial young prince, courageous

* The best introductions to it are J. P. Kenyon, 'Review Article: The Reign of Charles II', *Cambridge Historical Journal*, vol. XIII, 1957, and K. H. D. Haley, *Charles II*, Historical Association Pamphlet, 1966.

and determined, without much apparent difficulty, but then it was not on the surface a very difficult one to make. If royal princes had not been conducting the arts of war recently, there was a strong chivalric tradition that the Prince of Wales must be equipped to do so. Charles in Western England, the Scilly Islands and Jersey did as well as, or even better than, he could have been expected to do. The scars – for there must have been scars, as his whole secure world was reft asunder and his father murdered – did not as yet show.

The obvious ordeal began a few years before he inherited the crown. The ordeal, none the less burdensome for being nominal, came in the shape of months, then years and finally over a decade of expectation, despair, inertia all mixed – with a great deal of the last. It is surely impossible to over-estimate the effect of the exile upon his character. Charles II was like a soldier captured in his first youth, who spends the crucial span of his development as a prisoner-of-war. He was never in command of his own destiny at a time when he should have been flexing his muscles both as a man and a ruler.

In public the King survived all this admirably, putting out more flags. The second challenge to the monarchy, one more often faced in the twentieth century than in the seventeenth, that of enduring a protracted period of exile and then emerging *capax imperator*, was one which Charles II met better than most. He kept his nerve. He kept up his spirits. Like another more ferocious leader, Satan, he ever took the line in public: 'What though the field be lost? All is not lost ...' He also emerged in 1660 untainted. He had preserved himself against the 'slur of the Catholic religion', on the one hand, the rather different slur of a bad character on the other.

It was hardly surprising that ever after there was something different, pessimistic about him in private, a knowledge that this world is to be regarded with a cynical eye if one is not to be betrayed by it. The exile also bred other characteristics. They do not sound attractive on paper, although they were not without their uses in the tricky post-Restoration era. To dissimulate successfully was one essential lesson Charles had to learn – for there is no evidence that he was a born deceiver. Like vacillation, another quality which stole upon him in the exiled years, it was alien to the young Hotspur he once was. Nor, it seems, did he convince himself of the rightness of deception, even if he came to understand the necessity. Late in life – discussing his championship of the Queen – he told Burnet that he regarded falsehood and cruelty as 'the greatest of crimes in the sight of God'.[11] Cruelty at least he eschewed, as all his contemporaries testified.

Laziness, or at any rate a desire to concentrate on the pleasurable over the dutiful, was, on the other hand, more inherent. Everyone after the Restoration commented on the King's apparent sloth, from Madame his sister downwards. It should therefore be noted that the King was never actually let down by this laziness (except in so far as the low estimate of his contemporaries let him down). On the contrary, he was quite often successfully served by his powers of delay, or by what is sometimes termed a 'Negative Capability' – for which Queen Elizabeth I, another procrastinator, has been much praised. When the true moment of crisis came for the monarchy the King acted with despatch. The sovereign who disposed of the Oxford Parliament in 1681 was neither lazy nor irresolute.

The extent to which King Charles II overcame the third challenge to the monarchy, that embodied in the reign itself, is more debatable. Certainly by his last year the King had so shored up the hereditary monarchy that it gave every appearance of being secure, unthreatened in its traditional powers. The theory behind all his moves was the same: the traditional authority of the Crown, eroded in the past, was being properly upheld once more. This theoretical emphasis on the traditional is characteristic of the period, which takes its very name from an act of Restoration. It poses a problem concerning King Charles II himself. Given that many of these moves were practical encroachments, how far did he evolve a new theory of monarchy?

Here his reputation for indifference, even cynicism, was probably fully justified. Neither he, nor indeed his opponents, in the main the Whigs, had overcome the basic problem lurking at the heart of a hereditary office – and still for that matter lurking there today, if in a less extreme form. In the twentieth century memory the engine of our constitutional monarchy juddered at the hands of Edward VIII, needing a George VI to steady its forward progress. The central role of the monarch calls at least for an actor suited to the part, if a great actor is not available. But such casting can never be ensured by the hereditary couch. It was significant that both Tory and Whig philosophies depended upon a good king to make them work. Faced with such a need, it cannot be argued that Charles II ever came to grips with the problem of his own successor.

Pragmatic rather than lazy, he took the whole succession question only as it came along. This he dealt with in the short term, but never in the long. A mixture of deference to his much-betrayed Queen, and allegiance to the principle of legitimate monarchy embodied by his brother, kept him from the more ruthless settlement implied by a divorce on the one hand, legitimization of a bastard on the other. One emotion was a private weakness (where a less sympathetic man might have been stronger); the other fell into the Whigs' own trap of confusing the succession with the powers of the Crown. Because they spent so much energy in denouncing Catholic James, as though the constitution depended on it, the King too began to believe the two were synonymous.

Of course a far-seeing king can still leave behind him an unintentional legacy of succession troubles. It is peculiar to the case of Charles II that he seems to have been under little illusion about the consequences of his brother succeeding. The frame of mind of Charles II in his very last phase reminds one of Dryden's paraphrase of Horace:

> Happy the Man, and happy he alone,
> He, who can call today his own:
> He who, secure within, can say,
> Tomorrow do thy worst, for I have lived today.
> Be fair, or foul, or rain, or shine,
> The joys I have possessed, in spite of fate, are mine.

That kind of noble resolution, admirable in a private individual, is more complicated in a king with responsibilities to the next reign. Yet one has to face the fact that Charles II regarded his brother's succession not only as inevitable – but in a curious way right. Here, perhaps, the deep melancholy of the once-exiled King, the ex-prisoner-of-war, came into play.

In other ways, in a confused and transitional period, Charles II was a highly estimable king. Not every prince in a position to do so has practised the virtue of gratitude so thoroughly. The determined healing of the first ten years should be balanced against the more rigorous absolutism of the last five. The healing was policy. The absolutism, as King Charles saw it, was forced upon him. Indeed, so hand-to-mouth was the absolutism of this last period, so little was it based on a cunning philosophy, that the King has been criticized for not pursuing such policies rigorously enough.

The kind of propaganda exercise indulged in by Louis XIV, with every breath he drew every day of his life, was unthinkable to Charles II. The arts, for example, were there for enjoyment: a simple and even laudable view, but not one that has been shared by every monarch in history. The bewigged and padded creatures of his stage, the saucy mistresses in their boys' clothing, the graceful wielders of his garlanded violins, the shepherds and satyrs of his masques: none of these conspired to glorify the monarchy; if they did so, it was purely by accident. Dryden as Poet Laureate was given no great direction for his verse.[12] Satire – often of the monarchy itself – was a far more potent theme in the reign of Charles II than propaganda.

It would be going too far to say that the King enjoyed the satirical attacks on himself, his friends and his mistresses. Very few notable figures have enjoyed being satirized. But temperamentally the King was inclined to shrug his shoulders at personal lampoons (otherwise his friendship with Rochester, to say nothing of Buckingham, would have rapidly withered). Here again one is inclined to seek the explanation in the years of exile, as well as in Charles' natural affability. Charles II could hardly say with Charles I that a king and a subject were two quite different things – or, if he had said so, he could hardly have believed it. He came of a long line of kings, but he himself had once been Charles Stuart, the wanderer. Like Lear, he had experienced the storm on the heath. He had also watched how easily might could be turned into royalty in the case of Cromwell.

The lack of sheer interest in regal formality displayed by Charles was another topic of general comment among his contemporaries. Mulgrave, who knew Charles well, wrote of him as having a 'natural aversion' to it: 'He could not on premeditation act the part of a King for a moment, which carried him to the other extreme ... of letting all distinction and ceremony fall to the ground as useless and foppish.' He preferred, as Bruce tells us, to take off his hat to 'the meanest' as he strode through the royal galleries or the parks.[13]

Charles II would surely have found the propagandist pranks of his father and grandfather, virtually deifying themselves through the medium of art, deeply embarrassing. One can imagine the wisecracks with which he might have distanced himself from such practices. To that extent he was a highly modern monarch, if not a highly modern dictator. Such unconcern, attractive to contemplate from afar, was not the stuff of which a strong absolute monarchy, the magnet of the country, was made.

Two great institutions, one ancient and the other comparatively new, the English Church and the City of London, might have been moulded into pillars of support had Charles II had the Nietzschean will to do so. This will he singularly lacked. He took the situation as he found it, got on with it as best he could. Where the Church was concerned, he preferred toleration to repression, an admirable view, but against his time: one must never forget that Charles' personal tolerance, so attractive to us, was considered a liability by his contemporaries – be it for the Catholics or the Jews. As for the City of London, his attitude never extended much beyond a preference for low-interest loans, which was hardly surprising. All the interests of Charles II in scientific experiment and the way things worked went to make him a great pragmatist, not a political philosopher.

It was perfectly appropriate that he lived in an age when political theories were so chaotic. It left him free to follow his natural bent, which was to ignore such matters. He wished to incarnate that kind of monarch described by Dryden, 'who is just and moderate in his nature', and provides 'a government which has all the advantages of a liberty beyond a commonwealth, and all the marks of kingly sovereignty, without the danger of a tyranny'.[14] To many people who remembered the Commonwealth, it was a republic which 'gave that mock appearance of a liberty where all who have no part in government are slaves'. As these memories faded, so the unifying and unrestrained role of the King was no longer necessary. No-one, including the King, yet knew what was to be put in its place.

It was not that Charles II was ill served. In their different ways men such as Clarendon, Arlington and Danby, and on a lower level Williamson – and Pepys – were highly talented at home; in Scotland Lauderdale displayed strength and some national feeling; in Ireland one can go much further in praise of Ormonde and even Essex. Talented as they were, these men were, like their King, floundering in an age of change. The role of Parliament? The role of the *people*? Because the era of the Civil War ha ended in such a complete theoretical 'Restoration', such questions were still unresolved.

There is one charge which is constantly levelled against Charles II – lack of patriotism, based on his acceptance of secret French subsidies. But it is a charge which must lead directly to a question: what *was* the nature of patriotism then? No one can deny that Charles himself loved England (and things English) with a passion. He also equated the happiness of England with stable monarchical government. In a memorable phrase he told Lord Bruce: 'I would have everyone live under his own vine and fig-tree. Give me my just prerogative and I will never ask for more.' That was very far from being an outrageous view at the time: most of his subjects shared it for most of his reign and in 1660 virtually all of them did.

The next step, the employment of the French funds in order to do without the boa-constrictor's embrace of Parliament, is more controversial. The acceptance of such subsidies then was not of course the national scandal it would be today: let us remember not only the bribes administered by William of Orange to English MPs but also the guileful manner in which the Whig leaders, those showy enemies of absolutism, allowed themselves to receive similar payments from the absolute Louis XIV. Nevertheless, had Charles II intended to use these funds to change the religion of the country to Catholicism against its will it would be impossible to defend him as a patriot. But Charles II never even changed his own religion until it was too late to matter, let alone took any step to change that of the country as a whole.

His conception of the French money was as a support in his struggles with his Parliamentary enemies; without this support he feared, rightly or wrongly, that he would go the way of his father. And that, he sincerely believed, would lead to the perdition of his country once again. The receipt of foreign subsidies, far from being in contrast to such overtly (by our standards) patriotic actions as the maintenance of the Navy, the extension of the Empire, was part of the same process. One may therefore criticize Charles II for his Machiavellian policies, but not for lack of patriotism.

There is a comparison to be made with another popular charge: that Charles II was the political plaything of his mistresses. In fact, their opinions tended to echo his own predilections of the time rather than the other way round. One may criticize him for extravagance towards these ladies, or indeed for having mistresses in the first place – but not for succumbing to their political influence.

There must be 'condescensions from the throne, like kind showers from heaven', wrote Halifax. Of these condescensions, not to be confused with stiffer formalities, Charles II was a master. Dryden spoke of him awakening the English from the 'natural reservedness' of their dull and heavy spirits on his Restoration.[15] The enthusiasm with which his presence galvanized so many sides of English life was not assumed.

Both sport and the arts brought him towards his people. It was easy for him to discern the human being behind the office. He dined with the jockeys not only because of his passion for racing, but because he found jockeys good company. In the same way actors, and of course actresses, were for the first time treated with proper respect in English society during his reign, because of the King's love of the theatre. His love of a pretty face extended to a general respect for women: the position of women in the second half of the seventeenth century was in many ways preferable to their position in the nineteenth. Was it a complete coincidence that the climate of the Restoration led to a remarkable flowering of female playwrights not paralleled till our own day? Charles II was fascinated by science and patronized the Royal Society. Delight in his Navy and his Army extended to care for the welfare of his sailors and soldiers. His connection with Purcell has been mentioned, spreading out from his love of the new instrumental music brought from France which flourished during his era. Gardens and paths sprang up, as the King laid out and sauntered through his own.

Witty and kind, grateful, generous, tolerant, and essentially lovable, he was rightly mourned by his people, walking in the streets 'like ghosts' after his death, their faces suffused with tears. He had been their spirited young prince, their Black Boy, 'born the divided world to reconcile', in Waller's phrase, whose restoration brought about the return of ease. As a father to them in later years, he had incarnated so much of what they pined for in a ruler. Cynical and dissimulating, it can be argued that Charles II was not a king for all seasons. But he was the right king for that strange, demanding season in which he lived.

He was not a Merry Monarch – never has a popular catch-phrase been so deceiving. The age itself might be merry in many of its jollier public aspects: but the man who presided over it was in contrast marked by melancholy at the very heart. More important to his people was the fact that he understood one deep need of their nature. 'If he loved too much to lie upon his own down bed of ease,' wrote Halifax, 'his subjects had the pleasure during his reign of lolling and stretching upon theirs.' Many a monarch has had a worse epitaph than giving back peace to a torn nation.

Let his royal ashes lie soft upon King Charles II.

References

These have been kept to the minimum (except for MSS and where a point is controversial) on the grounds that the general reader will not want to know them, and the experts on the period already do. Authors and/or titles are given in the most convenient abbreviated form; full details will be found in the list of Reference Books alphabetically according to the first letter of the abbreviation used. '*Letters*' indicates *The Letters of King Charles II*, edited by Sir Arthur Bryant. 'Burnet' is a reference to the edition of O. Airy; 'Evelyn' to the edition of W. Bray, unless otherwise stated; 'Halifax' to the *Complete Works*, edited by J. P. Kenyon; 'Pepys' followed by a date is a reference to Pepys' *Diary*, edited by R. C. Latham and W. Matthews.

Chapter 1: Heaven was Liberal

1 Perrinchief, p. 8.
2 Horoscope cast by Julia Parker.
3 Cook, *Titus Britannicus*.
4 Strickland, v, p. 252.
5 Hartmann, *King My Brother*, p. 118; Hatton Correspondence, i, p. 44.
6 Kenyon, *Plot*, p. 55.
7 Burnet, i, p. 470.
8 Pepys, 25 May 1660.
9 *Motteville*, ii, p. 80.
10 Buckingham, *Works*, ii, p. 64.
11 Hamilton, *Henrietta Maria*, p. 187; Pepys, 22 November 1660.
12 Hamilton, *Henrietta Maria*, p. 96.
13 Petrie, *Letters*, p. 240.
14 Oman, p. 69.
15 Harris, i, pp. 3–4.

16 Chapman, *Charles II*, pp. 22–3; C. S. P. Domestic 1661–2, p. 221.
17 Wase, *Electra.*
18 Oman, p. 108.
19 Brett, p. 4.
20 Foxcroft, *Burnet*, p. 48.
21 Evelyn, II, p. 206; Hamilton, *Henrietta Maria*, p. 254.
22 *Hutchinson*, p. 3.
23 Millar, *Stuart Pictures*, No. 152, No. 151.
24 *Clarendon's History*, III, p. 381.
25 Ellis, 1st series, III, p. 288.
26 Strickland, V, p. 266.
27 *Letters*, p. 3.
28 Welwood, p. 90.
29 C. S. P. Domestic 1639, p. 509.

Chapter 2: 'I Fear Them Not!'

1 C. S. P. Clarendon, II, p. 254.
2 *Hutchinson*, p. 68.
3 Rushworth, p. 743.
4 Petrie, *Letters*, p. 116.
5 Warwick, p. 242.
6 Ellis, 1st series, IV, p. 2.
7 Plumb, *Royal Heritage*, p. 126; *Armouries of the Tower*, p. 28.
8 Young, *Edgehill*, pp. 107–26.
9 Hinton, *Memoires*, cit. Young, *Edgehill*, p. 300.
10 Chapman, *Villiers*, p. 35.
11 *Clarendon's History*, III, p. 449.
12 Earle, *Microcosmography*, pp. 1–2.

Chapter 3: Present Miseries

1 Morrah, p. 176.
2 Pepys, 11 November 1667.
3 *Clarendon's History*, IV, p. 22.
4 Hughes, *Boscobel*, p. 341.
5 *Clarendon's History*, IV, p. 23.
6 *Clarendon's History*, IV, pp. 21–2.
7 *Letters*, p. 4.
8 Bowle, p. 278.
9 Petrie, *Letters*, p. 174.
10 *Halifax*, p. 153.
11 *Fanshawe*, p. 74.
12 Strickland, V, p. 537.
13 Petrie, *Letters*, p. 175; Harris, I, p. 25.
14 *Société Jersiaise*, Bulletin 3, pp. 15–21.
15 Hoskins, I, p. 364 *et seq.*
16 *Fanshawe*, p. 42.
17 Dasent, pp. 20–28; Balleine, p. 49, note; Ogg, I, p. 203, note 1.
18 Balleine, p. 47.
19 Petrie, *Letters*, p. 205.
20 Hoskins, I, p. 446 *et seq.*

Chapter 4: Dependence

1 Sackville-West, p. 74; *Clarendon's History*, IV, p. 208.
2 *Motteville*, II, p. 85.
3 Halifax, p. 79.
4 Airy, *Charles II*, p. 23.
5 Burnet, I, p. 67.
6 *Motteville*, II, p. 80.
7 *Montpensier*, I, p. 139.
8 Geyl, p. 44.
9 Airy, *Charles II*, p. 29.
10 Clarke, *James II*, p. 48; Scott, *Exile*, p. 47.
11 Clarendon Mss, XXXI, fol. 242.
12 *Mercurius Britannicus.*
13 *Hamilton Papers*, p. 244.

Chapter 5: The King's Son

1 Geyl, p. 101.
2 Scott, *Lucy Walter*, pp. 36–9.
3 Almack, *Cavalier Soldier's Vade-Mecum.*
4 Oldmixon, p. 384.
5 Petrie, *Letters*, p. 239.
6 *Letters*, p. 6.
7 Cary, *Memorials*, II, pp. 101–102.
8 Wedgwood, *Trial*, p. 236, note 18; p. 238, note 24.
9 Nalson, pp. 105–107.
10 Harris, I, p. 40; Fraser, *Cromwell*, p. 289; but see Wedgwood, *Trial*, p. 170, note 2; p. 239 for correction.
11 Petrie, *Letters*, p. 261.
12 Gardiner, *Commonwealth*, I, p. 18.

Chapter 6: A Candle to the Devil

1 *Société Jersiaise*, Bulletin, 1952.
2 Osborn Collection.
3 *Newbattle*, II, S. R. O. GD/40/6, fol. XVI, 3, 7, 5, 6, 10, 11.
4 *Newbattle*, II, S. R. O. GD/40/6, fol. XVI, 16.
5 Gardiner, *Charles II and Scotland*, Introd.
6 Hoskins, II, p. 323.
7 Petrie, *Letters*, p. 262.
8 Hoskins, II, p. 329.
9 *Société Jersiaise*, Bulletin, 1952.
10 *Clarendon's History*, II, p. 535.
11 C. S. P. Domestic 1650, pp. 69–71 (Col. Herbert Price).
12 Cowan, p. 264.
13 Burnet, I, p. 47; *Clarendon's History*, V, p. 14.
14 R. A. SP Add. 1/19.
15 H. M. C. 10th Rept, App. IV, p. 174.
16 Gardiner, *Charles II and Scotland*, p. 106.
17 Gardiner, *Charles II and Scotland*, p. 57.
18 C. S. P. Clarendon, II, App. *li–liii.*
19 Scott, *Exile*, p. 135; Gardiner, *Charles II and Scotland* ('Briefe Relation', 21 April 1650).
20 *Clarendon's History*, V, p. 107.
21 Burghclere, *Buckingham*, p. 40.
22 Gardiner, *Last Campaign of Montrose*, but see Cowan, p. 294.
23 C. S. P. Clarendon, II, p. 528; III, p. 14.
24 Gardiner, *Charles II and Scotland*, p. 110 ('Briefe Relation', 30 May 1650).
25 *Mercurius Politicus*, 6 June 1650.
26 C. S. P. Clarendon, II, App. *lxiv.*
27 *Jaffray's Diary*, p. 55.
28 C. S. P. Domestic 1650, p. 265.
29 C. S. P. Domestic 1650, p. 265.
30 Gardiner, *Charles II and Scotland*, p. 317 ('Briefe Relation', 5 February 1651).
31 Gardiner, *Charles II and Scotland*, p. 138; Carte, *Letters*, I, p. 391.

32 Ancram Correspondence, I, p. 304.
33 Douglas, *Scotch Campaigns*, p. 130, note (*Mercurius Politicus*; 'Briefe Relation').
34 *Monarchy Revived*, p. 94.
35 Ancram Correspondence, II, p. 497.

Chapter 7: Ravished at Worcester

1 Scott, *Exile*, p. 190.
2 Ancram Correspondence, II, p. 306.
3 Scott, *Exile*, p. 187 for Buckingham's treachery; but see Burghclere, *Buckingham*, p. 44; Chapman, *Villiers*, p. 64 for a defence.
4 *Letters*, p. 18.
5 C. S. P. Domestic 1650, pp. 236, 271.
6 *Mercurius Politicus*, No. 50; Douglas, *Scotch Campaigns*, p. 210 and note.
7 Harris, I, p. 93; *Forme of the Coronation*, 1651.
8 Ancram Correspondence, I, p. 93.
9 *Morton Muniments*, S. R. O. GD 150/2949.
10 *Household Book*, 1651, S. R. O. E 31/19, fol. 32.
11 *Annals of Pittenweem*, pp. 68–70.
12 Carte, *Letters*, II, p. 13.
13 Hillier, *Narrative*, pp. 329–33; Willcock, p. 369.
14 Carte, *Letters*, I, p. 451.
15 Douglas, *Scotch Campaigns*, p. 260.
16 Underdown, p. 49 *et seq.*
17 Scott, *Exile*, p. 200.
18 Cary, *Memorials*, II, p. 305.
19 *Mercurius Politicus*, 7 August 1650, 21 August 1650.
20 *Ailesbury*, I, p. 5.
21 Underdown, p. 46 *et seq.*
22 Fraser, *Cromwell*, pp. 386–7.
23 Ollard, p. 22.
24 C. S. P. Domestic 1651, p. 437.
25 Hughes, *Boscobel*, p. 128.
26 Burnet, II, p. 466.
27 Fea, *After Worcester*, p. 69 (Blount, *Boscobel*).
28 Kingston, *Charles II in Staffs*, p. 9.

Chapter 8: Heroical Figure

1 *Exact Narrative and Relation of His Escape*; for post-Worcester sources in general see author's footnote p. 144 *ante*.
2 Fea, *After Worcester*, pp. 5–44; also *King Charles Preserved*.
3 Oldmixon, p. 398.
4 Lindley, *Catholics in the Civil War*.
5 *Letters*, p. 50; *Reresby*, p. 180.
6 Fea, *After Worcester*, p. 115 (Blount, *Boscobel*).
7 *Boscobel House*, p. 39 *et seq.*
8 Udal, Dorsetshire Folk-Lore, p. 42 *et seq.*
9 Fea, *After Worcester*, p. 155 *et seq.*; Kingston, *Charles II in Staffs*, p. 77.
10 See Matthews, *Charles II's Escape*, p. 100 *et seq.*
11 Fea, *After Worcester*, p. 213 *et seq.*
12 Fea, *After Worcester*, p. 173 *et*

seq.; Hughes, *Boscobel*, p. 117.
13 Mrs P. M. O'Connor to author.
14 Clarendon Mss, Vol. 92, fol. 176.
15 Fea, *After Worcester*, p. 152 (Blount, *Boscobel*).

Chapter 9: A Difficult Game

1 Scott, *Exile*, p. 334 ('English Spy in Paris').
2 *Letters*, p. 25.
3 *Clarendon's History*, v, p. 232.
4 Lyon, p. 290.
5 *James II's Memoirs, 1821*, p. 88.
6 R. A. SP Add. 5/2/3.
7 Geyl, p. 106.
8 C. S. P. Clarendon, III, p. 86.
9 Geyl, p. 116.
10 C. S. P. Clarendon, III, p. 171.
11 Clarendon Mss, Vol. 47, fol. 244.
12 Clarendon Mss, Vol. 52, fol. 87.
13 C. S. P. Clarendon, III, p. 173.
14 C. S. P. Clarendon, III, p. 218.
15 Clarendon Mss, Vol. 48, fol. 315.
16 Rawlinson Mss A, Vol. 16, fol. 483.
17 See Crist, *Taaffe*, Introd.; Macpherson, *James II*, p. 76; Scott, *Lucy Walter*, pp. 189–200, suggests Charles II was the father of Mary, but the evidence is not convincing.
18 Thurloe, II, pp. 601, 614.
19 Rawlinson Mss A, Vol. 42, fol. 176.
20 R. A. SP Add. 5/2/8.
21 *Letters*, pp. 30, 50.
22 *Clarendon's History*, v, p. 361.
23 *Clarendon's History*, v, p. 359.
24 *Letters*, p. 157.
25 Underdown, p. 73 *et seq.*
26 Underdown, p. 127 *et seq.*
27 C. S. P. Clarendon, III, p. 11.
28 *Nicholas*, II, p. 173.
29 Clarendon Mss, Vol. 49, fol. 402.
30 *Letters*, p. 37.

Chapter 10: The Courtesies and the Injuries

1 Fraser, *Cromwell*, p. 601.
2 R. A. SP Add. 5/2/5.
3 Clarendon Mss, Vol. 50, fol. 77; Carte, *Letters*, II, p. 219.
4 *Nicholas*, III, p. 15; Carte, *Ormonde*, II, p. 172; Thurloe, III, p. 465.
5 R. A. SP Add. 5/2/4.
6 Haley, *Shaftesbury*, p. 89.
7 R. A. SP Add. 5/2/19; Scott, *Exile*, p. 181.
8 *Letters*, p. 30; R. A. SP Add. 5/2/14; Summers, *Playhouse*, p. 115.
9 *Letters*, pp. 48, 46.
10 *Letters*, p. 45.
11 Clarendon Mss, Vol. 92, fols 21b–c.
12 Harris, II, p. 48.
13 Guildhall Mss, 10, 823; *Boddington Commonplace Book*, Vol. 1, pp. 38–9.
14 Harris, II, p. 281.
15 *Letters*, p. 31; Carte, *Letters*, II, p. 99.
16 *Letter farther evidencing the King's stedfastnesse*.

17 Carte, *Letters*, II, p. 264; *Royal Pilgrimage; True and Good News from Brussels.*
18 Foxcroft, *Burnet*, p. 139.
19 Pierpont Morgan, R. of G. box VIII, pt 2, fol. 8.
20 Clarendon Mss, Vol. 67, fol. 307–308.
21 Foley Mss.
22 Dasent, p. 66.
23 Thurloe, V, p. 645.
24 Crist, *Taaffe*, No. 20.
25 Thurloe, V, p. 645.
26 *Very curious story concerning Charles II.*
27 Thurloe, VII, p. 325.
28 *Mercurius Politicus*, 10–17 July 1656.
29 Scott, *Lucy Walter*, pp. 117–22; C. S. P. Clarendon, II, p. 419; Thurloe, I, p. 665.
30 Crist, *Taaffe*, No. 13.
31 Crist, *Taaffe*, No. 5.
32 Crist, *Taaffe*, Nos 7, 15.
33 Childs, p. 2; Clarendon, Mss, Vol. 54, fol. 189.
34 C. S. P. Clarendon, III, p. 374.
35 *Letters*, p. 54.
36 C. S. P. Clarendon, III, p. 364.
37 Underdown, p. 217.
38 Scott, *Exile*, p. 341.
39 C. S. P. Clarendon, III, p. 307.

Chapter 11: At the Waterside

1 C. S. P. Clarendon, IV, p. 75.
2 Crist, *Taaffe*, No. 20.
3 C. S. P. Clarendon, IV, p. 77.
4 *Clarendon's History*, VI, p. 98.
5 Thurloe, VII, p. 374.
6 Abbott, *Cromwell*, IV, p. 732; C. S. P. Clarendon, IV, p. 428.
7 *Letters*, p. 69.
8 See Underdown *passim* for a consideration of his character.
9 Carte, *Letters*, II, p. 207.
10 Habbakuk, p. 202; Ashley, *Monck*, p. 153 *et seq.*
11 Thurloe, IV, p. 88.
12 *Letters*, p. 65; Ashley, *Monck*, p. 160; C. S. P. Clarendon, IV, pp. 268–9.
13 Carte, *Letters*, II, p. 278.
14 Hartmann, *Madame*, p. 35.
15 *Motteville*, III, p. 244.
16 *Letters*, p. 80.
17 *Letters*, p. 89.
18 *James* II *(as Duke of York)*, p. 291.
19 Pepys, 11 February 1660.
20 Harris, I, p. 281.
21 *True and Good News from Brussels.*
22 Pepys, 7 February, 11 February, 5 March, 16 March 1660.
23 Clarendon Mss, Vol. 69, fol. 67.
24 Haley, *Shaftesbury*, pp. 132, 138; C. S. P. Clarendon, IV, p. 678.
25 *Letters*, p. 81.
26 *Letters*, p. 83.
27 *Letters*, p. 86 *et seq.*
28 C. S. P. Clarendon, IV, pp. 657, 678, 685.
29 Pepys, 1 May 1660.
30 See Lower, *Journal of the Voyage* for details of this journey.
31 Corfitz Braëm, Unpublished Diary, May 25, 1660.

Chapter 12: Noah's Dove

1 Pepys, 23 May 1660 *et seq.*
2 *Letters*, p. 92.
3 Bell, *Fire in 1666*, p. 25; Evelyn, I, p. 337.
4 Cook, *Titus Britannicus.*
5 *Earl of Manchester's Speech.*
6 *Earl of Manchester's Speech.*
7 Tuke, *Character of Charles II.*
8 Piper, *Age of Charles II*, No. 34; Pepys, 15 November 1660.
9 *Policy, no Policy*, 1660.
10 Pepys, 2 November 1663.
11 Guildhall Mss, 10, 823; *Boddington Commonplace Book*, Vol. I, pp. 38–9.
12 *Eikon Basilike of Charles II*; Tuke, *Character of Charles II.*
13 Ogg, p. 148.
14 Ashley, *Charles II*, p. 314.
15 Evelyn, I, p. 341; Wase, *Electra.*
16 Pepys, 26 February 1666; *King's Works*, p. 313.
17 Jusserand, p. 110.
18 Jusserand, p. 108.
19 Feiling, *Two Speeches.*
20 Cook, *Titus Britannicus.*
21 C. S. P. Domestic 1660–61, pp. *II*, 300.
22 C. S. P. Domestic 1660–61, pp. *V*, *IV*; R. A. *Establishment Book* 9.
23 Pierpont Morgan, R. of E. box IX, pt 3, fol. 3.
24 C. S. P. Domestic 1660–61, p. VIII; *Fanshawe*, p. 93.
25 Fitzmaurice, *Petty*, p. 104.
26 Jusserand, p. 100.
27 *Letters*, p. 101.
28 Childs, p. 7 *et seq.*; Havighurst, Pt I, p. 63.
29 Osborn Files: Charles II.
30 Ratcliff, *Savoy Conference*, p. 90 *et seq.*; see also Whiteman, *Restoration of the Church*, p. 21 *et seq.*
31 Ratcliff, *Savoy Conference*, p. 90.
32 Thirsk, *Sales of Royalist Land*; Thirsk, *Restoration Land Settlement*; Habbakuk.
33 C. S. P. Domestic 1660–61, *passim.*
34 Plumb, *Royal Heritage*, p. 128.
35 *King's Works*, p. 266.
36 Evelyn, I, p. 360.
37 McKie, *Royal Society*, p. 33.
38 Birch, *Royal Society*, I, p. 21 *et seq.*
39 McKie, *Royal Society*, p. 33 *et seq.*
40 de Beer, *Charles II Fundator*, pp. 43–4; Davis, *Shipping Industry*, p. 124; Hatton Correspondence, I, p. 142.
41 *Letters*, p. 103; Pepys, 30 September 1661.
42 Roth, p. 176; Clark, *Edward Backwell*, pp. 51–2.
43 Chandaman, p. 263.

Chapter 13: The Best of Queens

1 St George, *Coronation*, Osborn Files, fol. b.112.
2 Millar, *Lely*, p. 80.
3 Legg, *Coronation Records*, p. 276.
4 Evelyn, I, p. 349; Pepys, 22 April 1661.
5 Ogilby, *King's Coronation.*
6 Plumb, *Royal Heritage*, p. 128.

7 Legg, *Coronation Records*, pp. 276–86; R. A. Wardrobe 74653.
8 Osborn Files: Fagel.
9 Pepys, 23 April 1661.
10 Baker, *Chronicle*, p. 821; Cook, *Titus Britannicus*.
11 C. S. P. Domestic 1660–61, p. 580.
12 Fagel, *Foreigner at Court*.
13 Morrah, p. 409.
14 Miller, *James II*, pp. 44–5; Clarke, *James II*, I, p. 387.
15 Jusserand, p. 107.
16 Clarendon Mss, Vol. 74, fols 355–6.
17 Roth, p. 176.
18 Clarendon Mss, Vol. 74, fol. 298.
19 *Domiduca Oxoniensis*.
20 *Clarendon's Life*, I, p. 490.
21 Macray, *Privy Council*, p. 67.
22 Powys, *Lace of Charles II*.
23 *Letters*, p. 127.
24 *Clarendon's Life*, I, p. 490.
25 *Ailesbury*, I, p. 7; Grammont, p. 109.
26 R. A. Establishment Book 10; Latham, *Pepys*, VI, p. 172, note 4; Pepys, 13 July 1663.
27 *Domiduca Oxoniensis*; Evelyn, I, p. 363; Burnet, I, p. 307, note 4.
28 *Letters*, p. 126.
29 Evelyn, II, p. 57; Grammont, p. 109; Reresby, p. 10; Burnet, I, p. 168; Sergeant, p. 5.
30 Pepys, 21 May 1662.
31 Grammont, p. 118.
32 Jusserand, p. 91.
33 Jusserand, p. 95; Oldmixon, p. 577.
34 Evelyn, I, p. 367; Feiling, *Foreign Policy*, p. 51.
35 Hartmann, *Madame*, p. 49.
36 Hartmann, *King My Brother*, p. 47.
37 Latham, *Pepys*, IV, p. 107.
38 *Letters*, pp. 127, 149.
39 Pepys, 4 July 1663.
40 Strickland, V, p. 560; Pepys, 19 October 1663.

Chapter 14: The Dutch Business

1 Abbott, *Long Parliament*, p. 23; Witcomb, p. 175.
2 C. S. P. Clarendon, V, p. *xiv*; see also Whiteman, *Restoration of the Church of England* for a discussion of this; also Bosher, pp. 208–12, 275; Feiling, *Tory Party*, p. 104.
3 Barbour, p. 65, note 3.
4 H. M. C. 7th Rept, App. 484.
5 Roth, p. 167 *et seq*.
6 Samuel, *David Gabay's Letter*.
7 Wolf, *Jewry of the Restoration*, p. 32; Roth, p. 172, note; Sasportas letter quoted by permission of Professor I. Tishby (see Preface to *Sisath nobel Sebi*, Jerusalem, 1954, pp. 39–41) trans. Raphael Loewe.
8 Abbott, *Long Parliament*.
9 Kenyon, *Stuart Constitution*, p. 382; Robbins, *Triennial Act*, p. 135.
10 Turberville, Pt I, p. 402.
11 See Browning, *Parties and Party Organization*.
12 See Carlyle, *Clarendon and Privy Council*.
13 *Letters*, p. 155; Carlyle,

Clarendon and Privy Council; *Clarendon's Life*, III, p. 103.
14 Macray, *Privy Council*, p. 165; *Gracious Message*, 1660.
15 Heaton, *Yachting*, pp. 32–50.
16 Heaton, *Yachting*, p. 47.
17 R. A. Wardrobe 85631, 85650–1.
18 Evelyn, I, p. 354; C. S. P. Domestic 1671, p. 392.
19 Millar, *Queen's Pictures*, p. 71; Fitzmaurice, *Petty*, p. 110.
20 Burnet, I, p. 167.
21 *Letters*, p. 122.
22 Childs, p. 20; Hartmann, *King My Brother*, p. 296.
23 Davis, *Shipping Industry*, p. 14 *et seq.*
24 Geyl, p. 141.
25 Wilson, *Profit and Power*, p. 144 *et seq.*; Feiling, *Foreign Policy*, p. 83.
26 Wilson, *Profit and Power*, p. 19.
27 Hartmann, *King My Brother*, p. 53; Burnet, I, p. 301.
28 Hartmann, *King My Brother*, pp. 157; 21.
29 C. S. P. Clarendon, Vol. 75, fols 176–83.
30 *Letters*, p. 178.
31 *Letters*, p. 164.
32 Pepys, 22 February 1664.
33 Feiling, *Foreign Policy*, p. 131, who is, however, more favourable to Downing than Geyl, p. 190.
34 Pepys, 30 April 1664.
35 *Letters*, pp. 163, 164, 168, 173.
36 *Letters*, pp. 164, 170.
37 C. S. P. Clarendon, v, p. *xv*; Feaveryear, p. 100.

Chapter 15: Black Day

1 Pepys, 12 April 1665; Lee, *Cabal*, p. 15.
2 Evelyn, II, p. 5.
3 Ashley, *Charles II*, p. 84.
4 Ogg, p. 288 (Dryden, *Essay of Dramatic Poesy*).
5 Shrewsbury, p. 445 *et seq.*
6 Carlingford, II of III, 23 November 1665.
7 Oldmixon, p. 521; *Reresby*, p. 11.
8 Shrewsbury, p. 543; *Letters*, p. 189; Carlingford, II of III, 2 February 1666.
9 Burnet, I, p. 391.
10 Hartmann, *Belle Stuart*, p. 11; Pepys, 15 November, 25 November 1666.
11 Hartmann, *Belle Stuart*, p. 12 *et seq.*
12 Jusserand, App., p. 217.
13 *Letters*, p. 203.
14 Carlingford, II of III, 22 August 1665, 22 June 1666.
15 Carlingford, II of III, 11 January, 6 March, 27 April 1666.
16 *Letters*, p. 190.
17 Hartmann, *Clifford*, p. 111; Carlingford, II of III, 6 July 1666.
18 See Bell, *Fire in 1666*; also *Fire of London*, for references *passim*.
19 Evelyn, II, pp. 9–16.
20 Hamilton, *Henrietta Maria*, p. 255.
21 *Short but True Account of the Terrible Fire*.

22 Kenyon, *Plot*, p. 12.
23 *King's Works*, pp. 19–38 (Colvin, *Surveyorship of Sir Christopher Wren*).
24 *Letters*, p. 191.
25 *London's Roll of Fame*, p. x; Guildhall Library, to author.
26 Bell, *Fire in 1666*, p. 359 and note.
27 Kenyon, *Plot*, p. 13.
28 Pepys, 31 December 1666; Feiling, *Foreign Policy*, p. 202.
29 Margoliouth, II, p. 43.
30 Duffy, p. 86.
31 Evelyn, II, p. 25.

Chapter 16: This Revolution

1 Clayton Roberts, *Impeachment of Clarendon*, p. 11; Carlyle, *Clarendon and the Privy Council.*
2 Browning, *Danby*, I, p. 32.
3 *Clarendon's Life*, III, p. 183.
4 Browning, *Danby*, p.45; Pepys, 27 August 1667.
5 Clarendon Mss, Vol. 85, fol. 165–6.
6 Feiling, *Foreign Policy*, p. 229, note 3; Latham, *Pepys*, VIII, p. 404, note 1.
7 *Letters*, p. 205; but see Clayton Roberts, *Impeachment of Clarendon* for the view that Clarendon himself chose flight.
8 Clayton Roberts, *Impeachment of Clarendon*, p. 15.
9 *Letters*, p. 205.
10 Haley, *Shaftesbury*, p. 267.
11 Pepys, 10 September 1667.
12 Pepys, 18 February 1661; Burnet, I, p. 405.
13 Miller, *Popery and Politics*, p. 109; Miller, *James II*, pp. 58–9; Earle, *James II*, p. 85; Burnet, II, p. 217.
14 Burnet, II, p. 180.
15 Feiling, *Foreign Policy*, p. 268 and note 2; Dalrymple, II, pp. 94–9.
16 Huddleston, *Brief Account*.
17 Clarke, *James II*, I, p. 173.
18 Pepys, 19 February 1666; Hatton Correspondence, I, p. 48; *Clarendon's Life*, III, p. 60.
19 *Letters*, p. 219; Pepys, 7 May 1668.
20 *Letters*, p. 235; Pepys, 11 May, 19 May 1669.
21 *Letters*, p. 236.
22 *Letters*, p. 239; Burnet, I, p. 308.
23 Margoliouth, II, p. 317.
24 Shapiro, pp. 219, 288.
25 Feiling, *Foreign Policy*, p. 241 *et seq.*
26 Clark, *Edward Backwell*, pp. 51–4.
27 Millar, *Queen's Pictures*, p. 67; Renier, p. 45.
28 Feiling, *Foreign Policy*, p. 256.
29 *Letters*, p. 214.
30 Lee, *Cabal*, p. 132.
31 Pepys, 23 October 1668.
32 Browning, *Danby*, I, p. 74.
33 *Letters*, pp. 241, 242.
34 *Lauderdale Papers*, II, p. 164; Lee, *Cabal*, p. 52.
35 Lee, *Cabal*, pp. 30–69.

Chapter 17: A Very Near Alliance

1 Pepys, 5 November 1668.
2 See de Beer, *Charles II's own fashion.*

3 R. A. Wardrobe 79916; Jusserand, p. 87.
4 de Beer, *Charles II's own fashion*; Evelyn, II, p. 17.
5 Pierpont Morgan, R. of G. box VIII, pt 2, fol. 24.
6 Hartmann, *King My Brother*, p. 284; *Letters*, p. 211.
7 Feiling, *Foreign Policy*, p. 289; *Letters*, pp. 224, 229.
8 Hartmann, *King My Brother*, pp. 280, 283.
9 See Hartmann, *Madame*, App. III; Hartmann, *King My Brother*, pp. 284–7 and note p. 286 for this dating, refuting Feiling, *Henrietta Stuart*, who dates letter 1668.
10 Margoliouth, II, p. 316.
11 *Letters*, p. 242.
12 *Letters*, p. 242.
13 Pierpont Morgan, R. of G. box VIII, pt 2, fol. 28.
14 Rait, *Stuart Princesses*, p. 271.
15 Hartmann, *Madame*, p. 315.
16 Hartmann, *King My Brother*, p. 321.
17 Hartmann, *King My Brother*, p. 333 (Dr Jean Fabre, *Sur la vie et principalement sur la mort de Madame*).
18 Hartmann, *King My Brother*, p. 39; Fayette, p. 112.
19 Text still at Ugbrooke Park, in the care of Lord Clifford of Chudleigh, descendant of Thomas Clifford.
20 Chandaman, p. 274.
21 Barbour, p. 157.
22 Haley, *Shaftesbury*, p. 324; Browning, *Danby*, I, p. 81.
23 Dalrymple, II, Apps, p. *vii*.

Chapter 18: Virtues and Imperfections

1 Haley, *Shaftesbury*, p. 214.
2 Pepys, 17 February 1669.
3 Bryant, *Charles II*, p. 208.
4 Duffy, p. 126.
5 Grammont, p. 246.
6 Pepys, 30 July 1667.
7 Burnet, II, p. 28.
8 *Reresby*, p. 7.
9 Grammont, p. 450 (*Personal History*).
10 Pepys, 26 April 1667.
11 C. S. P. Domestic 1667–8, p. 306.
12 Harris, II, App., p. 398.
13 Pierpont Morgan, R. of E. box IX, pt 2, fols 55, 57, 62, 64; see Hart, *Nell Gwynne and Thomas Otway*.
14 First mentioned in *Lives of the most Celebrated Beauties*, 1715.
15 Wilson, *Nell Gwynn*, p. 55 (Celadon).
16 Wilson, *Nell Gwynn*, p. 119.
17 Delpech, p. 88; Osborn Files.
18 Delpech, p. 88.
19 Burnet, I, p. 475.
20 R. A. Wardrobe 79070–79184.
21 Aberdare, *Tennis*, pp. 70–79.
22 Blencowe, I, p. 20; II, p. 57.
23 Forwood, pp. 13–21.
24 C. S. P. Domestic 1661–2, p. 241.
25 Pepys, 25 May 1660; Evelyn, II, p. 206; R. A. Wardrobe 86381; Cunningham, II, p. 75.
26 *Letters*, p. 4; *Newcastle*, p. 120 and note 1.
27 C. S. P. Domestic 1661–2, p. 62; R. A. SP Add. 19.

28 *Letters*, p. 223.
29 Hore, *Royal Buckhounds*, *passim*.
30 R. A. Wardrobe 79830, 79832, 79836 verso; R. A. Establishment Book 10.
31 C. S. P. Domestic 1660–61, p. 208.
32 Hore, *Newmarket*, II, *passim*; Longrigg, *Horse-racing*.
33 Pepys, 8 March 1669.
34 Hore, *Newmarket*, II, p. 299.
35 Tozer, pp. 254–5; Hore, *Newmarket*, II, p. 326.
36 H. M. C., 6th Rept, p. 367.
37 Wheatley, p. 452; Brett-James, p. 1130.
38 Sykes, *Pleasures of the Park*.
39 Evelyn, II, p. 21.
40 Sykes, *Pleasures of the Park*.
41 Church, *Royal Parks of London*, pp. 7–12.
42 Cunningham, II, p. 70.
43 Crowne, Foreword to *Sir Courtly Nice*.
44 Millar, *Queen's Pictures*, p. 71; Crowne, Foreword to *Sir Courtly Nice*.
45 Summers, *Restoration Theatre*, p. 280.
46 Jusserand, p. 56.
47 Nicoll, I, p. 364; R. A. Wardrobe 85635–6.
48 Halifax, p. 340; Evelyn, II, p. 206.

Chapter 19: Subsisting Together?

1 *Letters*, p. 261.
2 Dalrymple, II (A), p. 80.
3 *Ailesbury*, I, p. 92; Oldmixon, p. 553; Clark, *Edward Backwell*, p. 53.
4 Feaveryear, p. 103.
5 Printed in Kenyon, *Stuart Constitution*, pp. 407–408.
6 C. S. P. Venetian 1671–2, p. 187; Havighurst, Pt I, pp. 72–4.
7 Haley, *Shaftesbury*, pp. 297–9.
8 *Letters*, p. 246; C. S. P. Domestic 1671, p. 220.
9 C. S. P. Venetian 1671–2, p. 244.
10 *Letters*, pp. 257, 259.
11 Renier, p. 49.
12 R. A. SP, Add. 1/18.
13 *Letters*, p. 258; Renier, p. 52.
14 Hatton Correspondence, I, p. 98.
15 Delpech, pp. 42–3.
16 Delpech, p. 82.
17 Hatton Correspondence, I, p. 76.
18 Ogg, I, p. 77.
19 Fea, *James II*, p. 95 (Diary of Lady Cowper, 10 March 1716).
20 *Reresby*, p. 24; Wilson, *Court Wits*, p. 119; Cunningham, II, p. 33.
21 Evelyn, I, p. 63; R. A. Wardrobe 79104 verso.
22 *King's Works*, p. 278; Evelyn, II, pp. 102, 107.
23 *Letters*, p. 255.
24 Petty, p. 8; Ogg, II, p. 400, note 3.
25 Bagwell, III, p. 112, note 1.
26 Bagwell, III, p. 115 and note 1; C. S. P. Domestic 1673, pp. 596–7, 12.
27 R. A. Wardrobe 85669.

28 *Letters*, pp. 260–62.
29 C. S. P. Domestic 1673, p. 126.
30 Essex Papers, I, p. 181.

Chapter 20: The Knot in the Comb

1 Miller, *Popery*, pp. 9–12; but see Kenyon, *Plot*, pp. 24–5 and note, for the much higher figure of 260,000.
2 Kenyon, *Plot*, p. 27; Childs, pp. 28–9.
3 Evelyn, II, p. 71.
4 Childs, pp. 219, 230, refers to 'little evidence' but cites no evidence.
5 Haley, *William and the Opposition*, *passim*.
6 Turner, *James II*, p. 109.
7 Miller, *James II*, pp. 71–3.
8 Pepys, 16 June 1665.
9 Hyde Correspondence, I, p. 45; Fraser, *Mary, Queen of Scots*, p. 123.
10 Foxcroft, *Burnet*, p. 143; Margoliouth, II, p. 338.
11 Miller, *James II*, p. 73.
12 Browning, *Danby*, I, p. 107.
13 Burnet, I, p. 470 *et seq.*
14 Haley, *Shaftesbury*, p. 346; Cunningham, II, p. 73.
15 Jones, *First Whigs*, p. 216.
16 *Letters*, p. 55; Hartmann, *King My Brother*, p. 134; *Letters*, p. 231.
17 Josten, *Ashmole*, I, p. 189; IV, pp. 1347–8.
18 Josten, *Ashmole*, I, p. 234 and note 4; IV, pp. 1350–1 and note 1, 1362.
19 *Letters*, p. 275; *Motteville*, II, p. 80.
20 *Letters*, p. 276.
21 C. S. P. Venetian 1673–5, p. 233.
22 Browning, *Danby*, I, p. 129 *et seq.*; Browning, *Parties and Party Organization.*
23 Chandaman, p. 235 *et seq.*
24 Chandaman, p. 271.
25 Bryant, *Charles II*, p. 192; See Shaw, *Treasury Books*, Introduction, for the view that the King was kept intolerably short by Parliament; recently upset by Chandaman.
26 Williamson, *Investigation*, pp. 182–4.
27 Millar, *Queen's Pictures*, p. 69.
28 Evelyn, II, pp. 53–5; *King's Works*, p. 28.
29 Millar, *Queen's Pictures*, p. 81.
30 Girouard, p. 130.
31 *King's Works* (*Windsor Castle*), pp. 313–41, *passim.*
32 North, p. 132.
33 Bryant, *Charles II*, p. 196 note.
34 Hamilton, *William's Mary*, p. 24; Strickland, V, p. 623.
35 R. A. Wardrobe 85774.
36 R. A. Wardrobe 85774.
37 Parry, p. 203 *et seq.*
38 Latham, *Pepys*, VIII, p. 73 and note 3.
39 Browning, *Danby*, I, pp. 147, 168.
40 *Letters*, p. 280.
41 *Letters*, pp. 281–2.
42 *Letters*, p. 282.
43 Browning, *Danby*, I, pp. 190–91.

Chapter 21: Peace For His Own Time

1 *Reresby*, p. 40; Halifax, p. 54.
2 Jones, *Green Ribbon Club*; Haley, *Shaftesbury*, p. 530.
3 Dalrymple, II, p. 117.
4 Chandaman, p. 35.
5 Dasent, p. 249.
6 Girouard, p. 130; Ailesbury, I, p. 95.
7 Halifax, p. 251.
8 Osborn Files, 50.17.
9 *Letters*, p. 221.
10 Hartmann, *Duchess*, p. 149 *et seq.*
11 *Mazarine's Memoires.*
12 C. A. 120, folio 227.
13 C. A. 123c, fol. 109 (Courtin).
14 Renier, p. 61.
15 Chapman, p. 240.
16 Browning, *Danby*, I, p. 214.
17 Burnet, II, p. 118.
18 North, p. 153; Havighurst, Pt 2, pp. 230–31.
19 Browning, *Danby*, I, p. 226; II, pp. 66–9.
20 Margoliouth, II, p. 355.
21 Robb, I, p. 88.
22 *Lake*, I, p. 9.
23 Robb, I, p. 98; *Letters*, p. 290.
24 Pepys, 1 May 1662; Hatton Correspondence, I, p. 151.
25 Oldmixon, p. 605; Robb, I, p. 101; Burnet, II, p. 132.
26 *Letters*, pp. 288–90.
27 Sitwell, p. 19.
28 Browning, *Danby*, I, p. 268; Haley, *Shaftesbury*, p. 415.
29 Clarke, *James II*, I, p. 259.
30 Clark, *Later Stuarts*, p. 90.
31 Browning, *Danby*, I, p. 282.
32 *Letters*, p. 295; Childs, p. 219.
33 R. A. Wardrobe 79612 verso.

Chapter 22: Against Exclusion

1 Kenyon, *Plot*, p. 51; for the course of these events see Kenyon, *Plot*, *passim.*
2 But see Kenyon, *Plot*, p. 53, for view that Charles believed there was some substance in the plot.
3 Kenyon, *Plot*, pp. 46–7 (F. J. Warner, *History of the English Catholics*).
4 Kenyon, *Plot*, pp. 34–7.
5 Evelyn, II, p. 131.
6 Kenyon, *Plot*, p. 114; *Letters*, p. 304.
7 Blencowe, I, p. 86.
8 Halifax, p. 203; Kenyon, *Plot*, p. 77.
9 *Letters*, pp. 329–30.
10 Jones, *First Whigs*, p. 23.
11 Jones, *Green Ribbon Club*; Evelyn, II, p. 152.
12 *Reresby*, p. 29; Elmes, p. 287.
13 *Letters*, p. 301.
14 Childs, p. 228.
15 Hatton Correspondence, I, p. 157; Miller, *Popery*, pp. 159, 184.
16 Kenyon, *Plot*, p. 93.
17 Haley, *Shaftesbury*, pp. 483–5.
18 Burnet, II, p. 180; Falkus, p. 101.
19 Grammont, p. 121.
20 Hatton Correspondence, I, p. 168; Harris, II, App., p. 393.
21 Browning, *Danby*, I, 309 and note 1.

22 Hatton Correspondence, I, p. 175; Summers, *Restoration Theatre*, p. 80.
23 Wilson, *Nell Gwynn*, p. 179 *et seq.*
24 Wilson, *Court Wits*, p. 119 *et seq.* (Rochester, *The Royal Angler*; Buckingham, *The Cabin Boy*).
25 Blencowe, I, p. 2.
26 *Letters*, p. 304.
27 *Lords' Journals*, p. 348 (31 Car. II, 1679).
28 Oldmixon, p. 578; Wheatley, I, p. 451.
29 Renier, p. 85.
30 Ogg, II, p. 585.
31 Clarke, *James II*, I, p. 555; Browning, *Danby*, I, p. 319.
32 Kenyon, *Sunderland*, p. 25.
33 Sitwell, p. 60.
34 Sitwell, p. 66.
35 Brett, p. 55.
36 Chapman, *Villiers*, p. 229 (Buckingham's *Commonplace Book*); *Ailesbury*, I, pp. 75–7.
37 Burnet, II, p. 353; Kenyon, *Plot*, p. 90.
38 Robb, I, p. 141.
39 Evelyn, II, p. 228.
40 Burnet, II, p. 216.
41 Mackenzie, *Lauderdale*, pp. 459–60.
42 Burghclere, *Ormonde*, II, p. 260.
43 Essex Papers, 28 March 1674 (Essex to Harbord).
44 Pierpont Morgan, R. of E. box IX, pt 3, fol. 96.
45 *Appeal from the Country to the City*, 1679.
46 *Reresby*, p. 66.

Chapter 23: A King at Chess

1 Jones, *First Whigs*, p. 63 *et seq.*
2 Burnet, II, p. 251, note 1.
3 Burnet, II, p. 213.
4 See Nutting, *The Most Wholesome Law.*
5 Haley, *Shaftesbury*, p. 536; Kenyon, *Sunderland*, p. 27; Blencowe, I, p. 36.
6 Hatton Correspondence, I, p. 196.
7 See Kenyon, *Acquittal of Wakeman*; but see Havighurst, pt 2, p. 234, for view that collusion possible.
8 Kenyon, *Acquittal of Wakeman.*
9 Mason, *Account of the death.*
10 Haley, *Shaftesbury*, p. 466; Western, *Monarchy and Revolution*, p. 35; Clarke, *James II*, II, p. 5; but see Turner, *James II*, p. 102, note 2, for Mary of Modena's contrary view.
11 See Siegel and Poynter, *Talbor and Cinchona.*
12 Kenyon, *Sunderland*, p. 30; Blencowe, I, pp. 99, 147; R. A. Wardrobe 79693.
13 Hatton Correspondence, I, p. 206.
14 Lauderdale Papers, III, p. 211–12; Halifax, p. 61.
15 Jones, *Green Ribbon Club*; Chapman, *Villiers*, pp. 257–9; *Domestick Intelligence*, 18 November 1679.
16 Kenyon, *Plot*, pp. 189–90.

17 *Letters to a Person of Honour concerning the King's disavowing Monmouth's mother.*
18 *Letter to a Person of Honour concerning the Black Box.*
19 Pierpont Morgan, R. of G. box VIII, pt 2, fols 52, 53.
20 Halifax, p. 319.
21 Kenyon, *Sunderland*, pp. 41–2.
22 See Sacret, *Municipal Corporations.*
23 North, p. 121; Furley, *Whig Exclusionists, passim.*
24 Miller, *James II*, p. 109; *James II's Memoirs, 1821*, p. 283, note.
25 Dalrymple, II, p. 282.
26 Halifax, p. 325.
27 Clark, *Later Stuarts*, p. 102.
28 *Letters*, p. 313.
29 *Letters*, p. 314.
30 Grey, *Debates of the House of Commons*, VIII, p. 11.
31 Kenyon, *Sunderland*, pp. 51, 66.
32 Burnett, I, p. 493.
33 de Beer, *House of Lords in 1680.*
34 Foxcroft, *Halifax*, pp. 246–7, 252–5.
35 Tate, *Poems by several hands*, p. 93.

Chapter 24: Bolder and Older

1 *Reresby*, pp. 110, 103.
2 Ashley, *Charles II*, p. 275, 342, note 22.
3 Welwood, p. 138.
4 Haley, *Shaftesbury*, p. 584.
5 *Letters*, p. 316.
6 Kenyon, *Plot*, p. 203.
7 *Stafford's Brief and Impartial Account.*
8 *Ailesbury*, I, p. 95.
9 Nicoll, I, p. 434.
10 Haley, *Shaftesbury*, p. 621; Pollock, *Plot*, pp. 390–91.
11 C. S. P. Domestic 1680–81, p. 178.
12 Summers, *Playhouse*, p. 129.
13 Childs, p. 229.
14 Dryden, VII, p. 5–7; Tate, *Poems by Several Hands*, p. 127.
15 *Letters*, p. 317, wrongly dated 20 March; H. M. C. Ormonde, V, p. 619.
16 *Ailesbury*, I, p. 57; Turberville, Pt I.
17 *Debates in the House of Commons*, 21 March 1680.
18 *Letters*, p. 319.
19 *Ailesbury*, I, p. 58.
20 Bryant, *Pepys*, *II*, p. 351, note.
21 Chandaman, p. 135; Ashley, *Charles II*, p. 278.
22 *Letters*, pp. 319–22.
23 Ogg, II, p. 620, note 1; Blencowe, I, p. 212.
24 Howell, *State Trials*, VIII, p. 246.
25 Howell, *State Trials*, VIII, pp. 591, 595, 602.
26 Hatton Correspondence, II, p. 10.
27 Kenyon, *Sunderland*, p. 66.
28 Haley, *Shaftesbury*, p. 667.
29 Airy, *Charles II*, p. 261.
30 Burnet, II, p. 176, note 3.
31 Foxcroft, *Burnet*, p. 136; *Ailesbury*, I, p. 86; *Reresby*, p. 133.
32 R. A. Wardrobe 86382; Pierpont Morgan, R. of E. box IX, Pt 2.

33 Sergeant, p. 209.
34 See Dillon, *Some familiar Letters, passim.*
35 Evelyn, II, p. 195; Hatton Correspondence, I, p. 96; *Letters*, p. 327; Dasent, p. 70; Dillon, *Some familiar Letters*, p. 188; Evelyn, II, p. 199.
36 Withycombe, *English Christian Names*; Hoskins, II, p. 352.
37 Dillon, *Some familiar Letters*, pp. 159–62.
38 Evelyn, II, p. 199; H. M. C., 7th Rept, App., Pt I, p. 373.
39 Halifax, p. 252.

Chapter 25: Another Way of Ruling

1 *Reresby*, p. 175; *Ailesbury*, I, p. 21.
2 Chandaman, p. 135.
3 R. A. SP Add. 1/69.
4 R. A. Wardrobe 79904 verso, 79781, 79785.
5 C. S. P. Domestic October 1683–April 1684, p. 365.
6 As did James himself; Clarke, *James II*, I, p. 746.
7 Turner, *James II*, pp. 213–15.
8 Dillon, *Some familiar Letters*, p. 160.
9 *Reresby*, p. 177; Clarke, *James II*, I, p. 746.
10 Western, *Monarchy and Revolution*, p. 10 *et seq.*
11 Dillon, *Some familiar Letters*, p. 181.
12 North, p. 251; Burnet, II, p. 180.
13 Havighurst, Pt 2, p. 247.
14 North, p. 141.
15 Havighurst, Pt 2, p. 246.
16 *Reresby*, p. 170.
17 C. S. P. Domestic May 1684–February 1685, pp. 216, 94, 20, 85, 292, 151–6.
18 Airy, *Charles II*, p. 266; C. S. P. Domestic May 1684–February 1685, p. *vii et seq.*
19 Burnet, II, p. 384, note 1.
20 C. S. P. Domestic May 1684–February 1685, p. 187.
21 Jones, *Green Ribbon Club.*
22 Haley, *Shaftesbury*, p. 707 *et seq.*; Wyndham, p. 105.
23 D'Urfey, I, pp. 246–9.
24 Burnet, II, p. 363.
25 Airy, *Essex*, D. N. B., where it is called 'flippant and cruel' – but more probably sincere.
26 Robb, I, p. 183.
27 C. S. P. Domestic October 1683–April 1684, p. 35.
28 C. S. P. Domestic October 1683–April 1684, p. 36; Kenyon, *Sunderland*, p. 95.
29 Miller, *James II*, p. 116.
30 Duffy, p. 216.
31 Turner, *James II*, p. 229.
32 C. S. P. Domestic May 1684–February 1685, p. 248; Burnet, II, p. 287.
33 North, p. 233.
34 Airy, *Charles II*, p. 385.
35 Havighurst, Pt 2, p. 246; H. M. C., 15th Rept, App., VIII, p. 200.
36 Ashley, *Charles II*, p. 289.
37 *King's Works*, p. 305.
38 *King's Works*, p. 308.
39 Evelyn, II, p. 186.
40 Plumptre, p. 158.

41 *Ailesbury*, I, p. 87.
42 Ascoli, pp. 40–75.
43 de Beer, *Charles II Fundator*, p. 44.
44 Foxcroft, *Burnet*, p. 75.

Chapter 26: The Dregs of Life

1 Chandaman, pp. 134–5.
2 H. M. C., 14th Rept, App., Pt IX, p. 400.
3 Havighurst, Pt 2, pp. 248–9 and note 16.
4 Browning, *Danby*, I, p. 363.
5 Ogg, II, p. 654; C. S. P. Domestic May 1684–February 1685, pp. 22–3, 39.
6 C. S. P. Domestic May 1684–February 1685, p. 187.
7 Clark, *Later Stuarts*, p. 110.
8 C. S. P. Domestic May 1684–February 1685, p. 187.
9 Kenyon, *Sunderland*, pp. 99–100.
10 Bagwell, III, p. 146.
11 Carte, *Ormonde*, II, App., p. 128.
12 Kenyon, *Sunderland*, pp. 108–109.
13 C. S. P. Domestic May 1684–February 1685, p. 168.
14 Foxcroft, *Halifax*, I, pp. 420–33; Browning, *Danby*, I, pp. 362–3.
15 H. M. C., 15th Rept, App., Pt VIII, I, p. 212.
16 Oldmixon, p. 691; Foxcroft, *Trimmer*, p. 209.
17 Burnet, II, p. 455.
18 Ogg, II, p. 453, note 1; Crowne, Foreword to *Sir Courtly Nice*; Bryant, *Charles II*, p. 283; *James II*, 1821, p. 177.
19 Tate, *Poems*, 1684, p. 69; Halifax, p. 98.
20 Burnet, II, p. 466; for sources in general, see Crawfurd, *Last Days*, Intro. pp. 1–11, and Narrative; references not given in Crawfurd listed below.
21 Evelyn, II, p. 210.
22 Mason, *Account of the death.*
23 Mason, *Account of the death.*
24 Morris, *Dryden, Hobbs, Tonson.*
25 Mason, *Account of the death.*
26 Mason, *Account of the death.*
27 Morris, *Dryden, Hobbs, Tonson.*
28 Mason, *Account of the death.*
29 Tate, *Poems by Several Hands*, p. 425; Mason, *Account of the death.*
30 Mason, *Account of the death.*
31 Welwood, p. 147.
32 Fraser, *Cromwell*, p. 671.
33 Muddiman, *Death of Charles II.*
34 Evelyn, II, pp. 237–8; de Beer, *Evelyn*, IV, pp. 476–9; *Copies of Two Papers, 1686*; Burnet, II, pp. 472–3; Halifax, p. 250.
35 Huddleston, *Brief Account*; Dalrymple, II, pp. 94–9 for Barrillon's despatch.
36 Ellis, 1st series, III, p. 333.
37 Macaulay, *History of England*, 1866, I, p. 342.
38 Mason, *Account of the death*; Evelyn, II, p. 206; Burnet, II, p. 461.

Chapter 27: His Royal Ashes

1 North, p. 253.
2 Wilson, *Nell Gwynn*, p. 218; C. S. P. Domestic February–December 1685, p. 8.

3 Stanley, pp. 499–500; details confirmed to author, 1978.
4 Evelyn, II, pp. 210–211.
5 Turner, *James II*, p. 244; Latham, *Pepys*, I, p. 249, note; C. S. P. Domestic February–December 1685, p. 8.
6 Fraser, *Cromwell*, pp. 680–85.
7 *The Quaker's Elegy*; Arwaker, *The Vision*.
8 Wilson, *Nell Gwynn*, p. 241; C. S. P. Domestic February–December 1685, p. 8.
9 Heaton, *Yachting*, p. 50.
10 Strickland, V, p. 682; Evelyn, II, p. 209.
11 Burnet, II, p. 180.
12 Plumb, *Growth of Political Stability*, p. 15.
13 Buckingham, *Short Character of Charles II*, p. 8; *Ailesbury*, I, p. 95.
14 Dryden, *Preface to All For Love*.
15 Halifax, p. 55; *Dryden Essays* (*Defence of the Epilogue*).

Reference Books

This list is not a bibliography, impracticable for reasons of space. It is merely intended to give details of works cited in brief in the references. For a full bibliography of the period the reader is referred to Godfrey Davis (1st edition) and Mary Frear Keeler (2nd edition) *Bibliography of British History, Stuart period 1603–1714* (Oxford, 1970). As a supplement: J. P. Kenyon, *Stuart England* (1978) includes a critical bibliography, and J. R. Jones, *Country and Court 1658–1714* (1978) appends a bibliographical essay, surveying recently published work on the period.

Abbott, W. C., *The Long Parliament of Charles II*, English Historical Review, Vol. 21, 1906.

Abbott, W. C., *Writings and Speeches of Oliver Cromwell*, 4 Vols, Cambridge, Massachusetts, 1937–47.

Aberdare, Lord, *The Story of Tennis*, 1959.

An Abstract of Provisions made in the Office of the Great Wardrobe for the use and Service of His Majestie King Charles the Second as well against his Royal Proceeding through the City of London the 22nd April 1661. As also for his Royall Coronation the day following, Royal Archives.

An Account of the Preservation of King Charles II, after the Battle of Worcester Drawn up by Himself to which are added His Letters to Several Persons, Glasgow, 1766.

Memoirs of Thomas, Earl of Ailesbury written by himself, 2 Vols, Roxburghe Club, 1890.

Airy, Osmund, *Charles II*, 1901.

Alden, John, *The Muses Mourn; A Checklist of Verse Occasioned by the Death of Charles II*, Charlottesville, Virginia, 1958.

Almack, Edward (ed.), *The Cavalier Soldier's Vade-Mecum*, 1900.

Correspondence of Sir Robert Kerr, 1st Earl of Ancram, and his son William, 3rd Earl of Lothian, Vols I and II, Edinburgh, 1871.

Anderson, Henry, *A Loyal Tear Dropt on the Vault of the High and Mighty Prince Charles II, Of Glorious and Happy Memory*, 1685.

Annals of Pittenweem, 1526–1793, ed. D. Cook, Anstruther, 1867.

An Appeal from the Country to the City by Junius Brutus, 1679.

The Armouries of the Tower of London, I, Ordnance, H. L. Blackmore, H.M.S.O., 1976.

Arwaker, Edmund M. A., *The Vision: A Pindarick Ode Occasion'd by the Death of Our Late Gracious Sovereign King Charles II*, 1685.

Ascoli, David, *A Village in Chelsea: An informal account of the Royal Hospital*, 1974.

Ashley, Maurice, *Charles II: Man and Statesman*, 1971.

Ashley, Maurice, *General Monck*, 1977.

Bagwell, Richard, *Ireland under the Stuarts*, 3 Vols, 1908 (reprinted 1963).

Baker, Sir Richard, *A Chronicle of the Kings of England ... with a continuation of the chronicle in this fourth edition to the coronation of his sacred majesty King Charles II*, 1665.

Balleine, G. R., *All for the King: The Life Story of Sir George Carteret (1609–1680)*, Société Jersiaise, St Helier, 1976.

Barbour, Violet, *Henry Bennet, Earl of Arlington*, 1914.

Baschet, A., *Transcripts of the despatches of French Ambassadors in London*, Public Record Office.

Beer, E. S. de, *The Diary of John Evelyn*, 6 Vols, Oxford, 1955.

Beer, E. S. de, *The House of Lords in the Parliament of 1680*, Bulletin of the Institute of Historical Research, Vol. XX, No. 59, November 1943.

Beer, E. S. de, *King Charles II, Fundator et Patronus*, Notes and Records of the Royal Society of London, ed. Sir Harold Hartley, Vol. 15, 1960.

Beer, E. S. de, *King Charles II's own fashion: An episode in English–French Relations* 1666–1670, Journal of the Warburg Institute, Vol. 2, 1938–9.

Beer, E. S. de, *Members of the Court Party in the House of Commons 1670–1678*, Bulletin of the Institute of Historical Research, Vol. XI, 1933–4.

Behrens, B., *The Whig Theory of the Constitution in the Reign of Charles II*, Cambridge Historical Journal, Vol. VII, 1941.

Bell, W. G., *The Great Fire of London in 1666*, 3rd edition, 1923.

Bell, W. G., *The Great Fire of London*, 1957.

Benson, Donald R., *Halifax and the Trimmers*, Huntingdon Library Quarterly, Vol. XXVII, February 1964.

Birch, Thomas, *The History of the Royal Society of London*, etc., Vol. I, 1761.

Blencowe, R. W. (ed. with notes), *Diary of the times of Charles II, by the Honourable Henry Sidney*, etc., 2 Vols, 1843.

Blount, Thomas, *Boscobel: or the Compleat History of His Sacred Majesties Most Miraculous Preservation after the Battle of Worcester, 3 Sept 1651*, 1660.

Boddington Commonplace Book.

Boscobel House and White Ladies Priory, Department of the Environment, H.M.S.O., 1965 (reprinted 1975).

Bosher, R. S., *The Making of the Restoration Settlement*, 1951.

Bowle, John, *Charles the First*, 1975.

Brett, A. C. A., *Charles II and his Court*, 1910.

Brett-James, G. N., *Growth of Stuart London*, 1935.

A Briefe Relation, 2 October 1649–22 October 1650.

Browning, Andrew, *Thomas Osborne, Earl of Danby and Duke of Leeds, 1632–1712*, 3 Vols, Glasgow, 1951.

Browning, Andrew, *Parties and Party Organization in the Reign of Charles II*, Transactions of the Royal Historical Society, 4th Series, Vol. XXX, 1948.

Bryant, Arthur, *King Charles II*, 1931 (revised edition, 1955, to which references are given).

Bryant, Arthur, *Samuel Pepys*; (I) *The Man in the Making*, new edition, 1947.

Bryant, Arthur, *Samuel Pepys*; (II) *The Years of Peril*, 1935.

Buckingham, John, Duke of, *A Short Character of King Charles II, King of England*, 6th edition, 1725.

Buckingham, John, Duke of, *Works*, 2 Vols, The Hague, 1726.

Burghclere, Winifred, Lady, *George Villiers, 2nd Duke of Buckingham, 1628–1687*, 1903.

Burghclere, Winifred, Lady, *The Life of James, 1st Duke of Ormonde, 1610–1688*, 2 Vols, 1912.

Burnet's History of my own time, new edition by Osmund Airy, 2 Vols, Oxford, 1897, 1900.

Calendar of the Clarendon State Papers, Vol. IV, 1657–60, and Vol. V, 1660–1726, F. J. Routledge, 1932.

(C. S. P. Domestic) Calendar of State Papers Domestic.

(C. S. P. Venetian) Calendar of State Papers Venetian.

Cardwell, Edward, *Documentary Annals of the Reformed Church of England*, Oxford, 1839.

Carlingford Papers, Osborn Collection.

Carlyle, E. I., *Clarendon and the Privy Council*, English Historical Review, Vol. 27, 1912.

Carte, Thomas, *A Collection of Original Letters and Papers ... Found among the Duke of Ormonde's Papers*, 2 Vols, 1739.

Carte, Thomas, *Life of James, Duke of Ormonde*, 3 Vols, 1735–6.

Cary, H., *Memorials of the Great Civil War in England, 1646–1652*, edited from original letters in the Bodleian Library, 2 Vols, 1842.

Chandaman, C. D., *The English Public Revenue, 1660–1688*, Oxford, 1975.

Chapman, Hester W., *Great Villiers; A Study of George Villiers, Second Duke of Buckingham, 1628–1687*, 1949.

Chapman, Hester, W., *The Tragedy of Charles II*, 1964.

Chevers, Norman, *An Enquiry into the Circumstances of the Death of King Charles the Second of England*, Calcutta, 1911.

Childs, John, *The Army of Charles II*, 1976.

Church, Richard, *Royal Parks of London*, H.M.S.O., 1956.

The History of the Rebellion and Civil Wars in England by Edward, Earl of Clarendon, ed. W. Dunn Macray, 6 Vols, Oxford, 1888.

The Life of Edward Earl of Clarendon ... in which is included a Continuation of his History of the Grand Rebellion, written by Himself, 3 Vols, new edition, Oxford, 1827.

Clarendon Mss, Bodleian Library, Oxford.

Clark, Dorothy K., *Edward Backwell as a Royal Agent*, Economic History Review, Vol. XI, 1938.

Clark, Sir George, *The Later Stuarts 1660–1714*, 2nd edition, Oxford, 1955.

Clarke, Rev. J. S. (ed.), *The Life of James the Second, King of England*, etc., 2 Vols, 1816.

Commons Journals, Vols VII–IX.

Cook, Aurelian, *Titus Britannicus: An Essay of History Royal in the Life and Reign of his Late Sacred Majesty Charles II of Ever Blessed and Immortal Memory*, 19 March 1685.

Copies of Two Papers Written by the late King Charles II, Together with a Copy of a Paper Written by the late Duchess of York, Henry Hills, 1686.

(C. A.), *Correspondence Politique, Angleterre*, Ministère des Affaires Etrangères, Paris.

Cowan, Edward J., *Montrose: For Covenant and King*, 1977.

Crawfurd, Raymond, *The Last Days of Charles II*, Oxford, 1909.

Crist, Timothy (ed. with Introd. and Notes), *Charles II to Lord Taaffe, Letters in Exile*, 1974.

Croft-Murray, Edward, Isaac Fuller's Paintings of Charles II's Escape after the Battle of Worcester, Society of Antiquaries, Oxford, 1971.

Crowne, John, *Sir Courtly Nice or It Cannot Be; A Comedy*, 1685.

Cunningham, Peter (related and collected by), *The Story of Nell Gwynn: and the Saying of Charles II*, 2 Vols, New York, 1883.

Dalrymple, Sir John, *Memoirs of Great Britain and Ireland*, 2 Vols, 1773.

Dasent, Arthur Irwin, *The Private Life of Charles the Second*, 1927.

Davies, Godfrey, *The Restoration of Charles II 1658–1660*, 1955.

Davis, Ralph, *The Rise of the English Shipping Industry in the Seventeenth and Eighteenth Centuries*, 1962.

The Debates in the House of Commons, Assembled at Oxford, 21 March 1680.

Debates of the House of Commons from the year 1667 to the year 1694, ed. Anchitel Grey, 1769.

Deedes, Cecil (ed.), *Royal and Loyal Sufferers*: 1903, includes: (1) Wase's *Electra* 1649; (2) *An Exact Narrative and Relation of his Sacred Majesties Escape from Worcester on the 3rd of September 1651*, etc.; (3) *Eikon Basilike or the True Portraiture of His Sacred Majestie Charles the II*, etc., *1630–1660*, by R. F., Esq., an eye-witness.

A Defence of the Papers Written by the late King of Blessed Memory and Duchess of York, Against the Answer Made to Them, by command H. Hills, 1686.

Delpech, Jeanine, *Life and Times of the Duchess of Portsmouth*, 1953.

Dillon, William, and Arthur, Harold, (transcribed and ed.), *Some familiar Letters of Charles II and James, Duke of York, addressed to their daughter and niece, the Countess of Lichfield*, Archaeologia, second series, Vol. VIII, Society of Antiquaries of London, 1902.

Domestick Intelligence.

Domiduca Oxoniensis: sive musae academicae gratulato ob auspicatissimum serenissimae principis Catharinae lusitanae regi suo desponsatae in Angliam appulsum, Oxoniae, 1662.

Donaldson, Gordon, *Scotland: James V to James VII*, Edinburgh, 1965.

Douglas, W. S., *Cromwell's Scotch Campaigns 1650–51*, 1898.

Downes, J. F., *The Strawberry Roan*, unpublished MS.

Works of John Dryden, ed. Sir Walter Scott, Vol. VII, 1808.

Dryden, John, *Essays*, ed. W. P. Kerr.

Duffy, Maureen, *The Passionate Shepherdess; Aphra Behn 1640–1689*, 1977.

D'Urfey, Thomas, *Wit and Mirth or Pills to Purge Melancholy*, Vol. I, 1719.

The Earl of Manchester's Speech to His Majesty in the name of the Peers, At his Arrival at Whitehall 29th May 1660. With his Majesties Gracious Answer, printed by John Macock and Francis Tyton, 1660.

Earle, John, *Microcosmography*, Pt I, 'The Child', 1628.

Earle, Peter, *James II*, 1972.

Eikon Basilike or the True Portraiture of His Sacred Majestie Charles the II, Beginning from his Birth 1630 into this present year 1660. Wherein is interwoven a Compleat History of the High-Born Dukes of York and Gloucester, in 3 books by R. F., Esq., an eye-witness, 1660. See Deedes, Cecil (ed.), *Royal and Loyal Sufferers*, 1903.

Ellis, Sir Henry, *Original Letters Illustrative of English History*, 1st and 2nd Series, Vols 3 and 4, 1824, 1827.

Elmes, James, *Sir Christopher Wren and his Times*, 1852.

Essex Papers (1672–7), ed. O. Airy and C. E. Pike, Camden Society, 1890, 1913.

Diary and Correspondence of John Evelyn, F. R. S., ed. William Bray, 4 Vols, 1850.

An Exact Narrative and Relation of his Sacred Majesties Escape from Worcester on the 3rd September 1651, etc., see Deedes, Cecil (ed.), *Royal and Loyal Sufferers*, 1903.

Fagel, Henry, *A Foreigner at the Court of Charles II*, 1661, Osborn Collection.

Falkus, Christopher, *The Life and Times of Charles II*, 1972.

The Memoirs of Ann, Lady Fanshawe, ed. E. J. Fanshawe, 1907.

Fayette, Madame de la, *The Secret History of Henrietta, Princess of England*, translated by J. M. Shelmerdine, 1929.

Fea, Allan, *After Worcester Fight*, 1904.

Fea, Allan, *The Flight of the King*, 1897.

Fea, Allan, *James II and his Wives*, 1908.

Feaveryear, A. E., *The Pound Sterling, A History of English Money*, Oxford, 1931.

Feiling, Keith, *British Foreign Policy, 1660–1672*, new impression, 1968.

Feiling, Keith, *A History of the Tory Party, 1649–1714*, Oxford, 1924.

Feiling, Keith, *Henrietta Stuart, Duchess of Orleans, and the Origins of the Treaty of Dover*, English Historical Review, Vol. 47, 1932.

Feiling, Keith, *Two Speeches of Charles II*, English Historical Review, Vol. 45, 1930.

Feiling, Keith, *Two Unprinted Letters of Henrietta Stuart, Duchess of Orleans*, English Historical Review, Vol. 43, 1928.

Fitzmaurice, Lord Edmond, *The Life of Sir William Petty 1623–1687*, 1897.

Foley, Mss, Jesuit Archives, Farm Street, London.

The forme and order of the Coronation of Charles the Second ... As it was acted and done at Scone, Jan. 1st 1651, Aberdeen, 1651.

Forwood, Mary Gwendoline, Lady, *The Cavalier King Charles Spaniel.*

Foxcroft, H. C. (ed.), *A supplement to Burnet's History of my own time*, Oxford, 1902.

Foxcroft, H. C., *A Character of the Trimmer*, 1946.

Foxcroft, H. C., *Life and Letters of Sir George Savile, Bart., first Marquis of Halifax*, with a new edition of his works, 2 Vols, 1898.

Fraser, Antonia, *Cromwell: Our Chief of Men*, 1973.

Fraser, Antonia, *Mary Queen of Scots*, 1969.

Furley, O. W., *The Whig Exclusionists: Pamphlet Literature in the Exclusion Campaign, 1679–81*, Cambridge Historical Journal, Vol. XIII.

Gardiner, S. R., *The Commonwealth and Protectorate*, 4 Vols, 1903.

Gardiner, S. R., *The Last Campaign of Montrose*, The Edinburgh Review, Vol. CLXXIX, 1894.

Gardiner, S. R. (ed. with Notes and Introduction), *Letters and Papers Illustrating the relations between Charles II and Scotland in 1650*, Edinburgh, 1894.

Geyl, Pieter, *Orange* and *Stuart 1641–72*, 1969.

Girouard, Mark, *Life in the English Country House*, 1978.

Grammont, Count, *Memoirs of the Court of Charles the Second*, also *The Personal History of Charles II* and *Boscobel Tracts* etc., ed. Sir Walter Scott, 1864.

Greene, Graham, *Lord Rochester's Monkey*, 1974.

Grey, A., *Debates of the House of Commons from 1667–1694*, 1769.

Guildhall Library Mss, London.

Habbakuk, Sir John, *Land Settlement and the Restoration of Charles II*, Transactions of the Royal Historical Society, 5th series, 28, 1978.

Haley, K. D. H., *Charles II*, Historical Association pamphlet, 1966.

Haley, K. D. H., *The First Earl of Shaftesbury*, Oxford, 1968.

Haley, K. D. H., *William of Orange and the English Opposition, 1672–4*, Oxford, 1953.

Halifax: Complete Works, ed. with an Introduction by J. P. Kenyon, 1969.

Hamilton, Elizabeth, *Henrietta Maria*, 1976.

Hamilton, Elizabeth, *William's Mary: A Biography of Mary II*, 1972.

Hamilton Papers, ed. S. R. Gardiner, Camden Society, 1880.

Harris, William, *An Historical and Critical Account of the Life of Charles II*, etc., 2 Vols, 1747.

Hart, W. H., *A Memorial of Nell Gwynne, the Actress, and Thomas Otway, the Dramatist*, 1868.

Hartmann, C. H., *La Belle Stuart*, 1924.

Hartmann, C. H., *Charles II and Madame*, 1934.

Hartmann, C. H., *Clifford of the Cabal: A Life of Thomas first Lord Clifford of Chudleigh, Lord High Treasurer of England 1630–1673*, 1937.

Hartmann, C. H., *The King My Brother*, 1954.

Hartmann, C. H., *The Vagabond Duchess*, 1926.

Correspondence of the Family of Hatton, 1601–1704, ed. E. M. Thompson, Camden Society, 2 Vols, 1878.

Havighurst, A. F., *The Judiciary and Politics in the Age of Charles II*, The Law Quarterly Review, Vol. 66, January and April 1950.

Hayward, John (ed.), *Collected Works of Rochester*, 1926.

Heaton, Peter, *Yachting: A History*, 1955.

Heraldic Visitations of Wales, ed. Sir Samuel Meyrick, 2 Vols, 1846.

Hillier, George, *A Narrative of the attempted Escapes of Charles I ... Including the letters of the King to Colonel Titus, now first deciphered and printed from the originals*, 1852.

Memoires by Sir John Hinton, Physician in ordinary to His Majestie's Person ... 1679.

His Majesties Gracious Message to all his loving Subjects in the Kingdom of Ireland upon their Exemplary Return to their Obedience, 30 March 1660.

(H. M. C.) Historical Manuscripts Commission, 1st Report.

(H. M. C.) Historical Manuscripts Commission, 6th Report.

(H. M. C.) Historical Manuscripts Commission, 7th Report, Part I, Report and Appendix, 1879.

(H. M. C.) Historical Manuscripts Commission, 10th Report, Appendix IV.

(H. M. C.) Historical Manuscripts Commission, 14th Report, Appendix, Part IX, *Mss The Earl of Lindsay*, 1895.

(H. M. C.) Historical Manuscripts Commission, 15th Report, Part VIII, *Mss of the Duke of Buccleuch and Queensberry*, Vol. I, 1897.

(H. M. C.) Historical Manuscripts Commission, *The Marquess of Ormonde*, new series, Vol. V.

Hore, J. P., *The History of Newmarket and the Annals of the Turf*, Vols II and III, 1886.

Hore, J. P. (compiled by), *The History of the Royal Buckhounds*, Newmarket, 1895.

Hoskins, S. Elliott, *Charles the Second in the Channel Islands*, 2 Vols, 1854.

Household Book: Minutes of the Board of Green Cloth during Charles II's residence in Scotland 1650–1, Scottish Record Office.

Howell, T. B., (compiled by), *1809 State Trials*, 8 Vols, London and Middlesex Archaeological Society, 1935.

Huddleston, John, *A Brief Account of Particulars occurring at the happy death of our late Sovereign Lord King Charles II, in regard to Religion ... Annexed to A Short and Plain Way to the Faith and Church by Richard Huddleston*, 1688.

Hughes, J. (ed.), *The Boscobel Tracts: relating to the Escape of Charles the Second after Worcester*, Edinburgh and London, 1830.

Correspondence of Henry Hyde, Earl of Clarendon, and of his brother Lawrence Hyde, Earl of Rochester, ed. S. W. Singer, 2 Vols, 1828.

Hutchinson, Lucy, *Memoirs of the Life of Colonel Hutchinson*, ed. James Satherland, repr. 1973.

The Diary of Alexander Jaffray, ed. J. Barclay, Aberdeen, 1856.

Memoirs of James II, 2 Vols, Colchester, 1821.

The Memoirs of James II: His Campaigns as Duke of York 1652–1660, trans. A. Lyton Sells from the Bouillon Manuscript, 1962.

Jones, J. R., *Country and Court: England 1658–1714*, 1978.

Jones, J. R., *The First Whigs: The Politics of the Exclusion Crisis, 1678–1683*, 1961.

Jones, J. R., *The Green Ribbon Club*, Durham University Journal, December 1956.

Josten, C. H. (ed. and with Introduction), *Elias Ashmole 1617–1692*, 5 Vols, Oxford, 1966.

Jusserand, J. J., *A French Ambassador at the Court of Charles II*, 1892.

Kenyon, John, *The Popish Plot*, 1972.

Kenyon, J. P., *The Acquittal of Sir George Wakeman 18 July 1679*, The Historical Journal, 1971.

Kenyon, J. P., *The Stuart Constitution, 1603–1688: Documents and Commentary*, Cambridge, 1966.

Kenyon, J. P., *Stuart England*, 1978.

Kenyon, J. P., *Robert Spence, Earl of Sunderland, 1641–1702*, 1958.

King Charles Preserved: An Account of his Escape after the Battle of Worcester dictated by the King himself to Samuel Pepys, Rodale Press, 1956.

The King's Coronation: Being an Exact Account of the Cavalcade, with a Description of the Triumphal Arches, and Speeches prepared by the City of London, etc., John Ogilby, 1685.

The History of the King's Works, Vol. v, 1660–1782, General Editor H. M. Colvin, H.M.S.O., 1976.

Kingston, H. P., *The Wanderings of Charles II in Staffordshire and Shropshire after the Worcester Fight*, Birmingham, 1933.

Diary of Dr Edward Lake, ed. G. P. Elliott, Camden Society Miscellany, I, 1847.

Latham, R. C., and Matthews, W. (eds), *The Diary of Samuel Pepys*, 9 Vols, 1970–76.

The Lauderdale Papers, ed. O. Airy, 3 Vols, Camden Society, 1884–5.

Lee, Maurice, Jr, *The Cabal*, Urbana, 1965.

Legg, L. G. W., *English Coronation Records*, 1901.

A Letter farther and more fully evidencing the King's stedfastenesse in the Protestant Religion, written by Monsieur de l'Angle, Minister of the Protestant Church at Rouen, to a friend in London, 1 June 1660.

A Letter to a Person of Honour Concerning the Black Box, 1680.

A Letter to a Person of Honour, concerning the King's disavowing the having been Married to the Duke of Monmouth's mother, Robert Ferguson, 1680.

The Letters, Speeches and Declarations of King Charles II (Letters) ed. Arthur Bryant, 1935.

Lindley, K. J. *The Part played by the Catholics in the English Civil War*, University of Manchester.

Lipscomb, F. W., *Heritage of Sea Power*, 1976.

Lives of the most Celebrated Beauties, 1715.

London's Roll of Fame 1885–1959, Introd. Irving B. Gare, 1960.

Longrigg, Roger, *A History of Horse-racing*, 1972.

Lords Journals, Vols IX–XIII.

Lower, Sir William, *A Relation In Form of Journal, Of The Voyage and Residence Which the most Excellent and most Mighty Prince Charles the II King of Great Britain*, etc., *hath made in Holland, from the 25th of May, to the 2nd of June 1660*, The Hague, 1660.

Lyon, C. J., *Personal History of King Charles the Second 1650–1651*, Edinburgh, 1851.

Mackenzie, W. C., *The Life and Times of John Maitland, Duke of Lauderdale 1616–1682*, 1923.

McKie, Douglas, *The Origins and Foundation of the Royal Society of London*, in *Notes and Records of The Royal Society of London*, ed. Sir Harold Hartley, Vol. 15, 1960.

MacLaurin, C., *Mere Mortals*, New York, 1925.

Macpherson, James, *Memoirs of King James II*, 1775.

Macray, W. D., (ed.), *Notes which passed at Meetings of the Privy Council between Charles II and the Earl of Clarendon 1660–1667*, Roxburghe Club, 1896.

Margoliouth, H. M. (ed.), *The Poems and Letters of Andrew Marvell*, 3rd edition revised by Pierre Legoirs, with E. E. Duncan-Jones, 2 Vols, Oxford, 1971.

Mason, Anne Margaret, Lady, *Account of the death of Charles II 'by a wife of a person about the Court at Whitehall'*, Household Words, 9, 1854.

Matthews, William (ed.), *Charles II's Escape from Worcester: A Collection of Narratives Assembled by Samuel Pepys*, Berkeley and Los Angeles, 1966.

Memoires of the Duchess of Mazarine: together with reasons for her coming into England, likewise a letter containing a true character ..., trans, P. Porter 1676.

Mercurius Britannicus.

Mercurius Politicus.

Millar, Oliver, *The Age of Charles I: Painting in England 1620–1649*, Tate Gallery, 1972.

Millar, Oliver, *The Queen's Pictures*, 1977.

Millar, Oliver, *Sir Peter Lely*, National Portrait Gallery, 1978.

Millar, Oliver, *The Tudor, Stuart and Early Georgian Pictures in the Collection of H. M. The Queen*, 1963.

Miller, John, *James II: A Study in Kingship*, Hove, 1977.

Miller, John, *Popery and Politics in England 1660–1688*, Cambridge, 1973.

Monarchy Revived: being the Personal History of Charles the Second from his earliest years to his Restoration to the throne, reprinted from 1661 edition, 1822.

Mémoires de Mademoiselle de Montpensier, ed. A. Cheruel, 4 Vols, Paris, 1892.

Morrah, Patrick, *Prince Rupert of the Rhine*, 1976.

Morris, G., *Dryden, Hobbs, Tonson and the Death of Charles II*, Notes and Queries, new series, Vol. 22, No. 12.

Morton Muniments, Scottish Record Office.

Memoirs of Madame de Motteville on Anne of Austria and her Court, trans. K. R. Wormsley, 3 Vols, 1902.

Muddiman, J. G., *The Death of Charles II*, The Month, 1932.

Nalson, John (taken by), *A true copy of the journal of the High Court of Justice for the Tryal of King Charles I*, 1683.

(Newbattle) *Inventory of Documents, State Papers and Letters belonging to the*

Marquess of Lothian and formerly preserved at Newbattle Abbey, Scottish Record Office.

The Life of William Cavendish Duke of Newcastle ... by Margaret Duchess of Newcastle, ed. C. H. Firth, 1886.

The Nicholas Papers: Correspondence of Sir Edward Nicholas, Secretary of State, ed. Sir G. F. Warner, Camden Society, 4 Vols, 1886–1920.

Nicoll, Allardyce, *A History of English Drama 1660–1900*, Vol. I, *Restoration Drama*, 1952.

North, Roger, *The Life of the Right Honourable Francis North, Baron of Guilford*, etc., 1742.

Notes and Records of the Royal Society of London, ed. Sir Harold Hartley, Vol. 15, 1960.

Nuttall, G. F., and Chadwick, Owen (eds), *From Uniformity to Unity*, 1962.

Nutting, Helen, A., *The Most Wholesome Law – The Habeas Corpus Act of 1679*, American Historical Review, Vol. LXV, April 1960.

Ogg, David, *England in the Reign of Charles II*, 2nd edition, 1963.

Oldmixon, John, *The History of England during the Reigns of the Royal House of Stuart*, 1730.

Ollard, Richard, *The Escape of Charles II after the Battle of Worcester*, 1966.

Oman, Carola, *Henrietta Maria*, 1936.

Osborn Collection, Yale University.

Parry, C. Hubert H., *The Music of the Seventeenth Century*, 2nd edition, with revisions and an Introductory Note by Edward J. Dent, 1938.

The Diary of Samuel Pepys, ed. R. C. Latham and W. Matthews, 9 Vols, 1970–76.

Perrinchief, R., *The Royal Martyr: Life and Death of King Charles I*, 1676.

Petrie, Sir Charles (ed.), *Letters of King Charles I.*

Petty, Sir William, *Political Anatomy of Ireland*, 1691.

Pierpont Morgan Library Mss, New York.

Piper, David, *The Age of Charles II*, Royal Academy Catalogue, 1960.

Plumb, J. H., *The Growth of Political Stability in England 1675–1725*, 1967.

Plumb, J. H., and Weldon, Huw, *Royal Heritage: The Story of Britain's Royal Builders and Collectors*, 1977.

Plumptre, E. H., *The Life of Thomas Ken, D. D.*, 2 Vols, 1888.
Policy, no Policy, the Devil Himself Confuted, 1660.
Pollock, John, *The Popish Plot*, 1903.
Powys, Marion, *The Lace of King Charles II*, Bulletin of the Needle and Bobbin Club, Vol. XII, No. 2.

The Quakers Elegy on the Death of Charles Late King of England, 'written by W. P., a sincere Lover of Charles and James', 1685.

Rait, R. S., *Five Stuart Princesses*, 1908.
Ratcliff, E. C., *The Savoy Conference and the Revision of the Book of Common Prayer*, in Nuttall, G. F., and Chadwick, Owen (eds), *From Uniformity to Unity*, 1962.
Rawlinson Mss, Bodleian Library, Oxford.
Receuil des instructions données aux ambassadeurs de France, Vols XXIV–XXV, *Angleterre*, 1648–90, ed. J. J. Jusserand, Paris, 1929.
Renier, G. J., *William of Orange*, 1952.
The Memoirs of the Honourable Sir John Reresby, Bart, etc., 1735.
Robb, Nesca A., *William of Orange, 1650–1673; A Personal Portrait*, 2 Vols, 1962.
Robbins, Caroline, *The Repeal of the Triennial Act 1664*, Huntingdon Library Quarterly, Vol. XII, 1948.
Roberts, Clayton, *The impeachment of the Earl of Clarendon*, Cambridge Historical Journal, Vol. XIII, 1957.
Roth, Cecil, *History of the Jews in England*, 3rd edition, Oxford, 1964.
(R. A.) Royal Archives, Windsor Castle.
The Royal Pilgrimage of the Progresse and Travels of King Charles the Second, Through the most and greatest Courts of Europe, by an Eye Witness, 26 March 1660.
Rushworth, John, *The Tryal of Thomas Earl of Stafford, Lord Lieutenant of Ireland*, etc., 1680.

Sackville-West, V., *Daughter of France: The Life of Anne-Marie Louise d'Orléans, duchesse de Montpensier 1627–1693*, 1959.
Sacret, J. H., *The Restoration Government and Municipal Corporations*, Economic History Journal, April 1930.

St George, Sir Thomas, *Coronation of King Charles II*, Osborn Collection.

Samuel, Edgar R., *David Gabay's 1660 Letter from London*, Transactions of the Jewish Historical Society, XXV.

Scott, Eva, *The King in Exile: The Wanderings of Charles II from June 1646 to July 1654*, 1904.

Scott, Eva, *The Travels of the King: Charles II in Germany and Flanders, 1654–1660*, 1907.

Scott, Lord George, *Lucy Walter – Wife or Mistress?*, 1947.

(S. R. O.) Scottish Register Office, Edinburgh.

The Secret History of the Reigns of King Charles II and King James II, 1690.

Sergeant, Philip W., *My Lady Castlemaine*, 1912.

Shapiro, Barbara J., *John Wilkins, 1614–1672: An Intellectual Biography*, Berkeley and Los Angeles, 1969.

Shaw, W. A. (ed.), *Calendar of Treasury Books*, 1904–62.

Short but True Account of the Cruel and Terrible Fire through which almost the whole of the City of London became Ashes, Rotterdam, 25 September 1666.

Shrewsbury, J. F. D., *A History of Bubonic Plague in the British Isles*, Cambridge, 1970.

Siegel, Rudolph E., and Poynter, F. N. L., *Robert Talbor, Charles II and Cinchona: A contemporary document*, Medical History, Vol. 6, 1962.

Sitwell, Sir George, *The First Whig*, Scarborough, 1894.

Société Jersiaise, Bulletin Annuel, Vol. 3, 1890–96.

Société Jersiaise, Bulletin Annuel, *Some letters of Charles II to Jersey*, 1952.

A Brief and Impartial Account of the Birth and Quality, Imprisonment, etc., *Last Speech and Final End of William, late Lord Viscount Stafford*, 1681.

Stanley, Dean, *Memorials of Westminster Abbey*, 7th impression with Appendix, 1867.

Strickland, Agnes, *Lives of the Queens of England*, Vols IV and V, 1851.

Summers, Montague, *The Playhouse of Pepys*, 1935.

Summers, Montague, *The Restoration Theatre*, 1934.

Sykes, Marjorie, *Pleasures of the Park*, History Today, Vol. XXVIII, April 1978.

Taaffe Letters, Osborn Collection.

Memoirs of the Family of Taaffe, Vienna, 1856.

Tate, Nahum (collected by), *Poems by Several Hands and on Several Occasions*, 1685.

Tate, Nahum, *Poems written on Several Occasions*, 2nd edition, 1684.

Tate, Nuham, *The History of King Richard Second*, 1681.

Thirsk, Joan, *The Restoration Land Settlement*, Journal of Modern History, Vol. XXVI, 1954.

Thirsk, Joan, *The Sales of Royalist Land during the Interregnum*, Economic History Reviw, Vol. X, 1952.

(Thurloe) *A Collection of the State Papers of John Thurloe*, ed. Thomas Birch, 7 Vols, 1742.

Tozer, Basil, *The Horse in History*, 1908.

True and Good News from Brussels: Containing a Sovereigne Antidote agst the Poysons and Calumnies of the present time, 2 April 1660.

Tuke, Sir Samuel, *A Character of Charles the Second written by an Impartial Hand*, etc., 1660.

Turberville, A. S., *The House of Lords under Charles II*, Parts I and II, English Historical Review, Vols 44 and 45, 1929 and 1930.

Turner, F. C., *James II*, 1948.

Udal, J. S., *Dorsetshire Folk-Lore*, With a fore-say by the late William Barnes, Hertford, 1922.

Underdown, David, *Royalist Conspiracy in England 1649–1660*, New Haven, 1960.

Van Doren, Mark, *The Poetry of John Dryden*, Cambridge, 1931.

A very curious and well attested story concerning King Charles II, Osborn Collection.

Walker, James, *The Secret Service under Charles II and James II*, Transactions of the Royal Historical Society, 4th Series, Vol. XV, 1932.

Warwick, Sir Philip, *Memoires of the reign of King Charles I with a continuation to the happy restoration of King Charles II*, 1701.

Wase's *Electra*, 1649, see Deedes, Cecil (ed.), *Royal and Loyal Sufferers*, 1903.

Wedgwood, C. V., *The Trial of Charles I*, 1964.

Welwood, James, M. D., *Memoirs of the most Material Transactions in England for the last Hundred Years*, etc., 7th edition, 1749.

Western, J. R., *Monarchy and Revolution: The English State in the 1680s*, 1972.

Wheatley, H., *London Past and Present*, based on the *Handbook of London* by P. Cunningham, 1891.

Whiteman, Anne, *The Restoration of the Church of England*, in Nuttall, G. F., and Chadwick, Owen (eds), *From Uniformity to Unity*, 1962.

Willcock, John, *The Great Marquess, Life and Times of Archibald 8th Earl and 1st (and only) Marquess of Argyll*, 1903.

Williamson, Audrey, *The Mystery of the Princes: An investigation into a supposed murder*, Dursley, 1978.

Wilson, Charles, *Profit and Power: A study of England and the Dutch Wars*, 1957.

Wilson, J. H., *The Court Wits of the Restoration: An Introduction*, Princeton, 1948.

Wilson, J. H., *Nell Gwynn: Royal Mistress*, 1952.

Witcomb, D. T., *Charles II and the Cavalier House of Commons*, Manchester, 1966.

Withycombe, E. G., *Oxford Dictionary of English Christian Names*, 2nd edition, Oxford, 1949.

Wolbarsht, M. L., Naval Medical Research Institute, Bethesda, and Sax, D. S., Psychiatric Institute, University Hospital Baltimore, *Charles II, A Royal Martyr*, Notes and Records of the Royal Society of London, Vol. 16, No. 2, November 1961.

Wolf, Lucien, *The Jewry of the Restoration 1660–1664*, Transactions of the Jewish Historical Society.

Wyndham, Violet, *The Protestant Duke: A Life of Monmouth*, 1976.

Young, Peter, *Edgehill*, 1972.

Index

In this index C= Charles II